COOK

WITH

JOY

Step-by-Step Directions

Also includes
"A JOURNEY THROUGH THE BIBLE"
and
A Large Section of Equivalents and Substitutions

By Ellen K. Benninger

TEN RULES FOR HAPPY LIVING

1. Read your Bible and talk to God about everything.
2. Never indulge in self-pity. Maybe you did not have opportunities as a child, but you can make them now.
3. When you go out, prepare to give a smile to everyone who will take it. "No one is properly clothed unless he wears a smile."
4. Cultivate a cheerful disposition and a sense of humor.
5. Put yourself out to help someone every day.
6. Fill your life with worthwhile things. Then should the light go out, you will have something to think about.
7. Appreciate people. Nothing gives more pay than appreciation.
8. Children are the hope of the world. Make at least one child happy every day.
9. Refuse to be discouraged. What should be done, can be.
10. Keep busy. One cannot always work strenuously, so have a hobby.

— The Railroad Evangelist

ISBN 0-938037-35-8

Cover By Victor Sanders

ALLEGHENY PUBLICATIONS SALEM, OHIO

COOK WITH JOY

by

ELLEN K. BENNINGER

Second Edition
2004

0-938-37-35-8

*We recommend that these pages be placed in a three-ring binder
in order to preserve the life of the cookbook.~The Publishers*

For additional copies, order from:

ALLEGHENY PUBLICATIONS
2161 WOODSDALE ROAD
SALEM, OH 44460
(800)672-7500

FOREWORD

Although I have collected thousands of recipes over the years, only the most practical are included in this cookbook. Names are given on some of the recipes. Because I have tested and revised constantly, the recipes may not appear exactly as they were given to me. Every recipe in this book, to the best of my knowledge, has been tested either by me, or in my kitchen. I have tried to make the directions easy to understand. Thus, a person who has never cooked before can try these recipes with confidence. Cooking is a happy experience for me and I hope it will be for you.

And now . . . cook with joy!

ELLEN K. BENNINGER

Motto: *"He who waits on God wastes no time."*

DEDICATION
and
EXPRESSION of APPRECIATION

To God, who has been my constant helper and loving guide through the years.

To my Mother, Anna Limber Stevenson, from whom I learned my first lessons in cooking when a child. Although paralyzed with rheumatoid arthritis, she was an excellent and patient teacher.

To my Husband, Jack Edward Benninger, who has given me his loyal support in this project and has endured many strange new dishes and experiments in the process.

To my Friend, Patricia Anne Swarts, who has tirelessly helped and encouraged me and has washed a "ton" of dishes for me. As the project was nearing completion, she tested some of the recipes in my kitchen.

TABLE OF CONTENTS

Chapter 1

Hydrogenated Fats & Trans Fatty Acids

ELLEN AND SPARKLE BERRY

REALLY IMPORTANT INFORMATION FOR YOUR HEALTH

This cookbook contains recipes that aim to limit hydrogenated fats, partially hydrogenated fats and trans fatty acids. That means that the recipes that had hydrogenated vegetable shortening or margarines in them have been changed. Why? Because many diseases, I believe, are being caused by some of the foods Americans have been eating in the last fifty years. So many people are being afflicted with diseases in the prime of their lives! It has been impossible to take out every ingredient in the recipes that have these fats in them, because they are so prevalent.

In the 1950's, margarine was proclaimed a healthy alternative to butter because it was made from vegetable oils. Sad to say, there is nothing healthy about margarine or other foods that contain partially hydrogenated oils and trans fatty acids. Read the labels on commercial foods such as margarine, shortening, some oils, cookies, crackers, desserts, snack foods, some peanut butter, some bread, some dry cereals, frozen whipped topping, cracker crumbs, ramen noodles, cake mixes, and many other things; you will see how prevalent the words "partially hydrogenated" are in the listed ingredients. French fries and doughnuts at restaurants are examples of foods loaded with trans fats.

What is wrong with hydrogenation and trans fatty acids? Hydrogenated fats are oils that have hydrogen reacting with the unsaturated parts of the oil molecule to stiffen them and make them spread more easily. Since the molecular structure changes from a "cis" into a "trans" structure when hydrogenation occurs, these oils are referred to as trans fatty. Hydrogenated fats contain harmful trans fatty acids that have been linked to cancer, heart disease, and other cardiovascular diseases.

Margarine, shortening and partially hydrogenated oils are prime examples of hazardous trans fatty acid compounds. Researchers believe that the hydrogenation process used in creating these products could be leading to many health problems. Trans fatty acids can increase production of cholesterol and promote arteriosclerosis (hardening of the arteries). Some day it may be proven that trans fatty acids promote the development of cancer and degenerative disease, increase inflammation, accelerate aging and obstruct immunity and healing.

In January 2006, the FDA will be requiring food labels to include artery-clogging trans fats. Until then, look for "hydrogenated oil" or "partially hydrogenated oil" on the label. These are code for trans fat, and we should try to avoid foods with these words in the ingredients as much as possible to reduce intake of trans fatty acids. I realize that avoiding these foods is not 100% possible at this time.

In the July 12, 2004 issue of *U.S. News & World Report* magazine a report was written about Dr. Walter C. Willett, M.D., who is a professor of epidemiology at the Harvard School of Public Health. The following is an excerpt from this article written by Amanda Spake:

Willett has never been a scientist who shrinks from controversy. "He upsets a lot of people," says Margo Wootan, director of nutrition policy at the Center for Science in the Public Interest. "He thinks about the implications of his research and advocates changes." The best example: his fight over trans fats in prepared foods.

Small amounts of trans fats occur naturally in some foods. But most result from cooking or baking with liquid vegetable oils that have been "hydrogenated," or formed into solids by the addition of hydrogen (think margarine). Their long shelf life made these oils the fat of choice for food makers and fast-food chains.

Early studies in animals indicated trans fats might lead to heart disease. They increased LDL, the "bad" cholesterol, while depressing "good" HDL cholesterol. In 1993, the Nurses' Health Study found a 50 percent increase in heart disease associated with trans fats in food. A year later, Willett dropped another bomb: People who ate the most trans-fat-rich food were two times as likely to have a heart attack as were people who ate less of these fats.

***Joint effort.** By the spring of 1994, Willett and CSPI had joined forces to persuade the U.S. Food and Drug Administration to require trans-fat labeling on food products. Willett's 1997 study estimated that use of hydrogenated oils was resulting in 30,000 heart-disease deaths per year, representing "the biggest food processing disaster in U.S. history."*

Hydrogenated Fats and Trans Fatty Acids

These efforts did not endear Willett to the food industry. Indeed, some companies refused to support conferences if Willett was invited to speak. But by 2002, the evidence was overwhelming: The Institute of Medicine reported that the safe amount of trans fat in the diet is zero. In July 2003, the FDA ruled that trans-fat food labeling must begin by January 2006. But Willett no longer believes labeling is enough. In May, he and 27 other scientists urged the FDA to remove hydrogenated oils from "the generally recognized as safe" list of food additives.

If we were to think about foods mentioned in the Bible, I believe we could eat more wisely. How many times olive oil is mentioned in the Bible! Grape juice is mentioned many times, and it is now confirmed that pure non-alcoholic purple grape juice (no sweetening added) is good for the heart. In the Bible, blood was not to be eaten. Rare steak with blood oozing out of it should be a no-no for the Christian. (Acts 15:29, "That ye abstain . . . from blood.") There was a good reason for this rule, because blood carries waste away from all tissues as well as carrying nutrients to the tissues.

Extra virgin olive oil is high in monounsaturated fatty acids, which have been found to help control cholesterol. Olive oil has been found by researchers to help lower LDL cholesterol levels (the bad cholesterol), while not affecting HDL (the good cholesterol). Also, olive oil may help protect against cardiac disease, according to studies at Stanford University. Researchers have found that olive oil can help reduce formation of unwanted blood clots that can lead to stroke and heart attack. Several studies on breast and colon cancer report that olive oil apparently does not promote tumors the way other oils can.

You may ask, "Why not use canola oil, since it has been promoted as a healthy monounsaturated fat also?" The answer is that commercial canola oil that is found in grocery stores is extracted in ways (heat, solvents and bleaching) that damage the oil; and pesticides are used heavily on the seeds.

There are spreads and shortenings that are not hydrogenated, and have no trans fatty acids in them. Two names are "Smart Balance" and "Earth Balance." Smart Balance Spread comes in light and regular. For cooking, frying and baking, the regular Smart Balance is the one to use, not "light." Smart Balance Shortening can be found at Meijer supermarkets in Indiana and in a few other states. Their email address is: consumermail@smartbalance.com. Earth Balance Spread and Shortening are easier to find because they are being carried by most of the major health food store distributors. If it is not readily available at your local health food store, request that the manager special-order it for you. You can get baking hints at their website at: www.earthbalance.net. Both Smart Balance and Earth Balance are owned and distributed by G.F.A. Brands, Inc., P.O. Box 397, Cresskill, NJ 07626-0397. The phone number for Earth Balance is 201-568-9300. Earth Balance is the all-natural version of Smart Balance. Whenever the words "Earth Balance Spread" appear, you know that you can use either that, or pure butter, or Smart Balance Spread (regular). Whenever the words "Earth Balance Shortening" appear, you know you can interchange with Smart Balance Shortening. Yes, these shortenings, spreads and extra virgin olive oil cost more than cheaper shortenings, margarines and oils, but if it would enhance your health, wouldn't it be worth it? (Smart Balance is cheaper than Earth Balance.)

A few more words about olive oil: cold-pressed or naturally pressed means no heat or chemicals were used to extract the oil from the olives. Extra virgin is the first pressing. If you don't want the taste of extra virgin olive oil in a cake or dessert, use extra light olive oil in those recipes.

Another food that is full of monounsaturated fat is the avocado. You can peel a ripe avocado, mash and season it, and use it as an alternative for butter or mayonnaise on bread and sandwiches.

It's always nice to end with some good news. You have probably all heard that a little dark chocolate can be good for you. The reason is that chocolate contains polyphenols called flavenoids that act as potent antioxidants. It has an acceptable fat content and protective phytochemicals with antioxidant activity. So, a little dark chocolate in moderation can actually be healthy . . . unless you have a gall bladder problem!

For healthier and happier cooking and baking, I wish you success!

ELLEN K. BENNINGER

Chapter 2

Journey Through The Bible

PASTOR JACK BENNINGER

Presented here is a portion of God's Word from every Book in the Bible (King James Version). You will find some of the most quoted verses of the Bible in this journey.

JOURNEY THROUGH THE BIBLE

Presented here is a portion of God's Word from every book in the Bible (King James Version). You will find some of the most quoted verses of the Bible in this journey.

Genesis

"In the beginning God created the heaven and the earth."

Genesis 1:1

"And God blessed the seventh day, and sanctified it: because that in it he had rested from all his work which God created and made."

Genesis 2:3

"And the Lord God formed man of the dust of the ground, and breathed into his nostrils the breath of life; and man became a living soul."

Genesis 2:7

"While the earth remaineth, seedtime and harvest, and cold and heat, and summer and winter, and day and night shall not cease."

Genesis 8:22

". . . Thou God seest me:"

Genesis 16:13b

"Is any thing too hard for the Lord?"

Genesis 18:14a

". . . and of all that thou shalt give me I will surely give the tenth unto thee."

Genesis 28:22b

Exodus

"The Lord shall fight for you, and ye shall hold your peace."

Exodus 14:14

"Thou shalt have no other gods before me."

Exodus 20:3

"Thou shalt not make unto thee any graven image. . . ."

Exodus 20:4a

"Thou shalt not take the name of the Lord thy God in vain;"

Exodus 20:7a

"Remember the sabbath day, to keep it holy."

Exodus 20:8

"Honour thy father and thy mother:"

Exodus 20:12a

"Thou shalt not kill."

Exodus 20:13

"Thou shalt not commit adultery."

Exodus 20:14

"Thou shalt not steal."

Exodus 20:15

"Thou shalt not bear false witness against thy neighbour."

Exodus 20:16

"Thou shalt not covet . . ."

Exodus 20:17a

"And the Lord said unto Moses, Come up to me into the mount, and be there: and I will give thee tables of stone, and a law, and commandments which I have written; that thou mayest teach them."

Exodus 24:12

"And he gave unto Moses, when he had made an end of communing with him upon mount Sinai, two tables of testimony, tables of stone, written with the finger of God."

Exodus 31:18

"And the tables were the work of God, and the writing was the writing of God, graven upon the tables."

Exodus 32:16

Leviticus

"It shall be a perpetual statute for your generations throughout all your dwellings, that ye eat neither fat nor blood."

Leviticus 3:17

"For the life of the flesh is in the blood: and I have given it to you upon the altar to make an atonement for your souls: for it is the blood that maketh an atonement for the soul."

Leviticus 17:11

"Thou shalt not go up and down as a talebearer among thy people:"

Leviticus 19:16a

"Thou shalt not avenge, nor bear any grudge against the children of thy people, but thou shalt love thy neighbour as thyself: I am the Lord."

Leviticus 19:18

"Ye shall keep my sabbaths, and reverence my sanctuary: I am the Lord."

Leviticus 19:30

"Regard not them that have familiar spirits, neither seek after wizards, to be defiled by them: I am the Lord your God."

Leviticus 19:31

"Thou shalt rise up before the hoary head, and honour the face of the old man, and fear thy God: I am the Lord."

Leviticus 19:32

"Sanctify yourselves therefore, and be ye holy: for I am the Lord your God."

Leviticus 20:7

Numbers

". . . hath he said, and shall he not do it? or hath he spoken, and shall he not make it good?"

Numbers 23:19c

". . . be sure your sin will find you out."

Numbers 32:23b

Deuteronomy

"Know therefore this day, and consider it in thine heart, that the Lord he is God in heaven above, and upon the earth beneath: there is none else."

Deuteronomy 4:39

"O that there were such an heart in them, that they would fear me, and keep all my commandments always, that it might be well with them, and with their children for ever!"

Deuteronomy 5:29

"And thou shalt love the Lord thy God with all thine heart, and with all thy soul, and with all thy might."

Deuteronomy 6:5

"And it shall be, if thou do at all forget the Lord thy God, and walk after other gods, and serve them, and worship them, I testify against you this day that ye shall surely perish."

Deuteronomy 8:19

"For the Lord your God is God of gods, and Lord of lords, a great God, a mighty, and a terrible, which regardeth not persons, nor taketh reward:"

Deuteronomy 10:17

"And ye shall rejoice before the Lord your God . . ."

Deuteronomy 12:12a

"For thou art an holy people unto the Lord thy God, and the Lord hath chosen thee to be a peculiar people unto himself, above all the nations that are upon the earth."

Deuteronomy 14:2

"Thou shalt be perfect with the Lord thy God."

Deuteronomy 18:13

"The woman shall not wear that which pertaineth unto a man, neither shall a man put on a woman's garment: for all that do so are abomination unto the Lord thy God."

Deuteronomy 22:5

"And the Lord, he it is that doth go before thee; he will be with thee, he will not fail thee, neither forsake thee: fear not, neither be dismayed."

Deuteronomy 31:8

"He is the Rock, his work is perfect: for all his ways are judgment: a God of truth and without iniquity, just and right is he."

Deuteronomy 32:4

"The eternal God is thy refuge, and underneath are the everlasting arms:"

Deuteronomy 33:27a

Joshua

". . . but as for me and my house, we will serve the Lord."

Joshua 24:15c

Judges

". . . And he wist not that the Lord was departed from him."

Judges 16:20c

Ruth

". . . for whither thou goest, I will go; and where thou lodgest, I will lodge: thy people shall be my people, and thy God my God:"

Ruth 1:16b

I Samuel

"Talk no more so exceeding proudly; let not arrogancy come out of your mouth: for the Lord is a God of knowledge, and by him actions are weighed."

I Samuel 2:3

"He will keep the feet of his saints . . ."

I Samuel 2:9a

". . . It is the Lord: let him do what seemeth him good."

I Samuel 3:18b

"Moreover as for me, God forbid that I should sin against the Lord in ceasing to pray for you:"

I Samuel 12:23a

". . . for the Lord seeth not as man seeth; for man looketh on the outward appearance, but the Lord looketh on the heart."

I Samuel 16:7d

". . . but as his part is that goeth down to the battle, so shall his part be that tarrieth by the stuff: they shall part alike."

I Samuel 30:24b

II Samuel

"Wherefore thou art great, O Lord God: for there is none like thee, neither is there any God beside thee . . ."

II Samuel 7:22a

"As for God, his way is perfect; the word of the Lord is tried: he is a buckler to all them that trust in him."

II Samuel 22:31

I Kings

"And he said, Lord God of Israel, there is no God like thee, in heaven above, or on earth beneath, who keepest covenant and mercy with thy servants that walk before thee with all their heart:"

I Kings 8:23

"Let your heart therefore be perfect with the Lord our God, to walk in his statutes, and to keep his commandments, as at this day."

I Kings 8:61

II Kings

". . . Fear not: for they that be with us are more than they that be with them."

II Kings 6:16b

I Chronicles

"Give thanks unto the Lord, call upon his name, make known his deeds among the people."

I Chronicles 16:8

". . . And all the people said, Amen, and praised the Lord."

I Chronicles 16:36b

"... for the Lord searcheth all hearts, and understandeth all the imaginations of the thoughts: if thou seek him, he will be found of thee; but if thou forsake him, he will cast thee off for ever."

I Chronicles 28:9b

"But who am I, and what is my people, that we should be able to offer so willingly after this sort? for all things come of thee, and of thine own have we given thee."

I Chronicles 29:14

II Chronicles

"If my people, which are called by my name, shall humble themselves, and pray, and seek my face, and turn from their wicked ways; then will I hear from heaven, and will forgive their sin, and will heal their land."

II Chronicles 7:14

"... The Lord is with you, while ye be with him; and if ye seek him, he will be found of you; but if ye forsake him, he will forsake you."

II Chronicles 15:2b

"For the eyes of the Lord run to and fro throughout the whole earth, to shew himself strong in the behalf of them whose heart is perfect toward him."

II Chronicles 16:9a

"... and their voice was heard, and their prayer came up to his holy dwelling place, even unto heaven."

II Chronicles 30:27b

"... but with us is the Lord our God to help us, and to fight our battles."

II Chronicles 32:8b

Ezra

"... The hand of our God is upon all them for good that seek him; but his power and his wrath is against all them that forsake him."

Ezra 8:22b

Nehemiah

"... for the joy of the Lord is your strength."

Nehemiah 8:10d

Esther

"... and who knoweth whether thou art come to the kingdom for such a time as this?"

Esther 4:14c

Job

"Also now, behold, my witness is in heaven, and my record is on high."

Job 16:19

"For I know that my redeemer liveth, and that he shall stand at the latter day upon the earth:"

Job 19:25

"But he knoweth the way that I take: when he hath tried me, I shall come forth as gold."

Job 23:10

"Doth not he see my ways, and count all my steps?"

Job 31:4

"I know that thou canst do every thing, and that no thought can be withholden from thee."

Job 42:2

Psalms

"Blessed is the man that walketh not in the counsel of the ungodly, nor standeth in the way of sinners, nor sitteth in the seat of the scornful."

Psalm 1:1

"My voice shalt thou hear in the morning, O Lord; in the morning will I direct my prayer unto thee, and will look up."

Psalm 5:3

"Let the words of my mouth, and the meditation of my heart, be acceptable in thy sight, O Lord, my strength, and my redeemer."

Psalm 19:14

"Give unto the Lord the glory due unto his name; worship the Lord in the beauty of holiness."

Psalm 29:2

"For I will declare mine iniquity; I will be sorry for my sin."

Psalm 38:18

"Great is the Lord, and greatly to be praised in the city of our God, in the mountain of his holiness."

Psalm 48:1

"Whoso offereth praise glorifieth me: and to him that ordereth his conversation aright will I shew the salvation of God."

Psalm 50:23

"Purge me with hyssop, and I shall be clean: wash me, and I shall be whiter than snow."

Psalm 51:7

"The sacrifices of God are a broken spirit: a broken and a contrite heart, O God, thou wilt not despise."

Psalm 51:17

"As for me, I will call upon God; and the Lord shall save me."

Psalm 55:16

"Evening, and morning, and at noon, will I pray, and cry aloud: and he shall hear my voice."

Psalm 55:17

"What time I am afraid, I will trust in thee."

Psalm 56:3

"Trust in him at all times; ye people, pour out your heart before him: God is a refuge for us. Selah."

Psalm 62:8

"O let the nations be glad and sing for joy:"

Psalm 67:4a

"Blessed be the Lord, who daily loadeth us with benefits, even the God of our salvation. Selah."

Psalm 68:19

"I will praise the name of God with a song, and will magnify him with thanksgiving."

Psalm 69:30

"Thou art the God that doest wonders:"

Psalm 77:14a

"For thou, Lord, art good, and ready to forgive; and plenteous in mercy unto all them that call upon thee."

Psalm 86:5

"Before the mountains were brought forth, or ever thou hadst formed the earth and the world, even from everlasting to everlasting, thou art God."

Psalm 90:2

"So teach us to number our days, that we may apply our hearts unto wisdom."

Psalm 90:12

"Thy testimonies are very sure: holiness becometh thine house, O Lord, for ever."

Psalm 93:5

"I will behave myself wisely in a perfect way."

Psalm 101:2a

". . . I will walk within my house with a perfect heart."

Psalm 101:2c

"I will set no wicked thing before mine eyes:"

Psalm 101:3a

"Oh that men would praise the Lord for his goodness, and for his wonderful works to the children of men!"

Psalm 107:8

"I will take the cup of salvation, and call upon the name of the Lord."

Psalm 116:13

"Precious in the sight of the Lord is the death of his saints."

Psalm 116:15

"It is better to trust in the Lord than to put confidence in man."

Psalm 118:8

[This is the halfway point through the Bible.]

"Thy word have I hid in mine heart, that I might not sin against thee."

Psalm 119:11

"Thy word is a lamp unto my feet, and a light unto my path."

Psalm 119:105

"I will lift up mine eyes unto the hills, from whence cometh my help. My help cometh from the Lord, which made heaven and earth."

Psalm 121:1, 2

"Behold, how good and how pleasant it is for brethren to dwell together in unity!"

Psalm 133:1

". . . thou hast covered me in my mother's womb."

Psalm 139:13b

"I will praise thee; for I am fearfully and wonderfully made: marvellous are thy works;"

Psalm 139:14a

"Search me, O God, and know my heart: try me, and know my thoughts: And see if there be any wicked way in me, and lead me in the way everlasting."

Psalm 139:23, 24

"Teach me to do thy will; for thou art my God: thy spirit is good; lead me into the land of uprightness."

Psalm 143:10

". . . happy is that people, whose God is the Lord."

Psalm 144:15b

"The Lord is nigh unto all them that call upon him, to all that call upon him in truth."

Psalm 145:18

"Sing unto the Lord with thanksgiving; sing praise upon the harp unto our God:"

Psalm 147:7

"The Lord taketh pleasure in them that fear him, in those that hope in his mercy."

Psalm 147:11

"For the Lord taketh pleasure in his people: he will beautify the meek with salvation."

Psalm 149:4

"Let every thing that hath breath praise the Lord. Praise ye the Lord."

Psalm 150:6

Proverbs

"In all thy ways acknowledge him, and he shall direct thy paths."

Proverbs 3:6

"The fear of the Lord is the beginning of wisdom:"

Proverbs 9:10a

"Hatred stirreth up strifes: but love covereth all sins."

Proverbs 10:12

"In the multitude of words there wanteth not sin: but he that refraineth his lips is wise."

Proverbs 10:19

"A talebearer revealeth secrets: but he that is of a faithful spirit concealeth the matter."

Proverbs 11:13

"The fruit of the righteous is a tree of life; and he that winneth souls is wise."

Proverbs 11:30

"There is a way which seemeth right unto a man, but the end thereof are the ways of death."

Proverbs 14:12

"Righteousness exalteth a nation: but sin is a reproach to any people."

Proverbs 14:34

"A soft answer turneth away wrath: but grievous words stir up anger."

Proverbs 15:1

"The eyes of the Lord are in every place, beholding the evil and the good."

Proverbs 15:3

"Better is little with the fear of the Lord than great treasure and trouble therewith."

Proverbs 15:16

"The way of life is above to the wise, that he may depart from hell beneath."

Proverbs 15:24

"The Lord is far from the wicked: but he heareth the prayer of the righteous."

Proverbs 15:29

"All the ways of a man are clean in his own eyes; but the Lord weigheth the spirits."

Proverbs 16:2

"Commit thy works unto the Lord, and thy thoughts shall be established."

Proverbs 16:3

"He that handleth a matter wisely shall find good: and whoso trusteth in the Lord, happy is he."

Proverbs 16:20

"A friend loveth at all times, and a brother is born for adversity."

Proverbs 17:17

"He that hath knowledge spareth his words: and a man of understanding is of an excellent spirit."

Proverbs 17:27

"A man that hath friends must shew himself friendly: and there is a friend that sticketh closer than a brother."

Proverbs 18:24

"Wine is a mocker, strong drink is raging: and whosoever is deceived thereby is not wise."

Proverbs 20:1

"Even a child is known by his doings, whether his work be pure, and whether it be right."

Proverbs 20:11

"Whoso keepeth his mouth and his tongue keepeth his soul from troubles."

Proverbs 21:23

"Withhold not correction from the child: for if thou beatest him with the rod, he shall not die. Thou shalt beat him with the rod, and shalt deliver his soul from hell."

Proverbs 23:13, 14

"Who hath woe? who hath sorrow? who hath contentions? who hath babbling? who hath wounds without cause? who hath redness of eyes? They that tarry long at the wine; they that go to seek mixed wine."

Proverbs 23:29, 30

"He that covereth his sins shall not prosper: but whoso confesseth and forsaketh them shall have mercy."

Proverbs 28:13

"He that giveth unto the poor shall not lack: but he that hideth his eyes shall have many a curse."

Proverbs 28:27

"The rod and reproof give wisdom: but a child left to himself bringeth his mother to shame."

Proverbs 29:15

"Every word of God is pure: he is a shield unto them that put their trust in him."

Proverbs 30:5

"Favour is deceitful, and beauty is vain: but a woman that feareth the Lord, she shall be praised."

Proverbs 31:30

Ecclesiastes

"Be not rash with thy mouth, and let not thine heart be hasty to utter any thing before God: for God is in heaven, and thou upon earth: therefore let thy words be few."

Ecclesiastes 5:2

".. . and the patient in spirit is better than the proud in spirit:"

Ecclesiastes 7:8b

"And so I saw the wicked buried, who had come and gone from the place of the holy, and they were forgotten in the city where they had so done:"

Ecclesiastes 8:10a

"Whatsoever thy hand findeth to do, do it with thy might;"

Ecclesiastes 9:10a

"Cast thy bread upon the waters: for thou shalt find it after many days."

Ecclesiastes 11:1

"Remember now thy Creator in the days of thy youth . . ."

Ecclesiastes 12:1a

".. . Fear God, and keep his commandments: for this is the whole duty of man."

Ecclesiastes 12:13b

"For God shall bring every work into judgment, with every secret thing, whether it be good, or whether it be evil."

Ecclesiastes 12:14

Song of Solomon

".. . jealously is cruel as the grave: the coals thereof are coals of fire, which hath a most vehement flame."

Song of Solomon 8:6c

Isaiah

"Come now, and let us reason together, saith the Lord: though your sins be as scarlet, they shall be as white as snow; though they be red like crimson, they shall be as wool."

Isaiah 1:18

"Woe unto them that are mighty to drink wine, and men of strength to mingle strong drink:"

Isaiah 5:22

"Also I heard the voice of the Lord, saying, Whom shall I send, and who will go for us? Then said I, Here am I; send me."

Isaiah 6:8

".. . Behold, a virgin shall conceive, and bear a son, and shall call his name Immanuel."

Isaiah 7:14b

"At that day shall a man look to his Maker, and his eyes shall have respect to the Holy One of Israel."

Isaiah 17:7

"O Lord, thou art my God; I will exalt thee, I will praise thy name; for thou hast done wonderful things; thy counsels of old are faithfulness and truth."

Isaiah 25:1

"He will swallow up death in victory; and the Lord God will wipe away tears from off all faces;"

Isaiah 25:8a

"Thou wilt keep him in perfect peace, whose mind is stayed on thee: because he trusteth in thee."

Isaiah 26:3

"Trust ye in the Lord for ever: for in the Lord JEHOVAH is everlasting strength:"

Isaiah 26:4

"Ye shall have a song, as in the night when a holy solemnity is kept;"

Isaiah 30:29a

"Thine eyes shall see the king in his beauty: they shall behold the land that is very far off. "

Isaiah 33:17

"Who hath measured the waters in the hollow of his hand, and meted out heaven with the span, and comprehended the dust of the earth in a measure, and weighed the mountains in scales, and the hills in a balance? "

Isaiah 40:12

"Behold, the nations are as a drop of a bucket, and are counted as the small dust of the balance: behold, he taketh up the isles as a very little thing. "

Isaiah 40:15

"It is he that sitteth upon the circle of the earth, and the inhabitants thereof are as grasshoppers; "

Isaiah 40:22a

"Hast thou not known? hast thou not heard, that the everlasting God, the Lord, the Creator of the ends of the earth, fainteth not, neither is weary? there is no searching of his understanding. "

Isaiah 40:28

"But they that wait upon the Lord shall renew their strength; "

Isaiah 40:31a

"Fear thou not: for I am with thee: be not dismayed; for I am thy God: I will strengthen thee; yea, I will help thee; "

Isaiah 41:10a

"I am the Lord: that is my name: and my glory will I not give to another, neither my praise to graven images. "

Isaiah 42:8

"Sing unto the Lord a new song, and his praise from the end of the earth, . . . "

Isaiah 42:10a

"I, even I, am the Lord; and beside me there is no saviour. "

Isaiah 43:11

"I, even I, am he that blotteth out thy transgressions for mine own sake, and will not remember thy sins. "

Isaiah 43:25

"I have blotted out, as a thick cloud, thy transgressions, and, as a cloud, thy sins: return unto me; for I have redeemed thee. "

Isaiah 44:22

"Look unto me, and be ye saved, all the ends of the earth: for I am God, and there is none else. "

Isaiah 45:22

"For the Lord God will help me; therefore shall I not be confounded: therefore have I set my face like a flint, and know that I shall not be ashamed."

Isaiah 50:7

"But he was wounded for our transgressions, he was bruised for our iniquities: the chastisement of our peace was upon him; and with his stripes we are healed."

Isaiah 53:5

"Seek ye the Lord while he may be found, call ye upon him while he is near:"

Isaiah 55:6

"For thus saith the high and lofty One that inhabiteth eternity, whose name is Holy; I dwell in the high and holy place, with him also that is of a contrite and humble spirit, to revive the spirit of the humble, and to revive the heart of the contrite ones."

Isaiah 57:15

"Is not this the fast that I have chosen? to loose the bands of wickedness, to undo the heavy burdens, and to let the oppressed go free, and that ye break every yoke?"

Isaiah 58:6

"Behold, the Lord's hand is not shortened, that it cannot save; neither his ear heavy, that it cannot hear:"

Isaiah 59:1

". . . When the enemy shall come in like a flood, the Spirit of the Lord shall lift up a standard against him."

Isaiah 59:19b

"Behold, my servants shall sing for joy of heart . . ."

Isaiah 65:14a

"And it shall come to pass, that before they call, I will answer; and while they are yet speaking, I will hear."

Isaiah 65:24

Jeremiah

". . . Obey my voice, and I will be your God, and ye shall be my people: and walk ye in all the ways that I have commanded you, that it may be well unto you."

Jeremiah 7:23b

"I the Lord search the heart, I try the reins, even to give every man according to his ways, and according to the fruit of his doings."

Jeremiah 17:10

"If that nation, against whom I have pronounced, turn from their evil, I will repent of the evil that I thought to do unto them."

Jeremiah 18:8

"Can any hide himself in secret places that I shall not see him? saith the Lord."

Jeremiah 23:24a

"And I will give them an heart to know me, that I am the Lord: and they shall be my people, and I will be their God: for they shall return unto me with their whole heart."

Jeremiah 24:7

"And ye shall seek me, and find me, when ye shall search for me with all your heart."

Jeremiah 29:13

"Ah Lord God! behold, thou hast made the heaven and the earth by thy great power and stretched out arm, and there is nothing too hard for thee:"

Jeremiah 32:17

"Behold, I am the Lord, the God of all flesh: is there any thing too hard for me?"

Jeremiah 32:27

"Call unto me, and I will answer thee, and shew thee great and mighty things, which thou knowest not."

Jeremiah 33:3

Lamentations

". . . great is thy faithfulness."

Lamentations 3:23b

"The Lord is good unto them that wait for him, to the soul that seeketh him."

Lamentations 3:25

"Let us search and try our ways, and turn again to the Lord."

Lamentations 3:40

"O Lord, thou hast pleaded the causes of my soul; thou hast redeemed my life."

Lamentations 3:58

Ezekiel

"The soul that sinneth, it shall die."

Ezekiel 18:20a

"When the righteous turneth from his righteousness, and committeth iniquity, he shall even die thereby."

Ezekiel 33:18

Daniel

". . . but the people that do know their God shall be strong, and do exploits."

Daniel 11:32b

"Many shall be purified, and made white, and tried;"

Daniel 12:10a

Hosea

"I will heal their backsliding, I will love them freely:"

Hosea 14:4a

Joel

"Multitudes, multitudes in the valley of decision: for the day of the Lord is near in the valley of decision."

Joel 3:14

Amos

"Can two walk together, except they be agreed?"

Amos 3:3

". . . prepare to meet thy God . . ."

Amos 4:12b

"Woe to them that are at ease in Zion . . ."

Amos 6:1a

Obadiah

"But upon mount Zion shall be deliverance, and there shall be holiness . . ."

Obadiah 1:17a

Jonah

". . . I will pay that that I have vowed. Salvation is of the Lord."

Jonah 2:9b

Micah

". . . and what doth the Lord require of thee, but to do justly, and to love mercy, and to walk humbly with thy God?"

Micah 6:8b

". . . I will look unto the Lord; I will wait for the God of my salvation: my God will hear me."

Micah 7:7

"Who is a God like unto thee, that pardoneth iniquity, and passeth by the transgression of the remnant of his heritage? he retaineth not his anger for ever, because he delighteth in mercy."

Micah 7:18

". . . and thou wilt cast all their sins into the depths of the sea."

Micah 7:19c

Nahum

"The Lord is good, a strong hold in the day of trouble; and he knoweth them that trust in him."

Nahum 1:7

Habakkuk

". . . but the just shall live by his faith."

Habakkuk 2:4b

Zephaniah

"The Lord thy God in the midst of thee is mighty; he will save, he will rejoice over thee with joy;"

Zephaniah 3:17a

Haggai

"Thus saith the Lord of hosts; Consider your ways."

Haggai 1:7

Zechariah

". . . Not by might, nor by power, but by my spirit, saith the Lord of hosts."

Zechariah 4:6b

". . . they shall call on my name, and I will hear them: I will say, It is my people: and they shall say, The Lord is my God."

Zechariah 13:9b

Malachi

"And I will come near to you to judgment; and I will be a swift witness against the sorcerers, and against the adulterers, and against false swearers, and against those that oppress the hireling in his wages, the widow, and the fatherless, and that turn aside the stranger from his right, and fear not me, saith the Lord of hosts."

Malachi 3:5

"For I am the Lord, I change not;"

Malachi 3:6a

"Will a man rob God? Yet ye have robbed me. But ye say, Wherein have we robbed thee? In tithes and offerings."

Malachi 3:8

"Bring ye all the tithes into the storehouse, that there may be meat in mine house, and prove me now herewith, saith the Lord of hosts, if I will not open you the windows of heaven, and pour you out a blessing, that there shall not be room enough to receive it."

Malachi 3:10

Matthew

"Blessed are they which are persecuted for righteousness' sake: for theirs is the kingdom of heaven."

Matthew 5:10

"Lay not up for yourselves treasures upon earth, where moth and rust doth corrupt, and where thieves break through and steal:"

Matthew 6:19

"But lay up for yourselves treasures in heaven, where neither moth nor rust doth corrupt, and where thieves do not break through nor steal:"

Matthew 6:20

"Judge not, that ye be not judged."

Matthew 7:1

Golden Rule of the Bible:

"Therefore all things whatsoever ye would that men should do to you, do ye even so to them:"

Matthew 7:12a

"Enter ye in at the strait gate: for wide is the gate, and broad is the way, that leadeth to destruction, and many there be which go in thereat: Because strait is the gate, and narrow is the way, which leadeth unto life, and few there be that find it."

Matthew 7:13, 14

". . . According to your faith be it unto you."

Matthew 9:29b

". . . there is nothing covered, that shall not be revealed; and hid, that shall not be known."

Matthew 10:26b

"But the very hairs of your head are all numbered."

Matthew 10:30

"But I say unto you, That every idle word that men shall speak, they shall give account thereof in the day of judgment."

Matthew 12:36

". . . If any man will come after me, let him deny himself, and take up his cross, and follow me."

Matthew 16:24b

"Again I say unto you, That if two of you shall agree on earth as touching any thing that they shall ask, it shall be done for them of my Father which is in heaven."

Matthew 18:19

"For where two or three are gathered together in my name, there am I in the midst of them."

Matthew 18:20

". . . What therefore God hath joined together, let not man put asunder."

Matthew 19:6b

". . . With men this is impossible; but with God all things are possible."

Matthew 19:26b

"And all things, whatsoever ye shall ask in prayer, believing, ye shall receive."

Matthew 21:22

"Watch therefore: for ye know not what hour your Lord doth come."

Matthew 24:42

"Watch and pray, that ye enter not into temptation:"

Matthew 26:41a

Mark

"For there is nothing hid, which shall not be manifested;"

Mark 4:22a

"... Be not afraid, only believe."

Mark 5:36c

"... Whosoever will come after me, let him deny himself, and take up his cross, and follow me."

Mark 8:34b

"For what shall it profit a man, if he shall gain the whole world, and lose his own soul?"

Mark 8:36

"Or what shall a man give in exchange for his soul?"

Mark 8:37

"Jesus said unto him, If thou canst believe, all things are possible to him that believeth."

Mark 9:23

"... What things soever ye desire, when ye pray, believe that ye receive them, and ye shall have them."

Mark 11:24

"... Go ye into all the world, and preach the gospel to every creature."

Mark 16:15

Luke

"For with God nothing shall be impossible."

Luke 1:37

"For every tree is known by his own fruit."

Luke 6:44a

"... for he that is least among you all, the same shall be great."

Luke 9:48c

"... blessed are they that hear the word of God, and keep it."

Luke 11:28b

"For there is nothing covered, that shall not be revealed; neither hid, that shall not be known."

Luke 12:2

"Therefore whatsoever ye have spoken in darkness shall be heard in the light; and that which ye have spoken in the ear in closets shall be proclaimed upon the housetops."

Luke 12:3

"But even the very hairs of your head are all numbered."

Luke 12:7a

"... Take heed, and beware of covetousness: for a man's life consisteth not in the abundance of the things which he possesseth."

Luke 12:15

"So is he that layeth up treasure for himself, and is not rich toward God."

Luke 12:21

"For where your treasure is, there will your heart be also."

Luke 12:34

"Be ye therefore ready also: for the Son of man cometh at an hour when ye think not."

Luke 12:40

". . . The things which are impossible with men are possible with God."

Luke 18:27

John

"But as many as received him, to them gave he power to become the sons of God, even to them that believe on his name:"

John 1:12

"Marvel not that I said unto thee, Ye must be born again."

John 3:7

Golden text of the Bible:

"For God so loved the world, that he gave his only begotten Son, that whosoever believeth in him should not perish, but have everlasting life."

John 3:16

"Search the scriptures;"

John 5:39a

". . . and him that cometh to me I will in no wise cast out."

John 6:37b

"Verily, verily, I say unto you, He that believeth on me hath everlasting life."

John 6:47

"Judge not according to the appearance, but judge righteous judgment."

John 7:24

". . . Jesus stood and cried, saying, If any man thirst, let him come unto me, and drink."

John 7:37b

". . . Jesus said unto her, Neither do I condemn thee: go, and sin no more."

John 8:11b

"Jesus said unto her, I am the resurrection, and the life: he that believeth in me, though he were dead, yet shall he live:"

John 11:25

"And I, if I be lifted up from the earth, will draw all men unto me."

John 12:32

"I am come a light into the world, that whosoever believeth on me should not abide in darkness."

John 12:46

"A new commandment I give unto you, That ye love one another;"

John 13:34a

"By this shall all men know that ye are my disciples, if ye have love one to another."

John 13:35

"Jesus saith unto him, I am the way, the truth, and the life: no man cometh unto the Father, but by me."

John 14:6

"If ye shall ask any thing in my name, I will do it."

John 14:14

"If ye love me, keep my commandments."

John 14:15

"Hitherto have ye asked nothing in my name: ask, and ye shall receive, that your joy may be full."

John 16:24

"I have given them thy word; and the world hath hated them, because they are not of the world, even as I am not of the world."

John 17:14

"But these are written, that ye might believe that Jesus is the Christ, the Son of God; and that believing ye might have life through his name."

John 20:31

Acts

"But ye shall receive power, after that the Holy Ghost is come upon you: and ye shall be witnesses unto me both in Jerusalem, and in all Judea, and in Samaria, and unto the uttermost part of the earth."

Acts 1:8

"Repent ye therefore, and be converted, that your sins may be blotted out, when the times of refreshing shall come from the presence of the Lord;"

Acts 3:19

"Neither is there salvation in any other: for there is none other name under heaven given among men, whereby we must be saved."

Acts 4:12

". . . We ought to obey God rather than men."

Acts 5:29b

"But if it be of God, ye cannot overthrow it; lest haply ye be found even to fight against God."

Acts 5:39

". . . Of a truth I perceive that God is no respecter of persons: But in every nation he that feareth him, and worketh righteousness, is accepted with him."

Acts 10:34b, 35

"And herein do I exercise myself, to have always a conscience void of offense toward God, and toward men."

Acts 24:16

"Then Agrippa said unto Paul, Almost thou persuadest me to be a Christian."

Acts 26:28

Romans

"For I am not ashamed of the gospel of Christ: for it is the power of God unto salvation to every one that believeth;"

Romans 1:16a

". . . The just shall live by faith."

Romans 1:17c

"For the wrath of God is revealed from heaven against all ungodliness and unrighteousness of men, who hold the truth in unrighteousness;"

Romans 1:18

"Wherefore God also gave them up to uncleanness through the lusts of their own hearts, to dishonour their own bodies between themselves:"

Romans 1:24

"Who changed the truth of God into a lie, and worshipped and served the creature more than the Creator, who is blessed for ever. Amen."

Romans 1:25

"For this cause God gave them up unto vile affections: for even their women did change the natural use into that which is against nature:"

Romans 1:26

"And likewise also the men, leaving the natural use of the woman, burned in their lust one toward another; men with men working that which is unseemly, and receiving in themselves that recompence of their error which was meet."

Romans 1:27

"For there is no respect of persons with God."

Romans 2:11

"For all have sinned, and come short of the glory of God;"

Romans 3:23

". . . Blessed are they whose iniquities are forgiven, and whose sins are covered."

Romans 4:7

"For the wages of sin is death; but the gift of God is eternal life through Jesus Christ our Lord."

Romans 6:23

". . . If God be for us, who can be against us?"

Romans 8:31b

"For whosoever shall call upon the name of the Lord shall be saved."

Romans 10:13

"And be not conformed to this world:"

Romans 12:2a

"Be kindly affectioned one to another with brotherly love; in honour preferring one another;"

Romans 12:10

"Rejoicing in hope; patient in tribulation; continuing instant in prayer;"

Romans 12:12

"Love worketh no ill to his neighbour:"

Romans 13:10a

"For none of us liveth to himself, and no man dieth to himself."

Romans 14:7

". . . for we shall all stand before the judgment seat of Christ."

Romans 14:10c

"For it is written, As I live, saith the Lord, every knee shall bow to me, and every tongue shall confess to God."

Romans 14:11

"So then every one of us shall give account of himself to God."

Romans 14:12

"Let us not therefore judge one another any more: but judge this rather, that no man put a stumblingblock or an occasion to fall in his brother's way."

Romans 14:13

I Corinthians

". . . He that glorieth, let him glory in the Lord."

I Corinthians 1:31b

"That your faith should not stand in the wisdom of men, but in the power of God."

I Corinthians 2:5

". . . Eye hath not seen, nor ear heard, neither have entered into the heart of man, the things which God hath prepared for them that love him."

I Corinthians 2:9

"For other foundation can no man lay than that is laid, which is Jesus Christ."

I Corinthians 3:11

". . . and the fire shall try every man's work of what sort it is."

I Corinthians 3:13c

". . . but ye are washed, but ye are sanctified, but ye are justified in the name of the Lord Jesus, and by the Spirit of our God."

I Corinthians 6:11b

"What? know ye not that your body is the temple of the Holy Ghost which is in you, which ye have of God, and ye are not your own?"

I Corinthians 6:19

"There hath no temptation taken you but such as is common to man: but God is faithful, who will not suffer you to be tempted above that ye are able; but will with the temptation also make a way to escape, that ye may be able to bear it."

I Corinthians 10:13

II Corinthians

"For our light affliction, which is but for a moment, worketh for us a far more exceeding and eternal weight of glory;"

II Corinthians 4:17

"For we know that if our earthly house of this tabernacle were dissolved, we have a building of God, an house not made with hands, eternal in the heavens."

II Corinthians 5:1

"For we must all appear before the judgment seat of Christ; that every one may receive the things done in his body, according to that he hath done, whether it be good or bad."

II Corinthians 5:10

"Therefore if any man be in Christ, he is a new creature: old things are passed away; behold, all things are become new."

II Corinthians 5:17

"Be ye not unequally yoked together with unbelievers:"

II Corinthians 6:14a

". . . God loveth a cheerful giver."

II Corinthians 9:7c

". . . bringing into captivity every thought to the obedience of Christ;"

II Corinthians 10:5c

"And he said unto me, My grace is sufficient for thee: for my strength is made perfect in weakness."

II Corinthians 12:9a

"Examine yourselves, whether ye be in the faith;"

II Corinthians 13:5a

Galatians

"And they that are Christ's have crucified the flesh with the affections and lusts."

Galatians 5:24

". . .for whatsoever a man soweth, that shall he also reap."

Galatians 6:7c

"And let us not be weary in well doing: for in due season we shall reap, if we faint not."

Galatians 6:9

"But God forbid that I should glory, save in the cross of our Lord Jesus Christ, by whom the world is crucified unto me, and I unto the world."

Galatians 6:14

Ephesians

"In whom we have redemption through his blood, the forgiveness of sins, according to the riches of his grace;"

Ephesians 1:7

"But now in Christ Jesus ye who sometimes were far off are made nigh by the blood of Christ."

Ephesians 2:13

". . . let not the sun go down upon your wrath:"

Ephesians 4:26b

"Neither give place to the devil."

Ephesians 4:27

"And grieve not the holy Spirit of God, whereby ye are sealed unto the day of redemption."

Ephesians 4:30

"And be ye kind one to another, tenderhearted, forgiving one another, even as God for Christ's sake hath forgiven you."

Ephesians 4:32

Philippians

"For to me to live is Christ, and to die is gain."

Philippians 1:21

". . . in lowliness of mind let each esteem other better than themselves."

Philippians 2:3b

"That at the name of Jesus every knee should bow . . ."

Philippians 2:10a

"Do all things without murmurings and disputings:"

Philippians 2:14

"Let us therefore, as many as be perfect, be thus minded: and if in any thing ye be otherwise minded, God shall reveal even this unto you."

Philippians 3:15

"Rejoice in the Lord alway:"

Philippians 4:4a

". . . in every thing by prayer and supplication with thanksgiving let your requests be made known unto God."

Philippians 4:6b

". . . whatsoever things are true, whatsoever things are honest, whatsoever things are just, whatsoever things are pure, whatsoever things are lovely, whatsoever things are of good report; if there be any virtue, and if there be any praise, think on these things."

Philippians 4:8

". . . I have learned, in whatsoever state I am, therewith to be content."

Philippians 4:11b

"I can do all things through Christ which strengtheneth me."

Philippians 4:13

"But my God shall supply all your need according to his riches in glory by Christ Jesus."

Philippians 4:19

Colossians

"In whom we have redemption through his blood, even the forgiveness of sins:"

Colossians 1:14

". . . having made peace through the blood of his cross . . ."

Colossians 1:20a

"Set your affection on things above, not on things on the earth."

Colossians 3:2

"And whatsoever ye do, do it heartily, as to the Lord, and not unto men;"

Colossians 3:23

"Continue in prayer, and watch in the same with thanksgiving;"

Colossians 4:2

I Thessalonians

"For God hath not called us unto uncleanness, but unto holiness."

I Thessalonians 4:7

"And that ye study to be quiet, and to do your own business, and to work with your own hands . . ."

I Thessalonians 4:11a

"For the Lord himself shall descend from heaven with a shout, with the voice of the archangel, and with the trump of God: and the dead in Christ shall rise first:"

I Thessalonians 4:16

"Then we which are alive and remain shall be caught up together with them in the clouds, to meet the Lord in the air: and so shall we ever be with the Lord."

I Thessalonians 4:17

"In every thing give thanks: for this is the will of God in Christ Jesus concerning you."

I Thessalonians 5:18

". . . hold fast that which is good."

I Thessalonians 5:21b

"Abstain from all appearance of evil."

I Thessalonians 5:22

"Faithful is he that calleth you, who also will do it."

I Thessalonians 5:24

II Thessalonians

". . . because they received not the love of the truth, that they might be saved."

II Thessalonians 2:10b

"Therefore, brethren, stand fast, and hold the traditions which ye have been taught, whether by word, or our epistle."

II Thessalonians 2:15

"But the Lord is faithful, who shall stablish you, and keep you from evil."

II Thessalonians 3:3

"And the Lord direct your hearts into the love of God, and into the patient waiting for Christ."

II Thessalonians 3:5

". . . be not weary in well doing."

II Thessalonians 3:13

I Timothy

"This is a faithful saying, and worthy of all acceptation, that Christ Jesus came into the world to save sinners; of whom I am chief."

I Timothy 1:15

"For there is one God, and one mediator between God and men, the man Christ Jesus;"

I Timothy 2:5

"But godliness with contentment is great gain."

I Timothy 6:6

"For we brought nothing into this world, and it is certain we can carry nothing out."

I Timothy 6:7

"For the love of money is the root of all evil:"

I Timothy 6:10a

"Charge them that are rich in this world, that they be not highminded, nor trust in uncertain riches, but in the living God, who giveth us richly all things to enjoy;"

I Timothy 6:17

II Timothy

"For God hath not given us the spirit of fear; but of power, and of love, and of a sound mind."

II Timothy 1:7

". . . for I know whom I have believed, and am persuaded that he is able to keep that which I have committed unto him against that day."

II Timothy 1:12c

"And the servant of the Lord must not strive; but be gentle unto all men, apt to teach, patient,"

II Timothy 2:24

"Having a form of godliness, but denying the power thereof: from such turn away."

II Timothy 3:5

"Yea, and all that will live godly in Christ Jesus shall suffer persecution."

II Timothy 3:12

Titus

"Teaching us that, denying ungodliness and worldly lusts, we should live soberly, righteously, and godly, in this present world;"

Titus 2:12

"Looking for that blessed hope, and the glorious appearing of the great God and our Saviour Jesus Christ;"

Titus 2:13

"Who gave himself for us, that he might redeem us from all iniquity, and purify unto himself a peculiar people, zealous of good works."

Titus 2:14

"To speak evil of no man . . ."

Titus 3:2a

Philemon

"I thank my God, making mention of thee always in my prayers,"

Philemon 1:4

Hebrews

"How shall we escape, if we neglect so great salvation;"

Hebrews 2:3a

"Take heed, brethren, lest there be in any of you an evil heart of unbelief, in departing from the living God."

Hebrews 3:12

"There remaineth therefore a rest to the people of God."

Hebrews 4:9

"For the word of God is quick, and powerful, and sharper than any twoedged sword . . . and is a discerner of the thoughts and intents of the heart."

Hebrews 4:12

"For we have not an high priest which cannot be touched with the feeling of our infirmities; but was in all points tempted like as we are, yet without sin."

Hebrews 4:15

"Let us therefore come boldly unto the throne of grace, that we may obtain mercy, and find grace to help in time of need."

Hebrews 4:16

"And being made perfect, he became the author of eternal salvation unto all them that obey him;"

Hebrews 5:9

"Which hope we have as an anchor of the soul, both sure and steadfast . . ."

Hebrews 6:19a

"By so much was Jesus made a surety of a better testament."

Hebrews 7:22

"Wherefore he is able also to save them to the uttermost that come unto God by him, seeing he ever liveth to make intercession for them."

Hebrews 7:25

". . . We have such an high priest, who is set on the right hand of the throne of the Majesty in the heavens;"

Hebrews 8:1b

"... by his own blood he entered in once into the holy place, having obtained eternal redemption for us."

Hebrews 9:12b

"And almost all things are by the law purged with blood; and without shedding of blood is no remission."

Hebrews 9:22

"For Christ is not entered into the holy places made with hands, which are the figures of the true; but into heaven itself, now to appear in the presence of God for us:"

Hebrews 9:24

"And as it is appointed unto men once to die, but after this the judgment:"

Hebrews 9:27

"Let us hold fast the profession of our faith without wavering; (for he is faithful that promised;)"

Hebrews 10:23

"Not forsaking the assembling of ourselves together, as the manner of some is;"

Hebrews 10:25a

"It is a fearful thing to fall into the hands of the living God."

Hebrews 10:31

"Now the just shall live by faith: but if any man draw back, my soul shall have no pleasure in him."

Hebrews 10:38

"But without faith it is impossible to please him: for he that cometh to God must believe that he is, and that he is a rewarder of them that diligently seek him."

Hebrews 11:6

"Follow peace with all men, and holiness, without which no man shall see the Lord:"

Hebrews 12:14

"... and be content with such things as ye have: for he hath said, I will never leave thee, nor forsake thee."

Hebrews 13:5b

"Jesus Christ the same yesterday, and to day, and for ever."

Hebrews 13:8

"By him therefore let us offer the sacrifice of praise to God continually, that is, the fruit of our lips giving thanks to his name."

Hebrews 13:15

James

"If any of you lack wisdom, let him ask of God, that giveth to all men liberally, and upbraideth not; and it shall be given him."

James 1:5

"But let him ask in faith, nothing wavering."

James 1:6a

"Blessed is the man that endureth temptation: for when he is tried, he shall receive the crown of life, which the Lord hath promised to them that love him."

James 1:12

"... and receive with meekness the engrafted word, which is able to save your souls."

James 1:21b

". . . If any man offend not in word, the same is a perfect man, and able also to bridle the whole body."

James 3:2b

". . . yet ye have not, because ye ask not."

James 4:2c

"Be ye also patient; stablish your hearts: for the coming of the Lord draweth nigh."

James 5:8

"Grudge not one against another . . ."

James 5:9a

"Confess your faults one to another, and pray one for another, that ye may be healed. The effectual fervent prayer of a righteous man availeth much."

James 5:16

I Peter

"But as he which hath called you is holy, so be ye holy in all manner of conversation;"

I Peter 1:15

"Seeing ye have purified your souls in obeying the truth through the Spirit unto unfeigned love of the brethren, see that ye love one another with a pure heart fervently:"

I Peter 1:22

"Being born again, not of corruptible seed, but of incorruptible, by the word of God, which liveth and abideth for ever."

I Peter 1:23

". . . love as brethren, be pitiful, be courteous:"

I Peter 3:8c

"For the eyes of the Lord are over the righteous, and his ears are open unto their prayers: but the face of the Lord is against them that do evil."

I Peter 3:12

"But the end of all things is at hand: be ye therefore sober, and watch unto prayer."

I Peter 4:7

"Use hospitality one to another without grudging."

I Peter 4:9

"And if the righteous scarcely be saved, where shall the ungodly and the sinner appear?"

I Peter 4:18

"Wherefore let them that suffer according to the will of God commit the keeping of their souls to him in well doing, as unto a faithful Creator."

I Peter 4:19

"Casting all your care upon him; for he careth for you."

I Peter 5:7

"But the God of all grace, who hath called us unto his eternal glory by Christ Jesus, after that ye have suffered a while, make you perfect, stablish, strengthen, settle you."

I Peter 5:10

II Peter

"Knowing this first, that no prophecy of the scripture is of any private interpretation."

II Peter 1:20

"The Lord knoweth how to deliver the godly out of temptations, and to reserve the unjust unto the day of judgment to be punished:"

II Peter 2:9

"Seeing then that all these things shall be dissolved, what manner of persons ought ye to be in all holy conversation and godliness,"

II Peter 3:11

". . . be diligent that ye may be found of him in peace, without spot, and blameless."

II Peter 3:14b

I John

"But if we walk in the light, as he is in the light, we have fellowship one with another, and the blood of Jesus Christ his Son cleanseth us from all sin."

I John 1:7

"If we confess our sins, he is faithful and just to forgive us our sins, and to cleanse us from all unrighteousness."

I John 1:9

"And hereby we do know that we know him, if we keep his commandments."

I John 2:3

"Love not the world, neither the things that are in the world. If any man love the world, the love of the Father is not in him:"

I John 2:15

"And the world passeth away, and the lust thereof: but he that doeth the will of God abideth for ever."

I John 2:17

"And this is the promise that he hath promised us, even eternal life."

I John 2:25

"He that committeth sin is of the devil;"

I John 3:8a

"Whosoever is born of God doth not commit sin;"

I John 3:9a

"And whatsoever we ask, we receive of him, because we keep his commandments, and do those things that are pleasing in his sight."

I John 3:22

"And this is his commandment, That we should believe on the name of his Son Jesus Christ, and love one another, as he gave us commandment."

I John 3:23

". . . God is love."

I John 4:8b

". . . if God so loved us, we ought also to love one another."

I John 4:11

". . . perfect love casteth out fear:"

I John 4:18b

". . . and this is the victory that overcometh the world, even our faith."

I John 5:4b

"... if we ask any thing according to his will, he heareth us:"

I John 5:14b

"And if we know that he hear us, whatsoever we ask, we know that we have the petitions that we desired of him."

I John 5:15

"We know that whosoever is born of God sinneth not; but he that is begotten of God keepeth himself, and that wicked one toucheth him not."

I John 5:18

II John

"... not as though I wrote a new commandment unto thee, but that which we had from the beginning, that we love one another."

II John 1:5b

"And this is love, that we walk after his commandments."

II John 1:6a

III John

"Beloved, follow not that which is evil, but that which is good."

III John 1:11a

"... He that doeth good is of God: but he that doeth evil hath not seen God."

III John 1:11b

Jude

"... that ye should earnestly contend for the faith which was once delivered unto the saints."

Jude 1:3c

"Keep yourselves in the love of God, looking for the mercy of our Lord Jesus Christ unto eternal life."

Jude 1:21

"Now unto him that is able to keep you from falling, and to present you faultless before the presence of his glory with exceeding joy, To the only wise God our Saviour, be glory and majesty, dominion and power, both now and ever. Amen."

Jude 1:24, 25

Revelation

"... Unto him that loved us, and washed us from our sins in his own blood,"

Revelation 1:5b

"I was in the Spirit on the Lord's day . . . "

Revelation 1:10a

"Remember therefore from whence thou art fallen, and repent, and do the first works;"

Revelation 2:5a

"... be thou faithful unto death, and I will give thee a crown of life."

Revelation 2:10d

"He that overcometh, the same shall be clothed in white raiment; and I will not blot out his name out of the book of life, but I will confess his name before my Father, and before his angels."

Revelation 3:5

"Behold, I stand at the door, and knock: if any man hear my voice, and open the door, I will come in to him, and will sup with him, and he with me."

Revelation 3:20

". . . and golden vials full of odours, which are the prayers of saints."

Revelation 5:8c

". . . and God shall wipe away all tears from their eyes."

Revelation 7:17c

". . . that he should offer it with the prayers of all saints upon the golden altar which was before the throne."

Revelation 8:3c

"And the smoke of the incense, which came with the prayers of the saints, ascended up before God out of the angel's hand."

Revelation 8:4

"And they overcame him by the blood of the Lamb, and by the word of their testimony;"

Revelation 12:11a

". . . Blessed are the dead which die in the Lord from henceforth: Yea, saith the Spirit, that they may rest from their labours; and their works do follow them."

Revelation 14:13b

"And I saw the dead, small and great, stand before God; and the books were opened:"

Revelation 20:12a

"And whosoever was not found written in the book of life was cast into the lake of fire."

Revelation 20:15

"And God shall wipe away all tears from their eyes; and there shall be no more death, neither sorrow, nor crying, neither shall there be any more pain:"

Revelation 21:4a

". . . I am Alpha and Omega, the beginning and the end. I will give unto him that is athirst of the fountain of the water of life freely."

Revelation 21:6b

"He that overcometh shall inherit all things; and I will be his God, and he shall be my son."

Revelation 21:7

"But the fearful, and unbelieving, and the abominable, and murderers, and whoremongers, and sorcerers, and idolaters, and all liars, shall have their part in the lake which burneth with fire and brimstone:"

Revelation 21:8a

"And the building of the wall of it was of jasper: and the city was pure gold, like unto clear glass."

Revelation 21:18

"And the twelve gates were twelve pearls; every several gate was of one pearl: and the street of the city was pure gold, as it were transparent glass."

Revelation 21:21

"And the city had no need of the sun, neither of the moon, to shine in it: for the glory of God did lighten it, and the Lamb is the light thereof."

Revelation 21:23

"And the gates of it shall not be shut at all by day: for there shall be no night there."

Revelation 21:25

"And there shall in no wise enter into it any thing that defileth, neither whatsoever worketh abomination, or maketh a lie: but they which are written in the Lamb's book of life."

Revelation 21:27

"And they shall see his face; and his name shall be in their foreheads."

Revelation 22:4

"And there shall be no night there; and they need no candle, neither light of the sun; for the Lord God giveth them light: and they shall reign for ever and ever."

Revelation 22:5

"Behold, I come quickly: blessed is he that keepeth the sayings of the prophecy of this book."

Revelation 22:7

"And, behold, I come quickly; and my reward is with me, to give every man according as his work shall be."

Revelation 22:12

"Blessed are they that do his commandments, that they may have right to the tree of life, and may enter in through the gates into the city."

Revelation 22:14

"I Jesus have sent mine angel to testify unto you these things in the churches. I am the root and the offspring of David, and the bright and morning star."

Revelation 22:16

"And the Spirit and the bride say, Come. And let him that heareth say, Come. And let him that is athirst come. And whosoever will, let him take the water of life freely."

Revelation 22:17

"He which testifieth these things saith, Surely I come quickly. Amen. Even so, come, Lord Jesus."

Revelation 22:20

"The grace of our Lord Jesus Christ be with you all. Amen."

Revelation 22:21

THE END

Chapter 3

Equivalents, Substitutions & Strange Recipes

ANNA LIMBER STEVENSON

1916

EQUIVALENTS, SUBSTITUTIONS & STRANGE RECIPES

EQUIVALENT MEASURES

A pinch or a dash	=	about $\frac{1}{16}$ teaspoon
1 tablespoon	=	3 teaspoons or $\frac{1}{2}$ fluid ounce
2 tablespoons	=	$\frac{1}{8}$ cup or 1 fluid ounce
4 tablespoons	=	$\frac{1}{4}$ cup or 2 fluid ounces
5 tablespoons + 1 tsp.	=	$\frac{1}{3}$ cup
8 tablespoons	=	$\frac{1}{2}$ cup or 4 fluid ounces
12 tablespoons	=	$\frac{3}{4}$ cup
14 tablespoons	=	$\frac{7}{8}$ cup or $\frac{3}{4}$ cup + 2 tablespoons
16 tablespoons	=	1 cup or 8 fluid ounces
2 cups	=	1 pint
2 pints	=	1 quart
4 cups	=	1 quart
4 quarts (liquid)	=	1 gallon (liquid)
8 quarts	=	1 peck (dry or solid)
4 pecks	=	1 bushel
1 liter	=	1.06 quarts (liquid) or 1 qt. + $\frac{1}{4}$ cup
1 jigger	=	3 tablespoons or $1\frac{1}{2}$ fluid ounces
1 pony	=	2 tablespoons or 1 ounce
1 wineglass	=	$\frac{1}{4}$ cup
1 gill	=	$\frac{1}{2}$ cup

CAN SIZES

4 ounce can	=	$\frac{1}{2}$ cup
6 ounce can	=	$\frac{3}{4}$ cup or 6 fluid ounces
8 ounce can	=	1 cup (also called buffet can)
#211 can	=	$1\frac{1}{2}$ cup (12 ounce can)

#300 can	=	1¾ cup (14 to 16 ounce can)
#303 can	=	2 cups (16 to 17 ounce can)
#2 can	=	2½ cups (1 lb. 4 oz. can)
#2½ can	=	3½ cups (1 lb. 13 oz. can)
46 oz. can	=	5¾ cups
#10 can	=	12 to 13 cups (6½ to 6¾ lb. can)

PAN SIZES

8-inch round pan	=	50.27 square inches
8 x 8-inch square pan	=	64 square inches
9-inch round pan	=	63.62 square inches
7 x 11-inch pan	=	77 square inches
10-inch round pan	=	78.6 square inches
9 x 9-inch square pan	=	81 square inches
11-inch round pan	=	95 square inches
10 x 10-inch square pan	=	100 square inches
12-inch round pan	=	113.1 square inches
9 x 13-inch pan	=	117 square inches
12 x 12-inch square pan	=	144 square inches
10 x 15-inch jellyroll pan	=	150 square inches
11 x 15-inch cookie sheet	=	165 square inches
11 x 17-inch pan	=	187 square inches
12 x 18-inch pan	=	216 square inches

ALCOHOLIC BEVERAGE SUBSTITUTIONS

Beer	= apple juice
Brandy, 2 tablespoons	= 2 tablespoons vanilla
Bourbon, 3 tablespoons	= 1 to 2 teaspoons vanilla
Bourbon, ½ cup	= ¼ c. unsweetened fruit juice or broth
Creme de cassis liqueur, 2 T.	= 2 tablespoons cranberry juice

Creme de menthe, 1 T.	= 4 to 6 drops peppermint flavor extract and 1 to 2 drops green food color
Creme de menthe, 2 T.	= 2 tablespoons melted mint jelly
Creme de menthe, white, 2 T.	= ⅛ teaspoon peppermint extract
Creme de menthe, green, 2 T.	= 1 T. water, ¾ tsp. mint extract and 3 drops green food color
Creme de menthe liqueur, 3 T.	= ¼ tsp. pure peppermint extract
Grand Marnier liqueur	= orange juice or lemon juice
Kahlua, ⅓ cup	= 2 T. hot water, ¼ c. instant coffee granules and ¼ c. corn syrup
Kirsch, ¼ cup	= 1 T. almond extract and 3 T. water
Kirsch, 1½ teaspoons	= ¼ tsp. almond extract
Kirsch, 1 tablespoon	= 1 tsp. almond extract + 1 tsp. vanilla extract
Orange liqueur, 1 tablespoon	= 1 T. orange juice
Rum, ¼ cup	= 1 tsp. vanilla flavoring
Rum, ½ cup	= ¼ c. unsweetened fruit juice or broth
Rum, light, ⅔ cup	= ⅔ c. water and 1 tsp. rum extract
Rum, light, 2 tablespoons	= ½ tsp. imitation rum extract
Rum, 2 tablespoons	= 1 tsp. imitation rum extract
Rum, 1 tablespoon	= 1 T. orange juice
Rum flavoring, 1 tablespoon	= 1 tsp. vanilla
Sherry	= orange pop
Sherry, dry	= orange juice
Whiskey, ½ cup	= ¼ c. unsweetened fruit juice or broth
Wine, red, ½ cup	= ½ c. unsweetened grape juice, orange juice or broth (recipe may need less sugar)
Wine, white (or dry white), ½ cup	= ½ c. apple juice, white grape juice, 7-Up, orange juice or broth (recipe may need less sugar)

EQUIVALENTS AND SUBSTITUTIONS (A TO Z)

—A—

Allspice	= ½ tsp. cinnamon and ⅛ tsp. ground cloves
Almonds, 1¼ lb. in shell	= 1 to 1¾ c. nutmeats
Almonds, 1 lb. shelled	= 3½ c. nutmeats
Apple, 1 medium	= 1 cup, sliced
Apples, 1 lb.	= 4 small or 3 medium or 2 large apples
Apples, 1 lb.	= 3 c., peeled and diced
Apples, 1½ lbs.	= 5 c., peeled and sliced
Apples, 1¾ lbs.	= 6 c., peeled and sliced
Applesauce, 1 (16-oz.) can	= 1 c. liquid in gelatin recipes

—B—

Baking powder, 1 tsp.　　= ¼ tsp. baking soda + ½ tsp. cream of tartar

Bananas, 3 large　　= 1¼ cups

Bananas, 1 lb.　　= 3 medium or 2 large (1 c. mashed)

Basil, ¼ c. chopped fresh　　= 2 T. dried basil

Beans, dry, 1 c.　　= 2½ to 3 c. cooked

Beans, kidney, dry, 1 lb.　　= 2½ c. uncooked or 6 c. cooked

Beans, lima, dry, 1 lb.　　= 2⅓ to 3 c. uncooked or 6 to 7 c. cooked

Beans, navy, dry, 1 lb.　　= 2 to 2¼ c. uncooked or 6 c. cooked

Beans, 1 (16-oz.) can　　= 2 c. cooked

Beef, ground, 1 lb.　　= 2 cups

Biscuit mix, 1 c.　　= 1 c. flour, 1½ tsp. baking powder, ½ tsp. salt and 1 T. shortening

Bread crumbs, ¼ c. fine dry　　= ¾ c. soft bread crumbs

Bread crumbs, ½ c. soft　　= 1 slice bread, approximately

Bread crumbs, 1 c. fine dry　　= ¾ c. cracker crumbs, cereal or rolled oats

Broccoli, 1 bunch　　= 1½ lbs. or 1 (20-oz.) pkg. frozen broccoli

Brown sugar, 1 c.　　= 1 c. white sugar + 2 tsp. molasses

Butter, 1 T.　　= 2 tsp. vegetable oil

Butter, 2 T.　　= 1 oz.

Butter, 1 c.　　= 1 c. shortening and ½ tsp. salt

Butter, 1 c.　　= ¾ c. olive oil

Butter, 1 lb.　　= 2 cups

Butter, ¾ stick　　= 6 tablespoons

Buttermilk, 1 c.　　= 1 c. sour milk or plain yogurt

Buttermilk, 1 c.　　= 1 c. sweet milk + 1 T. vinegar or lemon juice

—C—

Cabbage, 1 large head　　= about 2½ lbs.

Cabbage, 1 lb.　　= about 4 c. shredded

Cake flour, 1 c. sifted　　= 1 c. minus 2 T. all-purpose flour

Candied fruit, 8 oz.　　= 1 cup

Catsup, 1 c.　　= 1 c. tomato sauce, ½ c. sugar and 2 T. vinegar

Carrots, 1 lb.　　= 3 c. shredded or 2½ c. diced

Celery, ½ c. fresh　　= 2 T. dried celery leaves

Cheese, 4 oz. (¼ lb.)　　= 1 c. shredded cheese

Cheese, American, 1 lb.　　= 2⅔ c. cubed

Cheese, American, 1 lb.　　= 4 c. shredded

Cheese, bleu, 4 oz.　　= 1 c. crumbled

Cheese, cottage, 8 oz.　　= 1 cup

Cheese, cottage, 12 oz.　　= 1½ cup

Cheese, cottage, 1 lb.	= 2 cups
Cheese, cream, 8 oz.	= 1 cup
Cheese, cream, 3 oz.	= 6 tablespoons
Cheese, Parmesan, 4 oz. grated	= 1 cup
Cherry pie filling, 21 oz.	= 2¼ cup
Chicken, 3½ lb. fryer	= about 2 cups cooked, diced
Chives	= green onion tops
Chocolate, unsweetened, 1 square	= 1 oz.
Chocolate, unsweetened, 1 oz.	= 3 T. unsweetened cocoa + 2 to 3 tsp. oil, butter or shortening
Chocolate, unsweetened pre-melted, 1 envelope (1 oz.)	= 3 T. unsweetened cocoa + 1 T. oil
Chocolate chips, semisweet, 6 oz.	= 9 T. unsweetened cocoa + 7 T. sugar + 3 T. butter
Chocolate chips, 6 oz.	= 1 cup
Chocolate, semisweet, 3 squares (3 oz.)	= ½ c. semisweet chocolate chips
Chocolate, semisweet, 2 squares (2 oz.)	= ⅓ c. semisweet chocolate chips
Cilantro leaves, dried	= dried parsley leaves
Cilantro, 1 T. chopped fresh	= 1 tsp. dried cilantro leaves or parsley leaves
Coconut, 1 whole	= 2 to 3 c. shredded
Coconut, shredded or flaked, 4 oz. can	= 1⅓ c. approximately
Coffee, ground, 1 lb.	= will make 40 to 60 (6-oz.) cups
Coffee, instant, 2 oz.	= will make 25 (6-oz.) cups
Cornflakes, 1 c.	= ⅓ c. crushed
Cornflakes, 3 c.	= 1 c. crushed
Cornmeal, 1 lb.	= 3 cups
Cornstarch, 1 T.	= 2 T. flour for thickening
Cornstarch, 1 T.	= 1 T. quick tapioca
Corn syrup, 1 c.	= 1 c. sugar + ¼ c. liquid
Corn syrup, 16 fluid oz.	= 2 cups
Cottage cheese, 8 oz.	= 1 cup
Cracker crumbs, ¾ c.	= 1 c. bread crumbs
Cracker crumbs, graham, ⅓ lb. (1 pack)	= 1½ c. crumbs
Cranberries, 1 lb.	= 4 cups
Cranberry sauce, 1 (16-oz.) can	= 1 c. liquid in gelatin recipe
Cream, 1 c.	= 1 c. canned evaporated milk or evaporated skimmed milk

Cream, half and half, 1 c.	= ¾ c. milk and 3 T. butter
Cream, heavy, 1 c.	= ¾ c. milk and ⅓ c. butter
Cream, light	= Half 'n Half for baking
Cream, sour, 1 c.	= ⅞ c. buttermilk or yogurt + 3 T. butter
Cream, dairy sour	= 1 c. plain yogurt
Cream, sour, 1 c.	= 1 c. milk + 1 T. vinegar or lemon juice
Cream, whipping or heavy, 1 c. (½ pt.)	= 2 c. whipped cream
Cream cheese	= Neufchatel cheese or low-fat cream cheese
Currants	= raisins

—D—

Dates, 1 lb. pitted	= 2¼ c. finely chopped
Dates, 11 oz. pitted	= 1¾ c., cut up (approx.)
Dill, 2 T. chopped fresh	= 2 tsp. dried dill weed
Dream Whip, 1 envelope	= 2 c. whipped

—E—

Egg, ½	= 4 to 6 teaspoons
Egg white, 1	= 1½ tablespoons
Egg yolk, 1	= 1 tablespoon
Egg, 1 large	= ¼ c., scant
Egg, 1 whole	= 2 egg yolks and 1 T. water
Egg, 1 whole	= 2 egg yolks in custard
Egg, 1 whole	= 2½ T. sifted, dry egg powder + 2½ T. lukewarm water
Eggs, 2 medium	= ¼ to ⅓ cup
Eggs, 2 large	= ½ cup
Eggs, 2 large	= 3 small eggs
Eggs, 3 medium	= ½ cup
Eggs, 3 large	= ⅔ cup
Eggs, 3 whole	= ¾ c. egg whites
Eggs, 5 large	= 1 cup
Eggs, 6 to 7 small	= 1 cup
Eggs, 8 small	= 6 large eggs
Egg whites, 3	= ⅓ to ½ cup
Egg whites, 4 large	= ½ to ⅔ cup
Egg whites, 8 to 10	= 1 cup
Egg yolks, 5	= ⅓ cup
Egg yolks 12 to 16	= 1 cup
Egg substitute, ¼ c.	= 1 whole medium egg

Eggs, scrambled, 2 eggs	= 2 whites + 1 egg
Eggplant, 1 large	= 1½ lbs. (1 medium = ¾ lb.)
Escarole	= spinach or kale

—F—

Fish, boneless, 1 lb.	= 3 to 4 servings
Fish, Flounder	= sole, cod or halibut
Flour, 2 T. for thickening	= 1 T. cornstarch
Flour, 1½ T. for thickening	= 1 T. quick tapioca
Flour, all-purpose, 1 lb.	= 4 cups
Flour, all-purpose, 1 c. minus 2 T.	= 1 c. sifted cake flour
Flour, all-purpose, 1¾ c.	= 2 c. cake flour
Flour, cake 1 c.	= 2 T. cornstarch in a cup; fill cup with all-purpose flour and sift three times
Flour, self-rising, 1 c.	= 1 c. all-purpose flour, 1½ tsp. baking powder and ¼ tsp. salt

—G—

Garlic, 1 clove	= 5 drops liquid garlic
Garlic, 1 clove	= ⅛ to ¼ tsp. garlic powder
Garlic, 1 clove	= ¼ tsp. instant minced garlic
Garlic, 1 clove	= ½ tsp. garlic salt
Garlic salt, 1 tsp.	= ½ tsp. reg. salt & ¼ tsp. garlic powder
Gelatin, unflavored, 1 envelope & ¼ c. sugar	= 3 oz. pkg. gelatin
Gelatin, unflavored, ¼ oz. env.	= 1 tablespoon
Gelatin, unflavored, ¼ oz. env.	= enough to jell 2 c. liquid
Gingerroot, 1 to 2 slices fresh	= 1 T. ground ginger
Gingerroot, 2 tsp. grated, peeled	= ½ tsp. ground ginger
Graham cracker crumbs, 1 pkg. (⅓ lb.)	= 1½ cups
Green beans, 1 (16-oz.) can	= 2 c. cooked
Green pepper, 1 medium	= 1 c. chopped

—H—

Hamburger, 1 lb.	= 2 cups
Herbs, 1 T. fresh	= 1 tsp. dried
Honey, 1 c.	= 12 oz.
Honey, 1 c.	= 1 c. corn syrup or molasses
Honey, 1 c.	= 1¼ c. sugar + ¼ c. liquid

Honey, 1 lb.	= 1⅓ c.
Honey, ⅔ c.	= 1 c. sugar and ⅓ c. water
Ice cream, 1 c.	= 1 c. liquid in gelatin recipes
Italian spice, 1 tsp.	= ¼ tsp. each of oregano, basil, thyme, rosemary; + a dash of cayenne pepper

—J—

Jalapeno chili, one	= ⅛ tsp. red pepper
Jello, 3 oz. pkg.	= 6 to 6½ T. approx.
Jello, 3 oz. pkg.	= 1 env. unflavored gelatin + ¼ c. sugar

—K—

Karo, 16 fluid oz.	= 2 cups
Kasha	= bulgur or cracked wheat
Ketchup, 1 T.	= 1 T. tomato paste
Ketchup, 1 c.	= 1 c. tomato sauce + ½ c. sugar and 2 T. vinegar
Kohlrabi	= turnip

—L—

Leavening per c. of flour	= 1¼ tsp. baking powder
Leavening per c. of flour	= ½ tsp. baking soda + 2 T. vinegar
Leeks	= onions
Lemon, 1 medium	= 2 to 3 T. juice
Lemon, 1 medium	= 1 to 3 tsp. grated peel
Lemons, 5 to 8 medium	= 1 c. juice
Lemon juice, 1 tsp.	= ½ tsp. vinegar
Lemon rind, grated, of 1 lemon	= ½ tsp. lemon extract
Lime, 1	= 2 T. juice
Lime, 1	= 2 tsp. grated peel

—M—

Macaroni, 8 oz. (1¾ to 2 c.)	= 4 c. cooked
Macaroni, 1 c. uncooked	= 2 to 2¼ c. cooked
Macaroni, 1 lb. uncooked	= 8 c. cooked
Mace	= nutmeg
Margarine, 1 stick (¼ lb.)	= ½ cup or 8 tablespoons
Margarine, ¾ stick	= 6 tablespoons
Margarine, 1 c.	= 1 c. shortening + ½ tsp. salt
Marshmallows, 10 miniature	= 1 regular
Marshmallows, 10 oz.	= 4 c. miniature marshmallows
Marshmallows, 10 oz.	= 38 to 40 lg. marshmallows

Marshmallows, 16 large	= 1½ c. miniature marshmallows
Marshmallow creme, 7 oz.	= 1½ to 1¾ cups
Marshmallow creme, 2 c.	= 10 oz. large marshmallows or 4 c. miniature marshmallows
Meat, ground, 1 lb.	= 2 c. tightly packed
Milk, 1 cup	= ½ c. evaporated milk and ½ c. water
Milk, evaporated,	
1 (12-oz.) can	= 1½ c. undiluted
Milk, evaporated, 1 (5-oz.) can	= ⅔ c. undiluted
Milk, sour, 1 c.	= 1 c. sweet milk plus 1 T. vinegar or lemon juice; let stand 5 minutes.
Milk, sweet, 1 c.	= 1 c. sour milk or buttermilk plus ½ tsp. baking soda
Milk, sour, 1 c.	= 1 c. buttermilk
Milk, 1 c. skim	= 1 c. water + ⅓ c. nonfat dry milk powder
Mint, 2 T. chopped fresh	
mint leaves	= 1 tsp. dried mint flakes
Molasses, 12 oz.	= 1 cup
Molasses, 1 c.	= 1 c. honey
Mushrooms, 4 oz. canned	= ⅔ cup
Mushrooms, 8 oz. fresh	= about 1 c. sliced and cooked
Mustard, 1 T. prepared	= 1 tsp. dry mustard + 1 T. water
Mustard, 1 tsp. prepared	= ½ tsp. dry mustard + 2 tsp. vinegar

—N—

Noodles, Chinese	= angel hair pasta or vermicelli
Noodles, 8 oz. uncooked	= 4 to 4½ c. uncooked noodles
Noodles, 1 c. uncooked	= 1¼ c. cooked
Noodles, 8 oz. uncooked	= 4 to 4½ c. cooked
Nuts, 1 lb. almonds in the shell	= 1¾ c. shelled
Nuts, 1 lb. peanuts in the shell	= 2 c. shelled
Nuts, 1 lb. pecans in the shell	= 2¼ c. shelled
Nuts, 1 lb. walnuts in the shell	= 1⅔ c. shelled and chopped
Nuts, 1 lb. shelled walnuts	= 4 cups
Nuts, 1 lb. shelled pecans	= 4 cups

—O—

Oil, olive, ⅞ c.	= 1 c. butter
Onion, 1 small	= ¼ c. chopped
Onion, 1 small	= 1 tsp. onion powder
Onion, 1 small (¼ c.)	= 1 T. dried minced onion
Onion, 1 medium	= ½ c. chopped
Onion, 1 medium	= 4 shallots

Onion, 1 large = 1 c. chopped

Onion powder, 1 tsp. = ½ medium onion

Onion salt, 1 tsp. = flavor of 1 medium onion

Onion soup mix, dry, 1 pkg. = 4 T. approx.

Orange, 1 medium = ⅓ c. juice

Orange, 1 medium = 4 tsp. grated peel

Oreo cookies, 1 lb. = 42 cookies

—P—

Parsley, 1 T. dried = 3 T. freshly chopped

Pasta (except noodles), 2 c.
uncooked = 4 c. cooked

Pasta (except noodles), 1 lb.
uncooked = 9 c. cooked

Pasta, corkscrew or rotini,
8 oz. or 3 c. uncooked = 4 c. cooked

Pasta, rigatoni, 8 oz. or
3½ c. uncooked = 4½ c. cooked

Pasta, egg noodles,
1 c. uncooked = 1¼ c. cooked

Peaches, 1 lb. = 3 medium or 2 c., sliced

Peaches, frozen sliced, 1 lb. = 1¾ c. approx.

Pears, 1 lb. = 3 medium or 2½ c. sliced

Peas, 10 oz. box frozen = about 2 cups

Peas, split, dried, 1 lb. = 2 c. or about 5 c. cooked

Pecans, shelled, 1 lb. = 4 cups

Pecans in shell, 1 lb. = 2¼ c. nutmeats

Pepper, green bell, 1 large = 1 c. diced

Pepper, green or red sweet
pepper flakes, 1 T. = 2 T. fresh chopped green & red peppers

Pepperoni, 2 oz. = ½ c. sliced or shredded

Pineapple, crushed, 20 oz. can = 2½ c. undrained

Popcorn, 2 lbs. unpopped = 4½ c. unpopped

Potatoes, sweet, 1 lb. = 2 to 3 medium potatoes

Potatoes, white, 1 lb. = 3 to 4 medium potatoes

Potatoes, white, 2 lbs. = 6 cups

Prunes, pitted, dried, 1 lb. = 2½ cups

Prunes, pitted, dried, 12 oz. = 2 cups

Pumpkin pie spice, 2 tsp. = 1 tsp, cinnamon, ½ tsp. nutmeg, ¼ tsp. ginger and ¼ tsp. cloves

Rabbit   = chicken

Raisins, 1 lb.   = 2½ to 3 cups

Rhubarb, 1 lb.   = 1 qt. diced, uncooked rhubarb

Rice, reg. white, 1 c. uncooked = 3 to 3½ c. cooked

Rice, quick precooked instant,

1 c. uncooked   = 2 c. cooked

Rice, 1 lb. uncooked   = 2¼ c. uncooked

Ricotta, 1 c.   = 1 c. cottage cheese, pureed in blender

Roast (with bone in), 1 lb.   = 3 servings

Roast (boneless), 1 lb.   = 4 servings

Rutabaga   = use equal amount of turnip

—S—

Spaghetti, 8 oz. uncooked   = 4 c. cooked

Sugar, ¾ c. granulated + ¼ c.

molasses   = 1 c. brown sugar

Sugar, 1 c. granulated   = 1 c. packed brown

Sugar, 1 c. granulated   = ¾ c. honey

Sugar, 2 c. granulated   = 1 pound

Sugar, 1 c. granulated

(in baking)   = 1 c. honey + ¼ to ½ tsp. baking soda. Reduce liquid in recipe by ¼ cup.

Spareribs and short ribs, 1 lb.   = 2 servings

Steak, Porterhouse

or T-bone, 1 lb.   = 2 servings

Steak, round, 1 lb.   = 4 servings

Sweet One, 12 pts.   = 1 c. sugar

—T—

Tapioca, quick, 1 T.   = 1 T. cornstarch for thickening

Tapioca, quick, 1 T.   = 1½ T. flour for thickening

Thyme, 2 tsp. fresh leaves   = ¾ tsp. dried thyme leaves

Tomatoes, 1 lb.   = 3 to 4 medium tomatoes

Tomatoes, 16 oz. can   = 2 cups

Tomato juice, 1 c.   = ½ c. tomato sauce & ½ c. water

Tomato paste, 1 T.   = 1 T. ketchup

Tomato sauce, 29 oz. can   = 3½ cups

Tomato sauce, 8 oz. can   = 1 cup

Tomato sauce, 1 c.   = 6 T. tomato paste + ⅔ c. water + seasonings

Tomato sauce, 2 c.   = ¾ c. tomato paste + 1 c. water

—V—

Vanilla bean, ½   = 1 T. vanilla extract

Vinegar, ½ tsp.   = 1 tsp. lemon juice

Vinegar, red wine   = apple cider vinegar

—W—

Walnuts, 1 lb. in shell   = 1⅔ c. nutmeats, chopped

Walnut meats, 1 lb.   = 4 cups

Whipped topping, 12 oz. carton = 4½ to 5½ cups

Whipped topping, 8 oz. carton = 3½ cups

Whipping cream, 1 c. (½ pt.) = 2 c. whipped

—Y—

Yeast, 1 pkg. dry (¼ oz.)   = 1 cake (0.6) compressed fresh yeast

Yeast, 1 pkg. dry (¼ oz.)   = 2¼ tsp., level

Yeast, 3 pkg. dry (¼ oz. each) = One (2 oz.) compressed yeast cake

Yogurt, plain   = cottage cheese, blended until smooth

Yogurt, plain   = equal amt. of buttermilk or sour cream

—Z—

Zita, 8 oz. uncooked   = Penne pasta

Zita, 8 oz. uncooked   = about 2⅛ c. uncooked, or 3 to 3½ c. cooked

Zucchini, 1 large   = about 1⅔ lbs.

Zucchini, 1 medium   = about 10 oz.

Zucchini, 1 small   = about 6 oz.

Zwieback crumbs   = graham cracker crumbs

STRANGE RECIPES

BAKING POWDER, HOMEMADE

When you run out, here is an emergency recipe.

2 tsp. cream of tartar
1 tsp. baking soda
1 tsp. cornstarch

1. Mix together; store in airtight container. 2. Use 1½ teaspoons of this mixture for every cup of flour. 3. Do not use this recipe for any dough that has to be chilled.

BREAD CRUMBS

When a recipe calls for fine dry bread crumbs and you have none, try this.

Place bread slices on cookie sheet and heat in preheated 200° oven for 30 minutes; turn bread over and return to oven for 15 minutes longer. When cool, process into fine bread crumbs in food processor or blender. Six slices of bread makes approximately 2 cups fine crumbs.

BREAD CRUMBS, HERB-FLAVORED

2 c. finely crushed bread crumbs
2 T. crushed, dried parsley
2 T. dried chives (opt.)
1 T. garlic powder
1 T. dried minced onion
1 T. crushed, dried basil
1 T. paprika
½ T. dried or ground thyme
½ T. crushed, dried cilantro (opt.)
½ tsp. salt (opt.)

1. Air-dry leftover bread heels or slices; after bread is thoroughly dry, store in airtight container until ready to grind. 2. Grind bread in food processor or blender. 3. Mix 2 cups bread crumbs with remaining ingredients, stirring together. 4. Store in airtight container.

BROWN SUGAR

1 c. white granulated sugar
2 T. molasses

1. Mix sugar and molasses together thoroughly. 2. Store in airtight container or plastic bag.

BUBBLE SOLUTION

Mix your own bubble-blowing solution.

1 c. water
⅓ c. Joy dishwashing solution
2 T. light corn syrup

1. Mix solution well; allow to stand one hour before using. Tell young children this is not to be tasted. 2. Label any leftover solution and store in refrigerator.

CAKE FLOUR

Place 2 T. cornstarch in a cup; fill cup with all-purpose flour. Sift together 3 times.

CREAM CHEESE SUBSTITUTE

Amazingly like the real thing.

Drain a carton of plain yogurt (low-fat or nonfat) in a colander or sieve lined with coffee filters or several layers of dampened cheesecloth. Suspend over bowl and set in refrigerator overnight or for 24 hours. Discard liquid and use remainder as cream cheese. If desired, add a little salt to taste. Store in refrigerator; keeps about 1 week.

DOG BISCUITS, JUBIE (Red Star Jubilee)

Easy to make, and dogs love them.

1 c. all-purpose flour
1 c. whole-wheat flour
½ c. wheat germ or unprocessed wheat bran
⅓ to ½ c. nonfat milk powder
1 tsp. white or brown sugar
⅓ c. olive oil
1 egg
½ c. water

1. Turn oven dial to 325°. 2. Combine first 5 ingredients in mixer bowl, stirring together. 3. Add oil and mix on medium speed until mixture resembles cornmeal. 4. Add egg and water; mix together. If too sticky, add a little more flour. 5. Turn dough out onto lightly floured surface and knead for 1 minute, or until smooth. 6. Roll out in rectangular shape about ¼ inch thick; place in large ungreased cookie sheet or jellyroll pan and push dough with fingers to fit the bottom of pan. 7. With table knife, cut into 1-inch strips the long way; then cut into 3-inch strips the other way. (Cut clear through to bottom of pan.) 8. Bake in preheated 325° oven 45 minutes, or until golden brown; turn oven off and let dry in oven several hours or overnight. (Or follow baking directions for "Dog Biscuits, Shultz.") 9. When cool, break apart and store in airtight container.

DOG BISCUITS, SHULTZ

Easy to make, and dogs love them.

1¼ c. whole wheat flour, packed level
½ c. uncooked oatmeal, packed level
¼ c. cornmeal, packed level
¼ c. wheat germ or unprocessed wheat bran
⅛ c. olive oil
⅛ c. molasses
¾ c. water

1. Turn oven to 350°. 2. In mixer bowl, combine dry ingredients, oil and molasses. 3. Add water and mix together; if too sticky, add a little more flour. 4. Grease or spray large cookie sheet or 15 x 10 x 1-inch jellyroll pan. 5. Pat dough with floured fingers to fit prepared pan. (If needed, sprinkle a little flour over top dough while patting.) 6. With table knife, cut into 1-inch strips the long way and 3-inch strips across. (Cut clear through to bottom of pan.) 7. Bake in preheated 350° oven 30 to 35 minutes, or until medium brown in color. 8. When cool, break apart and store in tightly covered container. <u>Substitution</u>: If low on whole-wheat flour, use part all-purpose flour. (It may take more flour than the recipe calls for.)

DOG BISCUITS, SPARKLE BERRY

Easy to make, and dogs love them.

1½ c. quick or old-fashioned oatmeal, uncooked
1 c. whole-wheat flour
⅔ c. cornmeal
¼ c. wheat germ
2 large eggs
5 to 6 T. water

1. Preheat oven to 375°. In a bowl, mix all ingredients well. (It may need a tiny bit more water.) 2. Roll dough on a floured surface to ¼-inch thickness. (Don't roll all the dough at one time; divide it into several balls.) 3. With table knife, cut dough into desired pieces for dog biscuits. 4. Bake on greased cookie sheets for 40 minutes. 5. Remove and cool on rack.

DOG BISCUITS, ZIGGY

Easy to make, and dogs love them.

2 c. whole-wheat flour
2 T. (⅛ c.) olive oil
1 T. molasses, honey or corn syrup
3/4 c. water (or 1 c. commercial buttermilk)

1. Follow directions for "Dog Biscuits, Shultz."

DRAIN CLEANER

From Martha S. Bryan.

½ c. Arm & Hammer baking soda
1 c. boiling water

1. Mix soda and boiling water together; pour down drain, allowing to stand 15 minutes undisturbed. 2. After 15 minutes, run hot water down the drain.

EGG SUBSTITUTE I

When you need 1 egg; from Mary Trimble.

½ tsp. olive oil
1 T. all-purpose flour
¼ tsp. baking powder
1 egg white

1. Mix ingredients together. **When you need one egg yolk**: Use first 3 ingredients above; omit the egg white.

EGG SUBSTITUTE II

When you need 2 whole eggs.

4 egg whites
1 tsp. olive oil
2 drops yellow food coloring

1. Mix ingredients together. Makes ½ cup or equivalent to 2 eggs.

EGG SUBSTITUTION TO AVOID CHOLESTEROL

From Olive Holt.

Use 2 egg whites for 1 egg. Use 3 egg whites for 2 eggs. Use 4 egg whites for 3 eggs.

FLOUR, SELF-RISING

When you need 2 cups of self-rising flour.

2 c. all-purpose flour
3 tsp. baking powder
½ tsp. salt

1. Combine ingredients.

GELATIN, LEMON or LIME
(From "Scratch")

Equivalent to one small 3-ounce box gelatin.
Double recipe for 13 x 9-inch pan.

1 envelope unflavored gelatin (1 T.)
¼ c. sugar
2 c. boiling water
2 T. lemon juice
1 tsp. lemon extract
6 drops yellow food coloring

1. Stir together gelatin and sugar; add boiling water and stir until dissolved. **2.** Add remaining ingredients; refrigerate to set. <u>Lime Green Gelatin</u>: Substitute lime juice for lemon juice and green food coloring instead of yellow. <u>Note</u>: When adding drained fruit, decrease boiling water by ¼ cup.

GELATIN, ORANGE (From "Scratch")

Equivalent to one small 3-ounce box gelatin.

1 envelope unflavored gelatin (1 T.)
¼ c. sugar
2 c. boiling orange juice (or part water)
1 tsp. orange extract
3 drops red food coloring
3 drops yellow food coloring
2 T. lemon juice (opt.)

1. Stir together gelatin and sugar; add boiling liquid and stir until dissolved. **2.** Add remaining ingredients; refrigerate to set. <u>Note</u>: When adding drained fruit, decrease boiling liquid by ¼ cup.

GELATIN, ORANGE SUGAR-FREE
(From "Scratch")

1 envelope unflavored gelatin (1 T.)
¼ c. cold water
1 c. boiling water
1⁄16 tsp. salt (opt.)
½ tsp. orange extract
⅓ c. orange juice
⅓ c. powdered Sprinkle Sweet (or 2 tsp. liquid sweetener)

1. In small pan, sprinkle gelatin over cold water; place over medium-low heat, stirring constantly until gelatin dissolves (about 3 minutes). **2.** Add boiling water and salt, stirring together. **3.** Add remaining ingredients; chill.

ITALIAN HERB BLEND

6 T. dried basil
2 T. dried oregano
1 T. dried marjoram
1 T. dried thyme

ONION SOUP MIX, DRIED

½ tsp. onion powder
½ tsp. salt
¼ tsp. sugar
¼ tsp. Kitchen Bouquet browning sauce
½ c. chopped or minced dehydrated onions

1. In med.-small bowl, combine onion powder, salt and sugar. **2.** Add Kitchen Bouquet and stir until the seasonings are uniformly brown. **3.** Add dehydrated onions and mix thoroughly until the color is even again.

PEANUT BUTTER

Dry roasted peanuts require oil for this recipe.

1½ c. dry roasted peanuts
2 T. olive oil
⅛ tsp. salt (omit if using salted peanuts)

1. In food processor or blender, process peanuts briefly. **2.** Add oil and salt; process or blend to desired spreading consistency. (In blender, scrape down sides often with a rubber spatula.)

PUMPKIN PIE SPICE

Use when recipe calls for 1 tablespoon of pumpkin pie spice.

1½ tsp. cinnamon
½ tsp. nutmeg
½ tsp. ginger
¼ tsp. cloves

SALT SUBSTITUTE (Herb Blend)

2 tsp. black pepper
2 tsp. dried rosemary
2 tsp. dried thyme
½ tsp. garlic powder
2 tsp. dried instant chives (opt.)

1. Combine ingredients and store in an airtight jar.

SEASONED SALT

6 T. salt
2 tsp. paprika
1 tsp. dry mustard
½ tsp. dried thyme
½ tsp. garlic salt
½ tsp. curry powder
½ tsp. celery seed
½ tsp. marjoram (opt.)
¼ tsp. onion powder
⅛ tsp. dill seed

1. Put all ingredients in blender container and blend.

SEASONING, CREOLE

½ c. salt or light salt
¼ c. garlic powder
¼ c. black pepper
2 T. cayenne pepper
2 T. thyme
2 T. ground oregano

1. Mix together ingredients.

SESAME SEEDS, TOASTED

Cook and stir in a small dry skillet over medium heat until golden, about 5 minutes.

SOAP, HOMEMADE

From Henrietta Striegel.

1 (12-oz.) can lye
1 qt. (4 c.) cold water
3 T. Borax
½ c. cold water
2 T. sugar
¼ c. ammonia
5 lbs. clean melted lard

1. In a large granite pan, pour lye into 1 quart cold water; let cool. (The lye produces a surprising amount of heat when it is mixed with the water.) 2. In a separate container, combine Borax, 1/2 cup cold water, the sugar and ammonia. 3. When the lye-mixture is cool, add the Borax mixture. 4. Add melted lard, stirring all together in the large granite pan until its color turns from yellow to creamy white. 5. Later, when soap has begun to harden, cut into bars before it gets too hard. 6. Soap may be stored in paper-lined cardboard box. **Note**: This soap may be used for washing clothes and other cleaning purposes. It is not recommended for face washing.

SOUR CREAM SUBSTITUTE

Also called "Mock Sour Cream."
Makes 2 cups.

½ c. skim or 1% or 2% milk
1½ c. low-fat cottage cheese (12 oz.)
2 T. lemon juice
⅛ tsp. salt (opt.)

1. Place all ingredients in the container of a blender; blend until smooth. **Note**: If using in a hot dish, add at the last moment and do not boil or heat. Do not use this for baking.

SOUTHWEST SPICE BLEND

1 tsp. garlic powder
1 tsp. cumin
½ tsp. oregano
½ tsp. cilantro
⅛ tsp. red pepper

SWEEPING COMPOUND

Good for garage floors.

10 c. sand
3½ c. sawdust
1½ c. salt
1 c. mineral oil

1. Mix sand, sawdust and salt together well. 2. Add mineral oil and stir together.

SWEETENED CONDENSED MILK

Makes approximately the same amount as a 14-ounce can of sweetened condensed milk.

⅓ c. water + 1 tsp.
3 T. butter
Vanilla (a few drops)
1 c. nonfat dry milk powder (instant)
⅔ c. sugar

1. In small saucepan, bring water and butter to a boil. 2. Put all ingredients in blender or food processor container; blend or process until smooth. 3. Refrigerate in covered jar. Makes about 1¼ cups. **Note**: Can be refrigerated for 2 weeks, or frozen for up to six months.

TACO SEASONING MIX I

1 T. dried onion
1 T. garlic powder
4½ tsp. chili powder
2 tsp. paprika
1 tsp. cumin

TACO SEASONING MIX II

6 tsp. chili powder
4½ tsp. cumin
5 tsp. paprika
3 tsp. onion powder
2½ tsp. garlic powder
⅛ tsp. cayenne pepper

Chapter 4

Appetizers and Dips

STANDING: FRANCES (HILL), LAWRENCE, HAROLD, RUTH (CHESS)
SEATED: MARSHALL STEVENSON, LILLIAN (ROHLEDER), AND
SADIE STEVENSON

AROUND 1918

APPETIZERS AND DIPS

GRAPE TRUFFLES

Cream cheese, cold
Seedless red and/or green grapes
Coconut, flaked
Chopped peanuts, walnuts or pecans

1. Tear off small pieces of cream cheese and mold around grapes. 2. Roll half the truffles in flaked coconut and half in chopped nuts. 3. Serve on a tray with plain red and green seedless grapes.

GUS PUFFS (Hors d'Oeuvres)

*Multiply the recipe to make as many as wanted.
These are delicious hot or cold.*

½ c. mayonnaise (not salad dressing)
¼ c. grated Parmesan cheese (1 oz.), divided
⅓ c. finely minced onion (may be chopped in food processor)
Bread, day-old (20-oz. loaf of baker's bread)

1. In a small bowl, mix together mayonnaise, half the cheese and the minced onion; set aside. 2. With top of drinking glass or round cookie cutter, cut rounds from the bread (not using crusts). 3. Broil rounds on baking sheet until toasted on one side. Always leave oven door ajar in the broil-stop position (open about 4 inches) when broiling. 4. Turn rounds over and spread untoasted side with the mayonnaise mixture. 5. Sprinkle with remaining cheese. Return to oven and broil until the puffs are golden brown.

MUSHROOM CAPS, STUFFED

*From Jay Stevenson. Recipe may be doubled or tripled.
Also may be prepared ahead of time and frozen
until ready to bake.*

⅓ lb. (¾ c.) ground beef
⅓ lb. (¾ c.) regular sausage
1½ c. Pepperidge Farms herb stuffing
1½ c. Pepperidge Farms cornbread stuffing
1 med. onion, finely chopped
1 c. finely chopped celery
⅓ stick (2½ T.) butter, melted
⅔ c. beef broth
½ c. chicken broth
1 egg, beaten
¾ tsp. lemon juice
⅛ tsp. garlic powder
1½ lbs. mushrooms

1. Brown beef and sausage together, breaking into small pieces; drain off fat. 2. Combine meat, stuffing, onion and celery; add melted butter, the broths, beaten egg, lemon juice and garlic powder. 3. Refrigerate until ready to use. 4. Remove stems from mushrooms. (They can be used later in soups, scrambled eggs or sautéed as a side dish.) 5. Brush mushrooms clean and place 1 to 2 tablespoons stuffing mixture into each cap, depending on the size of mushroom. 6. Place onto lightly greased or sprayed cookie sheet; bake 20 minutes in preheated 350° oven. (If frozen, add 5 to 10 minutes to baking time.) **Note**: There are 16 to 30 mushrooms in 1 pound, depending on size.

VEGETABLE PIZZA

*Adapted from Jay Stevenson and Melodie Satterfield.
To cut this recipe in half, make it in 13 x 9-inch pan.
May be made a day in advance.*

2 tubes crescent rolls (8 oz, each)
2 pkgs. (8 oz. each) cream cheese
1 c. mayonnaise, salad dressing or sour cream
1 pkg. dry Hidden Valley Ranch dressing
1 c. chopped broccoli
1 c. chopped cauliflower
½ c. chopped or grated peeled carrots
½ c. chopped green pepper
¼ c. chopped onion (opt.)
4 oz. (1 c.) shredded Cheddar cheese (or less)

1. Turn oven dial to 350°. 2. Unroll crescent roll dough on bottom of lightly greased or sprayed large pizza pan, or large cookie sheet (or two 13 x 9-inch cake pans using 1 tube of rolls in each pan). 3. Pinch dough pieces together to form a seamless sheet, covering the entire bottom of pan; prick dough with fork. 4. Bake in preheated 350° oven 10 to 12 minutes, until lightly browned; cool. 5. Mix together cream cheese, mayonnaise and dry ranch dressing; spread over cooled crust. 6. Cover with cleaned, chopped vegetables; garnish with shredded cheese. 7. Cover with plastic wrap; press vegetables slightly into cream cheese mixture. 8. Refrigerate; at serving time, cut into pieces. **Note**: 1 package dried beef, chopped fine, may be added to cream cheese mixture, if desired.

WON TON CINNAMON CRISPS

12 won ton wrappers
1 T. butter, melted
1 T. granulated sugar
½ tsp. cinnamon

1. Turn oven dial to 375°. 2. Arrange won ton wrappers close together in a single layer on lightly greased or sprayed cookie sheet or jellyroll pan. 3. Brush won tons with melted butter. 4. With table knife cut each won ton wrapper in half to make a triangle; sprinkle with sugar and cinnamon which have been mixed together. 5. Bake in preheated 375° oven about 5 to 5½ minutes, until crisp and golden.

CHEESE BALL

Bits of red and green add color and flavor.

8 oz. cream cheese or light cream cheese, softened
10 oz. sharp Cheddar cheese, room temp.
2 T. drained pimiento, diced small
2 T. chopped green onion tops or chopped fresh
   chives or green pepper
½ c. nuts, finely chopped

1. In mixer bowl, beat cream cheese. 2. Shred Cheddar cheese on grater or in food processor; add to cream cheese and beat well. 3. Add pimiento and green onion tops and stir together. 4. Wet hands in cold water, shaking off excess; shape cheese into a ball and roll in chopped nuts, coating surface all around. 5. Place cheese ball on cheese board and cover with dome (or wrap in plastic wrap). 6. For easier spreading, leave cheese ball at room temperature in daytime and refrigerate overnight. <u>Substitutions</u>: Cooked or canned red sweet pepper, drained and diced, may be used instead of pimiento. Two teaspoons of chopped onion and two teaspoons dried parsley flakes may be used instead of green onion tops, chives, or ¼ t. dried onion flakes.

CHEESE BALL WITH DRIED BEEF

From Louise Sarber. Good on crackers.

2 (8 oz. each) pkgs. cream cheese, softened at room
   temperature
1 pkg. (2½ to 3 oz.) dried beef, diced
1 T. horseradish (or less)
½ tsp. garlic salt or garlic powder
¼ c. Parmesan cheese

1. Mix all ingredients together and form into a ball; wrap in plastic wrap and refrigerate. (Or just use as a dip.)

DIP, CHEESE-SALSA

A delicious recipe! Makes 3 cups.

1 lb. Velveeta pasteurized cheese product, cut up
1 c. (8-oz.) salsa, "med." hot

1. Combine in 1½-quart microwavable bowl on HIGH for 3 to 5 minutes, or until Velveeta is melted, stirring after 2 minutes. 2. Serve hot (or warm) with chips or cut-up vegetables. Also good on toast.

DIP, DILL WEED

Adapted from Flora McCreary and Jean Moyer.

8 oz. (1 c.) sour cream or low-fat or fat-free sour
   cream substitute
1 c. Hellmann's mayonnaise
3 tsp. dill weed
3 tsp. finely chopped onion or instant minced onion
   or ¼ c. green onions, chopped
1 tsp. seasoned salt (opt.)
⅛ to ¼ tsp. garlic powder or garlic salt (opt.)
3 tsp. dried parsley (opt.)

1. Mix all ingredients together; refrigerate in covered container. 2. Serve on baked potatoes or with crackers, chips or vegetable sticks. (Chill for at least 2 hours.)

DIP, DRIED BEEF

*Fills a small loaf of pumpernickel bread.
Double recipe for a large loaf.*

¾ c. sour cream or sour cream alternative
¾ c. mayonnaise
1 T. finely chopped onion
¼ tsp. dill weed
1 T. freshly chopped parsley (or 1 tsp. parsley
   flakes)
2½ oz. dried beef, chopped
1 sm. round loaf pumpernickel bread

1. Combine all ingredients, except bread and mix well; refrigerate several hours. 2. Cut center out of round loaf of bread; fill with dip. 3. Cube the cutout bread and place around loaf on serving plate or platter.

DIP FOR FRESH FRUIT

8 oz. cream cheese, softened
7 oz. jar marshmallow creme
Food coloring (opt.)
1 T. orange juice (opt.)
1 tsp. grated orange peel (opt.)
1/16 tsp. ground ginger (opt.)

1. Combine ingredients and beat with electric mixer until smooth; refrigerate. 2. Serve with fresh fruit which has been cut into pieces.

DIP, GREEN OLIVE

3 to 4 oz. cream cheese, softened
¼ c. mayonnaise
1 tsp. olive juice
1/16 tsp. pepper
⅓ to ½ c. olives, chopped or sliced
¼ c. chopped nuts (opt.)

1. Mix together cream cheese, mayonnaise, olive juice and pepper. **2.** Fold in olives (and nuts, if used).

DIP, GUACAMOLE (Avocado)

Serve with tortilla chips, corn chips, taco chips or on burritos.

1 med. or lg. ripe avocado
1 T. lemon or lime juice
⅓ c. mayonnaise, sour cream or softened cream cheese
1 sm. tomato, seeded and finely chopped
⅛ tsp. salt
⅛ tsp. pepper or cayenne pepper
1 T. finely chopped onion

Optional Ingredients:
1 clove garlic, finely minced
1 T. green chilies or green bell pepper, finely diced
5 drops bottled hot pepper sauce
3 slices bacon, cooked crisp, drained and crumbled

1. Peel avocado; cut in half and remove pit. **2.** Mash avocado with fork or in food processor; add lemon or lime juice and stir well. **3.** Add remaining ingredients and stir together; cover with plastic wrap pressed directly against the guacamole to prevent darkening. **4.** Chill. **Note**: Ripe avocados are soft to the touch when gently squeezed. If they are firm-fleshed, leave out on the counter as they will not ripen in refrigerator. When ripe, they can be refrigerated for up to 1 week.

DIP, PEPPERONI

¼ c. canned milk, chilled
6 oz. cream cheese, softened
1 c. ground pepperoni, or finely chopped in food
    processor
4 T. parsley flakes

1. Whip the chilled canned milk. **2.** Add cream cheese and blend together well. **3.** Stir in pepperoni and parsley flakes; serve with crackers.

DIP, REFRIED BEAN

1 (16-oz.) can refried beans (fat-free)
½ c. thick and chunky salsa (mild, medium or hot)
8 oz. shredded Cheddar cheese (opt.)
Tortilla chips

1. In saucepan, heat refried beans and salsa until warm. **2.** Serve with chips.

DIP, SALMON SPREAD (or Tuna)

Serve with crackers or pumpernickel bread.

15 to 16-oz. can salmon
8 oz. cream cheese
1 T. lemon juice
1 T. finely chopped onion
1 tsp. horseradish (opt.)
¼ tsp. salt
¼ tsp. liquid smoke (opt.)
3 T. chopped fresh parsley (or 1 T. dried parsley)
½ to 1 c. chopped pecans (opt.)

1. Drain salmon; remove skin and bones. **2.** Combine drained salmon with remaining ingredients. **3.** Chill for several hours. **Note**: If desired, parsley may be omitted and onion increased to ¼ cup sliced green onion. Two small cans tuna, drained, may be substituted for the salmon.

DIP, SHRIMP

Serve with crackers or veggies or fat-free baked tortilla chips.

1 (8-oz.) pkg. cream cheese, softened
½ c. mayonnaise or salad dressing
⅓ c. finely chopped onion or green scallions
½ c. finely diced celery
⅛ tsp. garlic salt or garlic powder
1 (4½-oz.) can tiny cocktail shrimp, drained and rinsed

1. Mix cream cheese and mayonnaise or salad dressing until well blended. **2.** Stir in remaining ingredients. **3.** Cover and store in refrigerator.

DIP, SPINACH

May be served with rye bread, crackers or veggies.

1 (10-oz.) pkg. frozen chopped spinach, thawed and drained
1½ to 2 c. dairy sour cream or low-fat or fat-free sour
    cream substitute
1 to 1½ c. mayonnaise (NOT salad dressing)
4 sm. green onions, finely chopped (opt.)
1 pkg. DRY vegetable soup mix

1. Squeeze excess liquid from spinach. **2.** Combine all ingredients in bowl, mixing well. **3.** Cover and chill several hours or overnight. **4.** Serve with fresh vegetable sticks, potato chips, crackers or pumpernickel bread. Makes 3 cups. **Note**: For a crunchy dip, add 1 can (8 ounces) water chestnuts, drained and chopped.

DIP, SPINACH (Fresh)

1 c. sour cream or sour cream alternative
1 c. mayonnaise
2 individual packets dried vegetable soup mix (Cup of
    Soup)
1 sm. onion, finely chopped
2 c. fresh spinach, washed, drained and finely chopped
    (don't cook)

1. In bowl, mix together all ingredients except spinach, blending well. 2. Add spinach; mix thoroughly. 3. Chill at least 1 hour.

DIP, TUNA

½ c. salad dressing or mayonnaise
8-oz. pkg. cream cheese, softened
6½-oz. can tuna, drained
2 T. sweet pickle relish
1 tsp. parsley flakes (opt.)

1. Gradually add salad dressing to softened cream cheese, mixing until well blended. 2. Add remaining ingredients, gently stirring together. 3. Chill; serve with crackers, bread rounds or veggies.

HORSERADISH I

Do not use cider vinegar as it turns the horseradish dark.

2 c. horseradish cubes (or ⅔ c. ground horseradish)
½ c. white or distilled vinegar
¼ tsp. salt
1½ tsp. sugar (opt.)

1. Scrape or peel roots as you would carrots. 2. Cut roots into ½-inch cubes. 3. In blender container, combine cubes, vinegar, salt and sugar; blend.

HORSERADISH II

½ c. finely ground horseradish root
1 tsp. packed brown sugar
1½ T. white vinegar
¼ tsp. salt

1. Combine ingredients and let stand overnight before using.

HORSERADISH III

¼ c. freshly ground horseradish
1 tsp. sugar
2 tsp. prepared mustard
2 tsp. white vinegar
½ tsp. salt

¼ tsp. pepper
4 T. light cream or evaporated milk

1. Combine ingredients in small saucepan; heat together, but do not boil.

Chapter 5

Beverages

JAMES AND LEOTA BENNINGER

BEVERAGES

BLACK COW

For each serving, put a scoop of vanilla ice cream in large glass. Fill glass with well-chilled root beer.

CHOCOLATE, HOT

Makes 8 big mugs full, or 9 to 11 regular cups full.

¾ to 1 c. sugar
5 T. unsweetened cocoa, level
¼ tsp. salt
½ c. hot water
6 c. milk
1 lg. can (1½ c.) evaporated milk
2 tsp. vanilla
1 c. miniature marshmallows (opt.)

1. In 3-quart saucepan, combine sugar, cocoa, salt and hot water. 2. Bring mixture to a boil; boil 1 minute. 3. Add milk and evaporated milk. 4. Heat until mixture is hot, but do not boil. 5. Remove from heat; add vanilla and marshmallows.

COCOA, ONE CUP (Microwave)

Delicious!

4 tsp. sugar, level
½ T. unsweetened cocoa powder, level (1½ tsp.)
Salt, tiny dash (opt.)
¾ c. milk, divided
¼ tsp. vanilla
Miniature marshmallows (opt.)

1. In 4-cup glass pitcher, mix together dry ingredients. 2. Add ¼ cup milk and stir. 3. Cook on HIGH 45 seconds. 4. Add remaining ½ cup milk, stirring together. 5. Cook on HIGH 1 minute, or until hot. 6. Add vanilla; serve with marshmallows, if desired. **Sugar-Free:** Omit sugar; when adding vanilla, add 2 packets Equal or Sweet 'n Low. Stir well.

COCOA, LARGER CUP (Microwave)

1½ to 2 T. sugar
1 T. unsweetened cocoa powder, level
Salt, tiny dash (opt.)
1 c. milk, divided
¼ to ½ tsp. vanilla
Miniature marshmallows (opt.)

1. In 4-cup glass pitcher, stir together dry ingredients. 2. Add ¼ cup milk and stir; don't worry about it not dissolving. 3. Cook on HIGH 45 seconds. 4. Add remaining ¾ cup milk, stirring together. 5. Cook on HIGH 1 minute or until hot.

6. Add vanilla; serve with marshmallows if desired. Makes 1 big mug. **Sugar-Free:** Omit sugar; when adding vanilla, add 3 packets Equal or Sweet 'n Low. Stir well.

EGGNOG, EASY

Makes 8 servings, 8 ounces each.

1 pkg. instant vanilla pudding (4-serving size)
⅓ c. sugar
½ c. Egg Beaters
1 tsp. vanilla
6 c. milk
Nutmeg

1. In large bowl, blend pudding mix, sugar, Egg Beaters and vanilla at high speed of electric mixer. 2. Add milk slowly while mixing. 3. Sprinkle nutmeg over each serving.

KOOL-AID FOR ADULTS

1 pkg. unsweetened Kool-Aid
⅔ c. sugar
5 c. cold water
OR:
2 pkgs. unsweetened Kool-Aid
1¼ to 1½ c. sugar
9 to 9½ c. cold water
OR:
3 pkgs. unsweetened Kool-Aid
2 c. sugar
3 qt. + 2 c. cold water (14 c.)

LEMONADE, ONE GLASS

1 c. water
2½ T. sugar, level (or to taste)
2 T. lemon juice
Ice cubes

1. Stir water, sugar and lemon juice together. 2. Add ice. **Note:** 1 tablespoon sugar and 3 packets Equal may be used.

LEMONADE, 1½ QUARTS

Very good.

⅔ to 1 c. sugar
5 c. cold water
⅔ to ¾ c. lemon juice
2 drops yellow food coloring (opt.)

1. In 2-quart pitcher, combine sugar and water, stirring until sugar is partially dissolved. 2. Add lemon juice and food coloring. 3. Refrigerate. **Note:** Part lime juice may be used in place of same amount lemon juice. Use 1 drop green food coloring instead of yellow.

LEMONADE, 3½ QUARTS

2⅔ c. sugar
2 c. lemon juice
Cold water
2 drops yellow food coloring (opt.)

1. In gallon container, combine sugar and lemon juice, stirring together. 2. Fill container with cold water to make 3½ quarts. 3. Add yellow food coloring. 4. Refrigerate. Serve with ice cubes. **Note**: If desired, a little more water may be added.

LEMONADE (Semi-Diet)

5 c. water
¼ c. sugar
½ c. lemon juice
1 T. liquid sweetener (or sweetener to equal ½ c. sugar)
1 drop yellow food coloring

1. Mix ingredients together and refrigerate.

LIMEADE

5 c. water
1 c. lime juice
⅔ c. sugar
2 T. honey
1 drop green food coloring (opt.)

1. In a 2-quart pitcher, combine all ingredients. 2. Stir to dissolve sugar; refrigerate.

MILK SHAKE, BANANA

Serves one.

½ lg. banana, sliced (or 1 med.-small banana)
½ c. milk
½ tsp. vanilla
2 tsp. sugar or 1 pkg. Equal
½ to 1 c. vanilla ice cream (for thick shake, use 1 c.)

1. Combine all ingredients in blender container; blend until smooth.

MILK SHAKE, BANANA (DIET)

Makes 2 big servings.

2 c. ice cubes or crushed ice
1 c. milk
2 sm. bananas (or 1 very lg. banana)
Sweetener equivalent to 3 T. sugar (or 4 to 5 pkts. Equal)
½ to 1 tsp. vanilla (opt.)

1. Blend together in electric blender. **Banana Chocolate Milkshake (Diet):** Add 1 teaspoon chocolate flavoring to above. (**Not** chocolate syrup.)

MILK SHAKE, BANANA-CHOCOLATE

Serves one.

½ ripe banana, cut into chunks
⅔ c. milk (or water with 3 T. nonfat dry milk powder)
1 T. chocolate syrup
2 lg. (or 3 med.) ice cubes
1 dip ice cream
½ tsp. vanilla
¼ tsp. orange rind (purely opt.)

1. Blend together in electric blender.

MILK SHAKE, CHOCOLATE

Thick and delicious. Makes 1 serving.

½ c. milk
2 T. chocolate syrup
¼ tsp. vanilla flavoring
1 c. vanilla or chocolate ice cream

1. Blend together in electric blender. **Note**: For thinner milk shake, use ⅔ cup milk.

MILK SHAKE, CHOCOLATE (Diet)

Delicious! Makes 1 serving.

½ c. low-fat milk
3 pkts. Equal or Sweet 'n Low
3 lg. ice cubes (or 6 med.)
2 tsp. unsweetened cocoa (level)
½ tsp. vanilla
½ tsp. chocolate extract (opt.)
½ to 1 T. sugar (opt.)

1. Blend together in electric blender.

MILK SHAKE, CHOCOLATE MALTED

Delicious!

½ c. milk
1 c. vanilla, chocolate or fudge-swirl ice cream or ice milk
1 T. chocolate-flavored malted milk powder
1 T. chocolate syrup

1. Blend together in electric blender.

MILK SHAKE, PEACH

⅓ c. milk
⅔ c. sliced fresh peaches (or drained, canned peaches)
½ c. vanilla or peach ice cream
1 T. sugar, level

1. Blend together in electric blender. Makes 1 serving (or two 6-ounce glasses).

MILK SHAKE, PURPLE COW

Delicious! Makes 3 glasses (or 2 huge glasses).

1 (6-oz.) can frozen grape juice concentrate
2 c. milk
1 lg. scoop vanilla ice cream
2 lg. (or 4 med.) ice cubes

1. Blend together in electric blender. **Smaller Recipe:** Blend together 3 to 5 tablespoons grape juice concentrate (frozen or partially thawed), 1 cup milk and 2 scoops vanilla ice cream. Makes 2 medium glasses.

MILKSHAKE, STRAWBERRY
(Or Raspberry)

The berries may be sweetened or unsweetened.

½ c. milk
½ c. sliced fresh strawberries (or thawed or partially frozen berries)
1 T. sugar
¾ to 1 c. vanilla or strawberry ice cream

1. Blend together in electric blender. (Sugar may be omitted if using sweetened berries.) Makes 1 large serving or 2 small servings.

MILK SHAKE, STRAWBERRY (Diet)

1 c. sliced fresh strawberries
½ c. skim milk
4 lg. (or 6 med.) ice cubes
1 T. nonfat dry milk powder
2 pkts. Equal (or 1 T. sugar)

1. Blend together in electric blender. Makes 2 servings.

MILK SHAKE, VANILLA

½ c. milk
1 c. vanilla ice cream
3 tsp. sugar, level
½ tsp. vanilla

1. Blend together in electric blender. Makes 1 large serving.

MILK SHAKE, VANILLA (Diet)

½ c. skim milk
2 pkts. Equal
3 lg. ice cubes (or 4 med.)
1 tsp. sugar (opt.)
1 tsp. vanilla

1. Blend together in electric blender. Makes 1 serving.

MILK SHAKE, VANILLA (Thin)

1 c. vanilla ice cream, rounded
1½ c. milk
⅛ c. sugar (2 T.)
1 tsp. vanilla extract

1. Blend together in electric blender.

ORANGE JULIUS

From Kelly Wells Crouch. Serves 3 to 4.

1 (6-oz.) can frozen orange juice concentrate
1 c. milk
1 c. water
¼ to ½ c. sugar
1 to 2 tsp. vanilla extract
6 lg. or 12 med. ice cubes
1 c. vanilla ice cream (opt.)

1. Mix all together in blender until ice cubes are crushed, adding half the ice cubes at a time. **2.** Serve immediately; refrigerate any that is leftover. Re-blend before serving again. **Strawberry Julius:** Substitute 2 c. fresh strawberries for the orange juice.

ORANGE JULIUS, SMALLER

From Janice Miller.

⅓ c. frozen orange juice concentrate
½ c. milk
½ c. cold water
¼ c. sugar
½ tsp. vanilla
1 rounded c. ice cubes (about 5 or 6)

1. Mix all together in blender until ice cubes are crushed. (1 cup milk may be used instead of using the cold water.) Makes enough for 2 medium glasses.

Beverages

PINA COLADA

A pineapple-coconut dairy drink.

½ c. crushed pineapple in its own liquid (or pineapple chunks)
½ c. milk
2 T. sugar, level
¼ tsp. coconut flavoring
2 lg. (or 3 med.) ice cubes
½ c. ginger ale

1. Blend together in electric blender. Makes 1 large glass or 2 medium glasses.

PUNCH, CITRUS SUPER

Fills 22 full-size (8-ounce) glasses.
Everyone will want seconds.

2 c. orange juice, fresh or reconstituted
1½ qt. (6 c.) cold water
1 (46-oz.) can pineapple juice or pink grapefruit juice
1 (6-oz.) can frozen lemonade or 1 c. lemon juice
1 c. sugar
1 c. hot water
2 qt. (2 liters) ginger ale

1. Freeze orange juice (to be added at serving time). 2. In 6 or 8-quart container, combine cold water, pineapple juice and lemonade (or lemon juice). 3. Dissolve sugar in 1 cup hot water and add to punch; refrigerate. 4. At serving time, add ginger ale and frozen block of orange juice. (This will completely fill a 6-quart punch bowl.)

PUNCH, CRANBERRY PINEAPPLE

A not-so-sweet punch; makes 3 tall glasses.

1½ c. cranberry juice cocktail
1½ c. unsweetened pineapple juice
1 (12-oz.) can ginger ale (1½ c.)
Crushed ice or ice cubes

1. Combine liquid ingredients; pour over ice.

PUNCH, JANELLE'S

Makes 20 full-size (8-ounce) glasses of punch.
(Plenty for 10 or 11 people.)

3 pkgs. unsweetened cherry, strawberry, orange or lemon Kool-Aid
2 c. sugar
12 c. water (3 qt.)
2 qt. (or 2 liters) ginger ale, chilled
1 (6-oz.) can frozen orange juice or lemonade (opt.)

1. In 6 or 8-quart container, combine Kool-Aid, sugar and water; refrigerate. 2. Just before serving, add ginger ale and frozen orange juice or lemonade. **Note**: 1 quart (or 1 liter) ginger ale and 1 (46-ounce) can pineapple juice may be substituted for 2 quarts ginger ale.

PUNCH, ORANGE BLUSH

Makes 8 to 12 servings.

2½ c. orange juice
½ c. lemon juice
2 c. pineapple juice
½ c. maraschino cherry juice
¼ c. honey
2 c. ginger ale

1. Mix together all ingredients, except ginger ale and chill. 2. Just before serving, add ginger ale. 3. Pour over ice in small punch bowl.

PUNCH, RASPBERRY-PINEAPPLE

Fills 10 full-size (8-ounce) glasses.

1 (46-oz.) can pineapple juice
4 c. Dole Pure & Light Country Raspberry Juice
1 pt. fresh or frozen raspberries
1 lemon, thinly sliced
Ice

1. Chill ingredients. 2. Combine in small punch bowl.

PUNCH, SHERBET

From Leota Reynolds and Sharon Close.

Pineapple or lime sherbet, any amount
Lemon-lime pop or 7-Up, any amount

1. Place sherbet in punch bowl or glasses. 2. Pour pop over the sherbet. **Note**: Orange sherbet with Canada Dry ginger ale is also good.

PUNCH, SPARKLE

From Barbara Benninger.
For a small 3-quart punch bowl.

1 (3-oz.) pkg. strawberry Jello
1 c. boiling water
1 (12-oz.) can frozen lemonade, slightly thawed
2 qt. (or 2 liters) ginger ale or 7-Up

1. Dissolve Jello in boiling water. 2. Add frozen lemonade, stirring until thawed. 3. Add ginger ale or 7-Up just before serving. 4. Serve with ice cubes. Makes over 2½ quarts. **Note**: Fresh strawberries, cut in half or pureed in blender, may be added if desired.

PUNCH, STRAWBERRY PINEAPPLE

From Shirley Stevenson.

1 (46-oz.) can pineapple juice
2 bottles (2 liters each) strawberry pop
2 bottles (2 liters each) 7-Up
Ice ring made of frozen pineapple juice

1. Place all ingredients in punch bowl.

PUNCH, TROPICAL

Fills 21 full-size (8-ounce) glasses; for 15 to 20 people, double the recipe.

2 pkgs. unsweetened red Kool-Aid
2 c. sugar
2 qt. (8 c.) water
1 (46-oz.) can Hawaiian Punch (red) or pineapple juice
1 (2-liter) bottle ginger ale (or 2 qt.)

1. Mix together Kool-Aid, sugar, water and the 46-ounce can of juice. 2. Put 2 cups of punch mixture into a small container, mold or ice cube trays and freeze. 3. Refrigerate remaining punch; at serving time, add ginger ale. 4. Place frozen punch in bottom of punch bowl and add punch (or serve in glasses with frozen punch ice cubes).

PURPLE COW

1 c. grape juice
1 c. vanilla ice cream

Fill glass ⅔ full with grape juice; add 2 scoops ice cream. Serve with iced teaspoon.

SLUSH, LIME PINEAPPLE

From Bonnie Swarts.

1 (3-oz.) pkg. lime gelatin
1 c. sugar
3 c. boiling water
1 (46-oz.) can pineapple juice
2 qt. (or 2 liters) ginger ale

1. Stir gelatin and sugar in boiling water until dissolved. 2. Add pineapple juice; freeze. 3. 2 to 3 hours before serving, let thaw until slushy. 4. Put in punch bowl and add ginger ale.

SLUSH, TROPICAL

*From Sarah Stevenson McIlhany.
Makes 20 (½-cup) servings.*

1½ c. sugar
3 c. water
3 c. unsweetened pineapple juice
1½ c. orange juice
2 T. lemon juice
3 ripe bananas, mashed
1 liter (4 c.) Sprite or lemon-lime pop, chilled

1. Combine sugar and water in saucepan and bring to a boil; reduce heat and gently boil 5 minutes. Cool. 2. In large plastic or glass container, combine sugar-syrup mixture, fruit juices and mashed bananas; mix well and freeze, covered. 3. Two hours before serving, remove from freezer and let stand at room temperature. 4. Just before serving, stir Sprite or pop into slushy mixture; serve immediately. (Or, put a scoop of frozen mixture in a glass with ice; fill up with Seven-Up or ginger ale.)

TEA, ICED

Makes a gallon. This can be ready to serve in 20 minutes, with ice cubes.

2 c. water, boiling
5 to 8 tea bags (or ⅓ c. loose tea leaves)
1 to 1¼ c. sugar, according to your taste (opt.)
Cold water

1. In small pan, bring 2 cups water to a full boil. 2. Add tea bags and set off burner; let steep 5 to 10 minutes. 3. Put sugar in gallon jar or gallon pitcher; add hot tea (discarding tea bags), stirring until sugar dissolves. If using loose tea, strain through sieve. 4. Add cold water to make one gallon of tea. 5. Refrigerate; serve with ice cubes.

TEA, ICED (Sugar-Free)

Makes 2 quarts.

2 c. water, boiling
4 regular-size tea bags
6 c. cold water
1 T. liquid sweetener or 4 to 6 envelopes Equal
    and ¼ tsp. Sweet 'n Low (opt.)

1. In small pan, bring 2 cups water to a full boil. 2. Add tea bags and set off burner; let steep 5 to 10 minutes. 3. Pour into pitcher, discard tea bags; add cold water and desired sweetener. 4. Refrigerate; serve with ice cubes.

TEA, SUN

5 to 8 regular-size tea bags
1 gal. cold water from tap
1 c. sugar (opt.)

1. Place tea bags in gallon jar and fill with cold water. 2. Cover jar and let it stand in the sun for 3 to 4 hours. (Sunlight isn't even necessary.) If desired, add sugar at this point (1 to 1¼ cups according to your taste), stirring until sugar dissolves. 3. Refrigerate.

Chapter 6

Quick Breads

LIMBER REUNION—1945

STANDING, L. TO R.: MAUDE LIMBER, EMILY MCKEAN KEEBAUGH, LEE LIMBER, JEAN HOCKETT, PHYLLIS LIMBER, PHYLLIS LAVER, BOB LIMBER, DORIS GOODRICH, ALDEN STEVENSON, EDDIE BEGGS, HELEN MCKEAN, REED MCCORMICK, MABEL GOODRICH HOLDING SCOTTY DOG, _____, EDNA GOODRICH, NEVIN LAVER, CARL LIMBER, ROY MCKEAN.

SEATED, L. TO R.: ANNA STEVENSON IN WHEELCHAIR, RUTH MCCORMICK, ELLEN STEVENSON, NOLA LIMBER, MARTY MCKEAN, SARAH STEVENSON, EDITH LIMBER, ALICE MCKEAN, DOROTHY LIMBER, AUDREY MCCORMICK, LAWRENCE STEVENSON, TOM MCCORMICK.

ON GROUND: JEAN LIMBER, _____, AND VIRGINIA MCCORMICK

QUICK BREADS

BISCUITS

2 c. all-purpose flour
3 tsp. baking powder
½ tsp. salt
⅔ c. milk
⅓ c. olive oil

1. Turn oven dial to 450°. **2.** Combine dry ingredients in medium bowl. **3.** In small bowl combine milk and oil, but do not stir; pour all at once over dry ingredients. **4.** Mix with fork only until dough clings together; knead lightly with floured hands 10 times. **5.** Place on waxed paper (on slightly wet surface to keep paper from sliding around); pat out to 1-inch thickness, making a 6-inch square. **6.** Cut into 9 square biscuits. (Or pat dough to ½-inch thickness and make 12 to 14 biscuits with cookie cutter or top of water glass.) **7.** With a pancake turner, place biscuits close together, sides touching, on ungreased baking sheet. **8.** Bake in preheated 450° oven 10 to 15 minutes, until golden. **For Drop Biscuits:** Increase milk to ¾ cup plus 2 tablespoons; mix dough and drop by spoonfuls on ungreased baking sheet.

BISCUITS, BUTTERMILK

Adapted from Shirley Triance.
Makes 10 to 12 biscuits, but may be doubled.

1½ c. all-purpose flour
3 tsp. baking powder
¼ tsp. baking soda
½ tsp. salt
¼ c. Earth Balance shortening
¾ c. commercial buttermilk

1. Turn oven dial to 450°. **2.** Grease or spray a small baking sheet or 11 x 7-inch shallow pan. **3.** In medium bowl, stir together dry ingredients. **4.** With pastry blender, work in shortening until mixture resembles coarse cornmeal. **5.** Add buttermilk all at once, mixing together lightly with fork just enough for dough to hold together. **6.** On lightly floured surface, pat dough to ¾-inch thickness. **7.** Cut out biscuits with floured 2½-inch cutter or top of water glass, floured; place on greased baking sheet, about ⅛-inch apart. **8.** Bake in preheated 450° oven 12 to 13 minutes or until golden brown.

BISCUITS, BUTTERMILK WHOLE WHEAT

Makes 10 biscuits.

1 c. whole-wheat flour
1 c. all-purpose flour
2 T. sugar
2 tsp. baking powder
¼ tsp. baking soda
½ tsp. salt
3 T. butter or reg. Smart Balance spread
¾ c. commercial buttermilk

1. Turn oven dial to 450°. **2.** In large bowl, mix together flours, sugar, baking powder, soda and salt. **3.** Cut in butter with pastry blender or fingers until mixture resembles coarse crumbs. **4.** Stir in buttermilk all at once with a fork, just until mixture forms soft dough that leaves side of bowl. **5.** Turn dough onto lightly floured surface; pat dough with floured fingers to 1-inch thickness. **6.** Cut into squares or diamonds (or with floured 2½-inch biscuit cutter); with pancake turner, place biscuits on lightly sprayed small baking sheet (1 inch apart for crusty biscuits or nearly touching for soft-sided ones.) **7.** Bake in preheated 450° oven 12 to 15 minutes, until golden.

BREAD, BANANA

Makes 1 loaf, but recipe may be doubled or tripled.
Quite ripe bananas may be used.

1¾ c. all-purpose flour
¾ c. sugar
2 tsp. baking powder
¼ tsp. baking soda
½ tsp. salt
2 eggs
1 tsp. vanilla
⅓ c. olive oil
1 c. (2 lg.) bananas, peeled and mashed (or use food processor)
¾ to 1 c. coarsely chopped nuts (opt.)

1. Turn oven dial to 325°. **2.** Grease 9 x 5-inch loaf pan (approximate size). **3.** In order given, put all ingredients in bowl; beat until smooth with spoon or mixer. **4.** Pour into prepared pan and bake in preheated 325° oven about 60 minutes, or until golden brown, and center top of loaf is no longer soft. **5.** Loosen around edges with a spatula; remove from pan and cool before slicing.

BREAD, CINNAMON SWIRL

From Kay Patterson; makes 2 loaves. Freezes well.

2 c. sugar
1 c. olive oil
4 eggs
3 c. all-purpose flour
2 tsp. baking powder
½ tsp. salt
1 c. milk

Cinnamon Mixture:
2 T. sugar
2 T. cinnamon

1. Turn oven dial to 350°; grease 2 bread pans. 2. In mixer bowl, cream together sugar and oil. 3. Add eggs, one at a time, beating well after each addition. 4. Add dry ingredients alternately with milk, beginning and ending with flour. 5. In small bowl or cup, mix together the cinnamon mixture. 6. Pour enough batter in each greased bread pan to cover bottom; sprinkle 2 teaspoons cinnamon mixture over batter. 7. Continue doing this several times until batter and cinnamon mixture are used, ending with batter. 8. Bake in preheated 350° oven 45 minutes, or until wooden pick comes out clean. 9. Let stand in pan 15 minutes before removing to cooling rack.

BREAD, COMMUNION

For religious services; from Mrs. Leota A. Benninger.

1 c. all-purpose flour, spooned lightly into cup
2 tsp. sugar, level
1/16 tsp. salt
1/4 c. pure butter (1/2 stick), cold
About 3 to 3 1/2 T. ice-cold water, approximately

1. In medium bowl combine flour, sugar and salt. 2. Add butter and mix with pastry blender or fingers until fine and crumbly. 3. Add cold water gradually, stirring with fork, using only as much as is needed to make like pie crust. Do not mix more than necessary. 4. Pat with fingers into 13 x 9-inch ungreased cake pan, evenly over the bottom. (It will be thin.) 5. Cut with dinner knife clear through to bottom of pan, making whatever size pieces desired. 6. Bake in preheated 350° oven for 15 to 20 minutes, or until light golden brown. 7. Let cool in pan. 8. Separate pieces and store in airtight container. **To cut in Half:** Pat into heavy pie pan or an 8 x 8-inch square pan.

BREAD, DATE-RAISIN

Delicious, baked in five soup cans!
From Betty Geneviva.

8-oz. pkg. dates, chopped
3/4 c. raisins
1 tsp. baking soda
1 c. boiling water
2 T. softened butter
1 c. sugar
1 tsp. vanilla
1 egg
1 1/3 c. all-purpose flour
3/4 c. chopped nuts

1. In bowl, combine dates, raisins, soda and boiling water; cover bowl with plate or lid. 2. Cream together butter, sugar and vanilla. 3. Beat in egg, then flour. 4. Fold in date mixture and nuts. 5. With pastry brush, butter five Campbell soup cans (10 3/4-oz. size) with soft butter. 6. Pour batter into soup cans; set cans on a cookie sheet. 7. Bake in preheated 325° oven 45 minutes. 8. Cool 5 minutes, then remove from cans to cooling rack.

BREAD, LEMON

Adapted from Carolyn Benninger Deets.

1/3 c. reg. Smart Balance spread or butter
1 c. sugar
2 eggs
1 1/2 c. all-purpose flour
1 tsp. baking powder
1/4 tsp. salt
2/3 c. milk
1/4 tsp. lemon extract or almond extract (opt.)
Grated rind from 1 lg. or 2 small lemons (opt.)
1/2 c. chopped nuts (opt.)

Glaze:
1/4 c. sugar
Juice from lemon(s) or 1/4 c. bottled lemon juice

1. Turn oven dial to 350°. 2. Grease and flour one loaf pan (or two tiny loaf pans). 3. Cream together butter and sugar until fluffy. 4. Add eggs and beat well. 5. In med.-small bowl, combine flour, baking powder and salt. 6. Add flour mixture to egg mixture alternately with milk, extract and lemon rind. 7. Fold in nuts; pour batter into prepared pan(s). 8. Bake in preheated 350° oven 45 to 60 minutes, until done; loosen around edges and remove from pan to a small platter, top side up. 9. In same med.-small flour bowl, combine the sugar and lemon juice for glaze. 10. Prick top of loaf or loaves with fork; drizzle glaze over hot bread. **Note**: When using 2 tiny loaf pans, bake 40 minutes.

BREAD, PUMPKIN

Makes 2 medium-size loaves; from Bonnie Bash.
May be frozen.

2 eggs
1 c. pumpkin
1/2 c. olive oil
1/3 c. water
1 2/3 c. all-purpose flour
1 1/4 c. sugar
1 tsp. baking soda
1/2 tsp. nutmeg
1/2 tsp. cinnamon
1/4 tsp. salt
1/2 c. chopped nuts or more (opt.)
1 c. candied fruit or candied cherries or fresh or frozen
    cranberries (opt.)

1. Turn oven dial to 350° and grease (or spray) and flour 2 medium-sized bread pans. 2. In mixer bowl, combine eggs, pumpkin, oil and water, beating together. 3. Add dry ingredients and mix together. 4. Stir in nuts and candied fruit or cranberries, if used. 5. Pour into prepared pans and bake in preheated 350° oven 45 minutes or until done.

BREAD, ZUCCHINI (2 Loaves)

Delicious! From Ruth Flick and Violet Crocker.

3 eggs, beaten until foamy
1 c. olive oil
2 c. sugar
2 tsp. vanilla
2 c. zucchini pulp
3 c. all-purpose flour
1 tsp. baking powder
1 tsp. baking soda
1 tsp. salt
3 tsp. cinnamon
½ to 1 c. chopped nuts (opt.)
1 c. raisins (opt.)
8 to 16 oz. crushed pineapple, well drained (opt.)
2 tsp. Durkee grated orange peel (opt.)

1. Prepare zucchini (and nuts and pineapple if used). **2.** Turn oven dial to 325° and grease and flour 2 loaf pans (large bread pans). **3.** In mixer bowl, beat eggs; add oil, sugar and vanilla, mixing well. **4.** Add zucchini which has been shredded or finely chopped in food processor, blender or grater. (I prefer to peel zucchini first and remove any large seeds.) **5.** Add remaining ingredients, mixing just until blended together. **6.** Pour batter into two well-greased and floured loaf pans and bake in preheated 325° oven for 1 to 1¼ hours (until wooden pick inserted in center comes out clean.) **7.** Cool in pans 10 minutes, then remove from pans and cool on cooling racks.

CORNBREAD

From Anna L. Stevenson.

1 c. all-purpose flour
1 c. yellow cornmeal
¼ to ⅓ c. sugar
4 tsp. baking powder
½ tsp. salt
1 c. milk
¼ c. olive oil (or melted butter)
1 lg. egg (or 2 med. eggs)

1. Turn oven dial to 400°. **2.** Combine dry ingredients in a bowl; stir well to blend. **3.** Add milk, oil and egg; beat until smooth, about 1 minute. (Do not over-beat.) **4.** Pour into greased or sprayed 8 x 8-inch or 9 x 9-inch square pan (or 13 x 9-inch or 11 x 7-inch pan). **5.** Bake in preheated 400° oven for 20 to 25 minutes or until golden brown. **Note**: If using self-rising flour, omit baking powder and salt. **For Corn Muffins:** pour into 12 greased muffin cups and bake 15 to 20 minutes, or until firm and golden brown.

CORNBREAD, HEALTH

No shortening or sugar in this cornbread.

1 c. yellow cornmeal
⅓ c. all-purpose flour
1 tsp. baking powder
¼ tsp. baking soda
¼ to ½ tsp. salt
1 egg
1 c. commercial buttermilk

1. Combine dry ingredients in a medium bowl. **2.** Add egg and buttermilk, mixing well. **3.** Pour batter into a greased 8 x 8-inch (or larger) pan. **4.** Bake in preheated 400° oven for 20 to 25 minutes or until golden brown.

HUSH PUPPIES

Adapted from a recipe that was 100 years old in 1999.

2 c. cornmeal
½ c. flour
3¾ t. baking powder
¾ t. salt
½ t. pepper
1½ c. chopped onion
Milk
Olive oil to fry (at least 3 inches deep)

1. Mix together, adding milk a little at a time; batter should be thick. **2.** Drop by teaspoons into boiling oil and cook to a golden brown. Makes approximately 25.

MUFFINS

1¾ c. all-purpose flour
⅓ c. sugar (or packed brown sugar)
2½ tsp. baking powder
¼ tsp. salt
1 egg (or 2 egg whites), beaten
¾ c. milk
¼ c. olive oil or melted butter
½ c. chopped nuts (opt.)

1. Turn oven dial to 425°. **2.** Grease or Pam-spray 12 medium (regular) muffin cups. **3.** In medium-large bowl, stir together flour, sugar, baking powder and salt. **4.** In small bowl, beat egg; add milk and oil and beat again. **5.** Add egg mixture and nuts all at once to dry ingredients; stir quickly just until dry ingredients are moistened. **6.** Spoon batter into 12 muffin cups (about ¾ full). **7.** Bake in preheated 425° oven about 18 to 25 minutes or until light golden brown and firm to the touch. **8.** Immediately remove muffins from cups; serve warm or cool.

MUFFINS, APPLE OATMEAL

Makes 12 muffins.

1¼ c. uncooked oats, quick or old-fashioned
1¼ c. all-purpose flour
½ c. FINELY CHOPPED apple (any kind)
⅓ c. packed brown sugar (or white sugar)
3 tsp. baking powder
1 tsp. cinnamon
¼ tsp. salt
1 c. milk
1 egg (or 2 egg whites)
¼ c. olive oil
½ to ¾ c. raisins (opt.)
½ c. chopped nuts (opt.)

Topping (Optional):
1 T. sugar
¼ tsp. cinnamon

1. Turn oven dial to 425°. 2. Grease or Pam-spray 12 medium (regular) muffin cups. 3. In mixing bowl, combine oats, flour, apple, brown sugar, baking powder, cinnamon and salt. 4. Add milk, egg, olive oil, raisins and nuts; stir just until dry ingredients are moistened. 5. Fill greased muffin cups, dividing batter equally. 6. For topping, mix together Topping ingredients and sprinkle scant ¼ teaspoon over each muffin. 7. Bake in preheated 425° oven 15 to 18 minutes or until golden brown and firm to the touch. 8. Loosen around edges and remove to cooling rack.

MUFFINS, APPLESAUCE BRAN

1½ c. all-purpose flour (white or whole-wheat)
½ c. oat bran or unprocessed wheat bran
2 tsp. baking powder
¼ tsp. salt
¾ tsp. cinnamon
¼ tsp. ginger
¼ c. sugar or honey
¼ c. olive oil
¾ c. applesauce, unsweetened or sweetened
¼ c. milk or apple juice
1 egg or 2 egg whites
¾ c. raisins or cut-up dates (opt.)
½ c. chopped nuts (opt.)

1. Turn oven dial to 400°. 2. In mixing bowl, stir together dry ingredients. 3. Add wet ingredients, stirring only until blended. 4. Fold in raisins and nuts. 5. Spoon batter into 12 greased or Pam-sprayed muffin cups. 6. Bake in preheated 400° oven on middle shelf 20 to 25 minutes or until golden brown and firm to the touch. 7. Immediately remove muffins from cups. **Note**: Bran may be omitted; in that case, use 1¾ cups flour.

MUFFINS, APPLESAUCE OATMEAL

Makes 12 delicious muffins.

1½ c. uncooked oats, quick or old-fashioned
1¼ c. all-purpose flour
1 tsp. baking powder
¾ tsp. baking soda
1 tsp. cinnamon
¼ tsp. salt (opt.)
1 c. unsweetened applesauce
½ c. packed brown sugar
½ c. milk
¼ c. olive oil
1 tsp. vanilla (opt.)
1 egg (or 2 egg whites)
¼ c. chopped nuts (opt.)
½ c. raisins (opt.)

1. Turn oven dial to 375°; grease or Pam-spray 12 medium (regular) muffin cups. 2. In mixing bowl, combine oats, flour, baking powder, baking soda, cinnamon and salt. 3. Add applesauce, brown sugar, milk, oil, vanilla and egg; mix just until dry ingredients are moistened. 4. Quickly stir in nuts and raisins, if used. 5. Fill muffin cups almost full, dividing batter equally. 6. Bake in preheated 375° oven 20 to 25 minutes or until golden brown and firm to the touch. 7. Loosen around edges and remove to cooling rack.

MUFFINS, BANANA BRAN

Uses bran cereal. Delicious!

1¼ c. oat bran or All-Bran cereal (or crushed Total or
    Bran Flakes)
¾ c. milk
¾ c. mashed ripe banana (2 med.-small bananas)
1 egg (or 2 egg whites)
½ c. packed brown sugar
¼ c. olive oil
½ tsp. vanilla
1 c. all-purpose flour
2½ tsp. baking powder
½ tsp. baking soda
½ tsp. cinnamon
¼ tsp. salt
¼ to ½ c. chopped nuts (opt.)

1. In large bowl combine bran and milk; let stand 5 to 10 minutes. 2. Turn oven dial to 400°. 3. Grease or Pam-spray 12 medium (regular) muffin cups. 4. To bran mixture, add bananas, egg, brown sugar, oil and vanilla. 5. Add dry ingredients and nuts, stirring just until moistened. 6. Fill greased muffin cups nearly full. 7. Bake in preheated 400° oven 20 minutes or until golden brown and firm to the touch. 8. Immediately remove muffins from cups; serve warm or cool.

MUFFINS, BLUEBERRY

2 lg. eggs
⅔ c. sugar
½ c. olive oil or soft butter
½ c. milk
1 or 2 tsp. vanilla
2½ c. all-purpose flour
3 tsp. baking powder
½ tsp. salt
1½ c. blueberries, fresh or frozen, drained
⅓ to ½ c. chopped nuts (opt.)

1. Turn oven dial to 400°. 2. Grease or Pam-spray 12 regular 2¾-inch muffin cups. 3. In medium-large bowl, combine eggs, sugar, oil and milk; whisk until smooth. 4. In another bowl, combine flour, baking powder and salt, stirring together. 5. Add dry ingredients all at once to egg mixture, stirring with rubber spatula just until combined. 6. Fold in blueberries and nuts gently. 7. Spoon batter into the prepared muffin cups. 8. Bake in preheated 400° oven about 20 minutes, or until golden brown and firm to the touch. 9. Immediately remove muffins from cups; serve warm or cool.

MUFFINS, BLUEBERRY (Smaller)

Makes 12 smaller muffins.

1¾ c. all-purpose flour
½ c. sugar
2½ tsp. baking powder
¼ tsp. salt
¾ c. milk
¼ c. olive oil
1 egg
1 c. blueberries, frozen or fresh, drained
1 T. flour
½ c. nuts (opt.)

1. Turn oven dial to 400° and grease or spray 12 regular muffin cups. 2. In medium bowl, combine first four dry ingredients, stirring together. 3. Make a well in the center; add milk, oil and egg to the well. 4. Break the egg with a fork; stir all together quickly with the fork, only until dry ingredients are moistened. 5. Toss drained blueberries with 1 tablespoon flour; fold gently into batter. 6. Spoon into prepared muffin cups, dividing batter equally. 7. Bake in preheated 400° oven 20 to 25 minutes or until golden brown and firm to the touch. 8. Immediately remove muffins from cups; serve warm or cool.

MUFFINS, BLUEBERRY OATMEAL

Makes 12 muffins.

1 c. uncooked oats, quick or old-fashioned
¾ c. milk or orange juice
1 c. whole-wheat or all-purpose flour
⅓ c. sugar (white or packed brown)

1½ tsp. baking powder
½ tsp. baking soda
¼ tsp. cinnamon
¼ tsp. salt (opt.)
¼ c. olive oil
1 egg (or 2 egg whites)
1 c. fresh or frozen blueberries, drained

1. Turn oven dial to 400°. 2. Grease or Pam-spray 12 medium (regular) muffin cups, or line with paper baking cups. 3. In mixing bowl, combine oats and orange juice or milk. 4. Add flour, sugar, baking powder, soda, cinnamon, salt, oil and egg, stirring just until dry ingredients are moistened. 5. Fold in blueberries. 6. Divide batter evenly in 12 muffin cups. 7. Bake in preheated 400° oven 18 to 22 minutes or until golden brown and firm to the touch. 8. Cool 5 minutes in pan; loosen edges and remove muffins from cups to cooling rack.

MUFFINS, BRAN FLAKE

Makes 12 muffins.

2½ c. bran flakes
1¼ c. milk
¼ c. olive oil
1 egg (or 2 egg whites)
1¼ c. all-purpose flour
3 tsp. baking powder
¼ tsp. salt
½ c. sugar (or packed brown sugar)
½ tsp. cinnamon (opt.)
½ c. raisins (opt.)
½ c. chopped nuts (opt.)

1. Mix bran flakes and milk in large bowl; let stand until cereal is softened, about 5 minutes. 2. Turn oven dial to 400°. 3. Grease or Pam-spray 12 regular 2¾-inch muffin cups. 4. Add oil and egg to cereal mixture and remaining ingredients, stirring only until moistened. 5. Divide batter into muffin cups. 6. Bake in preheated 400° oven for 18 to 23 minutes, until golden brown and firm to the touch. 7. Loosen around edges and remove to cooling rack.

MUFFINS, BRAN (High Fiber)

Makes 12 muffins.

2 c. 100% Bran cereal, or All-Bran or Bran Buds
1¼ c. milk
¼ c. olive oil
1 egg (or 2 egg whites)
1 c. all-purpose flour
⅓ c. packed brown sugar
2 tsp. baking powder
½ tsp. baking soda
¼ tsp. salt (opt.)
½ to ⅔ c. raisins (opt.)
⅓ to ½ c. chopped nuts (opt.)

1. In bowl, combine bran and milk; let stand 5 minutes. **2.** Turn oven dial to 400°. **3.** Grease or Pam-spray 12 medium (regular) muffin cups. **4.** Mix oil and egg into bran mixture. **5.** Stir in dry ingredients, mixing just until blended; fold in raisins and nuts. **6.** Spoon into 12 prepared muffin cups. **7.** Bake in 400° preheated oven 18 minutes or until golden brown and firm to the touch. **8.** Loosen around edges and remove to cooling rack.

MUFFINS, BRAN (No-Cholesterol)

Makes 12 muffins.

1 c. whole-wheat or all-purpose flour
1 c. All-Bran, Bran Buds or 100% Bran cereal
2 tsp. baking powder
¼ tsp. salt
½ c. raisins or nuts
2 egg whites
1 c. skim milk
¼ c. olive oil
¼ c. honey

1. Turn oven dial to 400°. **2.** Pam-spray 12 medium (regular) muffin cups. **3.** In large bowl, stir flour, bran cereal, baking powder, salt and raisins. **4.** In small bowl, stir egg whites, milk, oil and honey until well blended. **5.** Stir into flour mixture just until moistened; let stand 3 minutes. **6.** Divide batter into 12 muffin cups and bake in preheated 400° oven for 15 to 20 minutes, or until golden brown and firm to the touch. **7.** Loosen muffins around edges and remove to cooling rack.

MUFFINS, BRAN, PAT'S

Makes 12 delicious muffins.

1 c. unprocessed coarse bran, or All-Bran, Bran Buds or
    100% Bran cereal
1 c. boiling water
¼ c. olive oil
¼ c. honey or sugar
2 eggs
1½ c. all-purpose flour (or part whole-wheat flour)
1¼ tsp. baking soda
¼ tsp. salt
1 c. buttermilk, sour milk or yogurt
½ c. raisins (opt.)
½ c. chopped nuts or sunflower seeds (opt.)

1. Add bran to boiling water; let set 10 minutes. **2.** Grease or Pam-spray 12 regular 2¾-inch muffin cups. **3.** Turn oven dial to 350°. **4.** In large bowl, combine oil, honey and eggs; mix well. **5.** Add flour, soda and salt alternately with buttermilk. **6.** Stir in bran mixture, raisins and nuts. Do not over mix. **7.** Divide batter into muffin cups. **8.** Bake in preheated 350° oven 25 minutes or until golden brown and firm to the touch. **9.** Loosen around edges and remove to cooling rack.

MUFFINS, BRAN (Refrigerator)

Adapted from Betty Marcin. This batter keeps for four weeks in the refrigerator. Recipe may be doubled.

3 c. All-Bran, Bran Buds or 100% Bran cereal
1 c. raisins (opt.)
1 c. sugar
1 c. boiling water
¼ c. packed brown sugar
1 T. molasses
½ c. olive oil
2 c. commercial buttermilk
2 eggs
2½ c. all-purpose flour (or half whole-wheat flour)
2½ tsp. baking soda
½ tsp. salt
1 c. chopped nuts (opt.)

1. In large bowl, combine cereal, raisins, sugar and boiling water, stirring together; set aside for 10 minutes. **2.** Grease or spray as many muffin cups as desired. (The entire amount will make about 30 muffins.) **3.** Turn oven dial to 400°. **4.** Add brown sugar, molasses, oil, buttermilk and eggs to bran mixture; mix well. **5.** In med.-small bowl, combine flour, soda, salt and nuts, stirring together; add to bran mixture, stirring only enough to moisten dry ingredients. **6.** Fill prepared muffin cups about three-fourths full. **7.** Bake in preheated 400° oven 18 to 20 minutes or until golden brown and firm to the touch. **8.** Cool 3 to 5 minutes before loosening around edges and removing to cooling rack. **9.** Place remaining batter in covered container in refrigerator.

MUFFINS, OATMEAL & BRAN CRUNCHIES

1 c. all-purpose flour
¾ c. uncooked oats, quick or old-fashioned
¼ c. unprocessed wheat bran or oat bran or Bran Buds
3 tsp. baking powder
½ tsp. cinnamon
⅛ tsp. nutmeg
¼ tsp. salt
¼ c. packed brown sugar (opt.)
1 egg (or 2 egg whites)
1 c. milk
2 T. olive oil
½ tsp. vanilla
½ c. chopped walnuts or toasted chopped almonds
½ c. raisins or chopped dates (opt.)

1. Turn oven dial to 400°. **2.** Grease or Pam-spray 12 medium (regular) muffin cups. **3.** In mixing bowl combine flour, oats, bran, baking powder, cinnamon, nutmeg, salt and brown sugar. **4.** Add egg, milk, oil and vanilla; stir just until dry ingredients are moistened. **5.** Stir in nuts and raisins. **6.** Divide batter into greased muffin cups. **7.** Bake in preheated 400° oven 20 minutes or until golden brown and firm to the touch. **8.** Loosen around edges and remove to cooling rack.

MUFFINS, OATMEAL-RAISIN

Makes 12 muffins.

1 c. uncooked rolled oats
1 c. commercial buttermilk
1 c. whole-wheat flour (or half whole-wheat and half white)
1½ tsp. baking powder
½ tsp. baking soda
½ tsp. salt
¼ c. olive oil
¼ c. packed brown sugar
1 lg. egg, beaten
½ c. raisins
⅓ c. nuts, chopped

1. In large bowl, combine oats and buttermilk and let mixture stand at least 30 minutes. 2. Grease or Pam-spray 12 medium (regular) muffin cups. 3. Turn oven dial to 350°. 4. In small bowl, combine flour, baking powder, soda and salt; set aside. 5. Into the soaked oats, stir oil, sugar and egg; blend well. 6. Stir in flour mixture and raisins, mixing only until moistened. (Do not over mix.) 7. Spoon batter into 12 greased muffin cups (about ¾ full). 8. Bake in preheated 350° oven about 25 minutes or until golden brown and firm to the touch. 9. Loosen around edges and remove to cooling rack.

MUFFINS, PINEAPPLE-COCONUT

Very good.

2 c. all-purpose flour
1 c. quick oats (not instant)
3 tsp. baking powder
½ tsp. salt
½ c. sugar
½ c. shredded coconut, toasted or untoasted
1 egg
¼ c. olive oil
⅓ c. milk
1 tsp. vanilla
1½ c. crushed pineapple, undrained
½ c. chopped walnuts or pecans (opt.)

1. In bowl, stir together flour, oats, baking powder, salt, sugar and coconut. 2. Add egg, oil, milk, vanilla and pineapple; stir together, just until completely mixed. 3. Divide batter between 12 greased or sprayed muffin cups. 4. Bake in preheated 375° oven 25 to 30 minutes or until golden brown and firm to the touch. 5. Loosen around edges and remove from pan to cooling rack.

MUFFINS, ZUCCHINI

Makes 9 muffins.

1 c. shredded zucchini, pressed in cup
1 egg
⅓ c. sugar
¼ c. olive oil
1 c. all-purpose flour
¼ tsp. baking powder
¼ tsp. baking soda
¼ tsp. salt
¼ tsp. nutmeg
⅓ to ½ c. raisins
⅓ to ½ c. chopped nuts (opt.)

1. Turn oven dial to 375°. 2. Grease or Pam-spray 9 medium (regular) muffin cups. 3. Combine zucchini, egg, sugar and oil; mix well. 4. Add remaining ingredients, stirring just until mixed. Batter will be lumpy. 5. Fill greased muffin cups ¾ full. 6. Bake in preheated 375° oven about 20 minutes or until golden brown and firm to the touch. 7. Loosen around edges and remove to cooling rack.

SCONES, SCOTCH

Makes 12 scones.

2 c. all-purpose flour
3 tsp. baking powder
½ tsp. salt
2 T. sugar
2 eggs
¼ c. olive oil
¼ c. milk
½ c. raisins (opt.)
Sugar

1. Turn oven dial to 400°. 2. In medium-large bowl, combine dry ingredients. 3. In small bowl, beat eggs slightly; take out 1 tablespoon beaten eggs and set aside for brushing tops of scones. 4. In same small bowl with the eggs, add oil and milk, but do not stir; pour all at once into dry ingredients. Stir with a fork until mixture cleans sides of bowl and rounds up into a ball. (Do not over mix.) 5. Knead about 10 times; divide dough into three balls and pat each out into a ½-inch thick circle. 6. Cut each into four pie-shaped wedges; brush with remaining beaten egg and sprinkle with granulated sugar lightly. 7. Bake on ungreased baking sheet in preheated 425° oven 12 to 15 minutes or until golden brown.

Chapter 7

Yeast Breads

JIM AND MARTHA STEVENSON'S WEDDING

**LAWRENCE STEVENSON, ELLEN, ALPHA AND ELEANOR OSBORNE,
MILDRED AND MARGARET STEVENSON, MARTHA AND JIM STEVENSON, SHIRLEY
ARTMAN AND ALDEN STEVENSON**
1948

YEAST BREADS

BREAD-RAISING HINT

Turn oven dial to 150° or 170° for 1 minute, then turn off. Put bread dough in closed oven to rise.

BREAD, WHITE (BREAD MACHINE)

This makes 1 loaf of soft potato bread.

1¼ c. lukewarm water (70° to 80°)
2½ T. sugar
2 T. mashed potato flakes
1 tsp. salt
3 T. olive oil
3 c. all-purpose flour (or bread flour)
1½ tsp. active dry yeast

1. In bread machine pan, place all ingredients in order suggested by manufacturer. 2. Select "Basic Bread Setting." 3. Choose loaf size and crust color, if available. 4. Bake according to bread machine directions. (Check dough after 5 minutes of mixing; add 1 to 2 tablespoons of flour or water if needed.) Yields 1 loaf (1½ lbs.) **Optional ingredients:** 2 T. dry powdered milk, 2 T. ground flax seed, 1 T. wheat gluten, or raw or toasted wheat germ may be added, if desired.

BREAD, 1 LOAF (No-Knead)

Delicious and easy.

1¼ c. warm (not hot) water
1 pkg. active dry yeast (2¼ tsp. bulk dry yeast)
1½ T. sugar
1 tsp. salt
2 T. olive oil or softened butter
3 c. all-purpose flour, divided

1. In mixer bowl, dissolve yeast in warm water. 2. Add sugar, salt, oil or butter and 2 cups flour; beat 2 minutes at medium-high speed (or 300 vigorous strokes by hand). 3. Add remaining 1 cup flour and stir with large spoon until flour is well mixed. 4. Scrape batter down from sides of bowl; cover with damp cloth and let rise about 30 to 60 minutes. 5. Beat batter about 30 strokes and spread evenly in well-greased loaf pan (approximately 9¼ x 5¼ x 2¾ inches). 6. Let rise again, covered, until batter is to top of loaf pan (about 45 to 60 minutes), or even a bit above top of pan. 7. Bake in preheated 375° oven 45 to 50 minutes, until golden brown. 8. Remove from pan immediately; place on cooling rack or across top of empty loaf pan. 9. If desired, gently brush top with soft butter.

BREAD, 2 LARGE LOAVES

Or make three smaller loaves.

½ c. warm (not hot) water
2 pkgs. active dry yeast (5 tsp. bulk dry yeast)
1 c. milk or water
2 T. sugar
2½ tsp. salt
3 T. olive oil
1 c. cold refrigerator water
7 c. + ¼ to ⅓ c. all-purpose flour, divided

1. In large mixer bowl combine ½ cup warm water and yeast; set aside. 2. In small saucepan, bring milk, sugar and salt to almost boiling point; remove from heat and add oil. 3. Add refrigerator water, then feel liquid with finger; it should be warm but not hot. (If too hot, let it cool until it is warm, not hot.) 4. Add milk mixture to yeast mixture with 4 cups flour; beat 3 to 4 minutes on high or medium speed of mixer. 5. Into a large 8-quart stainless steel bowl (or dishpan), pour bread batter; with large spoon, stir in 3 cups flour. 6. Knead with hands 6 to 8 minutes, using the additional flour as needed, until dough is smooth and elastic. 7. Cover with cloth and let rise until double in bulk (about 1 to 1½ hours) in draft-free place. 8. Punch dough down; cover again and let rest 20 to 30 minutes. 9. Divide dough into 2 or 3 portions; shape each portion into a loaf and place in well-greased loaf pans. 10. Prick each loaf 8 to 10 times with fork, going clear to bottom of pan. 11. Cover with cloth and let rise until double in size (about 1 to 1½ hours). 12. Bake in center of preheated 375° oven 35 to 45 minutes, until golden brown and loaves sound hollow when tapped on bottom. 13. Remove from pans to cooling racks; brush tops of loaves lightly with softened butter, if desired. 14. Allow to cool at least 15 minutes before cutting. To cut, turn loaf on its side and cut slices with a serrated knife.

BREAD, 3 LOAVES

Recipe may be doubled, using 3 packages yeast.

2¾ c. warm (not hot) water
2 pkgs. active dry yeast (5 tsp. bulk dry yeast)
3 T. sugar
¼ c. olive oil
1 T. salt
8 c. all-purpose flour or bread flour, approximately (divided)

1. In large mixer bowl, combine all ingredients except flour. 2. Add 4 cups flour; beat on medium speed 3 minutes. 3. Remove bowl from mixer; with large spoon stir in 3½ cups flour. 4. With hands, knead on floured surface (or in a much larger bowl) 6 to 10 minutes, using another ½ cup flour only as needed. 5. Let dough rise in bowl, covered with a cloth, 1 to 1½ hours or until double in size (in a draft-free place). 6. Punch dough down; cover and let rise 30 to 45 minutes. 7. Shape dough into 3 loaves and place in greased loaf pans (or pie plates for round loaves). 8. Prick each loaf 8 to 10 times with fork, going clear through to bottom of pan. 9. Cover

and let rise until double in size (about 1 to 1½ hours). **10.** Lower oven rack so tops of pans will be in the center of oven. **11.** Bake in preheated 375° oven 40 to 45 minutes or until golden brown and loaves sound hollow when tapped on bottom. **12.** Remove from pans to cooling racks; brush tops of loaves lightly with softened butter, if desired. **13.** Allow to cool at least 15 minutes before cutting. To cut, turn loaf on its side and cut slices with a serrated knife. **To Freeze:** Double-bag in plastic bags when cool. **Substitution:** Use 1 c. whole-wheat flour for 1 c. of white flour, and add ½ c raw wheat germ.

BREAD, 3 LOAVES, QUICK (Potato)

Delicious and speedy. Four hours or less, from start to finish.

7 c. all-purpose flour, divided
3 T. dry (instant) mashed potato flakes
2 pkgs. dry yeast (5 tsp. bulk dry yeast)
2 tsp. salt
2½ c. water,125° (real hot)
⅓ c. sugar
⅓ c. olive oil
¼ c. additional flour or more

1. In large mixer bowl combine 3½ cups flour, the potato flakes, dry yeast and salt, stirring together. **2.** In small saucepan over medium heat, bring water, sugar and oil to 125° on candy thermometer. **3.** Add heated liquid mixture to flour mixture and beat 3 to 4 minutes on medium-high speed. **4.** Remove bowl from mixer and with a large spoon, stir in 3½ cups flour. **5.** Turn out onto floured surface or much larger bowl and knead with hands 5 to 6 minutes until smooth and elastic, using ¼ cup additional flour as needed. (Use a bit more, if needed.) **6.** Spray mixer bowl with cooking spray; return dough to bowl. Cover with cloth and let rise about 45 minutes (until double in size). **7.** Punch dough down; cover and let rest 20 minutes. **8.** Shape dough into 3 loaves and place in greased or sprayed loaf pans or round pie pans. **9.** Prick each loaf 8 to 10 times with fork, going clear through dough to bottom of pan. **10.** Cover with cloth and let rise 1 hour or until double in size. (If room is not warm, it might take 1½ hours.) **11.** Lower oven rack so tops of pans will be in center of oven. **12.** Bake in preheated 375° oven 35 to 40 minutes, or until golden brown and loaves sound hollow when tapped on bottom. **13.** Remove from pans to cooling racks; brush tops of loaves lightly with softened butter if desired. **14.** Allow to cool at least 15 minutes before cutting. To cut, turn loaf on its side and cut slices with a serrated knife. **To Freeze:** Double-bag in plastic bags when cool.

BREAD, 4 LOAVES

So good!

4 c. warm (not hot) water
2 pkgs. active dry yeast (or 2 T. bulk dry yeast)
¼ c. sugar

1½ T. salt, level
¼ c. olive oil
11½ to 11¾ c. all-purpose flour, approximately (divided)

1. In large mixer bowl, combine all ingredients except flour. **2.** Add 5 cups flour; beat on medium speed 3 minutes. **3.** Remove bowl from mixer; with large spoon, stir in an additional 6 cups flour. **4.** On floured surface (or in a much larger bowl), sprinkle ½ cup flour; scrape dough onto flour and knead with hands 7 to 10 minutes, using a little more flour if needed. **5.** With dough in bowl, cover with cloth and let rise 1½ hours or until double in size, in draft-free area. **6.** Punch dough down; cover and let rise again 30 to 45 minutes. **7.** Shape dough into 4 oblong loaves and place in greased loaf pans. **8.** Prick each loaf 8 to 10 times with fork, going clear to bottom of pan. **9.** Cover and let rise in draft-free area 1½ hours or until double in size. **10.** Lower oven rack so tops of pans will be in the center of oven. **11.** Bake in preheated 375° oven 40 to 45 minutes or until golden brown. **12.** Remove immediately from pans to cooling racks; brush tops of loaves lightly with softened butter, if desired. **13.** Allow to cool at least 15 minutes before cutting. To cut, turn loaf on its side and cut slices with a serrated knife. **To Freeze:** Double-bag in plastic bags when cool.

BREAD, 5 LOAVES

5 c. warm (not hot) water
2 pkgs. active dry yeast (5 tsp. bulk dry yeast)
⅓ c. sugar
2 T. salt, level
⅓ c. olive oil
15 to 15½ c. all-purpose flour or bread flour, approximately (divided)

1. In large mixer bowl, combine all ingredients except flour. **2.** Add 7 cups flour; beat on medium speed 3 minutes. **3.** Pour batter into a much larger bowl; spread a wet dishcloth under bowl to keep it steady. **4.** With large spoon, stir in 7½ cups flour; knead with hands 6 to 10 minutes, using another ½ to 1 cup flour, if needed. **5.** Cover dough with cloth and let rise 1½ hours or until double in size, in draft-free place. **6.** Punch dough down; cover and let rise 30 to 45 minutes. **7.** Shape dough into 5 oblong loaves and place in greased loaf pans. **8.** Prick each loaf 8 to 10 times with fork, going clear to bottom of pan. **9.** Cover and let rise until double in size, about 1½ hours. **10.** Lower oven rack so tops of pans will be in the center of oven. **11.** Bake in preheated 375° oven 40 to 45 minutes, or until golden brown and loaves sound hollow when tapped on bottom. **12.** Remove from pans to cooling racks; brush tops of loaves lightly with softened butter, if desired. **13.** Allow to cool at least 15 minutes before cutting. To cut, turn loaf on its side and cut slices with a serrated knife. **To Freeze:** Double-bag in plastic bags when cool.

BREAD, 7 LOAVES

6 c. warm (not hot) water (105° to 110°)
3 pkgs. active dry yeast or 1 lg. (2-ounce) cake com-
    pressed yeast or 7 tsp. active dry bulk yeast
½ c. sugar
½ c. olive oil
2½ T. salt
5-lb. bag all-purpose flour or bread flour, plus ½ to 1 c.
    additional flour, or more if needed

1. In large mixer bowl, combine all ingredients except flour.
2. Add 8 cups flour (or nearly half the 5-pound bag) and beat
on medium speed 3 minutes. 3. Pour batter into a much larger
bowl (or dishpan); with large spoon, stir in remaining flour
from bag. 4. Spread wet dishcloth under the bowl or dishpan; with hands, knead dough 7 to 10 minutes, using additional ⅓ to ½ cup flour gradually, or more if needed. 5. Cover
dough with cloth; let rise 1½ hours in draft-free place. Or
turn oven dial to 150° or 170° for 1 minute— no longer! **Turn
heat off immediately.** Put dough in oven to rise, with oven
door shut. 6. Punch dough down; cover and let rise again 30
to 45 minutes. 7. Shape dough into 7 oblong loaves (each
weighing a little over 1 pound) and place in greased loaf
pans, approximately 8½ x 4½ x 2½ inches (or can be larger). 8.
Prick each loaf 10 times with fork tines, going clear to bottom
of pan. 9. Cover and let rise in draft-free place 1½ hours or
until double in size. 10. Bake in preheated 375° oven (lower
the rack so that tops of pans are in center of oven). 11. Bake
40 to 45 minutes, or until golden brown and loaves sound
hollow when tapped on bottom. 12. Remove from pans to
cooling racks; brush top of loaves with softened butter, if
desired. **Note**: With most ovens, this is too many loaves to
bake at one time. While baking first load, uncover remaining
loaves. **To Freeze:** Double-bag in plastic bags when cool.

BREAD, CRACKED WHEAT (2 Loaves)

Delicious! Four hours or less from start to finish.

¾ c. bulgur or cracked wheat
¾ c. water
2 c. whole-wheat flour
3 c. all-purpose flour
2 pkgs. active dry yeast (or 4½ to 5 tsp. bulk dry yeast)
2 tsp. salt
1½ c. water
¼ c. olive oil
⅓ c. honey
½ c. additional flour or more, if needed (either kind)

1. In small saucepan over medium heat, bring bulgur and ¾
cup water to a boil; reduce heat to low and cook 5 minutes,
stirring occasionally (until water is absorbed). Remove pan
from heat and set aside. 2. In medium bowl mix together
whole-wheat flour and all-purpose flour; set aside. 3. In large
mixer bowl, combine 1½ cups of the flour mixture with yeast
and salt. 4. In small saucepan over medium heat, heat 1½
cups water with oil and honey until very warm (125° on candy
thermometer). 5. With mixer on low speed, slowly add warm

liquid to yeast mixture; beat 2 minutes on medium speed,
scraping bowl once with rubber scraper. 6. Add 1 cup flour
mixture and the bulgur mixture; beat 2 minutes on medium
speed. 7. With wooden spoon, stir in remaining flour mixture; turn dough out onto floured surface and knead until
smooth and elastic, about 6 minutes, working in the additional flour, as needed. 8. Place dough in greased or sprayed
bowl, turning dough over so top is greased; cover bowl with
cloth and let rise in draft-free place until doubled, about 1
hour. 9. Punch dough down; let rest 15 minutes. 10. Shape
into 2 loaves and place in greased or sprayed loaf pans; prick
each loaf 10 times with fork, going clear through to bottom
of pan. 11. Cover with cloth and let rise until doubled, about
1 hour. 12. Bake in preheated 400° oven 30 to 35 minutes,
until loaves sound hollow when tapped on bottom and are
golden brown. 13. Remove from pans to cooling rack; brush
tops of loaves with softened butter, if desired.

BREAD, ENGLISH MUFFIN

*From Marilyn Middleton, a quick and easy
recipe (no kneading).*

5½ to 6 c. flour, divided
2 pkg. dry yeast (2½ tsp. bulk dry yeast)
1 T. sugar
2 t. salt
¼ t. baking soda
2 c. milk
½ c. water
Cornmeal

1. Combine 3 c. flour, yeast, sugar, salt and soda in mixer
bowl. 2. Heat milk and water until very warm (120°-130°);
add to dry mixture and beat well for 3 minutes. 3. Stir in
enough more flour to make a stiff batter. (Do not knead.) 4.
Spoon into two loaf pans (8½ x 4½- inches) that have been
greased and sprinkled with cornmeal; sprinkle a little more
cornmeal over the tops. 5. Cover; let rise in warm place 45
minutes. 6. Bake in preheated 400° oven for 25 minutes;
remove from pans immediately and cool on wire racks. **To
Serve**: Slice and toast. (One loaf may be sliced, wrapped
and frozen for later use.)

BREAD, FRENCH

Makes two loaves.

1 pkg. active dry yeast (or 2¼ tsp.)
1½ c. warm water (105° to 115°)
1 T. sugar
1½ tsp. salt
1 T. butter, room temp.
4 c. all-purpose flour, divided
Cornmeal (opt.)

1. In large mixer bowl, sprinkle yeast over warm water; stir until dissolved. 2. Add sugar, salt, butter and 3 cups flour; beat at high speed one minute. 3. Remove bowl from mixer and stir in remaining 1 cup flour (or partially stir it in). 4. Empty contents of bowl on floured surface and knead until all the flour is absorbed and dough is smooth and elastic. 5. Leave dough on the kneading surface and cover with bowl. 6. Every 10 minutes knead dough 1 minute, re-covering with bowl. Do this 5 times. 7. Divide dough into 2 balls; let rest 10 minutes longer. 8. On lightly floured surface, roll each ball into a 12 x 9-inch rectangle. 9. Starting with long edge, roll each rectangle into a log (jellyroll fashion); press edges to seal. 10. Place loaves, edge side down, on ungreased cookie sheet. (If desired, sprinkle cornmeal on sheet first.) 11. Make 7 or 8 diagonal slices in top of each loaf with sharp knife. 12. Cover with cloth or towel and let rise 1½ hours or until double in size. 13. Bake in preheated 400° oven 30 minutes or until golden brown and hollow sounding when thumped on bottom. 14. Remove from oven and brush tops with soft butter while warm.

BREAD, GARLIC

1 loaf (16 oz.) French or Italian bread, unsliced
½ c. butter or reg. Smart Balance spread, softened
1 tsp. garlic powder or 2 to 3 cloves garlic, minced
¼ to ½ c. grated Parmesan cheese (opt.)
Basil or oregano
Paprika
Olive oil

1. Slice loaf of bread in half lengthwise. 2. In small bowl combine butter, garlic (and Parmesan cheese, if used); spread over cut sides of bread. 3. Sprinkle lightly with basil or oregano, then paprika. 4. Brush outside of loaf of bread lightly with oil; close loaf up. 5. Preheat oven to 350°; wrap loaf in foil and bake 20 minutes or until hot.

BREAD, GARLIC CHEESE

1 loaf of Italian or French bread, unsliced
4 T. (½ stick) softened butter (opt.)
¼ tsp. garlic powder
Sharp Cheddar cheese, sliced

1. Cut loaf of bread almost through to bottom crust in ¾ to 1-inch slices. 2. Mix together butter and garlic powder and spread between slices. 3. Add a slice of cheese between each slice of bread. 4. Wrap loaf in foil and heat in preheated 400° oven for 10 to 20 minutes (until cheese is melted). **Microwave**: Spread 2 slices of French bread with butter. Sprinkle with garlic powder; lay slices of Cheddar cheese on it. Put on a Corelle plate and microwave 1 minute on MED. (50%), uncovered.

BREAD, GARLIC (Microwave)

½ loaf Vienna, French or Italian bread
¼ c. melted butter
½ tsp. garlic powder
½ tsp. Italian seasoning (opt.)
1 T. Parmesan cheese

1. Cut bread, almost through to bottom crust, in 1-inch slices. 2. Combine melted butter, garlic powder, Italian seasoning and Parmesan cheese; brush mixture on each slice of bread and brush remainder over top of loaf. 3. Place on paper towel-lined, microwave-safe plate or platter. 4. Heat 45 seconds on BAKE (60% power), or until heated through.

BREAD, GARLIC MINI

4 T. butter or reg. Smart Balance Spread, softened
½ t. dill weed
½ t. garlic powder
½ t. Italian seasoning
4 hotdog buns, sliced in half the long way

1. In small bowl, combine butter, dill weed, garlic powder and Italian seasoning, stirring well. 2. Spread on cut sides of each bun. 3. Place on baking sheet; broil until golden brown. Makes 4 servings.

BREAD, GARLIC, FRIED

In skillet, melt 2 T. butter or Smart Balance Spread. Add ¼ tsp. garlic powder and stir together. Add 6 slices of bread, halved, and fry until golden brown on both sides.

BREAD, GARLIC TOAST

Brush 1-inch thick slices of bread with butter or olive oil; sprinkle with garlic powder or minced garlic and basil (optional). Bake in preheated 350° oven 10 to 15 minutes or until golden on topside. Or fry in large skillet until golden brown on each side. **Note**: May also be done in toaster oven, adding cheese toward the end.

BREAD, ITALIAN (3 Loaves)

Can also divide dough in half and bake in two greased bread pans for 45 minutes (after rising).

8 c. all-purpose flour, approximately, divided
2 pkgs. dry yeast (4½ to 5 tsp. bulk dry yeast)
3 T. sugar
1 T. salt
3 c. water, 125°(real hot)
3 T. olive oil

1. In mixer bowl, combine 4 cups flour; the yeast, sugar and salt. **2.** In saucepan, heat water with oil to 125° on candy thermometer (on medium heat). **3.** Add heated liquid to flour mixture and beat on high speed of electric mixer for 3 minutes. **4.** With large spoon, stir in 3 cups flour. **5.** In large 8-quart bowl, sprinkle ¾ cup flour over the bottom. **6.** Scrape dough into the large bowl; knead with hands 8 to 10 minutes, until smooth and elastic, using remaining ¼ cup flour if needed. **7.** Cover bowl with cloth and let rest 15 minutes. **8.** Divide dough into 3 portions; roll each portion out on floured surface. **9.** Roll up into loaves and place on greased or sprayed large cookie sheet. **10.** Prick loaves with fork 8 to 10 times, going clear through to bottom of cookie sheet. **11.** Cover and let rise 1½ hours. **12.** Bake in middle of preheated 350° oven for 30 minutes or until golden brown and loaves feel hollow when tapped on bottom. **13.** Remove from oven to cooling racks; brush lightly with oil or softened butter.

BREAD, MULTIGRAIN WITH FLAXSEED (BREAD MACHINE)

1 2/3 c. lukewarm water
3 T. nonfat dry milk powder
2 T. olive oil
2 T. honey
2 t. salt
¼ c. rolled oats, uncooked
¼ c. oat bran, uncooked
¼ c. flaxseed meal (flaxseed may be ground in a blender to make meal)
2 2/3 c. all-purpose flour
1 c. whole-wheat flour
1¼ t. dry yeast

1. In bread machine pan, place all ingredients in order given. **2.** Select Basic setting and 2-pound loaf. Check dough after 5 minutes of mixing; add 1 to 2 tablespoons of water or flour if needed. Yield: 1 loaf (2 pounds)

BREAD, OAT BRAN GOLDEN

Makes 2 loaves.

5¼ c. all-purpose flour, divided (approx)
2 pkgs. active dry yeast or quick-rise yeast
1 c. oat bran (hot cereal type, not cooked)
¼ c. wheat germ
2 tsp. salt
2 c. water
2 T. olive oil
¼ c. molasses (or half honey)
¼ c. raisins (opt.)

1. In large mixer bowl, combine 2 cups flour, yeast, oat bran, wheat germ and salt; mix well. **2.** In saucepan, heat water, oil and molasses until quite warm (125° to 130°), but not anywhere near boiling. **3.** Add warm liquid to flour mixture; blend at low speed until moistened. Scrape down sides. **4.** Beat 3 minutes at medium speed. **5.** Remove bowl from mixer

and with large spoon, stir in 3 cups flour (and raisins, if used). **6.** On floured surface, knead dough 5 minutes, using ¼ cup flour as needed. **7.** Place in greased or sprayed bowl, turning dough over to grease the top. **8.** Cover with cloth; let rise in draft-free place until doubled. (1 hour for active dry yeast; 30 to 35 minutes for quick-rise yeast.) **9.** Punch down dough; divide into 2 portions and shape into 2 oblong loaves. **10.** Place in greased 8½ x 4½-inch loaf pans; cover with cloth and let rise until doubled. (About 45 minutes for active dry yeast; 25 minutes for quick-rise yeast.) **11.** Bake in preheated 400° oven 25 to 30 minutes, until golden brown. **12.** Remove from pans to cooling rack; brush tops of loaves lightly with butter if desired. **To Freeze:** Double-bag in plastic bags when cool.

BREAD, OATMEAL (Light)

Makes 2 loaves. From Hazel Lewis.

1¾ c. warm (not hot) water
1 to 2 pkgs. active dry yeast (2¼ to 4½ tsp. bulk dry yeast)
⅓ c. packed brown sugar
3 T. olive oil
2 tsp. salt
2 c. rolled oats, uncooked
3¼ to 3½ c. all-purpose flour, approximately (divided)

1. In mixer bowl combine warm water, yeast, brown sugar, oil and salt. **2.** Add rolled oats and 1½ cups flour; beat well with electric mixer. **3.** Remove bowl from mixer; with large spoon, stir in 1½ cups additional flour. **4.** On floured surface, knead dough for 7 minutes, using ¼ to ½ cup flour as needed. **5.** Oil or spray bottom of bowl and return dough to bowl, turning once. **6.** Cover and let rise in draft-free place until double in size (about 1 to 1½ hours). **7.** Punch down and let rest 10 minutes. **8.** Shape into 2 loaves and place in greased or sprayed bread pans (or on cookie sheets for round loaves). **9.** Prick each loaf 9 times with fork, going clear to bottom of pan. **10.** Cover and let rise until double (1 to 1½ hours). **11.** Bake in preheated 350 oven for 40 minutes in middle of oven or until golden brown and loaves sound hollow when tapped on bottom. **12.** Remove from pans; brush top lightly with soft butter and cool on wire racks.

BREAD, OATMEAL (Dark)

Makes 2 loaves.

1½ c. boiling water
1 c. rolled oats, packed level (uncooked)
⅓ c. packed brown sugar
¼ c. molasses
2 tsp. salt
3 T. olive oil
¾ c. lukewarm water
2 pkgs. dry yeast (or 4½ tsp. bulk dry yeast)
2 c. whole-wheat flour
3½ c. all-purpose flour, divided

1. In mixer bowl, pour boiling water over oats, sugar, molasses and salt. **2.** Add oil; let cool to lukewarm or room temperature. **3.** In ¾ cup lukewarm water, dissolve yeast; add to oats mixture. **4.** Add 2 cups whole-wheat flour and beat for 2 minutes. **5.** With large spoon, stir in 3 cups white flour; let rest 10 minutes. **6.** On floured surface, knead dough for 7 minutes, using all remaining flour gradually. **7.** For remaining instructions, follow directions for previous recipe, "Light Oatmeal Bread," from step number 5 through to the end.

BREAD, RAISIN CINNAMON (2 Loaves)

5¼ to 5½ c. all-purpose flour, divided
2 pkgs. dry yeast (4½ tsp. bulk dry yeast)
1 c. milk
¾ c. water
¼ c. sugar
¼ c. olive oil
2 tsp. salt
1 egg
1 to 1½ c. raisins
⅔ c. sugar
1 T. cinnamon
2 T. butter, softened

1. In mixer bowl, combine 2 cups flour and yeast. **2.** In saucepan, heat milk, water, first sugar, oil and salt over low heat until very warm (120° to 130°). (Use a candy thermometer.) **3.** Add liquid to flour-yeast mixture and beat about 2 minutes on medium speed of electric mixer, or 300 strokes by hand. **4.** Blend in egg, then stir in raisins and 1 cup flour with large spoon. **5.** Stir in 2 cups additional flour with spoon. **6.** Turn out onto lightly floured surface and knead about 5 to 10 minutes, until smooth and satiny, using the last ½ cup flour, if necessary. **7.** Cover dough with bowl and let rest 40 minutes. **8.** Divide dough in half; combine ⅔ cup sugar and cinnamon in small bowl. **9.** On lightly floured surface, roll each portion of dough to 9 x 14-inch rectangle; spread with 1 tablespoon soft butter and sprinkle with half of cinnamon-sugar mixture. **10.** Beginning at narrow end, roll up <u>tightly</u>, as for jellyroll. **11.** Pinch seam and ends to seal; place in 2 greased 4½ x 8½-inch or 9 x 5 x 3-inch loaf pans, seam side underneath. **12.** Cover and let rise in draft-free area until doubled, about 45 to 60 minutes. **13.** Bake in preheated 375° oven for 35 to 40 minutes. **14.** Remove immediately from pans and cool on wire rack. **15.** If desired, frost with powdered sugar glaze: 1 c. powdered sugar, 1 T. softened butter, ¼ tsp. vanilla, 3 to 4 tsp. milk.

BREAD, WHEAT-HONEY

Makes 3 loaves.

3 c. warm (not hot) water
2 pkgs. active dry yeast (5 tsp. bulk dry yeast)
1 T. salt
½ c. honey or corn syrup
⅓ c. olive oil

4 c. whole-wheat flour (about 1⅛ lb.)
4½ to 4¾ c. all-purpose flour, approximately, divided

1. In mixer bowl, combine warm water, yeast, salt, honey and oil. **2.** Add whole-wheat flour and beat well. **3.** Add 2 cups all-purpose flour and beat. **4.** Remove bowl from mixer and stir in additional 2 cups all-purpose flour. **5.** In 8-quart bowl (or dishpan), sprinkle ½ cup all-purpose flour. **6.** Turn dough into the larger container and knead 10 minutes with hands, using small amount of additional flour, if necessary, until smooth and elastic. **7.** Remove dough long enough to grease or spray bottom of bowl; place dough in bowl, then turn dough over so greased side is up. **8.** Cover with cloth and let rise in warm place until double, 1 to 2 hours. (Dough is ready if indentation remains when touched.) **9.** Punch down dough; divide into 3 portions and let rest 10 to 15 minutes. **10.** Shape into 3 loaves; place in greased loaf pans and prick each loaf 9 times with fork, going clear to bottom of pan. **11.** Cover and let rise again in warm place until double in size, about 1 to 1½ hours. **12.** Place in preheated 375° oven (<u>lower the rack</u> so that tops of pans are in center of oven). **13.** Bake 30 to 40 minutes or until loaves are deep golden brown and sound hollow when tapped on bottom. **14.** Remove from pans and cool on wire rack.

BREAD, WHEAT-HONEY (Potato)

Makes 3 loaves. Very good!

4⅓ c. all-purpose flour, divided (a bit more may be needed)
1 c. dry mashed potato flakes
3 tsp. salt
2 pkgs. dry yeast (or 4½ to 5 tsp. bulk dry yeast)
1¾ c. water
1 c. milk
¼ c. olive oil
¼ c. honey
2 eggs
2½ c. whole-wheat flour

1. In large mixer bowl, combine 2 cups flour, the potato flakes, salt and yeast; stir together. **2.** In medium saucepan, heat water, milk, oil and honey to 125° (real hot), using a candy thermometer, on medium heat. **3.** Add liquid and eggs to flour-yeast mixture; beat 4 minutes on medium-high speed. **4.** Add whole-wheat flour and mix well. **5.** Remove bowl from mixer; with large spoon, stir in 2 cups all-purpose flour. **6.** On floured surface, knead with hands 5 to 7 minutes, until smooth and elastic, using remaining all-purpose flour as needed. **7.** Return dough to bowl which has been greased or sprayed; turn to grease both sides. **8.** Cover with cloth and let rise 1 hour (until double in size). **9.** Punch dough down; cover and let rest 20 minutes. **10.** Shape into 3 loaves and place in greased loaf pans (or pie plates for round loaves). **11.** Prick each loaf 8 to 10 times with fork, going clear through to bottom of pan. **12.** Cover and let rise 30 to 60 minutes (or until double in size). **13.** <u>Lower oven rack</u> so tops of pans will be in center of oven. **14.** Bake in preheated 375° oven 35 to 40 minutes, or until golden brown and loaves sound hollow when tapped on bottom. **15.** Remove from pans to cooling racks;

brush tops of loaves lightly with softened butter, if desired. **16.** Allow to cool at least 15 minutes before cutting. To cut, turn loaf on its side and cut slices with a serrated knife. **To Freeze:** Double-bag in plastic bags when cool.

BREAD, WHEAT-HONEY, ROBIN HOOD

Makes 2 loaves.

3 c. whole-wheat flour
2 pkgs. active dry yeast
1 T. salt
¼ c. olive oil
⅓ c. honey
2¼ c. very warm water (120° to 130°)
3½ c. all-purpose flour, approximately, divided

1. In large mixer bowl, mix together whole-wheat flour, dry yeast, salt, oil and honey. **2.** Add warm water, using candy or deep fat thermometer to check temperature. **3.** Beat on low speed for 1 minute, then on medium speed for 1 minute, scraping bowl once or twice. **4.** Remove bowl from mixer and with large wooden spoon, stir in 3 cups all-purpose flour, one cup at a time; stir until flour is mixed in. **5.** Turn dough onto lightly floured surface; knead until smooth and elastic, about 7 to 10 minutes, working in the ½ cup of flour while kneading (or as much of it as is needed). **6.** Place in greased bowl; turn greased side of dough up. **7.** Cover and let rise in draft-free place until double, 1 to 1½ hours. (Dough is ready if indentation remains when touched.) **8.** Punch dough down; let rest 15 minutes. **9.** Shape into 2 loaves and place in greased loaf pans, 8½ x 4½ x 2½ inches. **10.** Prick with fork 8 to 10 times, going clear to the bottom of pan. **11.** Let rise until double, 1 to 1½ hours. **12.** In preheated 375° oven, place loaves on lower rack so that tops of pans are in the center of the oven. **13.** Bake 40 to 45 minutes, until loaves are deep golden brown and sound hollow when tapped on bottom. **14.** Remove from pans; brush tops lightly with butter if desired. **15.** Cool on wire racks. **Note:** ¼ cup wheat germ may be added, if desired.

BREAD, WHOLE-WHEAT HONEY, NEOVI'S

Makes 3 medium-small loaves.
(A moist, firm, sweet bread..)

1 c. milk
2 T. sugar
1 T. salt
¼ c. olive oil (or butter)
½ c. honey
2 to 3 pkgs. (¼ oz. each) active dry yeast (or 5 to 6 tsp. bulk dry yeast)
1½ c. warm (not hot) water
2½ c. all-purpose flour
5 c. whole-wheat flour (or less)

1. Scald milk; add sugar, salt, oil or butter, and honey and stir. Cool to lukewarm. **2.** In large mixing bowl, sprinkle yeast over warm water, stirring until dissolved. **3.** Stir lukewarm milk mixture into yeast mixture. **4.** Add 2½ cups all-purpose flour and 2½ cups whole-wheat flour; beat with electric mixer or with large wooden spoon until smooth. **5.** Gradually stir in remaining whole-wheat flour with spoon; turn out onto lightly floured board. **6.** Cover with bowl and let rest 10 minutes. **7.** Knead until smooth and elastic, about 8 to 10 minutes. (1 to 2 tablespoons flour may be needed in the process.) **8.** Place in lightly greased or sprayed bowl, turning over to grease top; cover with towel and let rise in draft-free area until doubled, about 1½ hours. **9.** Punch dough down; divide in thirds and shape each portion into a ball. Let rest 10 minutes. **10.** Shape each ball into a loaf, place in greased bread pans and prick each loaf with fork 9 times; cover with towel. **11.** Let rise in draft-free area until doubled, about 1½ hours. **12.** Bake in preheated 375° oven 30 minutes, or until loaves are golden brown and sound hollow when tapped on bottom. **13.** Remove from pans; brush tops lightly with butter if desired. **14.** Cool on wire racks.

WELLS' MIXER BREAD

This recipe is from Jack Wells' Aunt Margaret Peters, who is 90 years young in 2004. No kneading, and _extra_ good! Uses an elctric mixer and makes 4 loaves of bread.

3⅓ c. water
3 T. sugar
3 T. shortening
1 tsp. salt
9 c. all-purpose flour, divided
4 tsp. active dry bulk yeast or 2 pkg. (¼ oz. each)

1. In saucepan, heat water, sugar, shortening and salt until warm, but not hot. **2.** In mixer bowl, mix together 5 cups flour and the dry yeast. **3.** Stir the warm water mixture into the flour mixture in mixer bowl. **4.** Let stand for five minutes; then stir in remaining 4 cups flour. **5.** Beat on low speed (#1) of mixer for five minutes, then on speed #2 for another five minutes. **6.** Put 1 cup water in a microwave-safe mug and place in the corner of microwave oven; heat this mug on HIGH for 2½ minutes. (Leave it there.) **7.** Put mixer bowl of dough in the microwave oven and shut the door, letting dough rise to the top of the bowl. **8.** Punch dough down and shut microwave door again; let dough rise again to the top of the bowl. **9.** Remove bowl of dough and shut door; with greased hands, shape dough into four loaves, placing them in greased or sprayed loaf pans. **10.** Prick each loaf 8 times with fork, going clear through dough to bottom of pans. **11.** Put the four loaves back in microwave oven and shut the door; let rise until they are double in size. **12.** Lower oven rack so tops of pans will be in center of oven; bake in preheated 375° oven 35 to 40 minutes, or until golden brown and loaves sound hollow when tapped on bottom. **13.** Remove from pans to cooling racks; brush tops of loaves lightly with softened butter, if desired. **To freeze:** Double-bag in plastic bags when cool. **Note:** Either regular dry active yeast or Quick-Rise dry yeast may be used in this recipe.

Chapter 8

Buns, Dinner Rolls & Sweet Rolls

CARL AND EDITH LIMBER

BUNS, DINNER ROLLS AND SWEET ROLLS

DOUGH-RAISING HINT

Turn oven dial to 150° to 170° for 1 minute, then turn off. Put dough or rolls in closed oven to rise.

BUNS OR ROLLS I (Makes 20)

Recipe may be doubled or tripled. If in a hurry, use 1½ packages dry yeast or 3 teaspoons dry yeast.

1 c. warm (not hot) water
1 pkg. (¼ oz.) active dry yeast or 2¼ tsp. bulk dry yeast
¼ c. sugar
¼ c. olive oil
½ tsp. salt
1 egg
3¼ to 3¾ c. all-purpose flour, divided (1 c. of this amount may be whole-wheat flour)

1. In mixer bowl, combine warm water and yeast. **2.** Add sugar, oil, salt, egg and 2 cups flour; beat 2 minutes. **3.** Remove from mixer and stir in 1¼ to 1½ cups flour with large spoon. **4.** Turn out on floured surface and knead until smooth and elastic, about 5 minutes or longer, adding ¼ cup flour gradually, as needed. **5.** Return dough to a greased or sprayed bowl, turning over to grease top; cover with cloth and let rise 1 hour. **6.** Shape dough into rolls and place on greased or sprayed baking sheet. **7.** Cover with cloth and let rise 1 to 1½ hours or until double in size, in warm draft-free area. **8.** Bake in preheated 375° oven 15 to 20 minutes, or until golden brown. **9.** Butter tops lightly if desired; remove from pan to cooling racks. **In 13 x 9-inch pan:** Put 20 buns close together in greased or sprayed pan. **For Sandwich Buns:** Shape 20 buns and flatten them with palm of hand or fingers on greased cookie sheet, leaving 2 inches between each one.

BUNS OR ROLLS II

For 28 rolls, shape dough into rolls the size of a small tangerine.

1½ c. warm (not hot) water
2 pkgs. dry yeast (5 tsp. bulk dry yeast)
⅓ c. sugar
⅓ c. nonfat dry milk powder
⅓ c. olive oil
1½ tsp. salt
2 eggs
6 c. all-purpose flour, divided (or less), or 4½ c. all-purpose flour and 1½ c. whole-wheat flour

1. In mixer bowl, combine warm water, yeast, sugar, dry milk powder, oil and salt, stirring together. **2.** Add eggs and 3 cups flour; beat on high speed of electric mixer for 2 to 3 minutes. **3.** Remove bowl from mixer and with large spoon, stir in 2¾ cups flour. **4.** Turn dough out onto floured surface and knead for 6 to 10 minutes, using the remaining ¼ cup flour gradually. (It may take a bit more flour.) **5.** Place dough in bowl which has been oiled or sprayed; turn dough over to grease both sides. **6.** Cover and let rise in warm draft-free area until double, about 1½ hours. **7.** Punch down dough; cover and let rest 30 minutes. **8.** Shape dough into rolls with buttered fingers; place on greased or sprayed cookie sheets. **9.** Cover and let rise in warm, draft-free area until double in size. **10.** Bake in middle of preheated 375° oven for 15 minutes or until golden brown. (Make sure they are done on the bottom.) **11.** Butter tops lightly, if desired; remove from cookie sheet to cooling racks.

Clover Leaf Rolls: For 24 large-sized cloverleaf rolls, follow directions through Step #7. **8.** Divide dough into 24 equal portions; divide each portion into 3 pieces and shape each piece into a ball, pulling edges under to make a smooth surface. **9.** Arrange 3 balls, smooth side up, in each muffin cup of greased or sprayed muffin pans. **10.** Cover and let rise until double in size in warm, draft-free area. **11.** Bake in preheated 375° oven for 12 to 15 minutes, or until golden brown. (Make sure they are done on the bottom.) **12.** Butter tops lightly, if desired; remove from pans to cooling racks.

HONEY WHOLE-WHEAT ROLLS

Makes 30 delicious rolls.

4 c. whole-wheat flour
1¾ c. all-purpose flour, divided
2 pkgs. dry yeast
1½ tsp. salt
2½ c. milk
⅓ c. honey
½ c. butter or reg. Smart Balance spread

1. Combine whole-wheat flour, 1 cup all-purpose flour, dry yeast and salt in mixer bowl. **2.** In saucepan, heat milk, honey and butter until very warm (120° to 130°). **3.** Add warm liquid gradually to flour mixture; beat on medium speed 2 minutes. **4.** Remove bowl from mixer; stir in ½ cup all-purpose flour. **5.** Turn dough onto lightly floured surface; knead 5 minutes, adding ¼ cup flour if necessary. **6.** Return dough to bowl; cover and let rise 1 hour, or until double. **7.** Punch dough down; form into smooth balls and place on greased baking pans. (10 rolls in 8-inch round cake pan and 20 rolls on cookie sheet.) **8.** Let rise, covered, for 1 to 1½ hours, or until double. **9.** Bake in preheated 400° oven for 20 minutes or until light golden brown and done on the bottom.

OVERNIGHT BUNS I

Start Saturday night; bake Sunday noon.
Makes 30 or 35.

1½ c. warm water, not hot (105° to 115°)
1 pkg. active dry yeast
⅓ c. sugar
⅓ c. olive oil
1½ tsp. salt
1 egg
4¾ to 5 c. all-purpose flour, divided (1¾ c. of the flour can
   be whole-wheat flour)

1. In large mixer bowl, combine all ingredients except flour; mix together. **2.** Add 3 cups flour; beat well 2 minutes. **3.** With large spoon, stir in about 1¾ cups flour. **4.** Turn dough onto floured surface; knead 4 to 5 minutes, adding a bit more flour, as needed, gradually. **5.** Grease bottom of same bowl; return dough to bowl, turning dough over to grease both sides. **6.** Cover bowl with plastic wrap loosely, then a cloth; refrigerate overnight. **7.** Next morning, about 8:00 or 8:30, make into buns with greased fingers (size of a large English walnut) and place in greased jellyroll pan, 15½ x 10½-inch, or large cookie sheet. Place 5 one way and 7 the other way, making 35 buns. **8.** Let rise, uncovered, at room temperature, for several hours. **9.** Between noon and 1:00 p.m., bake in preheated 375° oven 15 to 20 minutes or until golden brown. Make sure bottom of buns are done. **10.** Lightly butter tops of buns; remove to wire cooling rack.

OVERNIGHT BUNS II

Ready to bake when you awake (start them around 5:00
to 6:00 p.m. the night before).

½ c. lukewarm water
1 pkg. active dry yeast (2¼ tsp. bulk yeast)
1 tsp. sugar
2 c. lukewarm water
½ c. sugar
½ c. olive oil
1 egg
1½ tsp. salt
8½ c. all-purpose flour

1. In mixer bowl, combine ½ cup lukewarm water, yeast and 1 teaspoon sugar; let stand for 10 minutes. **2.** Add 2 cups lukewarm water, ½ cup sugar, the oil, egg, salt and 5 cups flour; beat well. **3.** Remove from mixer and stir in 3 cups flour with large spoon. **4.** Turn into a much larger bowl and knead with hands 5 minutes, adding ½ cup flour as needed. (May take a tiny bit more.) **5.** Let rise, covered, for 2 hours. **6.** Punch down; let rise again 1 to 2 hours. **7.** With greased hands, shape dough into buns the size of golf balls. **8.** Place about 1 inch apart on greased baking sheets. **9.** Let rise all night at room temperature, covered lightly with cloth. **10.** In the morning, bake in middle of preheated 375° oven for 14 to 15 minutes, or until golden brown on top and bottom. **11.** Lightly butter tops of buns; remove from cookie sheet to cooling racks. Makes 55 to 65 buns.

OVERNIGHT BUNS III (Larger)

Ready to bake when you awake;
start around 7:00 p.m. the night before.

1 pkg. active dry yeast
3 c. lukewarm water
¾ c. sugar
¾ c. olive oil
3 tsp. salt
3 eggs
11¼ c. all-purpose flour, approximately

1. In mixer bowl, dissolve yeast in 3 cups lukewarm water. (Start this after supper, around 7:00 p.m.) **2.** Add sugar, oil, salt and the eggs; beat together. **3.** Add 7 cups flour gradually, beating on medium speed. **4.** Remove bowl from mixer and stir in 4 cups flour with large spoon; turn out onto floured surface (or in 8-quart bowl), and knead until smooth and elastic (at least 5 minutes), adding small amounts of flour if necessary. **5.** Grease top of dough lightly; cover bowl with cloth and let rise 2 hours or until double in size. **6.** At this point, dough may be punched down to rest a little, or may be made into buns, using a piece of dough the size of an egg (greasing or buttering fingers frequently). Makes 60 to 90 buns, depending on the size. **7.** Place buns on greased cookie sheets or pizza pans, about 2 inches apart. Do not cover. **8.** Let buns rise all night at room temperature, uncovered. **9.** In the morning, bake in preheated 375° oven 15 to 20 minutes or until golden brown. Make sure buns are done on the bottom. **10.** Butter tops lightly, if desired; remove from pans to cooling racks.

OVERNIGHT ROLLS, LOUISE MCMINN'S

Ready to bake when you awake. These are eggless and
sweet; start at 4 p.m. the night before.

2 c. lukewarm water
1 pkg. active dry yeast
¾ c. sugar
½ c. olive oil
2 tsp. salt
7¼ to 7½ c. all-purpose flour, approximately

1. About 4:00 p.m., mix up rolls. Combine all ingredients in order given, adding flour gradually. **2.** Turn dough out onto floured surface and knead until smooth and elastic, adding small amounts of flour as necessary. **3.** Return dough to bowl; cover and let rise at room temperature until about 9:30 or 10:00 p.m. **4.** Punch down and make into rolls with greased fingers, using two greased 13 x 9-inch cake pans; put 12 rolls in each cake pan. (Or use greased cookie sheets.) **5.** Cover and let rise all night at room temperature. **6.** In the morning, bake in preheated 350° oven 20 minutes or until golden brown.

SANDWICH BUNS (Egg Rolls)

Makes 75 to 100 delicious hamburger buns that stay soft.

4½ c. warm water, not hot (105° to 115°)
3 pkgs. active dry yeast or 7½ tsp. dry bulk yeast
2½ tsp. salt
1 c. sugar
1⅓ c. olive oil
4 eggs, well beaten
5-lb. bag all-purpose flour, (about 15½ c.), divided

1. In mixer bowl, combine warm water and yeast; add salt, sugar, oil and beaten eggs; mix together. 2. Add about half the flour and beat on high speed. 3. In large bowl or dishpan, put remainder of 5-pound bag of flour, minus 2 cups which may not be needed. 4. Pour batter into flour and stir with large spoon until flour is pretty well mixed into batter. 5. Knead with hands 5 to 10 minutes, until dough is smooth and elastic. (If necessary, add more flour while kneading.) 6. Cover with cloth; let rise until double, about 1 to 2 hours, in warm, draft-free place. 7. Punch down and let rise again, covered, until double, about 1 hour or less. 8. Make into buns by using a piece of dough the size of an egg, with greased fingers. 9. Shape and flatten each bun about 2¼ inches in diameter and ¾ inch thick. 10. Place on greased cookie sheets, about 2 inches apart; cover and let buns rise until double, about 2 hours. 11. Bake in preheated 375° to 400° oven for 13 minutes or until golden brown on top and bottom. 12. If desired, brush tops gently with soft butter. 13. Remove from cookie sheets to cooling racks.

SWEET ROLL BASIC DOUGH

1 c. plus 2 T. (1⅛ c.) warm (not hot) water
1 to 2 pkgs. active dry yeast (2½ tsp. dry bulk yeast for each pkg.)
½ tsp. salt
⅓ c. sugar
⅓ c. olive oil
1 egg
4 c. plus 2½ T. all-purpose flour, approximately, divided

1. In mixer bowl combine water, yeast, salt, sugar, oil, egg and 2 cups flour; beat on high speed until well mixed. 2. Remove bowl from mixer; stir in 2 cups flour with large spoon. 3. Turn dough onto lightly floured surface; knead at least 5 minutes, adding a bit more flour as needed. 4. Place in greased or sprayed bowl, turning to grease top. 5. Cover and let rise 1 to 2 hours in draft-free area. (Or, refrigerate dough from 2 to 24 hours, covered.) 6. Use this dough for the recipes which call for Basic Sweet Roll Dough. (Or shape into 20 rolls, place on greased cookie sheet and let rise until double.) Bake in preheated 375° oven 12 to 15 minutes, until golden brown.

BUBBLE-RING PULL-APART SWEET ROLLS, CROWN

One recipe of Sweet Roll Basic Dough
⅓ c. butter, melted
¾ c. packed brown sugar
1 tsp. cinnamon
½ c. chopped nuts (or more)

1. Form dough into walnut-sized balls. 2. Dip each ball in melted butter, then roll in mixture of brown sugar and cinnamon. 3. Roll in chopped nuts; place balls in well-greased, one-piece angel food cake pan or bundt pan. 4. Cover pan with cloth and let rise until double (1½ to 2 hours). 5. Bake in preheated 350° oven 40 to 55 minutes or until well browned and done. Cool 10 minutes, then remove from pan.

BUBBLE ROLLS FROM FROZEN BREAD DOUGH

An easy way to defrost frozen bread dough is to put it in refrigerator overnight.

1 loaf (1 lb.) frozen bread dough, thawed
¼ c. (½ stick) butter, melted
1 sm. box (4-serving size) vanilla or butterscotch pudding mix (regular or instant)
½ c. packed brown sugar
½ c. chopped nuts (opt.)

1. Cut dough into 4 long pieces (lengthwise), then cut each piece into 8 pieces (total of 32 pieces). 2. Dip each piece into melted butter, then roll in combined mixture of dry pudding mix, brown sugar and nuts. 3. Put into greased or sprayed 8 x 8-inch or 9 x 9-inch pan or a bundt pan. 4. Drizzle any remaining butter over top. 5. Sprinkle remaining pudding mixture over top. 6. Let rise in warm place until double in size. 7. Bake in middle of preheated 350° oven 25 minutes, or until done. 8. Cool in pan 2 minutes, then invert onto platter or cookie sheet.

CARAMEL PECAN SWEET ROLLS

Bake in one 13 x 9-inch cake pan; makes 12 rolls.

One recipe Sweet Roll Basic Dough
1 T. softened butter
¼ c. packed brown sugar
Cinnamon

For Bottom of Pan:
¼ c. butter
⅓ c. packed brown sugar
⅓ c. light or dark corn syrup
1 to 1½ c. pecans or English walnuts (halves or coarsely chopped)

1. Follow Sweet Roll Basic Dough through step #5. 2. In small pan, combine ¼ cup butter, ⅓ cup brown sugar and ⅓ cup corn syrup; bring to a boil. 3. Reduce heat and gently simmer 1 minute; remove from heat and pour into 13 x 9-inch cake pan which has been greased on the sides only. 4. Sprinkle nuts over the syrup; set aside. 5. On lightly floured surface, pat or roll out dough to a 15 x 9-inch rectangle (about ½ inch thick). 6. Spread with 1 tablespoon softened butter. 7. Sprinkle with ¼ cup brown sugar, not quite to the edges. 8. Sprinkle lightly with cinnamon. 9. Starting at long side, roll as for jellyroll; push ends in gently until roll is 14 inches in length. 10. On cutting board, slice with sharp knife into 12 slices. 11. Carefully place slices of dough over nuts, cut side down. 12. Cover rolls with cloth and let rise in draft-free place about 1 hour or until double in size. 13. On lowest oven rack in preheated 375° oven, bake about 20 minutes or until light golden brown. (Make sure rolls are done in the center-top also.) 14. Loosen around edges and let set in pan 4 to 5 minutes. 15. Place a cookie sheet on top the pan of rolls, then turn upside down so rolls come out on cookie sheet.

Another Version for Bottom of Pan, "Sticky Nut":

¼ c. butter (½ stick), melted
½ c. packed brown sugar
2 T. cream or evaporated milk
1 to 1½ c. walnuts or pecans (halves or coarsely chopped)

1. In 13 x 9-inch cake pan, combine melted butter, brown sugar and cream; stir well. (Grease or spray sides of pan.) 2. Proceed with step #4 of above recipe.

CARAMEL PECAN SWEET ROLLS
(Overnight)

Bake for breakfast.

Follow recipe for "Caramel Pecan Sweet Rolls" with 2 exceptions: use only 1 package dry yeast, and in step #12, leave rolls uncovered. Let rise overnight (or up to 8 hours) at room temperature. Bake, as directed, for breakfast.

CHERRY SWEET ROLLS

Delicious sweet rolls topped with cherries and glaze.

One recipe of Sweet Roll Basic Dough
1 (21-oz.) can cherry pie filling
Powdered Sugar Glaze

1. Divide dough into 20 to 30 balls; place about 3 inches apart on lightly greased baking sheets. 2. Flatten each ball to ½-inch thickness; cover with cloth and let rise 1 hour or until double in size. 3. Make a depression in center of each roll with 2 fingers, pressing clear to bottom, and making an indentation about 1½ inches in diameter. 4. Spoon three cherries into each indentation. 5. In preheated 375° oven, bake 10 to 12 minutes, until light golden in color. 6. Remove to cooling racks and frost with Powdered Sugar Glaze around top edges, leaving cherries visible in center.

Powdered Sugar Glaze:

2 c. powdered sugar
2 T. soft butter
½ tsp. vanilla
2½ T. milk, approximately

1. Mix all together, stirring until smooth.

CINNAMON ROLLS

Bake in one 13 x 9 x 2-inch pan. Makes 12 big rolls.

One recipe Sweet Roll Basic Dough
2 T. (¼ stick) softened butter
½ c. packed brown sugar
2 to 4 tsp. cinnamon
Cinnamon Roll Icing

1. Grease or spray 13 x 9 x 2-inch pan. 2. On lightly floured surface, pat or roll out dough to a 15 x 9-inch rectangle (about ½ inch thick). 3. Spread with softened butter. 4. Sprinkle with brown sugar and cinnamon (not quite to the edges). 5. Starting at long side, roll as for jellyroll; lift roll gently onto cutting board and push ends in until roll is 14 inches in length. 6. Slice with sharp knife into 12 slices; carefully place in prepared pan. 7. Cover and let rise in draft-free area about 1 hour or until double in size. 8. In preheated 375° oven, bake on lower oven rack about 20 minutes, or until light golden brown. (Make sure rolls are light golden brown on bottom also.) 9. Loosen around edges; turn out onto cooling rack. 10. After rolls have cooled 10 minutes (or longer), frost with Cinnamon Roll Icing.

Cinnamon Roll Icing:

1 c. powdered sugar
1/16 tsp. salt
1 T. soft butter
1 T. hot water
¼ tsp. vanilla
⅛ tsp. maple flavoring (opt.)

1. Combine all ingredients and stir well. If too thick, add a few drops hot water; if too thin, add a little more powdered sugar.

CINNAMON ROLLS FROM FROZEN BREAD DOUGH

1 lb. loaf frozen bread dough, thawed
2 T. butter, softened
½ c. packed brown sugar
2 tsp. cinnamon

1. Roll out thawed bread dough on floured surface to ¼ to ½-inch thickness. 2. Spread softened butter over dough; sprinkle with brown sugar and cinnamon. 3. Roll up like jellyroll and cut with sharp knife into ¾-inch slices. 4. Place on greased or sprayed 11 x 7, 12 x 8 or 13 x 9-inch baking pan (or small cookie sheet); cover with cloth and let rise several hours or until

doubled in size. **5.** Bake in preheated 375° oven 12 to 15 minutes, or until light golden in color. **6.** Remove from pan; frost or glaze if desired. **Overnight:** To bake for breakfast, take dough out of freezer and thaw in refrigerator all day. At bedtime, follow first 4 steps and let rise all night, covered. (Not in too warm a place.) Bake for breakfast.

<u>Frosting:</u>
1 c. powdered sugar
1 T. butter, room temperature
1 T. hot water
¼ tsp. vanilla
⅛ tsp. maple flavoring (opt.)

1. Mix all together; if too thick, add a few drops hot water.

CINNAMON ROLLS, OVERNIGHT

Bake for breakfast.

1. Sometime during the day, make Sweet Roll Basic Dough, using only 1 package dry yeast; cover and refrigerate. **2.** Before going to bed, follow the first 6 steps for "Cinnamon Rolls." **3.** In step #7, leave rolls uncovered and let rise overnight at room temperature. Bake, as directed, for breakfast.

NUT ROLLS (Makes 6)

Rolled up like jelly rolls; slice to serve.

5½ c. all-purpose flour
1 tsp. salt
1½ c. (3 sticks) butter
1 lg. cake compressed yeast (or 2 pkgs. dry yeast)
1½ c. milk, heated to barely lukewarm
2 T. sugar
7 egg yolks
1 beaten egg for tops

<u>Nut Filling:</u>
7 egg whites
1 lb. (4 c.) powdered sugar
1 tsp. vanilla
2 lbs. shelled walnuts, ground or finely chopped in food processor

1. In large bowl, combine flour and salt; add butter and mix with pastry blender until mixture resembles cornmeal. **2.** Dissolve yeast in milk and 2 tablespoons sugar. **3.** In medium bowl, beat egg yolks; add yeast mixture and stir together. **4.** Add this liquid to flour mixture; mix together well. **5.** Cover with waxed paper and refrigerate 1 hour or longer. (Can be overnight.) **6.** Make filling by beating egg whites until foamy; add powdered sugar gradually, beating until stiff. **7.** Add vanilla and ground nuts; set aside. **8.** Divide dough into 6 pieces; on lightly floured surface, roll each piece quite thin. **9.** Spread with nut filling within ½ inch from edges; roll up as for jellyroll. **10.** Place (seam side down) on greased or sprayed cookie sheets; brush lightly with 1 beaten egg. **11.** Let rise

from 10 minutes to 1 hour; bake in preheated 350° oven 30 to 35 minutes or until light golden brown. Cool on wire racks.

Chapter 9

Cereal, French Toast, Pancakes and Waffles

DERRICK, JULIE AND RANDI MCILHANY

1957

CEREAL, FRENCH TOAST, PANCAKES AND WAFFLES

CORNMEAL MUSH

½ c. cornmeal
½ c. cold water
1½ c. boiling water
½ tsp. salt
1 T. butter

1. In small bowl, mix cornmeal and cold water together. 2. Add cornmeal mixture slowly to boiling water, salt and butter, stirring well. 3. Reduce heat to simmer and cook 5 to 10 minutes, stirring occasionally.

CORNMEAL MUSH, FRIED

From Hazel & Harvey Schreiner.

1⅓ c. cornmeal
1 tsp. salt
1 c. cold water
3 c. boiling water
Flour
Butter or olive oil

1. Combine cornmeal, salt and cold water in bowl. 2. Add to boiling water, stirring constantly; bring back to boiling point. 3. Reduce heat to low-simmer and cook, covered, 10 minutes longer, stirring frequently. 4. Pour into a wet dish or loaf pan and refrigerate overnight. 5. Cut into ½-inch slices; dip slices into flour (on both sides) and fry in hot butter or oil until golden brown on both sides. 6. Serve with syrup.

CREAM OF WHEAT

Serves 3 to 4 people.

3 c. water
½ tsp. salt
½ c. Quick Cream of Wheat (NOT instant)

1. In medium pan, bring water and salt to a boil. 2. Gradually add cream of wheat, stirring well. 3. Reduce heat to simmer and boil gently about 4 minutes, stirring frequently. Note: Raisins may be added to the water at the beginning.

Cream of Wheat for Two:
1⅓ c. water
¼ tsp. salt
¼ c. Quick Cream of Wheat (NOT instant)

1. Follow above directions.

GRITS (Hominy Grits)

3 c. boiling water
½ tsp. salt
¾ c. quick grits

1. Stir grits slowly into boiling water with salt. 2. When it boils, reduce heat to medium-low; cook 2½ to 5 minutes, stirring occasionally. 3. Remove from heat and cover pan to keep hot. 4. Serve with butter, salt and pepper, or gravy, or as a hot cereal with milk and sugar. Makes 3 large or 4 medium servings. Note: If grits are left over, chill; slice and fry in butter until golden brown.

One Serving:
1 c. boiling water
⅛ tsp. salt
¼ c. quick grits

OATMEAL CEREAL

For Two:
1⅓ c. water
⅛ tsp. salt (or less)
¾ c. oatmeal, quick or old-fashioned

1. In saucepan, bring water and salt to a boil; add oatmeal, stirring well. 2. Bring to a boil again; reduce heat and boil 1 to 3 minutes for quick oats or 5 minutes for old-fashioned oats. 3. Remove from heat; cover and let stand 3 to 5 minutes. 4. Stir and serve. Raisin-Spice: Add ¼ cup raisins, ⅛ teaspoon cinnamon and ¹⁄₁₆ teaspoon nutmeg.

For Three:
2⅓ c. water
¼ tsp. salt
1¼ c. oatmeal

OATMEAL & BRAN CEREAL

Adapted from Ruth and Clifford Hoien. Serves 2 to 3.

2 c. water
¼ tsp. salt
⅔ c. oatmeal (quick or old-fashioned)
⅔ c. oat bran

1. In saucepan, bring water and salt to a full boil. 2. Add oatmeal and bran, stirring. 3. Reduce heat and boil gently 2 to 5 minutes, stirring occasionally.

FRENCH TOAST

Recipe may be multiplied.
Triple recipe for 3 to 4 people.

1 lg. egg, slightly beaten (or 2 smaller eggs)
¼ c. milk
¹⁄₁₆ tsp. salt
1 T. olive oil (more if needed)
4 slices bread or more

1. In wide-bottom bowl, beat egg slightly with wire whip or fork. 2. Add milk and salt. 3. Heat oil in skillet. 4. Dip 2 slices bread quickly in and out of egg mixture and fry in skillet, browning each side. 5. Repeat until egg mixture is all absorbed. 6. Serve with butter and syrup (and bacon bits, if desired).

PANCAKE SYRUP, NEVER-FAIL

Makes a little over 3 cups.

½ T. cornstarch, packed level
1 c. sugar
1 c. packed brown sugar
1 c. corn syrup
1 c. water
⅛ tsp. salt
½ tsp. maple flavoring (or to taste)

1. In 2 or 3-quart saucepan, stir together cornstarch and sugar; add brown sugar, corn syrup, water and salt. 2. Bring to a boil, stirring occasionally; reduce heat and boil gently 5 minutes. 3. Remove from heat and add maple flavoring. When cool (or lukewarm) pour into an empty 24-ounce pancake syrup bottle.

PANCAKES, BASIC DELUXE

Makes enough for 4 to 5 people.
Good served with bacon flavor chips and syrup.

2 c. all-purpose flour (or half whole-wheat flour)
5 tsp. baking powder
¼ tsp. salt
3 T. sugar
2 c. milk* (or less)
2 eggs
¼ c. olive oil

1. In large mixing bowl, stir dry ingredients together. 2. Add remaining ingredients; mix until batter is fairly smooth. (If too thick, add a little more milk.) 3. Drop spoonfuls of batter on hot greased griddle or preheated electric skillet, 375°. 4. When pancakes bubble and are brown on bottom, turn over and cook other side until golden brown. **Apple Cinnamon Pancakes:** Add 1 cup finely chopped apples and 1 teaspoon cinnamon. (May take a little less milk.) **Blueberry Pancakes:** Add 1 cup frozen, sweetened blueberries, thawed and

drained. **Bran Pancakes:** Use ½ cup All-Bran, Bran Buds or crushed Bran Flakes in place of ½ cup flour. ***Note:** ⅔ cup nonfat dry milk powder may be added with dry ingredients and 1¾ to 2 cups water used instead of milk.

PANCAKES, BASIC DELUXE (Smaller)

Makes enough for 3 people.

1¼ c. all-purpose flour
3 tsp. baking powder
⅛ tsp. salt
2 T. sugar
1¼ c. milk
1 egg
2 T. + 1 tsp. olive oil, or melted butter

1. Follow directions for previous recipe. (If too thick, add a small amount more milk.)

PANCAKES, BRAN WHEAT

A good-health recipe. Enough for 3 people.

1 c. whole-wheat or all-purpose flour
¼ c. 100% unprocessed bran
1 tsp. baking soda
1 T. lecithin granules or liquid lecithin (opt.)
1½ c. buttermilk
1 T. molasses or honey
⅛ tsp. salt (opt.)
2 egg whites, stiffly beaten (or 2 whole eggs)

1. Place dry ingredients in medium-large bowl; add buttermilk and molasses. 2. Fold in stiffly beaten egg whites (or whole eggs). If a thinner batter is desired, add a little more buttermilk. 3. Drop spoonfuls of batter on hot greased griddle or preheated electric skillet (375°). 4. When pancakes bubble and are brown on bottom, turn over and bake other side until golden brown.

PANCAKES, BUCKWHEAT, OLD-FASHIONED

Overnight buckwheat cakes.

2½ c. lukewarm water
1 pkg. dry yeast
1 c. all-purpose flour
2 c. buckwheat flour (NOT self-rising)
½ tsp. salt
2 T. white or brown sugar

Next Morning:
2 T. olive oil or melted butter
2 T. molasses
½ tsp. soda dissolved in 2 T. warm water

1. In large bowl, dissolve yeast in lukewarm water. **2.** Add flour, buckwheat flour, salt and sugar; mix together with large spoon or electric mixer until well blended. **3.** Cover and let set at room temperature overnight or for 2 to 8 hours. **4.** When ready to use, stir in molasses, oil and the soda which has been dissolved in the warm water. **5.** Bake on preheated, greased griddle (375° or 400°) until brown on both sides. <u>For Less Buckwheat:</u> Use 2 cups all-purpose flour and 1 cup buckwheat flour. **Note**: If you use this leftover batter later, add a little sugar or molasses so they will brown.

PANCAKES, BUTTERMILK

Enough for 2 or 3 adults.

1 egg
1¼ c. commercial buttermilk
2 T. olive oil
1 c. all-purpose flour
2 tsp. sugar
1 tsp. baking powder
½ tsp. baking soda
¼ tsp. salt

1. In medium bowl, beat egg. **2.** Add buttermilk and oil; mix together to blend. **3.** Add remaining ingredients, stirring only until all moistened. (Batter will be lumpy.) **4.** Put spoonfuls on hot greased griddle and turn as soon as brown on one side (375° or 400° on preheated electric skillet).

PANCAKES, CORN GRIDDLE CAKES

1½ c. all-purpose flour
4 tsp. baking powder
½ tsp. salt
1 tsp. sugar
⅛ tsp. pepper
1 egg
1¼ c. milk
1 c. cream-style corn
2 T. olive oil

1. Combine dry ingredients in bowl, stirring together. **2.** Add remaining ingredients; mix only until dry ingredients are moistened. **3.** Bake on hot greased griddle, on both sides. Makes about 12 pancakes.

PANCAKES, FEATHER

For 2 or 3 adults.

1 c. all-purpose flour
¼ tsp. salt
1 to 2 T. sugar
1 to 2 T. baking powder
1 c. milk
1 egg
1 T. olive oil

1. In med.-small bowl, stir together dry ingredients. **2.** Add milk, egg and oil; beat with wire whip until fairly smooth. **3.** Lightly grease hot griddle or preheated electric skillet (375° to 400°) before baking each batch. **4.** Drop by spoonfuls; cook on one side until batter is puffed and full of bubbles. **5.** Turn pancakes and brown on bottom. Makes 8 or 9 pancakes.

PANCAKES, OATMEAL

For 2 or 3 adults.

¾ c. all-purpose flour
1 c. quick rolled oats, uncooked (not instant)
1 tsp. baking powder
1 tsp. baking soda
½ tsp. salt
1 to 2 T. sugar or honey
1 to 2 T. olive oil
1 lg. or medium egg
1½ c. milk

1. In mixer bowl, combine dry ingredients, stirring together. **2.** Add remaining ingredients; beat until well mixed. (Batter will be thin.) **3.** Drop spoonfuls of batter on hot greased griddle, stirring from bottom of bowl each time. **4.** When pancakes bubble and are brown on bottom, turn over and cook other side until golden brown.

WAFFLES, BELGIAN (Yeast-Raised)

Batter stands 45 minutes before using.
For a lot of waffles, double recipe.

1 c. lukewarm milk
½ pkg. active dry yeast (1⅛ to 1¼ tsp.)
2 egg yolks
½ tsp. vanilla
1¼ c. all-purpose flour
¼ tsp. salt
½ T. sugar
¼ c. melted butter (or half olive oil)
2 stiffly beaten egg whites

1. In mixing bowl, sprinkle yeast over lukewarm milk; stir to dissolve. **2.** In small bowl, beat egg yolks; add to milk. **3.** Add vanilla, flour, salt and sugar. **4.** Stir in melted butter thoroughly. **5.** Carefully fold stiffly beaten egg whites into batter. **6.** Let mixture stand in draft-free place about 45 minutes. **7.** Lightly spray (or grease with olive oil) grids of Belgian waffle iron; close lid and preheat. **8.** When preheat light goes out, raise lid and pour ¾ to ⅞ cup batter on lower grid; close lid. (If using a regular waffle iron, use ½ cup batter.) **9.** When steaming has stopped, gently lift lid to check for brownness. **10.** Before making another waffle, wait until preheat light goes off.

WAFFLES, CLASSIC

This makes plenty of waffles for four people.

2 lg. eggs, separated (or 3 smaller eggs)
1¼ c. milk, approximately
⅓ c. olive oil (or melted butter)
1½ c. all-purpose flour
3 tsp. baking powder
¼ tsp. salt
2 tsp. sugar (omit sugar for very crisp waffles)

1. In mixer bowl, beat egg whites stiff; set aside. **2.** In medium bowl, beat egg yolks; add milk and oil, stirring together well. **3.** Add dry ingredients, stirring together quickly. **4.** Fold in egg whites. **5.** Add a little more milk if batter is too thick to pour. **6.** In heated waffle iron, put 1 tablespoon batter in each compartment. Cover and leave closed until no more steam appears. **7.** Lift lid. If waffle is golden brown, lift from iron with fork. (If not done, close lid and bake a little longer.) **Note**: Do not grease waffle grids; if necessary, spray them lightly with non-stick spray.

WAFFLES, EASY (For 4 to 5 People)

Cut recipe in half for 2 to 3 people.

2 eggs, well beaten
1¾ to 2 c. milk
¼ c. olive oil
2 c. all-purpose flour (or half whole-wheat flour)
4 tsp. baking powder
½ tsp. salt
1 T. sugar (opt.)

1. In mixer bowl or container for electric blender, beat eggs. **2.** Add remaining ingredients in order given; stir just until blended. **3.** In preheated waffle iron, put 1 tablespoon batter in each compartment. (Use more for Belgian waffle iron.) **4.** Cover and leave closed until steaming stops and waffle is golden brown. **Note**: These waffles may be baked in regular or Belgian waffle iron.

WAFFLES, YEAST (Overnight)

Batter will keep 2 to 3 days in refrigerator.

2 c. milk, scalded and cooled
1 pkg. active dry yeast
¼ c. lukewarm water
2 c. all-purpose flour
½ tsp. salt
2 T. sugar
3 eggs, beaten
¼ c. olive oil

1. In small bowl, dissolve yeast in lukewarm water. **2.** In mixing bowl, combine flour, salt and sugar; add cooled milk and yeast mixture. **3.** In empty yeast bowl, beat eggs; add to batter. **4.** Add oil; beat until batter is smooth. **5.** Cover and refrigerate overnight. **6.** Next morning, stir before using; bake in hot waffle iron.

Chapter 10

Eggs

STONEBORO WESLEYAN METHODIST SCHOOL

1964-1965

FROM BACK, L. TO R.: WILLIAM EASTLICK, DONALD CLEVENGER, MR. ANDREW YOUNGBLOOD, LUCINDA GREENLEE, MISS LEOTA BENNINGER, REV. DAVID PHELPS, RHETTA SMITH, MRS. RUTH HOIEN, RUTH SLOZAT, REV. C. A. HOIEN, GLORIA JEAN FOLTZ

SHARON DEETS, DEBBIE VOGT, LINDA SHORTS, RUTH EICHORN, LINDA BELL

JOHN BOUGHNER, LARRY SLOZAT, CLARENCE BENNINGER, MARK DEETS, ROBERT ALTER

BARBARA VOGT, DONNA ALTER, NAOMI EICHORN, DONALD BOUGHNER, JEFFRY SHORTS, DANIEL ALTER, SAM DEETS

KATHY ALTER, DARLA ALEXANDER, DIANE BOUGHNER, ROGER THAWLEY, PHILIP DEETS, ENOCH EICHORN, MARK EICHORN

EGGS

EGGS, BOILED HARD I

Cover eggs with cold water in saucepan. Bring to a boil on HIGH, then reduce heat a little and boil 15 minutes with no lid (20 minutes for extra-large eggs). Remove from heat; drain and rinse under cold water.

Hint to shell hard-boiled eggs: **1.** Put several eggs in a pan and cover with cold water. **2.** Bring to a full rolling boil; turn heat off and cover with lid for 15 to 20 minutes. **3.** Drain water off; cover eggs with cold water. (If in a hurry, cover the eggs and cold water with ice cubes.) **4.** Let stand until eggs are cold. **5.** Drain water and ice off; with lid on, shake pan back and forth vigorously for a few seconds. The egg shells will be all cracked and should come off easily.

EGGS, BOILED HARD II

Cover eggs with cold water in saucepan. Bring to a full, rolling boil. Cover with lid and remove pan from heat; let stand for 20 minutes. Then drain water off.

EGGS, BOILED SOFT

1. Place eggs in single layer in saucepan. Add enough cold water to cover eggs completely. Cover with lid and quickly bring water to a boil. **2.** Turn off heat and remove pan from burner. **3.** Let eggs stand, covered, in hot water for 3 to 4 minutes, depending on desired doneness. (Three minutes is the average for a large egg.) **4.** Immediately run cold water over eggs until cool enough to handle. **5.** To serve, cut shell through middle with knife. With a teaspoon, scoop egg out of each shell half onto serving dish. (Or serve in eggcup by placing egg in cup, small end down; slice off large end of egg with knife and eat from shell.)

EGG BREAKFAST STRATA I

Adapted from Homer Patterson and Shirley Kaufman. To double this recipe, bake in a 13 x 9-inch pan.

3 slices white bread, cubed (including crusts)
4 oz. (1 c.) shredded Cheddar or Swiss cheese
4 oz. (¾ c.) ham or Canadian bacon cubes (or ½ lb. sausage, browned and drained)
4 eggs
2 c. milk
½ tsp. salt
½ tsp. dry mustard
¼ tsp. pepper

1. Grease or spray 8 x 8 x 2-inch baking pan. **2.** In bottom of pan, layer bread cubes, cheese and meat. **3.** In bowl, beat together eggs, milk and seasonings; pour over strata. **4.** Cover and refrigerate overnight or bake immediately. **5.** Bake in preheated 350° oven, uncovered, 45 to 60 minutes or until top is browned and knife inserted in center comes out clean. Let stand 5 minutes before cutting. Serves 5 or 6. **Note**: 5 to 6 slices cooked bacon, crumbled, may be substituted for the meat. Sprinkle some of it over the top. **Optional ingredients**: Red sweet pepper strips and 2 T. sliced green onion tops.

EGG BREAKFAST STRATA II

8 slices bread (several days old)
8 slices "light" cheese (or regular)
Ham or Spam cubes
3 eggs
2 c. milk
½ tsp. salt
¼ tsp. dry mustard
1 T. butter, melted

1. Lightly butter or spray 8 x 8-inch baking dish. **2.** Trim crusts off bread; place 4 slices in bottom of dish. (Reserve crusts.) **3.** Place 4 slices cheese over the bread; sprinkle half the ham or Spam cubes over top. **4.** Repeat layers of bread, cheese and meat. **5.** In med.-small bowl, beat eggs; add milk, salt and dry mustard. **6.** Pour egg mixture over all; let stand, covered, overnight in refrigerator (or at least 4 hours) before baking. **7.** In saucepan, melt butter; tear crusts into bite-sized pieces and add to butter, stirring. **8.** Sprinkle crust-crumbs over top strata; bake, covered with foil, in preheated 350° oven 45 minutes. Uncover and bake 15 minutes longer.

EGGS, DEVILED

7 to 8 eggs, hard-boiled and shelled
¼ c. mayonnaise or salad dressing
1 tsp. prepared mustard or ⅓ tsp. dry mustard (opt.)
½ tsp. sugar (opt.)
½ tsp. vinegar
⅛ tsp. salt or onion salt
Paprika or pepper for top

1. Halve eggs and remove yolks. **2.** Mash yolks with fork or press through sieve or use food processor. **3.** Add mayonnaise, mustard, sugar, vinegar and salt to mashed yolks; mix well. **4.** Pile egg yolk mixture into egg white cavities. **5.** Sprinkle with paprika; cover with plastic wrap, holding it above eggs by sticking a wooden pick into several of the deviled eggs. **6.** Refrigerate. **Note**: Vinegar may be omitted; use ¼ teaspoon sugar.

EGGS FRIED, EASY OVER

½ T. butter
2 to 3 eggs
Salt and pepper

1. In skillet, melt butter over medium heat. 2. Add eggs and lightly salt and pepper them. 3. Fry 3 minutes on one side. 4. Turn over gently with spatula; turn heat off and fry just until the white of egg is cooked. 5. Lift out carefully with spatula.

EGGS, FRIED-STEAMED

Butter
Eggs
Salt and pepper
1 tsp. water

1. Place skillet over medium heat for ½ minute. 2. Add ½ teaspoon butter for each egg. 3. When butter is melted, add eggs. 4. Salt and pepper each egg lightly. 5. Add 1 teaspoon water to skillet and cover with tight lid. 6. Turn burner to low; complete cooking to desired stage. (It doesn't take long!)

EGG OMELET BASIC

Do not double this recipe.

3 eggs
1 T. water
½ T. olive oil
½ T. butter
⅛ tsp. salt
Pepper
1 T. bacon flavor chips (opt.)
Parsley for garnish (opt.)

1. In small bowl, beat eggs with a table fork; add water and beat again. 2. To hot 10-inch skillet, add oil and butter and melt; tilt skillet to coat bottom and sides. 3. When butter stops foaming, beat eggs again with fork or whisk and pour into skillet; reduce heat. 4. With an inverted pancake turner, carefully push cooked portions at edge toward center so uncooked portions can reach hot pan surface (tilt pan so uncooked egg will flow underneath). Allow 2 or 3 minutes cooking time. 5. Sprinkle salt and pepper over omelet. 6. Sprinkle bacon chips (or other desired fillings) over half the omelet, while omelet is still moist and creamy. 7. Slip pancake turner under unfilled side and fold over filling. 8. Slide omelet onto heated plate; garnish with parsley, if desired, and serve immediately.

EGG OMELET WITH MUSHROOMS & CHEESE

Made the easy way.

2 T. butter
6 eggs, slightly beaten
⅓ c. milk
Salt and pepper
2½-oz. jar mushrooms, drained
1 tsp. finely chopped chives
¾ c. shredded Monterey Jack cheese (or most any kind of cheese)

1. Melt butter in skillet over low heat. 2. Combine eggs, milk, salt and pepper; pour into skillet. Cook slowly. 3. As egg mixture sets, lift slightly with spatula so uncooked portion flows underneath. 4. Cover with mushrooms, chives and cheese; fold in half and cut into 3 or 4 pieces. Makes 3 to 4 servings.

EGGS, PICKLED WITH BEETS

Very easy and delicious.

6 to 8 hard-boiled eggs, shelled
1 (16-oz.) can beets, cut, sliced or small whole
½ c. sugar
¼ c. vinegar
½ stick cinnamon and/or 6 whole cloves (opt.)

1. Drain beets, reserving juice; measure ¾ cup beet juice, adding water if there is not enough. 2. In small pan, combine the ¾ cup beet liquid, sugar, vinegar and spices (if used); bring to a full boil, then remove from heat immediately. 3. Place shelled eggs in bottom of bowl; place drained beets over them. 4. Pour hot beet syrup over all. 5. Cover or use a wide-mouth glass jar and refrigerate several hours or overnight.

EGGS, POACHED

Water or milk
Eggs
Salt
Pepper

1. Grease or spray pan or skillet. 2. Add enough water or milk to fill nearly 1 inch deep; heat liquid to boiling. 3. Reduce heat to keep liquid simmering. 4. Break eggs, one at a time, into saucer, then slip each into the simmering liquid, holding saucer close to liquid surface. 5. Simmer 2½ to 5 minutes, depending on desired doneness and size of eggs (until white is firm). 6. When done, lift eggs out with slotted spoon or spatula, draining off liquid. (Trim edges if desired.) 7. Salt and pepper lightly, before serving.

EGGS, POACHED (Steam-Basted)

This requires a skillet with a tight lid.

½ T. butter
2 eggs
Salt
Pepper
½ T. water

1. In medium skillet over high heat, melt butter. 2. Break eggs into saucer and slip into skillet; reduce heat to low. 3. Salt and pepper eggs lightly and cook until edges of eggs turn white. 4. Add water; cover skillet with tight lid to hold steam. 5. Cook to desired doneness. (For soft eggs, it doesn't take long!) <u>Note</u>: If cooking more than 2 eggs, use larger skillet and add ½ teaspoon water for each egg.

EGGS (2), SCRAMBLED (Microwave)

This recipe may be doubled, doubling time also.

1 tsp. butter
2 lg. eggs
⅛ tsp. salt
Pepper
2 T. milk or cream

1. Melt butter in 2-cup glass pitcher or bowl on HIGH for 25 seconds. 2. Break eggs into pitcher; add salt, pepper and milk; mix with fork to scramble eggs. 3. Cook on HIGH for 60 seconds; stir. 4. Cook on HIGH for 60 seconds longer. 5. Let stand 1 to 3 minutes.

EGGS (5), SCRAMBLED (Range-Top)

Recipe may be cut in half.

5 lg. eggs (or 6 to 7 sm. eggs)
½ c. milk
¼ to ½ tsp. salt
⅛ tsp. pepper
½ to 1 T. butter

<u>Optional Ingredients:</u>
Shredded cheese
Leftover ham
Chopped green pepper
Chopped chives or onion
Bacon flavor chips
Cooked shrimp
Mushrooms, sliced*

1. Beat eggs slightly with fork in bowl. 2. Add milk, salt and pepper; stir together. 3. Heat skillet with butter; pour egg mixture into skillet and cook until creamy, stirring and scraping from bottom of skillet. (Don't overcook.) 4. While cooking, add any desired optional ingredients. Serves 3 to 4. *If using fresh mushrooms, sauté them in the butter before proceeding with recipe.

EGGS, SCRAMBLED, SPANISH STYLE

Serves 4 to 5 people..

2 T. olive oil, divided
1 to 2 med.-sized green bell peppers, cut in ¼-inch thick slices
1 med-sized onion, thinly sliced
1 sm. garlic clove, minced
¼ tsp. dried thyme
½ tsp. salt
1 to 2 med.-sized tomatoes, coarsely chopped
¼ tsp. hot pepper sauce
8 lg. eggs
½ tsp. salt
½ c. water

1. In 12-inch skillet over medium-high heat, in 1 tablespoon hot oil, cook green peppers, onion, garlic, thyme and first salt until vegetables are tender-crisp. 2. Add tomatoes and hot pepper sauce; cook 2 to 3 minutes until tomatoes are softened. 3. Spoon mixture onto a warm platter; keep warm. 4. In bowl, beat eggs, second salt and water with wire whisk or fork until blended. 5. In same skillet, heat 1 tablespoon oil until hot; add egg mixture. As eggs begin to set, stir slightly so uncooked egg flows to bottom. 6. Continue cooking until egg mixture is set but still moist, stirring occasionally. 7. Spoon scrambled eggs over vegetables on platter.

EGGS, TOAD-IN-A-HOLE

Egg fried inside a slice of bread.
From Kelly Wells Crouch.

1 tsp. butter
1 slice bread, buttered on both sides
1 egg
Salt and pepper

1. Melt butter in small skillet. 2. Cut a hole in center of buttered bread with a round cookie cutter or top of water glass. 3. Lay bread in skillet; break egg into a saucer and gently slip it into the hole. 4. Salt and pepper egg; cook for 2 or 3 minutes on medium heat. 5. Turn with spatula and fry 1 minute longer, or until done. (Center of bread may also be browned in skillet on both sides, at the same time.)

EGGS & ZUCCHINI

Adapted from Ruth Melichar. Serves 2.

1 sm. to med. zucchini
1 T. chopped onion (or more)
1 clove garlic, chopped (opt.)
½ T. butter
½ T. olive oil
3 eggs
3 T. milk
⅛ tsp. salt
Black pepper

1. Cut unpeeled zucchini in quarters lengthwise, then cut into slices. **2.** Fry zucchini, onions and garlic in melted butter and oil, stirring frequently. **3.** In small bowl, beat eggs, milk, salt and pepper together; pour over zucchini. **4.** On low heat, scramble as for scrambled eggs (or put lid over skillet and let cook until firm, like omelet.)

Chapter 11

Sandwiches

JIM AND MARTHA STEVENSON, PATRICIA, DAVID AND MARSHALL
1965

SANDWICHES

SANDWICH, BEEF (Roast beef)

Cold roast beef, sliced
Lettuce
Tomatoes, sliced
Onion, sliced (opt.)
Buns or bread

<u>Horseradish Dressing:</u>
½ c. mayonnaise
1 T. drained white horseradish

1. Make sandwiches, spreading one side of bun or bread with Horseradish Dressing. (If desired, salt tomato slices lightly.)

SANDWICH, B.L.T.

Bacon, lettuce and tomato.

Hot toast, buttered
Bacon, fried and drained
Sliced fresh tomatoes
Lettuce
Mayonnaise

1. On one slice of hot buttered toast, layer bacon, tomatoes, lettuce and mayonnaise. 2. Top with another slice of hot buttered toast; serve immediately. **Note**: No bacon? Sprinkle Bacos (bacon flavor chips) between the tomatoes and lettuce.

SANDWICH, CHEESE-PIMIENTO SPREAD

Multiply recipe as needed.

1 c. ground or shredded yellow cheese, any kind (4 oz.)
¼ c. mayonnaise or salad dressing
1 T. (or more) canned pimiento with juice, chopped

1. Combine ingredients, stirring well; refrigerate in covered container. **Note**: Red or green bell pepper (either cooked and drained or raw, chopped) may be substituted for pimiento.

SANDWICH, CORNED BEEF BUNS

1 (12-oz.) can corned beef
4 T. chili sauce or barbecue sauce
1 T. ketchup
½ T. prepared mustard (or less)
8 to 10 sandwich buns
8 to 10 slices of American cheese

1. Mix together corned beef, chili sauce, ketchup and mustard. 2. Put meat filling and a slice of cheese in each bun. 3. Wrap in aluminum foil; heat in preheated 350° oven for 20 minutes.

SANDWICH, CORNED BEEF & ONION

A good cold sandwich.

1 c. canned corned beef, mashed
½ c. chopped celery
2 T. chopped onion
2 tsp. prepared mustard
Sweet pickle, diced (opt.)
¼ c. mayonnaise
Butter
10 slices rye bread (or other bread)

1. Combine corned beef, celery, onion, mustard, pickle and mayonnaise, stirring together. 2. Butter bread on one side. 3. Spread corned beef mixture over half the bread slices; top with remaining slices. Makes 5 sandwiches.

SANDWICH, CORNED BEEF REUBENS, DILLED

Makes 4 delicious sandwiches.

1 c. (8 oz.) sauerkraut, rinsed and drained
¼ c. mayonnaise (Hellmann's Light)
1½ tsp. dried dill weed
2 T. chopped onion (opt.)
4 rye buns or 8 slices rye bread
½ of 12-oz. can corned beef
4 oz. (4 slices) Muenster cheese

1. Mix sauerkraut, mayonnaise and dill weed in small bowl. 2. Spread corned beef over one side of bun, or one slice of bread. 3. Spread ¼ of sauerkraut mixture over corned beef; lay cheese slice over sauerkraut and top with bun or bread slice. 4. Repeat with remaining sandwiches. 5. Wrap each sandwich in paper towel and microwave separately, on HIGH for 30 to 45 seconds per sandwich (until cheese melts). **To Heat in Conventional Oven**: Wrap in foil and bake in preheated 350° oven 10 to 15 minutes (or until cheese melts).

SANDWICH, CORNED BEEF REUBEN, GRILLED

Rye or pumpernickel bread, sliced
Corned beef lunch meat, sliced very thin
Sauerkraut, drained
Swiss cheese slices
Thousand Island dressing (or mix 2 parts mayonnaise with 1 part chili sauce)
Chopped onion (opt.)
Butter

1. For each sandwich, cover one bread slice with approximately 1 ounce chipped corned beef, ¼ cup sauerkraut, 1 slice Swiss cheese, 1 tablespoon dressing, a little chopped onion if desired and second bread slice. 2. Lightly butter both sides of sandwich on outside. 3. On low heat, grill sandwiches slowly in skillet (until golden brown on both sides and cheese is melted). Note: If buying at the deli, have the corned beef chipped fine; otherwise it will be hard to chew.

SANDWICH, CRABMEAT

1 (12-oz.) pkg. fully-cooked imitation crabmeat, thawed
½ c. mayonnaise or Miracle Whip salad dressing
2 T. finely chopped onion
Dash of garlic salt or garlic powder
2 T. finely chopped celery
Several radishes, chopped
¼ tsp. dried dill weed
¼ tsp. black pepper
Buns or bread

1. Combine crabmeat, mayonnaise, onion, garlic salt, celery, radishes, dill weed and pepper. 2. Put between buns or bread slices.

SANDWICH, CREAMY ORANGE SPREAD

A good spread for bagels.

4 oz. cream cheese, softened
2 to 3 T. orange marmalade

1. Mix together well.

SANDWICH, EGG SALAD FILLING

For 6 to 8 slices of bread.

4 hard-boiled eggs, shelled
¼ c. mayonnaise or salad dressing
⅛ to ¼ tsp. salt, onion salt or celery salt
¼ tsp. sugar
½ tsp. prepared mustard

Optional Ingredients:
⅛ to ½ c. chopped celery
2 T. diced sweet pickle or relish
½ T. fresh chives, chopped
¼ to ½ tsp. fresh or instant minced onion or 1/16 tsp. onion powder

1. Chop eggs or mash with fork or pastry blender (or put through ricer or food processor). 2. Add remaining ingredients and mix well. **Variations:** Add sliced or chopped olives, green pepper, dried chives or crumbled fried bacon.

SANDWICH, EGG SALAD FILLING WITH CARROTS

3 hard-boiled eggs, shelled
½ c. grated carrot
¼ c. chopped celery, green pepper or sweet pickles
2 T. mayonnaise or salad dressing
1 tsp. sugar or less
½ tsp. prepared mustard
¼ tsp. salt
1/16 tsp. pepper

1. Chop eggs or mash with fork. 2. Add remaining ingredients and mix well. 3. Put ⅓ cup of mixture between 2 slices of bread. (Makes enough for 6 to 8 slices bread.)

SANDWICH, GARDEN SPREAD

Adapted from Leota A. Benninger. Recipe may be doubled, if desired.

3 green bell peppers
3 red sweet peppers
1 med. carrot (not large)
2 onions
1½ c. sugar
¼ c. flour
¼ c. water
½ c. vinegar
1 tsp. salt
½ c. prepared mustard
1 pt. Miracle Whip salad dressing

1. Grind peppers, carrot and onion. 2. Pour boiling water over ground vegetables; let stand 2 minutes, then drain and squeeze water out. 3. In saucepan, stir together sugar and flour; add water, vinegar, salt and prepared mustard. 4. Boil gently 15 minutes; add drained vegetables and boil an additional 15 minutes. 5. Remove from heat and cool 15 minutes. 6. Stir in Miracle Whip salad dressing. 7. Pour into jar; cover and refrigerate.

SANDWICH, HAM BARBECUE (CHIPPED HAM) I

From Betty Marcin and Johann Morris.

1 lb. chipped ham
1 c. ketchup
⅓ c. relish including juice
1 med. onion, finely chopped
1 sm. green bell pepper, chopped
2 T. sugar
1 T. vinegar
1 tsp. prepared mustard
⅛ tsp. pepper
8 to 10 sandwich buns (Kaiser buns, preferably)

1. Combine all ingredients (except buns) in saucepan and bring to boiling point, uncovered. **2.** Reduce heat and simmer 30 to 60 minutes, uncovered.

SANDWICH, HAM BARBECUE (CHIPPED HAM) II

This recipe is for 6 buns, but may be multiplied.

8 oz. (1 c.) tomato sauce
2 T. packed brown sugar
2 tsp. vinegar
1 tsp. prepared mustard
½ tsp. Worcestershire sauce
½ lb. chipped ham (if ham is in slices, dice it)
6 sandwich buns

1. In saucepan, combine all ingredients except ham and buns; simmer 5 minutes. **2.** Add chipped ham; simmer 5 minutes longer. **3.** Serve hot in buns. <u>Note</u>: For a spicier, sharper ham barbecue, use chili sauce in place of tomato sauce.

SANDWICH, HAM BARBECUE (CHIPPED HAM) III

Crock-pot version fills 20 to 24 buns.

2 c. ketchup
¼ c. packed brown sugar
2 tsp. prepared mustard or 1 tsp. dry mustard
1 T. vinegar (opt.)
3 T. water
1 med. onion, finely chopped (½ c.)
2 lbs. chipped ham (if ham is in slices, dice it)

1. In crock-pot, combine all ingredients and stir well. **2.** Cover with lid and cook 1 hour on HIGH. **3.** Reduce heat to LOW and cook 2½ to 3 hours, covered.

SANDWICH, HAM, CHIPPED (Hot)

½ lb. chipped ham
4 slices American or Velveeta cheese, diced (about ½ c.)
4 green scallions, diced, or ⅛ c. chopped onion
¼ c. mayonnaise
2 T. chili sauce or barbecue sauce
8 wiener buns or 6 hamburger buns

1. If chipped ham is in slices, cut it up with sharp knife. **2.** Mix all ingredients, except buns. **3.** Heap in buttered buns and wrap in foil individually. **4.** Store in refrigerator if making ahead of time. **5.** Heat in preheated 350° oven about 15 minutes.

SANDWICH, HAM SALAD FILLING

1 lb. bologna (or chicken franks)
½ c. mayonnaise or salad dressing
3 T. relish
½ T. instant minced onion or 1 to 2 T. fresh onion, chopped
Sweet pickles, diced or chopped
1 T. sweet pickle syrup (or to taste)

1. Put bologna or franks through food grinder or food processor. **2.** Add remaining ingredients, mixing well.

SANDWICH, HAM & SWISS CHEESE, GRILLED

2 slices bread
2 T. Catalina dressing (or a similar dressing)
1 slice cooked ham
1 slice Swiss cheese
2 T. butter

1. Spread dressing on each slice of bread. **2.** Place ham and Swiss cheese between bread slices. **3.** Melt 1 tablespoon butter in skillet. **4.** Spread remaining butter on each side of sandwich. **5.** Cook on each side until golden brown and cheese is melted.

SANDWICH, HORSERADISH SPREAD

Spread for meat sandwiches.

3 oz. cream cheese, softened (or ½ c. mayonnaise)
1 T. prepared horseradish or horseradish sauce

1. Mix together cream cheese and horseradish.

SANDWICH, MARSHMALLOW PEANUT BUTTER

Delicious!

Bread slices
Marshmallow creme
Peanut butter

1. Spread one slice of bread with marshmallow creme. **2.** Spread another slice of bread with peanut butter; put both slices together.

SANDWICH, PEANUT BUTTER-ORANGE SPREAD

½ c. peanut butter
¼ c. orange marmalade
¼ c. raisins

1. Mix ingredients together.

SANDWICH, PITA POCKETS

Pita pocket halves
Mayonnaise, salad dressing or bottled dressing

<u>Optional Ingredients:</u>
Cooked meat, sliced or diced
Cooked bacon or bacon flavor chips
Cheese, shredded or sliced
Lettuce, shredded
Tomato, diced or cut in strips
Green bell pepper, chopped (or red or yellow bell pepper)
Sweet onion, chopped or in rings
Broccoli florets, raw
Sprouts
Cucumber, sliced or chopped

1. Warm pita bread in toaster, toaster oven or microwave oven. (Or warm it in a preheated 350° conventional oven for 10 minutes). 2. Stuff pitas with any of the desired optional ingredients; put a little mayonnaise or dressing on it.

SANDWICH, PITA POCKETS, MEXICAN

Delicious!

½ pita pocket
2 to 3 T. refried beans
1 to 2 T. salsa or taco sauce
1 slice cheese or 3 T. shredded cheese
1 green scallion, sliced (opt.)

1. Stuff ingredients into one pita half. 2. Place pita on Corelle plate and microwave on High for 30 seconds, or until cheese is slightly melted.

SANDWICH, SALAMI BAGEL

From Stephanie Swarts Smith.

Bagel, split
Cream cheese
Salami slice

1. Spread cream cheese on split bagel; top with slice of salami. 2. Wrap in foil; warm in toaster oven.

SANDWICH, SALMON SALAD

1 (14¾ to 16-oz.) can salmon, drained
¼ c. chopped celery
¼ c. chopped onion
¼ c. mayonnaise
2 tsp. lemon juice
½ tsp. dill weed
⅛ to ¼ tsp. pepper
Lettuce leaves (opt.)

Cucumbers, thinly sliced (opt.)
Bread or buns

1. Break drained salmon into chunks. 2. Add celery, onion, mayonnaise, lemon juice, dill weed and pepper. 3. Place lettuce leaf, cucumber slices and salmon mixture between bread slices or buns. (Or make open-faced sandwiches.)

SANDWICH, SALMON SALAD, BROILED

Makes 4 open-faced sandwiches.

1 (7¾-oz.) can salmon, drained (or ½ of 15-oz. can, about ¾ c.)
2 hard-boiled eggs, chopped
¼ c. shredded or chopped cheese (most any kind)
1 T. finely chopped onion
1 T. chopped ripe olives (opt.)
¼ c. mayonnaise or tartar sauce
2 tsp. lemon juice
¼ tsp. celery salt
⅛ tsp. dry mustard
4 slices bread, buttered on one side

1. Mix all ingredients, except bread, together; spread over buttered bread. 2. In preheated broiler, broil 2 to 3 minutes or until cheese melts (4 to 6 inches from heat).

SANDWICH, SLOPPY JOES, BAKED

For 8 to 10 buns.

½ T. olive oil
1 lb. lean ground beef
1 onion, chopped (½ c.)
1 c. chopped celery
½ green bell pepper, diced
⅛ tsp. black pepper
½ c. ketchup
½ c. chili sauce
⅛ to ¼ c. hot water (opt.)

1. In hot oil, brown beef and onion; drain off all fat. 2. In greased or sprayed 1½-quart baking dish or casserole, combine meat and remaining ingredients; cover with lid or foil. 3. Bake 1½ hours in 325° oven. <u>Note</u>: For top-of-stove version, simmer on low heat in skillet or pan about 30 minutes, stirring occasionally.

SANDWICH, SLOPPY JOES, CROCK-POT

Makes about 1½ quarts when cooked.

1 tsp. olive oil
1½ to 2 lbs. lean ground beef
1 to 1¼ c. finely chopped onion
1 c. finely chopped celery
1 c. ketchup
8 oz. (1 c.) tomato sauce

½ c. water
1 tsp. salt
1 tsp. chili powder
1 tsp. dry mustard
1 tsp. Worcestershire sauce
1 tsp. vinegar
½ tsp. sugar (opt.)
¼ tsp. pepper
¼ tsp. garlic powder

1. Heat oil in skillet and brown ground beef; drain off all fat. 2. Put meat in crock-pot along with uncooked onion and celery; add remaining ingredients. 3. Cook, covered, on HIGH for 1 hour, then on LOW for 2½ to 4 hours. **Alternative Cooking Method:** Cook on LOW the whole time, for 8 to 10 hours, in crock-pot.

SANDWICH, SLOPPY JOES, DEBBIE'S

From Debra Patterson.

1 lb. ground beef
1 tsp. olive oil
1 tsp. salt
3 tsp. sloppy Joe seasoning mix (1 env.)
1 (6-oz.) can tomato paste
1¼ c. water
1 to 3 T. sugar or 3 T. packed brown sugar (opt.)

1. Brown ground beef in skillet with oil; drain off all fat. 2. Stir in remaining ingredients, adding water gradually. 3. Bring to a boil; reduce heat and simmer 10 minutes, stirring occasionally. **Note:** ½ to 1 cup chopped onions and/or celery may be cooked with the ground beef, if desired.

SANDWICH, SLOPPY JOES, ELSIE'S

From Elsie Croyle; makes enough to fill 8 buns.

1 lb. ground beef
1 onion, chopped
1 tsp. olive oil
1 (15½-oz.) can Manwich Sloppy Joe Sauce
⅓ c. water
1 T. sugar (or to taste)
¼ tsp. salt
¼ tsp. pepper

1. Brown ground beef and onion (green bell pepper may also be added) in olive oil; drain off all fat. 2. Add sauce, water, sugar, salt and pepper; heat thoroughly.

SANDWICH, SLOPPY JOES FOR A CROWD

2 T. olive oil
8 lbs. lean ground beef
2 c. finely chopped onion
2 c. finely chopped celery
1½ c. ketchup or chili sauce

1 (1 lb. 13-oz.) can tomato puree (4½ c.)
2 T. sugar (or less)
⅓ c. Worcestershire sauce (or less)
½ c. prepared mustard
4 tsp. salt (or less)
1 tsp. Tabasco (opt.)
3 to 4 tsp. chili powder (or to taste)

1. Heat oil in skillet (or use 2 skillets) and brown ground beef; drain off all fat. 2. In cooking pot, put meat and uncooked onion and celery; add remaining ingredients. 3. Bring to a boil; reduce heat and simmer for 1 hour, uncovered, stirring occasionally. 4. Serve in 65 to 70 buns. (Serves 35 people, 2 sandwiches each.)

SANDWICH, TUNA FISH FILLING I

1 (6½-oz.) can tuna, drained
¼ c. celery, diced small (or more)
3 T. mayonnaise or salad dressing
1 T. relish (opt.)
1 T. chopped onion or ½ tsp. instant minced onion (opt.)
1 to 2 hard-boiled eggs, shelled and diced (opt.)
⅛ tsp. salt, onion salt or onion powder (opt.)
⅛ tsp. black pepper (opt.)
1 tsp. dried parsley flakes (opt.)
½ to 1 tsp. lemon juice (opt.)

1. Mix all ingredients together. Makes enough to fill 3 sandwiches (6 slices bread) or 4 sandwich buns.

SANDWICH, TUNA FISH FILLING II

Recipe is for small food processor.

1 stalk celery, cut in 1-inch pieces
½ small onion or less
3-oz. can drained tuna
⅛ t. pepper (opt.)
2 T. mayonnaise

1. Pulse a few times to mix; this recipe is for 2 sandwiches. This can also be doubled in some small food processors.

SANDWICH, TUNAWICHES, BAKED

Adapted from Laura Robison.

1 (6⅛-oz.) can tuna, drained
¼ c. Velveeta or other cheese, cubed
2 T. finely chopped celery
1 sm. green onion, finely chopped
Mayonnaise or salad dressing the size of a small egg
¼ tsp. prepared mustard
4 hamburger buns or 8 slices bread

1. Turn oven dial to 350°. 2. Combine first 6 ingredients; spread between buns or bread slices. 3. Wrap each sandwich in foil; place in preheated 350° oven 15 minutes.

SANDWICH, TURKEY SALAD FILLING
(or CHICKEN)

2 c. cooked turkey, diced small (remove all bones, skin and
    fat before dicing)
½ c. diced celery
½ c. mayonnaise
1 T. milk or cream
2 to 3 tsp. lemon juice
¼ tsp. salt
⅛ tsp. pepper

Optional Ingredients:
2 T. finely chopped onion (or 1 T. instant minced onion)
1 hard-boiled egg, chopped
½ T. sugar
½ t. dill weed
1 T. green bell pepper, finely chopped
Fresh parsley, chopped
Olives, chopped

1. Combine ingredients and mix well. **2.** Put filling between
slices of bread or stuff inside pita bread.

SUB, SAMPSON'S DELIGHT

From Carol Wells comes the best sub I have ever eaten.
Serves 6.

1 loaf (1 pound) French bread, split lengthwise
Shredded lettuce
½ lb. turkey lunch meat, sliced (or cooked turkey)
½ lb. baked ham, sliced
½ lb. salami, sliced
¼ lb. Swiss cheese, sliced
2 medium tomatoes, sliced

Dressing:
1 pkg. (3 oz.) cream cheese, softened
2 T. ranch salad dressing
1 tsp. poppy seeds
⅛ tsp. garlic powder

1. In a small bowl, beat cream cheese, ranch salad dressing,
poppy seeds and garlic powder until smooth. **2.** Spread on
both cut surfaces of bread. **3.** Layer lettuce, turkey, ham,
salami, cheese and tomatoes on bottom half of bread; top
with the other half. **4.** Wrap in plastic wrap ahead of time
and refrigerate (or make and serve at once).

Chapter 12

Dumplings, Noodles and Rice

ALDEN AND SHIRLEY STEVENSON, JAY, JANICE, JOELLEN AND JEFFRY
1969

DUMPLINGS, NOODLES AND RICE

DUMPLINGS

Makes 12 large dumplings.

2½ c. all-purpose flour
3 tsp. baking powder
1 tsp. salt
3 T. olive oil
1¼ c. milk

1. In bowl, mix together dry ingredients; combine oil and milk. **2.** With fork, stir in liquid until moistened. Do not over mix. **3.** Drop by large spoonfuls on top of simmering stew. **4.** Simmer for 5 minutes, uncovered; then cover and simmer 15 to 20 minutes longer. Serve immediately.

DUMPLINGS, DELICIOUS

Enough for 3 people.
Recipe may be doubled to make more.

1 c. all-purpose flour
2 tsp. baking powder
½ tsp. salt
½ c. milk
2 T. (⅛ c.) extra light olive oil

1. In medium bowl, combine dry ingredients; make a nest or depression in the middle. **2.** Add milk and oil in the nest; stir together only until combined. **3.** Drop from tablespoon atop gently bubbling mixture, making 9 to 10 dumplings. **4.** Cover tightly with lid; simmer 15 minutes without lifting the lid.

NOODLES & CHICKEN BROTH

7 c. chicken broth
1 med. onion, finely chopped
¼ c. celery, finely chopped (opt.)
2 T. chopped fresh parsley (or 2 tsp. dried parsley flakes) (opt.)
2 tsp. chicken bouillon
1 tsp. olive oil
⅛ tsp. pepper
8 oz. uncooked noodles (4 to 4½ c.)

1. Combine all ingredients except noodles in cooking pot; bring to a boil. **2.** Stir noodles into boiling mixture and simmer 20 minutes or until noodles are tender. **West Bend slow cooker**: Set dial on #5 and cook for 1 hour or until tender.

NOODLES, CONFETTI

A pretty side dish.

6 to 8 oz. medium egg noodles
3 T. butter
¼ c. peeled, grated or shredded carrot
3 T. chopped fresh parsley or chives
⅛ to ¼ tsp. salt (opt.)
Pepper

1. Cook noodles in 2 quarts boiling water and 2 teaspoons salt until tender; drain. **2.** Add remaining ingredients to noodles, stirring together until butter is melted.

NOODLES, DIXONVILLE

Adapted from Mrs. Della Long.

2 egg yolks
2 T. milk or cream
¼ tsp. salt
½ c. plus 2 tsp. all-purpose flour, approximately

1. In med.-small bowl, mix together egg yolks, milk and salt. **2.** Add flour, enough to make a rather stiff dough, but not real stiff. **3.** On floured surface, roll half of dough at a time as thin as possible, turning over often and flouring surface each time. **4.** Sprinkle top of noodle dough lightly with flour; roll up like jellyroll and slice with sharp knife into noodles. Repeat with second piece of dough. **5.** Unroll noodles; can use immediately or let dry. **Note**: Mrs. Long's directions: for each egg yolk, use 1 tablespoon milk or cream, ⅛ teaspoon salt and enough flour to make a rather stiff dough.

NOODLES, KELLY'S

From Kelly Wells Crouch.

3 lg. egg yolks
1 whole egg
3 T. cold water
1 T. vinegar
1 tsp. salt
2 c. flour
Flour to roll

1. In med.-small bowl, beat eggs. **2.** Add cold water, vinegar, salt and flour, stirring together. **3.** Divide dough in 3 parts. **4.** Roll each part very thin on floured surface. **5.** Dry 1 hour or longer, then sprinkle with a little extra flour and roll up like jellyroll. **6.** Cut into desired size; unroll noodles and spread out to dry. **7.** To cook, drop into boiling broth; boil until tender. **Note**: Cook ½ of these noodles in 4 cups of boiling broth (or water with bouillon cubes) until tender.

NOODLES, PARSLEY

Serves 3 people.

4 c. water
4 bouillon cubes or 4 tsp. instant bouillon
4 oz. (2½ c.) wide egg noodles
1 T. butter
½ T. dried parsley flakes

1. Combine water and bouillon in 3-quart saucepan; bring to a rapid boil. 2. Crush bouillon cubes with spoon or potato masher, if necessary. 3. Add noodles, butter and parsley flakes to boiling liquid. 4. Boil 12 to 15 minutes, or until noodles are tender, stirring occasionally. **Note:** Broth may be used instead of water and bouillon. (Taste for salt.)

NOODLES, POLISH

Cook all these noodles in 5 cups boiling broth.

3 lg. egg yolks
½ tsp. salt
¼ c. cold water
Flour, about 1 c. plus 3 T. additional flour for rolling

1. Mix egg yolks, salt and water together; stir in enough flour to make stiff dough (about 1 cup). 2. Divide dough into 3 pieces and roll each piece out on floured surface. 3. Follow directions for either Dixonville Noodles or Kelly's Noodles.

RICE

1 cup raw rice makes 3 cups cooked rice.

1 c. regular white rice
1¾ c. cold tap water
¾ to 1 tsp. salt
1 T. olive oil (opt.)

1. Combine all 4 ingredients in 2-quart saucepan and bring to a full boil; stir well. 2. Cover pan with tight lid and turn heat to LOW; cook 15 minutes. 3. Turn heat off and do not lift lid for another 5 to 10 minutes. **For Brown Rice:** Increase water to 2½ cups; follow above directions except cook for 45 minutes, or until tender.

RICE & BROTH

Serves 3 people.

3 c. beef broth or chicken broth (fat removed)
⅔ c. uncooked rice
¼ tsp. salt (or 1 to 2 beef or chicken bouillon cubes)
1 T. butter

1. Bring broth to a full boil. 2. Add rice, salt or bouillon cubes and butter; stir. 3. Reduce heat to low simmer; cook, covered, stirring occasionally, until rice is tender. (Or pres-sure at 15 pounds pressure for 10 minutes, according to manufacturer's directions.) **Note:** If needed, add more broth or water during or after cooking period.

RICE-ONION PILAF

A really good recipe from Wanda Marshall.

1 stick butter or 1/3 to 1/2 c. regular Smart Balance Spread (not *light*)
1 c. regular long grained rice (not instant or Minute Rice)
1 can cream of mushroom soup, undiluted
1 can Campbell's French Onion Soup
1 cup water
1 can water chestnuts, drained (opt.)

1. Turn oven dial to 350°; melt butter in ovenproof casserole. 2. Add remaining ingredients and stir together. 3. Bake, uncovered, for 1 hour in 350° oven, or until rice is tender.

RICE PILAF, BAKED

¾ c. regular rice, uncooked
2 T. olive oil or butter
½ c. shredded carrot
⅛ c. chopped onion
½ c. chopped celery
¼ c. chopped parsley (fresh) or 1 T. dried parsley
1¾ c. chicken broth or water
1 T. chicken granules (bouillon)
⅛ t. black pepper
¼ tsp. salt (opt.)

1. Combine all ingredients in greased 8-inch square baking dish. 2. Cover with tight lid or foil and bake in preheated 375° oven 40 to 45 minutes or until rice is tender. 3. Stir once after 25 minutes. Serves 4.

RICE PILAF, TOP OF STOVE

1 c. regular rice, uncooked (white or brown)
2 c. water
2 beef or chicken bouillon cubes
¼ c. chopped onion or 1 T. dried onion flakes
¼ c. celery, diced small
½ tsp. salt
¼ tsp. pepper
1 to 2 T. butter
1 (4-oz.) can mushroom stems and pieces, drained (opt.)
1 T. parsley leaves, fresh or dried

1. Combine all ingredients in 2-quart saucepan and bring to a full boil, stirring occasionally. 2. Reduce heat to low; cover with tight lid and cook for 20 minutes (45 minutes for brown rice), or until tender. 3. Let stand, covered, 10 minutes before serving; fluff rice lightly with fork.

RICE, RED HOT (Chicken House)

Great served with fried chicken. If a hot pepper is not available, the cayenne pepper is satisfactory. This freezes well.

2 T. butter
2 onions, diced
1 raw hot pepper, sliced (opt.)
½ c. uncooked rice
3½ to 4 c. canned tomatoes or 2 cans (1 lb. each) stewed
    tomatoes
1 T. sugar
¼ to ½ tsp. salt
¼ tsp. paprika
¼ tsp. red cayenne pepper (opt.)
¼ tsp. black pepper

1. In 2-quart saucepan, cook onions and hot pepper in butter; add rice and stir well. **2.** Add remaining ingredients and bring to a boil. **3.** Cover with lid; reduce heat and cook slowly until rice is tender (about 40 to 45 minutes), stirring occasionally. Add a little water if necessary. **4.** Remove pepper slices before serving.

Chapter 13

Salads

**AKRON WESLEYAN METHODIST SCHOOL
1970-1971**

FRONT ROW: (L TO R) LYNN PATTERSON, JONATHAN GEE, RONNIE WEST, WESLEY
GOCH, RONALD PATTERSON, KENNY FILLER, RUSSELL PATTERSON, STEPHEN HAMMONS

SECOND ROW: MRS. BENNINGER, MISS HICKS, DAVID SWARTS, LINDA McHUGH, LORA
WOODRING, REBEKA GEE, RANDY GOCH, MRS. GEHO, MRS. WOLFE

THIRD ROW: COLLENE STEESE, BONNIE MESSNER, KATHY KOOSED, REBECCA McHUGH,
KATHY WEST, JANE MARCIN, RUTH ELLEN McHUGH, FRANCES YEAGER, CONNIE
YAEGER, MISS MARVIN, MRS. UREY

FOURTH ROW: TOMMY WEST, DON O'BRIEN, CYNTHIA WOODRING, CAROLYN UREY,
KATHY GOCH, CONNIE DeHASS, KATHLEEN STEESE, NANCY GOCH, RENEE BRINK,
THELMA KOOSED, EDWARD WOODRING

SALADS

APPLE CINNAMON JELLO SALAD

1 (3-oz.) pkg. cherry gelatin (sugar-free)
1 c. boiling water
¼ c. red cinnamon candies dissolved in ½ c. boiling
    water
1 to 2 c. chopped or diced apples
½ c. chopped or diced celery
½ c. chopped pecans or walnuts

1. Dissolve gelatin in 1 cup boiling water. 2. Combine cinnamon candies and ½ cup boiling water, stirring over low heat until candies dissolve. Add enough cold water to make 1 cup liquid. 3. Add cinnamon liquid to gelatin; chill until partially set. 4. Add remaining ingredients; pour into 6 individual molds (or into a serving dish). 5. Chill until firm.

APPLE-LEMON JELLO SALAD

1 (3-oz.) pkg. lemon gelatin
1½ c. boiling water
1 c. chopped apples
1 T. lemon juice
½ c. chopped celery
¼ c. chopped nuts

1. Dissolve gelatin in boiling water; chill in 8 x 8-inch glass pan until it begins to set. 2. Combine apples and lemon juice, stirring together; add to gelatin. 3. Add celery and nuts; refrigerate.

APPLE OPTION SALAD

*This apple salad is good even without
any of the options.*

6 to 8 med. apples (4 to 5 c.), diced
⅓ to ½ c. mayonnaise or salad dressing
3 T. sugar
1 to 2 T. lemon juice

Optional Ingredients:
2 to 3 oranges, peeled and diced
1 to 3 bananas, sliced
½ to 1 c. raisins
½ to 1 c. miniature marshmallows
½ c. celery, diced
⅓ to ½ c. nuts, coarsely chopped
¼ to ½ c. flaked coconut
Dash of nutmeg

1. Mix apples, mayonnaise, sugar and lemon juice together. 2. Add any (or all) of the optional ingredients; stir well. 3. Serve in dessert dishes or on lettuce leaves.

APPLE WALDORF SALAD

Serves 3 people. Recipe may be multiplied.

2 c. diced apples, peeled or unpeeled
½ c. diced celery (opt.)
1 banana, sliced (opt.)
¼ to ½ c. walnuts, coarsely chopped
½ tsp. lemon juice
1 T. sugar
2 T. (⅛ c.) mayonnaise or salad dressing

1. Mix all ingredients together, stirring well.

APPLESAUCE

Recipe may be cut in half.

2 qt. (8 c.) peeled and cored apples
1 c. water
¼ to ⅔ c. sugar or more, depending on tartness of
    apples (or ⅓ c. Sprinkle Sweet)
¼ tsp. cinnamon

1. Wash apples and cut in quarters; core and peel, then cut each quarter in half. 2. Place in heavy saucepan with water; bring to a boil. 3. Lower heat to simmer or med.-low and cover pan; cook until apples are soft, about 20 to 25 minutes, stirring occasionally. 4. For chunky applesauce, partially mash with potato masher. For smooth applesauce, put through food mill, colander, food processor or blender. 5. Add sugar and cinnamon (to taste); stir well. 6. Serve warm or cold, with an additional sprinkle of cinnamon.

APPLESAUCE, GOLDEN OR
RED DELICIOUS

3 lbs. Golden or Red Delicious apples
½ c. water
⅓ c. sugar
⅓ c. packed brown sugar
1 T. lemon juice
½ tsp. cinnamon

1. Wash and core apples and cut in quarters or eighths. 2. Place in large pot; add water. 3. Cover and cook slowly, about 20 to 25 minutes, or until apples are tender, stirring occasionally. 4. If apples are unpeeled, put through food mill to remove skins. 5. Add sugars, lemon juice and cinnamon. 6. If apples were peeled before cooking, blend in blender for a smooth applesauce; partially mash with potato masher for a chunky sauce.

APPLESAUCE (Microwave)

Makes almost 2½ cups applesauce.

5 c. quartered, cored and peeled apples
1 T. lemon juice
2 T. water
¼ c. sugar
⅛ tsp. cinnamon
⅛ tsp. nutmeg (opt.)

1. In 2 to 3-quart casserole or microwave-safe bowl, combine apples, lemon juice and water. 2. Cover with lid or plastic wrap (vented); microwave on HIGH 5 minutes. 3. Stir; microwave an additional 4 to 5 minutes, or until apples are soft. 4. Combine apples, sugar and spice. If a smooth consistency is desired, use food processor, blender, electric mixer, food mill or potato masher. **Note**: Spices may be omitted or increased, according to taste. If apples are extremely sour, replace lemon juice with water.

APPLESAUCE RED JELLO SALAD

Tangy and delightful.

6 oz. strawberry or red raspberry gelatin (large box)
2 c. boiling water
¼ c. cinnamon red-hots (opt.)
1¾ to 2 c. applesauce (or 16-oz. can)
¼ c. walnuts
2 T. lemon juice
1 T. vinegar (opt.)
1 c. finely chopped celery (opt.)

1. Dissolve gelatin and red hots in boiling water. 2. Add remaining ingredients, mixing together with wire whip. 3. Pour into 8 x 8-inch or 7 x 11-inch pan or loaf pan, or into eight individual molds, or into a 4 or 5-cup mold. 4. Refrigerate; serve on lettuce, if desired. **For a Christmas Topping**: Combine ½ c. whipped topping or whipped cream, ½ c. mayonnaise, 1 drop green coloring and ¼ tsp. cinnamon (opt.)

APRICOT ICE CREAM SALAD

This is not a frozen salad. From Bonnie Bash.

6 oz. apricot gelatin
3 c. boiling water
1 c. vanilla ice cream
1 (29-oz.) can apricot halves, well drained

Optional Ingredients:
1 can (any size) crushed pineapple, well drained
1 c. chopped celery
½ c. chopped nuts

1. Dissolve gelatin in boiling water; set aside until lukewarm. 2. When lukewarm, blend in ice cream until completely melted and blended in. 3. Add drained apricots and any of the optional ingredients desired. 4. Chill until firm.

APRICOT JELLO SALAD

From Jean Moyer.

6 oz. apricot gelatin
2 c. boiling water
1 (20-oz.) can crushed pineapple (reserve juice)
8 oz. cream cheese, softened
8 oz-carton whipped topping, thawed
Crushed nuts (for top)

Optional Ingredients:
1 can mandarin oranges or cut-up apricots, drained (or both)
1 c. diced celery
½ c. chopped nuts (for top)

1. Dissolve gelatin in boiling water. 2. Drain pineapple, reserving juice; add drained pineapple to gelatin mixture and set aside. 3. In mixer bowl, beat cream cheese; add reserved pineapple juice gradually to cream cheese. 4. Combine gelatin and cream cheese mixture; chill until rather thick, stirring twice. 5. Fold in whipped topping; add any desired optional ingredients. 6. Pour into 12 x 8-inch or 13 x 9-inch dish or pan; sprinkle crushed nuts over top. 7. Cover with lid or plastic wrap; chill.

AVOCADO SALAD

A delicious salad.

6 oz. cream cheese, softened
2 ripe avocados, peeled and mashed
6 oz. lime gelatin
⅔ c. boiling water
½ c. cool tap water
¾ c. crushed pineapple, partially drained
½ c. chopped pecans and/or walnuts

1. Cream the cream cheese; add mashed avocado and mix well. 2. Dissolve gelatin in boiling water; add cool tap water. 3. Add gelatin to cream cheese mixture, then crushed pineapple and nuts. 4. Pour into glass or Tupperware pan and refrigerate 6 hours or overnight. 5. Cut in squares and serve on lettuce leaf.

BANANA NUT SALAD

Makes 6 salads.

3 ripe bananas
½ c. chopped nuts
6 lettuce leaves
6 slightly rounded T. mayonnaise or salad dressing

1. Peel bananas and cut lengthwise into quarters, making a total of 12 pieces. 2. Dip in cool water and roll in nuts. 3. Place 2 pieces of banana on a lettuce leaf and garnish with 1 slightly rounded tablespoon mayonnaise for each salad.

BEAN SALAD (Four-Bean)

From Martha Rough and Judy Dunn.

1 (15 to 16-oz.) can green beans, drained
1 (15 to 16-oz.) can yellow wax beans, drained
1 (15 to 16-oz.) can red kidney beans, drained
1 (15 to 16-oz.) can navy, great northern or baby lima
    beans, drained
½ c. minced or diced onion
½ c. chopped green pepper (opt.)

Dressing:
1 c. sugar
½ c. olive oil
½ c. vinegar
1 tsp. salt
½ tsp. pepper

1. Place drained beans in glass bowl; add onion and green pepper. **2.** Combine dressing ingredients, stirring or shaking until sugar dissolves; pour over bean mixture and toss. **3.** Cover and refrigerate at least 2 hours or overnight. This will keep for a week or longer in refrigerator.

BEAN SALAD, LIGHT

Follow recipe for Bean Salad, using this dressing:

⅓ c. sugar
⅓ c. olive oil (or less)
⅓ c. vinegar
¼ tsp. salt (opt.)
¼ tsp. pepper

BEET MOLDED SALAD

1 (16-oz.) can beets, diced small
½ c. sugar
¼ c. vinegar
1 (3-oz.) pkg. raspberry gelatin
½ c. chopped pecans or walnuts

1. Drain beets, reserving ⅔ cup beet juice. **2.** In saucepan, bring beet juice, sugar and vinegar to a boil; remove from heat and stir in gelatin until dissolved. Set aside. **3.** When gelatin mixture is cool (or lukewarm), add nuts and the beets which have been diced small. **4.** Chill until firm in refrigerator in 8 x 8-inch dish. **Optional ingredients**: 1 to 1½ c. diced celery <u>or</u> ¼ c. sliced stuffed olives.

BLACKBERRY TWO-LAYER SALAD

Bottom Layer:
6 oz. blackberry gelatin
2 c. boiling water
1 (15 to 16-oz.) can blackberries
1 (8-oz.) can crushed pineapple with juice (1 c.)

Top Layer:
8 oz. cream cheese
1 c. powdered or granulated sugar
2 to 3 c. whipped topping, thawed
Chopped nuts for top (opt.)

1. Dissolve gelatin in boiling water. **2.** Drain berries, reserving juice; add enough water to the blackberry juice to make 1 cup. Add to gelatin and refrigerate. **3.** When slightly thickened, add blackberries and crushed pineapple, stirring carefully. **4.** Pour into 13 x 9-inch dish or cake pan; chill until firm. **5.** In mixer bowl, mix together cream cheese and sugar; fold in whipped topping. **6.** Spread mixture over blackberry layer; sprinkle nuts over top, if desired. Chill.

BLUEBERRY TWO-LAYER SALAD

Adapted from Shirley Kaufman.

Bottom Layer:
6 oz. grape, black cherry, blackberry or black rasp-
    berry gelatin
2 c. boiling water
1 (21-oz.) can blueberry pie filling
1 (20-oz.) can crushed pineapple with juice

Top Layer:
4 to 8 oz. cream cheese, room temp.
8 oz. (1 c.) sour cream or sour cream alternative
½ c. sugar
1 tsp. vanilla
2 c. whipped topping, thawed (opt.)
Chopped nuts (opt.)

1. Dissolve gelatin in boiling water; cool at room temperature for 15 minutes. **2.** Add pie filling and undrained pineapple. **3.** Pour into 13 x 9-inch dish or cake pan; chill until firm. **4.** Combine cream cheese, sour cream, sugar and vanilla in mixer bowl; mix well, scraping sides of bowl once. **5.** Fold in whipped topping, if used; spread mixture over blueberry layer. **6.** Sprinkle top with chopped nuts, if desired. Chill. <u>Note</u>: Top layer can be omitted; just spread whipped topping over salad.

BROCCOLI SALAD

Delicious!

3 c. fresh broccoli, cut in sm. pieces
2 T. chopped onion
2 T. bacon flavor chips
½ c. diced cheese (Monterey Jack or most any kind),
    opt.

Dressing:
½ c. mayonnaise
3 T. sugar
2 tsp. vinegar

1. Combine broccoli, onion, bacon chips and cheese. 2. In small bowl, combine dressing ingredients, stirring well; pour over broccoli and mix together. 3. Refrigerate several hours or overnight, or serve immediately.

BROCCOLI SALAD (Larger)

2 bunches fresh broccoli, cut in sm. pieces (should measure 6 to 9 c.)
¼ c. chopped onion
1 c. shredded cheese (Cheddar or most any kind)
½ lb. bacon, fried crisp and crumbled
½ c. sunflower seeds (opt.)

Dressing:
¾ to 1 c. mayonnaise
¼ to ½ c. sugar
2 T. vinegar

1. Combine broccoli, onion and cheese. 2. In small bowl, mix together dressing ingredients; pour over broccoli and mix together. 3. Refrigerate several hours or overnight. 4. Add crumbled bacon just before serving; otherwise it does not stay crisp.

BROCCOLI & CAULIFLOWER SALAD

Adapted from Marie Leyda; a terrific salad.

1 lg. bunch broccoli
1 head cauliflower
1 sm. or med. onion, chopped
½ c. sharp or med. Cheddar cheese, shredded (opt.)
½ lb. bacon, fried crisp or !/3 c. bacon bits

Dressing:
1 c. Miracle Whip salad dressing
½ c. sugar
 2 T. vinegar
⅛ tsp. salt (opt.)

1. Cut broccoli and cauliflower into small bite-sized pieces, discarding the tough part of stem. (Should measure about 8 to 10 cups broccoli and cauliflower together). 2. Combine broccoli, cauliflower, onion and cheese in bowl. 3. Combine dressing ingredients, stirring well; pour over vegetables and mix together. 4. Refrigerate several hours or overnight. 5. At serving time, add crumbled bacon or bacon bits.

CARROT SALAD, SHREDDED

Keeps well for several days in refrigerator.

3 to 4 c. shredded carrots
½ c. mayonnaise or salad dressing
1 to 3 T. sugar
¼ tsp salt
½ c. raisins (opt.)

½ to 1 c. flaked coconut (opt.)
½ to 1 c. crushed pineapple (opt.)

1. Mix ingredients together well; refrigerate.

Larger Recipe (serves 8 or more):
5 c. shredded carrots
⅔ c. mayonnaise or salad dressing
2 to 4 T. sugar
½ tsp. salt
¾ c. raisins (opt.)
1 c. flaked coconut (opt.)
1 (20-oz.) can crushed pineapple (opt.)

CHERRY SWIRL SALAD

From Deloris Dunkle.

6 oz. black cherry gelatin
2 c. boiling water
1 c. cold water
1 (21-oz.) can cherry pie filling
2 env. Dream Whip whipped topping mix, whipped separately (or 8 oz. whipped topping, thawed and divided)

1. Dissolve gelatin in boiling water in large bowl; add cold water. 2. Refrigerate until nearly firm. 3. Fold in cherry pie filling and 1 envelope Dream Whip, whipped according to package directions. 4. Blend together well; pour into 13 x 9-inch glass or Tupperware dish. 5. Whip second envelope of Dream Whip according to package directions; marbleize it through the gelatin mixture. 6. Refrigerate. **Note**: Red cherry gelatin in this recipe does not work well.

CHERRY TWO-LAYER JELLO SALAD

This recipe may be doubled in a 13 x 9-inch pan.

1 (3-oz.) pkg. cherry gelatin
1 c. boiling water
1 (21-oz.) can cherry pie filling
1 (3-oz.) pkg. lemon gelatin
1 c. boiling water
3 to 4 oz. cream cheese, softened
¼ c. mayonnaise
1 (8-oz.) can crushed pineapple (about 1 c. with juice)
1 to 2 c. whipped topping, thawed, or Dream Whip
Chopped nuts for top (opt.)

1. Dissolve cherry gelatin in 1 cup boiling water; stir in pie filling. 2. Pour into 8 x 8-inch or 9 x 9-inch glass dish; chill until set or partially set. 3. Dissolve lemon gelatin in 1 cup boiling water; cool to room temperature. 4. Beat together cream cheese and mayonnaise; gradually add the cooled lemon gelatin. 5. Stir in undrained pineapple; fold in whipped topping. 6. Spread mixture over cherry gelatin; sprinkle nuts over top, if desired. 7. Chill until set.

CHICKEN SALAD (Or Turkey)

Makes 4 individual salads.

2 c. diced or chopped cooked chicken or turkey
⅔ c. diced or chopped celery
1 (8-oz.) can water chestnuts, drained (opt.)
1 T. finely chopped onion (or 1 tsp. instant onion flakes)
½ sm. green bell pepper, chopped (opt.)

Dressing:
½ c. mayonnaise
1 to 1½ tsp. sugar
1 T. milk
2 tsp. lemon juice
¼ tsp. salt
¹⁄₁₆ tsp. pepper

1. Combine chicken or turkey with celery, onion and green pepper in bowl. **2.** In small bowl, combine dressing ingredients; mix well and pour over chicken. **3.** Stir gently together; refrigerate. **4.** To serve, line salad plates with lettuce leaves and top with chicken salad.

Chicken Fruit Salad: Instead of using the onion and green pepper, add 1 cup halved red or green seedless grapes, 1 cup drained pineapple chunks and ½ cup slivered almonds. If needed, add a little more mayonnaise. (Almonds are optional.)

CHICKEN & FRUIT SALAD

From Sarah Baxter.

3 c. cooked, cubed chicken breast
1 c. chopped celery
1 c. chopped apple, sprinkled with 1 t. lemon juice
1 c. halved green or red grapes
¼ c. pecan halves

Dressing:
¾ c. mayonnaise
½ t. sugar
⅛ t. salt
⅛ t. white pepper
¼ t. dry mustard
1 t. vinegar

1. Combine chicken, celery, fruit and pecans in bowl. **2.** In another small bowl, combine dressing ingredients; mix well and pour over chicken. **3.** Stir gently and refrigerate, covered.

CHICKEN & RICE SALAD

From Jay Stevenson. Serves 4 to 6 people.

¾ c. uncooked rice
1½ c. boiling water
2 T. olive oil
¾ tsp. salt
2 c. cubed cooked chicken (white meat)

1 c. halved seedless grapes (red or green)
½ c. chopped celery
¼ c. thinly sliced green onions, including green tops
¼ c. chopped pecans or walnuts for garnish (opt.)

Dressing:
½ c. sour cream or light sour cream
½ c. mayonnaise
½ tsp. celery seed
1 tsp. Dijon or spicy mustard

1. Add rice to 1½ cups boiling water with the oil and salt; stir well. Reduce heat to low; cover pan with tight lid and cook 15 minutes. **2.** Remove from heat and let stand 5 minutes before removing lid; rinse rice in cold water and drain well. **3.** In large bowl, combine drained rice, chicken, grapes, celery and onions. **4.** In small bowl, combine dressing ingredients, stirring together; add to rice mixture and stir all together. **5.** Garnish with nuts and chill before serving.

CHICKEN TACO SALAD

Serves 4.

2 chicken breast halves, boned, skinned and cubed
1 T. olive oil
½ c. salsa
½ c. mayonnaise or Miracle Whip salad dressing
1 ripe avocado, peeled and mashed
¼ to ½ tsp. hot pepper sauce
2 c. shredded lettuce (or more)
1 (15-oz.) can kidney beans, drained and rinsed
½ c. chopped tomato
Tortilla chips
Shredded cheddar cheese

1. Stir-fry chicken in oil over medium-high heat for 5 minutes or until tender. **2.** Reduce heat to medium; stir in salsa. Cover and simmer 5 minutes. **3.** Combine salad dressing, avocado and hot pepper sauce, stirring together. **4.** Serve on 4 individual salad plates, making layers of lettuce, beans, chicken, chopped tomato and avocado mixture. **5.** Put tortilla chips all around each salad at base and sprinkle cheese over top. **Note**: 1½ cups cooked chicken, skinned and cubed, may be used instead of stir-frying uncooked chicken.

CHRISTMAS LAYERED JELLO SALAD

The layers are green, white and red.

2 pkg. (3-oz. each) lime gelatin
2 c. boiling water
2 c. cold water
1 pkg. (3 oz.) lemon gelatin
1 c. boiling water
½ c. miniature marshmallows
8 oz. cream cheese, softened
1 c. mayonnaise
1 c. (8 oz.) crushed pineapple, undrained
2 pkg. (3-oz. each) cherry gelatin

2 c. boiling water
2 c. cold water

1. In a bowl, dissolve lime gelatin in 2 cups boiling water; add 2 cups cold water and pour into a 13 x 9 x 2-inch pan. Refrigerate until set. 2. In a bowl, dissolve lemon gelatin in 1 cup boiling water; stir in marshmallows until melted. Cool for 20 minutes. 3. In a small mixing bowl, beat cream cheese and mayonnaise together until smooth; gradually beat in lemon gelatin. Stir in pineapple. Carefully spoon over the lime layer. Chill until set. 4. Dissolve cherry gelatin in 2 cups boiling water; add 2 cups cold water. Spoon over the lemon layer. Refrigerate overnight. Cut into squares to serve. Serves 8 to 12. **Note**: Two other colors of gelatin may be used instead of green and red.

COLESLAW I

To double this recipe, use a 2-pound head of cabbage.

2 to 2½ c. shredded cabbage, firmly measured (or squeezed-out blender cabbage)
⅓ c. mayonnaise or salad dressing
2 T. sugar
⅛ tsp. salt
½ tsp. vinegar or lemon juice

1. Mix ingredients together thoroughly; cover and refrigerate. 2. Sprinkle top with paprika when serving, if desired. Serves 2 to 3. **With Carrot:** Add 1 medium carrot, peeled and shredded or grated, and ⅛ teaspoon celery seed (optional).

COLESLAW II

Recipe may be doubled, or cut in half.

3 to 3½ c. shredded cabbage, firmly measured (or squeezed-out blender cabbage)
½ c. mayonnaise or salad dressing
3 T. sugar
¼ tsp. salt
1 tsp. vinegar or lemon juice

1. Mix ingredients together thoroughly; cover and refrigerate. 2. Sprinkle top with paprika when serving, if desired.

COLESLAW, BLENDER

Blender coleslaw is more easily digested than shredded cabbage.

1. Cut a head of cabbage into quarters or eighths and remove core; slice cabbage coarsely. 2. Fill blender container ½ to ⅔ full with cabbage. 3. Add cold water to the maximum liquid level, or to cover cabbage. 4. Cover container and blend for 2 or 3 seconds; drain cabbage in sieve. 5. Squeeze water out of cabbage with hand. (This step is very important!) 6. Measure squeezed-out cabbage firmly in measuring cup, and proceed with recipe for Coleslaw I or II, doing as many blenderfuls as needed.

COLESLAW (Oil)

This keeps well in the refrigerator. Cabbage may be chopped in food processor.

1 med. head cabbage, shredded (1½ to 2 lbs. or 6 to 8 c.)
1 sm. carrot, peeled and shredded (about ⅓ c.) or 1 green pepper, chopped
2 T. chopped onion
2 T. chopped fresh parsley (opt.)

Dressing:
⅔ c. sugar
⅓ c. vinegar
⅓ c. olive oil
½ tsp. salt
¼ tsp. pepper
½ tsp. celery seed (opt.)

1. In large bowl, combine cabbage, carrot, onion and parsley. 2. In saucepan, bring dressing ingredients to a full rolling boil. 3. Pour boiling syrup over cabbage mixture; stir together well. 4. Store in refrigerator, covered.

COLESLAW, OIL (For Freezer)

Cabbage remains crisp after thawing.

3 lbs. cabbage
2 med. onions
2 green bell peppers
2 carrots

Dressing:
1½ c. sugar
1 c. vinegar (or less)
½ c. olive oil
1 T. salt
1 T. whole mustard seed
2 tsp. celery seed

1. Shred (or chop in food processor) all vegetables. 2. Combine dressing ingredients in a saucepan and bring to a boil; pour over vegetables and mix well. 3. Freeze in freezer containers. Before using, let thaw in refrigerator.

COLESLAW WITH GREEN PEPPER

2 c. shredded cabbage
1 sm. green bell pepper, cored, seeded and thinly sliced
1 tsp. chopped onion (opt.)
1 T. pimientos, drained and diced (opt.)

Dressing:
2 to 3 T. sugar
2 T. olive oil
2 T. vinegar
1 T. lemon juice (opt.)
¼ tsp. salt

1. In bowl, combine cabbage, green pepper and parsley or onion. **2.** In jar, shake together dressing ingredients until sugar is dissolved. **3.** Pour over cabbage and toss to coat; cover and chill.

COTTAGE CHEESE & CHIVES

Mix together cottage cheese, chopped fresh chives and a dash of salt and pepper. Serve on lettuce leaf, if desired.

COTTAGE CHEESE FLUFFY SALAD I

A pastel pink or yellow salad.

1 (3-oz.) pkg. strawberry or lemon gelatin (add dry)
12 to 16 oz. (1½ to 2 c.) cream-style cottage cheese
1 (20-oz.) can crushed or chunk pineapple, drained
8 oz. carton whipped topping, thawed (or 1 env. whipped topping mix, prepared)
2 c. miniature marshmallows (opt.)

1. In bowl, sprinkle dry gelatin over cottage cheese and stir together. **2.** Add drained fruit (other drained fruit may also be added, if desired). **3.** Fold in whipped topping. **4.** May be eaten immediately, or chill 1 to 3 hours or overnight.

COTTAGE CHEESE FLUFFY SALAD II

So easy!

1 (3-oz.) pkg. orange gelatin (add dry)
1 c. small curd cottage cheese
1 (11-oz.) can mandarin oranges, drained
1 can pineapple chunks or tidbits (any size), drained (opt.)
8-oz. carton whipped topping, thawed (or 1 env. whipped topping mix, prepared)
½ c. chopped walnuts (opt.)
2 c. miniature marshmallows (opt.)

1. In bowl, sprinkle dry gelatin over cottage cheese and stir together. **2.** Add drained fruit, then fold in whipped topping and nuts. **3.** May be eaten immediately, or chill several hours or overnight.

COTTAGE CHEESE FLUFFY SALAD III

From Florence Youngblood; makes a lot!

6 oz. orange or pineapple gelatin (add dry)
16 oz. cottage cheese (2 c.)
1 (20-oz.) can crushed pineapple, drained, or pineapple chunks, drained
1 can mandarin oranges, drained
12 to 16 oz. carton whipped topping, thawed (or 2 env. whipped topping mix, prepared)

1. In large bowl, sprinkle dry gelatin over cottage cheese and stir together. **2.** Add drained fruit, then fold in whipped topping. **3.** May be eaten immediately, or chilled overnight.

COTTAGE CHEESE FRUIT SALAD

Cottage cheese
Canned fruit, drained
Lettuce leaves (opt.)

1. Gently stir together equal amounts of cottage cheese and **drained** canned peaches, fruit cocktail, pineapple chunks or crushed pineapple. (Just partially drain crushed pineapple.) **2.** Chill; may be served on a lettuce leaf if desired.

COTTAGE CHEESE GARDEN SALAD

Recipe may be multiplied. Best when made ahead of time and refrigerated.

1 c. cottage cheese
1 tsp. mayonnaise
2 T. shredded carrot
2 T. chopped green bell pepper (opt.)
2 T. chopped celery
2 T. chopped green onions, chives or leeks
1/16 to 1/8 tsp. salt
1/16 tsp. pepper
¼ tsp. sugar (opt.)

1. Combine ingredients and refrigerate. **2.** Serve on lettuce leaf, if desired. Serves 2 or 3.

COTTAGE CHEESE-TOMATO SALAD

Makes 4 individual salads.

4 med. tomatoes
½ c. cottage cheese
½ c. chopped celery
½ c. chopped cucumber (opt.)
1 T. chopped onion
1 T. chopped green bell pepper
2 T. mayonnaise
¼ tsp. salt
1/8 tsp. pepper

1. Cut stems from tomatoes; cut each tomato into 8 wedges, leaving wedges attached at bottom. Fan wedges slightly. **2.** In med.-small bowl, combine cottage cheese and remaining ingredients; stir well. **3.** Spoon evenly into tomatoes; serve immediately.

CRANBERRY BANANA SALAD

From Betty Edwards. Delicious.

6 oz. strawberry gelatin (or 3 oz. strawberry and 3 oz. raspberry)
3 c. boiling water
3 bananas
1 (16-oz.) can cranberry sauce
3 to 4 apples, peeled and diced or 1 (16-oz.) can crushed pineapple, drained
½ to 1 c. nuts, coarsely chopped

1. Dissolve Jello in boiling water and allow to cool to room temperature, but not set. (Do not add any cold water.) 2. Whip bananas and cranberry sauce together in blender or mixer; add to Jello. 3. Add apples (or drained pineapple) and nuts. 4. Pour into pan mold(s) and chill.

CRANBERRY JELLO SALAD I

So easy and so good.

6 oz. red raspberry gelatin
2 c. boiling water
1 (16-oz.) can whole berry cranberry sauce with juice
1 (20-oz.) can crushed pineapple with juice
1 orange, peeled and diced (or 1 can mandarin oranges, drained and diced)
½ to 1 c. chopped pecans or walnuts
Lettuce leaves (opt.)

1. Dissolve gelatin in boiling water. 2. Add remaining ingredients, except lettuce. 3. Chill until firm in 13 x 9-inch or 12 x 8-inch glass dish. 4. Cut into squares and serve on lettuce leaf, if desired.

CRANBERRY JELLO SALAD II

So good with turkey or chicken.

2 sm. pkgs. (3 oz. each) strawberry or cherry gelatin
2 c. boiling water
1 (16-oz.) can jellied cranberry sauce
½ c. cold water
1 can crushed pineapple, drained (or 1 can mandarin oranges, drained)
½ c. nuts, coarsely chopped
½ c. diced celery
2 c. diced apples
1 to 2 T. lemon juice

1. Dissolve gelatin in boiling water. 2. Add cranberry sauce, blending in with rotary eggbeater or large wire whip. 3. Add cold water, crushed pineapple with its liquid, nuts, celery, apples and lemon juice. 4. Pour into mold(s) or 13 x 9-inch (or 12 x 8-inch) glass or Tupperware container.

CRANBERRY JELLO SALAD III

Larger version of Salad II.

3 sm. boxes (3 oz. each) strawberry or cherry gelatin
3 c. boiling water
1 (16-oz.) can jellied cranberry sauce
1 (20-oz.) can crushed pineapple
¾ c. nuts, coarsely chopped (opt.)
1 c. diced celery
3 c. diced apples
2 to 3 T. lemon juice

1. Dissolve gelatin in boiling water. 2. Add cranberry sauce, blending in with rotary eggbeater or large wire whip. 3. Add crushed pineapple with its liquid, nuts, celery, apples and lemon juice. 4. Pour into mold(s) or 13 x 9-inch (or 12 x 8-inch) glass or Tupperware container.

CROUTONS

5 slices bread
¼ c. (½ stick) butter or olive oil
¼ tsp. garlic powder
½ T. Italian seasoning

1. Cut bread into ½-inch squares, approximately. 2. Melt butter in large skillet, stirring in seasonings. 3. Add bread, tossing to coat well. 4. Spread croutons evenly on ungreased baking sheet. 5. Bake in preheated 325° oven 20 minutes, stirring occasionally. Watch that croutons do not get too brown. 6. Cool before storing.

CUCUMBERS & ONIONS IN DRESSING

From Mrs. Leota A. Benninger.
For 1 cucumber, cut recipe in half.

2 lg. cucumbers, peeled and sliced (3 to 4 c.)
1 to 2 onions, sliced
½ c. sour cream, mayonnaise, salad dressing or evaporated milk
2 T. sugar
1½ T. vinegar
¼ tsp. salt
Black pepper

1. Place cucumbers (sliced ⅛-inch thick or less) and sliced onion in serving dish. (Onion may be separated into rings if desired.) 2. Combine sour cream, sugar, vinegar and salt in small bowl; stir well with wire whip or whisk. 3. Pour dressing over cucumbers and onion. 4. Sprinkle with black pepper; cover and refrigerate.

CUCUMBERS IN SWEET 'N SOUR DRESSING

From Lola Cramer.

½ c. sugar
¼ c. vinegar
⅓ c. cold water
1 T. olive oil
3 to 4 c. cucumbers, peeled and sliced
Onion slices (opt.)
Salt and pepper

1. In deep bowl, combine sugar, vinegar, water and oil; stir with wire whisk to dissolve sugar. 2. Slice cucumbers ⅛ to ¼ inch thick and add to dressing; add onions, separated into rings. 3. Sprinkle with salt and pepper; refrigerate. (Will keep several days in refrigerator.)

DARK RED FROSTED SALAD

1 (3-oz.) pkg. black cherry gelatin
1 (3-oz.) pkg. raspberry gelatin
2 c. boiling water
1½ c. cold water
1 (29-oz.) can peaches, or 1 qt. home-canned, drained and sliced (reserve juice)
1 lg. tart apple, peeled and finely diced (or 2 med. apples)

Frosted Topping:
¼ c. sugar
2 T. flour, level
1 c. peach juice
2 tsp. lemon juice
1 egg
1 env. Dream Whip, prepared (2 c.)
Chopped nuts or graham cracker crumbs (opt.)

1. Dissolve gelatin in boiling water; add cold water, drained peaches and diced apple. 2. Pour into long glass pan; refrigerate until set. 3. To make topping, mix together sugar and flour in medium saucepan; add peach juice, stirring well. 4. Add lemon juice and egg and beat with wire whip. 5. Bring to a boil, stirring constantly; remove from heat; cover with lid and set aside to cool. 6. When cool, fold whipped topping into egg mixture. 7. Spread topping over the set gelatin; sprinkle with nuts or cracker crumbs, if desired. 8. Cover with plastic wrap or lid and chill.

EGG & PEA SALAD

A good recipe for hard-boiled eggs after Easter.

¼ c. mayonnaise or salad dressing
1 T. sweet pickle relish or chopped sweet pickle
¼ tsp. celery salt
½ tsp. chopped onion (or ¼ tsp. instant minced onion)
4 hard-boiled eggs, peeled and coarsely chopped
1 c. frozen peas, not cooked

2 T. diced celery
Milk, if needed
Lettuce leaves

1. In medium bowl, stir together mayonnaise, relish, celery salt and onion. 2. Add eggs, uncooked peas and celery, stirring gently. 3. If too dry, add a few drops milk; cover and refrigerate. 4. Serve on lettuce leaves. Serves 4.

FIVE-CUP SALAD

Makes 5 to 6 servings.

1 c. pineapple chunks, drained
1 c. orange sections, seeded and cut in pieces (or 11-oz. can mandarin oranges, drained)
1 c. miniature marshmallows
1 c. flaked coconut or green grapes, halved (no seeds)
1 c. whipped topping, thawed (or half sour cream or sour cream alternative)

1. Combine ingredients and fold together. 2. Chill 3 hours or longer.

FROZEN CHERRY SALAD

If preferred, this fluffy pink salad may be chilled and eaten without freezing. From Olive Holt.

1 (21-oz.) can cherry pie filling
1 (14-oz.) can sweetened condensed milk
1 (20-oz.) can crushed pineapple, drained
8 to 12 oz. carton whipped topping, thawed
½ to 1 c. pecans or walnuts, chopped (opt.)
1 c. miniature marshmallows (opt.)

1. In large bowl, stir all ingredients together. 2. Pour into long Tupperware or glass 13 x 9-inch baking dish; cover and freeze. 3. Remove from freezer 10 minutes before serving; cut into squares. 4. If not freezing, pour into fancy bowl and chill. Note: Blueberry or strawberry pie filling may be substituted for cherry pie filling. Note: Spray dish with cooking spray before using, if freezing.

FROZEN CREAMY CRANBERRY SALAD

From Shirley Stevenson.

1 (16-oz.) can whole berry cranberry sauce
1 (14-oz.) can sweetened condensed milk
1 (20-oz.) can crushed pineapple, drained
12-oz. carton whipped topping, thawed
1 T. lemon juice
1 c. chopped pecans
5 drops red food coloring (opt.)

1. In large bowl, stir all ingredients together. 2. Pour into long Tupperware or glass 13 x 9-inch baking dish or a loaf pan; cover and freeze. 3. Remove from freezer 10 minutes before serving.

FROZEN FRUIT SALAD

Makes 24 to 28 servings.

8 oz. cream cheese, softened
1 (14-oz.) can sweetened condensed milk
12-oz. carton whipped topping, thawed
2 to 3 bananas, mashed
1 (20-oz.) can crushed pineapple, drained
1 (21-oz.) can cherry pie filling
1 can fruit cocktail, drained
1 c. chopped pecans or walnuts (opt.)
1 c. miniature marshmallows (opt.)
1 c. flaked coconut (opt.)

1. Mix together cream cheese and sweetened condensed milk in mixer bowl. 2. Add whipped topping, blending well. 3. Add remaining ingredients; fill paper-lined muffin cups and freeze. 4. When frozen, remove from muffin pans and store in freezer bag in freezer. (Or, freeze in one long Tupperware or glass 13 x 9-inch baking dish and cut into squares at serving time, having removed from freezer 10 minutes previously.)

FROZEN ORANGE PINEAPPLE SALAD
(Or Dessert)

From Leota Reynolds.

1 (14-oz.) can sweetened condensed milk
¼ c. lemon juice
1 (12-oz.) carton whipped topping, thawed
1 (20-oz.) can crushed or chunk pineapple, drained
1 can mandarin oranges, drained
Maraschino cherries, drained and sliced (opt.)
Chopped nuts (opt.)
½ c. flaked coconut (opt.)

1. Combine first 2 ingredients in large bowl; mix well. 2. Fold in whipped topping. 3. Fold in drained fruit. 4. Add cherries, nuts and coconut as desired. 5. Pour into oblong or square dish; cover and freeze. 6. Remove from freezer 10 minutes before serving; cut into squares.

FROZEN STRAWBERRY SALAD

Also called "Banana Split Salad."

8 oz. cream cheese, softened
½ to ⅔ c. sugar
10 to 16 oz. frozen strawberries, partially thawed
1 (16 to 20-oz.) can crushed pineapple, drained
2 bananas, diced in small pieces
½ to 1 c. chopped pecans or walnuts
8-oz. carton whipped topping, thawed

1. Mix together cream cheese and sugar in large mixer bowl. 2. Add strawberries, pineapple, bananas and nuts. 3. Fold in whipped topping. 4. In glass container, greased lightly with mayonnaise, pour mixture. 5. Freeze overnight, or at least 3 hours. Remove from freezer 30 minutes before serving.

FRUIT BOWL

Serves 20. Delicious!

1 (20-oz.) can pineapple chunks with juice
1 can peaches (any size) with juice, cut up
1 can pears (any size) with juice, cut up
1 can green grapes, DRAINED (or fresh green seedless grapes)
1 can mandarin oranges, DRAINED
1 sm. jar maraschino cherries, DRAINED (opt.)
1 cantaloupe or honeydew melon, made into melon balls or cubes
3 lg. bananas (or more), sliced

1. In large bowl, combine fruit, except bananas. (Add bananas at serving time.) Refrigerate. **Note**: If watermelon or fresh strawberries are available, 2 cups watermelon balls (or cubes) or halved strawberries may be used in place of maraschino cherries.

FRUIT BOWL (LARGER)

Fills a punch bowl and makes a lot.

3 honeydew melons
3 cans (20 oz. each) pineapple chunks with juice
3 cans (11 oz. each) mandarin oranges and juice
2 cans (29 oz. each) peaches with juice
2 cans (16 oz. each) green grapes, drained
1 (29-oz.) can pears with juice
2 jars (10 oz. each) maraschino cherries, drained
5 to 6 lbs. bananas

1. Make melon balls and put in punch bowl. 2. Add canned fruit, cutting peaches and pears into small pieces. 3. Just before serving, add sliced bananas.

FRUIT BOWL SYRUP

When you don't have enough pineapple juice to put raw fruit in.

1 c. sugar
3 c. water

1. Bring sugar and water to a boil; cool.

FRUIT CUP

Serves 8 to 12, depending on which amounts are used.

1 (16 to 20-oz.) can pineapple chunks with juice
2 to 3 c. diced apples
3 to 4 bananas, sliced
2 oranges, peeled and sectioned or 1 (11-oz.) can mandarin oranges with juice
1 to 1½ c. green or red seedless grapes (or peeled and sliced kiwi fruit)

1. Combine all ingredients; chill, if desired. 2. Serve in fruit cups, dessert dishes or on lettuce leaves.

FRUIT SALAD, CREAMY

Uses cooked pudding and fresh fruit.
Makes 6 to 8 servings.

1 (20-oz.) can pineapple chunks in natural juices, drained and juice reserved
1 pkg. cook 'n serve vanilla pudding (4-serving size)
⅓ c. flaked coconut (opt.)
4 c. mixed fresh fruit chunks (apples, pears, peaches, bananas, oranges, etc.)
½ c. chopped pecans or walnuts

1. In saucepan, combine reserved pineapple juice and pudding mix; cook over medium heat until thickened and bubbly. 2. Cool pudding; add pineapple chunks, coconut, fruit chunks and nuts. 3. Chill until serving time.

FRUIT SALAD, FLUFFY

Uses instant pudding and canned fruit, drained.

1½ c. milk
1 (4-serving size) pkg. vanilla instant pudding
8-oz. carton whipped topping, thawed
1 to 2 cans (16 oz. each) fruit cocktail or sliced peaches, drained (or pineapple chunks, drained)

Optional Ingredients:
Mandarin oranges, drained
Miniature marshmallows
Bananas, sliced
½ c. flaked coconut
½ c. chopped nuts

1. In mixer bowl, combine milk and instant pudding; beat together. 2. Fold in whipped topping, then drained fruit and any optional ingredients desired. 3. Pour into serving dish or long Tupperware pan and chill.

FRUIT SALAD, GRACE ROUGH'S

May be eaten immediately, or chilled.
So easy and good!

1 (20-oz.) can crushed pineapple, undrained
1 large or 2 small (4-serving size) boxes instant pudding (vanilla or lemon)
1 (8 to 12-oz.) carton whipped topping, thawed
1 to 2 cans mandarin oranges, drained
Miniature marshmallows (opt.)
Maraschino cherries, drained (opt.)
Chopped nuts (opt.)

1. In mixer bowl, combine undrained crushed pineapple and dry instant pudding; beat together on low speed 2 min. 2. Fold in whipped topping, then drained mandarin oranges and any other optional ingredients desired.

FRUIT SALAD, INSTANTLY FABULOUS

From Louise McMinn. Serves 6 to 8.

1 (20-oz.) can pineapple chunks WITH JUICE
1 can fruit cocktail or mandarin oranges, DRAINED
1 sm. box (4-serving size) INSTANT pudding (vanilla, pistachio or lemon)
2 sliced bananas or 1 to 2 diced apples
Miniature marshmallows (opt.)
⅓ c. chopped nuts (opt.)
Lettuce leaves (opt.)

1. Mix together pineapple chunks with juice, the other drained fruit and the dry instant pudding. 2. Add bananas, marshmallows and nuts. 3. Refrigerate or serve immediately on lettuce leaves or in salad dishes. Note: When using vanilla instant pudding, 2 to 3 tablespoons lemon juice may be added, if desired.

FRUIT SALAD & LEMON SAUCE

From Geraldine Patterson. Makes a lot.

Sauce:
4 eggs, beaten well
¼ c. sugar
¼ c. lemon juice
¼ c. (½ stick) butter
½ pt. (1 c.) whipping cream
2 T. sugar or powdered sugar
¼ tsp. vanilla

Fruit Salad:
1 c. red grapes, no seeds
1 c. green grapes, no seeds
2 c. sliced peaches, drained
2 c. chunk pineapple, drained
2 c. mandarin oranges, drained
1 bag miniature marshmallows (opt.)

1. In heavy saucepan, combine eggs, sugar, lemon juice and butter; cook, stirring almost constantly over low heat until it thickens. Set aside to cool. 2. Drain fruit; combine fresh fruit and drained canned fruit. 3. When sauce is cool, fold into the fruit gently. 4. Whip cream with sugar and vanilla until stiff; fold gently into the fruit mixture (with marshmallows, if used). 5. Pour into 3-quart fancy dish; refrigerate.

FRUIT SALAD, ORANGE CREAM

So good!

1 (20-oz.) can pineapple chunks, drained (or slices, cut up)
1 (16-oz.) can sliced peaches, drained
2 med. bananas, sliced
2 med. apples, cored and diced (leave part of the red skin on)
1½ c. milk
½ of 6-oz. can orange juice concentrate, thawed (⅓ c.)
1 (4-serving size) pkg. vanilla instant pudding

1. In large bowl, combine drained fruit, bananas and apples. 2. In small bowl, combine milk, orange juice concentrate and dry pudding mix; beat with rotary beater 1 to 2 minutes, until well blended. 3. Fold into fruit mixture; cover and refrigerate several hours.

FRUIT SALAD, QUICK

Simple and delicious.

1 can chunk pineapple with juice
1 can mandarin oranges with juice
2 apples, peeled or unpeeled, and diced
2 bananas, sliced

1. Mix the fruits together and serve.

FRUIT SALAD, SEVEN FRUITS

Makes a gallon or more, and is delicious.

1 qt. (or 29-oz. can) pears, with juice, diced
1 qt. (or 29-oz. can) peaches, with juice, diced
1 (20-oz.) can pineapple chunks with juice
3 bananas, sliced
3 or 4 apples with red skin, diced
Some fresh strawberries, sliced (or fresh raspberries or fresh blueberries)
3 kiwi, peeled and sliced (or green seedless grapes)

1. In large bowl, combine everything except kiwi. Add kiwi last, stirring in very gently. Substitution: 2 or 3 cans mandarin oranges may be substituted for peaches. Note: Frozen berries of any kind do not work well because they discolor the fruit salad.

GOLDEN GLOW SALAD

With cabbage and carrots.

2 sm. boxes (3 oz. each) lemon or pineapple gelatin
2 c. boiling water
1 (20-oz.) can crushed pineapple, including juice
⅛ tsp. salt
1 c. shredded cabbage
½ to ¾ c. shredded carrots
¼ to ½ c. celery, sliced thin (opt.)

1. Dissolve gelatin in boiling water; add remaining ingredients in order given. 2. Pour into 13 x 9-inch or 12 x 8-inch oblong pan or glass loaf pan. 3. Chill until firm.

GOLDEN GLOW SALAD, LARGER

With apples and carrots; from Erma Blair.

1 sm. box (3 oz.) orange gelatin
1 sm. box (3 oz.) lemon gelatin
1 sm. box (3 oz.) pineapple gelatin
3 c. boiling water
1½ c. cold water
Diced red apples
Celery, finely diced
Carrots, finely shredded (4 med.)
Walnuts, chopped (opt.)
1 (20-oz.) can crushed pineapple, including juice

1. In mixing bowl, dissolve gelatins in boiling water. 2. Add cold water; chill until partially set. 3. Add remaining ingredients; pour into 13 x 9-inch or 12 x 8-inch oblong dish or pan. 4. Chill until firm.

GOLDEN GLOW SALAD, SMALLER

With carrots and nuts. Also called "Sunshine Salad."

1 sm. box (3 oz.) orange or lemon gelatin
1 c. boiling water
1 (8½-oz.) can crushed pineapple (RESERVE JUICE)
1/16 tsp. salt
½ tsp. lemon juice or vinegar
1 c. shredded carrots
⅓ c. chopped nuts (opt.)

1. Dissolve gelatin in boiling water. 2. Drain pineapple, reserving juice; add water to juice to make ¾ cup. 3. Combine gelatin, ¾ cup liquid, crushed pineapple, salt and lemon juice. 4. Chill until partially set; fold in carrots and nuts. 5. Pour into mold(s), loaf pan or 8 x 8-inch square pan; chill until firm. Note: This recipe may be doubled, using 20-ounce can crushed pineapple; put in 12 x 8-inch or 13 x 9-inch oblong pan.

GRAPE JELLO SALAD

Adapted from Ruby Gurnee; also a dessert.

6 oz. grape gelatin
2 c. boiling water
2 c. vanilla ice cream
Tokay grapes (seeds removed)
Bananas, sliced

1. Dissolve gelatin in boiling water; add ice cream and stir until melted. 2. Add fruit; chill. Note: Any flavor of gelatin may be used, and any drained fruit.

JELLO THREE-RIBBON SALAD (CHRISTMAS)

Red, green and white for Christmas. Serves 12 to 15.

1 sm. box (3 oz.) lemon Jello
1 c. white miniature marshmallows (or 10 lg., halved)
1 c. boiling water
6 to 8 oz. cream cheese, softened
½ c. mayonnaise
1 (20-oz.) can crushed pineapple, drained
1 c. Cool Whip or prepared Dream Whip
1 sm. box (3 oz.) lime Jello
1 c. boiling water
¾ c. cold water
1 sm. box (3 oz.) red raspberry Jello
1 c. boiling water
¾ c. cold water

1. Dissolve lemon Jello and marshmallows in 1 cup boiling water. (Marshmallows may not dissolve completely.) 2. Add softened cream cheese and beat until blended (or use blender). 3. Chill until slightly thickened; add mayonnaise, drained pineapple and Cool Whip. Chill until very thick. 4. Dissolve lime Jello in 1 cup boiling water; add ¾ cup cold water; pour into 13 x 9-inch pan and chill until almost set, but still a little sticky to the touch. 5. Spoon white pineapple mixture gently over lime Jello; chill while continuing next step. 6. Dissolve raspberry Jello in 1 cup boiling water; add ¾ cup cold water; refrigerate until it begins to thicken. 7. Pour over white layer; chill until firm. 8. To serve, cut into 12 to 15 squares. Put a wooden pick through the center of each square so layers won't slide apart, if necessary. Note: Any color combination of Jello may be used.

KIDNEY BEAN SALAD

1 (15 to 16-oz.) can kidney beans or red beans, drained and rinsed
1 sm. onion, diced (⅛ c.)
¼ c. finely diced celery (or more)
⅛ to ¼ c. mayonnaise, salad dressing or French dressing
½ to 1 tsp. sugar
⅛ tsp. salt
⅛ tsp. pepper
1 to 2 hard-cooked eggs, sliced or chopped (opt.)
¼ c. diced green bell pepper (opt.)
¼ c. chopped sweet or dill pickle, not relish (opt.), or black olives

1. Rinse kidney beans and drain well; combine with remaining ingredients. 2. Chill; serve on lettuce leaf, if desired.

LEMON JELLO-COTTAGE CHEESE SALAD

Also called "Snow Flake Salad."

1 (3-oz.) pkg. lemon Jello
2 c. boiling water
1 c. crushed pineapple, well drained
1 c. cottage cheese
Diced celery (opt.)
¼ c. chopped nuts (opt.)
Lettuce leaves (opt.)

1. Dissolve Jello in boiling water; cool in refrigerator until Jello is slightly thickened, but not set. 2. Add drained pineapple, cottage cheese and celery and/or nuts, if desired. 3. Pour into 8 or 9-inch square pan or dish and chill. 4. Cut in squares and serve on lettuce, if desired.

LEMON JELLO FROSTED SALAD

A wonderful salad from Berniece Cordial.

6 oz. lemon Jello (large box)
3 T. sugar
2 c. boiling water
1½ c. cold water or 7-Up
1 (20-oz.) can crushed pineapple, well drained (save juice)
3 bananas, sliced or diced
3 apples, peeled or unpeeled, diced in small pieces
Nuts, chopped (opt.)

Frosted Topping:
½ c. sugar
3 T. flour, level
¾ to 1 c. reserved pineapple juice
1 egg, beaten well
1 env. Dream Whip, prepared, or ½ of an 8-oz. carton whipped topping, thawed (about 2 c.)
Chopped nuts (opt.)

1. Dissolve Jello and sugar in boiling water. 2. Add cold water and drained pineapple; pour into 12 x 8-inch or 13 x 9-inch dish or pan and refrigerate. 3. When Jello begins to set, stir in bananas and apples (and nuts, if used); refrigerate until firm. 4. To make topping, mix together sugar and flour in medium saucepan; add pineapple juice, stirring well. 5. Add beaten egg and beat with wire whip. 6. Bring to a boil, stirring constantly; cover and set aside to cool. 7. When cool, fold whipped topping into egg mixture. 8. Spread topping over the set Jello; sprinkle with chopped nuts, if desired. 9. Cover with plastic wrap or lid and chill.

LEMON OR LIME PERFECTION SALAD

A classic recipe.

2 sm. boxes (3 oz. each) lemon or lime gelatin (or one of
    each kind)
2 c. boiling water
1 c. cold water
⅛ tsp. salt
2 c. shredded cabbage or less
1 c. shredded carrots
½ c. chopped celery
¼ c. chopped green pepper (opt.)
2 T. chopped pimiento (opt.)
1 T. lemon juice or vinegar

1. Dissolve gelatin in boiling water; add remaining ingredients. 2. Pour into 6-cup mold or glass loaf pan or 7 x 11-inch
or 8 x 8-inch pan. 3. Chill until firm. **Note**: A 20-oz. can of
crushed pineapple, well drained, may also be added. Do not
use 12 x 8-inch pan, as salad will be too thin.

LEMON-LIME PERFECTION SALAD (Diet)

2 env. Knox gelatin
1 c. cold water
¼ tsp. salt
2 c. cold water
1 T. liquid sweetener
3 packets Equal sweetener
1 pkg. UNSWEETENED lemon lime Kool-Aid
1½ c. shredded cabbage
½ c. shredded carrots

1. Dissolve Knox gelatin in 1 cup cold water. 2. Add salt, 2
cups cold water, liquid sweetener, Equal and Kool-Aid; stir
until Kool-Aid is dissolved. 3. Add cabbage and carrots;
pour into 7 x 11-inch or 9 x 9-inch pan, or glass loaf pan. 4.
Chill until firm.

LETTUCE-CAULIFLOWER SALAD

*From Shirley Stevenson; make
12 to 24 hours before serving.*

1 med. or med.-lg. head iceberg lettuce (7 to 8 c.)
1 sm. or med. head cauliflower (3½ c.)
10 oz. (about 2 to 2¼ c.) frozen peas, or less
1 sm. bunch green onions, sliced, or 1 med.-sm. onion,
    chopped or 1 T. instant minced onion
3 to 4 T. bacon bits (or ½ lb. bacon, fried crisp)
2 tsp. dry Good Seasons Italian salad dressing mix (½
    env.)
1 to 2 c. mayonnaise
Parmesan cheese or shredded Cheddar cheese (opt.)

1. In large bowl, break lettuce into bite-sized pieces. 2. Cover
lettuce with cauliflower cut into spriglets or small pieces. 3.
Cover cauliflower with frozen peas (thawed just enough to

separate). 4. Add layer of onions (just the white part of green
onions). 5. Add layer of bacon bits or crumbled crisp bacon.
6. Sprinkle dry Italian dressing over top. 7. Cover all with
mayonnaise, spreading to edges of bowl. 8. Sprinkle cheese
over top. 9. Seal tightly with lid, foil or plastic wrap; refrigerate several hours or overnight. 10. Just before serving, toss
together lightly. Serves 12 or more. **Note:** If preferred, fried
bacon may be stirred in at serving time.

LETTUCE & FRUIT SALAD I

Serves 2 to 3 people.

Iceberg lettuce, cut up or chopped
Apples, diced (opt.)
Seedless grapes (opt.)
Bananas, sliced (opt.)
Canned pineapple chunks, drained (opt.)
Orange or tangerine sections (opt.)
3 to 4 T. mayonnaise or salad dressing (the size of a lg.
    egg)
½ to 1 T. sugar (or 1 pkt. Equal and 1 tsp. sugar)

1. Measure lettuce and fruit to make a total of 3 to 3½ cups.
2. Add mayonnaise and sugar (use only ½ tablespoon sugar
if the only fruit is bananas); mix well.

LETTUCE & FRUIT SALAD II

No mayonnaise or salad dressing in this recipe.

¼ head lettuce, chopped (or 2 c.)
1 orange, peeled and cut into chunks
1 to 1½ c. seedless grapes, halved
1 sm. can pineapple chunks, drained
1 Red Delicious apple, diced (peeled or unpeeled)
1 banana, sliced
¼ c. peanuts or pecans, coarsely chopped (or more)
2 T. sugar
1 T. lemon juice

1. Mix all ingredients together.

LETTUCE (LEAF) WITH
OLD-FASHIONED DRESSING

A wonderful recipe.

1 colanderful leaf lettuce or homegrown lettuce, cleaned
    and cut up (about 4 to 5 c.)
Sliced scallions or 2 T. chopped onion or ⅛ tsp. onion
    powder

Dressing
¼ c. mayonnaise or salad dressing
2 T. sugar
2 T. milk
⅛ tsp. salt or onion salt
½ tsp. vinegar (use 1 tsp. vinegar if using mayonnaise)

1. Combine cut-up lettuce and onion in bowl. **2.** In small bowl, combine mayonnaise with remaining ingredients, stirring well with small whisk. **3.** Add dressing to lettuce, stirring together. <u>Note</u>: For an extra-large colanderful of lettuce, double the dressing ingredients.

LETTUCE & PEAS LAYERED SALAD

7 to 8 c. iceberg lettuce, broken into bite-size pieces (or part or all fresh spinach)*
1½ to 2 c. frozen peas (do not cook)
2 to 4 T. chopped onions or little green onions, sliced
2 to 4 hard-boiled eggs, peeled and sliced
2 T. bacon flavor chips (or 5 to 8 slices bacon, fried crisp and crumbled)

<u>Dressing:</u>
1 c. mayonnaise
1 to 1½ tsp. dry Good Seasons Italian or Hidden Valley Ranch dressing mix

<u>Top:</u>
Parmesan cheese or shredded cheese (opt.)

1. In 13 x 9-inch long dish, layer salad ingredients in order given. **2.** In small bowl, mix together dressing ingredients; spread over top of salad. **3.** Sprinkle with cheese and cover with plastic wrap; refrigerate overnight (or for 4 to 24 hours). <u>Note</u>: Salad may be sprinkled with croutons at serving time, if desired. *If spinach is used, remove stems.

LETTUCE SALAD

A favorite salad.

3 to 4 c. iceberg lettuce, cut up or torn into bite-sized pieces
¼ c. mayonnaise or salad dressing
2 to 3 tsp. sugar, level or 1 pkg. Equal and 1 tsp. sugar
⅛ tsp. salt or onion salt
1 to 2 hard-boiled eggs, shelled and coarsely chopped (opt.)
Green onions, sliced, or sweet onion, chopped (opt.)
Radishes, sliced (opt.)
Chopped celery and/or celery leaves (opt.)
1 tomato, diced, or cherry tomatoes, cut in half (opt.)

1. Combine ingredients, using any or all of the options; stir together well.

LETTUCE, WILTED, WITH BACON (or SPINACH)

A Pennsylvania Dutch meal, delicious served over hot, boiled potatoes.

1 lg. colanderful LEAF lettuce (6 to 7 c.), torn or cut up
5 little green onions, sliced thin, or 1 med. onion, thinly sliced and separated into rings
5 slices bacon, fried crisp (or more)
4 T. bacon drippings (or part olive oil)
¼ c. vinegar
3 T. sugar
1 T. water
¼ tsp. salt
¼ tsp. pepper

1. In large salad bowl, combine lettuce and onion. **2.** After frying bacon, lift bacon out with slotted spoon to drain on paper towels. **3.** Discard some of the bacon drippings, leaving 4 tablespoons (or part oil) in the skillet. **4.** Add vinegar, sugar, water; salt and pepper to the skillet and bring to a boil. **5.** Immediately pour over lettuce and onions. **6.** Crumble bacon and add to lettuce; toss together a few times until lettuce is slightly wilted. **7.** Serve immediately over hot, boiled potatoes. <u>Note</u>: A 12-oz. pkg. of spinach may be used in place of the leaf lettuce and 2 hard-boiled eggs, sliced (opt.)

LIME JELLO-COTTAGE CHEESE SALAD

1 (3-oz.) pkg. lime Jello
1 c. boiling water
3 to 4 oz. cream cheese, softened
½ c. finely chopped celery (opt.)
8-oz. can crushed pineapple, including juice (1 c.)
1 c. low-fat cottage cheese
Chopped nuts for top, if desired

1. Dissolve Jello in boiling water. **2.** Add cream cheese and beat together with electric mixer or wire whip. **3.** Fold in celery, pineapple and cottage cheese. **4.** Sprinkle with nuts and cover with plastic wrap. **5.** Refrigerate.

LIME JELLO, PEARS & CREAM CHEESE SALAD I

From Hazel Schreiner.

6 oz. lime gelatin
2 c. boiling water
2 c. cold water
1 (29-oz.) can pear halves (or 1 qt. home-canned), drained
8 oz. cream cheese, softened
1 c. whipped topping, thawed
Crushed or finely chopped walnuts or pecans

1. Dissolve gelatin in boiling water; add cold water and refrigerate (just until it starts to congeal) in 13 x 9-inch glass pan. 2. Drain pears and set aside. 3. Beat cream cheese; add whipped topping and nuts, mixing well. 4. Fill pear cavities with cream cheese mixture; when gelatin is starting to congeal, place the pear halves (filled-side down) in the gelatin.

LIME JELLO, PEARS & CREAM CHEESE SALAD II

From Frances Craig.

1 (29-oz.) can pears, or 1 qt. home-canned pears, drained (reserve liquid)
2 c. pear juice (add water to make 2 c.)
6 oz. lime gelatin
3 oz. softened cream cheese
2 env. Dream Whip, prepared (or 8-oz. carton whipped topping, thawed)

1. Heat the 2 cups pear juice (and water) to boiling; add gelatin and stir to dissolve. 2. Add hot mixture to softened cream cheese gradually, beating well. 3. Refrigerate until it begins to thicken. 4. Mash pears and add to green mixture. 5. Fold in whipped topping; pour into long glass or Tupperware dish and refrigerate.

LIME JELLO PERFECTION SALAD

Very good. To double, put in 13 x 9-inch dish.

1 (3-oz.) box lime gelatin
1 c. boiling water
¼ c. cold water
1 (8-oz.) can crushed pineapple with juice (1 c.)
⅔ c. shredded carrots
⅓ c. shredded cabbage
1/16 tsp. salt (opt.)

1. Dissolve gelatin in boiling water. 2. Add remaining ingredients; pour into 8 x 8-inch square dish or pan. 3. Chill until firm.

LIME MIST JELLO SALAD

Marshmallows used in this recipe may be rather old.

1½ c. miniature marshmallows (or 16 lg. marshmallows)
1 c. milk
1 sm. pkg. (3 oz.) lime gelatin
3 to 4 oz. cream cheese, softened
½ c. walnuts, coarsely chopped (opt.)
1 (20-oz.) can crushed pineapple, including juice
¼ c. mayonnaise
2 c. whipped topping or 1 env. prepared Dream Whip

1. In top of double boiler over boiling water, melt marshmallows in milk. 2. When melted, dissolve gelatin in mixture; stir until dissolved. 3. Add softened cream cheese and beat

with electric mixer on high speed (or blender) until smooth. 4. Add nuts, crushed pineapple and mayonnaise; beat well with wire whisk. 5. Fold in whipped topping; pour into 12 x 8 2-inch or 13 x 9 2-inch glass or Tupperware dish, cover and chill. <u>Note</u>: At Christmas time, red Jello stars may be placed on top each serving. (Combine 1 small 3-ounce package red Jello with 1 cup boiling water; add ¾ cup cold water. Pour into 13 x 9 x 2-inch dish and let set. Cut out stars with cookie cutter.)

LIME TWO-TONE GELATIN SALAD

Adapted from Betty Rowan.

<u>Bottom Layer:</u>
1 (3-oz.) pkg. lemon gelatin
¾ c. boiling water
¾ c. cold water
4 oz. cream cheese, softened
1 (20-oz.) can crushed pineapple, well-drained
⅓ c. pineapple liquid

<u>Top Layer:</u>
1 or 2 (3-oz.) pkgs. lime gelatin, made according to pkg. directions

1. Dissolve lemon gelatin in ¾ cup boiling water; add ¾ cup cold water. Place in refrigerator until it starts to jell. 2. In mixer bowl, mix together cream cheese, drained crushed pineapple and ⅓ cup pineapple liquid. (Use remaining pineapple liquid for other purposes.) 3. Add lemon gelatin, which has just started to jell, to the cream cheese mixture; mix well and pour into 13 x 9-inch glass or Tupperware dish. 4. Prepare lime gelatin as directed on package; chill in refrigerator until it just barely begins to thicken. Pour over top the lemon-cream cheese mixture. 5. Refrigerate.

LINGUINE (OR SPAGHETTI) SALAD

Adapted from Carol Wells. Recipe may be doubled.

8 oz. linguine (or spaghetti), broken in half or smaller
½ c. (4 oz.) Italian oil dressing (like Kraft's Zesty)
1 tomato (or more), diced
½ green bell pepper, diced
½ purple, sweet or regular onion, chopped

<u>Optional Ingredients:</u>
1 T. McCormick's Salad Supreme seasoning (or Schilling Salad Seasonings)
½ can black olives, sliced
½ cucumber, chopped or sliced
2 oz. pepperoni, thin-sliced
1 clove garlic, minced
1 T. sugar

1. Cook broken linguine or spaghetti according to package directions. (Do not overcook.) Rinse with cold water and drain. 2. In serving bowl, combine pasta, Italian oil dressing and remaining ingredients. 3. Refrigerate overnight or at least

a few hours. Serves 4 to 6 generously; keeps 1 week in refrigerator. If needed, add a little more Italian oil dressing. **Substitution**: Instead of ½ cup Italian oil dressing, use 1 packet Good Seasons Italian salad dressing mix (mixed according to package directions with ¼ cup vinegar, 2 tablespoons water and ½ cup oil). Just use half of this for the salad.

MACARONI B.L.T. SALAD

Bacon, lettuce and tomato macaroni salad from Nancy Chess.

2 c. to 2½ c. uncooked macaroni (cook as directed in salted water until tender)
5 green onions, finely chopped (or 1 small onion)
1 or more large tomatoes, diced (or 1 to 2 cups of cherry tomatoes, halved)
1¼ c. diced celery
½ to 1 lb. bacon, diced and fried crisp
Lettuce

Dressing:
1¼ c. mayonnaise
1 T. white vinegar
¼ c. sugar (or to taste)
¼ tsp. salt (or to taste)
⅛ tsp. pepper

1. Rinse cooked macaroni in cold water and drain; in large bowl, combine macaroni, onion, tomato and celery. 2. In small bowl, combine dressing ingredients, mixing well. 3. Add dressing to macaroni and toss to coat; chill 2 hours. 4. Just before serving, toss in bacon; serve on a bed of lettuce.

MACARONI SALAD I

This recipe takes 4 to 5 cups cooked macaroni.

2 c. uncooked macaroni (7 to 8 oz.)
2 qt. boiling water
2 tsp. salt
2 to 4 hard-boiled eggs, diced
½ to 1 c. chopped celery
¼ c. sliced radishes or more
¼ c. finely chopped onion or sliced green scallions (opt.)
1 or 2 fresh tomatoes, diced (opt.)
¼ c. diced sweet pickles (opt.)
Sliced olives or diced green pepper (opt.)

Dressing:
¾ c. salad dressing or mayonnaise
½ to 2 tsp. prepared yellow mustard or ½ tsp. dry mustard (opt.)
3 to 5 T. sugar
3 T. evaporated milk
2 T. vinegar
½ tsp. salt (may need a bit more)
Few drops yellow food coloring (opt.)

1. Cook macaroni in boiling water with 2 teaspoons salt until tender; drain and rinse with cold water. Drain again. 2. Combine macaroni, eggs, celery, radishes and any other optional vegetables. 3. In small bowl, combine dressing ingredients, mixing well. 4. Add dressing to macaroni mixture, mixing gently. 5. Put in 2-quart bowl; sprinkle paprika over top, if desired. 6. Cover and refrigerate several hours. Makes 6 cups. Note: 1 tablespoon chopped chives or instant minced onion (or ½ teaspoon onion powder) may be substituted for the fresh onion, if desired.

MACARONI SALAD II (Larger)

From Carol Wells. Makes a lot.

3 c. uncooked macaroni (6 to 9 c. cooked macaroni)
1 med. onion, chopped (½ c.)
4 to 6 hard-boiled eggs, cut up
½ c. sweet pickles, diced
1 c. chopped celery
Sliced radishes (opt.)

Dressing:
1¼ c. mayonnaise or salad dressing
¼ c. sugar
¼ c. evaporated milk or milk
3 T. vinegar
¾ tsp. salt
Few drops yellow food coloring (opt.)

1. Cook macaroni in 3 quarts boiling water and 1 tablespoon salt, until tender; drain and rinse with cold water. Drain again. 2. In large bowl, combine cooked macaroni, onion, boiled eggs, pickles, celery and radishes. 3. In small bowl, combine mayonnaise, sugar, milk, vinegar, salt and coloring; mix well. 4. Add dressing to macaroni mixture; stir together gently. 5. Sprinkle with paprika if desired. 6. Refrigerate, covered.

ORANGE FLUFF SALAD

From Leota Benninger Reynolds.

6 oz. apricot or orange gelatin
2 c. boiling water
1⅔ c. cold water
2 c. whipped topping, thawed
2 sm. cans mandarin oranges, drained
Chopped nuts (opt.)

1. In medium bowl dissolve gelatin in boiling water; add cold water and refrigerate until set. 2. Whip with mixer or rotary eggbeater. 3. Fold in whipped topping and drained mandarin oranges. 4. Pour into 8 x 8-inch dish; sprinkle nuts over top, if desired. 5. Cover and refrigerate.

ORANGE JELLO KANSAS SALAD

From Wanda Marsh.

1 (3-oz.) pkg. orange gelatin
1 c. boiling water
¾ c. cold water
1 c. cream, whipped or 1 pkg. Dream Whip, prepared (or 2
    c. thawed whipped topping)
½ c. drained crushed pineapple (or fresh orange sections)
½ c. shredded Longhorn or sharp Cheddar cheese
¼ to ½ c. chopped nuts

1. Dissolve gelatin in boiling water; add cold water and refrigerate in bowl until firm. 2. Beat with electric mixer or
rotary beater. 3. Fold in remaining ingredients.

ORANGE or LIME MIST SALAD

6 oz. orange or apricot or lime gelatin
2 c. boiling water
1½ c. cold water
1 env. Dream Whip, prepared (or 2 c. whipped topping,
    thawed)
3 oz. cream cheese, softened
2 c. drained peaches, diced (or other canned fruit,
    drained)
2 to 3 bananas, sliced, or apples, peeled and diced
Flaked coconut (opt.)

1. Dissolve gelatin in boiling water; add cold water and refrigerate until slightly thickened. 2. Combine whipped topping with
softened cream cheese, blending well. 3. Add slightly thickened
gelatin and fold together. 4. Add drained fruit, fresh fruit and
coconut. 5. Pour into long glass pan; chill.

PASTA SALAD

From Robin McNutt. Double recipe for a big bowl.

8 oz. (3 c.) uncooked spiral corkscrew pasta or rotini
½ to ¾ c. Wishbone Italian or Kraft Zesty Italian
    dressing
½ to 1 tsp. dill weed
1 tomato, diced
¼ c. onion, chopped (or sliced green onions or chopped
    chives) or ¼ tsp. onion powder
¼ c. diced or sliced pepperoni
½ green bell pepper, diced
½ c. sliced radishes or cucumbers (opt.)
Broccoli florets, raw (opt.)
Black or green olives, sliced
1 c. diced Monterey Jack cheese or sharp cheese

1. Cook pasta in 2 quarts boiling water and 2 teaspoons salt,
until tender (about 18 minutes); drain, then rinse with cold
water and drain again. 2. Add remaining ingredients; put in 2-
quart bowl or casserole. 3. Cover and refrigerate overnight, or
at least 2 hours. Serves 6. **To Make Your Own Oil Dressing**

for this recipe: Shake together ½ cup olive oil, ¼ cup vinegar,
1 teaspoon Italian seasoning, ½ teaspoon garlic powder, ½
teaspoon salt and ¼ teaspoon pepper. (1 T. sugar is optional.)

PASTA SALAD, ANTIPASTO

From Lois Kok; makes a large bowl.

1 lb. spiral corkscrew pasta or rotini (6 c. before cooking)
1 c. hard salami, sliced or diced
1 c. pepperoni, sliced or diced
1 c. (4 oz.) diced or shredded cheese (most any kind)
1 med. onion, diced small or green onions, sliced
½ to 1 green bell pepper, diced
Black and/or green olives, drained and sliced
3 stalks celery, diced
1 to 3 tomatoes, diced (or cherry tomatoes, halved)

Dressing:
¾ c. olive oil
⅓ c. vinegar
1½ tsp. salt (or less)
1 tsp. oregano
1 tsp. pepper
2 T. sugar (opt.)

1. In 3½ quarts boiling water and 4 teaspoons salt, cook
pasta until tender, about 18 minutes; drain, then rinse with
cold water and drain again. 2. Shake together dressing ingredients in a jar; add to pasta along with remaining ingredients.
3. Chill in refrigerator, covered, overnight or several hours.

PASTA SALAD, ORIENTAL SWEET & SOUR

*From Jay Stevenson. If you like Chinese food,
you'll love this.*

6 to 8 oz. snow pea pods
½ lb. (8 oz.) thin spaghetti
½ lb. (8 oz.) mushrooms, cleaned and sliced
½ to 1 T. olive oil

Dressing:
¼ c. olive oil
3 T. sesame oil
3 T. honey
3 T. Chinese plum sauce (duck sauce)
2 T. soy sauce
½ tsp. salt (opt.)

1. Clean pea pods and remove stem, tips and strings, if any;
cut pods in two unless small. 2. Blanch pea pods in 3 quarts
(12 cups) boiling water for 45 seconds in large pan (save
boiling water); cool in ice water, then drain well. 3. In the
same boiling water, add 2 teaspoons salt and the spaghetti;
cook until tender, but not mushy. Rinse in cold water and
drain. 4. In skillet, lightly sauté mushrooms in ½ to 1 tablespoon oil; set aside. 5. To make dressing, heat olive oil and
sesame oil in saucepan over low heat 5 minutes. 6. Stir in
honey, plum sauce, soy sauce and salt if used. (If plum sauce

has large pieces in it, cut into small pieces.) Mix well. **7.** In large bowl, combine drained pea pods, drained spaghetti, mushrooms and dressing, stirring together. **8.** Chill before serving.

PASTA SALAD, SEAFOOD

Very good.

8 oz. small seashell, spiral or rotini pasta (3 to 3½ c. before cooking) or 2 c. uncooked elbow macaroni
1 c. mayonnaise or salad dressing
¼ c. chopped onion or sliced green onions
½ tsp. salt or seasoned salt
¼ tsp. pepper
2 sm. cans tuna, or 1½ c. crabmeat or tiny shrimp, drained, or 1 (15-oz.) can salmon, drained

Optional Ingredients:
1 to 2 tomatoes, chopped, or cherry tomatoes, halved
Radishes, sliced
Black or green olives, sliced
Chopped sweet pickles or cucumbers, diced
½ c. celery, chopped
¼ c. red or green bell pepper, diced
2 hard-boiled eggs, diced
Peas, fresh or frozen, uncooked
1 c. broccoli florets, uncooked
1 tsp. Italian seasoning
½ tsp. garlic salt or powder
½ tsp. dill weed
2 T. sugar

1. Cook pasta in 2 quarts boiling water and 2 teaspoons salt until tender; drain, rinse with cold water and drain again. **2.** Add remaining ingredients, gently stirring in drained seafood last. (Use at least 3 of the optional ingredients.) **3.** Chill or serve immediately. **Substitutions**: Instead of 1 cup mayonnaise, use ½ cup mayonnaise and ¼ cup bottled Italian dressing. Or omit mayonnaise completely and use 1 cup bottled Italian dressing.

PASTA SALAD (Sweet)

⅓ c. sugar
¼ c. vinegar
¼ c. olive oil
8 oz. rotini (spiral) pasta (3 to 3½ c. before cooking)
¼ c. chopped onion
1 tomato, diced
6 black or green olives, sliced
¼ tsp. garlic salt
1/16 tsp. pepper
1 cucumber or ½ green bell pepper, diced

1. In saucepan, bring to a full boil sugar, vinegar and oil, stirring to dissolve sugar; cool. **2.** Cook and drain pasta; in large bowl, combine pasta and remaining ingredients. **3.** Pour cooled dressing over salad, stirring gently together. **4.** Refrigerate. This will keep a week in refrigerator.

PEA SALAD

Salad and vegetable all in one. Serves 4.

1 (10-oz.) pkg. frozen peas (about 2 c.) broken apart or thawed
1 c. celery, diced extremely small
¼ c. chopped sweet onion or little green onions, thinly sliced
¼ c. sour cream or sour cream alternative
¼ c. crisply cooked bacon, crumbled
¼ c. salted cashews

1. Combine uncooked peas, celery, onion and sour cream. **2.** Just before serving, add crumbled bacon and nuts. (If desired, serve on lettuce leaf.)

PEACH JELLO SALAD

Fluffy and delicious.

6 oz. peach Jello
1 c. boiling water
1 c. cold water
½ of an 8-oz. carton whipped topping, thawed (about 2 c. or more)
Canned peaches, drained (sliced or diced)

1. Dissolve Jello in boiling water; add cold water and refrigerate in large bowl until firm. **2.** Add whipped topping; beat with electric mixer until well blended. **3.** Add drained peaches and pour into serving dish or long glass pan; chill.

PEACH TWO-LAYER GELATIN SALAD

1 sm. (3-oz.) box lemon or peach gelatin
1 c. boiling water
1 c. cold orange juice
2 c. whipped topping, thawed (or 1 env. Dream Whip, prepared)
3 oz. cream cheese, softened

Top Layer:
1 sm. (3-oz.) box peach or lemon gelatin
1 c. boiling water
¾ c. cold water
1 qt. canned peaches, drained well (or 29-oz. can, drained)

1. Dissolve first box of gelatin in first cup of boiling water; add orange juice and chill until it thickens slightly. **2.** Combine whipped topping and softened cream cheese, blending together; add thickened gelatin, beating well. **3.** Pour into long glass or Tupperware pan; chill until firm. **4.** Dissolve second box of gelatin in second cup of boiling water; add cold water and well-drained peaches. **5.** Carefully pour over first layer; chill until top layer is firm.

PERFECTION SALAD

When you have no Jello. Makes 8 to 10 servings.

2 env. unflavored gelatin
½ c. sugar
¼ tsp. salt
1½ c. boiling water
1½ c. cold water
¼ c. lemon juice
1 drop yellow food coloring or 5 drops green food
    coloring
½ T. vinegar
1½ c. shredded cabbage
1 c. diced celery
½ c. shredded carrot
¼ to ½ c. chopped green pepper (opt.)

1. Mix gelatin, sugar and salt together. **2.** Add boiling water, stirring until gelatin dissolves. **3.** Add cold water, lemon juice, coloring and vinegar; chill until partially set. **4.** Add vegetables; pour into mold(s), loaf pan, 9 x 9-inch or 7 x 11-inch pan. **5.** Chill until firm.

PINEAPPLE MIST GELATIN SALAD

1 (20-oz.) can crushed pineapple
2 boxes (3 oz. each) orange-pineapple or pineapple or
    orange gelatin
1 c. cold water
8 oz. cream cheese
½ c. hot or boiling water
8-oz. carton whipped topping, thawed (or 2 pkgs.
    Dream Whip, prepared)
1 c. chopped nuts

1. Drain crushed pineapple, reserving juice; add enough water to juice to make 2 cups. **2.** Heat juice to boiling; add gelatin, stirring until dissolved. **3.** Add 1 cup cold water; refrigerate until partially set. **4.** In mixer bowl, combine cream cheese and ½ cup hot or boiling water; beat until smooth. **5.** Add drained pineapple, whipped topping, nuts and partially-set gelatin, blending carefully all together. **6.** Pour into 13 x 9 x 2-inch dish; sprinkle additional chopped nuts over top, if desired. **7.** Refrigerate.

PISTACHIO FLUFF SALAD

*Also called 'Watergate Salad.' Very quick and easy;
from Mary Stevenson.*

1 (20-oz.) can crushed pineapple and juice
1 sm. box instant pistachio pudding mix (4-serving size)
8-oz. carton whipped topping, thawed

Optional Ingredients:
1 c. miniature marshmallows

Maraschino cherries, drained (or mandarin oranges,
    drained)
⅓ c. coarsely chopped nuts (or more)

1. In medium large bowl, stir crushed pineapple and dry pudding mix together. **2.** Fold in remaining ingredients, using any or none of the optional ingredients. **3.** Refrigerate. This salad can be eaten immediately.

POTATO SALAD, AMISH (Shredded)

*A 3-quart serving bowl is perfect for this amount.
This is a very <u>sweet</u> potato salad.*

6 c. potatoes (6 lg.)
6 hard-boiled eggs
⅔ c. finely chopped celery
½ c. finely chopped onion
Paprika (for top)

Dressing:
1½ c. Miracle Whip salad dressing
¾ c. sugar
1½ T. vinegar
1 T. prepared mustard
1 tsp. salt

1. Boil potatoes (peeled or unpeeled) with water and 1 teaspoon salt, until tender. Do not overcook. **2.** Put potatoes (skins removed) and eggs through coarse shredder or slicing side of coleslaw cutter; add celery and onions. **3.** In small bowl, mix dressing ingredients together; add to potato mixture and mix well. Put in serving bowl and sprinkle with paprika. **4.** Refrigerate several hours or overnight. Keeps well in refrigerator.

POTATO SALAD, CLASSIC

*Adapted from Hazel Schreiner and Carol Wells.
Makes enough for a 2½-quart bowl.*

6 c. cooked, diced potatoes
3 to 4 hard-boiled eggs, cut up (opt.)
1 sm. to med. onion, finely diced or chopped
½ to 1 c. diced celery
½ c. diced sweet pickles
Radishes, sliced (opt.)
1 c. mayonnaise or Miracle Whip salad dressing
1 to 3 tsp. yellow prepared mustard
2 T. milk or evaporated milk
2 T. vinegar
6 T. sugar, level
¾ tsp. salt
Paprika over top (opt.)
Fresh parsley garnish (opt.)

1. Mix all ingredients, except paprika and parsley, in order given. **2.** Put potato salad in 2 or 2½-quart bowl or casserole;

sprinkle with paprika and garnish with parsley. **3.** Cover and refrigerate. <u>Note</u>: Cook about 10 cups scrubbed potatoes, cut in quarters, in water with 1 level tablespoon salt until tender. Drain, cool and remove skins. Dice potatoes and measure 6 cups, gently pressed in cup. This recipe may be tripled, using 10 lbs. of potatoes with 1 level T. of salt. Makes an 8-quart bowl full.

POTATO SALAD FOR A SMALL CROWD

Serves 20 or more; from Patricia Swarts.

5 lbs. potatoes
1 med.-large onion, diced
1 c. celery, diced
Paprika
1 c. sweet pickles, diced
6 hard-boiled eggs, peeled and diced

<u>Dressing:</u>
2 c. Miracle Whip salad dressing or mayonnaise
1 to 1⅛ c. sweet pickle relish, including juice
¼ c. milk
1½ tsp. salt
½ tsp. pepper
2 T. sugar
1 T. yellow mustard (opt.)

1. Scrub potatoes and boil in water with ½ to 1 tablespoon salt, until tender but not overcooked; drain and cool. **2.** Remove skins and dice or cube potatoes into a 5-quart bowl. **3.** Add onion, celery, sweet pickles and boiled eggs; stir together. **4.** Combine dressing ingredients in med.-small bowl, mixing well; pour over potatoes. **5.** Stir all together; put into a <u>4-quart serving bowl</u> and sprinkle with paprika. **6.** Cover and refrigerate. <u>Note</u>: If desired, boil 1 extra egg to slice over the top.

POTATO SALAD, HOT GERMAN

*Delicious! Serves 3 to 4 people,
but recipe could be doubled.*

4 med. potatoes (4 c.)
⅛ to ¼ lb. bacon, cut into ½-inch pieces
1 T. olive oil
¼ c. chopped onion
¼ c. sugar
1 T. flour, packed level
½ c. cold water
¼ c. vinegar
½ tsp. salt
⅛ tsp. pepper
Fresh parsley, chopped (opt.)
Sliced radishes (opt.)

1. Scrub potatoes; boil until tender. Remove skins, if desired, and dice. **2.** Fry bacon in large skillet until crisp; remove bacon with slotted spoon and drain on paper towels. **3.** Pour off all but 1 tablespoon bacon fat from skillet. (Discard all but the 1 tablespoon.) Add 1 tablespoon oil to the skillet. **4.** Add onions to skillet and sauté until transparent. **5.** Add sugar and flour, stirring together. **6.** Add cold water all at once, stirring. **7.** Add vinegar, salt and pepper; cook until mixture thickens and boils, stirring almost constantly. Turn off heat. **8.** In large bowl, combine potatoes and bacon; pour hot dressing over potatoes, stirring gently to coat. (If potatoes were cooked without salt, ¼ teaspoon salt may be stirred in now.) **9.** Sprinkle with parsley (if desired) and serve warm, or may be served at room temperature.

RASPBERRY JELLO SALAD

A delicious salad.

1 red raspberry gelatin, prepared according to package
    directions
Apples, diced small
Pears, diced
Bananas, diced

1. Let gelatin cool; when beginning to set, add fruit. Chill.

RASPBERRY TWO-LAYER SALAD

If you like red raspberries, you'll love this!

1 sm. box (3 oz.) lemon Jello
1½ c. boiling water
3½ c. miniature marshmallows
1 (20-oz.) can crushed pineapple, drained
½ c. chopped nuts
2 c. whipped topping
8 oz. cream cheese, softened
1 lg. box (6 oz.) raspberry Jello
2 c. boiling water
2 pkgs. (10 oz. each) frozen red raspberries, partially
    thawed (with juice)

1. Dissolve lemon Jello in 1½ cups boiling water. **2.** Add marshmallows; stir until partially melted. **3.** Add drained crushed pineapple and nuts. **4.** Combine whipped topping and cream cheese; fold into lemon Jello mixture. **5.** Pour into 13 x 9-inch pan or dish; chill until firm. **6.** Dissolve raspberry Jello in 2 cups boiling water and cool to room temperature or lukewarm. **7.** Add raspberries (and juice) which are nearly thawed; stir very gently to separate berries. **8.** Pour raspberry Jello mixture over first layer; chill until firm.

RHUBARB SAUCE

7 c. rhubarb, cut up in 1-inch pieces
1 c. sugar
1 c. water
1 T. tapioca, level
7 drops red food coloring (opt.)

1. Put rhubarb, sugar, water and tapioca in a 3-quart pan and stir together. 2. Cook until rhubarb is tender, stirring occasionally. 3. When done, remove from heat and add food coloring if desired. 4. Taste for sweetness; more sugar may be added while it is hot, if needed.

SALMON SALAD

Makes 4 to 5 individual salads.

1 (14 to 16-oz.) can salmon, drained
A few radishes, sliced (opt.)
1 c. diced celery
1 to 2 T. chopped onion
½ T. lemon juice
¼ tsp. seasoned salt (opt.)
¼ tsp. pepper
¼ c. mayonnaise or salad dressing
Lettuce leaves

1. In bowl, break salmon into bite-sized chunks and remove or crush bones. 2. Add remaining ingredients (except lettuce) and stir gently together. 3. Spoon salmon mixture on lettuce-lined salad plates. **Optional Ingredients:** For added crunch, add 1 can Chinese noodles just before serving. Also frozen peas, 2 hard-boiled eggs (coarsely chopped), and/or canned pimiento, drained, can be added.

SAUERKRAUT SALAD OR RELISH

1 (16-oz.) can sauerkraut (2 c.), drained
1 med. onion, sliced or chopped
½ c. chopped celery
½ c. chopped green bell pepper (or part red bell pepper)
⅔ c. sugar
2 T. vinegar
2 T. water
2 T. olive oil

1. Combine drained sauerkraut, onion, celery and green pepper in bowl. 2. In small saucepan, heat remaining ingredients until sugar is dissolved; pour hot syrup over sauerkraut. 3. Mix well; cover and refrigerate 6 hours or overnight. **Note:** A little shredded carrot or chopped red pimiento may be added. Also more sugar or vinegar may be added, if desired.

SPINACH SALAD

Raw spinach with a delicious dressing.

1 (10-oz.) pkg. fresh spinach, washed and drained
2 to 3 hard-boiled eggs, shelled and sliced or coarsely chopped
3 T. bacon bits (or 6 slices bacon, fried crisp and crumbled)
¼ c. chopped or sliced onion
Croutons

Dressing:
¼ c. sugar
⅓ c. olive oil
2 T. vinegar
¼ tsp. salt
½ tsp. celery seed
¼ tsp. pepper

1. Remove stems from spinach; if leaves are whole, break or cut up. 2. Put spinach in large salad bowl and refrigerate. 3. Combine dressing ingredients and shake well; refrigerate. 4. Just before serving, add eggs, bacon and onion to spinach. 5. Pour dressing over salad; toss gently together. 6. Serve with croutons, if desired.

STAINED GLASS SALAD

*Also called 'Prism Jello Dessert;'
it is beautiful and delicious.*

1 (3-oz.) pkg. lime Jello
1 (3-oz.) pkg. orange or apricot Jello
1 (3-oz.) pkg. raspberry or cherry Jello
1 c. pineapple juice
¼ c. sugar
1 (3-oz.) pkg. lemon Jello
1 c. graham cracker crumbs
¼ c. butter, melted
8-oz. carton whipped topping, thawed or 2 env. Dream Whip, prepared

1. Prepare first 3 packages Jello separately, using 1 cup boiling water to dissolve each one, and adding ½ cup cold water to each. 2. Pour into separate 8 x 8-inch pans and chill until firm. 3. Combine pineapple juice and sugar in saucepan; heat until sugar is dissolved and juice is almost boiling. 4. Remove from heat and add lemon Jello, stirring to dissolve; add ½ cup cold water and pour into a large bowl. Chill until syrupy. 5. Mix graham cracker crumbs with melted butter; press into 13 x 9-inch cake pan or 9-inch springform pan. 6. Fold whipped topping into syrupy, partially-set lemon Jello. 7. Cut the firm green, orange and red Jello in ½-inch squares; lift out with wide spatula and gently fold into whipped topping mixture. 8. Pour into crumb-lined pan; chill several hours or overnight.

STRAWBERRY PRETZEL DELIGHT

Use as a salad or a dessert.

¾ c. (1½ sticks) butter, melted
Pretzels, coarsely crushed (or part graham cracker crumbs) to make 2 c.
3 T. sugar
6 oz. strawberry gelatin (large box)
2 c. boiling water
2 pkgs. (10 oz. each) frozen strawberries (or 2 c. strawberries)
8 oz. cream cheese

¾ c. powdered or granulated sugar
2 to 3½ c. whipped topping, thawed (8-oz. container)

1. Combine melted butter, pretzels and sugar, mixing well; press into 13 x 9-inch baking dish. 2. Bake in preheated 400° oven for 8 minutes; cool. 3. Dissolve gelatin in boiling water; immediately add frozen strawberries. Let set 10 minutes, then gently break berries apart. 4. In mixer bowl, mix together cream cheese and sugar until blended well. 5. Fold in whipped topping; spread over the cooled pretzel crust. 6. Pour strawberry mixture over white layer; cover with lid or plastic wrap and refrigerate.

STRAWBERRY SALAD

From Jean Moyer.

6 oz. strawberry gelatin
2 c. boiling water
2 pkgs. (10 oz. each) frozen strawberries
3 bananas, sliced
1 c. chopped walnuts or pecans
1 can (any size) crushed pineapple, drained (opt.)
Miniature marshmallows (opt.)
Flaked coconut (opt.)

1. Dissolve gelatin in boiling water; immediately add frozen strawberries. Let set 10 minutes, then gently break berries apart. 2. Add remaining ingredients and pour into long glass pan or serving bowl; chill.

TACO DIP SALAD

From Bonnie Swarts.

White corn chips, nacho chips or tortilla chips

Base:
8 oz. cream cheese, softened
¼ c. sour cream
¼ c. taco sauce (mild, medium or hot)

Toppings:
Lettuce, shredded
Green bell peppers, chopped
Shredded cheese (Colby, Longhorn or Cheddar)
Sweet onions, chopped
Tomatoes, chopped

1. Mix together cream cheese, sour cream and taco sauce; spread on plate or platter. (Or if taking it somewhere, spread in 13 x 9-inch Tupperware or glass pan.) 2. Top with shredded lettuce. 3. Layer green peppers, cheese, onions and tomatoes on top lettuce. 4. Refrigerate 2 to 3 hours. 5. If desired, serve with chips surrounding the bottom layer on plate or platter.

TACO SALAD

Adapted from Sarah McIlhany.

½ T. olive oil
1 to 1½ lbs. ground beef
1 packet taco seasoning mix
1 c. water
1 head iceberg lettuce
1 med. onion, chopped (or 4 to 6 little green onions, sliced)
1 to 2 med. tomatoes, diced
1 avocado, peeled and diced (opt.), or black olives, drained
1 to 2 cans (16 oz. each) kidney beans, drained (opt.)
4 to 8 oz. (1 to 2 c.) shredded Cheddar or Longhorn cheese
8 to 10-oz. bag tortilla chips, taco chips or corn chips, broken
8 oz. Catalina, French, Italian or Western dressing (or desired amount)

1. Heat oil in skillet and brown beef, breaking it into bite-sized chunks; drain off all fat. 2. Stir in taco seasoning mix and water; simmer until liquid is nearly all gone. Cool. 3. In large 6 to 8-quart bowl, tear or cut lettuce into bite-sized pieces; add onion, tomatoes, avocado, drained beans, cheese and cooled meat mixture; stir together and refrigerate. 4. Just before serving, stir in dressing; lay chips all around edge of bowl (or serve chips in separate bowl) to prevent chips from getting soggy. Or toss chips in at the last minute. Corn chips don't get soggy.

TOMATO SALAD

Adapted from Betty Geneviva.

2 tomatoes, cut into chunks, or 2 c. cherry tomatoes, cut in half
1 to 2 garlic cloves, chopped
Onion slices
Dried oregano, ¼ tsp.
2 T. olive oil
1 T. vinegar (opt.)
Salt and pepper, ⅛ tsp. of each
1 T. sugar (opt.)

1. Mix ingredients together.

TUNA & LETTUCE SALAD (or SALMON)

A delicious salad.

3 to 4 c. lettuce, cut up or torn into bite-sized pieces
Mayonnaise or salad dressing the size of a lg. egg (¼ c.)
1 tsp. sugar
⅛ tsp. salt or onion salt
1 boiled egg, shelled and sliced (opt.)
Chopped onion (opt.)
Chopped celery or celery leaves (opt.)
4 radishes, sliced (opt.)

1 tomato, diced, or cherry tomatoes, cut in half (opt.)
1 to 2 (6 to 7-oz.) cans tuna, drained, or 1 can salmon,
    drained

1. Combine lettuce, mayonnaise, sugar, salt and any of the optional ingredients desired; stir together. **2.** Fold in tuna or salmon gently.

TWELVE (OR 24) HOUR FRUIT SALAD

From Ruth Campbell and Laura Stevenson.

1 sm. pkg. instant vanilla pudding, prepared as directed (4-
    serving size)
1 c. whipping cream, whipped, or 1 pkg. Dream Whip,
    prepared (2 c.)
1 (11-oz.) can mandarin oranges, drained
1 (20-oz.) can pineapple chunks, drained (cut chunks in
    half)
2 c. white cherries or white grapes, drained (or fresh
    red or green seedless grapes, halved), or bananas or
    apples
2 oranges, peeled, diced and seeds removed, (opt.)
2 c. miniature marshmallows (opt.)

1. Fold whipped cream or whipped topping into prepared instant pudding. **2.** Add remaining ingredients; chill 12 to 24 hours. Serves 8. <u>Note</u>: 1 pkg. regular cook-type pudding may be used with 1¾ c. milk; let cool.

Chapter 14

Salad Dressings

BACK ROW: LAWRENCE STEVENSON, JAMES PATTERSON,
JACK BENNINGER
MIDDLE ROW: DEBRA AND CLARENCE BENNINGER
FRONT ROW: LAURA STEVENSON, BETH BENNINGER,
GERALDINE PATTERSON, AND ELLEN BENNINGER

1971

SALAD DRESSINGS

AVOCADO DRESSING

Toss with salad greens, tomatoes, onions and ripe olives.

1 med.-sized ripe avocado, peeled and seeded
2 T. lemon juice
½ c. sour cream
¼ c. olive oil (or milk)
½ tsp. seasoned salt
¼ to ½ tsp. dried red pepper flakes (or ⅛ tsp. cayenne
    pepper), opt.
½ tsp. sugar
1 clove garlic, chopped

1. In small bowl, mash avocado with fork. **2.** Stir in remaining ingredients.

BLEU CHEESE DRESSING

2 oz. (½ c.) crumbled bleu cheese, divided
¾ c. sour cream or low-fat or fat-free sour cream substitute, divided
2 T. olive oil
1 T. lemon juice
⅛ to ¼ tsp. salt
1/16 tsp. pepper
1 tsp. sugar (opt.)

1. In small bowl, mash half the bleu cheese with fork. **2.** Add 2 tablespoons sour cream; beat with fork until quite smooth. **3.** Stir in remaining crumbled blue cheese and other ingredients. Yield: 1 cup. **Note**: Less bleu cheese may be used in this recipe, but for bleu cheese lovers, use it all.

CREAMY SALAD DRESSING

1 c. mayonnaise
¼ c. olive oil
1 tsp. onion salt
¼ tsp. salt (opt.)
1 tsp. paprika
1 tsp. vinegar
4 to 6 T. sugar, level

1. Beat mayonnaise and oil together. **2.** Add remaining ingredients and beat together.

FRENCH DRESSING

Recipe may be doubled. Adapted from Kay Anderson.

½ c. sugar
½ c. ketchup
½ c. olive oil
¼ c. vinegar
1 sm. onion or 1 tsp. onion powder
1 lg. clove garlic or ⅛ tsp. garlic powder
¼ tsp. salt
¼ tsp. pepper
6 stuffed olives (opt.)

1. Put all ingredients in blender container and blend 3 minutes. Makes 1¾ to 2 cups. **Note**: For a less sweet dressing, reduce sugar by at least one half.

FRENCH DRESSING (Sweet 'n Sour)

Makes about 2 cups.

½ c. sugar
½ c. olive oil
⅓ c. ketchup
¼ c. vinegar
¼ c. water
1 tsp. instant minced onion
¼ tsp. salt
¼ tsp. Italian seasoning
⅛ tsp. garlic powder or garlic salt

1. Blend together 3 to 5 minutes in blender container.

FRENCH DRESSING, TOMATO SOUP

Adapted from Mabel Wagner.

1 (10¾-oz.) can tomato soup
½ c. sugar
1 c. olive oil
½ c. vinegar
1 tsp. salt
1 tsp. dry mustard or 1 T. prepared mustard
½ tsp. pepper
½ tsp. Worcestershire sauce (opt.)
¼ tsp. garlic powder or 1 clove garlic, minced or
    pressed
1 sm. onion, chopped fine

1. Place all ingredients in jar with tight lid; shake well. (Or, blend in blender without chopping onion and garlic.) **2.** Store in refrigerator.

GREEN-GREEN DRESSING

¾ c. coarsely chopped parsley
3 little green onions with tops (or 3 T. chopped fresh
    chives)
1 tsp. sugar
½ tsp. dried basil
⅛ tsp. garlic powder
1 T. vinegar
1 c. mayonnaise

1. Blend all ingredients together in blender.

HERB SALAD DRESSING

Makes 6 servings.

¼ c. sugar
¼ c. vinegar
½ c. olive oil
¼ tsp. salt
¼ tsp. thyme
¼ tsp. rosemary or oregano
¼ tsp. marjoram or basil
¼ tsp. pepper
1 clove garlic, minced

1. Combine ingredients in a jar; shake well and chill.

HONEY VINAIGRETTE SALAD DRESSING

Delicious over salad greens or a fresh fruit salad.

2 T. vinegar
1 T. lemon juice
¼ c. honey
¼ c. olive oil
1 tsp. dry mustard
¼ tsp. salt
2 T. pineapple juice

1. Combine all ingredients in a jar and shake vigorously, or blend in blender. Stir with spoon to see if honey is well blended. (If desired, more vinegar or lemon juice may be added to taste.)

ITALIAN CREAMY SALAD DRESSING

1 c. mayonnaise
1 T. sugar
1 to 2 T. vinegar
1 tsp. Italian seasoning
¼ tsp. salt
¼ tsp. pepper

Optional Ingredients:
2 T. minced parsley
1 T. chopped onion
1 clove garlic, minced or pressed (or ¼ tsp. garlic powder)

1. Stir together (or put in electric blender or food processor without mincing and chopping vegetables). 2. Chill in covered jar.

MARSHMALLOW DRESSING

Fluffy topping for fruit salads.

½ of 7-oz. jar marshmallow creme
1 T. orange juice

1 T. lemon juice
¼ c. mayonnaise or salad dressing

1. Whip marshmallow creme, orange juice and lemon juice together with electric or rotary beater until very fluffy. 2. Fold in ¼ cup mayonnaise or salad dressing. Makes about 1¼ cups.

OIL-FREE SALAD DRESSING I

Very low in calories and zero fat.

1 T. powdered fruit pectin (like Sure-Jell)
¼ tsp. crushed dried oregano, basil, thyme, tarragon, savory or dill weed
½ to 1 tsp. sugar
⅛ tsp. dry mustard
⅛ tsp. salt
⅛ tsp. pepper
¼ c. water
½ to 1 T. vinegar
1 sm. clove garlic, minced or crushed

1. In small bowl, combine pectin, desired herb, sugar, dry mustard, salt and pepper. 2. Stir in water, vinegar and garlic; cover and store in refrigerator.

OIL-FREE SALAD DRESSING II

Very low in calories and zero fat.

1 T. cornstarch
1 tsp. sugar
½ tsp. dried dill weed
¼ tsp. dried basil, crushed
¼ tsp. salt
⅛ tsp. garlic powder
1 c. cold water
¼ c. ketchup
2 T. vinegar
1 tsp. Worcestershire sauce

1. In small saucepan, combine dry ingredients, stirring together. 2. Add remaining ingredients; cook and stir over medium heat until thickened and bubbly. 3. Reduce heat; cook and stir 2 minutes. 4. Cover and chill.

POPPY SEED DRESSING

Omit the onion for fruit salads.

½ c. sugar
1 tsp. salt (or less)
1 tsp. dry mustard
2 tsp. finely chopped onion (opt.)
⅓ c. white vinegar
1 c. olive oil
1 T. poppy seed

1. In blender container, combine all ingredients except oil. (Can also be done in mixer bowl with electric mixer.) 2. Add oil slowly, while blending or beating on medium speed, until well mixed and thick. 3. Add poppy seed. 4. Store in covered container in refrigerator; stir well before using. Makes about 1½ cups.

SOUR CREAM DRESSING

1 c. sour cream or sour cream alternative
½ c. mayonnaise
1 tsp. vinegar
¼ tsp. salt
¼ tsp. pepper
¼ tsp. paprika
¼ tsp. onion powder
¼ tsp. dill weed
1 T. chopped fresh chives (opt.)
1 clove garlic, cut in half

1. Mix together all ingredients; let stand 2 hours or longer. 2. Remove the garlic halves before serving.

SWEET VINAIGRETTE SALAD DRESSING

¾ c. sugar (or less)
1 tsp. dry mustard
½ tsp. salt
⅓ c. vinegar
1½ T. grated onion
1 c. olive oil

1. In medium bowl, mix ingredients together; beat until thick. 2. Chill.

THOUSAND ISLAND DRESSING

¾ c. mayonnaise or salad dressing
2 tsp. lemon juice or vinegar
3 T. chili sauce, ketchup or salsa
2 T. sweet pickle relish
⅛ tsp. salt

Optional Ingredients:
1 hard-cooked egg, chopped
1 tsp. paprika
1 T. chopped onion
1 T. chopped red or green bell pepper
1 T. chopped celery
1 T. chopped stuffed olives

1. Mix all ingredients together; keep refrigerated.

Chapter 15

Soup and Chili

THE MCNUTT FAMILY

**TOM, DON, CLARK AND PAUL
RUSTY HOLDING DANIEL, AUDREY, RUTH AND CAROL**

1972

SOUP AND CHILI

ASPARAGUS SOUP

¼ to ⅓ c. chopped onion
2 T. butter
1 can condensed cream of mushroom soup or cream of
    chicken soup
1 (14½ to 16-oz.) can asparagus
1 c. milk, divided
⅛ tsp. pepper

1. In saucepan, fry onion in butter until soft. 2. In blender container, combine onion-butter mixture, soup, asparagus (not drained) and ½ cup milk. 3. Cover and blend until smooth. 4. Pour back into saucepan; add remaining ½ cup milk and the pepper. 5. Simmer 10 minutes. (Do not boil.)

BEAN SOUP

If using salty ham broth, omit salt in recipe!

1 lb. (2 to 2¼ c.) dried navy, great northern, lima or pinto
    beans
8 c. hot water or broth
1 onion, chopped or whole
1 tsp. salt
⅛ to ¼ tsp. black pepper
Ham bone or ham hock or cubed fully cooked ham
    (opt.)

1. Wash beans in cold water. (Watch for tiny stones or pieces of dirt the size of a bean.) 2. Drain; repeat until beans are clean. **Crock-Pot Method:** Put all ingredients in crock-pot and cook on HIGH for 3 to 3½ hours, covered; or 9 to 10 hours on LOW, if they have been soaked overnight in water. **Stove-Top Method:** In soup pot, simmer for 1½ to 3 hours, uncovered, until beans are tender. Add more water or broth, if necessary, to make soup desired consistency. **Note:** Beans may be covered with cold water and soaked overnight, if desired. Drain and discard water. Beans cook quicker this way. **Quick Soak:** Rinse and sort beans. In large pan bring 1 lb. beans and 6 to 8 cups hot or cold water to a rapid boil; boil for 2 minutes. Remove from heat, cover and let stand for 1 hour. Drain and rinse, then proceed with recipe.

BEAN SOUP, MANY BEANS

From Pat Swarts.

16 to 20-oz. bag "15-Bean Soup" beans (mixed dried
    beans)
2 qt. (8 c.) cold water
½ lb. smoked sausage, kielbasa or ham, diced (fat
    removed)
1 lg. onion, chopped (opt.)
1 clove garlic, minced (opt.)

1. Wash beans thoroughly. 2. Place beans in cooking pot; cover with water 2 inches above beans and add 2 tablespoons salt; soak overnight. 3. Next morning, drain; add 2 quarts cold water, meat, onion and garlic. 4. Bring to a boil; reduce heat, cover and simmer slowly 2 hours or until tender. (Add water, if needed, while cooking.) **Crock-Pot:** Cook 3 hours on HIGH, or 5 hrs on LOW.

BROCCOLI CHEESE SOUP

Simple and good.

4 c. chicken broth (may be made with bouillon)
2 c. noodles, uncooked
1 c. chopped broccoli
8 slices Velveeta cheese
1 c. milk

1. Heat broth to boiling; add noodles and boil for a few minutes. 2. Add broccoli and cook until broccoli is tender. 3. Add milk and bring just to a simmer. 4. Turn off heat and add cheese; when melted, stir together and serve.

BROCCOLI & CHEESE NOODLE SOUP

Quick and easy. Adapted from Geraldine Frazer.
Recipe may be doubled.

¼ to ⅓ c. finely chopped onion
1 to 1½ T. olive oil
3 c. water
3 chicken or beef bouillon cubes
4 oz. (2 c.) thin noodles or 3-oz. pkg. Ramen noodles,
    broken up
½ tsp. salt
⅛ tsp. pepper
⅛ tsp. garlic powder
1 (10-oz.) pkg. frozen chopped broccoli, thawed, (or ½
    to 1 bunch fresh broccoli, cut in small bite-size
    pieces, discarding tough stem)
3 c. milk
½ lb. Velveeta or Velveeta Light cheese, cut into small
    cubes (or more)

1. In 3-quart (or larger) saucepan, fry onion in oil for 3 minutes. 2. Add 3 cups water and bring to a boil; add bouillon cubes, mashing them with potato masher. 3. Add noodles, salt, pepper and garlic powder; simmer on reduced heat 8 to 10 minutes. 4. Add broccoli and simmer 5 minutes longer. 5. Add milk and cheese; heat only until cheese is melted. 6. Makes 2 to 2½ quarts and serves 4 to 6. **Note:** If Ramen noodles and the flavoring packet are used, omit salt, pepper and garlic powder.

BROCCOLI (CREAM OF BROCCOLI) CHEESE SOUP (or CAULIFLOWER)

A terrific recipe!

½ stick (¼ c.) butter
1 med. onion, chopped
⅓ c. flour, packed level
2 c. milk
2 c. chicken broth (can be made with chicken bouillon)
1 med. carrot, chopped (opt.)
10-oz. pkg. frozen broccoli cuts (about 3 to 4 c.) or 1 head fresh broccoli, cut bite-size, or 3 c. cauliflower
½ c. chopped celery with leaves (opt.)
1 to 1½ c. Velveeta Light cheese, diced, or American cheese, diced (or ½ lb.)

1. Melt butter in 2 to 4-quart heavy saucepan and cook onion in it until translucent. 2. Blend in flour carefully. 3. Add milk and broth; stir until mixture boils. 4. Add broccoli and celery and bring to a boil again; reduce heat to very low and barely simmer for 10 to 15 minutes. 5. Add cheese; stir gently until melted. Do not boil.

BROCCOLI, HAM & CHEESE CHOWDER

From Adele Crognale. Delicious.

1 lg. onion, chopped
1 c. fresh mushrooms, sliced (opt.)
3 T. butter
2 T. flour
1 (14-oz.) can chicken broth
2 c. milk or half 'n half
½ to 1 lb. extra sharp Cheddar cheese, shredded (or reg. Cheddar)
½ to 1 tsp. Worcestershire sauce
1 c. cooked whole-kernel corn, drained (opt.)
2 c. cubed, cooked ham
2 c. carrots, sliced, cooked and drained
1 bunch broccoli, cut into 2-inch chunks (cooked and drained)

1. Sauté onion and mushrooms in butter; add flour and stir together. 2. Add chicken broth and milk; stir together and bring to a boil. Lower heat and simmer 2 minutes. 3. Turn off heat and add cheese; stir until melted. 4. Add cooked and drained carrots and broccoli, and cooked ham. 5. Keep warm but do not boil. 6. Add salt and pepper to taste (if needed).

CHEESE POTATO SOUP I

Serves 3 to 5.

1 chicken bouillon cube
¾ c. water
2 T. chopped onion
⅓ c. celery, diced small
⅓ c. carrots, diced small (opt.)
2 c. potatoes, peeled and diced small

½ tsp. salt
2 c. milk
1 T. flour, packed level
1 to 1½ c. American cheese or Velveeta cheese, cubed (4 to 6 oz.)

1. In medium saucepan, dissolve bouillon in water. 2. Add remaining ingredients except cheese. 3. Simmer until vegetables are tender, about 15 to 20 minutes. 4. Add cheese and heat over low heat until melted. Do not boil.

CHEESE POTATO SOUP II

Serves 4 to 5 people.

2 T. butter
⅓ c. chopped celery
⅓ c. chopped onion
3½ to 4 c. peeled, diced potatoes (or less)
3 c. chicken broth (or 3 c. water and 3 chicken bouillon cubes)
2 c. milk
½ tsp. salt
¼ tsp. pepper
⅛ tsp. paprika
8 oz. (2 c.) shredded Cheddar cheese
Fresh parsley, chopped (opt.)

1. In large heavy saucepan, melt butter over medium heat; fry celery and onion until tender. 2. Add potatoes and broth; cover, bring to a boil, then reduce heat and simmer until potatoes are tender, about 15 minutes. 3. Puree potato mixture in food processor or blender in batches; return to saucepan. 4. Stir in milk, salt, pepper, paprika and cheese; heat on medium or medium-low heat only until cheese melts. 5. Garnish with parsley, if desired; serve immediately.

CHICKEN NOODLE SOUP

Serves 4 to 5 people.

1 whole (or cut-up) broiler-fryer chicken
10 c. water
1 med. or lg. onion, chopped
2 to 3 ribs celery, including leaves, sliced or diced
2 to 3 carrots, scrubbed or peeled and sliced
2 tsp. salt
¼ tsp. pepper (or 6 peppercorns)
A few drops yellow food coloring (opt.)
Chicken bouillon cubes or instant chicken bouillon (opt.)
2 to 3 c. uncooked thin or med. egg noodles

1. Remove giblets from chicken (discard liver); wash chicken in cold water and remove fat from chicken cavity opening. 2. Place chicken, giblets and water in large soup pot and bring to a boil; reduce heat and simmer 15 minutes. 3. Skim off foam and scum; add vegetables, salt and pepper. Cover and simmer gently over low heat 1 to 1½ hours, until meat is tender. 4. Remove chicken from broth and set aside until cool enough

to handle. Skin chicken and remove meat from bones; discard skin, fat and bones, cutting meat in bite-size pieces. Set aside. **5.** Remove fat from top of broth and discard peppercorns, if used. (Broth may be strained and vegetables discarded, if desired.) Add food coloring and chicken bouillon, if desired. **6.** Bring broth to a boil; stir in noodles and simmer gently 20 minutes or until noodles are tender. **7.** Add chicken and stir gently together.

CHILI, ELLEN'S

Scrumptious.

½ T. olive oil
½ to 1 lb. ground beef or ground turkey
½ to 1 c. chopped onion
1 (28 to 32-oz.) can (3½ to 4 c.) tomatoes or tomato
    juice
1 (6-oz.) can tomato paste
2 c. water
1 (14 to 16-oz.) can kidney beans, drained and rinsed
½ green bell pepper, chopped (opt.)
1 tsp. salt
¼ tsp. pepper or ¹⁄₁₆ tsp. cayenne pepper
¼ tsp. garlic powder
1 to 3 tsp. chili powder (or to taste)
2 to 4 T. sugar (or more to taste)
½ tsp. cumin (opt.)
1 bay leaf (opt.)

1. In cooking pot or large skillet, fry meat and onions in oil until lightly browned, stirring occasionally; rinse with hot water and drain. **2.** Add remaining ingredients, stirring together. **3.** Bring to a boil; reduce heat and simmer, uncovered, 20 minutes, stirring occasionally. **4.** Remove bay leaf before serving. **Crock-Pot:** After step #2, cook in crockpot, covered, on HIGH for 3 to 4 hours, or on LOW for 10 to 12 hours. (Recipe may be doubled.)

CHILI FOR A CROWD

Serves 25 or more. Makes about 10 quarts (or 40 cups).

1 to 2 T. olive oil
6 lbs. ground beef (or part deerburger)
3 c. chopped onion
4 qt. tomato juice (14 to 16 c.)
24 oz. tomato paste
6 to 8 c. water
⅓ c. sugar
4 (15 to 16 oz.) cans kidney beans, rinsed and drained
4 tsp. salt
2 tsp. garlic salt
1 tsp. black pepper
4 tsp. chili powder (or more to taste)

1. In two large skillets, fry meat and onions in oil until lightly browned, stirring frequently; drain off fat. **2.** Rinse meat and onions with very hot water (to remove more fat); drain. **3.** In large cooking pot, combine all ingredients, stirring together in order given. **4.** Bring to a boil; reduce heat and simmer on low heat, uncovered, for 1 hour, stirring occasionally.

CHILI, JOHNSTOWN (Crock-Pot)

½ T. olive oil
1 to 2 lbs. ground beef
1 c. chopped onion
1 (28-oz.) can tomatoes or 3½ to 4 c. canned tomatoes or
    tomato juice
3½ to 4 c. spaghetti sauce
2 cans (14 to 16 oz. each) kidney beans, drained and
    rinsed
2 to 4 T. sugar (or to taste)
2 tsp. chili powder (or to taste)
1 to 2 tsp. salt
½ tsp. pepper
½ tsp. cumin (opt.)
¼ tsp. garlic powder (opt.)

1. In a skillet, fry meat and onions in oil until lightly browned, stirring occasionally; drain off excess fat. **2.** Put meat in crockpot; add remaining ingredients and stir together. **3.** Cover and cook on HIGH 4 to 5 hours, or on LOW 10 to 12 hours. **Note**: Or follow directions for Chili, Ellen's.

CHILI, MILDLY HOT & DELICIOUS

½ T. olive oil
1 med. onion, chopped
½ green pepper, chopped (opt.)
1 lb. ground beef
1 (28-oz.) can (3½ c.) canned tomatoes
8 oz. (1 c.) tomato sauce
1 (14 to 16-oz.) can kidney beans, drained and rinsed
1 teaspoon salt
¼ tsp. garlic powder
¼ tsp. red cayenne pepper
¼ tsp. black pepper
¼ tsp. red-hot sauce
2 T. sugar (or to taste)
½ to 1 tsp. chili powder, or more to taste

1. In hot oil, cook onion and green pepper until tender, about 5 minutes, over medium low heat. **2.** Add ground beef; cook until browned, stirring frequently. **3.** Drain excess fat, if any. **4.** Add remaining ingredients to meat and bring to a boil. **5.** Reduce heat and simmer, uncovered, 30 minutes or until chili reaches desired thickness, stirring occasionally. **Note**: More red-hot sauce and cayenne pepper may be added (sparingly).

CHILI, PAT'S

From Pat Swarts.

3 lbs. ground beef
2 lg. onions
1½ tsp. salt
1 tsp. pepper
2 (28-oz.) cans tomatoes (7 to 8 c. canned tomatoes)
2 (15-oz.) cans tomato sauce (about 4 c.)
1 (28-oz.) can kidney beans
Sugar to taste (or ¼ c.)
Chili powder to taste

1. In large skillet, brown beef and onions; drain off all fat. 2. In large pan, combine all ingredients; bring to a boil. 3. Reduce heat and simmer, uncovered, 1 hour or longer.

CREAM OF SOUP (GENERIC)

This equals one can (10½ to 10¾ oz.) of condensed cream soup.

2 T. butter or olive oil
3 T. flour, packed level
¼ t. salt
⅛ t. pepper
1⅓ c. milk (reconstituted skim milk is fine)
1 to 2 t. chicken bouillon powder or bouillon cubes
1 to 2 t. dried onion flakes or ¼ t. onion powder
⅛ t. garlic powder
½ t. dried basil

Optional Ingredients:
¼ c. chopped celery
1 (4-oz.) can mushrooms, drained, or ½ c. sliced mushrooms
Cooked broccoli, chopped and drained
Cooked chicken, diced

1. Melt butter in saucepan over low heat; blend in flour, salt and pepper. 2. Add milk all at once; cook, stirring constantly, until mixture bubbles and thickens. 3. Add remaining ingredients, if desired, making sure bouillon cubes have dissolved, if used.

EGG DROP SOUP I

Serves one.

1 c. chicken broth
1 egg, slightly beaten
Salt
Pepper

1. Bring chicken broth to a slow boil. 2. Slowly pour egg into chicken broth while stirring constantly; continue to cook for 1 to 2 minutes until egg is fully cooked. 3. Season to taste with salt and pepper.

EGG DROP SOUP II

Serves 3.

¼ c. thinly sliced celery
1 green onion, thinly sliced, or 1 T. chopped onion
2 T. thinly sliced mushrooms (opt.)
3 c. chicken broth (no fat)
¼ tsp. salt
1⁄16 to ⅛ tsp. pepper
1 egg, slightly beaten

1. Combine vegetables and chicken broth in saucepan; add salt and pepper. 2. Bring to a boil; lower heat and simmer 5 minutes. 3. Slowly drizzle egg into broth while stirring constantly. 4. Simmer 1 minute longer.

FISH CHOWDER (Crock-Pot)

½ c. chopped onions
2 T. butter
4 c. diced raw potatoes
1 (15-oz.) can cream-style corn
2 c. water
1 tsp. dried parsley flakes
½ c. sliced celery (opt.)
1 carrot, sliced very thin, (opt.)
1 tsp. salt
¼ tsp. black pepper
1 lb. fresh or frozen cod, haddock or whiting fish
1 c. milk
½ c. evaporated milk or half & half cream

1. Sauté onions in butter in skillet until transparent but not brown. 2. Combine onions, potatoes, corn, water, vegetables and seasonings in crock-pot. 3. Cook on HIGH for 2 hours. 4. Add fish which has been diced or cubed; cook 30 minutes. 5. Add milk and evaporated milk or cream; cook another 30 minutes. Turn heat off, or put on LOW until it is served. Note: This recipe takes 3 hours on HIGH, but it may be cooked on LOW the whole time for 6 hours, adding the evaporated milk or half & half during the last hour.

HAMBURGER CABBAGE SOUP

Recipe may be cut in half for smaller amount.

1 T. olive oil
½ to 1 lb. lean ground beef
2 med. onions, chopped
½ c. diced celery
½ c. diced green pepper (opt.)
1½ tsp. salt
2 to 3 T. sugar
¼ tsp. pepper
½ tsp. paprika
4 c. canned tomatoes or 1 (28-oz.) can tomatoes
1 (6-oz.) can tomato paste
8 c. hot water

2 beef bouillon cubes
3 T. chopped parsley (or 1 T. dried)
1 c. diced or sliced raw carrots
2 c. diced raw potatoes
6 to 8 c. chopped or diced green or red cabbage (approximately 1 sm. head)
Some frozen peas at end of cooking (opt.)

1. Heat oil in cooking pot; lightly brown beef, onion, celery and green pepper. (If ground beef is not lean, drain off fat.) 2. Add remaining ingredients. 3. Bring soup to a boil, then simmer for 1 hour, uncovered, or until vegetables are tender, stirring occasionally. Makes about 5 quarts. <u>Note</u>: More water may be added if a thinner soup is desired.

HAMBURGER VEGETABLE SOUP

Serves 6.

1 lb. lean ground beef
1 T. olive oil
1 c. chopped onion
½ green pepper, chopped (opt.)
4 c. hot water
1 c. diced carrots, peeled, (or green beans)
1 to 2 c. diced potatoes, peeled
1 c. diced celery
1½ tsp. salt
¼ tsp. pepper
6 c. canned tomatoes (or whole fresh tomatoes, skins removed)
1 T. sugar
1 T. parsley flakes (opt.)

1. Fry beef in oil in heavy kettle or 6-quart stockpot, stirring occasionally. 2. Add onion and green pepper and cook 5 minutes longer; drain off all fat. 3. Add remaining ingredients; bring to a boil. 4. Reduce heat and simmer 30 minutes.

MUSHROOM SOUP

2 T. butter
8 oz. mushrooms, washed and brushed clean
¼ c. finely chopped onion
1 T. minced fresh parsley or ½ T. dried parsley flakes
1 clove garlic, minced
1 T. flour, packed level
2 c. broth or cold water
2 beef bouillon cubes
1 c. milk or light cream

1. Heat butter in 2-quart saucepan. 2. Add mushrooms which have been chopped or minced, onion, parsley and garlic. 3. Sauté until mushrooms soften (at least 5 minutes). 4. Sprinkle flour over mixture and stir together; add broth and bouillon cubes, stirring well. 5. Bring to a boil, stirring frequently; reduce heat and simmer 15 minutes, covered. 6. Add milk or cream; reheat but do not boil.

OYSTER STEW

More oysters may be added to this recipe if desired.

2 to 4 T. butter
8 oz. (½ pt. or 1 c.) oysters (reserve liquid)
4 c. milk (or part cream or part evaporated milk)
½ tsp. salt
½ tsp. celery salt (opt.)
1/16 to 1/8 tsp. pepper
1/8 tsp. paprika (opt.)

1. In 2-quart pan, melt butter. 2. Add oysters, reserving liquid; cook oysters in butter about 3 minutes, until the oysters plump and the edges begin to curl. 3. Add oyster liquid, milk and remaining ingredients. 4. Heat over medium heat until very hot, but <u>**do not let boil**</u>. Serves 3 (or makes 7 single servings); serve with oyster crackers or soda crackers. <u>Note</u>: 1 can (8 ounces) Chicken of the Sea whole oysters may be used when fresh or frozen oysters are not available.

POTATO SOUP

Delicious with homemade bread.

4 to 5 c. peeled, diced potatoes
1 med. or lg. onion, diced or chopped (½ to 1 c.)
5 c. water
2 tsp. salt
1/8 to ¼ tsp. pepper
2 T. butter
1 sm. can (5 oz.) evaporated milk (⅔ c.), or cream or milk

1. Put all ingredients, <u>except milk</u>, into pan and cook, uncovered, until potatoes are tender (about 20 minutes after coming to a boil). 2. Remove from heat and add milk just before serving. <u>Note</u>: May be cooked in pressure cooker, processing 7 minutes after pressure comes to 15 pounds, according to manufacturer's directions. <u>Note</u>: May be cooked in crockpot, covered with lid, for 2½ hours on HIGH.

SALMON SOUP

From Adrienne Hepfner–a delicious soup.

1 (15 to 16-oz.) can salmon, including juice
4 c. milk
2 T. dried onion, level
1 T. butter
Salt and pepper to taste

1. Put all ingredients in saucepan and heat to simmering, but do not boil.

SOY BEAN STEW

From Dr. R. E. Carroll.

1 c. dry soybeans
1 (8-oz.) can tomato sauce
⅓ c. chopped onions
1 clove garlic, crushed or minced
1 stalk celery, chopped
½ tsp. salt
½ tsp. ground cumin
1/16 tsp. cinnamon
1/16 tsp. cloves
1/16 tsp. nutmeg
1/16 tsp. allspice
½ c. chopped green pepper
⅔ c. grated cheese

1. Cook dry soybeans in water until tender; save the liquid from beans. **2.** Combine drained soybeans with remaining ingredients except green pepper and cheese (they are added last) in cast iron Dutch oven skillet. **3.** Cook stew over low heat about 30 minutes, adding liquid from beans if mixture becomes dry. **4.** Remove from heat and stir in green peppers and cheese. The residual heat will warm peppers and melt the cheese.

SPLIT PEA SOUP I

1 lb. green split peas (2 to 2½ c.)
10 c. boiling water
Ham bone, ham pieces or bacon rind
1 med. onion, chopped
½ c. chopped celery
½ c. shredded or chopped carrots (or 1 carrot, shredded)
1½ tsp. salt
¼ tsp. pepper
¼ tsp. garlic powder (opt.)
1 bay leaf (opt.)
1 tsp. ground thyme (opt.)

1. Wash split peas and drain; remove anything that looks like a little stone. **2.** Combine all ingredients in kettle and bring to a boil. **3.** Reduce heat and simmer, covered, for 1½ hours, stirring occasionally. (If soup gets too thick, add a little water.) **4.** Remove bones, rind and bay leaf before serving. **Note**: If a smooth soup is desired, puree (half at a time) in blender or food processor.

SPLIT PEA SOUP II (CROCK-POT)

Use ingredients for Split Pea Soup I, except use 8 cups boiling water instead of 10 cups. Cook on HIGH for 2½ hours in crock-pot, covered. (For thicker soup, remove lid and let simmer another 30 minutes on HIGH.) Remove bones, rind and bay leaf before serving.

VEGETABLE BEEF SOUP, CROCK-POT

1 to 2 lbs. chuck boil, stewing beef or round steak (all fat removed)
1 tsp. salt per pound of meat
⅛ tsp. pepper
4 c. canned tomatoes or tomato juice (or fresh tomatoes, peeled)
2 c. water
1 med. onion, chopped
½ to 1 c. chopped celery
1 to 2 c. diced or sliced raw carrots
1 to 2 c. peeled potatoes or turnips, diced
2 c. green beans, fresh or canned, undrained
1 tsp. dried parsley flakes or 3 T. fresh parsley, chopped (opt.)
½ T. sugar, or to taste (opt.)

1. Combine all ingredients in crock-pot in order given, stirring together. **2.** Cover and cook on HIGH for 5 to 7 hours (or on LOW for 12 to 18 hours), until meat is tender. **3.** Before serving, remove meat and bones; cut meat into bite-sized pieces and return to soup.

VEGETABLE BEEF SOUP, QUICK

This recipe uses leftover roast beef.

3½ to 4 c. canned tomatoes, tomato juice or fresh tomatoes, peeled, or 1 (28-oz.) can
5 c. water, vegetable juices or beef broth
3 beef bouillon cubes, crushed (opt.)
3 med. potatoes, diced
3 med. carrots, diced
3 med. turnips, diced (opt.)
1 med. onion, diced
½ c. celery or celery leaves, chopped (or 2 T. dried celery leaves)
3 T. chopped fresh parsley (or 1 tsp. dried parsley flakes)
1½ c. (or more) leftover roast beef, diced
2 c. green beans, drained
Leftover peas, corn and/or lima beans, drained
Leftover cauliflower, drained (opt.)
1 T. butter
1 tsp. salt
⅛ tsp. pepper
1 to 2 T. sugar (opt.)

1. In 5 or 6-quart pan, combine all ingredients. **2.** Bring to a boil; reduce heat and simmer gently for 30 to 40 minutes, or until potatoes and carrots are tender. **Note**: Frozen, sliced carrots may be used. More water may be added, if desired.

VEGETARIAN VEGETABLE SOUP

Delicious every time!

3½ to 4 c. canned tomatoes or tomato juice (or fresh
   tomatoes, peeled)
5 c. water or vegetable juices
1 to 3 c. potatoes, peeled and diced
1 to 3 c. carrots, peeled and diced
1 to 2 c. turnips, peeled and diced (opt.)
1 to 2 c. cauliflower, broccoli or cabbage, diced
1 c. diced celery
1 onion, diced (any size)
1 to 2 c. green beans, fresh or canned, cut small
1 c. corn, peas or lima beans, fresh or canned
¼ c. chopped fresh parsley or 1 to 2 tsp. dried parsley
   flakes
1 clove garlic, minced, or ⅛ tsp. garlic powder
1½ tsp. salt
¼ tsp. pepper
½ T. sugar (or more to taste)
¼ c. barley (opt.)

1. Combine all ingredients in 5 or 6-quart cooking pan; bring
to a boil. 2. Reduce heat and boil gently, covered or uncovered, until potatoes and carrots are tender. **Note**: If frozen
peas are used, add just before serving (to keep their bright
green color).

VEGETARIAN VEGETABLE SOUP, QUICK

1 (46-oz.) can tomato juice (or about 6 c.), or part canned
   tomatoes
6 c. water or beef broth
2 med. onions, chopped
4 potatoes, peeled and diced
½ c. barley
1 to 2 c. celery, diced
1 tsp. parsley flakes
1 tsp. salt
⅛ tsp. pepper
1 (15 to 17-oz.) can whole kernel corn (or ½ can),
   undrained
1 (15 to 17-oz.) can peas, undrained
1 (15 to 17-oz.) can green beans, undrained
3 c. chopped cabbage (opt.)
1 T. sugar (opt.)

1. Combine all ingredients in soup pot and cook over medium heat until potatoes and barley are tender, stirring occasionally. **Note**: Makes a 6-quart pan almost full.

WEDDING SOUP

Adapted from Rita Stevenson.
Some of this soup can be frozen in containers.

1 to 2 lbs. chicken breasts
1 to 1½ lbs. beef roast (opt.)
6 quarts water
2 tsp. salt
¼ t. pepper
2 tsp. celery salt
4 stalks celery
4 carrots, peeled
1 large onion, whole
2 to 4 bunches escarole (depending on size)
1 c. fine, small pasta (opt.)
Meatballs (recipe follows)

1. Bring to a boil chicken breasts, beef roast, salt, pepper and
celery salt in 6 quarts of water, then add celery, carrots and
onion; cook 3 hours. 2. Remove meat; cool, then discard any
fat, skin or gristle; shred meat with a fork. 3. Remove celery and
carrots and finely slice; set aside. 4. Discard the onion and
strain broth through a sieve. With gravy ladle, remove any fat
from top of broth. 5. Wash escarole and cook in salted water
about 15 minutes at a rapid boil (until tender); drain and cool,
then chop escarole, discarding the large white stems if desired.
6. Return shredded meat, diced vegetables, meatballs, chopped
escarole and pasta to the pot of strained broth; bring to a boil,
then simmer for 15 minutes. If soup is too thick, add chicken
broth or beef broth, (canned or made from bouillon is okay).

Meatballs:
1½ lbs. meatloaf mix (mixture of ground beef and
   ground pork)
2 eggs
¾ c. fine dry breadcrumbs (plain)
1 t. salt
¼ t. pepper
1 T. dried parsley flakes
½ t. garlic salt.

1. Mix all ingredients together and roll into marble-sized meatballs (or a bit larger). 2. Lay on greased baking sheet (with
sides) and bake in preheated 350° oven 30 min.

WONTON SOUP

½ lb. (1 c.) ground beef or finely diced frying chicken,
   uncooked
⅛ tsp. garlic powder
2 T. fine dry bread crumbs
2 T. finely minced onion
½ tsp. salt
1 tsp. dried parsley flakes
2 tsp. soy sauce
1 egg
48 wonton skins
6 c. beef broth or chicken broth
Green onions, sliced

169

1. Combine meat, garlic powder, bread crumbs, onion, salt, parsley, soy sauce and egg, mixing well. **2.** In each wonton skin, put 1 level teaspoon of meat mixture. **3.** Dip fingers in water and wet edges of wonton skin. **4.** Fold wonton in half; seal edges together. Overlap edges and press to seal. **5.** Drop about 5 wontons into boiling broth and simmer for 5 minutes; repeat until desired number are cooked. **6.** To serve, pour boiling broth over wontons; add sliced green onions for garnish. **Note**: Wontons may be deep-fried until golden brown, if preferred. Also filled wontons may be frozen before cooking, if desired.

Chapter 16

Vegetables

SHELLY, SAM AND CAROLYN DEETS

1975

VEGETABLES

ASPARAGUS

8 to 16 oz. asparagus, after trimming off tough ends
⅛ tsp. salt
2 T. water

1. Cut off tough ends of asparagus, which may be several inches; cut tender asparagus into 1-inch lengths. 2. In microwave-safe dish, combine asparagus, salt and water; cover with glass lid or plastic wrap. 3. Microwave on HIGH for 6 minutes; let stand, covered, for 3 minutes. **Note**: If asparagus is very young and tender, it may take only 4 minutes on HIGH. (Or it may take longer, especially if cooking 16 oz.)

BAKED BEANS, CROCK-POT

4 to 5 cans (13½ to 16 oz. each) pork and beans
2 T. dried onion (or fresh)
¾ c. brown sugar
¾ c. ketchup
1 tsp. mustard, prepared or dry
½ tsp. liquid smoke (opt.)
Bacon Bits (opt.)

1. Cook in crock-pot on HIGH for 2 hours.

BAKED BEANS (Range-Top)

1 (16-oz.) can pork and beans
⅛ c. brown sugar, packed
⅛ c. ketchup (2 T.)
1 tsp. dehydrated onion or ⅛ c. finely chopped fresh onion (opt.)
1 tsp. prepared yellow mustard
1 tsp. bacon-flavor chips (opt.)
½ tsp. liquid smoke (opt.)

1. Heat in saucepan and bring to a boil; reduce heat and simmer 5 to 10 minutes.

BAKED BEANS, SWEET

From Pat Crocker and Violet Hilliard.
Very sweet, but people love them.

3 cans (16 oz. each) Great Northern beans
1 c. sugar
½ c. brown sugar
½ c. white corn syrup
3 T. ketchup
1 T. prepared mustard
6 to 8 slices bacon, diced (not cooked)

1. Mix all ingredients together in a baking dish or casserole and bake in preheated 350° oven, uncovered, for 2 ½ to 3 hours.

BEAN CASSEROLE

From Shirley Stevenson. This freezes well.

8 slices bacon, cut up
4 lg. onions, sliced and separated into rings
¾ c. packed brown sugar
1 tsp. dry mustard
1 tsp. salt (or less)
½ tsp. garlic powder
½ c. cider vinegar
1 (15 to 16-oz.) can lima beans, drained
1 (16-oz.) can green beans, drained
1 (16-oz.) can red kidney beans (do not drain)
1 (1 lb. 11-oz.) can New England baked beans (do not drain)

1. Fry bacon; remove bacon and cook onions in the drippings. Drain off fat. 2. Add sugar, seasonings and vinegar; cook slowly 20 minutes. 3. Add beans and fried bacon. 4. Bake, uncovered, in 3-quart casserole 1 hour in 350° oven.

BEETS, HARVARD

1 (16-oz.) can beets (or 1 pt. home-canned)
⅓ c. sugar
1½ T. cornstarch
⅛ tsp. salt
2 T. lemon juice (or 1 T. vinegar)
1 T. butter

1. Drain beets, reserving juice. If beets aren't diced, cut smaller or dice. 2. In medium saucepan, mix together sugar, cornstarch and salt. 3. Add 1 cup beet juice (add water to beet juice if necessary, or use all water); stir together. 4. Bring mixture to a boil; boil gently ½ minute, stirring. 5. Add lemon juice or vinegar, butter and diced beets; cover with lid. 6. Turn heat off and leave pan on burner for 20 to 30 minutes; before serving, bring just to boiling point. (If in a hurry, omit standing time and bring to a boil.)

BROCCOLI-CAULIFLOWER, WONDERFUL (Stove-Top)

Frozen vegetables may be substituted for fresh.
Double recipe for a big family.

½ bunch broccoli
½ head cauliflower
½ can condensed cream of chicken or cream of mushroom soup
1 c. (4 oz.) cubed Velveeta Light, American cheese or shredded Cheddar cheese
1 T. milk
1 T. butter

1. Cut up broccoli and cauliflower and cook in 1 to 2 inches boiling water with ¼ teaspoon salt, covered, until tender, about 10 minutes; drain off liquid. 2. In med.-small saucepan, combine remaining ingredients and cook over med.-low heat,

173

Vegetables

stirring constantly, until cheese melts. **3.** Put drained vegetables in serving dish; pour hot cheese sauce over top. **Note**: One whole bunch broccoli or one whole head of cauliflower may be used instead of mixing the vegetables (or one 16-ounce package frozen broccoli or cauliflower).

BROCCOLI CHEESE BAKE
(or CAULIFLOWER)

1 bunch (about 1½ lbs.) fresh broccoli (or part cauliflower)
    or 20 oz. frozen broccoli
½ c. water
¼ tsp. salt
2 T. butter
½ tsp. lemon juice
2 c. (8 oz.) cubed Velveeta Light cheese
¼ tsp. dry mustard
Cracker crumbs

1. Cook broccoli with the water and salt until tender; drain liquid off and place in greased baking dish. **2.** In medium saucepan, melt together butter, lemon juice and cheese, stirring constantly over medium heat. **3.** Add dry mustard and stir well; pour over drained broccoli. **4.** Sprinkle cracker crumbs over top. **5.** Bake in preheated 375° oven 25 to 30 minutes.

BROCCOLI, EASY

Serves 4 to 5 adults.

1 bunch (about 1½ lbs.) fresh broccoli
1 (11-oz.) can Campbell's cheddar cheese soup
½ c. milk
Pepper (opt.)

1. Divide broccoli into spears; cut off tough ends of stalks. Peel the stems and cut into 2-inch lengths. Rinse in cold water. **2.** Cook broccoli in 1 inch of water and ¼ teaspoon salt, covered, for 10 to 15 minutes after it comes to a boil. **3.** Drain broccoli and set aside. **4.** In small saucepan, mix soup and milk thoroughly with wire whip; heat until almost boiling, stirring often. **5.** Place broccoli in serving dish; pour cheese soup mixture over it. **6.** Sprinkle lightly with pepper.

BROCCOLI (Microwave)

Clean and trim 1 bunch broccoli (1 to 1½ pounds); cut into chunks. Peel the stems and cut into 2-inch lengths. Sprinkle with ¼ tsp. salt. Cook in microwave-safe dish with no liquid (2 to 3-quart casserole), covered with lid or vented plastic wrap. Microwave 6 to 8 minutes on HIGH (until fork-tender). Let stand 3 minutes, covered. **Note**: For ¾ lb. broccoli, add ⅛ tsp. salt and microwave on HIGH for 5 minutes.

BROCCOLI-MINUTE RICE CASSEROLE

1 (10¾-oz) can cream of chicken soup
½ c. milk
1 c. Minute Rice (uncooked)
2 c. cooked and drained chopped broccoli
1 small onion (⅛ to ¼ cup), chopped
1 T. butter
½ c. diced Velveeta Cheese

1. Combine the soup and milk until smooth; add remaining ingredients, stirring all together. **2.** Bake in preheated 350° oven for 35 minutes, covered.

BROCCOLI-RICE CASSEROLE

Adapted from Mary Trimble. Frozen broccoli may be thawed in microwave oven for a few minutes on 30% power (DEFROST).

1 med. onion, chopped
½ c. chopped celery or green bell pepper
¼ c. (½ stick) butter
1 (10¾-oz.) can cream of mushroom or cream of
    chicken soup (not diluted)
4 oz. (½ c.) Cheez Whiz or Velveeta
1 (10-oz.) box thawed chopped broccoli (or partially
    thawed)
1 to 1½ c. cooked rice
1 can sliced water chestnuts, drained (opt.)

1. Sauté onion and celery in butter until vegetables are transparent or soft. **2.** In 1½-quart round casserole, combine soup and Cheez Whiz, blending well. **3.** Add the onion mixture, broccoli, cooked rice and water chestnuts (if used), stirring together gently. **4.** Bake, uncovered, in preheated 350° oven 25 to 35 minutes. **Note**: Recipe may be doubled and baked in 13 x 9-inch glass baking dish.

BROCCOLI STIR-FRY

Makes 4 terrific servings.

1 bunch fresh broccoli (about 1½ lbs.)
2 to 3 onions, sliced
1 sm. carrot, thinly sliced diagonally
3 T. olive oil

Sauce:
2 T. soy sauce
1 tsp. cornstarch
1 T. honey
½ tsp. freshly grated ginger root (or ¼ tsp. ground
    ginger)
¼ tsp. hot pepper sauce

1. Wash broccoli and cut off broccoli florets; peel stems and slice ½-inch thick. **2.** In large skillet or wok, heat oil. **3.** Stir-fry broccoli, onions and carrot slices in hot oil 5 minutes, until crisp-tender. **4.** In small bowl, combine soy sauce and cornstarch. **5.** Add remaining ingredients; pour over broccoli. **6.** Cook until sauce thickens slightly.

BROCCOLI WITH SESAME SEEDS

1 lb. fresh broccoli, cut up
1 c. water
1 t. olive olil
1 T. sesame seeds
½ T. sugar
1 T. lemon juice
1 T. soy sauce
1 T. olive oil

1. In small sauce pan, bring broccoli and water to a boil; reduce heat, cover and simmer until crisp-tender. **2.** In small skillet, fry sesame seeds in 1 teaspoon olive oil until lightly browned; remove from heat. **3.** Add sugar, lemon juice, soy sauce and 1 tablespoon olive oil to the seeds. **4.** Drain broccoli, then add the sesame seed mixture.

CABBAGE BACON CASSEROLE

From Hazel Belle Deemer. Recipe may be cut in half.

1 head cabbage, cut up
½ lb. bacon, fried crisp and crumbled (or less)
1 c. Velveeta cheese, diced, or other diced cheese (4 oz.)
2 to 3 slices buttered bread, torn into crumbs

White Sauce:
4 T. (½ stick) butter
¼ c. all-purpose flour, level
½ tsp. salt
2 c. milk

1. Cook cabbage with 1 cup water (no salt) for 7 minutes after it comes to a boil, covered. **2.** Drain off liquid; add crumbled bacon and diced cheese. Set aside. **3.** To make white sauce, melt butter in saucepan over low heat. **4.** Blend in flour and salt; add milk all at once. **5.** Cook quickly, stirring constantly, until mixture thickens and bubbles. **6.** In casserole, combine cabbage and white sauce; sprinkle buttered bread crumbs over top. **7.** Bake in preheated 350° oven, uncovered, for 30 minutes, or until bubbly.

CABBAGE, BOILED

2½ qt. (10 c.) sliced cabbage
1 c. water
½ tsp. salt
2 T. butter (opt.)

1. Combine and cook, covered, until tender. **Microwave:** (For cabbage wedges) Add ¼ cup water to cabbage wedges in microwave-safe container; cover. For each pound of cabbage wedges, cook on HIGH 10 to 12 minutes. (¼ tsp. salt for 1 lb.)

CABBAGE CHEESE CASSEROLE, SCALLOPED

1 med. head cabbage (about 6 to 8 c.), cut up
1 T. butter
¼ c. milk
½ lb. Velveeta cheese
2 T. flour

1. Cut cabbage in quarters and discard core; chop into pieces. **2.** Boil cabbage in water with ½ teaspoon salt until tender; drain and put cabbage in 1½-quart round casserole, greased or sprayed. **3.** In small saucepan, combine butter, milk and cheese which has been chunked or cubed; on low heat, stir together until cheese is melted. **4.** Sprinkle flour over cabbage in casserole. **5.** Pour cheese sauce over cabbage and stir all together. **6.** Bake, covered, in preheated 325° oven for 45 minutes; remove cover and bake an additional 15 to 20 minutes.

CABBAGE, FRIED

Serves 2 to 3 adults (cabbage shrinks when cooked).

1 to 2 T. olive oil
6 c. cabbage, sliced about ¼ inch thick with sharp knife
¼ tsp. salt
⅛ tsp. pepper

1. In large skillet, heat oil. **2.** Add cabbage, salt and pepper; fry over medium to medium-high heat, turning and stirring occasionally, uncovered, for 5 minutes. **3.** Reduce heat to medium-low and fry 15 minutes longer, turning occasionally.

CABBAGE, RED (Sweet & Sour)

Also called "German Cabbage."

1 med. head red cabbage (about 1½ lbs.), cored and shredded or thinly sliced
1 c. water or beef broth
¾ tsp. salt
¼ c. sugar (or packed brown sugar)
1 T. butter or olive oil (opt.)
⅛ tsp. pepper
1 or 2 apples, peeled, cored and chopped (opt.)
1 onion, chopped (opt.)
4 slices bacon, fried crisp and crumbled (opt.)
2 to 4 T. vinegar (to taste)

1. Cook all ingredients, covered, until cabbage is tender, stirring occasionally. Makes 5 to 6 servings.

CABBAGE WEDGES

Cut 1 medium head of cabbage into 8 wedges, leaving a portion of core on each wedge. Cook in boiling water with 1 t. salt for 15 minutes; drain. Place wedges carefully in serving dish. If desired, pour White Sauce over them.

CARROTS, GLAZED

1 (16-oz.) can carrots, drained
2 T. butter
2 T. packed brown sugar
1 tsp. grated orange rind (opt.)

1. Melt butter in heavy skillet; add brown sugar and orange rind, if desired, and stir until mixture thickens. 2. Add drained carrots; stir until carrots are glazed and heated through.

CARROTS, SWEET 'N SOUR

Also called "Copper Coins" and "Gold Coins."
These are good served hot, warm or cool.
Even better the next day. From Berniece Cordial.

2 to 3 lbs. raw carrots or 2 to 3 cans (16 oz. each) sliced
   carrots, drained
1 onion, sliced and separated into rings (or diced or
   coarsely chopped)
½ to 1 green bell pepper, diced
1 (10¾-oz.) can tomato soup
1 c. sugar
¼ tsp. salt
⅛ tsp. pepper
1 tsp. dry mustard (or prepared mustard)
½ c. vinegar
½ c. olive oil

1. Peel and slice raw carrots (about 4 to 6 cups), and cook with water and 1 teaspoon salt until tender but not mushy; drain. 2. In 2½-quart serving dish or casserole, combine drained carrots, onion and green pepper; set aside. 3. In saucepan, combine tomato soup and remaining ingredients, mixing well with whisk; bring to a full boil, then pour immediately over carrots. **Note**: As carrots are eaten, more carrot slices may be added as long as liquid remains.

CAULIFLOWER

1 inch boiling water in pan
1 lb. cauliflower florets, approx.
1 T. lemon juice (opt.)
¼ tsp. salt

1. Combine all ingredients and bring to a boil. 2. Reduce heat and cover pan; boil gently 10 minutes (or until as tender as desired). 3. Cauliflower may be seasoned with butter and pepper, or drained and served with a cheese sauce. **Micro-**

wave: Core 1 medium head cauliflower (1 to 2 pounds) leaving head intact; place in microwave-safe bowl. Add 2 tablespoons water. Cook, covered, on HIGH 6 to 9 minutes or until tender-crisp; drain. Pat ½ cup shredded Cheddar cheese on top of cauliflower. Cook on HIGH 1 to 3 minutes, or until cheese is melted. To serve, cut into wedges. (Or, cut into florets before cooking.)

CHINESE CABBAGE STIR-FRY

Very good!

2 T. olive oil
1 onion, sliced
½ green bell pepper, cut into 2-inch strips
½ Chinese cabbage, sliced (about ½ lb.)
1 (5-oz.) can water chestnuts, drained (opt.)
½ carrot, shredded
Salt and pepper to taste

1. Heat oil in large skillet and stir-fry onion slices and green pepper. 2. Add remaining ingredients and stir-fry until crisp-tender. **Note**: Mushrooms, fresh or canned and drained, may be used in place of water chestnuts.

CORN, BAKED I

From Kay Patterson. Serves 4 to 6.
To double recipe, put in glass 13 x 9-inch dish.

2½ c. corn, drained (16-oz. bag of frozen corn, thawed, is
   good)
2 T. flour
1 T. sugar
½ to ¾ tsp. salt
½ tsp. baking powder
⅛ tsp. pepper
2 eggs, beaten
1½ c. milk
2 T. butter

1. Turn oven dial to 350°. 2. In 2-quart casserole, place drained corn. 3. In a cup, mix together flour, sugar, salt, baking powder and pepper. 4. In med.-small bowl, beat eggs; add milk and flour mixture, stirring together well. 5. Pour over corn; dot with butter. 6. Bake in preheated 350° oven 1 hour, uncovered (or until knife inserted in center comes out clean).

CORN, BAKED II

From Dorothy Bowser.

2 eggs, beaten
1 can (15- or 16-oz.) whole kernel corn (do not drain)
1 can (15- or 16-oz.) cream-style corn
1 box (8½-oz.) Jiffy Corn Muffin Mix
½ c. butter or regular Smart Balance Spread, softened

1 c. sour cream (can be low fat)
¼ c. sugar

1. Grease or spray a 9x13 baking dish; turn oven dial to 350°. **2.** In mixing bowl, beat eggs; add remaining ingredients and mix together well. **3.** Pour into prepared dish and bake, uncovered, for 35-40 minutes (until top is light golden brown).

CORN, CREOLE

1 can (15 to 16-oz.) whole kernel corn
¼ c. chopped green pepper
¼ c. chopped onion
2 T. butter
2 tsp. sugar
¼ tsp. salt
1 large fresh tomato, cut up

1. Cook all ingredients, except tomato, over medium heat until butter is melted. **2.** Cover and cook on low heat 10 minutes. **3.** Stir in tomato; cover and cook 5 minutes longer.

CORN, DRIED

Serves 3 to 4.

1 c. dried corn
2 c. cold water
½ tsp. salt
1 T. honey or sugar
Dash of pepper
1 T. butter
2 T. milk (opt.)

1. In saucepan, soak dried corn in cold water 2 hours; do not drain. **2.** Add salt, honey and pepper; cover and cook slowly until kernels are tender (40 to 60 minutes). **3.** Add butter and milk.

CORN ON THE COB (Boiled)

Husk corn and remove silk; plunge ears of corn into large kettle of rapidly boiling water. Cover with lid and cook over high heat 10 minutes. Remove from water; drain well and put on warm platter.

CORN ON THE COB (Microwave)

In Corning casserole or any microwave-safe oblong dish with lid, place ears of corn (which have been husked, silk removed and washed). Cover with lid. (Add no water.)

Cook on HIGH:
1 large ear – 4 minutes (3 minutes for medium ear)
2 ears – 5 to 6 minutes (depending on size)
3 ears – 7 to 8 minutes

4 ears – 9 to 11 minutes
5 ears – 9 to 11 minutes
6 ears – 12 minutes
7 ears – 13 minutes
8 ears – 14 minutes

In Plastic Wrap: Husk corn, remove silk, rinse and wrap each ear tightly in plastic wrap or waxed paper. Use time chart above.

EGGPLANT, BREADED & FRIED

Serves 4.

1 eggplant (about 1 lb.), cut into ¼-inch slices
⅓ c. all-purpose flour
⅓ c. cornmeal
½ tsp. salt (or less)
⅛ tsp. pepper
¼ c. grated Parmesan cheese
1 egg, beaten with 2 T. water
Butter or olive oil

1. Combine flour, cornmeal, salt and pepper; stir in Parmesan cheese. **2.** Roll eggplant slices in flour mixture. **3.** Dip slices in egg-water mixture, then roll again in breading. **4.** Pan-fry in butter over medium heat, turning only once (about 5 minutes per side).

EGGPLANT PARMESAN

Makes 8 servings.

1 lg. eggplant (about 1½ lbs.), peeled
3 T. olive oil, divided
1 c. chopped onion
3 garlic cloves, minced
1 (28-oz.) can crushed tomatoes (3½ c.)
1 tsp. dried basil
1 tsp. dried oregano
¼ tsp. salt
¼ tsp. pepper
3 T. grated Parmesan cheese
1 c. shredded low-fat Mozzarella cheese

1. Cover broiler pan with foil; cut eggplant into ½-inch slices and place on broiler pan. **2.** Brush both sides of slices with 2 tablespoons olive oil. **3.** Broil 4-5 inches from heat until medium brown, turning once; set aside. **4.** In heavy saucepan, heat remaining 1 tablespoon oil; add onion and cook until onion just begins to brown. **5.** Add garlic and cook ½ minute more. **6.** Stir in tomatoes and bring to simmer; add basil, oregano, salt and pepper. **7.** Preheat oven to 400°. **8.** Spoon a thin layer of tomato sauce over bottom of 11 x 7-inch baking dish; cover with single layer of eggplant slices. **9.** Sprinkle with half the Parmesan cheese; cover with remaining sauce. **10.** Add remaining eggplant and Parmesan cheese; sprinkle mozzarella over top. **11.** Bake in preheated 400° oven 20 minutes.

EGGPLANT PATTIES

Makes 4 fried patties, but recipe may be doubled.

½ med. eggplant, peeled and cubed
½ c. cracker crumbs (or 12 soda crackers, 2 x 2 inches
    each, crushed)
1 T. chopped onion
1 T. chopped green pepper or minced fresh parsley
¼ tsp. salt
⅛ tsp. garlic powder
⅛ tsp. pepper
1 egg
½ c. shredded sharp Cheddar or American cheese (opt.)
1½ T. olive oil

1. In covered saucepan, cook eggplant until tender in boiling water (about 5 to 8 minutes after it comes to a boil). 2. Drain well and mash; drain again. 3. Stir in all remaining ingredients, except oil. 4. Shape into 4 patties and fry in hot oil about 3 minutes on each side, or until golden brown.

ENDIVE OR DANDELION GREENS, WILTED

A Pennsylvania Dutch-German dish, delicious served over boiled or mashed potatoes.

4 to 8 slices bacon, fried crisp
1 T. bacon drippings
1 T. olive oil
2 T. butter
⅓ c. sugar
3 T. flour, packed level
2 c. cold tap water
¾ tsp. salt
⅛ tsp. pepper
2 T. vinegar
4 to 6 c. endive or dandelion greens, washed and
    drained (1 colanderful, or about ½ to 1 lb.)

1. Drain bacon on paper towel; set aside. 2. In large skillet, combine measured bacon drippings, oil, butter, sugar and flour; stir well, letting butter melt. 3. Add cold water all at once, and salt, pepper and vinegar. 4. On medium-high heat, cook, stirring frequently, until sauce comes to a full boil. 5. Chop greens or slice with sharp knife; add to sauce. Cook 2 to 3 minutes, removing skillet from heat while greens are still bright green in color (unless further cooking is desired). 6. Crumble bacon over top when serving (or crumble and stir into sauce).

GREEN BEAN BAKE, CLASSIC

Makes 6 servings.

1 (10¾-oz.) can cream of mushroom soup
½ to ¾ c. milk

⅛ tsp. pepper
4 c. cooked cut green beans, drained
1 (2.8-oz.) can French-fried onions, divided (1⅓ c.)*

1. Turn oven dial to 350°. 2. In 1½-quart casserole, combine soup, milk and pepper. 3. Stir in green beans and ½ can onions. 4. Bake, uncovered, in preheated 350° oven 25 to 30 minutes, or until heated. 5. Top with remaining onions; bake, uncovered, until golden, 5 to 10 minutes. **Beans to Use:** 1 quart home-canned green beans or 1½ pounds fresh green beans, or 2 cans (16 ounces each) or 1 bag (16 to 20 ounces) frozen green beans, or 2 packages (9 ounces each) frozen green beans, thawed and drained. *__Substitution:__ Use 98% fat-free Kielbasa, sliced.

GREEN BEANS, BAKED, NELL'S

*A delicious way to serve green beans
(or yellow wax beans).*

2 cans (16 oz. each) or 1 qt. canned green beans, drained
1 (4-oz.) can mushroom stems and pieces, drained (opt.)
½ can cream of mushroom soup or Cheddar cheese soup
⅓ c. milk
⅛ tsp. salt
⅛ tsp. pepper
1 tsp. minced onion or ⅛ tsp. onion powder (opt.)
¼ c. shredded cheese, any kind (opt.)
1 slice bread, buttered (cut into cubes)

1. Put drained green beans and mushroom pieces in microwave-safe casserole. 2. In med.-small bowl, blend together soup, milk, salt, pepper, onion and cheese; pour over green beans. 3. Place casserole in microwave oven, covered, and cook on REHEAT (80% power) 10 minutes, until cheese is melted and beans are bubbly. 4. Remove from microwave oven and sprinkle with buttered bread crumbs. 5. Place in conventional oven, preheated to 450° (uncovered); bake 10 minutes or until bread is golden brown. **Note**: Double recipe for 9 to 10 adults.

GREEN BEANS, MAMA'S FAMOUS

From Shirley Kaufman.

1 qt. canned green beans (3½ to 4 c.), drained (reserve
    liquid)
¾ c. green bean liquid
2 T. sugar
1½ tsp. vinegar, or more to taste (opt.)
½ tsp. basil
⅛ to ¼ lb. bacon, fried crisp (or some Baco Bits)
1 T. bacon fat (or butter)

1. Combine all ingredients and cook together. (Can be cooked either short or long time.)

GREEN BEANS, QUICK

From Jean Alexander.

2 (16-oz.) cans or 1 qt. canned green beans
½ can cream of mushroom soup, undiluted
¼ c. green bean liquid
4 oz. (1 c.) diced or shredded cheese (or less)

1. Drain beans, reserving ¼ cup liquid. 2. Combine soup and liquid in saucepan; add beans and heat thoroughly. 3. At almost serving time, add cheese; turn heat off and let cheese melt.

LIMA BEANS, BARBECUED BAKE

For less-sweet beans, use only ½ cup brown sugar.

1 lb. dry lima beans (lg. or baby)
8 c. cold water
1½ tsp. salt
1 c. ketchup
¾ c. packed brown sugar
½ c. chopped onion
1 tsp. dry mustard
½ tsp. Liquid Smoke (opt.)
3 to 4 strips bacon, fried crisp (opt.)

1. Soak beans in 8 cups cold water overnight; drain and rinse. Or, use alternate method: In large pan, combine beans and 8 cups cold water. Bring to boiling; reduce heat and simmer 2 minutes. Remove from heat; cover and let stand 1 hour. Drain and rinse. 2. To cook, combine beans with 8 cups fresh cold water and the salt; bring to boiling, then reduce heat and simmer, covered, until beans are tender, stirring occasionally. (About 1 to 1¼ hours for large limas, or 45 to 60 minutes for baby limas.) 3. Drain beans, reserving 1 cup liquid. 4. Combine beans, 1 cup bean liquid and remaining ingredients; pour into a small roaster or 2½ to 3-quart casserole. 5. Cover with lid and bake 1 to 2 hours in 325° oven (or bake at 350° for 45 minutes); then uncover and bake 10 min. longer. Alternate Method for Bacon: Omit bacon during baking period. The last 10 minutes place crisp-fried bacon on top beans; bake, uncovered, in 350° oven.

MUSHROOMS, SAUTÉED

Recipe may be cut in half. Delicious!

4 to 6 T. butter or olive oil
1 tsp. lemon juice or vinegar
¼ tsp. salt
⅛ tsp. pepper
1 lb. fresh mushrooms, cleaned and sliced

1. Melt butter in large skillet. 2. Add remaining ingredients and sauté five minutes, stirring occasionally. Makes 4 servings.

MUSHROOMS, STIR-FRIED

Recipe may be cut in half. Delicious!
Makes 4 to 6 servings.

¼ c. olive oil
1 lb. fresh mushrooms, whole or sliced
1 T. soy sauce
¼ tsp. sugar
½ c. water
2 tsp. cornstarch
2 tsp. cold water

1. In 10-inch skillet over medium-high heat, in hot oil, cook mushrooms, soy sauce, sugar and ½ cup water, stirring quickly and constantly, until well coated. 2. Reduce heat to medium and continue to stir-fry 5 to 6 minutes (until tender). 3. In a cup, stir cornstarch and 2 teaspoons cold water until smooth; stir into mushroom mixture. 4. Cook, stirring, until mixture thickens.

OKRA, FRIED

Okra should be less than 4 inches long.

½ lb. fresh okra
¼ c. fine dry bread crumbs or yellow or white cornmeal
    or a mixture of crumbs and cornmeal
¼ tsp. onion salt or onion powder
⅛ tsp. pepper
¼ c. olive oil

1. Wash okra; remove ends and cut into ½-inch slices. 2. In bowl, combine crumbs, onion salt and pepper; add okra and stir together to coat okra. 3. Heat oil in skillet; add okra mixture and cook and stir until golden brown. Serves 2.

ONION RINGS, FRENCH FRIED

Serves 4 to 6.

1 egg
1 c. milk
1 T. olive oil
1 c. flour
1 tsp. baking powder
¼ tsp. salt
3 onions
Olive oil for frying

1. Combine egg, milk and 1 tablespoon oil in medium bowl. 2. Add flour, baking powder and salt; beat until smooth. 3. Peel and slice onions in ¼ to ⅓-inch thick slices; separate into rings. 4. Pour about 1½ inches of oil in a heavy kettle or electric skillet; heat to 365° or 370° on a deep-fry thermometer (or electric skillet). 5. Dip rings, a few at a time, in batter; fry in hot oil until golden brown on both sides. 6. Drain on paper towels.

Vegetables

ONIONS, FRIED

4 to 6 c. sliced onion
3 to 4 T. butter or regular Smart Balance spread

1. In skillet, melt butter. 2. Add onions, stirring often; fry until tender (or tender-crisp).

PARSNIPS, FRIED

Peel parsnips (if large, slice lengthwise). Boil in lightly salted water until tender. Drain and cool. Melt some butter (or part oil) in skillet; dip parsnips in flour and fry until golden brown on both sides.

PEAS, CREAMED

1 T. flour, level
¼ t. salt
⅔ c. milk
1 (10-oz.) pkg. frozen peas (or 2 c. fresh peas)

1. Mix flour, salt and milk together well in a saucepan; add peas and bring to a boil. 2. Reduce heat and simmer until peas are tender. Makes 4 servings.

POTATO BAKE, ITALIAN

No need to peel the potatoes unless you want to.

3 T. olive oil
5 to 8 potatoes, scrubbed, then sliced, diced or cut into chunks (6 c.)
1 pkg. dry onion soup mix (or 1 env. Good Seasons Italian salad dressing mix)

1. Turn oven dial to 350°. 2. Put oil in long 13 x 9-inch baking dish or casserole in oven. 3. Add potatoes and remaining ingredients, stirring all together. 4. Cover with lid or foil and bake 1 hour in 350° oven. Uncover last 10 minutes of baking time. Stir before serving. Note: If using salad dressing mix, 1 onion, sliced, may be placed over potatoes.

POTATO CASSEROLE AU GRATIN I

Adapted from Bonnie Swarts and Kathleen Churchill. Especially good made with Longhorn cheese.

½ c. butter or reg. Smart Balance spread
32-oz. bag frozen hash brown potatoes, partially thawed (6 c.)
2 c. (8 oz.) shredded Longhorn, Colby, American or Monterey Jack cheese
⅓ c. finely chopped onion or sliced green onions
1 (10¾-oz.) can cream of chicken soup, undiluted
1 to 2 c. dairy sour cream or sour cream alternative
½ tsp. salt
¼ tsp. pepper

Topping: (can be omitted)
4 T. (½ stick) butter, melted (opt.)
Bread crumbs, soda crackers or Ritz crackers, crushed

1. In large saucepan, melt butter; remove from heat. 2. Add potatoes, cheese, onion, soup, sour cream, salt and pepper; stir together well. 3. Pour into sprayed 13 x 9 x 2-inch baking dish. 4. Combine topping ingredients and sprinkle over potatoes. 5. Bake in preheated 350° oven 1 hour, uncovered, until golden and bubbly.

POTATO CASSEROLE AU GRATIN II

No frozen hash browns or soup in this recipe.
To make half this recipe, put in 8 x 8-inch pan.

6 c. cooked and peeled potatoes, shredded coarsely or sliced. (Salt the potatoes when cooking.)
¼ c. chopped onion or green onions
¼ c. butter, melted
8 oz. (2 c.) shredded cheddar cheese, sharp or regular, or longhorn or Colby cheese
1 c. sour cream (can be the fat-free kind if desired)
1 tsp. salt
¼ tsp. pepper
2 T. butter for top
Paprika

1. Mix ingredients (except the last two) together and spoon into a greased or sprayed 13 x 9 x 2-inch baking dish or pan. 2. Dot with 2 T. butter and sprinkle with paprika. This may be refrigerated 3 to 4 hours (or overnight, covered); or may be baked immediately, uncovered, in a preheated 350° oven 40 minutes (50 to 60 minutes if it was refrigerated), or until bubbly and golden brown. Note: If desired, 2 c. (before crushing) crushed potato chips or corn flakes may be sprinkled over top before baking. Serves 6 to 9.

POTATO CHEESE CASSEROLE

From Betty Marcin.

3 T. butter
3 T. flour
½ tsp. salt
⅛ tsp. pepper
1½ c. milk
1 c. shredded or diced yellow cheese
3 c. boiled potatoes, peeled and diced
1 T. chopped onion
3 T. diced canned pimiento (opt.)
Paprika

1. Turn oven dial to 350°. 2. In saucepan, melt butter; add flour, salt and pepper, stirring well. 3. Add milk all at once; cook, stirring, until it thickens and bubbles. 4. Remove from heat and add cheese; stir until cheese is nearly all melted. 5.

Place potatoes, pimiento and onion in greased or sprayed 1½-quart casserole. **6.** Pour cheese mixture over potatoes and stir together; sprinkle paprika over top. **7.** Bake in preheated 350° oven 30 minutes or until bubbly and golden brown. **Range-Top Method:** Potatoes and onion can be added to the cheese mixture in saucepan; heat together but <u>do not let boil</u>. Omit baking.

POTATO, CHEESE & PIMIENTO BAKE

Also called 'Pittsburgh Potatoes.' This dish can be made the night before and baked next day.

4 c. peeled, diced potatoes
1 sm. onion, finely chopped
½ tsp. salt
2 T. butter
2 T. flour, packed level
2 c. milk
1 tsp. salt
6 to 8 oz. (1½ to 2 c.) mild Cheddar cheese, cubed (or other mild cheese) or Velveeta
½ can drained pimientos, diced
4 to 6 slices bread, cubed
3 to 4 T. butter

1. Cover potatoes, onion and ½ teaspoon salt with boiling water; boil 5 minutes, then drain. **2.** Make white sauce by melting first butter in saucepan; add flour, stirring well. **3.** Add milk and 1 teaspoon salt; cook until thick and bubbly, stirring constantly. Turn heat off. **4.** Add cheese and stir until melted; remove from burner and add diced pimiento. **5.** Put potatoes in greased or sprayed 13 x 9 x 2-inch baking pan; pour white sauce over potatoes. **6.** In skillet, brown cubed bread in second butter; sprinkle bread cubes over top potatoes. **7.** Bake in preheated 350° oven 35 minutes, or until bubbly hot. (If potatoes have been in refrigerator overnight, baking time will be longer.)

POTATO CHIPS, FAT-FREE, MICROWAVE

Delicious!

12 unpeeled potato slices (sliced very thin)
Salt

1. On microwave cooking rack, arrange 12 potato slices in a circle; sprinkle lightly with salt. **2.** Cook on HIGH 5½ to 6½ minutes, until golden brown. **3.** Let stand 1 minute. **Note:** If a microwave-cooking rack is not available, lightly spray a microwave-safe bacon rack with non-stick vegetable spray and cook potato chips on it.

POTATO LATKES (Hash Brown Patties)

Sometimes called potato pancakes; cut recipe in half for 2 people.

3 c. shredded raw potatoes
½ tsp. lemon juice
2 T. finely chopped onion
1 egg (or 2 egg whites)
1 T. flour
1 tsp. salt
⅛ tsp. pepper
2 tsp. dried parsley flakes (or 2 T. fresh parsley, minced)
3 T. olive oil or butter

1. Drain shredded potatoes in colander or sieve and add lemon juice; squeeze between paper towels to remove excess moisture. **2.** In medium bowl, beat egg with fork. **3.** Add potatoes, onion, flour, salt, pepper and parsley flakes; mix well. **4.** In large skillet, heat oil to sizzling. **5.** Drop potato mixture, ¼ cupful for each patty, into hot oil; flatten somewhat with back of measuring cup. **6.** Fry over medium-high heat (or 375° in electric skillet) until golden brown, about 4 to 5 minutes on each side. **7.** Drain on paper towel. Keep warm in oven at lowest setting. Makes 8 potato patties. **Note:** Hot Latkes are traditionally served with applesauce.

POTATOES, BACON & CHEESE CASSEROLE

3 to 3½ c. boiled potatoes, peeled and cubed
6 slices bacon, fried
1 c. yellow cheese, cubed or 8 slices cheese, cut up
½ c. salad dressing or mayonnaise
1½ c. milk
⅛ tsp. pepper

1. Turn oven dial to 375°. **2.** Combine potatoes, bacon, cheese and salad dressing. **3.** Pour into greased or sprayed 2-quart casserole or baking dish. **4.** Pour milk over mixture; sprinkle with pepper. **5.** Bake, uncovered, in preheated 375° oven about 30 minutes, or until hot and bubbly. **Note:** If in a hurry, heat milk before adding to casserole.

POTATOES, BAKED

1. Pierce skin of each scrubbed potato in several places with tines of a fork. **2.** Place directly on oven rack or on cookie sheet. (Do not wrap in foil.) **3.** Bake at 400° for 45 to 60 minutes, depending on size. (Or, adjust time with heat anywhere from 325° to 450°.) **4.** Test for doneness with a fork. **Note:** Larger potatoes will take longer.

POTATOES, BAKED (Jo-Jo Lites)

No shortening or oil; serves 3 to 4 people.

5 to 6 med. potatoes, unpeeled
1 egg white, slightly beaten
Salt
Pepper
Paprika

Optional Ingredients:
Oregano
Garlic powder
Onion powder
Parmesan cheese, grated

1. Turn oven dial to 450°. 2. Scrub potatoes and cut into quarters lengthwise. 3. Line a cookie sheet with foil, then grease or spray the foil. 4. Dip each potato wedge in slightly beaten egg white. 5. Place wedges, skin side down, on foil in a single layer. 6. Sprinkle lightly with salt, pepper, paprika and any or all of the optional ingredients. 7. Bake, uncovered, in preheated 450° oven 20 to 30 minutes, or until tender and golden brown. **Slower Heat:** Bake 1 hour (uncovered) in 350° oven, or until tender.

POTATOES, BAKED (Microwave)

Scrub potatoes and pat dry; prick several times with a fork. Arrange in microwave oven on paper towels at least 1 inch apart. (If baking more than 2, arrange in a circle.) Microwave on HIGH until tender. Let potatoes stand 5 minutes. To keep hot for up to 30 minutes, wrap in foil after baking. These times are approximate and vary with size of potatoes:

1 potato – 3 to 6 minutes
2 potatoes – 5 to 8 minutes
3 potatoes – 7 to 10 minutes
4 potatoes – 11 to 14 minutes
6 potatoes – 16 to 18 minutes

POTATOES, BAKED (Oven-Fried Chips)

These potatoes bake in 15 to 20 minutes!
Allow about 1 potato per person.

2 med.-size potatoes, scrubbed
1 T. olive oil
1 T. melted butter
Salt
Pepper
Paprika
Garlic powder or onion powder
Grated Parmesan cheese (opt.)

1. Turn oven to 425°. 2. Cut scrubbed potatoes into ⅛-inch slices; place on lightly sprayed large cookie sheet or 15 x 10-inch jellyroll pan in a single layer. 3. Combine oil and butter; brush lightly over potatoes. 4. Sprinkle very lightly with salt,

pepper, paprika and garlic or onion powder. 5. Bake, uncovered, in preheated 425° oven for 15 to 20 minutes, or until potatoes are tender and golden. 6. If desired, sprinkle potatoes with Parmesan cheese after removing from oven; serve immediately.

POTATOES, BAKED TWICE I (Stuffed)

From Mrs. Helen Kuhn.

6 medium potatoes
½ c. sour cream
3 T. butter or reg. Smart Balance Spread
½ t. salt and ⅛ t. pepper
2 T. finely chopped onion
1 c. shredded Cheddar cheese, divided
3 T. crumbled, cooked bacon (opt.)
1½ c. cooked, chopped broccoli
Paprika

1. Bake the potatoes until tender. 2. Cut slice from top of each one; scoop out insides and mash. 3. Add sour cream, butter, salt, pepper, onion, ¾ c. cheese and bacon, mixing together; gently stir in broccoli last of all. 4. Refill potato shells and top with remaining cheese; sprinkle with paprika. 5. Place potatoes on greased baking sheet and bake at 425° for 20 to 25 minutes or until heated through.

POTATOES, BAKED TWICE II (Stuffed)

From Barb Johnson.

4 med.-large baking potatoes, scrubbed
½ c. butter
1 c. shredded low-fat Cheddar cheese, divided
1 c. shredded low-fat Mozzarella cheese, divided
¼ c. chopped chives
¼ tsp. paprika
Additional paprika

1. Prick scrubbed potatoes with fork. Microwave on HIGH 12 to 14 minutes or until fork-tender. Wrap in foil and let stand 5 to 10 minutes. (Or bake potatoes in conventional oven.) 2. Meanwhile combine butter, ¾ cup Cheddar cheese and ¾ cup Mozzarella cheese. 3. Cut potatoes in half lengthwise; scoop out insides, leaving ¼-inch shell. 4. Using an electric mixer, beat potato insides and butter-cheese mixture until well blended. 5. Spoon mixture into potato shells. 6. Combine remaining ¼ cup of each of the cheeses with chives and ¼ teaspoon paprika; divide over top stuffed potatoes. 7. Microwave on HIGH 3 to 4 minutes, or until cheese is melted and potatoes are heated through. 8. Sprinkle with additional paprika and serve.

POTATOES, BOILED (Microwave)

6 med. potatoes, peeled and cut in half lengthwise (3½ to 4 c.)
¼ c. water
½ tsp. salt

1. Put all ingredients in 2-quart covered microwave-safe casserole. 2. Microwave on HIGH 6 minutes, then stir. 3. Microwave 6 to 10 minutes longer; let stand, covered, 3 to 5 minutes.

POTATOES, BOILED (Crock-Pot)

From Betty Jo Cochran.

1. Cut peeled potatoes in half or quarters, according to size, and put in crock-pot; cover potatoes with water. 2. Add 2 **level** tsp. salt for 6 cups of potatoes. 3. Turn crock-pot on HIGH, cover with lid, and cook for 3 or 4 hours. 4. On Sunday morning they can cook while you are at church. 5. Drain water off and mash, if desired.

POTATOES, BOSTON (Microwave)

Adapted from Adele Crognale. Serves 4.

3½ to 4 c. potatoes (1½ lbs.), cut into 1½-inch chunks
2 med. onions, each cut into 8 wedges
1 to 2 green or red bell peppers, cut into 1½-inch chunks (opt.)
2 to 3 garlic cloves, minced (opt.)
Parsley flakes, fresh cut chives or ½ tsp. dried rosemary, oregano or Italian seasoning
¾ tsp. salt
¼ tsp. pepper
⅛ tsp. crushed red pepper (opt.)
2 T. olive oil (or butter)

1. Potatoes may be scrubbed or peeled; combine all ingredients in microwave-safe bowl or casserole. 2. Toss and stir together to coat vegetables with oil. 3. Cook, covered, in microwave on HIGH 15 to 18 minutes, or until tender, stirring once or twice during cooking. 4. Let stand, covered, 3 to 5 minutes.

POTATOES, BUTTERED (Microwave)

6 med. potatoes (peeled or unpeeled), sliced ¼ inch thick or cut into chunks
½ tsp. salt
2 T. butter
Pepper

1. Put potatoes in 2-quart microwave-safe casserole; sprinkle with salt and dot with butter. 2. Microwave, covered, on HIGH 10 minutes, then stir. 3. Microwave 5 to 6 minutes longer <u>or until tender</u>. 4. Let stand 5 minutes. Stir before serving and sprinkle with pepper.

POTATOES, CREAMED, WITH PARSLEY

Serves 4 to 5 people.

4 c. potatoes, peeled and cut in quarters
1 c. water
1¼ tsp. salt
2 T. butter
3 T. flour, level
½ tsp. salt
¼ tsp. pepper
2 c. milk
¼ c. chopped fresh parsley (or more)

1. Cook potatoes with water and 1¼ teaspoon salt until tender; drain and set aside. 2. Melt butter in saucepan; stir in flour. 3. Add ½ teaspoon salt, the pepper and milk; stir well. 4. Bring to a boil, stirring constantly; reduce heat and simmer gently 3 minutes. 5. Add drained potatoes and heat together 2 or 3 minutes; just before pouring into serving dish, stir in fresh parsley.

POTATOES, FRIED, FROM BOILED POTATOES

Use any size potatoes for this.

4 c. small whole potatoes, scrubbed (or larger potatoes, cut up)
1 c. water
1 to 1½ tsp. salt
3 T. olive oil or butter
Pepper

1. In covered pan, boil potatoes with water and salt until tender; drain. (If desired, remove skins.) 2. Cut each potato in quarters or smaller. 3. Heat oil or butter in large skillet. When hot, add potatoes and sprinkle with pepper. 4. Fry on medium-high heat until golden brown, turning potatoes two or three times.

POTATOES, HOME FRIES (HASH BROWNS) I

Makes enough for two people.

1 to 2 T. olive oil
2 to 2⅓ c. (firmly pressed) shredded raw potatoes or sliced boiled potatoes
1 to 2 T. chopped onion or ¼ tsp. onion powder (opt.)
⅓ tsp. salt
Pepper and paprika

1. Heat oil in medium to large skillet. 2. (Potatoes may be chopped in food processor.) Add potatoes, onion and seasonings to skillet. (Paprika helps in browning potatoes.) 3. Fry on medium heat, turning potatoes over when brown; brown on both sides. (Or turn several times.) **Note**: Double recipe for 3 adults; triple recipe for 4 adults. When making recipe larger be sure to use large 12-inch skillet.

POTATOES, HOME FRIES (HASH BROWNS) II

Serves 2 to 3 adults. Double recipe for 5.

3 T. olive oil
3 c. peeled and shredded raw potatoes (or chopped fine in food processor)
1 sm. onion, chopped (about ¼ c.), opt.
⅓ to ½ tsp. salt
Pepper and paprika

1. Heat oil in large 12-inch skillet until hot, but not smoking. 2. Add potatoes, onion and seasonings. 3. Put lid on skillet and brown potatoes on one side; turn potatoes over. 4. Cook, uncovered, turning several times, frying on medium heat until potatoes are tender. **Note**: For one person, cut recipe in half and use 10-inch skillet.

POTATOES, HOME FRIES (HASH BROWNS) III

Serves 3 adults.

2 T. olive oil
4½ c. potatoes, peeled and thinly sliced
½ tsp. salt
1 med. onion, chopped or thin sliced (opt.)
1 T. butter
Pepper

1. Heat oil in 11 or 12-inch skillet until hot, but not smoking. 2. Add potatoes; sprinkle salt over them. 3. Lay onion over top. 4. Dot with butter and sprinkle with pepper. 5. Cover with tight lid; cook on low heat 15 minutes. 6. Turn potatoes and cook, **uncovered**, about 10 minutes longer, increasing heat if needed. **Note**: To double, use two large skillets; do not make this recipe any larger in the same skillet.

POTATOES, MASHED

6 c. potatoes, peeled and cut into quarters
3 c. water
2 tsp. salt, level
¾ to 1 c. milk
1 T. butter (opt.)

1. In pan, bring potatoes, water and salt to a boil; lower heat and cover pan, boiling potatoes about 20 minutes, or until tender. (Make sure water continues to boil gently.) Or cook in pressure cooker with 1½ cups water 7 to 8 minutes, at 15 pounds pressure, following manufacturer's directions. 2. Drain potatoes and mash. 3. Add milk (heated milk is best) and butter; whip until fluffy.

Smaller Recipe I:
5 c. potatoes, peeled and cut into quarters
2½ c. water
1¾ tsp. salt, level
⅔ c. milk

2 tsp. butter (opt.)

Smaller Recipe II:
4 c. potatoes, peeled and cut into quarters
2 c. water
1½ tsp. salt, level
½ to ¾ c. milk
½ T. butter (opt.)

Mashed Potato Statistics: Cook at least 1 cup cut-up raw potatoes for each adult; cook ½ cup for each small child when making mashed potatoes. Mashed potatoes may be prepared in advance and reheated in microwave oven. Heat 3 minutes on HIGH, stirring once during heating. OR, put in crock-pot on LOW after mashing. Cover with lid.

Mashed Potatoes, New Method: I love this way, and use this method all the time now. Cook potatoes, water and salt as instructed above. When potatoes are tender, drain them, saving some of the hot potato liquid. Mash the potatoes a little, then add dry powdered milk and hot potato liquid and mash until fluffy. For 6 c. potatoes, I use 2 T. dry powdered milk and 1/3 cup hot potato liquid or as much as needed. For 5 cups and 4 cups of potatoes, use lesser amounts (as much hot potato liquid as is needed). This makes fluffy potatoes.

POTATOES, MASHED, CREAMY BAKE

This recipe revives leftover mashed potatoes.

1 egg
3 to 4 c. leftover mashed potatoes (or make up instant mashed potatoes for 8 servings, omitting butter)
3 to 4 oz. cream cheese, softened
¼ c. sour cream or sour cream substitute (opt.)
1 to 2 tsp. instant minced onion (or 1 to 1½ T. finely chopped fresh onion)
¼ tsp. salt
1 T. butter
Paprika

1. In mixer bowl, beat the egg. 2. Add potatoes and whip together. 3. Add cream cheese, sour cream, onion and salt; beat on high speed of electric mixer until well mixed. 4. Put potato mixture in 1½-quart greased or sprayed casserole (or 8 x 8-inch baking dish). 5. Dot with butter and sprinkle lightly with paprika. 6. Bake in preheated 350° oven for 45 minutes (or 400° for 30 minutes), uncovered.

POTATOES, MASHED (Make-Ahead)

Serves 12.

5 lbs. potatoes, peeled and quartered
6 to 8 oz. cream cheese
1 c. sour cream (light or regular)
1 egg (or 2 egg whites)
2 tsp. salt, level
1 to 1½ tsp. onion powder or instant minced onion or chopped chives

¼ tsp. pepper (opt.)
2 T. butter
Paprika

1. Cook potatoes in boiling water until tender; drain. 2. Mash until there are no lumps. 3. Add all remaining ingredients except butter and paprika; beat until smooth consistency. 4. If preparing ahead, cover and refrigerate (for several days, if desired). 5. To use, place in buttered or sprayed 13 x 9-inch baking dish (or casserole). If only using part of it, place in smaller casserole. 6. Dot with butter; sprinkle lightly with paprika. 7. Bake in preheated 350° oven for 40 to 45 minutes or until heated through. (If it has been refrigerated, bake 60 minutes for whole amount, or else bring to room temperature before baking.)

POTATOES, MASHED POTATO PATTIES, FRIED

2 c. leftover mashed potatoes
¼ c. milk
3 T. fine dry bread crumbs
2 T. (⅛ c.) finely chopped onion
½ egg (⅛ c. scant), slightly beaten
¼ t. salt
⅛ t. pepper
1/16 t. garlic powder

1. Mix all ingredients together; shape into six patties. 2. Fry on a skillet that has been greased with oil for 4 to 5 minutes on each side, or until brown. **Note:** to keep these warm, put in a 250° oven.

POTATOES, NEW, WITH NEW PEAS

12 sm. new potatoes or about 3 c.
2 to 3 c. freshly shelled peas
1½ c. milk or half & half
Salt and pepper
2 T. flour
2 T. butter

1. Scrape skin off new potatoes. (If not real small, cut up.) 2. Cook separately the potatoes and the peas, with 1 cup water and ½ teaspoon salt in each pan, until tender. 3. Drain off any remaining liquid from each vegetable. 4. Combine vegetables in a 2 or 3-quart pan. 5. Pour milk over vegetables and bring to boiling point; add ¼ teaspoon salt and ¼ teaspoon pepper. 6. In small bowl, stir together flour and butter until blended; add to hot vegetables, stirring gently. 7. Cook until mixture comes to a boil again; remove from burner. **Note:** Peas and potatoes which are not new may also be used in this recipe. A 10-ounce package frozen peas may be used instead of fresh peas, cooked with ¼ teaspoon salt.

POTATOES, OVEN-ROASTED WEDGES

Serves 5 to 6; potatoes are done in 30 minutes.

2 lbs. unpeeled potatoes (or 4 large or 6 medium)
2 T. olive oil
2 garlic cloves, minced
1 med. onion, chopped (opt.)
1 tsp. dried rosemary or 1 T. chopped fresh rosemary
½ tsp. salt
¼ tsp. pepper

1. Turn oven dial to 400°. 2. Scrub potatoes; cut small potatoes into wedges. (Cut larger potatoes in half across the middle, then into wedges.) 3. Place potato wedges in 13 x 9 x 2-inch baking pan; drizzle oil over top. 4. Sprinkle with garlic, onions (if used), rosemary (crushed), salt and pepper; stir gently. 5. Bake, uncovered, in preheated 400° oven 45 to 50 minutes, or until tender, turning once. **Slower Heat**: Bake, uncovered, in preheated 375° oven 1 hour.

POTATOES & RUTABAGA, MASHED

This is very good.

6 c. water
1⅓ c. peeled and diced rutabaga (8 oz.)
4 c. peeled potatoes, cut in 1-inch pieces
¼ c. milk
1 tsp. salt
¼ tsp. pepper
2 T. butter

1. Bring water and rutabaga to a boil in a 5 or 6-quart saucepan over high heat; lower heat to medium and boil 15 minutes. 2. Add potatoes and bring to a boil again; reduce heat and boil 20 minutes longer, or until vegetables are tender. 3. Drain water off; add remaining ingredients and mash until smooth.

POTATOES, SCALLOPED (Classic)

Adapted from Hazel Schreiner. Serves 6.

5 to 6 c. peeled and sliced potatoes
4 T. butter
2 T. flour
1½ tsp. salt or onion salt
3 c. milk
2 T. chopped onion (opt.)
¼ c. diced pepperoni (opt.)
Pepper

1. Put potatoes in greased 2 to 2½-quart casserole. 2. Turn oven dial to 350°. 3. Melt butter in saucepan; add flour and salt, stirring well. 4. Add milk all at once and stir well. 5. Add onion and pepperoni, if used; bring to a boil, stirring frequently. 6. Pour over potatoes; sprinkle with pepper. 7. Bake in preheated 350° oven, uncovered, 1½ hours or until done. **Cheese Scalloped Potatoes:** Add 4 to 5 slices of Ameri-

185

can cheese or shredded Cheddar cheese to hot milk mixture. **Ham or Spam Scalloped Potatoes:** Add diced or chunked ham or Spam to the sliced potatoes.

POTATOES, SCALLOPED
(For 6 to 7 People)

6½ to 7 c. peeled and sliced potatoes
1 (10¾-oz.) can cream of mushroom or cream of chicken
    soup
2¾ c. milk
1½ tsp. salt
½ tsp. onion powder (opt.)
2 to 3 T. butter
Pepper

1. Put potatoes in greased or sprayed <u>3-quart baking dish</u>. **2.** Turn oven dial to 350°. **3.** In bowl, combine soup, milk, salt and onion powder with wire whip; pour over potatoes. **4.** Dot with butter and sprinkle with pepper. **5.** Bake, uncovered, 2 hours in 350° oven. **<u>Slower Heat</u>:** Bake, covered, in 275° oven 3 hours. Then remove lid and bake 30 minutes in 350° oven. **<u>In West Bend Cooker</u>:** 3½ hours on #3½; reduce milk to 1½ c.

POTATOES, SCALLOPED
(For 9 to 10 People)

9 c. peeled and sliced potatoes (2¾ lb.)
6 T. butter
3 T. flour
2 tsp. salt
4½ c. milk
¼ c. finely chopped onion (opt.)
¼ c. diced pepperoni (opt.)
Pepper

1. Put potatoes in greased or sprayed 3-quart baking dish. **2.** Turn oven dial to 350°. **3.** Melt butter in 2-quart saucepan; add flour and salt, stirring well. **4.** Add milk all at once and stir well. **5.** Add onion and pepperoni, if used; bring to a boil, stirring frequently. **6.** Pour over potatoes; sprinkle with pepper. **7.** Bake in preheated 350° oven, uncovered, 1¾ to 2 hours.

POTATOES, SCALLOPED
(For 15 to 20 People)

Bake these for 2 to 3 hours.

14 c. peeled and sliced potatoes (weighing 4½ to 5 lbs.
    AFTER peeling)
2 cans (10¾-oz. each) cream of mushroom soup
4 soup cans of milk (5½ c. milk)
1½ tsp. salt
2 tsp. onion salt
½ c. reg. Smart Balance spread or butter
Pepper

1. Put potatoes in greased or sprayed roaster or deep baking pan. **2.** In large bowl, combine soup, milk, salt and onion salt; mix well. **3.** Pour over potatoes; dot butter over top. **4.** Sprinkle with pepper. **5.** Cover with lid and bake in preheated 350° oven 1 hour; remove from oven and stir well. **6.** Bake 1 hour longer, uncovered, or until potatoes are tender. **<u>Note</u>:** 2% milk is better in this recipe than skim milk.

POTATOES, SCALLOPED (Microwave)

Serves 4 to 5.

¼ c. butter
2 T. flour, packed level
2 tsp. instant minced onion
1 tsp. salt
½ tsp. dry mustard
⅛ tsp. pepper
1¾ c. milk
5 med. potatoes, sliced (or 4 c., sliced)

1. Microwave butter in covered 2-quart casserole on HIGH 45 seconds to 1¼ minutes, or until melted. **2.** Stir in flour, onion, salt, dry mustard and pepper; blend in milk. **3.** Microwave on HIGH 5 to 7 minutes, or until thickened, stirring every other minute. **4.** Mix in potatoes; cover with glass lid or waxed paper. Microwave on HIGH 15 to 20 minutes, or until potatoes are tender, stirring 2 or 3 times. **<u>Au Gratin</u>:** Add ¾ to 1 cup shredded cheese to sauce; stir until melted. **<u>Ham</u>:** Add 2 to 3 cups cubed cooked ham or some Spam with potatoes.

POTATOES, SCALLOPED (No Milk)

From Martha Rough.
These cheesy potatoes never curdle.

1 (10¾-oz.) can cream of chicken, cream of mushroom or
    cream of celery soup
1 c. water
1 tsp. salt
⅛ tsp. pepper
½ tsp. onion powder
3 slices American cheese or more
5 to 6 c. potatoes, peeled and sliced

1. In saucepan, combine soup, water, salt, pepper; onion powder and cheese; heat just enough to melt cheese. **2.** Pour over potatoes in buttered or sprayed 2½-quart casserole. **3.** Bake in 275° oven, covered with lid or foil, for 3 hours. **4.** Uncover potatoes and turn oven dial to 350°; bake until potatoes brown a little on top. **<u>In West Bend slow cooker</u>:** Grease pan. Set dial at 3½; cook, covered, for 3 hours.

POTATOES, SCALLOPED, SMALL

Adapted from Irma Chess. Serves 5. A really good recipe.

5 c. peeled and sliced potatoes
2 tsp. instant minced (or fresh) onion (opt.)
2 tsp. flour
2 T. butter
1 can cream of celery, cream of mushroom or cream of
    chicken soup
1 c. milk
½ tsp. salt
Pepper

1. Turn oven to 350° after preparing potatoes. 2. Put half the potatoes in buttered 2-quart casserole. 3. Sprinkle with half the onion and half the flour. 4. Dot with half the butter. 5. Repeat entire process again. 6. In med.-small bowl, add milk gradually to soup. 7. Add salt to soup and mix well. 8. Pour soup mixture over potatoes. (Add a little more milk, if needed.) 9. Sprinkle with pepper and cover. 10. Bake in preheated 350° oven 1½ to 2 hours, removing lid or foil the last 30 minutes. **In West Bend slow cooker**: Grease pan. Set dial on #4 for 2 hours or on #3½ for 3 hours.

POTATOES, SCALLOPED WITH CHEESE
(Quick)

2 c. milk
4 c. potatoes (about 2 lbs. before peeling), peeled and
    sliced ⅛ to ¼ inch thick
⅛ tsp. dried thyme
¼ tsp. dried rosemary (opt.)
¼ tsp. garlic powder
½ tsp. salt
⅛ tsp. pepper
1 c. shredded Cheddar cheese
1 c. milk or light cream

1. Heat milk in large, heavy saucepan; add potatoes and seasonings. 2. On medium-low heat, cook about 20 minutes, stirring often. 3. In greased or sprayed baking dish, layer potato mixture with shredded cheese. 4. Pour milk or cream over all. 5. Bake in preheated 350° oven 30 minutes, uncovered (or until potatoes are tender).

SNOW PEAS

3 to 4 c. fresh snow peas
½ to 1 c. water
¼ tsp. salt
½ tsp. sugar or more
2 T. butter(opt.)

1. Remove tips and strings from fresh snow pea pods. 2. In saucepan, combine peas, water, salt and sugar; cover and bring to a boil. 3. Boil 2 to 3 minutes or until tender-crisp. 4. Drain most of liquid off peas; add butter.

SPINACH RICE CASSEROLE

¼ c. (½ stick) butter
1 med. onion, chopped
½ c. celery, chopped (or green bell pepper)
1 (10¾-oz.) can cream of chicken soup
1 sm. (4-oz.) jar Cheez Whiz (½ c.)
1½ c. cooked rice
1 (10 to 16-oz.) pkg. frozen chopped spinach, thawed and
    drained

1. Sauté onion and celery in butter. 2. Add soup and Cheez Whiz, blending well. 3. Add cooked rice and drained spinach; gently mix all together. 4. Pour into greased or sprayed 1½-quart casserole. 5. Bake, uncovered, in preheated 375° oven 25 minutes. Serves 5 to 6.

SQUASH, ACORN, BUTTERCUP OR BUTTERNUT, BAKED

Cut squash in half; remove seeds and stringy portions. Brush the cut surfaces with softened or melted butter. Sprinkle lightly with salt and pepper. Place in baking dish, cut side up. Bake in 400° oven for 45 to 60 minutes (until fork-tender on the inside).

SQUASH, SPAGHETTI

This is a low-calorie squash.

Cook 1 spaghetti squash in one of the following ways (boiling water, oven or microwave). When hard shell can be pierced easily with a fork, it is done. Cool squash a few minutes, then cut in half lengthwise. Remove seeds and stringy interior from the cavity. Then with a fork, comb the flesh lengthwise to separate into strands. Serve hot with butter, salt, pepper, Parmesan cheese, fresh chopped parsley, dried basil or spaghetti sauce and meatballs. **To Boil:** Lower whole spaghetti squash into a kettle of boiling water and boil about 30 minutes (20 to 60 minutes, depending on size), or when a fork goes easily into the flesh. Then split it lengthwise and remove seed and stringy interior from the cavity. **To Bake:** Prick whole spaghetti squash with a fork and bake in 350° oven for 45 minutes to 1½ hours, depending on size. **To Microwave:** Pierce spaghetti squash in several places with a fork. A 3½-pound squash will cook at HIGH power in 15 minutes. Or, cut uncooked squash in half, scoop out seeds and fiber, and brush with butter. Cover tightly with plastic wrap and microwave on HIGH about 7 minutes for each half. (May take 12 minutes if large size.) Remove from microwave and cool 4 minutes. Comb flesh lengthwise to separate into strands.

SQUASH (WINTER), MASHED

1. Cut winter squash in pieces and remove stringy portion and seeds; peel. **2.** Cut peeled squash into chunks and cook on a rack in pressure cooker with ¾ cup water and a sprinkling of salt for 4 minutes after pressure has reached jiggling point (at 15 lbs. pressure), following manufacturer's directions. **3.** Drain in sieve or colander. Mash with potato masher. If desired, add a little butter and a little brown sugar.

SUMMER SQUASH, CARROT & STUFFING BAKE

Adapted from Carolyn Benninger Deets;
a delicious company-size casserole.

2 c. water
2 lbs. zucchini and/or yellow summer squash, sliced
   (about 7 c.)
1 med. onion, chopped (up to ½ c.)
¼ to ½ tsp. salt
1 (10¾-oz.) can cream of chicken soup (or cream of celery
   or cream of mushroom soup)
1 c. (8 oz.) sour cream or sour cream alternative
1 c. shredded carrots
6-oz. pkg. Stove-Top Stuffing Mix (or 2 c. herb-seasoned
   stuffing mix or seasoned croutons)
¼ c. (½ stick) butter, melted

1. In large pan, bring to boil 2 cups water; add sliced, unpeeled squash, onion and salt. Cook for 5 minutes, stirring twice; drain well. **2.** In a large bowl, combine soup, sour cream and shredded carrots; gently fold in zucchini. **3.** Combine stuffing mix with melted butter (disregard package directions); sprinkle half the stuffing mixture in a 12 x 8 x 2-inch baking dish. **4.** Spoon vegetable mixture atop; sprinkle with remaining stuffing mixture. **5.** Bake, uncovered, in preheated 350° oven 30 to 35 minutes or until heated through. (Or microwave, uncovered, on HIGH for 7 minutes, or until heated through.) **Optional Ingredients**: 8 oz. shredded cheese, layered in the casserole, and I green pepper, diced.

SUMMER SQUASH, DELECTABLE

2 T. butter or olive oil
1 med. onion, sliced
½ to 1 green bell pepper, diced (or celery, sliced or
   diced)
3 to 3½ c. sliced yellow summer squash or zucchini
1 tomato, sliced (opt.)
½ tsp. salt
½ tsp. Italian seasoning (opt.)
Black pepper
½ c. diced or shredded cheese (Colby, Cheddar, American, Velveeta, etc.)
A handful of snow peas (opt.)

1. In 10-inch skillet, fry onion and green pepper or celery in melted butter until crisp-tender. **2.** Add sliced squash, tomato, salt and pepper; cook, uncovered, turning often until crisp-tender. **3.** Sprinkle cheese over top of squash and turn off heat, leaving skillet on burner. **4.** When cheese is nearly all melted, serve immediately. (Do not lift into a serving dish, but serve from skillet.)

SUMMER SQUASH FRITTERS

Adapted from Mary Elbertson. Squash may be
prepared in food processor.

1½ c. all-purpose flour
2 tsp. baking powder
½ tsp. salt
¼ tsp. sugar
1 c. grated white or yellow summer squash (or zucchini)
1 egg
1 c. milk

Optional Ingredients:
½ c. shredded Mozzarella cheese
½ c. pepperoni, finely chopped
3 T. onion, chopped
3 T. Parmesan cheese

1. In bowl, stir together dry ingredients. **2.** Add squash, egg and milk and any of desired optional ingredients; mix just until moistened. **3.** Heat a little oil or butter in skillet; drop batter by tablespoon and fry until brown; turn over and brown on other side. (Or deep fry in hot oil, 375°, a few at a time, 3 to 4 minutes, until golden brown.) **4.** Drain on paper towel; serve hot. **Serving Suggestions:** Serve with syrup or gravy; or eat as a hot bread.

SUMMER SQUASH SKILLET, STEAMED

Delicious.

2 T. butter (or part olive oil)
1 med. onion, chopped
¼ c. celery, chopped
4 c. summer squash or zucchini, diced
½ sm. red, yellow or green bell pepper, diced
¼ c. water
½ tsp. salt
¼ tsp. pepper
4 oz. (1 c.) cubed Velveeta cheese (or sliced or shredded
   American cheese)

1. In large skillet, fry onion and celery in butter until tender. **2.** Add diced squash, red pepper, water, salt and pepper. **3.** Cook (covered with tight lid) just until crisp-tender. **4.** Remove lid and add cubed cheese; turn burner off and let stand until cheese melts.

SUMMER SQUASH STIR-FRY

Delicious for breakfast, lunch or supper, this recipe serves 1 to 2 adults. Recipe may be doubled in large skillet.

½ to 1 T. olive oil
2 c. sliced summer squash, unpeeled (8 to 9 oz.)
½ to 1 onion, thinly sliced
1 sm. green pepper, chopped (opt.)
¼ tsp. salt
⅛ tsp. pepper
¼ tsp. Italian seasoning or basil (opt.)
1 clove garlic, crushed (opt.)

1. In skillet on medium heat, bring oil to hot temperature (not smoking). **2.** Add remaining ingredients and fry, stirring frequently, uncovered, until cooked to desired tenderness (crisp-tender). **To Steam:** Omit oil and use 2 tablespoons water. Cover vegetables with tight-fitting lid.

SUMMER SQUASH & VEGETABLE STIR-FRY

2 T. olive oil
1½ c. broccoli or sliced cauliflower florets, or snow peas (strings removed) or Chinese cabbage, sliced
1½ c. sliced summer squash or zucchini
1 sm. onion, sliced
¼ to ½ c. red or green bell pepper, cut into 2-inch strips
¼ tsp salt
Pepper
½ c. Velveeta cheese, cubed (opt.)

1. On medium-high heat, stir-fry all the vegetables in large skillet until crisp-tender. (Sprinkle with salt and pepper.) **2.** Lay cheese over top and cook, uncovered, over low heat until cheese melts. **Microwave Method:** Decrease oil to 1 tablespoon. Microwave vegetables and oil in 2-quart microwave-safe casserole on HIGH 4 to 6 minutes, or until crisp-tender, stirring every 2 minutes. Sprinkle with salt and pepper. Add cheese and microwave 1 minute, or until cheese is melted.

SUMMER ZUCCHINI & BROCCOLI STIR-FRY

2 T. olive oil
1 lb. broccoli or cauliflower, cut up
1 med. zucchini, sliced (about 10 oz. or 2 to 3 c.)
½ med. onion, sliced

Sauce:
1½ tsp. cornstarch
1 tsp. sugar
1½ T. soy sauce (lite or regular)
1 c. water
1 chicken bouillon cube, crushed, or 1 tsp. instant chicken bouillon

1. Heat oil in large skillet; fry broccoli, zucchini and onion for 3 minutes, stirring occasionally. **2.** In small bowl, combine sauce ingredients; add to vegetables and cook until vegetables are crisp-tender.

SUMMER ZUCCHINI & EGGS, SCRAMBLED

Adapted from Hazel Workman; serves 2.

½ T. olive oil or butter
1 c. unpeeled diced zucchini
¼ c. diced green bell pepper
1 to 2 T. chopped onion (or 2 cloves garlic, minced)
⅛ tsp. salt
Pepper
2 to 4 eggs, lightly salted

1. In skillet, heat oil or butter. **2.** Add vegetables, salt and pepper; stir-fry until crisp-tender. **3.** Add lightly salted eggs and scramble together, cooking just until eggs are done.

SUMMER ZUCCHINI & GREEN TOMATOES

A good way to use green tomatoes.

1 T. olive oil or butter
2 c. unpeeled, diced zucchini
1½ c. diced green tomatoes
1 med. or lg. onion, diced or chopped
½ tsp. salt
Pepper
1 tsp. sugar (opt.), or more

1. In large skillet, heat oil or butter. **2.** Add remaining ingredients and stir-fry until tender-crisp, uncovered.

SUMMER ZUCCHINI ROUNDS

Something like fritters, these are a good side dish for 3 to 4 people.

1½ c. grated or chopped unpeeled zucchini (about 10 oz.)
2 T. grated or chopped onion
¼ c. flour, packed level
¼ c. Parmesan cheese
1 egg
2 T. (⅛ c.) mayonnaise
¼ tsp. salt
¼ tsp. oregano
⅛ tsp. pepper
1 T. olive oil or butter

1. Zucchini and onion may be chopped in food processor. Press zucchini between paper towels to absorb moisture, then measure. **2.** Mix all ingredients, except oil, together. **3.** Heat oil in large skillet. **4.** Drop rounded tablespoons of batter into hot skillet; flatten somewhat with spoon. **5.** Cook over medium heat until brown; turn over and brown other side.

SUMMER ZUCCHINI SKILLET, LAYERED

Adapted from Grace Cwynar.

2 to 4 T. butter or olive oil
4 to 5 med. onions, sliced ¼ inch thick
3 cloves garlic, chopped, or ¼ tsp. garlic powder
3½ c. sliced, unpeeled zucchini
½ to ¾ tsp. Italian seasoning (opt.)
2 med. tomatoes, sliced
½ tsp. salt
Black pepper
3 to 5 slices American cheese (or other cheese)

1. In large skillet that has a tight lid, heat butter or oil. **2.** Layer remaining ingredients in order given. (Do not stir.) **3.** Cover with lid and cook 15 minutes on low or medium-low heat.

SUMMER ZUCCHINI SOUFFLÉ

Adapted from Marie Stonebraker.

3 eggs
1 c. Bisquick or biscuit mix
¼ to ⅓ c. chopped onion
2 c. grated or shredded zucchini
⅓ c. olive oil
1 c. (4 oz.) shredded Cheddar cheese
Paprika or pepper

1. Turn oven dial to 350°. **2.** Beat eggs well; add remaining ingredients, stirring together. **3.** Pour into greased or sprayed 9 or 10-inch pie pan; sprinkle paprika or pepper over top. **4.** Bake in preheated 350° oven about 35 to 40 minutes. **5.** To serve, cut in wedges.

SUMMER ZUCCHINI & TOMATO SCALLOP (Baked)

Adapted from Ruth Melichar.

3 T. butter, divided
1 sm. onion, chopped
½ lb. zucchini
2 firm-ripe tomatoes
1 T. sugar
¾ tsp. salt
⅛ tsp. pepper
¼ tsp. oregano
2 T. grated Parmesan cheese (opt.)

1. Melt 2 tablespoons butter in shallow 6-cup (1½-quart) baking dish in 350° oven. **2.** Sprinkle onion over melted butter. **3.** Wash zucchini and trim ends. Quarter each zucchini lengthwise to make 4 sticks. **4.** Wash tomatoes and cut out stems; cut each tomato into 8 wedges. **5.** Arrange zucchini and tomatoes over onion in baking dish. **6.** Sprinkle sugar, salt, pepper and oregano over vegetables. **7.** Dot with remaining 1 tablespoon butter; cover and bake in preheated

350° oven 1 hour or until zucchini is tender. **8.** Sprinkle with Parmesan cheese before serving. Serves 4.

SUMMER ZUCCHINI WITH STEWED TOMATOES

3½ to 4 c. canned or fresh tomatoes, peeled
½ lb. (2 c.) zucchini, unpeeled, cut in cubes
1 med. onion, chopped
1 green bell pepper, diced (opt.)
⅓ c. chopped celery (opt.)
2 T. sugar
1 tsp. salt
½ tsp. oregano (opt.)
⅛ tsp. black pepper
2 T. butter

1. In saucepan, cook all ingredients together until zucchini and onion are tender.

SWEET POTATO CASSEROLE

3 c. cooked and mashed sweet potatoes
⅓ c. Smart Balance 67% Buttery Spread
½ c. sugar
¼ c. milk
2 eggs, beaten a little
1 t. vanilla extract

<u>Topping:</u>
½ c. brown sugar
½ t. cinnamon
¼ c. flour
3 T. Smart Balance 67% Buttery Spread
½ to ¾ c. chopped walnuts or pecans
1. Combine mashed sweet potatoes with Smart Balance, sugar, milk, eggs and vanilla; mix well. **2.** Pour into a 1½-quart casserole that has been lightly coated with Smart Balance Spread. **3.** In a small bowl, combine topping ingredients and sprinkle over sweet potato mixture. **4.** Bake in preheated 350° oven for 30 minutes.

SWEET POTATOES OR YAMS, CANDIED I

1 (29 to 40-oz.) can yams (or several sweet potatoes or yams, boiled, then peeled)
4 to 5 T. butter
1 c. packed brown sugar
⅔ c. water (or syrup from canned yams)

1. Drain canned yams, saving ⅔ cup syrup or liquid. If using boiled yams, cut into chunks or thick slices. **2.** Melt butter in skillet; add brown sugar and ⅔ cup water or syrup from yams. Bring to a boil. **3.** Reduce heat and add potatoes; simmer gently (uncovered) 30 minutes, basting occasionally with syrup or turning potatoes over several times.

SWEET POTATOES OR YAMS, CANDIED II

A company-sized recipe from Pat Swarts.

3 lbs. sweet potatoes or yams
½ c. reg. Smart Balance spread or butter
1½ c. packed brown sugar
2 T. water

1. Scrub potatoes; boil with skins on in water with 1 teaspoon salt, until tender. 2. Drain, cool, then remove skins; cut potatoes into chunks or thick slices. 3. Melt butter in large skillet; add remaining ingredients. 4. Bring to a boil; add sweet potatoes. 5. Reduce heat to low and simmer, uncovered, 30 minutes or longer, basting potatoes occasionally with syrup in skillet.

TOMATOES, FRIED (Green)

1 T. packed brown sugar
1 c. all-purpose flour
4 to 6 med.-size green tomatoes, sliced ½ inch thick (don't peel)
1 egg, beaten
¼ c. milk
1 c. seasoned dry bread crumbs
3 T. butter
1 T. olive oil

1. Combine brown sugar and flour; place on a shallow plate. 2. Dip both sides of each tomato slice into flour mixture. 3. Combine egg and milk. 4. Dip each tomato slice into milk mixture, then into bread crumbs. 5. In large skillet, heat butter and oil over medium heat. 6. Fry tomato slices until brown on both sides, but still firm enough to hold their shape. **Easier Method:** Slice green tomatoes ½ inch thick; sprinkle lightly with sugar and dip in cornmeal or flour seasoned with salt and pepper. Fry in small amount of butter until browned on both sides (in single layer); drain on paper towels. **Another Breading:** 1 cup cornmeal, ½ cup flour and 1 tablespoon sugar.

TOMATOES, FRIED (Red)

From Violet Crocker Hilliard.

Firm red tomatoes, not real ripe
Flour
Olive oil or butter
Salt
Pepper
Sugar (opt.)

1. Slice tomatoes about ½ inch thick; dip in flour. 2. Fry in skillet in hot olive oil or butter; sprinkle lightly with salt, pepper (and sugar, if desired). 3. Turn over and brown other side.

TOMATOES, STEWED WITH BREAD

This is an old-fashioned recipe.

1 (16-oz.) can tomatoes (or 2 c. cooked)
1 to 2 T. sugar or more
1 to 2 T. chopped onion, fresh or instant dried
1 T. butter (opt.)
1 to 2 slices bread or leftover toast, cubed

1. Combine all ingredients, except bread, in saucepan. 2. Bring to a boil; lower heat and simmer 10 minutes. 3. Add bread and cook 2 minutes longer.

TURNIPS, CREAMED (or Onions)

A delicious recipe for those who like turnips.

Turnips or onions, peeled
2 T. butter
2 T. flour
Milk
Pepper (and salt to taste)

1. Cut vegetables into chunks or slices; cook in boiling salted water until tender. 2. Drain, reserving liquid. 3. In skillet or saucepan, heat together butter and flour. 4. Into flour mixture, pour part vegetable liquid and part milk, using a total of about 1½ cups liquid (or until sauce is of desired consistency). Stir constantly during process. 5. Add drained vegetables; add pepper and taste to see if more salt is needed. 6. Cook on low heat a few minutes.

TURNIPS (Microwave)

2 to 3 turnips (1 lb.), peeled and cubed
3 T. water
¼ tsp. salt

1. In 1½-quart glass casserole, microwave turnips with water and salt on HIGH, covered, 7 to 9 minutes. 2. Let stand 3 minutes, covered.

TURNIPS & POTATOES, MASHED

Very good!

3 c. turnips, peeled and quartered
2 c. potatoes, peeled and quartered
2 c. water
1½ tsp. salt
¼ c. milk
1 to 2 T. butter

1. Cook turnips and potatoes together in water and salt until tender. 2. Drain and mash with potato masher or electric mixer. 3. Add milk and butter, mixing well.

VEGETABLE STIR-FRY (Microwave)

*This same recipe may be stir-fried on stove in large skillet
with 2 tablespoons olive oil instead of water.*

2 carrots, peeled and diagonally sliced
½ lb. broccoli
½ lb. cauliflower
4 oz. (about 2 c.) snow peas
1 green or red bell pepper, cut into thin strips
1 onion, sliced thin
2 cloves garlic, chopped (opt.)
¼ tsp. salt
⅛ tsp. pepper
¼ c. bottled salad dressing or Chinese Stir-Fry Sauce
    (opt.)

1. Slice carrots; cut broccoli into bite-sized flowerets, discarding tough end of stem. Peel remaining broccoli stems
and slice ½ inch thick. **2.** Cut cauliflower into bite-size flowerets; wash and remove strings from snow peas. **3.** In 2½-
quart covered casserole, cook carrots with 2 tablespoons
water on HIGH 2 minutes (with lid). **4.** Add broccoli, cauliflower and snow peas; cook, covered, 4 minutes, stirring halfway through cooking. **5.** Add green pepper, onion, garlic,
salt and pepper; cook, covered, 4 to 8 minutes, stirring halfway through cooking. **6.** If desired, toss with ¼ cup dressing
or sauce.

VEGETABLES, STIR-FRY

2 T. olive oil
**8 c. vegetables (sliced zucchini, sliced onion, sliced
    cabbage, sliced green pepper, cut-up broccoli,
    carrots (thinly sliced), snow peas, sliced mushrooms,
    etc.)**
½ tsp. salt
1 tsp. Italian seasoning

1. Heat oil in largest skillet. **2.** Add vegetables (any combination), and fry until crisp-tender, stirring often.

YELLOW WAX BEANS, CREAMED

1 qt. (or 2 cans, 16 oz. each) canned yellow wax beans
2 T. butter
2 T. flour
¼ tsp. salt
⅛ tsp. pepper
1 c. milk
¾ to 1 c. (4 oz.) sharp Cheddar cheese, shredded (opt.)

1. Drain beans, reserving bean liquid. (If home-canned beans
are used, boil 5 to 10 minutes in liquid before draining.) **2.** In
saucepan, melt butter; stir in flour, salt and pepper. **3.** Remove from heat; add milk all at once, plus ¼ cup bean liquid.
4. Cook, stirring constantly, until mixture thickens and comes
to a boil. (If using cheese, add now.) **5.** Add drained beans;
stir gently together. **6.** Heat thoroughly; if too thick, add a
little more bean liquid or milk.

192

Chapter 17

Sauces for Vegetables and Meat

VIC AND BETTY MARCIN
JANE AND MARY
1978

SAUCES FOR VEGETABLES AND MEAT

BARBECUE SAUCE

2 to 3 T. packed brown sugar
2 T. vinegar (or less)
1½ c. ketchup
½ c. chopped celery
1 onion, chopped
2 T. Worcestershire sauce
½ tsp. dry mustard
1/16 to 1/8 tsp. cayenne pepper (opt.)

1. Combine all ingredients in saucepan over medium heat and bring to a boil. **2.** Reduce heat; cover pan and simmer 30 minutes, stirring occasionally. **3.** Remove lid and simmer 15 minutes longer.

BARBECUE SAUCE, PAT'S

From Pat Swarts.

3 to 4 strips bacon, finely diced
1 lg. onion, chopped
1 (32-oz.) bottle ketchup
1 T. Worcestershire sauce
1 tsp. prepared mustard
½ c. packed brown sugar (or to taste)

1. Fry bacon and onion together, drain off grease and add remaining ingredients. **2.** Simmer 30 minutes on low heat, uncovered.

BASIC WHITE SAUCE (1 Cup)

1 to 2 T. butter
2 T. flour or 1 T. cornstarch
¼ tsp. salt
1/8 tsp. pepper
1 c. milk

1. Melt butter in small saucepan over low heat. **2.** Blend in flour or cornstarch, salt and pepper. **3.** Add milk all at once; bring to boil over medium heat, stirring constantly until mixture thickens and bubbles. Reduce heat and cook, stirring, about 1 minute longer.

Cream Sauce for Vegetables: Add 3 cups cooked or canned vegetables, drained, to above sauce. Heat. 1 cup (4 ounces) shredded sharp Cheddar or Colby cheese and ¼ teaspoon dry mustard may be added after step #3. Stir until cheese melts, then add drained vegetables.

BASIC WHITE SAUCE, MICROWAVE

Makes 1 cup.

1 to 2 T. butter
2 T. flour, packed level
¼ tsp. salt
1/8 tsp. pepper
1 c. milk

1. In 1-quart microwave-safe bowl or pitcher, melt butter on HIGH for 30 to 60 seconds. **2.** Stir in flour, salt and pepper until smooth. **3.** Blend in milk; microwave on HIGH 2 minutes, then stir. **4.** Microwave until mixture thickens, stirring after every 60 seconds. <u>For Thin White Sauce:</u> Use 1 tablespoon flour, level.

CHEESE SAUCE

A wonderful sauce for cauliflower, broccoli, green beans or Brussels sprouts.

2 T. butter
2 T. flour
¼ tsp. salt or seasoned salt
1/8 tsp. pepper (or less)
1/8 tsp. dry mustard (opt.)
1 c. milk
1 c. sharp Cheddar or plain yellow cheese, shredded or cut-up

<u>Stove-Top Method:</u> **1.** Melt butter in saucepan. **2.** Add flour, stirring well; heat and allow to bubble 1 minute. **3.** Add salt, pepper and dry mustard. **4.** Add milk; cook, stirring almost constantly, until it boils. **5.** Stir in cheese; with heat turned off, stir until cheese melts.

<u>Blender Method:</u> **1.** Put all ingredients, except cheese, in blender; blend a few seconds until smooth. **2.** Pour into saucepan and heat on stove until it boils, stirring almost constantly. **3.** Stir in cheese; with heat turned off, stir until cheese melts.

CHEESE SAUCE (Microwave)

2 T. butter
2 T. flour
1 tsp. chopped chives (opt.)
¼ tsp. dry mustard
¼ tsp. salt
1/8 tsp. pepper
1 c. milk
2 to 4 oz. (½ to 1 c.) shredded Cheddar, Colby or American cheese (or Velveeta, diced)

1. In 1-quart microwave-safe bowl or pitcher, melt butter on HIGH for 30 to 60 seconds. **2.** Stir in flour, chives, dry mustard, salt and pepper until smooth. **3.** Blend in milk; microwave on HIGH 2 minutes, then stir. **4.** Microwave until mixture thickens, stirring after every 60 seconds. **5.** Add cheese, stirring until it melts; microwave 30 seconds. Stir before serving.

CHINESE STIR-FRY SAUCE

5¼ tsp. cornstarch, level
1 to 2 tsp. sugar
¼ tsp. ground ginger
1 c. water or broth
⅛ c. soy sauce (regular or "lite")

1. In small pan, mix together cornstarch, sugar and ginger. **2.** Add 1 cup liquid and soy sauce; cook, stirring, until it comes to a full boil.

HOLLANDAISE SAUCE, EASY

No cholesterol. Makes about 1 cup.

½ c. (4 oz.) egg substitute (like "Egg Beaters")
2 T. lemon juice
¼ tsp. salt
Dash of cayenne pepper
⅓ c. butter, melted (very hot)

1. Put egg substitute, lemon juice, salt and cayenne pepper into a blender or food processor; blend. **2.** Pour hot melted butter through opening in blender lid; blend. (Sauce should thicken slightly.) **3.** For additional thickening (or reheating), pour sauce into small microwave-safe bowl and microwave on HIGH 10 seconds. **4.** Stir; repeat if necessary.

OSCAR SAUCE (Chili Sauce)

From Marilyn England; may be added to meatloaf or hamburger to replace liquid, onions, and seasoning.

24 large tomatoes (peel, if desired), washed and chopped
6 red sweet peppers, chopped
6 green peppers, chopped
8 large onions, chopped
6 c. sugar
4 c. white vinegar
1 c. water
4 T. salt
1 T. black pepper
A few cloves of garlic, chopped (opt.)

1. Put all ingredients in a soup pot and cook them on low heat, uncovered, for several hours. Stir occasionally, making sure it does not stick to bottom of pan. **2.** If not thick enough, add a 6 oz. can tomato paste. **3.** May be frozen or canned.

PICANTE SALSA (or Taco Sauce)

Also for burritos, etc. Mildly hot.

1 (16-oz.) can or 2 c. whole tomatoes, undrained
1 (4-oz.) can diced green chilies, well drained

1 tsp. cornstarch
1 tsp. sugar
1 tsp. ground coriander (opt.)
⅛ tsp. salt (opt.)

1. Combine all ingredients in container of food processor or blender; process until smooth. **2.** Pour mixture into small saucepan; bring to a boil. **3.** Reduce heat; simmer 2 minutes, stirring occasionally.

SPAGHETTI SAUCE, GARDEN FRESH

Makes 3 quarts from fresh tomatoes.

1 gal. (4 qt) washed, cut-up, ripe tomatoes
½ to ¾ lb. onions, peeled and diced
1 green or red bell pepper, de-seeded and diced
1 hot banana pepper, de-seeded and diced (opt.)
2 cloves garlic, peeled and sliced, or ½ tsp. garlic powder
12 oz. tomato paste
3 to 4 tsp. salt
1 tsp. dried oregano
1 tsp. dried basil
1 tsp. dried parsley flakes (opt.)
¼ to ½ c. olive oil
⅓ c. sugar (or to taste)

1. In large stainless steel or enamel pot, simmer tomatoes, onions, pepper and garlic until soft and well cooked. **2.** Put cooked tomatoes through food mill or sieve. **3.** Add remaining ingredients to tomatoes; simmer 1 to 2 hours, until thick.

Chapter 18

Main Dishes and Meat

RICHARD AND PATRICIA SWARTS
1978

MAIN DISHES & MEAT

BACON

Baked: Place single layer of slices in greased or sprayed shallow baking pan. Bake in 400° oven for 10 to 14 minutes, or to desired crispness. No turning necessary. (The time depends also on the thickness of bacon slices.) It does not splatter the oven. **Pan Fried:** Place slices in cold skillet. Cook over medium-low heat to desired crispness, turning frequently. Drain on paper towels. **Microwaved:** Microwave on HIGH to desired crispness, approximately 1 minute per slice, on a microwave-safe plate or platter lined with a paper towel and covered with a paper towel. Microwave ovens vary, so experiment with the time. **Broiled:** Place bacon strips on broiling rack in preheated broiler 3 to 5 inches from heat. Broil several minutes on each side, turning slices once or twice. (Leave oven door open about 4 inches.) Place cooked bacon on paper towel to drain. **Note**: I read that if you microwave bacon, it will have only one-tenth of the cancer-causing nitrosamines of fried bacon.

BAKED BEANS WITH HAMBURGER (CALICO)

From Martha Rough; uses four different kinds of beans.

1 lb. ground beef
1 med. onion, chopped
½ T. olive oil or butter
1 (15 to 16-oz.) can pork & beans
1 (15 to 16-oz.) can kidney beans, drained (preferably dark red)
1 can butter beans or lima beans, drained
1 (15 to 16-oz.) can pinto or great northern beans, drained
1 c. ketchup
1 c. packed brown sugar
1 tsp. dry mustard
¾ to 1 lb. bacon, (or less) fried crisp (opt.)

1. Fry ground beef and onion in ½ tablespoon oil, stirring frequently, until cooked; drain off fat. **2.** In 2½-quart roaster, combine browned beef with remaining ingredients. **3.** Bake in 350° oven, covered, 45 minutes. Uncover and bake 15 to 20 minutes longer.

BAKED BEANS WITH WIENERS (CALICO)

Uses three different kinds of beans.

1 onion, finely chopped
1 T. olive oil
2 (14 to 17-oz.) cans pork & beans
1 (14 to 17-oz.) can kidney beans
1 can butter beans (or lima or great northern beans), drained

1 (6-oz.) can tomato paste
⅔ c. packed brown sugar
½ T. prepared mustard
1 lb. wieners, cut in halves or quarters

1. Fry onion in olive oil until soft. **2.** In large bowl, combine pork & beans and kidney beans, including liquid. **3.** Add drained butter beans (discarding liquid). **4.** Add tomato paste, brown sugar, mustard, cooked onion and wieners; stir well. **5.** Pour into a 13 x 9 x 2-inch baking dish (grease top edge of dish about 1 inch down, all around the inside). **6.** Bake in preheated 350° oven for 1 hour, uncovered. **Substitution**: 5 slices of bacon, fried crisp, drained and crumbled, may be added instead of wieners.

BAKED BEANS WITH WIENERS, LARGE RECIPE

7 or 8 cans (14 to 16 oz. each) pork and beans, undrained
1½ c. packed brown sugar
1½ c. ketchup
1½ t. dry mustard (or 1 T. prepared mustard)
1 to 1½ c. chopped onion, fried in 1 T. olive oil
10 to 12 wieners, each cut in eight slices

1. Put all ingredients in large roaster. **2.** Bake, uncovered, in 350° oven for 2 hours.

BEANS & HOT DOGS, STOVE TOP

A quick and simple recipe which may be doubled or tripled.

1 (11 to 16-oz.) can baked beans
2 to 4 hot dogs, sliced
2 T. packed brown sugar
2 T. ketchup
1 tsp. prepared mustard

1. Combine all ingredients in medium saucepan; cook over medium heat until mixture begins to boil. **2.** Reduce heat to low and simmer 10 minutes, stirring occasionally.

BEEF POT ROAST, POTATOES & CARROTS

From Eileen Bell. Scrumptious!

1 beef roast (any size)
½ tsp. salt per pound of meat
Pepper
½ to 1 env. dry onion soup mix (or fresh onions, quartered)
1 bay leaf (opt.)
Water
Potatoes, peeled and cut in chunks
Carrots, peeled and cut in chunks
Cabbage wedges (opt.)
½ c. cold water
⅓ c. flour, packed level
1 tsp. Gravy Master or Kitchen Bouquet

1. Place beef roast in roaster and sprinkle with the salt, pepper, onion soup mix (or fresh onions) and bay leaf. 2. Add water ⅓ to ½ way up the roast; cover and roast in preheated 400° oven 1 hour. 3. Lower oven dial to 300° and roast meat 3 hours, covered, or until tender. 4. Cook vegetables in salted water, each separately, until nearly tender; drain and set aside. 5. Remove meat from roaster and cut into chunks, discarding all fat. 6. Pour broth into wide-mouthed jar and skim off all fat with gravy ladle. 7. Put 4 cups of beef broth back in roaster and heat on stove burner. 8. Shake together ½ cup cold water and the flour; add to hot broth, stirring constantly. Bring to a boil. 9. Add Gravy Master or Kitchen Bouquet, making a dark, thin gravy; add beef and partially cooked vegetables. Cover and return to 300° oven for 1 hour. **Sunday Morning Easy Way:** Follow steps 1 and 2. Then add uncooked vegetables, cover and roast in 300° oven for 3 hours or until meat is tender.

BEEF POT ROAST, SMALL

Serves 3 adults. Recipe may be doubled in a larger roaster.

1¼ to 1½ lbs. beef roast
4 to 5 med. potatoes, peeled
5 to 6 med. carrots, peeled
1 beef bouillon cube (opt.)
1 to 2 onions or leeks, sliced
2 c. water
1½ tsp. salt
Pepper

1. Put roast in 2½ to 3-quart baking dish or small roaster. 2. Add whole potatoes and carrots, crushed bouillon cube and onions. 3. Pour water around meat and vegetables. 4. Sprinkle 1 teaspoon salt over meat and ½ teaspoon salt over the vegetables. 5. Sprinkle with pepper. 6. Cover with tight lid or foil; roast 3 to 3½ hours in 350° oven or until meat is tender. If there is not enough broth, add a little hot water. **Note:** 1 envelope Lipton's onion soup mix may be sprinkled over meat and vegetables instead of using salt, pepper and onions.

BEEF POT ROAST, VEGETABLES & BROTH

*Delicious dinner in the oven;,
adapted from Dorothy Patterson.*

Potatoes, peeled (whole or cut in half)
Carrots, peeled (whole or cut in half)
Celery, cut in ½-inch chunks (opt.)
Onions, sliced
Water to nearly cover vegetables (4 c., approx.)
½ to 1 tsp. salt over vegetables
Beef roast (any kind)
Salt (½ tsp. per pound of beef)
Pepper

1. Put all ingredients in roasting pan in order given, placing beef roast on top of vegetables. 2. Cover with lid or foil and roast in 325° oven 3 to 4 hours, or until tender (or in 300° oven for 4 to 5 hours). If necessary to brown, remove lid and roast 15 to 30 minutes longer. 3. When ready to serve, lift meat onto platter; lift vegetables into serving bowl. 4. Pour broth into a wide-mouth tall jar and skim fat off top of broth with gravy ladle, discarding fat. 5. Pour broth over vegetables in bowl. **Note:** If oven is slow, roast at 350° or 375° for 3 to 4 hours, or until tender.

BEEF ROAST I

*Old-fashioned method and delicious!.
This is my favorite recipe for roast beef.*

Beef roast, frozen or thawed (or venison roast)
3 c. water
Salt (½ tsp. for each pound of meat)
Pepper
Onion slices (opt.)
2 tsp. beef flavor powdered bouillon or 2 beef bouillon
    cubes (or 2 T. onion soup mix)

1. Preheat oven to 400°. 2. Place meat in roaster pan; add water. 3. Sprinkle with salt and pepper. If cooking venison, lay onion slices over top. 4. Add beef bouillon to water around meat. 5. Cover roast and put meat in oven; lower oven dial to 300°. Roast about 5 hours (give or take), until tender (or if in a hurry, set dial at 325° and roast 3 to 3½ hours, or until tender). **Gravy:** 1. Pour broth from beef roast into a wide-mouthed quart jar; skim off fat with gravy ladle (discard fat). Taste broth; if necessary, add some water. 2. Shake together ½ cup water and 1/3 cup flour. 3. Return broth to pan and bring to a boil; remove pan from heat and add as much thickening as is needed, stirring. 4. Return gravy to burner and bring to a full boil, stirring almost constantly. **For Pot Roast:** Omit making gravy. One hour before serving, add potatoes, carrots and onion to broth around meat. (Cover pan again with lid.)

BEEF ROAST II

This recipe is also very good!

Beef roast, frozen or thawed
2 c. water
1 beef bouillon cube
Salt (½ tsp. for each pound of meat)
Pepper

1. Turn oven dial to 250°. 2. Place meat in roaster pan; add water and bouillon cube. 3. Sprinkle with salt and pepper. 4. Cover roaster with lid and roast 6 hours.

BEEF ROAST or DEER ROAST (CROCK-POT)

For Sunday dinner, turn crock-pot on LOW at 11:15 P.M.

Beef or venison roast, 3 lbs. or larger, thawed (all fat removed)
½ tsp. salt for each pound of meat
Pepper
Garlic powder or onion powder (opt.)
Some low-sodium beef bouillon or 2 bouillon cubes
½ c. water

For browning paste:
1 T. flour, packed level
2 T. cold water
½ tsp. Kitchen Bouquet or Gravy Master

1. Put roast in bottom of crock-pot; sprinkle with salt, pepper, and garlic powder. 2. Add bouillon and !/2 c. water. 3. Make a paste of 1 tablespoon flour, 2 tablespoons water and the browning sauce; spread over the top of meat with pastry brush. 4. Cover and cook on LOW for 13 hours (or on HIGH for 8 hours). With vegetables: Put peeled potatoes, carrots and onions around and over the meat when starting the crock-pot. (Sprinkle vegetables with a little bit of salt.)

BEEF STEW, JULIE'S (CROCK-POT)

A wonderful recipe. Plug in at 7:00 A.M. on LOW and it is done at 5:00 P.M. for supper.

1½ lbs. beef stew meat, cubed (all fat removed)
2 c. raw potatoes, peeled and cut in chunks
2 c. carrots, peeled and cut in ½-inch slices
1 env. dry onion soup mix
1 (10¾-oz.) can golden mushroom soup (do not substitute)
1 bay leaf
1 c. water
1 beef bouillon cube

1. Combine all ingredients in crock-pot. 2. Cook all day on LOW, (10 hours); remove bay leaf. Serves 6.

BEEF STEW, OVEN

So easy! Bake 4 to 5 hours.

1½ c. cold water
¼ c. flour (level)
1 (10¾-oz.) can tomato soup, not diluted
2 tsp. powdered beef bouillon or 2 beef bouillon cubes
½ tsp. salt
¼ tsp. pepper
1 to 2 lbs. beef stew meat, fat removed, and cut in 1 to 2-in. cubes
4 c. potatoes, peeled and cut in 1½-inch chunks

4 med. carrots, cut in 1-in. diagonal slices
2 onions, sliced
1 c. celery, sliced
1 bay leaf
1 tsp. dried rosemary (opt.)

1. Turn oven dial to 350°. 2. In a jar, shake together water and flour. 3. In roaster pan, combine soup, water-flour mixture, beef bouillon, salt and pepper; mix well. 4. Add remaining ingredients and stir together. 5. Cover with lid or foil and place in preheated oven. 6. **Immediately turn oven dial to 275°** and bake 4 to 5 hours (until beef is tender). 7. Remove bay leaf before serving.

BEEF STEW, PRESSURE COOKER

1 to 1½ lbs. boneless beef stew meat, cut into cubes
1 T. butter
1 T. olive oil
2 c. water
2 tsp. salt, divided
¼ tsp. pepper
¼ tsp. paprika
1 c. onion (1 lg.) or leeks, sliced or diced
3 c. potatoes, peeled and cut in chunks
3 c. carrots, peeled and cut in chunks
1 to 2 c. frozen lima beans or frozen peas

1. Trim all fat from beef and brown beef in pressure cooker on all sides, in butter and oil; drain off all fat. 2. Add water, 1½ teaspoons salt, the pepper and paprika. 3. Cover; pressure meat according to manufacturer's directions at 10 pounds pressure for 15 to 20 minutes. 4. Remove from burner and let stand 5 minutes; then reduce pressure as directed by manufacturer. 5. Add onions, potatoes, carrots and ½ teaspoon salt; cover and cook for 8 minutes at 10 pounds pressure. 6. Reduce pressure; add frozen green vegetable. 7. If a thickened stew is desired, shake together ⅓ cup water and 2 tablespoons flour; add to beef stew and bring to a boil, stirring. 8. Reduce heat and simmer gently 5 minutes (no pressure) or until frozen vegetable is done.

BEEF STEW, RANGE-TOP

Simply delicious. Makes 6 servings or more.

1 to 2 lbs. boneless beef stew meat, cut into cubes
1 T. butter
1 T. olive oil
2 lg. onions, sliced or chopped
2 cloves garlic, minced (or ¼ tsp. garlic powder)
3 c. water
2 to 3 c. tomato juice or canned tomatoes, broken up
2 lg. ribs celery, sliced
2 tsp. salt
½ tsp. oregano or thyme
¼ tsp. pepper

1 bay leaf
1 to 2 c. raw carrots, peeled and sliced
3 c. raw potatoes or turnips, peeled and cut in chunks
10 oz. frozen peas or baby limas or green beans

1. Trim all fat from beef and discard. 2. In soup kettle, melt butter with oil; brown beef well. Drain off fat. 3. Push beef to one side (or remove); add onions and garlic; cook 5 minutes, stirring occasionally. 4. Add water, tomatoes, celery, salt, oregano or thyme, pepper and bay leaf. 5. Bring to a boil; reduce heat, cover and simmer 1 to 1½ hours or until meat is almost tender. (If necessary, add more water.) 6. Add carrots and potatoes; bring to a boil; reduce heat, cover and simmer 30 minutes longer or until beef and vegetables are tender. 7. Add final green frozen vegetable; cook 10 to 15 minutes longer. 8. Discard bay leaf before serving. Add 1 T. sugar, if needed. Note: Sliced mushrooms, raw or canned (drained), may be added with the final vegetable. Note: If a thickened stew is desired, mix together 3 tablespoons cornstarch and ½ cup water; add with the final vegetable. Bring to a boil, stirring. Note: If planning to freeze, use turnips instead of potatoes.

BEEF STIR-FRY

Serves 3 adults generously.

½ to ¾ lb. sirloin steak
¼ c. olive oil
1 onion, sliced and separated into rings
¾ c. very thinly sliced carrots
1½ c. diagonally sliced celery
1 (4-oz.) can sliced mushrooms, drained
1 med.-small green pepper, cut in thin strips
1 T. cornstarch
¼ c. low-sodium soy sauce
1 (8-oz.) can (1 c.) tomato sauce
1 to 2 tsp. sugar
¼ tsp. ground ginger
Cooked rice or noodles

1. Trim all fat from steak; cut steak into thin strips, 2 inches long. 2. Sear meat in hot oil in a large skillet or wok over high heat, stirring constantly. 3. Add onion rings, carrots and celery; continue to stir and fry over high heat just until crisptender. 4. Add drained mushrooms and green pepper strips, cooking and stirring 1 minute. 5. Blend together cornstarch and soy sauce in small bowl; add tomato sauce, sugar and ginger. 6. Add tomato sauce mixture to meat and vegetables; stir and cook 3 to 4 minutes longer, until sauce thickens and bubbles. 7. Serve over hot cooked rice or noodles.

BEEF STIR-FRY & BROCCOLI

From Roberta Wells. Serves 4.

1 lb. round steak, cut in very thin slices
½ c. water, divided
⅓ c. soy sauce (lite or reg.)
2 T. packed brown sugar

1 tsp. cornstarch
1 tsp. ginger
1 clove garlic, pressed or ⅛ tsp. garlic powder
3 T. olive oil
1 bunch broccoli florets
1 lg. onion, cut in sm. wedges

1. Marinate steak in mixture of ¼ cup water, the soy sauce, brown sugar, cornstarch, ginger and garlic for 10 minutes. 2. Drain steak, reserving marinade. 3. Heat the oil in large skillet or wok; add steak pieces and brown over high heat. 4. Remove steak from skillet. 5. Add broccoli and onion to skillet; stir-fry for 1 to 3 minutes. 6. Add remaining ¼ cup water; cover and steam 3 minutes. 7. Return meat and reserved marinating sauce to broccoli in skillet; heat thoroughly until sauce bubbles and boils. 8. Serve over cooked rice, hot buttered noodles or Chinese noodles. Note: Steak may be cut while either frozen or fresh.

BEEF STIR-FRY & SNOW PEAS

*Serve over hot cooked rice, thin spaghetti
or angel hair pasta. Serves 4.*

¾ to 1 lb. beef steak (or deer steak or chops), cut into thin
  strips
1 med. onion, thinly sliced
2 cloves garlic, minced
½ c. beef broth (may be made with bouillon)
1 sweet red or green pepper cut into thin strips (or 2 c.
  sliced fresh mushrooms)
2 to 3 c. fresh snow peas

Sauce:
1 T. cornstarch
1 c. beef broth
⅛ tsp. black pepper
⅛ tsp. (scant) crushed red pepper flakes
½ T. sugar (opt.)
2 T. balsamic vinegar or "lite" soy sauce

1. Prepare meat and vegetables; set aside. 2. In a large non-stick skillet, stir-fry the onion and garlic in 1 tablespoon olive oil over low heat until tender. 3. Add meat and an additional tablespoon olive oil, and stir-fry over medium heat 8 minutes, or until meat is no longer pink. 4. Remove meat and onions from skillet and set aside. 5. Add broth to skillet; add peppers or fresh mushrooms. Stir-fry over high heat until peppers are crisp-tender. 6. In a bowl, combine the sauce ingredients; add to the skillet and bring to a boil. (Add snow peas at this time.) Cook and stir until thickened (about 2 minutes). 7. Add meat and onions; heat through.

BEEF TIPS & GRAVY

So easy and so good. Do not add any salt.

1 to 1½ lbs. sirloin tip steak or lean stewing beef
1 (10¾-oz.) can condensed golden mushroom soup or
  cream of chicken soup

1 (10½-oz.) can condensed French onion soup
¼ c. water

1. Turn oven dial to 350°. 2. Remove any fat from meat; cut into cubes or bite-size pieces and put in baking dish or small roaster. 3. In bowl, mix together soups and ¼ cup water; pour over meat. 4. Cover with foil or tight lid; bake in preheated 350° oven for 2½ to 3 hours (until tender). 5. Serve over cooked noodles, rice or mashed potatoes. Crock-Pot: Cook on LOW for 10 hours.

CABBAGE HAMBURGER CASSEROLE

Tastes similar to cabbage rolls, only easier!

1 med. -large head cabbage, coarsely chopped (2 to 2½ lbs.)
1 to 1½ lbs. ground beef
½ c. reg. rice, uncooked, or 1½ c. Minute Rice, uncooked
½ tsp. salt
½ tsp. garlic salt
⅛ to ¼ tsp. black pepper
½ c. chopped onion
½ c. tomato juice
1 egg
1 (10¾-oz.) can tomato soup
⅔ c. water
2 c. tomato juice
1 T. sugar (opt.)

1. Precook chopped cabbage in 1 cup water just until wilted, stirring together well; drain. 2. Cook ground beef until lightly browned; drain off fat. 3. To drained meat, add rice, seasonings, onion, ½ cup tomato juice and egg; mix well. 4. Place half the cabbage in 13 x 9-inch baking pan (or roaster pan). 5. Spoon meat mixture over cabbage. 6. Top with remaining cabbage. 7. To soup, gradually add water; add 2 cups tomato juice and sugar. Pour over cabbage. 8. Cover tightly with foil or lid; bake in 350° oven for 1½ hours. (When using regular rice, make sure rice is done.)

CABBAGE ROLLS

Makes 12 or 14 cabbage rolls.

1 head cabbage (med. to lg.)
1 to 1½ lbs. lean ground beef
1 sm. or med. onion, chopped
1 lg. egg (or 2 sm. eggs)
1 to 1½ tsp. salt
⅛ tsp. pepper
3 T. raw rice (do not use Minute Rice)
3½ to 4 c. spaghetti sauce or tomato juice or 2 (10¾-oz.)
    cans tomato soup mixed with 2 cans water

1. Make some deep cuts with sharp knife around base of cabbage core, and completely remove core. 2. Microwave head of cabbage for 5-10 minutes, depending on size of head. After it cools somewhat, the leaves separate easily. 3. In bowl, combine ground beef, onion, egg, salt, pepper and rice, mixing well. 4. Using scant ¼ cup measure, form 12 oblong

rolls of meat mixture. 5. Place meat on thick end of cabbage leaf; fold sides of leaf over meat and roll up. 6. Lay unused cabbage leaves (or wedges of unused cabbage) in bottom of roaster (or serve remaining cabbage another time). 7. Lay cabbage rolls in roaster, seam side down; pour tomato liquid over all. 8. Cover with lid or foil and bake in preheated 350° oven for 2 hours (or in 250° oven for 3 to 4 hours). Note: If using tomato juice, 2 tablespoons sugar may be added, if desired. Stove-Top Method: Simmer on low heat 2 hours. Crock-Pot Method: Cook, covered, 6 to 10 hours on low setting, using only 2 cups tomato liquid. West Bend Slow Cooker: Set dial on #4 and cook 4 to 5 hours, using 1 quart home-canned tomato soup.

CAVATINI

8 oz. small shell macaroni, uncooked
½ lb. ground beef
½ lb. Italian sausage
1 med. onion, chopped
½ green pepper, chopped
1 (15-oz.) jar spaghetti sauce (or about 2 c.)
1 tsp. Italian seasoning (or basil or oregano)
1 tsp. sugar (opt.)
2 c. canned tomatoes
½ to 1 c. tomato sauce (4 to 8 oz.)
1 (4-oz.) can mushrooms, drained (opt.)
8 oz. (2 c.) shredded Mozzarella or sharp cheese
½ c. diced pepperoni (or more)

1. Cook pasta in 10 cups boiling water and 2 teaspoons salt for 12 minutes after coming to a boil again (or until tender, but not overcooked). Drain, rinse and drain again. 2. Fry beef, sausage, onion and green pepper together until meat is cooked; drain off all fat. 3. Add meat mixture to pasta and all remaining ingredients, stirring gently together. 4. Pour into sprayed 2½ to 3-quart casserole or baking dish; cover. 5. Bake in preheated 350° oven for 40 minutes, covered with lid or foil. Uncover and bake 10 to 15 minutes longer.

CHINESE ANGEL HAIR STIR-FRY

Serves 4. So good!

6 ounces angel hair pasta, broken in half (or spaghetti,
    broken)
½ to 1 lb. boneless, skinless chicken breast (or beef or
    pork), cut into ¼-inch strips
1 T. cornstarch
3 T. olive oil, divided
¼ tsp. salt
⅛ tsp. pepper
6 oz. snow peas, trimmed
1 sweet red or green pepper, cut into ¼-inch wide strips

Sauce:
4 tsp. cornstarch, level
2 tsp. sugar (opt.)
¼ tsp. ground ginger

203

¼ tsp. garlic powder (opt.)
1 c. water or chicken broth (can be made with chicken
    bouillon)
3 T. "lite" soy sauce
⅛ tsp. crushed red pepper flakes (opt.)

1. Cook pasta according to package directions; drain. Rinse with water and drain again. Set aside. **2.** Cut meat into ¼-inch thick slices; combine with cornstarch, 1 tablespoon olive oil, salt and pepper, and stir together. **3.** Heat 1 tablespoon olive oil in large skillet over high heat; add meat strips and stir-fry 4 minutes, until browned. **4.** Add last tablespoon olive oil and the snow peas and pepper strips; stir-fry 3 to 4 minutes. **5.** To make sauce, combine sauce ingredients in a small saucepan, stirring to dissolve cornstarch; cook, stirring until it comes to a full boil. **6.** Pour sauce over meat and vegetables; add pasta and stir all together. Cook and stir until heated through. <u>**Substitutions**</u>: 2 cups broccoli florets and 2 cups julienned carrots and/or 2 cups shredded Chinese cabbage may be substituted for the snow peas and sweet pepper. Also, 2 c. sliced zucchini squash may be substituted for one of the vegetables. Cooked turkey pieces may be used instead of frying meat.

CHINESE FRIED RICE

3 tsp. olive oil, divided
2 large eggs, lightly beaten
8 oz. mushrooms, thinly sliced (fresh or canned and
    drained)
1 medium red or green bell pepper, finely chopped
2 garlic cloves, minced
½ tsp. ground ginger
4 to 4½ c. cooked and cooled white rice (not Minute Rice)
1 c. frozen peas, thawed
2 green onions, thinly sliced (or 2 T. finely chopped onion)
½ c. chicken broth
2 T. soy sauce
1 tsp. sesame oil
½ c. loosely packed fresh parsley or cilantro, chopped
    (opt.)

1. In 10- or 12-inch nonstick skillet, put 1 teaspoon olive oil over medium heat until hot; add eggs and cook about 2 minutes, stirring with wooden spoon until eggs are scrambled. Transfer to a plate and set aside. **2.** In same skillet, heat remaining 2 teaspoons olive oil over medium heat; add mushrooms and bell pepper and cook until tender, stirring occasionally. **3.** Add garlic and cook, stirring, 1 minute. **4.** Add ginger, rice, peas, onions, chicken broth, soy sauce, sesame oil and the scrambled eggs; cook about 3 minutes or until heated through, stirring with spoon. **5.** Toss in parsley just before serving.

CHINESE STIR-FRY I

1 lb. steak, chicken or pork (fat removed), cut into ⅛-in.
    slices
2 T. olive oil
1 lg. onion, sliced or coarsely chopped
2 c. sliced Chinese cabbage
1 green pepper, cut into strips
Fresh mushrooms, sliced
1½ T. cornstarch
¾ c. water
3 T. soy sauce
¼ tsp. dry mustard
½ tsp. grated fresh ginger (or ground ginger)
⅛ to ¼ tsp. crushed red pepper
Hot cooked rice

1. Stir-fry meat in hot oil just until done; remove from wok or skillet. **2.** Stir-fry onion for 2 minutes; remove. **3.** Repeat procedure with Chinese cabbage, green pepper and mushrooms. **4.** Return meat and vegetables to wok; push to sides. **5.** In small bowl, combine cornstarch, water, soy sauce, dry mustard, ginger and red pepper. **6.** Add to center of wok and bring to a boil. **7.** Stir meat and vegetables into boiling sauce. **8.** Serve over hot cooked rice.

CHINESE STIR-FRY II

Delicious.

3½ T. cornstarch
2 tsp. sugar
½ tsp. ground ginger
2 c. water or broth
½ c. soy sauce (reg. or lite)
Hot cooked rice
Chow mein noodles (opt.)
1 to 2 cans bean sprouts, drained (or fresh bean sprouts)
1 to 2 sm. cans mushrooms, drained (unless using fresh
    mushrooms)
1 (8-oz.) can sliced water chestnuts, drained
1 (6 to 8-oz.) can bamboo shoots, drained (opt.)
1 to 2 onions, sliced and separated into rings (or 5 green
    onions with tops, sliced)
1 clove garlic, minced (opt.)
Olive oil for stir-frying
1 to 2 c. celery, sliced diagonally in 1-in. pcs.
1 to 2 red or green bell peppers, cut in ½-in. strips, then in
    2-in. chunks
1½ c. (or more) sliced fresh mushrooms (opt.)
1 c. fresh carrots, peeled and sliced very thin (opt.)
1 (6-oz.) pkg. frozen snow peas, thawed (or 1 c. frozen
    peas)
½ to 1 lb. uncooked lean pork, beef or chicken, cut
    diagonally into thin strips or slices

1. In small pan, mix together cornstarch, sugar, ginger, water and soy sauce; set aside without cooking. **2.** Start cooking rice according to package directions. **3.** Preheat oven to 250°.

4. In large casserole, place drained bean sprouts, drained mushrooms, drained water chestnuts and drained bamboo shoots; place casserole in oven, uncovered. **5.** In heated wok or large skillet, stir-fry onion slices and minced garlic in 1 tablespoon oil; add to casserole in oven. **6.** Stir-fry each of the remaining vegetables, separately in ½ to 1 tablespoon oil (or less) until slightly cooked (2 to 4 minutes) over quite high heat; add each vegetable to casserole in oven. (Frozen peas do not need stir-fried.) **7.** Stir-fry meat in 1 tablespoon oil, just until done; remove to casserole in oven. **8.** Cook soy sauce mixture until it comes to a full boil; pour sauce over casserole ingredients and very gently stir all together. (It may be transferred to the wok for serving, if desired.) **9.** Serve immediately with hot rice and chow mein noodles. **Note**: If using smaller amounts of vegetables and meat, cut sauce ingredients in half. **To Use Cooked Meat**: Use 2 cups cooked chicken, turkey or cubed roast pork. Omit stir-frying the cooked meat.

CHINESE STIR-FRY, SHRIMP

Follow preceding recipe, using ½ pound cleaned, deveined shrimp, cut into bite-size pieces. Stir-fry shrimp in 1 tablespoon oil until firm and pink. (Omit other meat in recipe.)

CITY CHICKEN

Pork and veal on wooden skewers; delicious!
(Or sometimes City Chicken is all pork.)

2 lbs. (6 to 8 pcs.) city chicken on wooden skewers
1 egg, slightly beaten
1 T. milk
¾ c. cracker crumbs or seasoned bread crumbs
1½ tsp. salt
¾ tsp. paprika
⅛ tsp. black pepper (opt.)
½ tsp. ground sage or poultry seasoning (opt.)
1½ T. olive oil
1½ T. butter
2 chicken bouillon cubes
1 c. boiling water

1. If making your own "City Chicken," cut 1 pound pork steak and 1 pound veal steak into pieces 1½ inches square and about ¾-inch thick. Alternate pieces of pork and veal on wooden skewers, spearing through middle of meat squares (remove all fat first). **2.** In med.-small bowl, combine egg and milk. **3.** In medium bowl, combine cracker crumbs, salt, paprika, pepper and sage. **4.** Dip City Chicken in milk mixture, then in cracker crumb mixture. **5.** Brown on all sides in hot oil and butter in skillet. **To Bake In Oven:** Place meat in baking dish or roaster. Dissolve bouillon cubes in boiling water and pour around meat. Cover with tight lid or foil and bake in 350° oven for 1¼ to 1½ hours or until tender. If meat is not brown, remove lid and bake 15 minutes longer. If desired, gravy may be made from drippings and liquid in pan. (Skim fat off top of

liquid.) Add water to make enough gravy, then thicken. **To Cook On Stove Top:** Dissolve bouillon cubes in boiling water and add to meat in skillet. Cover with tight lid and simmer 1 to 1½ hours, adding water several times, if needed. If desired, gravy may be made from drippings and liquid in pan. (Skim fat off top of liquid.) Add water to make enough gravy, then thicken. Serves 4 adults or more.

CITY CHICKEN, LARGER

12 City Chicken (3 to 4 lbs.) on wooden skewers
1 lg. egg, slightly beaten
2 T. milk
1¼ c. cracker crumbs or seasoned bread crumbs
2¼ tsp. salt
⅛ tsp. pepper
¾ tsp. sage or poultry seasoning (opt.)
2 T. olive oil
2 T. butter
1½ c. boiling water
3 chicken bouillon cubes

1. Follow directions for City Chicken. Serves 6 or more adults.

CORN DOGS

Inserting Popsicle sticks in the wieners
before dipping in batter is optional.

1 egg
1 c. all-purpose flour
⅔ c. cornmeal
1 tsp. baking powder
2 T. dry onion soup mix (opt.)
¼ tsp. salt
Milk
1 lb. wieners
Olive oil for deep-frying

1. Beat egg; add dry ingredients with just enough milk to make a stiff batter. **2.** Roll wieners in batter and fry in oil heated to 375°; cook until golden brown. **3.** Drain on paper towels and serve hot. (Ketchup and mustard may be brushed on before eating.)

CORNED BEEF & CABBAGE

Adapted from Beverly Lucich. Add no extra seasoning.
Always better the next day.

1 corned beef flat-cut brisket
Cold water
1 head cabbage, cut into wedges
Small potatoes, peeled
2 or 3 onions, sliced

1. Remove fat from corned beef, as much as possible. Put corned beef in roaster pan along with contents of packet that comes with it; cover with cold water. 2. Bake, covered, in 350° oven for 3 hours or until tender. 3. Remove meat from roaster and when cool enough, cut any remaining fat off. Cut meat into chunks. 4. Pour broth into wide-mouth jars and skim fat off the top. 5. Put meat, broth, uncooked cabbage wedges, uncooked potatoes and sliced onions back into roaster; cover and bake in 350° oven until cabbage and potatoes are tender.

CORNED BEEF & POTATO BAKE

From Dorothy Bowser.

Potatoes, boiled, peeled and diced to make 4 cups
1 onion, diced or chipped
1 (12-oz.) can corned beef, diced
3 T. butter
3 T. flour
¼ tsp. salt
⅛ tsp. black pepper
1 c. milk
1 c. half 'n half (or part evaporated milk and water)

1. In a greased 2- or 2½-quart baking dish, combine diced potatoes, onion and corned beef (gently). 2. Melt butter in saucepan and add flour, salt and pepper, stirring together; add 1 cup milk all at once, and bring to a boil, stirring. 3. Pour this white sauce over the potato mixture, stirring together a little; then pour 1 cup of half 'n half (or milk) over the top. 4. Bake 1 hour in preheated 350° oven, uncovered.

CORNED BEEF BOILED DINNER

Serves 3 adults.

3 to 4 c. potatoes, peeled and quartered
2 to 2½ c. carrots, peeled and quartered (opt.)
1 to 2 onions, sliced
1 clove garlic, minced (opt.)
1 bay leaf (opt.)
1½ tsp. salt
⅛ tsp. pepper
3 c. water
1 (12-oz.) can corned beef
1 sm. head cabbage, cut into 6 wedges (or cauliflower)

1. Place all ingredients, except meat and cabbage, into cooking pot. 2. Bring to a boil; cover and boil gently 10 minutes. 3. Add corned beef (in one whole piece to reduce disintegration) and cabbage wedges over top potatoes and carrots; cook, covered, 20 minutes longer or until vegetables are tender. (Do not boil hard, but simmer.) 4. Remove bay leaf.

CORNED BEEF REUBEN CASSEROLE

10 slices rye bread, cubed
1 (16-oz.) can (or 2 c.) sauerkraut, drained
1 (12-oz.) can corned beef, shredded with fork
8 to 12 oz. sliced or shredded Mozzarella or Monterey Jack cheese
8 oz. sliced or shredded Swiss cheese
1 c. sour cream or sour cream alternative
1 sm. onion, chopped
¼ c. butter, melted

1. Combine sour cream and chopped onion; set aside. 2. Turn oven dial to 350°. 3. Put 4 slices cubed rye bread over bottom of 13 x 9-inch pan. 4. Place remaining ingredients (except butter) in layers in order listed: sauerkraut, corned beef, the 2 cheeses, sour cream and onion mixture and the remaining 6 slices cubed rye bread. 5. Drizzle melted butter over bread cubes. 6. Bake in preheated 350° oven for 30 to 35 minutes or until hot and bubbly, and top bread cubes are toasty.

DRIED BEEF & CREAMED CABBAGE CASSEROLE

Adapted from Shirley Kaufman. Serves 4.

½ lg. head cabbage
1 (2.25-oz.) jar or pkg. dried beef, rinsed in warm water
White Sauce recipe
½ c. buttered crumbs

<u>White Sauce:</u>
3 T. butter
3 T. flour
¼ tsp. salt
⅛ tsp. pepper
1½ c. milk

1. Cut cabbage coarsely, removing core; cook in unsalted boiling water (about 5 minutes after coming to a boil). Drain. 2. Place cabbage and dried beef in alternate layers in greased or sprayed 1½ to 2-quart casserole. 3. To make white sauce, melt butter in saucepan; add flour, salt and pepper, stirring well. 4. Add milk all at once; cook quickly, stirring constantly until mixture thickens and bubbles. 5. Pour white sauce over cabbage and beef. 6. Top with buttered crumbs. 7. Bake, uncovered, in preheated 350° oven for 25 minutes.

DRIED BEEF OR CHIPPED HAM GRAVY, CREAMED

Blender method is easy. Serves 4 or 5.

4 c. milk
5 T. flour, packed level
2 T. butter (or half olive oil)
2¼ to 5 oz. dried beef, diced (or 8 oz. chipped ham)
Black pepper
Toast

1. In blender container, combine milk and flour; blend on low a few seconds until smooth. 2. In skillet, melt butter; lightly brown dried beef. 3. Add milk mixture all at once; bring to a boil, stirring almost constantly. 4. Lower heat and simmer gently 2 minutes. (It will be thin, but continues to thicken as it sets.) 5. Pour into serving dish, sprinkle with pepper and serve over toast. **Note**: If using chipped ham, a little salt may be needed, according to taste. If dried beef or chipped ham is limited, try adding some diced bologna. **Conventional Method:** Melt butter in skillet; lightly brown dried beef. Add flour and stir together. Add milk all at once; stir constantly until it comes to a boil. Lower heat and simmer 2 minutes.

GREEN PEPPERS, STUFFED

So good!

1 lb. lean ground beef (2 c.)
1 tsp. salt
⅛ tsp. pepper
1¼ c. soft bread crumbs
2 eggs (can be small)
1 onion, chopped
15 to 16 oz. tomato sauce, divided
6 green peppers

1. Mix together beef, salt, pepper, bread crumbs, eggs, onion and ¼ cup tomato sauce. 2. Wash peppers and cut in half; remove seeds and membrane. 3. Fill pepper halves with meat mixture; place in baking dish, pan or roaster. 4. Pour remaining tomato sauce around peppers; bake, uncovered, in 350° oven 1½ hours. **To Serve With Baked Potatoes:** Put scrubbed and pricked potatoes in the same oven the last 60 minutes (or the whole time if the potatoes are large).

GREEN PEPPERS, STUFFED (Cooked Rice)

From Pat Swarts. Recipe may be doubled.

6 to 7 med.-lg. green bell peppers
1 to 1¼ lbs. extra-lean ground beef
1 onion, chopped
¾ c. cooked rice
¾ tsp. salt
⅛ tsp. pepper
2 (8-oz.) cans tomato sauce, divided

1. Cut tops from peppers and remove seeds and membrane. 2. Combine beef, onion, cooked rice, salt, pepper and ¼ cup of the tomato sauce; mix well. 3. Fill peppers with meat mixture and place in small roaster or baking dish. 4. Pour remaining tomato sauce over and around peppers. 5. Bake, covered, in preheated 325° oven for 2 to 3 hours. Or, bake in 350° oven for 1½ hours, uncovered. (Spray pan with non-stick spray.)

GREEN PEPPERS, STUFFED (Large Recipe)

Recipe may be cut in half. Very good!

Green peppers (10 approx.)
1½ to 2 lbs. extra-lean ground beef
1½ tsp. salt
¼ tsp. black pepper
2 eggs
1 med.-lg. onion, chopped
1½ c. tomato juice, tomato sauce or canned tomatoes
¼ c. uncooked oats
¼ c. uncooked rice
1 c. soft bread crumbs (2 slices reg. bread)
3½ to 4 c. spaghetti sauce or tomato sauce or thick tomato juice

1. Wash and drain peppers; cut in half lengthwise or remove stem end, leaving whole. Remove seeds and membrane. 2. Combine meat, salt, pepper, eggs, onion, 1½ cups tomato liquid, oats, rice and bread crumbs. 3. Fill peppers with meat mixture and place in roaster or baking dish. 4. Pour spaghetti sauce or tomato sauce over and around peppers. Cover with lid or foil. 5. Bake 1½ hours in 350° oven, or 2 hours in 300° or 3 hours in 275° oven, or 3½ to 4 hours in 250° oven. (Toward the end of baking, uncover and turn the oven up to brown peppers a little.)

GREEN PEPPERS, STUFFED (Microwave)

4 lg. green peppers
1 lb. lean ground beef or ground turkey
1 sm. or med. onion, chopped
1 clove garlic, minced (opt.)
2 T. celery, chopped (opt.)
8 oz. (1 c.) tomato sauce
1 to 1¼ c. quick-cooking (Minute) rice
1 tsp. salt
½ tsp. basil leaves
⅛ tsp. black pepper

1. Cut peppers in half (horizontally); wash, remove seeds and pulp. Set aside. 2. In 1½ or 2-quart casserole, combine crumbled meat, onion, garlic and celery; cover with glass lid and microwave on HIGH 4 to 6 minutes, stirring after each minute. (If needful, drain off fat.) 3. Add tomato sauce, rice, salt, basil and pepper; mix well with meat. 4. Fill each pepper-half with mixture. Place in microwave-safe baking dish. 5. Cover with plastic wrap; microwave at HIGH 10 to 12 minutes or until peppers are tender and rice is cooked. 6. Let stand, covered, 3 minutes.

GREEN PEPPERS, STUFFED (Oatmeal)

If extra sauce is unwanted around the peppers, omit step 4.

6 (or more) green peppers
1½ lbs. extra-lean ground beef (3 c.)
1 to 1½ tsp. salt
¼ tsp. black pepper
1 extra-large egg (or 2 small eggs)

1 med. onion, chopped (½ c. approx.)
⅔ c. uncooked oatmeal
3½ to 4 c. spaghetti sauce or tomato sauce, divided

1. Wash and drain peppers; cut in half lengthwise or remove stem end, leaving whole. Remove seeds and membrane. **2.** Combine meat, salt, pepper, egg, onion, ⅔ cup of the spaghetti sauce or tomato sauce and oatmeal. **3.** Fill peppers with meat mixture and place in roaster or baking dish. **4.** Pour remaining spaghetti sauce or tomato sauce over and around peppers. Cover with lid or foil. **5.** Bake 1½ hours in 325° oven, or 2 hours in 300° oven, or 3 hours in 275° oven, or 3½ to 4 hours in 250° oven. **Note**: Remove lid last 15 to 20 minutes and bake at 350°. Ladle off any excess fat before serving.

GREEN PEPPERS, STUFFED (Small Recipe)

4 green bell peppers (6 to 8 halves)
½ lb. lean ground beef (1 c.)
½ tsp. salt
⅛ tsp. pepper
1 egg
2 T. raw rice (level)
1 T. fine dry bread crumbs
1 T. wheat germ (opt.)
2 to 4 T. chopped onion
16 oz. (2 c.) tomato sauce (or spaghetti sauce or pizza sauce), divided
2 T. water
2 tsp. sugar (opt.)

1. Wash and drain peppers; cut in half lengthwise or remove stem end, leaving whole. Remove seeds and membrane. **2.** Combine meat, salt, pepper, egg, rice, bread crumbs, onions and 2 tablespoons tomato sauce. **3.** Fill peppers with meat mixture and place in small roaster. **4.** Pour remaining tomato sauce around peppers; sprinkle water and sugar over sauce. **5.** Cover with lid or foil and bake in preheated 350° oven 1 to 1½ hours, or 2 hours in 300° oven, or 3 hours in 275° oven, or 3½ to 4 hours in 250° oven. **Note**: Remove lid or foil last 15 to 20 minutes. **West Bend Slow-Cooker**: Set dial on #3 and cook for 4 to 6 hours, or set dial on #5 and cook for 2 hours.

GUISO AND RICE

From Nick Melendez. Pronounced "Geese-so."

1 lb. hamburger
Small amt. of hot sausage (opt.)
1 onion
½ med. head of cabbage, coarsely chopped
1 t. salt
1 green pepper, coarsely chopped
Celery, sliced (opt.)
1 quart canned tomatoes (3½ to 4 cups), divided
½ t. garlic powder
½ t. Italian seasoning
⅛ t. black pepper

⅛ t. red cayenne pepper
Cooked rice

1. Fry hamburger, sausage and onion together; if there is grease, drain off. **2.** Add chopped cabbage, 1 t. salt and ½ c. tomatoes. Steam together until cabbage is somewhat wilted (with or without a lid). **3.** Add green pepper, celery, remaining tomatoes and seasonings; cook 20 minutes. **4.** Serve over hot cooked rice.

HAM, BAKED I

Make sure it is a fully cooked ham.

1 (3 to 8-lb.) pc. fully-cooked ham
3 to 4 c. water, depending on size of ham

1. Place ham and water in roaster. (Do not add salt.) **2.** Bake, covered, in 325° oven 2 to 2½ hours. Or, ham may be baked with no water and no lid, in 325° oven, allowing 30 minutes per pound. **Sunday Morning Baked Ham:** Bake in 275° oven with 3 cups water covered, for 3½ to 4½ hours (3 hours for the 3 to 3½-pound piece). **Ham Gravy:** Skim fat off broth in wide-necked quart jar. Measure 2½ cups skimmed ham broth into saucepan. Shake together ½ cup cold water and ⅓ cup flour; add flour mixture to boiling broth, stirring constantly. Add 2 to 3 drops Kitchen Bouquet or Gravy Master (just for color). Let gravy boil gently a few minutes. **Note**: Taste the broth. If too salty, add more water. Noodles may be cooked in the skimmed broth instead of making gravy.

HAM, BAKED II

9 to 10½ lb. piece of ham, not fully cooked; bake for 1½ hours at 325°, then lower heat to 275° and bake for 3 ½ hours.

HAM BALLS

From Martha Rough and Judy Dunn. Delicious!

2 lbs. ham loaf mix (ground ham and ground pork)
2 lg. Shredded Wheat biscuits, crumbled
2 eggs
1 c. milk

Syrup:
1½ c. packed brown sugar
⅔ c. water
¼ c. + 2 T. vinegar
¾ tsp. dry mustard

1. Mix together meat, Shredded Wheat, eggs and milk with hands or electric mixer. **2.** Form into 18 to 20 balls; place in 13 x 9-inch baking dish. **3.** Meanwhile, bring syrup ingredients to a boil; reduce heat and boil gently 4 minutes. **4.** Pour syrup over ham balls. **5.** Bake, uncovered, in 350° preheated oven 1 hour and 10 minutes, or until brown. (No need to baste or turn over.) **Longer Baking:** Bake in 200° or 250° oven for 3 to 4 hours. **Note**: 2 Shredded Wheat biscuits,

crushed in food processor, equals ⅔ cup. **To Cut Recipe in Half**: Bake in 8 x 8-inch or 9 x 9-inch square baking dish.

HAM LOAF, ADELE'S

From Adele Crognale.

1 lb. ground ham
1 lb. ground pork
2 eggs
1 c. milk
1 c. fine dry bread crumbs (plain)

Topping:
¼ c. packed brown sugar
¼ c. ketchup

1. Mix together ham, pork, eggs, milk and bread crumbs; form into a loaf. 2. Place in small or medium roaster. 3. Combine brown sugar and ketchup; spread over top ham loaf. 4. Bake in 350° oven 1½ hours, covered. (Remove lid the last 10 to 15 minutes.) **Note**: 2 pounds ham loaf mix may be substituted for the ground ham and ground pork.

HAM LOAF, HILLTOP

Adapted from Martha Rough and Jean Alexander.

2 lbs. ham loaf mix (ground ham and ground pork)
2 eggs
½ c. milk
2⅓ c. Wheaties, Bran Flakes or similar cereal, before
    crushing in food processor (1 c. after crushing,
    approx.)

1. Mix together all ingredients and form into a loaf. 2. Place in small or medium roaster; put 1 cup water around loaf and cover with lid. 3. Bake 1½ hours in 350° oven. **Sunday Morning Ham Loaf:** Bake in 250° oven for 3 to 4 hours.

HAM, POTATOES & CABBAGE
(or SMOKED SAUSAGE)

Ham pieces
1 ham bone (opt.)
4 c. water or ham broth (no fat)
4 c. raw potatoes, peeled and cut in quarters or smaller
Cabbage wedges
1 onion, sliced (opt.)

1. If ham and ham bone are not fully cooked, cook before adding remaining ingredients. 2. Combine ham, ham bone, 4 cups liquid and potatoes; boil 10 minutes. 3. Add cabbage wedges; cover with lid and boil gently 20 minutes longer or until both potatoes and cabbage are tender. 4. Taste to see if salt is needed. (When using ham broth, it is not usually necessary to add salt.) **Substitution for Ham:** Use ½ to 1 pound kielbasa or smoked sausage, sliced. (Add 1½ to 2 teaspoons salt.) **West Bend Slow-Cooker:** Set dial at 3½ and cook for 3 to 4 hours. Reduce water to 3 cups.

HAM, POTATOES & GREEN BEANS
(or KIELBASA)

Serves 4 hungry people or more.

6 c. fresh green beans (or canned green beans, drained)
4 to 5 c. potatoes, peeled and cut into pieces
3 c. water, green bean liquid or ham broth without fat
1 to 2 onions, sliced
2 tsp. salt (unless ham or broth is extra salty)
¼ tsp. black pepper (opt.)
Ham pieces (fat removed)

1. Combine all ingredients in pot and bring to a boil; reduce heat and simmer, covered, until both green beans and potatoes are tender. **Substitution for Ham:** Use ½ to 1 pound kielbasa or smoked sausage, sliced.

HAMBURGER CABBAGE CASSEROLE

1 lb. ground beef
¾ c. diced fresh onion
3 c. coarsely chopped cabbage
1 (10½-oz.) can cream of mushroom soup
1 soup can full of warm water
½ c. uncooked rice (not instant or minute rice)
1 can drained mushrooms (opt.)
1 tsp. salt
½ tsp. black pepper
¼ tsp. garlic salt
1 T. brown sugar
1 T. lemon juice

1. Brown ground beef and onion; drain off fat. 2. Place cabbage in a greased 2- or 2½-qt. casserole. 3. In a bowl, combine mushroom soup and warm water; mix together until smooth. 4. Combine ground beef, soup mixture, rice, drained mushrooms, salt, pepper, garlic salt, brown sugar and lemon juice all together and mix well; pour over cabbage. 5. Cover and bake in preheated 350° oven for 1 hour.

HAMBURGER CHINESE DINNER

Recipe may be doubled.

1 lb. ground beef
1 T. olive oil
1 (10½-oz.) can cream of mushroom soup
¾ c. warm water
¾ c. chopped fresh onion
¾ c. celery, thinly sliced
1 can bean sprouts, drained
¼ c. uncooked rice (not instant or minute rice)
⅛ c. soy sauce

1. Brown beef in oil; drain off fat. 2. In a large bowl, combine mushroom soup and warm water; mix together until smooth. 3. Add beef, the onion, celery, drained bean sprouts, rice and soy sauce; mix well and pour into a casserole. (If doubling

recipe, put into a 9x13 baking dish.) **4.** Cover and bake in preheated 350° oven for 1 hour.

HAMBURGER GRAVY

*This makes enough for 2 hungry adults;
serve over potatoes, toast, etc. Very good.*

1 tsp. olive oil or butter
½ lb. (1 c.) ground beef or ground venison
1 sm. onion, chopped
½ to 1 tsp. salt
⅛ tsp. pepper (or less)
1½ c. water
¼ tsp. Gravy Master or Kitchen Bouquet
⅓ c. water
¼ c. flour
1/16 tsp. oregano (opt.)

1. Heat oil in skillet and lightly brown meat and onion. (Leave meat in bite-size chunks.) **2.** In colander or sieve, drain fat off meat; rinse with very hot water. Return meat to skillet. **3.** Add salt, pepper, 1½ cups water and the Gravy Master; bring to a simmering boil. **4.** In jar, shake together ⅓ cup water and the flour. **5.** Turn heat off and add as much of the flour mixture as is needed for gravy consistency. **6.** Bring gravy to a boil, stirring; add oregano, if desired.

HAMBURGER-GREEN BEAN CASSEROLE

*Fresh green beans, cooked and
drained, may also be used.*

2 (16-oz.) cans or 1 qt. green beans, drained (saving ½ c. liquid)
½ to ¾ lb. ground beef
1 med. or lg. onion, chopped
1 tsp. butter or olive oil
½ tsp. salt
¼ tsp. pepper
1 (4-oz.) can mushrooms, drained
1 (10¾-oz.) can cream of mushroom soup, undiluted
Croutons or buttered bread crumbs

1. Put drained green beans in 2-quart casserole; set aside. **2.** In skillet, brown beef and onion in butter, adding salt and pepper; drain off fat, if any. **3.** Add mushrooms, soup and ½ cup bean liquid to beef, stirring together. **4.** Pour meat mixture over green beans; sprinkle top with croutons or bread crumbs. **5.** Bake in preheated 350° oven for 30 to 45 minutes, uncovered, or until bubbly.

HAMBURGER LAYERED CASSEROLE

Recipe from Greenville, PA.

1 lb. ground beef
2 onions, chopped or sliced
1 tsp. salt, divided

¼ tsp. pepper, divided
3½ to 4 c. raw potatoes, peeled and sliced thin
1 (15 to 16-oz.) can kidney beans or green beans or carrots or peas, drained
1 (10¾-oz.) can tomato soup or cream of mushroom soup, undiluted
½ c. water
1 tsp. sugar, if using tomato soup (opt.)

1. In skillet, cook beef and onions until meat is no longer pink; drain off all fat. **2.** Butter or spray 2 to 2½-quart casserole; turn oven dial to 350°. **3.** Layer ½ the meat mixture in bottom of casserole; sprinkle with ½ teaspoon salt and ⅛ teaspoon pepper. **4.** Layer all the sliced potatoes over meat. **5.** Layer remaining meat mixture over potatoes. **6.** Sprinkle with remaining ½ teaspoon salt and ⅛ teaspoon pepper. **7.** Layer the drained can of vegetables. **8.** Mix together soup, ⅓ cup water and the sugar, if used; pour soup mixture over all. **9.** Cover with lid or foil and bake in preheated 350° oven 1½ hours, or until potatoes are tender.

HAMBURGER-MASHED POTATO CASSEROLE I

A delicious casserole from Mary Trimble. Serves 4 to 5.

1 lb. lean ground beef
1 med. onion, chopped (½ c.)
½ tsp. salt
¼ tsp. pepper
½ T. olive oil
1 (15 to 16-oz.) can stewed tomatoes, drained
2 to 4 c. leftover mashed potatoes
4 to 6 cheese slices (thin)

1. Brown ground beef, onion, salt and pepper in hot oil; drain, discarding grease. **2.** In a casserole, alternate layers of meat and drained stewed tomatoes. **3.** Cover with mashed potatoes. **4.** Top with slices of cheese; bake in preheated 375° oven for 30 to 35 minutes, uncovered.

HAMBURGER-MASHED POTATO CASSEROLE II

*From Margaret Evans.
Leftover mashed potatoes may be used.*

1 tsp. olive oil
1 lb. ground beef
1 onion, chopped
1 tsp. salt
⅛ to ¼ tsp. pepper
1 (16-oz.) can whole kernel corn, drained (or 2 c. corn, cut off the cob)
2 tsp. sugar, divided
1 (10¾-oz.) can tomato soup, not diluted
4 to 5 c. peeled, cut-up potatoes
2 c. water
1½ tsp. salt

½ to ¾ c. milk
1 to 2 T. butter
Paprika

1. In skillet in hot oil, brown beef, onion, salt and pepper; drain off all fat. **2.** Grease sides of a 2 or 2½-quart casserole; put meat in bottom. **3.** Put drained corn over meat; sprinkle with 1 teaspoon sugar. **4.** Spoon tomato soup over corn; sprinkle with remaining sugar. **5.** Cook potatoes with water and second salt until tender (after coming to a boil, boil 20 minutes). **6.** Drain potatoes and mash, adding milk and butter. **7.** Spoon mashed potatoes over top of casserole; sprinkle with paprika. **8.** Bake in preheated 375° oven for 30 minutes, covered with lid or foil; remove cover and bake 5 to 10 minutes longer. <u>Note</u>: Drained green beans may be used instead of whole kernel corn.

HAMBURGER PASTA ITALIAN CASSEROLE

8 oz. penne, ziti, spirals or mostaccioli, uncooked (2⅓ c.)
2 qts. water, boiling
1 tsp. salt
¾ to 1 lb. lean ground beef
½ c. chopped onion or 2 T. dried onion
1 tsp. chopped garlic
½ c. chopped green pepper (opt.)
3 c. canned tomatoes or tomato juice or spaghetti sauce
1 (8-oz.) can tomato sauce (1 c.)
1½ to 2 T. sugar (opt.)
¾ tsp. salt
½ tsp. oregano
⅛ tsp. black pepper
10 to 12 oz. shredded Mozzarella cheese or part Provolone, divided (2½ to 3 cups or more)
Grated Parmesan cheese (opt.)

1. In large pan, cook pasta in 2 quarts boiling water and 1 teaspoon salt until tender (15 minutes, approx.); drain in colander and rinse. **2.** Meanwhile, in large skillet cook beef, onions, garlic and green pepper over medium heat until meat is no longer pink; if there is any excess fat, drain and discard. **3.** Put meat mixture in the large pan in which pasta was cooked; add tomatoes, tomato sauce, sugar, salt, oregano, pepper, 2 cups shredded cheese, and cooked pasta. Stir all together. **4.** Pour into greased or sprayed 13 x 9-inch baking dish; top with remaining cheese and sprinkle with Parmesan cheese. **5.** Bake, uncovered, in preheated 350° oven for 30 to 40 minutes, or until hot and bubbly.

HAMBURGER PIE WITH RICE

Extra-lean ground beef makes the crust, and rice is in the filling. Serves 5 or 6.

<u>Crust:</u>
⅞ to 1 lb. extra-lean ground beef

½ c. dry bread crumbs (Italian style or reg.)
¼ c. chopped onion
¼ c. chopped green pepper
½ c. (4 oz.) tomato sauce
1 tsp. salt
⅛ tsp. pepper
¼ tsp. oregano or Italian seasoning

<u>Filling:</u>
3 c. cooked rice (cook 1 c. raw rice)
1½ c. (12 oz.) tomato sauce
¼ tsp. salt (opt.)
1 c. shredded Cheddar cheese, divided

1. Turn oven dial to 350°. **2.** In bowl, combine all crust ingredients, mixing well; pat into bottom and sides of greased or sprayed 10-inch pie plate (<u>do not use a 9-inch pie plate</u>). **3.** Combine cooked rice, remaining tomato sauce, salt and ½ cup shredded cheese; spoon mixture into meat shell. **4.** Bake in preheated 350° oven for 30 minutes; sprinkle top with remaining cheese and bake 10 minutes longer, or until cheese is melted.

HAMBURGER-RICE HAPPY STUFF

From Adele Crognale.

1 lb. ground chuck
1 onion, chopped
1 (10¾-oz.) can cream of mushroom soup
½ soup can water
1⅓ c. Minute Rice, cooked according to pkg. directions

1. Brown ground chuck and onion; drain off fat. **2.** Add mushroom soup and ½ can water (or more water if needed to make proper consistency). **3.** Add cooked Minute Rice and heat through.

HAMBURGER-RICE RUSSIAN FLUFF CASSEROLE

1 med. or lg. onion, chopped
2 T. olive oil
1 to 1½ lbs. ground beef
3 c. cooked rice (cook 1 c. rice)
½ tsp. salt
⅛ tsp. black or cayenne pepper
1 (10¾-oz.) can tomato soup
1 (15 to 16-oz.) can peas with liquid

1. Sauté onion in oil; add ground beef, cooking 10 minutes. Drain off all excess fat. **2.** Add remaining ingredients; put in 2-quart casserole (can be covered or uncovered). **3.** Bake in preheated 350° oven for 45 minutes (or 1 hour at 325°).

HAMBURGER-RICE SUPPER, KATHLEEN'S

A top-of-the-stove meal; very good with a salad.

½ to 1 lb. ground beef
1 T. olive oil, if needed
1 c. raw reg. rice
2½ c. water
1 lg. onion, diced (1 c.)
1 green bell pepper, coarsely chopped
Fresh or canned mushrooms, drained (opt.)
1 beef bouillon cube
½ T. soy sauce
¾ tsp. salt

1. Brown ground beef in saucepan, Dutch oven or large skillet with oil; drain off excess fat. **2.** Add remaining ingredients; bring to a boil. **3.** Reduce heat to low and cover with tight lid. **4.** Cook on low heat 25 minutes or until rice is tender.

HAMBURGER SHIPWRECK CASSEROLE

Serves 4 to 5 people.

½ c. uncooked reg. rice (white or brown)
2 c. tomato juice or canned tomatoes
2½ c. raw potatoes, peeled and sliced
½ T. olive oil
¾ to 1 lb. ground beef (or more)
1 onion, chopped (any size)
1 tsp. salt
1 rib celery, sliced thin
1 carrot, peeled and sliced thin (1 c.)
1 (15 to 16-oz.) can kidney beans, lima beans or green
    beans, drained (or all three)
1 (10¾-oz.) can tomato soup or cream of mushroom soup
1 c. water
¼ tsp. Worcestershire sauce
1 T. sugar
¼ tsp. salt
⅛ tsp. pepper
½ tsp. chili powder (opt.)

1. Lay rice in bottom of greased or sprayed 2½ to 3-quart casserole or roaster or 13 x 9-inch cake pan. **2.** Add tomato juice and sliced potatoes over rice. **3.** In hot oil, lightly brown ground beef and onion; drain off fat and lay meat over potatoes. **4.** Sprinkle 1 teaspoon salt over meat. **5.** Layer celery, carrots and beans over top. **6.** In same meat skillet, heat soup with 1 cup water, Worcestershire sauce, sugar, ¼ teaspoon salt and the pepper, blending together well; pour over vegetables. **7.** Cover with lid or foil and bake in 275° oven for 3 to 4 hours, or 350° oven for 2 hours, or 375° oven for 1½ hours.

HEART (CROCK-POT)

1 (2½ to 3-lb.) beef heart
5 c. water
1 onion, sliced
1 tsp. salt
1 bay leaf (opt.)

1. Wash heart; cut out gristle and veins. **2.** Soak in cold salt water for 15 minutes; drain. **3.** Cook all ingredients in crock-pot 8 hours on HIGH, or 10 to 11 hours on LOW.

HEART, PRESSURE-COOKED

½ or 1 beef heart
2 T. butter
1 bay leaf (opt.)
1 onion (whole) or 1 T. instant minced onion
2 c. hot water
Salt and pepper

1. Wash heart; cut out gristle and veins. **2.** Soak in cold salt water for 15 minutes; wipe dry. **3.** Brown heart in melted butter. **4.** Add hot water and sprinkle heart with salt and pepper. **5.** Cover with lid and pressure-cook at 15 pounds for 45 minutes; let pressure drop of its own accord.

HEART, STUFFED & BAKED

½ or 1 beef or deer heart
2 T. butter
1 med. onion (½ c.), chopped
3 c. soft bread crumbs (about 6 slices bread)
¼ tsp. rubbed sage or poultry seasoning
¼ tsp. salt
⅓ c. lukewarm water
1 onion, cut in half
1 c. hot water

1. Wash heart and cut out gristle and veins. **2.** Soak in cold water with 1 teaspoon salt for 15 minutes; drain. **3.** Slowly cook chopped onion in melted butter 5 minutes. **4.** Combine bread crumbs, sage, salt and lukewarm water; mix together with cooked onion. **5.** Make an opening in the heart with sharp knife for stuffing. (Or cut it in half.) **6.** Sprinkle inside of heart with salt and pepper; fill with stuffing and sew up opening or use wooden picks or skewer to fasten. (Or fill each heart-half with stuffing.) **7.** Place on a rack in baking dish or roaster; add 1 cup hot water and onion halves. **8.** Cover tightly with lid or foil and bake in preheated 350° oven about 2 hours, or until tender. (Or pressure at 15 pounds for 45 minutes; let pressure drop of its own accord.)

LASAGNA, CLASSIC

Makes 8 to 12 servings.

½ lb. (8 oz.) lasagna noodles
1 to 1½ lbs. ground beef (or part sausage, plain or Italian)
½ to 1 c. chopped onion
2 cloves garlic, minced or pressed (or ¼ tsp. garlic powder)
1 (28-oz.) can tomatoes, broken up (3½ c.)
12 oz. tomato paste
1 tsp. salt
½ tsp. oregano
1½ tsp. dried basil
¼ tsp. pepper
1 to 2 T. sugar
1 egg (or 2 sm. eggs)
15 to 16 oz. cottage cheese or Ricotta cheese (2 c.)
1 T. dried parsley leaves
1 lb. (4 c.) Mozzarella cheese, divided
½ lb. Provolone), shredded
¾ c. grated Parmesan or Romano cheese, divided

1. Cook lasagna noodles in 3 quarts boiling water with 1 tablespoon salt and 1 tablespoon olive oil until tender (about 15 to 20 minutes); drain and rinse with cold water. 2. While noodles are cooking, lightly brown meat in large skillet or cooking pot; drain off fat and rinse in colander with very hot water; drain again. 3. Return meat to cooking pot and add onions and minced garlic or garlic powder; cook 5 minutes, stirring frequently. 4. Add tomatoes, tomato paste, salt, oregano, basil, pepper and sugar. 5. On very low heat, simmer 15 minutes, stirring occasionally. 6. Combine egg, cottage cheese, parsley flakes and 1 cup shredded Mozzarella cheese (in food processor or blender container, if desired), mixing well. 7. In bottom of ungreased lasagna pan or 13 x 9-inch baking dish (should be at least 2 inches deep), spread a thin layer of meat sauce. 8. Layer ⅓ of noodles in dish. 9. Layer ⅓ of meat sauce over top. 10. Layer ⅓ of cottage cheese mixture. 11. Layer 1 cup Mozzarella or Provolone cheese. 12. Layer ¼ cup Parmesan cheese. 13. Repeat procedure 2 more times. 14. Cover with foil and bake in preheated 375° oven for 25 to 30 minutes. 15. Remove foil and bake, uncovered, 25 to 30 minutes longer. 16. Let stand 10 minutes before cutting. **Note**: Lasagna may be assembled the day before, or several hours ahead of time, and refrigerated. Allow 10 to 15 minutes longer in oven. **Note**: Pepperoni-lovers may sprinkle ⅛ to ¼ cup diced pepperoni over top. **Note**: To cut this recipe in half, bake in an 8 x 8 x 2-inch dish.

LIVER & ONIONS, BAKED IN GRAVY

Recipe may be doubled. Serve with mashed or boiled potatoes. This makes enough for 3 to 4 people.

1 to 1¼ lbs. beef liver, cut in serving-size pcs.
¼ c. flour
2 T. butter
3 to 4 onions, sliced
3½ c. water
1 tsp. salt
⅛ tsp. pepper
½ c. cold water
⅓ c. flour

1. Wash liver pieces in cold water and drain; dip in flour and brown on both sides in hot butter. (Use large skillet.) 2. Lay browned liver in baking dish or small roaster. 3. Arrange sliced onions over liver. 4. Bring 3½ cups water to boiling in the skillet, adding salt and pepper. 5. Shake together ⅓ cup cold water and cup flour in covered jar. 6. Remove skillet from heat and add all the thickening while stirring. 7. Bring gravy to a boil, stirring constantly. 8. Pour gravy through a sieve over the liver and onions. (Gravy will thicken more during baking.) 9. Bake, covered, in 350° oven for 2 hours (or in 250° oven for 3 hours). **Crock-Pot:** Reduce water to 2 cups; cook on HIGH for 2 hours, then turn to LOW and cook 3 additional hours (covered).

MACARONI & CHEESE, BAKED I

Serves 4 to 6.

8 oz. (2 c.) uncooked elbow macaroni (about 4 c., cooked)
1½ T. olive oil or butter
2 T. finely chopped onion
¾ tsp. salt
¼ tsp. pepper
1½ T. flour, packed level
2 c. milk
8 oz. (2 c.) shredded or diced American, Velveeta, Colby or sharp Cheddar cheese

1. Cook macaroni in 2 quarts boiling water and 2 teaspoons salt until tender (about 12 minutes); drain and put in buttered or sprayed 2-quart casserole. 2. Melt butter in saucepan; add onion and cook until tender. 3. Add salt, pepper and flour, stirring well. 4. Add milk all at once and blend together; cook, stirring constantly, until bubbly. 5. Turn off heat and add cheese; stir until melted. 6. Pour cheese mixture over macaroni and stir gently together. 7. Bake in preheated 375° oven for 30 minutes, until hot and bubbly. **Note**: 10 ounces of cheese may be used, if desired. **Broiler Version:** Follow directions through step 6. Sprinkle with 1 tablespoon grated Parmesan cheese and ¼ cup shredded Cheddar cheese. Preheat broiler; broil 4 inches from heat source for about 5 minutes, until golden. (Leave oven door ajar while broiling.)

MACARONI & CHEESE, BAKED II

From Patricia Swarts. To double this recipe, bake in 13 x 9-inch baking pan or 3½ to 4-quart baking dish.

1½ c. uncooked elbow macaroni
3 T. butter
3 T. flour (level)
½ tsp. salt
2 c. milk

8 oz. (2 c.) shredded or diced Colby, Longhorn or American cheese
2 oz. (½ c.) shredded sharp Cheddar cheese
Pepper

1. Cook macaroni in 1½ quarts boiling water and 2 teaspoons salt until tender (about 12 minutes); drain and put in buttered or sprayed 2-quart casserole. 2. Melt butter in saucepan; remove from heat and stir in flour and ½ teaspoon salt until blended together. 3. Add milk all at once; return to heat and bring to a boil, stirring constantly. 4. Reduce heat and simmer 1 minute, stirring. 5. Turn heat off and gradually stir in cheese; beat with large spoon until cheese is nearly all melted. 6. Pour cheese sauce over macaroni; stir together. 7. Sprinkle pepper lightly over top. 8. Bake in preheated 375° oven for 30 minutes, covered; remove cover and bake 15 minutes longer or until golden brown on top. Serves 4 to 5.

MACARONI & CHEESE, EASY

From Ruth Melichar.

7 to 8 oz. (or 2 c.) macaroni, uncooked
16 oz. Longhorn or sharp Cheddar cheese, cubed or shredded
1 T. butter
2 T. finely chopped onion (or less)
3 eggs, beaten
2 c. milk
2 T. butter

1. Cook macaroni in 2 quarts boiling water and 2 teaspoons salt until tender (about 12 minutes); drain. 2. In buttered or sprayed 2 or 2½-quart casserole, layer half the macaroni. 3. Layer half the cheese. 4. Dot with 1 tablespoon butter and sprinkle onion over top. 5. Add remaining macaroni, then remaining cheese. 6. In bowl, combine beaten eggs with milk; pour over macaroni. 7. Top with 2 tablespoons butter, cut in chunks; bake, uncovered, in preheated 350° oven 45 minutes.

MACARONI & CHEESE, ELECTRIC SKILLET

Serves 4 or more.

8 oz. (2 c.) macaroni, uncooked
2 T. butter
⅓ c. fine dry bread crumbs
2 T. butter
1 T. minced onion
1 T. flour (level)
¾ tsp. salt
¼ tsp. dry mustard
⅛ tsp. pepper
2 c. milk
8 oz. (2 c.) shredded cheese, divided
Paprika

1. Cook macaroni in 2 quarts of boiling water and 2 teaspoons salt until tender (about 12 minutes); drain. Set aside. 2.

Preheat electric skillet to 300°. 3. Melt 2 tablespoons butter in electric skillet; add bread crumbs and brown, stirring. 4. Remove crumbs and set aside. 5. Melt second 2 tablespoons butter in electric skillet; add onion and sauté at 275°. 6. Blend in flour, salt, dry mustard and pepper. 7. Add milk and stir until smooth and bubbly at 300°. 8. Stir in 1½ cups shredded cheese and the drained macaroni. 9. Stir frequently with wooden spoon until cheese is melted. 10. Turn heat to 225°; sprinkle remaining ½ cup cheese and the crumb mixture over top. 11. Cook about 25 minutes, covered, at 225°.

MACARONI, CHEESE & MUSHROOM CASSEROLE

From Adele Crognale; for mushroom lovers.

8 oz. (2 c.) uncooked elbow macaroni (cook and drain)
1 (10¾-oz.) can cream of mushroom soup, undiluted
1 (4-oz.) can mushroom stems and pcs, including liquid
8 oz. (2 c.) shredded Cheddar cheese
1 c. mayonnaise
½ c. chopped onion
1 sm. green bell pepper, chopped
1 T. chopped pimiento

Topping:
2 slices bread, buttered and cubed

1. Mix all together (except topping); pour into greased or sprayed casserole. 2. Bake, uncovered, in preheated 375° oven for 30 minutes; then sprinkle buttered bread crumbs over top and bake 15 minutes longer.

MACARONI & CHEESE, QUICK

A top-of-the-stove recipe which is surprisingly good.

7 to 8 oz. (1¾ c. uncooked) elbow macaroni, cooked and drained
¼ c. milk
8 oz. cheese, diced or shredded (or less)
2 T. butter
⅛ tsp. salt
⅛ tsp. pepper

1. In heavy saucepan (or deep black iron skillet), combine milk, cheese, butter, salt and pepper; melt into a sauce. 2. Add hot, drained macaroni.

MACARONI, CHEESE & SMOKED SAUSAGE

*Serves 6. Leftovers? This is delicious
warmed up (fried) in a Pam-sprayed skillet.*

2⅔ to 3 c. elbow macaroni, uncooked
1 to 2 tsp. olive oil
1 lb. smoked sausage or kielbasa
1 med. onion, chopped
½ green bell pepper, diced (opt.)

3 T. butter
3 T. flour
2 c. milk
8 oz. (2 c.) shredded sharp Cheddar cheese
¼ c. grated Parmesan cheese (opt.)
½ to 1 tsp. salt

1. Cook macaroni according to package directions; drain. Rinse with cold water and drain again. 2. Meanwhile, in large skillet with oil, cook sausage (cut into sections) until well browned on all sides. (If sausage is not "fully cooked," cook and fry until thoroughly cooked.) 3. Remove sausage from skillet; over medium heat, add onion and green pepper to skillet drippings and cook until tender, about 5 minutes, stirring occasionally. 4. Drain off all fat; add vegetables to macaroni along with the sausage which has been cut into ½ to 1-inch thick slices. 5. In small saucepan, melt butter; stir in flour. 6. Add milk all at once; heat to boiling, stirring frequently. 7. Remove from heat and stir in both cheeses and salt, until cheese melts. 8. Add to macaroni-sausage mixture and stir together. 9. Pour into greased or sprayed 12 x 8-inch or 13 x 9-inch baking dish. 10. Bake in preheated 375° oven for 25 to 30 minutes, until hot and bubbly.

MACARONI & HAMBURGER MEAL

Top-of-the-stove Johnny Marzetti (or goulash).
Serves 4 adults or more.

2 tsp. olive oil
¾ to 1 lb. (1½ to 2 c.) ground beef
½ tsp. salt
⅛ tsp. black pepper
½ c. chopped onion (or 1 onion, chopped)
1 to 2 cloves garlic, chopped (opt.)
2 c. tomato juice or canned tomatoes
8 oz. (1 c.) tomato sauce
¼ c. water
½ tsp. Italian seasoning, basil or oregano
1 to 2 T. sugar (opt.)
½ to 1 green bell pepper, diced (opt.)
2 c. uncooked macaroni

1. In oil, lightly brown beef with salt, pepper, onions and garlic; drain off excess fat, if any. 2. Add tomato juice, tomato sauce, water, Italian seasoning, sugar and green pepper; bring to a boil. On low heat, simmer 15 minutes, covered. 3. Meanwhile, cook macaroni in 2 quarts boiling water and 2 teaspoons salt about 12 minutes, or until tender; drain. 4. Add drained macaroni to tomato-meat mixture; on low heat, cook just long enough to heat macaroni. **Kelly Crouch's Version:** Substitute 2¼ cups V-8 juice in place of the tomato juice and water. Add 1 (15 to 16-oz.) can kidney beans, drained and rinsed. **Ken Dilley's Version**: Cook 1 lb. macaroni. Instead of the tomato juice, tomato sauce and ¼ c. water, he uses 1 qt. canned tomatoes, mashed somewhat with a fork, and adds some butter to the recipe.

MACARONI OVERNIGHT CASSEROLE, EASY

From Carolyn Benninger Deets.

1 c. uncooked elbow macaroni
1 (10¾-oz.) can cream of chicken, cream of mushroom or cream of celery soup
1 c. milk
1 med. onion, chopped (or less)
4 oz. (1 c.) diced American or Cheddar cheese
1 c. cooked meat (chicken, turkey, ham, pork, tuna, Spam, sliced wieners or ½ pkg. dried beef, cut up)
Croutons (opt.)

1. In 2-quart casserole, combine all ingredients, except croutons. 2. Cover and refrigerate overnight. (The macaroni absorbs the milk and softens overnight.) 3. Microwave on HIGH, covered, for 15 minutes. 4. Top with croutons just before serving. **Conventional Oven:** Bake in preheated 350° oven for 1¼ hours, uncovered. Recipe may be doubled for conventional oven.

<u>Optional Ingredients:</u>
3 c. cooked, diced chicken
½ jar pimientos
1 c. celery, chopped
¼ tsp. salt
½ green pepper, chopped
¼ lb. Velveeta cheese, diced

MANICOTTI, CHEESE-FILLED

<u>Sauce:</u>
1 med. onion, chopped (½ c.)
1 sm. clove garlic, crushed (or ⅛ tsp. garlic powder)
2 T. (⅛ c.) olive oil
3 c. tomato juice or canned tomatoes, undrained
1 c. water or tomato sauce (8 oz.)
1 (6-oz.) can tomato paste
2 T. chopped parsley or 2 tsp. dried parsley flakes
½ tsp. salt
¼ tsp. pepper
½ tsp. oregano
½ tsp. basil or Italian seasoning
1 T. sugar
7 drops bottled hot pepper sauce (opt.)

<u>Shells:</u>
1 c. all-purpose flour
1 c. cool water
¼ tsp. salt
4 eggs (room temp.)

<u>Cheese Filling:</u>
1 lb. ricotta cheese
4 oz. Mozzarella cheese (1 c.), diced or shredded
3 T. grated Parmesan cheese
1 egg
½ tsp. salt

⅛ tsp. pepper
1 T. chopped parsley or 1 tsp. dried parsley flakes
2 T. grated Parmesan cheese for top

1. Fry onion and garlic in hot oil for 5 minutes. **2.** Add remaining sauce ingredients, stirring well. If using canned tomatoes, mash with fork. **3.** Bring to a boil; reduce heat and simmer, covered, for 30 to 60 minutes, stirring occasionally. **4.** Meanwhile, make manicotti shells; mix flour, water and salt until smooth. **5.** Beat in eggs, one at a time. **6.** Slowly heat 8-inch nonstick skillet; pour in 3 tablespoons batter, rotating skillet quickly to spread batter evenly over bottom. **7.** Cook over medium heat until top is dry, but bottom is not brown. **8.** Turn out on a wire rack to cool; continue until all batter is used. As manicotti cools, stack with waxed paper between them. **9.** Make Cheese Filling: combine all filling ingredients, mixing well. **10.** Spread about ¼ cup filling down the center of each manicotti and roll up. **11.** In 13 x 9-inch (or 12 x 8-inch) baking dish, spoon 1½ cups sauce over bottom. **12.** Place rolled manicotti, seam side down, in single layer. If any remains, lay on top. **13.** Pour remaining sauce over all; sprinkle with 2 tablespoons grated Parmesan cheese. **14.** Bake in preheated 350° oven, uncovered, for 30 to 40 minutes, or until bubbly.

MANICOTTI, QUICK (With Sausage Links)

12 manicotti shells (store bought)
12 pork sausage links (not small breakfast links) or 12 pieces of string cheese
4 (1½-oz.) slices Mozzarella cheese
2 (15-oz.) cans tomato sauce or 3½ to 4 c. spaghetti sauce
½ tsp. oregano
½ tsp. basil
1 tsp. salt
⅛ tsp. pepper
¼ c. grated Parmesan cheese

1. Cook manicotti shells in 4 quarts boiling water and 1 tablespoon salt for 10 minutes, stirring occasionally; drain. Rinse in cold water and drain. **2.** Brown sausage links; drain on paper towels. **3.** Wrap each sausage in ⅓ slice cheese and stuff into shell or stuff with string cheese. **4.** Arrange manicotti in buttered 12 x 8-inch shallow baking dish. **5.** Combine tomato sauce and seasonings; pour over manicotti on each shell. **6.** Sprinkle with Parmesan cheese. **7.** Cover and bake in preheated 400° oven for 30 minutes.

MEATBALLS, BASIC

Makes 20 or more small meatballs.

1 lb. ground beef
½ c. fine dry bread crumbs
⅛ c. finely chopped onion
1 egg
¼ c. milk
1 tsp. salt
⅛ tsp. pepper (opt.)
1 T. freshly chopped parsley or 1 tsp. dried parsley flakes (opt.)
½ tsp. Worcestershire sauce

1. Mix together all ingredients with hands or electric mixer. **2.** Shape into meatballs, using ⅛-cup measure. **3.** Brown in skillet, turning occasionally. (Or place on ungreased cookie sheet with sides, or on shallow cake pans; line with foil, then spray with non-stick spray and bake in preheated 375° oven for 25 minutes, or until light brown.) **4.** Lift meatballs onto paper towel to drain; use as desired. Meatballs may be frozen. **Crock-Pot Meatballs & Spaghetti Sauce:** Put meatballs and 4 cups spaghetti sauce into crock-pot. Turn on HIGH for 45 minutes, or until sauce is bubbly hot; then turn on LOW to keep hot as long as desired.

MEATBALLS IN TOMATO SOUP (or MUSHROOM GRAVY)

1 lb. lean ground beef
1 T. instant minced onion (or 3 T. fresh chopped onion)
½ c. fine dry bread crumbs, seasoned or plain
½ c. water
1 egg
¾ tsp. salt
⅛ tsp. pepper
Flour to roll balls in
1 T. olive oil
1 (10¾-oz.) can condensed tomato soup
⅓ c. water
½ to 1 T. sugar

1. Mix together ground beef, onion, bread crumbs, ½ cup water, egg, salt and pepper. **2.** Shape into 12 balls using a ¼-cup measure (level) for each. **3.** Roll balls in flour and brown in hot olive oil; drain meatballs on paper towel. **4.** In med.-small bowl, combine soup, ⅓ cup water and the sugar; mix well. **5.** Place meatballs in 1½ to 2-quart casserole; pour soup mixture over balls. **6.** Bake, covered, in 275° oven for 3 hours, or in 300° oven for 2 hours, or in 350° oven for 1½ hours. **Stove-Top Method:** In cooking pan, pour soup mixture over meatballs. Simmer on low heat, covered, for 30 minutes. **Mushroom Gravy Version:** Use mushroom soup and ⅛ teaspoon Kitchen Bouquet or Gravy Master. Omit sugar.

MEATBALLS, OVEN-BARBECUED

Makes 30 meatballs.

1½ lbs. ground beef (3 c.)
¼ to ⅓ c. chopped onion
2 eggs
1 c. fine dry bread crumbs (plain)
⅔ c. milk
1½ tsp. salt
⅛ tsp. pepper
¼ tsp. allspice
¼ tsp. nutmeg

Sauce:
1 c. ketchup
2 T. packed brown sugar
2 T. Worcestershire sauce
1 T. vinegar

1. Combine all ingredients for meatballs in bowl and mix well; shape into balls. **2.** Place in 13 x 9-inch baking dish or pan and bake, uncovered, in preheated 375° oven 25 to 30 minutes or until lightly browned. **3.** Pour off excess fat. **4.** Combine sauce ingredients and pour over meatballs; cover with foil and continue baking 25 to 30 minutes longer. **5.** Remove foil and bake 10 to 15 minutes longer, uncovered. **Crock-Pot:** after step # 3, cook in crock-pot on LOW 4 hours, covered.

MEATBALLS, YUMMY (Baked)

Makes about 30 meatballs in sauce.

1½ lbs. lean ground beef, deerburger or ground turkey
1 sm. onion, chopped
⅓ c. raw rice
⅓ c. cracker crumbs
1 egg
1 tsp. salt
¼ tsp. pepper
2 to 3 c. spaghetti sauce or home-canned tomato soup

1. Combine meat, onion, rice, cracker crumbs, egg, salt and pepper, mixing well. **2.** Shape into meatballs the size of golf balls; brown lightly in skillet with 1 tablespoon olive oil. **3.** Drain meatballs on paper towel, then place in greased or sprayed casserole. **4.** Pour spaghetti sauce or home-canned tomato soup over meatballs. **5.** Bake, covered, in 350° oven for 1½ hours.

MEAT LOAF, BLENDER OR FOOD PROCESSOR

2¾ to 3 lbs. ground beef
2¼ tsp. salt
¾ c. cracker crumbs or 6 slices bread, diced
3 eggs
1 onion, quartered
½ c. celery tops and leaves
¼ c. milk
Ketchup for top

1. In large bowl, combine beef, salt and cracker crumbs or diced bread. **2.** In blender or food processor container, blend eggs, onion, celery and milk until smooth; add to meat mixture and mix all together. **3.** Shape into loaf and place in greased or sprayed roaster; add 1 cup water around loaf. **4.** Gently crisscross top of loaf with table knife; spread ketchup over top. **5.** Bake, uncovered, in 400° oven for 30 minutes; reduce heat to 375° and bake 30 minutes longer. **Slower Heat:** Bake in 250° or 275° oven for 3 to 4 hours.

MEAT LOAF, DARLINGTON

1½ lbs. ground beef
1½ c. soft crumbled bread
1½ tsp. salt
⅛ to ¼ tsp. pepper
1 egg
¼ c. milk
¼ c. chopped onion
¼ c. chopped green pepper
¼ c. finely shredded carrot

1. Mix all ingredients together (egg, milk and vegetables may be blended in blender, if desired; then added). **2.** Shape into loaf and wrap in foil. **3.** Place meat loaf in baking pan and bake in preheated 350° oven 1½ hours. (Loosen foil and uncover top the last 15 minutes.)

MEAT LOAF, EASY

Serves 5 to 6 people.

1½ lbs. ground beef or ground venison
2 eggs
½ c. oatmeal, uncooked
⅓ c. chopped onion
2 to 4 T. milk
1¼ tsp. salt
⅛ tsp. garlic powder
⅛ tsp. pepper
3 T. ketchup for top of meat loaf

1. Turn oven dial to 350°. **2.** Combine all ingredients, except ketchup and mix well. **3.** Shape into loaf and place in small roaster with ½ cup water around it. **4.** Crisscross top of loaf with knife and spread with ketchup. **5.** Bake in preheated 350° oven, covered, 1½ hours, removing lid the last 20 minutes. **Slower Temperature:** Bake in 250° oven, covered, for 4 hours. (Spray bottom of roaster with non-stick spray.) **Note:** Half ground beef and half ground turkey may be used, adding ½ teaspoon thyme.

MEAT LOAF, INDIVIDUAL LOAVES IN MUFFIN CUPS

These are speedy! Recipe can be cut in half.

1 lb. ground beef (2 c.)
1 egg
⅛ c. (2 T.) milk or evaporated milk or canned tomatoes
⅛ c. (2 T.) ketchup
1 c. soft bread crumbs
⅓ c. chopped onion (or part chopped celery)
1 tsp. salt
½ tsp. dry mustard
½ T. horseradish (opt.)
Ketchup for tops of meat loaves

1. Turn oven dial to 375°. 2. Combine meat loaf ingredients; divide into 8 little round loaves. 3. Place in 8 greased or sprayed muffin cups. 4. Spread about ½ tablespoon ketchup over the top of each loaf. 5. Bake in preheated 375° oven for 30 minutes. <u>Italian Flavor:</u> Substitute ¼ cup tomato sauce, tomato soup or spaghetti sauce for the milk and first ketchup. Add ½ teaspoon oregano.

MEAT LOAF, LILLIAN'S

Adapted from Lillian Stevenson Rohleder.

1 egg, beaten
1½ lbs. ground chuck
1 c. canned tomatoes or milk
¼ c. chopped onion
½ c. uncooked oats
1½ tsp. salt
1 tsp. dry mustard
⅛ tsp. garlic powder (opt.)
½ tsp. Worcestershire sauce
Ketchup for top

1. Turn oven dial to 350°. 2. Combine all ingredients, except ketchup, and mix well. 3. Shape into loaf and place in shallow baking pan. 4. Crisscross top of loaf with knife and spread with ketchup. 5. Bake in preheated 350° oven, uncovered, 1 to 1½ hours.

MEAT LOAF, MICROWAVE I

Do not use diet bread.

1 lb. ground beef
1 c. soft bread crumbs (2 slices bread)
1 med. onion, chopped (about ½ c.)
⅓ c. milk
1 egg
¾ tsp. salt
⅛ tsp. pepper
1 T. Worcestershire sauce or Heinz 57 Sauce
2 T. ketchup for top

1. In bowl, combine all ingredients, except ketchup. 2. Pack mixture into ungreased glass loaf pan; spread ketchup over top. 3. Cover with waxed paper and microwave on HIGH 13 minutes. 4. Let stand 5 minutes. 5. Microwave 2 minutes longer, uncovered. 6. Let stand another 5 minutes before serving.

MEAT LOAF, MICROWAVE II (Larger)

Do not use diet bread.

1½ lbs. ground beef
1½ c. soft bread crumbs (3 slices bread)
¼ c. chopped onion or 1 T. instant minced onion
¼ c. milk
2 eggs

1 tsp. salt
⅛ to ¼ tsp. pepper
1 T. Worcestershire sauce or Heinz 57 Sauce
¼ c. ketchup for top

1. In bowl, combine all ingredients, except ketchup. 2. Pack mixture into ungreased glass loaf pan. 3. Microwave, uncovered, on 70% (medium-high) 20 minutes. 4. Spread ketchup over top and microwave on 70% (medium-high) 5 minutes longer. (Center of meat loaf should be firm and should have lost its pink color.) 5. Let stand 5 to 10 minutes. Serves 4 to 6 people.

MEAT LOAF, OLD-FASHIONED I

Recipe may be cut in half or doubled.

1⅔ to 2 lbs. ground beef
1½ to 2 tsp. salt
2 lg. (or 3 sm.) eggs
⅓ c. uncooked rolled oats
⅓ to ½ c. fine dry bread crumbs or finely crushed cracker crumbs (15 soda crackers, 2 x 2-in. each)
1 med. onion, chopped (⅓ to ½ c.) or ½ c. finely chopped celery, or both
⅓ c. milk, tomato juice, canned tomatoes or tomato sauce
2 to 3 T. ketchup for top of meat loaf

1. Combine all ingredients, except ketchup, in large bowl, using hands or electric mixer. 2. Form into a loaf and place in greased or sprayed baking pan or roaster. 3. Put ⅔ cup water around meat loaf. 4. Score top of loaf with knife in crisscross fashion; spread ketchup over top. 5. Bake in preheated 350° oven, uncovered, 1½ hours. <u>Slower Heat:</u> Bake in 250° or 275° oven in covered roaster for 3 to 4 hours, removing lid the last 30 minutes. <u>Substitution</u>: 2 cups (4 to 4½ slices) soft crumbled bread may be substituted for cracker crumbs and oatmeal. (Or use 2 slices soft crumbled bread and ¼ cup oatmeal.) <u>To Reheat:</u> Cover with aluminum foil and heat in preheated 350° oven 15 minutes, or until thoroughly heated. <u>Note</u>: This can also be baked at 325° for 2 hours, removing lid the last 30 minutes.

MEAT LOAF, OLD-FASHIONED II (Larger)

2¾ to 3 lbs. ground beef (5½ to 6 c.)
2 tsp. salt
½ c. cracker crumbs
½ c. uncooked oatmeal, packed
1 med. to lg. onion, chopped (½ to ⅔ c.)
¼ c. celery, chopped
3 lg. or 4 med. eggs (or 5 egg yolks)
¾ c. tomato juice, tomato sauce or canned tomatoes
3 T. ketchup for top

1. In large bowl, combine all ingredients, except ketchup; mix well. 2. Form into loaf and place in greased or sprayed baking pan or roaster. 3. Add ½ cup water around meat loaf. 4. Gently crisscross top of loaf with table knife; spread ketchup

over top. **5.** Bake, covered, in 325° oven 2 hours, removing lid the last 30 minutes. <u>Slower Heat:</u> Bake in 275° oven for 3½ hours, removing lid the last 30 minutes and turning oven dial higher. <u>Blender:</u> The onions, celery, eggs and tomato liquid may be pureed in blender or food processor until smooth, if desired. <u>Substitution</u>: ¾ cup cracker crumbs may be used, omitting oatmeal.

MEAT LOAF, ONION SOUP MIX

2 lbs. ground beef
1½ c. soft bread crumbs (3 slices)
1 env. dry onion soup mix (about 4 T. bulk onion soup mix)
⅓ c. ketchup
⅔ c. water
2 eggs

1. Turn oven dial to 350°. **2.** In large bowl, combine all ingredients. **3.** In large shallow baking dish, shape into loaf. **4.** Bake 1 hour and 15 minutes, uncovered.

MEAT LOAF (Picante Sauce)

Also called "Everyday Meat Loaf."

⅔ c. dry bread crumbs
1 c. milk
1½ lbs. ground beef
2 eggs
¼ c. chopped onion
1 tsp. salt
½ tsp. ground or rubbed sage
¼ tsp. pepper

Picante Sauce:
3 T. brown sugar
¼ c. ketchup
¼ tsp. nutmeg
1 tsp. dry mustard (or 1 T. prepared mustard)

1. <u>Soak crumbs in milk.</u> **2.** Add remaining meat loaf ingredients; mix well. **3.** Form into loaf and place in a baking pan or dish (or form into individual loaves and place in 12 greased muffin cups). **4.** Make picante sauce by combining the four ingredients and mixing well. **5.** Cover meat with the sauce and bake in 350° oven for 1 hour for loaf (45 minutes for muffin cups).

MEAT LOAF, POTATOES & CARROTS

Meat Loaf, Old-Fashioned, I or II
1½ c. water
6 med. potatoes (or more), peeled
3 c. carrot chunks (or more), peeled
1 to 2 whole onions, peeled (opt.)
Salt and pepper

1. Place water around meat loaf in greased or sprayed roaster pan. **2.** Add raw vegetables around meat loaf. **3.** Sprinkle vegetables with salt and pepper. **4.** Bake, covered, in 325° oven for 2 hours, removing lid the last 15 minutes. **5.** When serving broth with vegetables, pour broth into wide-mouthed jar; skim and discard fat. <u>Note</u>: If using more vegetables, increase water to 2½ to 3 cups. <u>Slower Heat:</u> Bake in 275° oven for 3 to 4 hours, removing lid the last 30 minutes.

MEXICAN BURRITOS

Recipe may be doubled.

½ lb. (1 c.) ground beef
¼ c. chopped onion
½ tsp. olive oil
¼ tsp. salt
¼ tsp. garlic powder
¼ tsp. ground cumin (opt.)
¼ tsp. ground coriander (opt.)
½ c. salsa, taco sauce or tomato sauce
¾ c. (½ of 16-oz. can) refried beans or mashed kidney
    beans or other canned beans, mashed
5 to 6 flour tortillas
Shredded lettuce
Fresh tomatoes, chopped
Shredded Cheddar cheese
Sour cream or low-fat or fat-free sour cream substitute
    (opt.)

1. Brown ground beef and onion in oil; drain off fat. **2.** Add salt, seasonings, salsa and beans; stir together and heat thoroughly. **3.** Warm tortilla shells in microwave oven, toaster oven or conventional oven (or lightly grill both sides of tortilla in a frying pan). **4.** On each tortilla, place a portion of meat mixture; follow with a layer of shredded lettuce, chopped fresh tomato, shredded Cheddar cheese and 1 tablespoon sour cream, (if desired). **5.** Roll up each tortilla to make burrito and serve immediately.

MEXICAN BURRITOS, BAKED (BLUE SPRINGS)

Serve with salsa, if desired.

1 lb. hamburger
1 onion, chopped
1 (11-oz.) can condensed cheddar cheese soup
1 (16-oz.) can refried beans
1 (4-oz.) can chopped green chilies
1 pkg. taco seasoning
12 (7-in.) flour tortillas
Cheddar cheese, shredded (1 T. over each burrito)

1. Brown meat and drain off fat. **2.** Add onion, soup, refried beans, green chilies and taco seasoning; mix well. **3.** Spread about ⅓ cup meat mixture on one tortilla; roll up and place, seam side down, on foil-lined cookie sheet. **4.** Repeat with remaining tortillas, having sides touching each other. **5.** Bake in preheated 350° oven about 15 minutes, or until hot. **6.** Top with shredded Cheddar cheese and return to oven until cheese melts.

MEXICAN BURRITOS, BAKED CRISPY

Makes 10 burritos.

1 lb. ground chuck
½ c. chopped onion
4 oz. (1 c.) Monterey Jack cheese or softened Neufchatel cheese
½ tsp. dried oregano
½ tsp. cumin
¼ tsp. garlic powder
10 (6 or 7-in.) flour tortillas
5 c. shredded lettuce
Picante Salsa (recipe below) or mild taco sauce
Sour cream or nonfat sour cream alternative (opt.)

1. Combine ground chuck and onion in large skillet; cook until beef is browned. Drain off fat. **2.** Add cheese and seasonings, stirring together. **3.** Fill each tortilla with ¼ cup beef mixture; roll up. **4.** Place, seam side down, on lightly-greased or sprayed 12 x 8-inch or 13 x 9-inch baking dish. **5.** Cover and bake in preheated 350° oven for 20 minutes. **6.** Place each burrito on ½ cup shredded lettuce; serve with salsa or taco sauce (and a tablespoon of sour cream, if desired). **Note**: To cut recipe in half, place 5 rolled-up tortillas in greased or sprayed 8 x 8-inch baking dish or pan.

Picante Salsa (mildly hot):
1 (16-oz.) can or 2 c. whole tomatoes, undrained
1 (4-oz.) can diced green chilies, well drained
1 tsp. cornstarch
1 tsp. sugar
1 tsp. ground coriander (opt.)
⅛ tsp. salt (opt.)

1. Combine all ingredients in container of food processor or blender; process until smooth. **2.** Pour mixture into a saucepan; bring to a boil. **3.** Reduce heat and simmer 2 minutes, stirring occasionally.

MEXICAN BURRITOS, BEAN & CHEESE BAKE

Serves 4 people with 2 burritos each.

1 (16-oz.) can refried beans
1 med. tomato, coarsely chopped or ½ c. drained canned tomatoes
1 tsp. chili powder
4 oz. (1 c.) shredded sharp Cheddar cheese, divided
8 (7-in.) flour tortillas
1 (12-oz.) jar mild thick and chunky salsa (1½ c.)
Sour cream or nonfat sour cream alternative (opt.)

1. Turn oven dial to 400°. **2.** In saucepan, over medium heat, cook refried beans, tomato and chili powder until heated through; remove from heat. **3.** Stir in ¾ cup cheese; reserve ¼ cup cheese for topping. **4.** Spread ⅓ cup bean-cheese mixture onto center of 1 tortilla; roll up and place in lightly-greased or sprayed 13 x 9-inch baking dish. **5.** Repeat with remaining tortillas. **6.** Spoon salsa over burritos; sprinkle with reserved cheese. **7.** Cover dish with foil and bake 10 minutes in preheated 400° oven. **8.** Remove foil and bake 5 minutes longer, or until cheese melts and burritos are heated through. **9.** Serve with sour cream, if desired.

MEXICAN BURRITO, QUICK & EASY

A delicious bean burrito, ready in a few minutes.

1 (7-in.) flour tortilla
2 to 3 T. refried beans or mashed kidney beans
1 to 2 T. salsa or taco sauce
1 slice Cheddar, Colby or Monterey Jack cheese (or 3 T. shredded Cheddar cheese)
Avocado guacamole dip or sour cream (opt.)

1. Place tortilla on Corelle plate. **2.** Spread beans over tortilla. **3.** Spread salsa over beans; lay cheese over all. **4.** Roll up tortilla and microwave on HIGH for 40 to 50 seconds, or until cheese is slightly melted. **5.** Serve immediately with guacamole or sour cream, if desired.

MEXICAN CHIMICHANGAS

Makes 12. Serve with salsa and a tossed salad.

2 T. olive oil
1 med. onion, diced or chopped
1 to 2 cloves garlic, minced or pressed
2 med. tomatoes, peeled and chopped
1 (4-oz.) can chopped green chilies, drained (or more)
1 lg. potato, peeled, boiled and chopped
1 tsp. salt
1 tsp. dried oregano
1 tsp. chili powder (or more to taste)
2 tsp. dried cilantro or parsley flakes
2 c. cooked beef, pork or chicken, chopped, shredded or sliced very thin
12 flour tortillas, warmed
8 oz. (1 c.) Cheddar cheese, diced small
Olive oil
Salsa

1. In skillet, heat oil over medium heat; add onion and garlic, frying until onion softens. **2.** Add tomatoes, chilies, potato, salt, oregano, chili powder and cilantro or parsley flakes; simmer a few minutes. **3.** Add meat and stir together; simmer on low heat 2 minutes longer. **4.** In middle of each warmed tortilla, place ¼ cup meat filling; sprinkle 1 rounded tablespoon cheese over filling. (Tortillas roll up easier when warmed.) **5.** Wrap each way, envelope style, like a burrito, and hold together with a toothpick. **6.** Fry, seam side down, in ¼ to ½ inch hot oil (360°-375°) until golden brown; turn and brown other side, removing toothpicks. **7.** Drain on paper towel and serve immediately with salsa, guacamole, and sour cream.

MEXICAN ENCHILADA CHEESE BAKE

From Janice Stevenson Martinovic. Delicious!

10 flour tortillas
1 pt. sour cream or low-fat or fat-free sour cream substitute
8 oz. shredded Monterey Jack cheese
8 oz. shredded Cheddar cheese (mild or med.-sharp)
1 sm. onion, chopped
Black olives, sliced or chopped (opt.)
1 (12-oz.) jar enchilada sauce or picante salsa (mild or med., 1½ c.)

1. In each tortilla, spread some sour cream over the surface. **2.** Sprinkle a handful of both kinds of cheese (⅛ cup of each) down the center of each tortilla. **3.** Sprinkle 1 teaspoon chopped onion and a little of the black olives over the cheese; roll up tortillas lightly. **4.** Spray bottom and sides of long glass baking dish or 13 x 9-inch baking pan with nonstick cooking spray; spread half the sauce (¾ cup) in a thin layer over bottom of pan. **5.** Place tortillas, seam side down, in a single layer in pan. **6.** Pour remaining sauce (¾ cup) over tortillas (some sauce on each one). **7.** Sprinkle remaining cheese (both kinds) over top. **8.** Bake in preheated 375° oven 20 to 25 minutes, uncovered, until bubbly and browned on top a little.

MEXICAN TACO CASSEROLE

From Laura Stevenson.

1 to 1¼ lbs. ground chuck
1 med. onion (½ c.), chopped fine
1 (10¾-oz.) can cream of mushroom soup
1 c. (8 oz.) tomato sauce
1 (7-oz.) can whole kernel corn, drained (¾ c.)
½ to 1 pkg. taco seasoning mix (or use less, if desired)
10 taco shells, broken up
1 to 1½ c. grated sharp or mild Cheddar cheese

1. Brown ground chuck and onion together. **2.** Add soup, tomato sauce and corn; stir together. **3.** Add ½ package (2 tablespoons) taco seasoning mix; add more only if desired. **4.** Cook on low heat for 10 minutes. **5.** In bottom of greased or sprayed 8 x 8-inch baking dish or casserole, place a layer of crushed taco shells. **6.** Add meat mixture over top. **7.** Sprinkle remaining crushed taco shells over meat mixture; bake in preheated 350° oven for 20 minutes, covered. **8.** Sprinkle grated cheese over top; return, uncovered, to oven for 8 minutes, or just until cheese melts.

MEXICAN TACO LUNCH

A delicious lunch for 3 people.

½ to ¾ c. ground beef
½ onion, chopped
1 can red kidney beans, rinsed and drained
½ pkg. taco mix
2 c. tomato juice
¼ tsp. salt
¼ tsp. pepper
Tortilla chips or corn chips
Shredded lettuce
Shredded cheese (opt.)
Diced fresh tomatoes

1. Fry beef and onion together until no pink remains in beef; drain off fat. **2.** Add drained and rinsed beans, taco mix, tomato juice, salt and pepper. **3.** Simmer mixture 15 minutes, stirring occasionally, until it thickens somewhat. **4.** To serve, put chips around outer edge of each dinner plate. **5.** Cover middle of plate with shredded lettuce. **6.** Cover lettuce with meat sauce. **7.** Sprinkle with cheese and diced tomatoes.

MEXICAN TORTILLA BAKE

To serve, slice like a pie.

1 lb. ground beef, browned and drained
1 pkg. taco mix
Water as required on packet of taco mix
½ c. green bell pepper, chopped
¼ c. chopped onion
1 (16-oz.) can refried beans
1 (8-oz.) jar taco sauce (1 c.)
1 pkg. flour tortillas
8 oz. (2 c.) shredded Cheddar cheese
Chopped lettuce
Chopped tomato

1. After browning and draining beef, add taco seasoning mix and the required water on packet (in 10-inch skillet). **2.** Add green peppers, onion, refried beans and taco sauce; heat, stirring, until hot. **3.** In a greased or sprayed 10-inch pie plate, layer tortillas, meat mixture and Cheddar cheese. (Make 3 or 4 layers of the 3 items, ending with tortillas.) Use the whole package of tortillas; they may have to be overlapped. **4.** Heat in preheated 425° oven for 15 minutes. **5.** Top with lettuce, tomatoes and a little shredded cheese; slice like a pie.

MEXICAN TORTILLA CASSEROLE

Serves 4, using corn tortillas and no beans.

1 lb. lean ground beef
1 med. onion, chopped
¼ tsp. garlic powder
1 T. olive oil
1 (8-oz.) can tomato sauce
¼ to ½ c. sliced ripe olives
⅔ c. water
1 to 3 tsp. chili powder
1 tsp. salt
¼ tsp. black pepper
6 corn tortillas, torn into pcs.
2 c. shredded Cheddar cheese, divided

1. Brown beef, onion and garlic powder in oil; drain off fat. 2. Add tomato sauce, sliced olives, water, chili powder, salt and pepper. 3. In round casserole, alternate layers of tortilla pieces, beef mixture and 1½ cups shredded cheese. 4. Sprinkle remaining ½ cup cheese over top. 5. Cover and bake in preheated 400° oven for 25 minutes. 6. Uncover and let stand 5 minutes. To serve, cut into wedges.

PASTA, FETTUCCINI ALFREDO

8 oz. fettuccini
3 qt. boiling water
½ T. salt
⅓ c. butter
¾ c. whole milk, cream or light evaporated skimmed milk
¾ c. freshly grated Parmesan cheese
¼ tsp. salt
⅛ tsp. pepper
¼ c. Parmesan cheese, grated
Coarsely ground pepper (opt.)
Fresh parsley, chopped (opt.)

1. In large kettle, add fettuccini to boiling water with ½ tablespoon salt; boil, uncovered, stirring occasionally, until tender, about 15 minutes. 2. Drain; keep fettuccini warm while making sauce. 3. Heat butter and milk until butter is melted; remove from heat and add ¾ cup Parmesan cheese, salt and pepper. Stir until sauce is blended and fairly smooth. 4. Add to drained fettuccini and toss until well coated. 5. Sprinkle with remaining Parmesan cheese, coarsely ground pepper and chopped parsley; serve immediately.

PASTA SHELLS STUFFED WITH MEAT

6 to 8 oz. lg. pasta stuffing shells (about 17 to 20 shells)
1 T. butter
½ lb. ground pork
1 lb. ground beef
1 med. onion, chopped (⅓ to ½ c.)
¼ c. finely chopped celery
1 clove garlic, minced

⅓ c. grated Parmesan or Romano cheese
⅓ c. cranberry juice or tomato juice
1 tsp. salt
⅓ to ½ c. bread crumbs
1 qt. (4 c.) spaghetti sauce
Mozzarella cheese, shredded (opt.)

1. To 3 quarts boiling water, add 2 teaspoons salt; gradually add shells so water does not stop boiling. Boil, uncovered, 12 to 15 minutes, gently stirring occasionally. Do not overcook. 2. Drain; then partially cover with warm water and set aside. 3. Melt butter in large skillet; add pork and beef; cook until lightly browned. 4. Add onion, celery and garlic; cover with lid, reduce heat to low and cook 10 to 15 minutes, until celery is tender. 5. Drain off all fat; add cheese, cranberry juice, salt and bread crumbs, mixing together. Cool slightly. 6. Stuff each shell with meat mixture. 7. Pour half the spaghetti sauce into a 13 x 9-inch baking dish; arrange stuffed shells in dish and top with remaining spaghetti sauce. 8. Cover with foil or lid and bake in preheated 375° oven for 30 minutes. 9. Uncover and sprinkle with Mozzarella cheese, if desired; bake, uncovered, 10 minutes longer, or until bubbly.

PASTA SPIRALS WITH HAMBURGER

Recipe may be cut in half.

1 lb. ground beef
1 med. onion, chopped (¼ to ½ c.)
1 tsp. salt
1 T. olive oil
5 c. (48-oz. jar) spaghetti sauce or more, if desired
1 T. Italian seasoning
1 lb. spiral corkscrew pasta (4 c., uncooked or 8 to 10 c., cooked)
4 qt. boiling water
4 tsp. salt

1. Fry ground beef, onion and 1 teaspoon salt in the oil until meat is no longer pink, stirring frequently. 2. Drain grease off meat; add spaghetti sauce and bring to a boil on medium heat, stirring often. 3. Reduce heat to low; simmer 10 minutes. 4. Meanwhile, cook pasta in boiling water with 4 teaspoons salt until nearly tender; drain and rinse with a little warm water. Drain again and set aside. 5. About 5 minutes before serving, add drained pasta to meat sauce. Stir very little to avoid breaking pasta. (Or combine pasta and sauce in a roaster and place in 350° oven until hot.) Serves 12.

PIEROGIS STUFFED SHELLS

1½ lbs. potatoes, peeled and quartered
4 oz. sharp Cheddar or Colby cheese, shredded (1 c.)
½ tsp. salt
¼ tsp. pepper
¼ c. (½ stick) butter
3 c. sliced onions
½ (12-oz.) box jumbo stuffing shells

1. Cook jumbo stuffing shells according to package directions; drain and cool immediately under cold running water. 2. Cook potatoes in boiling water until tender; drain and return to pot. 3. Add cheese to hot potatoes and mash until cheese melts and potatoes are smooth; stir in salt and pepper. 4. Melt butter in large skillet; add onions and cook 10 to 15 minutes, stirring frequently, until tender, but not browned. 5. Heat oven to 350°. 6. Spread half the onions over bottom of 13 x 9-inch baking dish. 7. Gently stuff each shell with a heaping tablespoon of potato mixture, bringing sides of shells together over filling. 8. Arrange in a single layer on onions; spread remaining onions over top. 9. Bake, uncovered, in preheated 350° oven 15 to 20 minutes, until heated through.

PIZZA I (One 14-inch Pizza)

Make and bake immediately. Serves 2 to 3 people.

1 pkg. active dry yeast (or 2½ tsp. dry bulk yeast)
⅔ c. warm (not hot) water
½ tsp. sugar
½ tsp. salt
1 T. olive oil
1¾ c. all-purpose flour
¾ c. pizza sauce
8 oz. (2 c.) shredded Mozzarella cheese (or Provolone)
1 to 2 oz. (¼ to ½ c.) sliced pepperoni or ½ lb. sausage, browned and drained

1. Turn oven dial to 425° and grease a 14-inch round pizza pan (or a large cookie sheet). 2. In medium bowl, dissolve yeast in warm water. 3. Stir in sugar, salt, oil and flour; beat with mixer (or spoon or fork vigorously). 4. Turn dough out on floured surface and knead 2 minutes. 5. Place bowl upside down over dough and let rest 5 minutes. 6. Press dough into a 13 or 14-inch circle over bottom of pan, forming a little rim around the edge. (If dough is sticky, flour fingertips.) 7. Spread pizza sauce over dough to the rim. 8. Sprinkle cheese over top. 9. Place pepperoni slices or browned, drained sausage over top. 10. Bake on lowest shelf of preheated 425° oven (2 to 4 inches from bottom of oven) for 15 to 20 minutes or until golden brown on bottom. **Note:** 2 c. bread dough that has risen can be used. **Note:** To double this recipe, it is not necessary to double the amount of yeast.

PIZZA II (Two 10 or 11-inch Pizzas)

Make and bake immediately, or bake one and freeze one.

1 pkg. active dry yeast (or 2½ tsp. dry bulk yeast)
1 c. warm (not hot) water
1 tsp. salt
1 tsp. sugar
2 T. (⅛ c.) olive oil
2½ c. all-purpose flour
1⅓ c. pizza sauce
12 oz. (3 c.) Mozzarella cheese, shredded
2 to 4 oz. (½ to 1 c.) sliced pepperoni (or less)

1. Oil or lightly grease two 12 or 14-inch round pizza pans. 2. In medium bowl, dissolve yeast in warm water. 3. Stir in salt, sugar, oil and 2 cups flour; beat vigorously with large spoon, about 30 strokes. 4. Stir in remaining ½ cup flour; let dough rest while making pizza sauce. 5. Turn oven dial to 425°. 6. Divide dough in half; pat dough on prepared pans with floured hands and fingertips to 10-inch circles (for thick crust) or 11-inch circles (for medium crust) or 12-inch circles (for thin crust). 7. Spread ⅔ cup pizza sauce on each pizza to within ½ or ¾ inch of edge. 8. Sprinkle 1½ cups cheese over sauce on each pizza. 9. Arrange ¼ to ½ cup pepperoni slices over each pizza. 10. Bake on lowest shelf of preheated 425° oven (2 to 4 inches from bottom of oven) for 16 to 20 minutes, or until underneath side of crust is light golden brown. **Note:** Dough may be patted out on one large cookie sheet to make one large pizza. **Note:** Recipe may be doubled without doubling yeast.

PIZZA III (Two 12 or 13-inch Pizzas)

Dough rises 1 hour.

1 pkg. dry yeast (or 2½ tsp. dry bulk yeast)
1 c. warm water (about 110°)
2 T. olive oil
1 tsp. salt
3 c. all-purpose flour (approx.)
1⅓ to 2 c. pizza sauce
2 to 3 c. (8 to 12 oz.) shredded Mozzarella or Provolone cheese
1 c. (4 oz.) sliced pepperoni

1. Dissolve yeast in warm water and set aside for about 10 minutes. 2. Add oil, salt and most of the flour; mix with large spoon until ingredients cling together and can be gathered into a ball of dough. 3. Turn dough onto floured surface and knead for 10 minutes, adding a little more flour as necessary, until dough is smooth and elastic. 4. Place dough in lightly oiled bowl, cover with cloth and set aside to rise until doubled, about 1 hour. 5. Dough is now ready to use, or it may be wrapped in plastic and stored in refrigerator (or frozen). 6. When ready to bake, turn oven to 425°. 7. Punch dough down; divide into 2 pieces (weighing is the most accurate). 8. On 2 lightly oiled 12 to 14-inch pizza pans, pat and press dough to the edges. (Make a tiny rim around edge.) 9. Spread half the pizza sauce on each pizza. 10. Sprinkle half the cheese over each pizza. 11. Place half the pepperoni over each pizza. 12. Bake on lowest shelf of preheated 425° oven (2 to 4 inches from bottom of oven) for 18 to 20 minutes, or until underneath side of crust is golden brown.

PIZZA IV

Subs, hoagie buns, flour tortillas, etc.
Pizza sauce
Mozzarella cheese, sliced or shredded
Pepperoni slices

1. Preheat oven to 450°. **2.** Place open bun halves on ungreased cookie sheet; spread with pizza sauce. **3.** Top with cheese, then pepperoni. **4.** Bake 6 minutes or until cheese is melted and bubbly.

PIZZA, CLARENCE'S

1 recipe "Pizza II" dough
1 recipe "Pizza Sauce I" (1⅓ c. pizza sauce)
½ to 1 lb. extra-lean ground beef or lean sausage
Garlic powder
Pepper
8 oz. (2 c.) shredded American cheese
4 oz. (1 c.) shredded sharp Cheddar cheese

1. In 1 large 17 x 14-inch cookie sheet, lightly greased with oil, pat all the dough evenly with fingertips to the edges. (Dip fingertips in flour, if necessary.) **2.** Spread all the pizza sauce over the dough, almost to the edges. **3.** Sprinkle uncooked meat over sauce in small chunks, about the size of peas. **4.** Sprinkle lightly with garlic powder and pepper. **5.** Mix both kinds of cheese together; sprinkle over all. **6.** Bake on lowest shelf of preheated 425° oven (2 to 4 inches from bottom of oven) for 15 to 18 minutes or until underneath side of crust is light golden brown.

PIZZA, COOKIE SHEET (Crisp Crust)

1 recipe "Pizza II" dough
1 recipe "Pizza Sauce I" (1⅓ c.)
12 oz. (3 c.) Mozzarella cheese, shredded
Sliced pepperoni

1. Let dough rise 30 minutes. **2.** Spread on large greased cookie sheet, patting out with fingertips; let rise 15 to 20 minutes. **3.** Bake in preheated 400° oven for 10 minutes. **4.** Remove from oven and cover with pizza sauce, shredded cheese and sliced pepperoni. **5.** Bake 15 to 20 minutes longer or until cheese is melted and bottom of crust is light golden brown (on lowest rack, 2 to 4 inches from bottom of oven).

PIZZA, ENGLISH MUFFIN

English muffin
1 to 1½ T. pizza sauce or spaghetti sauce
2 T. shredded Mozzarella or pizza cheese

Optional Toppings:
3 slices pepperoni, diced
Sliced mushrooms, drained
Sliced olives
Sweet onion, diced
Green bell pepper, diced
Light sprinkle of oregano

1. For each split English muffin half, layer with sauce, cheese and optional toppings. Heat in 1 of the following ways. **Toaster Oven:** Heat until cheese melts. **Broiler Oven:** Broil 3 minutes, or until cheese melts. **Conventional Oven:** Place on cookie sheet and bake in preheated 400° oven 8 to 9 minutes, or until cheese melts. **Microwave Oven:** Heat on HIGH power (100%) 20 to 30 seconds for 1 half muffin, or until cheese melts.

PIZZA FROM FROZEN BREAD DOUGH

Adapted from Toy Coleman.
Makes one pizza in a jellyroll pan.

1 loaf frozen bread dough, thawed
1 to 2 c. pizza sauce or spaghetti sauce
6 oz. (1½ c.) shredded Mozzarella cheese (or Provolone)
2 oz. (½ c.) sliced pepperoni
Any other toppings desired

1. Turn oven dial to 425°. **2.** Pat dough out on 15 x 10 x 1-inch jellyroll pan or cookie sheet which has been greased or sprayed. **3.** Spread with desired amount of pizza sauce or spaghetti sauce. **4.** Sprinkle 1½ cups shredded cheese over top evenly. **5.** Add pepperoni slices over top (and any other desired toppings). **6.** Bake on bottom shelf of preheated 425° oven 18 to 20 minutes or until golden on the bottom. **Note:** Frozen bread dough, if placed in refrigerator overnight, will be thawed by morning. (Cover dough with oiled plastic wrap when leaving in refrigerator to thaw.) **Note:** For a thick crust, let dough rise slightly in jellyroll pan before baking.

PIZZA FROM HOT ROLL MIX

This pizza has a thick, tender crust.

1 (16-oz.) box Pillsbury hot roll mix
1¼ c. water
2 T. olive oil
1⅓ to 2 c. pizza sauce
2 c. shredded Mozzarella (or part Monterey Jack or Provolone) cheese
Pepperoni slices (thin)
1 (4-oz.) can mushroom pcs., drained (opt.)
¼ c. chopped green pepper (opt.)
¼ c. chopped onion (opt.)

1. Mix and knead hot roll dough as directed on package, except use 1¼ cups water, 2 tablespoons oil and **omit egg**; cover with bowl and let rest 5 minutes. **2.** Grease or spray 15 x 10-inch jellyroll pan; with greased hands, pat dough into pan, forming a little rim around edges. **3.** Prick dough generously with fork; cover and let rise 15 minutes. **4.** Uncover dough and spread pizza sauce evenly over top. **5.** Sprinkle cheese over pizza sauce; top with desired topping ingredients. **6.** Bake in preheated 425° oven on lowest oven rack for 20 to 25 minutes.

PIZZA, PITA

1 (6 to 7-in.) pita (or 1 flour tortilla)
½ c. salsa, pizza sauce, taco sauce or spaghetti sauce
2 T. grated Parmesan cheese
6 T. shredded Mozzarella (or 2 slices Provolone cheese)
Pepperoni slices
Oregano (opt.)

1. Split pita in half, making 2 round circles; place each half on a dinner plate. 2. On each half, spread ¼ cup sauce, 1 tablespoon grated Parmesan cheese, 3 tablespoons Mozzarella cheese, pepperoni slices and a light sprinkle of oregano, if desired. 3. Place on plate in microwave oven and bake on HIGH 1 minute, or until Mozzarella cheese is melted. Repeat for second plate. <u>Note</u>: 1 flour tortilla may be used for this recipe. Roll up on plate.

PIZZA, PITA POCKET

1 pita half
Pizza sauce
Pepperoni, sliced or Canadian-style bacon
¼ c. (about 1 oz.) shredded Mozzarella cheese
Thin onion rings, halved
Green pepper rings, halved
Black olives, pitted and sliced
Mushrooms, sliced (opt.)

1. Inside the pita half, put whatever ingredients are desired. 2. To heat, cook in microwave oven on HIGH for 30 seconds, or until cheese is melted.

PIZZA SAUCE I (Makes 1⅓ Cups)

Makes enough for 2 (10 to 12-inch) pizzas.

1 (6-oz.) can tomato paste
¾ c. warm water (1 paste can)
2 tsp. sugar
1 tsp. oregano
1 tsp. Italian seasoning or basil (opt.)
⅛ tsp. salt
⅛ tsp. pepper
⅛ tsp. garlic powder
⅛ tsp. crushed red pepper or dash (1/16) red pepper (opt.)

1. In small bowl, gradually add warm water to tomato paste, blending together well. 2. Add remaining ingredients and stir together.

PIZZA SAUCE II (Makes About 2½ Cups)

Makes enough for 3 (12 to 14-inch) pizzas.

1 (8-oz.) can tomato sauce (1 c.)
1 (6-oz.) can tomato paste
¾ c. warm water
2¼ tsp. sugar

2 tsp. oregano
½ tsp. Italian seasoning (opt.)
⅛ tsp. salt
¼ tsp. pepper
¼ tsp. garlic powder

1. Combine ingredients in saucepan, stirring well; bring to a boil. 2. Reduce heat and simmer 5 minutes.

PIZZA SAUCE III (Makes About 2¾ Cups)

1 (16-oz.) can tomatoes, cut up (with juice)
1 (6-oz.) can tomato paste
1 tsp. sugar
1 tsp. basil
1 tsp. oregano
¼ tsp. salt

1. Combine all ingredients and stir well.

PORK CHOPS, BAKED

From Mrs. Idella McConnell.

Remove excess fat from pork chops; brown them on both sides in skillet (salt and pepper them while frying). Put browned chops in roaster pan and add 1½ cups water. Cover with lid. Bake in 350° oven for 1 hour; then reduce heat to 250° and bake another hour or two. If necessary, add more water during baking period. (Especially if you want to make gravy.)

PORK CHOPS, BARBECUED (Oven)

Easy oven dish.

Pork chops
1 (10¾-oz.) can cream of mushroom soup
1 c. ketchup
1 tsp. Worcestershire sauce
½ c. chopped onion

1. Trim all fat off pork chops; lay chops in baking pan. 2. Combine soup, ketchup, Worcestershire sauce and onions; pour over chops. 3. Bake 2 hours in 350° oven, covered.

PORK CHOPS, BARBECUED (Skillet)

Top-of-stove recipe.

¾ c. ketchup
¾ c. water
2 T. vinegar
½ T. Worcestershire sauce
1 tsp. salt
1 tsp. paprika
½ tsp. pepper

1 tsp. chili powder or less
⅛ tsp. cayenne pepper (or less) opt.
⅓ c. packed brown sugar
Pork chops, fat removed

1. Combine all ingredients, except pork chops; set aside. 2. Brown pork chops on both sides in small amount of oil. 3. In a skillet or large pan that has a tight lid, spread 1 tablespoon sauce on each chop; cover with lid and cook 8 minutes on medium-low heat. 4. Turn chops over and pour remaining sauce over all. 5. Cover with lid and cook slowly 30 to 40 minutes, turning chops occasionally.

PORK CHOPS & HOMINY

From Mrs. Janet Holley.

3 or 4 pork chops (fat removed)
2 (15 to 16-oz.) cans hominy, drained (or a 29-oz. can, drained)
1 (10¾-oz.) can cream of mushroom or cream of celery soup

1. Brown pork chops in skillet, salting and peppering them lightly. 2. Grease or spray 1¼ to 1½-quart casserole around the sides. 3. Place drained hominy in casserole; spoon undiluted soup over top. 4. Top with browned pork chops. 5. Cover and bake in preheated 350° oven for 1 hour. Serves 3.

PORK CHOP-RICE DINNER

3 to 6 pork chops (1 to 1½ in. thick), fat removed
1 to 2 T. olive oil
1 c. uncooked reg. rice
1 env. dry onion soup mix
3½ c. hot water
1 (4-oz.) can mushrooms, drained (opt.)

1. Turn oven dial to 350°. 2. Brown pork chops on both sides in hot oil. 3. Spread rice on bottom of ungreased 13 x 9-inch baking pan or dish. 4. Reserve 1 tablespoon of dry soup mix; sprinkle remaining soup mix over rice. 5. Pour hot water over rice; arrange mushrooms over rice, if used. 6. Place pork chops over rice and sprinkle with reserved tablespoon of dry soup mix. 7. Cover tightly with foil; bake in preheated 350° oven for 45 to 60 minutes, depending on thickness of chops. 8. Remove foil and bake another 10 minutes, or until excess liquid evaporates.

PORK CHOP, RICE & TOMATO DINNER

Makes 3 to 5 servings.

3 to 5 pork chops
2 T. olive oil
Salt and pepper
½ c. diced celery

½ c. diced onion (1 med.)
1 c. (8-oz.) tomato sauce
3 c. COOKED rice
1 T. sugar (opt.)

1. Brown pork chops on both sides in skillet with oil. (Season them with salt and pepper.) 2. Remove chops from skillet; fry celery and onions in drippings. 3. Stir in tomato sauce and cooked rice. 4. Pour rice mixture into baking dish. 5. Arrange chops on top of rice; bake, uncovered, in preheated 350° oven for 45 minutes.

PORK CHOP SUPPER (Range-Top)

1 med. to lg. onion, sliced
3 T. olive oil
2 T. flour, packed level
1 tsp. salt
¼ tsp. pepper
4 pork chops, fat removed
2 lg. potatoes, sliced (2½ to 3 c.)
1 to 2 large carrots, sliced
1 (16-oz.) can tomatoes (2 c.) with liquid
¼ tsp. basil or oregano (opt.)
1 c. frozen peas (or frozen or canned green beans, drained)

1. In large skillet, sauté onion slices in hot oil until tender; remove onion with slotted spoon and set aside. 2. In shallow bowl, combine flour, salt and pepper; coat pork chops in mixture and brown on both sides in the oil. 3. Add sliced potatoes, carrots, tomatoes, basil or oregano, and reserved onions. 4. Bring to a boil; reduce heat, cover with tight lid and simmer on low for 50 to 60 minutes (until potatoes and carrots are tender). 5. Add frozen peas (or green beans) the last 10 minutes.

PORK CHOPS, STUFFING & GRAVY

Serves 4 adults.

4 lg. (or 8 sm.) pork chops, all fat removed
1 T. olive oil
1 (10¾-oz.) can cream of chicken or cream of mushroom soup
1 c. water

Stuffing:
8 oz. soft bread crumbs (about 5 c.)
¼ c. chopped celery
2 T. chopped onion
¼ tsp. salt
⅛ tsp. pepper
½ tsp. poultry seasoning or sage
½ c. reg. Smart Balance spread or butter, melted
1 sm. egg (or ½ lg. egg)
¼ c. milk

1. Brown chops in hot oil on both sides. (Do not salt.) 2. Place chops in roaster or baking dish in single layer. 3. In

bowl, combine bread crumbs, celery, onion, salt, pepper and poultry seasoning. **4.** Pour melted butter over bread crumbs, stirring with fork. **5.** In small bowl, beat egg and milk together with fork or wire whip; pour over bread crumbs, stirring together. **6.** Place a mound of stuffing on top of each chop. **7.** Discard fat from skillet in which chops were browned; add soup and water, stirring until well blended. **8.** Pour soup mixture around chops; cover tightly with foil or lid. **9.** Bake 1 hour in preheated 350° oven (or 250° for 3 to 4 hours).

PORK CHOPS, TOP-OF-STOVE

From Ida Berlin.

Brown pork chops in heavy skillet. Add a little water and a tight lid. Cook 45 minutes, watching that it doesn't go dry. (Add water as needed.) Make gravy after lifting pork chops out.

PORK ROAST

Old-fashioned method. Delicious.

Pork roast
3 c. water
Salt (½ tsp. for each pound of meat)
Pepper
2 tsp. chicken flavor powdered bouillon (or 2 chicken
    bouillon cubes)

1. Preheat oven to 400°. **2.** Place meat in roaster pan; add water. **3.** Sprinkle with salt and pepper; add chicken bouillon around meat. **4.** Cover and roast 1 hour in 400° oven. **5.** <u>After 1 hour, turn oven dial to 300°</u>. **6.** Roast 3 to 4 hours, covered, or until tender. If browner roast is desired, remove lid the last 30 to 45 minutes. **Gravy: 1.** Pour broth from pork roast into a wide-mouthed quart jar; skim off fat with gravy ladle. (Discard fat.) **2.** Shake together ½ cup water and ⅓ cup flour. **3.** Return broth to pan, adding more water if necessary; bring broth to a boil. Remove pan from heat and add thickening as needed, stirring. **4.** Return gravy to burner and bring to a full boil, stirring almost constantly.

PORK & SAUERKRAUT, BAKED I

Drain and rinse sauerkraut if it is in tin cans.

Pork roast
1 (2-lb.) bag fresh sauerkraut or 27 to 32 oz. canned
    sauerkraut (about 4 c.)
2½ to 3 c. water or broth
Salt (½ tsp. per pound of meat)
3 chicken bouillon cubes
Pepper

1. Preheat oven to 400°. **2.** Remove excess fat from pork; lay meat in roaster, cover with lid and roast 1 hour. **3.** Drain off all

fat and use paper towels to wipe out remaining fat from roaster. **4.** Put undrained sauerkraut in bottom of roaster; add water and bouillon cubes. **5.** Lay meat on top of sauerkraut and sprinkle with salt and pepper. **6.** Cover with lid and return to oven, <u>turning oven dial to 300° to 325°</u>. **7.** Bake for 3 hours or until meat is tender. If browner roast is desired, remove lid for last 30 minutes. **Slower Heat:** In step 6, turn oven dial to 275° and bake for 4 hours or until tender. **Note:** Recipe may be doubled, using 7 pounds of boneless rolled pork roast and 4 pounds sauerkraut.

PORK & SAUERKRAUT, BAKED II

Pork chops, pork steak or pork spareribs
2 lb. bag fresh sauerkraut or about 4 c. canned
    sauerkraut
3 to 4 c. water or chicken broth
Salt (½ tsp. per pound of meat)
Pepper
1 onion, chopped
3 chicken bouillon cubes
½ T. olive oil

1. Preheat oven to 350°. **2.** Remove fat from meat and brown in ½ tablespoon olive oil. (If using spareribs, no need to brown.) **3.** Put meat in bottom of roaster; sprinkle with salt and pepper. **4.** Cover with sauerkraut. **5.** Add water, onion and bouillon cubes. **6.** Cover with lid or foil and bake for 2 hours at 350°. (If you like it brown, remove lid the last hour.)

RIGATONI WITH MEATBALLS

Serves 4 to 6.

<u>Sauce:</u>
½ c. chopped onion
2 cloves garlic, crushed
2 T. (⅛ c.) olive oil
4 c. tomato juice
1 (6-oz.) can tomato paste (⅔ c.)
2 T. sugar
1½ tsp. salt
1 tsp. parsley flakes
½ tsp. basil
½ tsp. Italian seasoning
¼ tsp. black pepper
8 oz. rigatoni (3½ c.), uncooked (or about 4½ c., cooked)

<u>Meatballs:</u>
1 lb. lean ground beef
1 tsp. salt
⅛ tsp. black pepper
3 T. chopped onion
1 egg
3 slices bread, soaked in ½ c. milk
1 tsp. olive oil for frying meatballs

1. Fry onion and garlic in 2 tablespoons oil until tender, but not brown; stir in remaining sauce ingredients and bring to a boil. 2. Reduce heat and simmer gently while making meatballs. 3. Combine meatball ingredients and form into balls; fry in 1 teaspoon oil, turning to brown all sides. 4. Add meatballs to sauce and simmer gently while cooking rigatoni. 5. In 10 to 12 cups boiling water and 2 teaspoons salt, boil rigatoni for 15 to 16 minutes, or until tender; drain. 6. Add rigatoni to sauce; pour into 3-quart serving bowl.

SAUERKRAUT, MEAT & DUMPLINGS

Serves 4. Dumplings may be omitted.

1 (2-lb.) bag sauerkraut or 1 (27 to 32-oz.) can or 3 to 4 c.
    sauerkraut, drained
2½ to 3 c. water
1 lb. wieners, Smokie Links, smoked sausage,
    knockwurst or kielbasa, cut into chunks
Dumpling recipe

1. Put drained and rinsed sauerkraut in cooking pot; add water. 2. Lay meat over top; cover and bring to a boil. 3. Reduce heat and simmer, covered, 30 to 40 minutes, on low heat. 4. Drop dumpling batter by spoonfuls on top gently boiling sauerkraut and meat. (Sauerkraut should be just barely covered with liquid. If not, add water.) 5. Replace lid and cook 20 minutes without peeking, on low heat. (Or follow directions given in dumpling recipe.) **Crock-Pot**: Cook sauerkraut, water and meat (no dumplings) on HIGH, covered, for 2 hours. **Baked**: Bake sauerkraut, water and meat (no dumplings) in 350° oven, covered, for 2 hours. Or for slower oven, bake in 250° oven for 4 hours. (Or 275° for 3 hours.)

SAUSAGE GRAVY

Serves 5 to 6. Recipe may be cut in half for 3 people.

1 lb. Bob Evans or Jimmy Dean sausage
½ to 1 tsp. salt
¼ tsp. pepper
¼ tsp. sage (opt.)
⅔ c. flour, packed level
5 c. milk (or water) or a little more for thinner gravy

1. Crumble sausage into skillet and brown over medium heat with salt, pepper and sage, stirring frequently. 2. Sprinkle flour over meat and stir well to coat meat and soak up sausage drippings. 3. Over low heat, slowly add 5 cups milk (or water), stirring constantly; continue cooking and stirring until thickened and bubbly. 4. If a thinner gravy is desired, add a little more milk or water until gravy reaches desired consistency. 5. Serve with biscuits, toast or boiled potatoes.

SAUSAGE STIR-FRY

Serves 3 people.

¾ lb. smoked sausage or kielbasa, sliced (reg., lite or
    turkey)
3½ to 4 c. raw vegetables (onions, mushrooms, green bell
    pepper, carrots, broccoli, cabbage, snow peas, celery,
    etc.)
Salt and pepper
1 to 2 T. olive oil
½ c. cashew nuts (opt.)

1. Brown sausage in skillet; remove from skillet and discard any grease. 2. Add oil; when hot, add raw vegetables, appropriately sliced. 3. Sprinkle with salt and pepper; stir-fry until crisp-tender. 4. Add sausage and cashews; cook 2 minutes until warm.

SHEPHERD'S PIE I

Serves 5 people.

4 c. raw potatoes, peeled and cut in chunks
1½ tsp. salt
2½ c. water
1 to 2 T. olive oil
1 med. onion, chopped
¼ c. green bell pepper, chopped (opt.)
1 to 1½ lbs. lean ground beef
1 tsp. salt
¼ tsp. pepper
2 T. flour
1 (10¾-oz.) can tomato soup, undiluted
½ T. dried parsley flakes (opt.)
1 egg
⅓ c. milk
1 T. butter
½ to 1 c. shredded sharp Cheddar cheese or American
    process cheese

1. Cook potatoes with 1½ teaspoons salt and 2½ cups water until tender; drain. 2. While potatoes are cooking, heat oil in large skillet; add onion and green pepper; fry for 2 minutes. 3. Add ground beef and cook, stirring occasionally, for 5 minutes; drain off excess fat. 4. Add 1 teaspoon salt, the pepper and flour; stir together. 5. Add tomato soup and parsley; bring to a simmering boil. 6. Grease or spray a 10-inch pie pan or 8 x 8 x 2-inch square baking pan; pour beef mixture into pan. 7. Mash potatoes; add egg, milk and butter, whipping well. 8. Spread mashed potatoes over beef mixture; sprinkle with shredded cheese. 9. Bake in preheated 400° oven for 15 minutes. **Note**: If using leftover mashed potatoes, don't use more than 3 cups.

SHEPHERD'S PIE II

Serves 5 people. No tomato soup in this one.

1 to 1½ T. olive oil
1 med. onion, chopped
¼ c. green bell pepper, chopped (opt.)
1 lb. lean ground beef or ground turkey
1 tsp. Kitchen Bouquet browning and seasoning sauce
1 c. cold water or beef broth
2 T. flour, packed level
½ tsp. salt
¼ tsp. pepper
Mashed potatoes (either freshly made or leftover)
Paprika or pepper

1. Heat oil in large skillet; add onion and green pepper; fry for 2 minutes. **2.** Add ground beef and cook, stirring occasionally, for 5 minutes; drain off excess fat. **3.** Sprinkle Kitchen Bouquet over meat; stir together. **4.** In a covered jar, shake together water, flour, salt and pepper; add to meat mixture and cook, stirring constantly, until gravy thickens and comes to a boil. **5.** Place in 10-inch pie pan, 12 x 8-inch, 11 x 7-inch or 8 x 8-inch baking dish, or shallow casserole. **6.** Cover with mashed potatoes; sprinkle lightly with paprika or pepper. **7.** Bake in preheated 375° oven for 20 to 25 minutes. <u>Note</u>: 2 c. leftover diced roast beef or venison can be used in place of ground beef.

SPAGHETTI, BAKED

From Ron Churchill.

12 oz. thin spaghetti, cooked
1 lb. ground beef
1 c. chopped onion
1 c. chopped or diced green pepper
1 T. olive oil or butter
1 (28-oz.) can tomatoes with liquid, cut up (3½ c.)
1 (4-oz.) can mushroom stems and pieces, drained
1 (2¼-oz.) can sliced ripe olives, drained (opt.)
2 tsp. dried oregano
1 tsp. salt or garlic salt
1 T. sugar
8 oz. (2 c.) shredded cheddar cheese
1 (10¾-oz.) can condensed cream of mushroom soup, undiluted
¼ c. water
¼ c. grated Parmesan cheese

1. Cook and drain spaghetti; rinse with a little hot water and set aside. **2.** In large skillet, brown ground beef; drain off any fat and remove meat from skillet. **3.** In same skillet, cook onion and green pepper in olive oil or butter until tender. **4.** Add tomatoes, mushrooms, olives, oregano, salt, sugar and the ground beef; simmer, uncovered, for 10 minutes. **5.** Place half the spaghetti in greased 13 x 9 x 2-inch baking dish; top with half the vegetable mixture, then sprinkle with 1 cup cheddar cheese. **6.** Repeat layers. **7.** Mix soup with ¼ c. water until smooth; pour over all; sprinkle with Parmesan cheese.

8. Bake, uncovered, in preheated 350° oven for 35 minutes, or until heated through. Serves 10 to 12.

SPAGHETTI & CHEESE, BAKED

8 oz. spaghetti
2 T. butter
8 oz. sliced or shredded cheese
2 c. milk
Additional butter
Pepper

1. Cook spaghetti in 2 quarts boiling water, 2 teaspoons salt and 1 teaspoon olive oil until tender; drain. **2.** Stir butter through hot, drained spaghetti. **3.** In buttered casserole or baking pan, alternate layers of spaghetti and cheese. **4.** Pour milk over all; dot with additional butter and sprinkle with pepper. **5.** Bake, covered, for about 30 minutes in preheated 350° oven.

SPAGHETTI & MEATBALLS

For 9 to 10 adults or more.

2 lbs. spaghetti

<u>Meatballs:</u>
2 lbs. ground beef
2 tsp. salt
¼ tsp. pepper
⅓ c. cracker crumbs or ½ c. fine, dry bread crumbs
1 onion, chopped (½ to 1 c.)
2 eggs

<u>Sauce:</u>
3 qt. tomato juice (10½ to 12 c.)
18 oz. tomato paste
¾ tsp. salt
¾ c. sugar (or to taste)
2 cloves garlic, cut in half or ¼ tsp. garlic salt

1. Combine meatball ingredients with electric mixer or hands; form into meatballs. **2.** In skillet with 1 tablespoon olive oil, brown meatballs on all sides. **3.** Meanwhile, in large cooking pot, combine sauce ingredients; stir well and bring to a simmering boil. **4.** Add meatballs, discarding the fat. **5.** Simmer sauce and meatballs on low heat gently for 30 to 60 minutes, stirring occasionally. **6.** Cook spaghetti in large pot of 6 quarts boiling water, 2 tablespoons salt and 2 tablespoons oil until tender (about 12 to 15 minutes after coming to a boil). **7.** Drain spaghetti and rinse briefly with hot water; drain again.

<u>Smaller Recipe (for 6 to 7 adults):</u>
1½ lbs. spaghetti

<u>Meatballs:</u>
1½ lbs. ground beef
1½ tsp. salt
⅛ tsp. pepper
¼ c. cracker crumbs (8 soda crackers, 2 x 2 in. each, in food processor)

1 onion, chopped (¼ to ½ c.)

2 eggs

Sauce:

2 qt. tomato juice (7 to 8 c.)

12 oz. tomato paste

½ tsp. salt

½ c. sugar (or to taste)

1 to 2 cloves garlic, cut in half or ¼ tsp. garlic powder

1 tsp. Italian seasoning (opt.)

1. Follow above directions.

SPAGHETTI & MEATBALLS, SPICY

For 4 to 6 adults.

1 to 1¼ lbs. spaghetti

Meatballs:

¾ to 1 lb. ground beef

¾ to 1 tsp. salt

⅛ tsp. pepper

¼ c. cracker crumbs (8 soda crackers, 2 x 2 in. each, in food processor) or ⅓ c. fine dry bread crumbs

1 med. onion, chopped (about ½ c.)

2 T. uncooked oats

1 egg

1 T. olive oil

Sauce:

2 (28-oz.) cans tomatoes or 7 c. tomato juice or canned tomatoes

12 oz. tomato paste (1⅛ to 1½ c.)

½ tsp. salt

1 tsp. basil

½ tsp. ground thyme

¼ tsp. oregano

½ c. sugar

1 bay leaf (opt.)

⅛ to ¼ tsp. crushed red pepper or cayenne pepper (opt.)

2 cloves garlic, minced or ¼ tsp. garlic powder

1. Combine meatball ingredients (not oil) with electric mixer or hands; form into 16 to 20 meatballs. (Makes 21 meatballs using a level ⅛-cup measure for each one.) **2.** In skillet with the oil, brown meatballs on all sides; discard all fat. **3.** Meanwhile, combine sauce ingredients in cooking pot; with a potato masher or wire whip, blend tomatoes and tomato paste together, breaking up the tomatoes. **4.** Bring sauce to a boil; reduce heat to low. **5.** Add meatballs and simmer, covered, for 30 minutes, stirring occasionally. **6.** In 6-quart cooking pot, cook spaghetti in 4 quarts boiling water, 1 tablespoon salt and 1 tablespoon oil for about 12 to 15 minutes, or until tender. **7.** Drain spaghetti and rinse quickly with hot water; drain again. **8.** Remove bay leaf from sauce. **9.** Serve spaghetti in one bowl and sauce with meatballs in another bowl. **West Bend Slow-Cooker**: Set dial on #5 at first; then lower to #3 and cook sauce and meatballs for several hours.

SPAGHETTI SKILLET

No boiling of spaghetti ahead of time.

1 tsp. olive oil

¾ to 1 lb. ground beef

2¾ c. tomato juice

1 (6-oz.) can tomato paste

3 c. water

2 T. dried minced onion

1½ tsp. dried oregano

2 to 3 tsp. chili powder (opt.)

2 T. sugar

1¼ tsp. salt

½ to 1 tsp. chopped garlic

7 to 8 oz. thin spaghetti, broken

Grated Parmesan cheese (opt.)

1. In large skillet that has a tight-fitting lid, crumble beef into olive oil and cook until no longer pink. (If there is visible grease, drain off.) **2.** Combine tomato juice and tomato paste in a bowl and beat until smooth; add to meat. **3.** Add water, onion, oregano, chili powder, sugar, salt, garlic and spaghetti; bring to a boil. **4.** Cover with tight lid and simmer for 30 minutes, or until spaghetti is tender, stirring occasionally. **5.** When serving, sprinkle with Parmesan cheese if desired. Makes 4 to 6 servings.

SPAGHETTI WITH MEAT SAUCE

Serves 4 hungry people.

Meat sauce:

2 tsp. olive oil

1 lb. ground beef

½ to 1 c. chopped onion

1 tsp. salt

¼ tsp. pepper (or less)

3 c. tomato juice

1 c. (8 oz.) tomato sauce

1 (6-oz.) can tomato paste

½ tsp. Italian seasoning or oregano or basil

¼ tsp. garlic powder or garlic salt

2 T. sugar (or to taste)

Spaghetti:

3 qt. boiling water

1 T. salt

1 T. olive oil

1 lb. spaghetti

1. In 2 teaspoons olive oil, combine beef, onions, salt and pepper; brown lightly, leaving some of the beef in chunks the size of strawberries. **2.** Put beef mixture in colander or sieve, draining off fat. **3.** In empty meat skillet, combine tomato juice, tomato sauce and tomato paste; mix together well with wire whip. **4.** Add seasonings and beef; bring to a boil; then reduce heat and simmer gently 10 or 15 minutes. **5.** In boiling water, add salt, 1 tablespoon olive oil and spaghetti; boil until tender; then drain. **6.** Serve spaghetti individually on plates and spoon sauce over top. **Alternative:** After step 2, commercial spaghetti sauce (4 to 6 cups) may be added to the ground beef instead of using the remaining ingredients.

SPAGHETTI WITH MEAT SAUCE, LARGER

From Pat Swarts. Serves 10 to 11 adults. 11½ cups home-canned tomato juice may be substituted in this recipe.

1 to 2 T. olive oil
2 lbs. ground beef
2 to 3 onions, chopped
4 cloves garlic, minced or ½ tsp. garlic powder or garlic salt
2 tsp. salt
1 tsp. black pepper
2 (46-oz.) cans tomato juice (11½ c.) or 1 can tomato juice and 1 can V-8 juice
18 oz. tomato paste
½ c. sugar (or to taste)
2 lbs. spaghetti

1. In heavy pot, lightly brown beef, onions, garlic, salt and pepper with the oil. 2. Drain off all fat. 3. Add tomato juice, tomato paste and sugar; stir well. 4. Bring sauce to a boil; reduce heat to low and simmer 30 to 60 minutes, stirring occasionally. 5. Cook spaghetti in large pot of 6 quarts boiling water, 2 tablespoons salt and 2 tablespoons oil until tender (about 12 to 15 minutes after coming to a boil). 6. Drain spaghetti and rinse briefly with hot water; drain again. 7. Serve spaghetti and meat sauce in separate bowls.

SPANISH RICE WITH CHEESE

From Mrs. Leota A. Benninger.

1 (28-oz.) can tomatoes or 3½ to 4 c. tomato juice
¼ c. water
⅓ c. reg. white rice, uncooked
1 onion, chopped (or 2 T. instant minced onion)
½ tsp. salt
¼ tsp. garlic salt or garlic powder
⅛ tsp. pepper
2½ T. sugar (level)
4 oz. (1 c.) shredded sharp Cheddar cheese
3 T. butter

1. Turn oven to 350° and grease or spray 1½ to 2-quart casserole. 2. Put all ingredients into casserole in order given; stir together. 3. Bake, uncovered, in 350° oven 1 hour and 45 minutes, stirring once or twice during the last hour.

SPANISH RICE WITH CHEESE, LARGER

5 c. canned tomatoes or tomato juice
½ c. + 1 level T. reg. rice, uncooked
½ c. water
1 lg. onion, chopped (about ¾ c.)
¾ tsp. salt

¼ tsp. garlic powder
⅛ tsp. pepper
3 T. sugar (level)
7 to 8 oz. grated sharp Cheddar cheese
2 to 4 T. butter

1. Turn oven dial to 350°. 2. Grease 2½ to 3-quart casserole. 3. Put all ingredients into casserole in order given. 4. Bake, uncovered, for 1 hour and 30 minutes, stirring once or twice during the last hour, or until rice is tender.

SPANISH RICE WITH CHEESE (Microwave)

From Barbara Clark Benninger.

¾ c. reg. rice, uncooked
1 (8-oz.) can tomato sauce
2 cans (2 c.) water
1 tsp. salt
Dash of pepper
¼ c. sugar
1 med. onion, diced or chopped
4 (¾-oz.) slices cheese, torn into pcs. (Velveeta cheese may be used instead.)

1. Place all ingredients in greased or sprayed 1½ to 2-quart casserole; cover with lid or plastic wrap. 2. Microwave on HIGH for 5 minutes; stir. 3. Microwave on 60% (bake) for 40 minutes, covered, stirring occasionally.

SPANISH RICE WITH HAMBURGER I

Uses regular rice.

1 T. olive oil
1 onion, thinly sliced or chopped
½ med. green pepper, chopped or diced (opt.)
¾ to 1 lb. extra-lean ground beef
¾ to 1 c. reg. rice, uncooked
1 clove garlic, minced or ⅛ tsp. garlic powder (opt.)
15 to 16 oz. (2 c.) tomato sauce or spaghetti sauce or stewed tomatoes
1¾ c. hot water
1 tsp. salt
⅛ tsp. pepper
1 to 2 T. sugar (opt.)
¼ tsp. oregano or basil (opt.)

1. Heat oil in large skillet. 2. Add onion, green pepper, ground beef, rice and garlic; stir over medium-high heat until lightly browned. 3. Add tomato sauce, water, salt, pepper and sugar, if used; mix well. 4. Bring quickly to a boil; cover tightly and reduce heat. Cook on low heat 25 minutes, covered, stirring occasionally (or until rice is tender). Serves 4 or more.

SPANISH RICE WITH HAMBURGER II

Uses Minute Rice.

1 tsp. olive oil
¾ to 1 lb. ground beef
1 sm. to med. onion, chopped or 1 T. instant minced onion
½ med. green pepper, chopped (opt.)
1 clove garlic, minced (opt.)
1 tsp. salt
⅛ tsp. pepper
8 oz. (1 c.) tomato sauce
1 c. canned tomatoes
1 c. water
1 to 1½ T. sugar
1½ c. Minute Rice, uncooked

1. In skillet, brown beef and onion in oil; drain off excess fat, if there is any. 2. Add remaining ingredients, except Minute Rice; boil 1 minute. 3. Reduce heat; add Minute Rice. 4. Simmer on low heat, uncovered, for 10 minutes, stirring often.

SPARERIBS, BARBECUED I

A delicious recipe from Adrienne Hepfner.

2 to 3 lbs. Western or Country Style pork spareribs or pork loin back ribs
2 cloves garlic, chopped
1 (10¾-oz.) can tomato soup
¾ c. water
½ c. ketchup
¼ c. vinegar
1 T. lemon juice
2 T. prepared mustard
1 T. dried chopped onion
⅓ to ½ c. packed brown sugar
⅛ tsp. cayenne red pepper
¾ tsp. salt
¼ tsp. black pepper
1 T. Worcestershire sauce
1 T. liquid smoke (opt.)
1 tsp. chili powder (opt.)

1. Trim extra fat from spareribs; parboil ribs and garlic in water until tender, about 40 to 60 minutes after water begins boiling. 2. Drain ribs, discarding liquid, and place in roaster. 3. Make sauce by combining remaining ingredients in saucepan; simmer for 10 to 15 minutes, uncovered. 4. Pour boiling sauce over meat; cover with lid and bake in 350° oven for 1½ hours.

SPARERIBS, BARBECUED II

Allow 1 pound ribs per person. This recipe serves 3. Adapted from Mrs. Debbie Griggs.

2¾ to 3 lbs. pork spareribs or country-style ribs
Salt
Pepper
Garlic powder
Liquid smoke (opt.)
⅓ c. chopped onion
⅓ c. olive oil
⅓ c. vinegar
½ c. ketchup
2 T. sugar
1 T. chili powder
¼ tsp. hot pepper sauce (opt.)

1. Trim extra fat from spareribs; cut into serving-size pieces. 2. Parboil ribs in water until tender (about 30 minutes after water comes to a boil, or longer). 3. Drain ribs, discarding liquid; cool. 4. Sprinkle ribs with salt, pepper, garlic powder and a little liquid smoke; rub in with fingers. 5. Fry onion in the oil in small saucepan or skillet. 6. Add vinegar, ketchup, sugar, chili powder and hot pepper sauce; bring to a full boil, stirring constantly. 7. Reduce heat and boil a few minutes, stirring, until sauce is thick enough that it will not run off meat. 8. Place ribs in shallow pan in single layer; pour sauce over ribs and bake in preheated 350° oven for 30 to 40 minutes.

SPARERIBS, JOE'S BARBECUED HONEY RIBS

From Joe Morris.

Pork short ribs, pork spareribs or beef short ribs
Hot water
Barbecue sauce
Honey
Several cloves garlic, finely minced
Salt and pepper

1. Turn oven dial to 350°. 2. If ribs are in a rack, cut into serving-size pieces; if desired, remove some of the fat. 3. Place ribs in glass 13 x 9-inch baking dish; add hot water to ½-inch depth. 4. Cover dish tightly with aluminum foil; bake in preheated 350° oven for 30 minutes. 5. Remove pan from oven and drain off all water. 6. Pour honey over ribs, then barbecue sauce (about half and half of each). 7. Sprinkle minced garlic over ribs; sprinkle with salt and pepper (or ribs can be salted individually at the table). 8. Cover with foil again and return to oven; bake 30 to 45 minutes longer, or until tender.

STEAK, COUNTRY ROASTED

From Clara Irvin.

1 round steak (½ to ¾ in. thick) or thick deer steak
Flour
Salt and pepper
Butter or olive oil
Water (hot)

1. Cut steak into serving-size pieces; trim off all fat. 2. Pound flour, salt and pepper into steak on both sides with rim of saucer. 3. Heat butter in big iron skillet (or a skillet that is oven proof); brown steak on both sides. 4. Add about 1 inch of hot water to skillet; cover tightly with lid or foil. 5. Bake in

350° oven for 1½ hours or until steak is tender. <u>Stove Top:</u> After step 4, simmer 2 hours on low heat, adding more water, if necessary. (Or less time if it is deer.)

STEAK FINGERS

From Adrienne Hepfner.

Cubed steak or deer tenderloin steak, sliced
Salt, pepper and garlic powder
Flour
1 med. onion, chopped
Green pepper, chopped (opt.)
Olive oil or reg. Smart Balance Spread

1. Season the cubed steak with salt, pepper and garlic powder. 2. Cut steak into strips or "fingers;" flour the strips and fry in hot oil or Smart Balance until brown and tender along with onion (and pepper if desired).

STEAK MEAL, LEOTA'S

From Leota Benninger Reynolds.

1¼ to 2 lbs. round steak (beef or venison)
1 env. dry onion soup mix (4 T.), divided
1 (10¾-oz.) can cream of mushroom or cream of chicken
    soup
½ c. water
6 to 8 med. potatoes, peeled
5 large carrots, peeled and cut in half

1. Remove all fat from steak; cut into serving-size pieces. 2. Grease or spray casserole or small roaster; sprinkle ½ envelope (2 T.) dry onion soup mix over bottom. 3. Lay steak over bottom; sprinkle with remaining onion soup mix. 4. If using potatoes and carrots, lay them over steak. 5. Combine soup with ½ cup water, stirring until smooth; pour over all. 6. Cover with lid or foil; bake in 250° oven for 3½ to 4 hours (or 275° for 3 hours). <u>Crock-Pot Method</u>: Cook on LOW for 6 to 8 hours, covered. <u>West Bend Slow-Cooker</u>: Use ¼ cup water instead of ½ cup. Set dial on #5 for 2 to 3 hours, or on #4 for 3 hours or on #3½ for 4 to 5 hours.

STEAK & ONION PIE

From Joanna Pears. Delicious! Serves 4 to 5.

1 c. onions, sliced
¼ c. olive oil
¼ c. flour, packed level
1¼ tsp. salt
½ tsp. pepper
½ tsp. paprika
1 lb. round steak, cut into cubes (weight after all fat and
    bone removed)
2½ c. boiling water

2 c. diced, peeled potatoes

<u>Pastry:</u>
1 c. all-purpose flour
¼ tsp. salt
⅓ c. Earth Balance shortening
3 to 3½ T. ice water
1 egg, beaten (for top)
Dill weed, garlic powder or onion powder (opt.)

1. Cook onions in hot oil on medium heat until soft; remove onions from oil with slotted spoon. Set aside. 2. Combine flour, salt, pepper and paprika, stirring together; roll steak cubes in flour mixture, reserving any flour that is not used. 3. Brown steak cubes in hot oil on all sides. 4. Add boiling water; cover with tight lid and simmer gently 1 hour. 5. Add potatoes and reserved flour mixture, stirring together well; cover and cook 15 to 20 minutes (until potatoes are almost tender). 6. Meanwhile, make pastry for top of pie by combining flour and salt in bowl; cut in shortening with pastry blender. 7. Sprinkle, 1 tablespoon at a time, ice water over all, stirring gently with fork until dough can be shaped into a ball. 8. On floured surface, roll out crust to fit a 2-quart 12 x 8-inch oblong baking dish or 1½-quart round casserole, or deep 10-inch pie pan. (Roll out a little larger so edges can be turned under and fluted.) 9. Pour meat filling into pan; top with crust, fluting edges. 10. Brush crust with beaten egg; sprinkle with dill weed, garlic powder or onion powder. 11. Bake in preheated 400° oven for 30 to 35 minutes, until crust is light golden brown.

STEAK, PEPPER

From Sophie Calderone.

1½ lbs. round steak
½ c. flour
½ tsp. salt
⅛ tsp. pepper
¼ c. olive oil
1 (28-oz.) can tomatoes (or 3½ c.)
½ c. chopped onion
1 garlic clove, minced
1 T. Kitchen Bouquet
1½ tsp. Worcestershire sauce
3 med. green bell peppers, cut into ½-in. strips
Hot cooked rice or mashed potatoes

1. Cut steak into ½-inch strips, discarding all fat; set aside. 2. Combine flour, salt and pepper; coat meat with flour mixture. 3. Brown meat in hot oil. 4. Drain tomatoes, reserving both pulp and liquid; add water to the liquid to make 2 cups. 5. In large deep skillet, add liquid, onion, garlic, Kitchen Bouquet and the browned meat; cover with lid and simmer 1½ hours on low heat. 6. Add Worcestershire sauce, reserved tomato pulp and pepper strips; simmer, covered, 10 minutes or until pepper strips are tender-crisp. 7. Serve over rice or mashed potatoes.

STEAK, SALISBURY (Baked)

Makes 20 pieces or more. Delicious! Also called "Poor Man's Steak." From Mrs. Horst.

2 to 3 lbs. lean ground beef
1 c. fine cracker or bread crumbs
1 c. water or milk
1 onion, chopped
1 to 1½ tsp. salt (depending on which amount of meat is used)
¼ tsp. pepper
Flour for browning meat
1 (10¾-oz.) can condensed cream of mushroom or cream of celery soup
1 soup can of water

1. Mix together beef, crumbs, 1 cup water, onion, salt and pepper. 2. Press into large shallow 15 x 10-inch pan or cookie sheet; refrigerate overnight or several hours. 3. Cut into squares, roll in flour and brown both sides in skillet with small amount of olive oil; place browned squares in roaster. 4. Combine soup with 1 soup can of water until well blended; pour over meat. 5. Cover and bake in preheated 350° oven for 1 hour, or in 300° oven for 1½ hours, or at 250° for 2 hours. Note: For thicker pieces, press meat into a 13 x 9-inch cake pan.

STEAK, SALISBURY (Stove-Top)

Make these immediately. Very good!

1 lb. lean ground beef
1 egg
½ c. quick oats, uncooked
2 T. ketchup
2 T. water
1 to 2 tsp. Worcestershire sauce
1 tsp. dried onion
½ tsp. salt
Dash of pepper
Flour
1 (10¾-oz.) can condensed cream of mushroom soup, tomato soup, or cream of celery soup
1 soup can of water

1. Combine beef, egg, oats, ketchup, 2 tablespoons water, Worcestershire sauce, onion, salt and pepper; mix well. 2. Form into 5 or 6 oval patties; roll in flour to cover. 3. Brown patties on both sides in small amount of butter; pour off grease. 4. Combine soup and 1 soup can of water until well blended; pour over patties. 5. Simmer, covered, 45 minutes. (Or bake in preheated 350° oven 1 hour, or 2 hours at 250°.)

STEAK, SWISS, CAROLYN'S

From Carolyn Benninger Deets.

2 round steaks
2 cans (10¾-oz. each) cream of celery or cream of mushroom soup
2 env. dry onion soup mix
2 c. ginger ale

1. Remove all fat from steak; cut into serving-size pieces and lay in roaster or baking casserole. 2. Combine soup, onion soup mix and ginger ale until smooth; pour over steak. 3. Cover and bake in 300° oven for 3 to 4 hours. **West Bend Slow-Cooker**: Cut recipe in half, using round steak or deer chops. Set dial at # 3½ for 4 to 5 hours, covered.

STEAK, SWISS, DELECTABLE

Serves 4 to 6 adults, depending on which amount of steak is used.

2¼ to 3½ lbs. beef steak, deer steak or deer chops
½ c. flour (approx.)
3 to 4 T. olive oil or butter
2 env. dry onion soup mix
3½ c. warm tap water
¾ c. cold tap water
¼ c. flour, packed level

1. Remove all fat from steak; cut into serving-size pieces. 2. Roll steak in first flour, flouring both sides well; lightly brown in large skillet in oil or butter. Do not salt steak. 3. Put browned steak in 2½-quart baking dish, 13 x 9-inch glass baking dish or roaster. 4. Sprinkle dry onion soup mix over steak. 5. In same skillet, bring the warm tap water to a boil. 6. Meanwhile, shake together cold tap water and ¼ cup flour in covered jar. 7. Add all at once to boiling water, stirring constantly; bring to a boil again. 8. Through a sieve, pour gravy over steak; cover with tight lid or foil. 9. Bake in 250° oven 3 to 4 hours.

STEAK, SWISS, PRESSURED

Quick and very good, from Adrienne Hepfner. No need to pound the steak.

Steak or deer chops, all fat removed
Salt and pepper
Garlic powder or onion powder (opt.)
Flour
2 c. water or more
Olive oil
2 tsp. or 2 cubes of beef bouillon

1. Season the meat on one side only with salt and pepper. 2. Sprinkle lightly with garlic powder. 3. Flour pieces of meat on both sides and brown in hot olive oil on high heat. 4. Pour off any extra oil. 5. Place meat on a rack in pressure cooker; add 2 cups water (or 2½ to 3 cups if more gravy is wanted). 6. Follow directions for pressure cooker and pressure 20 minutes. 7.

Bring pressure down to zero, and open cooker; remove meat to warm platter and make gravy by adding thickening. (Shake together ½ cup water and ⅓ cup flour.) Use as much as is needed, stirring and bringing to a boil. **8.** Boil 2 or 3 minutes.

STEAK SWISS, SUPERB, WITH TOMATOES

This is so good! A top-of-stove recipe.

½ c. flour
½ tsp. salt
½ tsp. pepper
1¾ to 2¼ lbs. boneless round steak (beef or venison), cut into serving pieces
2 to 3 T. olive oil (more if needed)
1 (14½ oz.) can stewed tomatoes (about 1¾ c.)
1 (10¾ oz.) can tomato soup, undiluted
1 large onion or 2 to 3 medium onions, sliced
¼ tsp. each of paprika, thyme, marjoram and salt
1 bay leaf (optional)

1. In a vegetable bowl, combine flour, first salt, and the pepper. **2.** Remove all fat, skin and gristle from steak; add the meat, one piece at a time, to flour mixture and coat both sides. **3.** In large skillet that has a tight lid, brown steak in oil over med.-high heat on both sides. **4.** In another bowl, combine stewed tomatoes, tomato soup, onion, paprika, thyme, marjoram, remaining salt and bay leaf; pour over steak. **5.** Bring to a boil; reduce heat and simmer, covered, on low heat for 1½ to 1¾ hours, or until meat is tender. Discard bay leaf.

STEAK, SWISS, TRADITIONAL

From Pat Swarts.

2 to 2½ lbs. round steak
½ c. flour (approx.)
3 T. olive oil
3 T. butter
2 to 2½ tsp. salt
¼ tsp. pepper
2 med. onions, sliced
4 c. water

1. Cut steak into serving-size pieces; cut off all fat and discard. **2.** Put oil and butter in large skillet (or divide it into 2 skillets) over medium-high heat and melt butter. **3.** Dip steak pieces into ½ cup flour, coating both sides. **4.** Place steak in skillet(s), browning on both sides. **5.** Lay steak in roaster or 2½-quart baking dish; sprinkle with the salt and pepper. **6.** Lay onion slices over the steak. **7.** Measure remaining flour in ¼-cup measure; if necessary, add more flour to make ¼ cup full. **8.** Add the ¼ cup flour to drippings in skillet. (If using 2 skillets, pour drippings all into 1 skillet.) Stir well. **9.** Add 4 cups water to flour mixture all at once; bring to a boil, stirring. **10.** Pour this thin gravy through a sieve over the steak and onions. (Gravy will get thicker as it bakes.) **11.** Cover and bake in 250° oven for 3 hours.

STEAK, SWISS, WITH TOMATOES

Cut recipe in half for 2 adults.

2 lbs. round steak or deer steak
½ c. flour
1 tsp. salt
¼ to ½ tsp. pepper
⅓ c. butter or olive oil
2 c. sliced onions (or less)
1 (16-oz.) can (2 c.) tomatoes
2 c. tomato juice
½ c. water
1 T. sugar (level)

1. Trim all fat from steak and discard. **2.** Mix flour, salt and pepper together; pound into steak with rim of saucer. **3.** Cut steak into serving-size pieces; brown lightly in melted butter. **4.** Place steak in 2½-quart baking dish or roaster. **5.** Brown onions lightly in same skillet in which meat was browned; place on top steak. **6.** Pour canned tomatoes over steak. **7.** Add remainder of flour mixture to butter in skillet; blend together. **8.** Add tomato juice and water to skillet; cook until mixture boils, stirring constantly. **9.** Pour this tomato gravy over steak. **10.** Bake, covered, in 250° oven for 3 hours or in 350° oven 2 hours (or until tender). Serves 4. **Note:** ¼ teaspoon each of basil, oregano and thyme may be used, if desired.

STROGANOFF, BEEF

From Carol Wells. Serves 6.

8 oz. fresh mushrooms, thinly sliced (or 8-oz. can, drained)
1 lg. or 2 med. onions, chopped
¼ c. (½ stick) butter
2 lbs. round steak (approx., or less)
Flour for dredging
2 T. additional butter
1 tsp. salt
2 c. beef broth (or use water and beef bouillon cubes)
8 oz. (1 c.) sour cream or low-fat or fat-free sour cream substitute
Cooked noodles

1. Sauté mushrooms and onion in ¼ cup butter; remove with slotted spoon from skillet and set aside. **2.** Remove fat and bone from steak; cut into bite-size pieces and dredge in flour. **3.** Melt additional 2 tablespoons butter in same skillet; brown meat on both sides. **4.** Add salt and broth or bouillon mixture; cover with lid and simmer until meat is tender, approximately 1¼ hours, stirring occasionally. **5.** Add mushrooms, onion and sour cream; heat, but do not let boil. **6.** Serve over hot noodles or rice.

STROGANOFF, HAMBURGER

1 lb. ground beef
1 med. or lg. onion, chopped
½ T. olive oil, if needed
1 c. water
2 beef bouillon cubes or 2 tsp. instant beef bouillon
3 T. butter
1 tsp. Worcestershire sauce
1 (4-oz.) can mushrooms, including liquid
1 tsp. salt
¼ tsp. pepper
¼ tsp. garlic powder (opt.)
8 oz. egg noodles, uncooked
½ c. (4 oz.) sour cream or low-fat or fat-free sour cream
    substitute

1. In skillet, cook ground beef and onion, using oil if needed; drain off all fat. 2. Add water, beef bouillon cubes, butter, Worcestershire sauce, mushrooms and liquid, salt and pepper; simmer on low heat 15 minutes. 3. Meanwhile, in large pot, cook noodles in 3 quarts boiling water and 2 teaspoons salt for 10 to 12 minutes or until tender; drain; then return to pot. 4. Pour beef mixture over hot noodles, add sour cream and gently stir together; heat, but do not boil.

STROGANOFF, POOR MAN'S

From Adele Crognale. So easy!

1 lb. stewing beef (do not brown) or round steak, cut up
1 (10¾-oz.) can cream of mushroom soup, undiluted
½ env. Lipton onion soup mix (2 T.)
Cooked noodles or rice

1. Combine beef, mushroom soup and onion soup mix in casserole or small roaster. 2. Bake, covered, in 275° oven 2 to 2½ hours (or until tender). 3. Serve over hot noodles or rice. Crock-Pot: Cook in crock-pot on LOW 6 to 8 hours.

STROMBOLI, DOROTHY PATTERSON'S

This recipe will serve 8 to 10 people.

2 loaves frozen bread dough, thawed
½ lb. baked ham or turkey ham, sliced thin
½ lb. Provolone cheese, sliced thin
½ lb. hard Salami, sliced thin
½ lb. Mozzarella cheese, sliced thin
½ lb. sandwich pepperoni, sliced thin
1 sm. onion, chopped
1 med. green pepper, chopped
1 can mushrooms, drained (opt.)

1. Thaw bread dough, but do not let rise. (An easy way to thaw it is to leave it in refrigerator overnight.) 2. Grease 2 cookie sheets lightly with oil. 3. Turn oven dial to 350°. 4. Spread 1 loaf of dough onto 1 cookie sheet, pressing with fingertips until it nearly covers sheet. 5. Layer meats and cheeses on the bread dough in order given. (Do not go clear to edges.) 6. Top with onion, green pepper and mushrooms. 7. Spread second loaf of dough on the other cookie sheet; then lift the dough off and place over top the stromboli. 8. Seal edges by pressing top and bottom doughs together. 9. Bake in preheated 350° oven 30 minutes or until golden brown; let cool 5 minutes before cutting.

STROMBOLI, ROLLED

From Louave Hopper.

1 loaf frozen bread dough, thawed
2 egg yolks (reserve whites)
1 T. Parmesan cheese
1 tsp. parsley
1 tsp. garlic powder
1 tsp. oregano
¼ tsp. black pepper
4 to 8 oz. pepperoni, sliced thin
8 to 12 oz. Mozzarella or Provolone cheese, sliced thin

1. Turn oven dial to 350°. 2. On greased cookie sheet, spread thawed bread dough with palm of hand, about 10 x 14 inches. (Or homemade bread dough equivalent to 1 loaf.) 3. Combine egg yolks, Parmesan cheese and the seasonings together and spread on dough, like butter, to ½ inch of edge of dough. 4. Cover top with pepperoni and cheese; roll like jellyroll, placing seam side down. 5. Brush top of loaf with egg whites. 6. Bake in preheated 350° oven 30 to 40 minutes. 7. After cooling a little, slice and serve. (May be dipped in side dish of pizza sauce, if desired.) Note: Chopped green pepper, mushrooms, thinly sliced onions, black olives and ham (or any combination you wish) may be added.

STROMBOLI, SAUSAGE

From Adele Crognale.

1 (1-lb.) loaf frozen bread dough, thawed
¾ to 1 lb. Jimmy Dean sausage
1 med. onion, chopped
1 med. green pepper, chopped
½ c. chopped fresh mushrooms (opt.)
1 c. (4 oz.) shredded Cheddar cheese
1 c. (4 oz.) shredded Mozzarella cheese
1 egg, beaten
Heated spaghetti sauce or picante sauce (opt.)

1. Let bread thaw and rise according to package directions. 2. In skillet, brown sausage, onion, green pepper and mushrooms (brown well); drain all liquid off. 3. On lightly floured surface, roll out bread dough to rectangle shape (approximately 14 x 10 inches); lay on a slightly greased cookie sheet. 4. Spread ½ of sausage mixture down center of dough. 5. Combine Cheddar cheese and Mozzarella cheese; sprinkle ½

the cheese over sausage. **6.** Layer remaining sausage mixture over cheese. **7.** Sprinkle remaining cheese over top. **8.** Put left side of dough over center, then right side of dough over center; tuck ends under and brush with beaten egg. **9.** Bake in preheated 375° oven until brown, about 20 minutes. **10.** Serve with heated spaghetti sauce or picante sauce to dip stromboli in.

TEXAS HASH

½ T. butter or olive oil
¾ to 1 lb. ground beef
2 lg. onions, chopped or sliced
1 green pepper, chopped (opt.)
2 c. canned tomatoes (16 oz. can)
½ c. uncooked reg. rice
½ to 2 tsp. chili powder
1 tsp. salt
⅛ tsp. pepper
1 to 2 T. sugar

1. Put butter or oil in large skillet and brown ground beef, onions and green pepper. **2.** If there is excess fat, drain off. **3.** Add tomatoes, rice, chili powder, salt, pepper and sugar. **4.** Bring to a boil; then reduce heat and simmer, tightly covered, for 25-30 minutes, until rice is done. Serves 3 to 5 people.

TONGUE, BEEF

1 fresh beef tongue, washed well
Boiling water
1 lg. onion, peeled and sliced
1 carrot, peeled and sliced
1 c. celery, including leaves
½ to 1 T. dried parsley flakes
7 peppercorns
1 tsp. salt
1 bay leaf (opt.)

1. Cover tongue with boiling water; add remaining ingredients. **2.** Simmer until tender, 2½ hours or longer. (Or cook in crock-pot on HIGH for 4 to 4½ hours.) **3.** Discard vegetables and broth; peel skin and fat off tongue and serve hot or cold, sliced. <u>Note</u>: Cooked tongue freezes well, but freeze some of the liquid with it to keep the tongue moist.

VEAL ROAST

Veal roast
2½ c. water
2 chicken bouillon cubes
½ tsp. salt per pound of meat
Pepper

1. Preheat oven to 400°. <u>Turn down to 275°</u> when putting roast in oven with the water, bouillon cubes, salt and pepper. **2.** Cover with lid and roast 4 to 4½ hours.

WIENERS, BARBECUE SKILLET

"Delicious! From Sarah Stevenson McIlhany."

½ to 1 T. butter or olive oil
1 lb. wieners (10 to 16 oz.)
1 sm. onion, finely chopped (or 1 T. dried onion flakes)
1 sm. green pepper, chopped (opt.)
⅔ c. ketchup
⅓ c. water
2 T. packed brown sugar
2 T. prepared mustard

1. Melt butter in skillet. **2.** Slash tops of wieners diagonally with sharp knife; brown on all sides in skillet. **3.** In small bowl, blend together remaining ingredients; pour over wieners. **4.** Simmer gently 15 minutes, uncovered, or cook in crock-pot on LOW for 2 hours.

WIENERS & BEANS, STOVE TOP

"Recipe may be multiplied. Delicious!"

2 to 4 wieners, cut into ¼-in. thick slices
½ med. onion, chopped
1 T. olive oil
1 (15 to 16-oz.) can pork & beans
2 T. packed brown sugar
2 T. ketchup
1 tsp. prepared mustard or ½ tsp. dry mustard
½ tsp. liquid smoke (opt.)
1 tsp. bacon flavor chips (opt.)

1. Fry sliced wieners and chopped onion in oil. **2.** Stir in remaining ingredients. **3.** Heat through, but do not boil.

WIENERS & BUNS (Microwave)

Pierce wiener in several places to prevent bursting during cooking. Place in bun and wrap in napkin or paper towel. Cook 1 hot dog on HIGH for 30 to 45 seconds; 2 hot dogs for 45 seconds to 1 minute; 4 hot dogs for 1½ to 2½ minutes.

WIENERS & CONEY SAUCE

½ lb. (1 c.) ground beef
1 tsp. olive oil, if needed
1 med. onion, chopped
1 (8-oz.) can (1 c.) tomato sauce
1 tsp. chili powder
¼ tsp. Worcestershire sauce
1 to 2 tsp. sugar
Red Hot pepper sauce to taste
8 to 10 wieners
8 to 10 hot dog buns

1. Cook beef in oil with onion in skillet on medium heat, stirring well to break up meat into very small pieces. **2.** Drain off all fat. **3.** Combine meat, tomato sauce, chili powder, Worcestershire sauce, sugar and hot pepper sauce; bring to a boil. **4.** Reduce heat and simmer 5 to 10 minutes. **5.** Serve wieners in buns; top with Coney Sauce.

ZUCCHINI HAMBURGER BOATS

1½ to 2 lbs. zucchini (about 6 sm.)
½ lb. ground beef or bulk Italian sausage
1 sm. onion, chopped
1 clove garlic, minced
⅓ c. dry bread crumbs
½ tsp. salt
½ tsp. oregano (opt.)
¼ tsp. pepper
1 egg
2 T. grated Parmesan or Romano cheese
⅔ c. spaghetti sauce

1. Cut off each end of zucchini, but do not peel; leave whole. **2.** Drop into a pot of boiling water; when water boils again, boil 5 minutes (or 10 minutes if zucchini are medium sized). **3.** Drain and cut in half lengthwise; carefully spoon out centers, leaving ¼-inch shell. **4.** Chop spooned-out pulp and reserve. **5.** Fry meat, onion and garlic in skillet; drain off fat. **6.** To the meat, add reserved zucchini pulp, bread crumbs, seasonings, egg and cheese; mix together. **7.** Stuff meat mixture into zucchini boats; place in greased or sprayed shallow baking dish and top with spaghetti sauce. **8.** Bake, uncovered, 30 to 40 minutes in preheated 375° oven.

Chapter 19

Fish

Bob & Barbara Benninger

Debbie Patterson

Dan + Pat, Laura + Eric Benninger

Patricia Swarts

Nick, Shelly, Shannon, Kurtis

Sarah McElhany '81

Erla Hoobler

Leota Reynolds

Alden Stevenson

FISH

CRAB CAKES I

A Maryland recipe. Serves 4.

1 egg
3 to 4 T. mayonnaise
1 tsp. dry mustard
1 tsp. Old Bay seasoning (or ¼ tsp. salt)
½ tsp. black pepper
⅛ tsp. Red Hot pepper sauce
1 T. minced onion
1 tsp. Worcestershire sauce
1 lb. crab meat (2 to 2½ c.), picked over for shells, drained
¼ c. cracker crumbs or 1 slice white bread, crumbled
Olive oil for frying

1. In bowl, combine egg, mayonnaise, mustard, Old Bay seasoning, pepper, hot pepper sauce, onion and Worcestershire sauce; mix until frothy. 2. In another bowl, place crabmeat; pour egg mixture over the top. 3. Sprinkle the cracker crumbs over all; gently toss together, trying not to break up the lumps of crabmeat. 4. Form into 4 cakes by hand, making about 1 inch thick. Keep crab cake batter as loose as possible, yet still holding form. 5. Fry crab cakes in hot olive oil (375°) until golden brown on all sides (3 or 4 minutes on each side). 6. Remove with slotted utensil to paper towels to drain. **Note**: Crab cakes may also be browned under a preheated broiler, turning to cook evenly. **Substitution for crab meat**: 3 cans (6 oz. each) crab meat, drained, flaked (and cartilage removed).

CRAB CAKES II

¼ c. finely chopped red or green bell pepper
¼ c. finely chopped green onions or regular onion
¼ c. mayonnaise
1 T. lemon juice
¼ tsp. seasoned salt
½ tsp. garlic powder
⅛ tsp. red cayenne pepper
2 cans (6-oz. each) Chicken of the Sea Crab
1 egg, beaten
1 c. seasoned or plain bread crumbs, divided
3 T. butter or olive oil

1. In bowl combine bell peppers, onion, mayonnaise, lemon juice, seasoned salt, garlic powder and red pepper, mixing well. 2. Stir in crab meat, egg and ⅓ c. bread crumbs. (Mixture may be sticky.) 3. Divide and form into four balls; roll in remaining bread crumbs, then flatten into cakes about ½-inch thick. 4. In skillet, melt butter over medium heat; fry crab cakes 3 to 4 minutes per side or until golden brown. Makes 4 servings.

FISH, BAKED

No need to turn fish in oven.

1 to 1¼ lbs. haddock, trout, cod or pollock fillets, thawed
Vegetable spray
Salt and pepper
2 T. butter, melted
1 T. lemon juice
1 tsp. grated or minced onion (opt.)
Paprika

1. Rinse fish in cold water; pat dry with paper towel. 2. Spray 13 x 9-inch shallow baking pan with vegetable spray. 3. Lay fish, single layer, in pan; sprinkle with salt and pepper. 4. Combine melted butter, lemon juice and onion; pour over fish. 5. Sprinkle with paprika. 6. Bake, uncovered, in preheated 450° oven 10 to 12 minutes, or can bake at 400° for 35 minutes, or until fish flakes easily. Garnish with snipped fresh parsley. Serves 3 adults. <u>Note</u>: To double recipe, use 15 x 11-inch jellyroll pan.

FISH, BAKED CRISPY

Easy, quick and delicious.

1 lb. fish fillets
3 T. lemon juice
¼ tsp. salt (opt.)
Pepper
1½ to 2 T. olive oil
½ c. cornflake crumbs or Wheaties crumbs

1. Wash and dry fillets and cut into serving-size pieces. 2. Pour lemon juice into a platter or large plate; add fish and let set in lemon juice 10 to 15 minutes. 3. Turn oven dial to 475°. 4. Drain fish and season with salt and pepper. 5. Dip in oil in shallow dish; then coat with crumbs. 6. Arrange in one layer in lightly greased or sprayed shallow baking dish or pan. 7. Bake in preheated 475° oven, without turning, for 10 to 14 minutes. Serves 3 adults.

FISH, BAKED FIESTA

This is a good recipe for strong-flavored fish.

½ to 1 c. chopped green bell pepper
½ to 1 c. chopped sweet onion
1 to 2 lbs. fish (any kind)
⅓ c. water
⅓ c. melted butter
Garlic powder or minced garlic
Salt
Pepper
Paprika

1. In bottom of oblong baking dish or pan, sprinkle green pepper and onion. 2. Lay fish, skin side down, on top of vegetables. 3. Add water around fish. 4. Pour melted butter over fish. 5. Sprinkle fish lightly with garlic, salt, pepper and paprika. 6. Cover and bake in preheated 400° oven for 35 minutes. Serves 3 to 4 adults.

FISH, BROILED (or SALMON)

2 T. butter
1 T. lemon juice
1 tsp. minced onion (opt.)
½ tsp. salt
¼ tsp. pepper
1 tsp. dill weed or 1 T. chopped fresh dill (opt.)
1 lb. cod, perch, salmon or other fish fillets (fresh or thawed)
1 T. fresh parsley or chives, chopped (opt.)

1. In small saucepan, melt butter; add next 5 ingredients, stirring well. 2. Place fish in lightly greased or sprayed 11 x 7 x 2-inch shallow baking pan. 3. Spoon half the butter mixture over fish. 4. Broil 5 to 6 inches from heat for 10 minutes or until fish flakes easily with a fork. 5. Transfer fish to a serving platter; pour remaining butter mixture over fish. 6. Sprinkle with parsley. Serves 3. **Note**: Always broil with the oven door in the broil-stop position (open about 4 inches).

FISH CAKES, GOLDEN

This recipe makes two rather large fish cakes. It may be multiplied to make as many as needed.

¼ to ⅓ lb. fish, cooked and flaked (haddock, cod, whitefish, etc.)
½ c. soft bread crumbs
¼ to ⅓ med. onion, chopped
1 egg
½ T. mayonnaise
½ tsp. dry mustard
¼ tsp. salt
½ tsp. dried parsley flakes
1 T. water (if needed)
1 T. olive oil
½ c. seasoned dry bread crumbs (approx.)

1. In a bowl, combine first 9 ingredients; mixing well; shape into 2 patties. 2. Heat olive oil in skillet. 3. Coat fish patties with the seasoned dry bread crumbs and fry on each side until lightly browned. Serve with tartar sauce and lemon wedges, if desired.

FISH, DEEP-FRIED & CRISPY

Serves 2 adults. Recipe may be multiplied. From Jill Cline.

Olive oil
¾ to 1 lb. cod fillets (fresh or frozen)
⅓ c. all-purpose flour
¼ tsp. salt
½ T. vinegar
¼ tsp. baking soda
⅓ c. water

1. Heat oil (2 or 3 inches deep) in heavy pan or deep-fat fryer to about 375°. (Use candy thermometer if necessary.) 2. Cut fish fillets into serving pieces. (If frozen, thaw completely.) Pat dry with paper towel. 3. Combine flour and salt in med.-small bowl. 4. In a cup, combine vinegar and soda; stir into flour. 5. Stir in water and beat until smooth. 6. Dip fish into batter, allowing excess batter to drip back into bowl. 7. When oil is 375°, remove thermometer and fry fish until brown, turning once (about 3 to 5 minutes or less). 8. Drain fish on paper towels, using a slotted spoon. 9. Immediately put thermometer back in the oil and bring to 375° again. Then remove thermometer and fry more fish. Repeat process until finished, placing fried fish in preheated 300° oven on baking sheets to keep warm. **Note**: Do not crowd fish; fry only 1 or 2 pieces at a time.

FISH, FRIED CRISPY

¼ c. flour or cornmeal (or 2 T. of each)
½ tsp. salt
⅛ tsp. pepper
⅛ tsp. paprika (opt.)
1 lb. perch, flounder, haddock, trout or pollock fillets
1 T. olive oil

1. Combine first 4 ingredients; stir well. 2. Dip fish in mixture, coating both sides. 3. Fry in hot oil, turning when golden brown; fry on second side until golden brown. 4. Drain on paper towel. Serves 2 to 3.

FISH, FRIED FLOUNDER OR CATFISH

This recipe may be used for other fish, also.

1 egg
⅛ tsp. hot pepper sauce
¼ c. yellow cornmeal
2 T. flour
½ tsp. salt
1 T. cooked, crumbled bacon (opt.)
4 flounder or catfish fillets (about 6 oz. each)
¼ c. olive oil

1. In pie plate, with fork, beat egg and hot pepper sauce. 2. On waxed paper, mix cornmeal, flour, salt and crumbled bacon (if used). 3. Dip fish fillets into egg mixture, then into cornmeal mixture to coat. 4. In 10-inch skillet over medium heat in hot oil, fry fish, 2 fillets at a time, until golden brown on both sides and fish flakes easily when tested with fork (about 6 minutes). 5. Drain on paper towels. Yield: 4 servings.

FISH PACKETS, STEAM-BAKED

Makes 4 servings.

1 c. thinly sliced celery
1 c. thinly sliced bell pepper (red or green)
½ c. thinly sliced scallions or finely chopped onion
1 to 1¼ lbs. fish fillets or steaks

4 tsp. lemon juice
1 tsp. dill weed (NOT dill seed)
Salt
Pepper
Butter

1. Turn oven dial to 350°. 2. Cut 4 pieces of aluminum foil about 14 inches long. 3. Divide vegetables equally on each piece of foil. 4. Arrange fish over vegetables; sprinkle 1 teaspoon lemon juice, ¼ teaspoon dill weed, ⅛ teaspoon (or less) salt and pepper over each. 5. Dot each fish steak with 1 tablespoon butter (or less). 6. Seal foil tightly around fish and vegetables. 7. Place packets on baking sheet; bake 30 minutes in preheated 350° oven.

FISH STEAKS, BAKED

2 salmon, halibut or haddock steaks, fresh or thawed (8 oz. each)
2 T. butter or olive oil
1 T. lemon juice (or more)
1 green onion, sliced, or !/2 small onion, chopped
1 T. minced fresh parsley
!/4 tsp. garlic salt
!/8 tsp. lemon-pepper

1. Place fish in a lightly greased or sprayed 8 x 8-inch square baking dish. 2. Saute onions and parsley in butter or olive oil until vegetables are tender; pour over fish. 3. Sprinkle with lemon juice, garlic salt and lemon pepper. 4. Bake, uncovered, in preheated 400° oven for 15 or 20 minutes (until fish flakes easily with a fork).

OYSTERS, FRIED

1 (12-oz.) can oysters, drained
2 eggs, slightly beaten
2 T. milk
¼ to ½ tsp. salt
⅛ tsp. pepper
1 c. cracker crumbs, fine dry bread crumbs or cornmeal
Olive oil for frying

1. In med.-small bowl, mix eggs, milk, salt and pepper together. 2. Dip oysters in egg mixture; then roll in crumbs. 3. Fry in deep-fat fryer at 375° for 2 minutes or until brown. Or, to pan-fry, heat ¼ inch of oil in skillet; place oysters in single layer and fry until golden brown. 4. Drain on paper towel; serve hot.

SALMON CAKES, FRIED

1 (14 to 16-oz.) can salmon, partially drained (save ¼ c. liquid)
1 egg, large
1 c. soft bread crumbs

½ T. dried parsley flakes
2 T. onion, finely chopped or ½ T. dried onion
¼ c. celery, finely chopped (opt.)
¼ c. salmon liquid
1 T. butter or olive oil

1. Mix together all ingredients, except butter; shape into 4 to 6 patties. 2. Melt butter in skillet; fry patties for 5 minutes on each side or until golden brown.

SALMON, CREAMED (Or Tuna)

Serve over biscuits, toast or cooked noodles.

2 T. butter
¼ c. chopped celery
1 T. chopped onion
1 T. chopped green or red pepper
5 T. flour, packed level
3 c. milk
1 tsp. salt
¼ tsp. pepper
2 c. (1-lb. can) flaked salmon, drained, or 1 to 2 (6⅛-oz.) cans chunk tuna, drained
1 T. chopped pimiento (opt.)
Frozen peas (or cooked peas, drained)

1. Melt butter in large skillet; add celery, onion and green pepper. Fry until tender. 2. Add flour and mix well. 3. Add milk all at once and stir together. Add salt and pepper. 4. Bring to a boil, stirring frequently. 5. Reduce heat; add drained salmon or tuna, pimiento and peas. 6. Simmer on low heat 5 minutes.

SALMON LOAF, BAKED

This mixture may also be used to make 8 salmon patties, 1 inch thick, pan-fried on both sides in a little oil until golden brown.

1 (14 to 16-oz.) can salmon
2 c. soft bread crumbs (not packed)
¼ c. finely chopped onion
¼ c. milk
2 eggs (or 4 egg yolks + 2 T. water)
1 T. lemon juice
1 tsp. dried parsley flakes or 2 T. freshly chopped parsley
¼ tsp. salt
¼ tsp. dill weed
⅛ tsp. pepper
Paprika (opt.)

1. Grease or spray loaf pan or baking dish. 2. Turn oven dial to 350°. 3. Drain salmon, reserving 2 tablespoons of the liquid. 4. Put salmon in bowl; flake salmon, removing bones and skin, if desired. 5. Add remaining ingredients (except paprika) and the 2 tablespoons salmon liquid; stir together. 6. Shape into loaf and place in greased pan; sprinkle top lightly with paprika. 7. Bake, uncovered, in preheated 350° oven 45 minutes, or until firm. Serves 4. **Note**: Recipe may be doubled, putting all in 1 loaf pan and baking 1 hour, or until loaf is set in the center.

SALMON LOAF (Microwave)

Good hot or cold. Serves 4.

1 (14 to 16-oz.) can salmon, drained and flaked (reserve liquid)
2 eggs (or 4 egg yolks + 2 T. water)
1 c. soft bread crumbs (2 slices)
Milk combined with reserved salmon liquid to make ½ c.
1 T. fresh or instant minced onion
½ c. chopped celery
½ T. dried parsley flakes or 1 T. freshly chopped
1 T. lemon juice
¼ tsp. salt
⅛ tsp. pepper
Paprika

1. Grease or spray glass loaf pan or 4-cup microwave-safe casserole. 2. In bowl, combine all ingredients, except paprika, stirring well. (If desired, remove bones and skin from salmon.) 3. Spoon mixture into prepared pan, spreading evenly; cover with glass lid or plastic wrap, venting one corner. 4. Microwave on MEDIUM (50%) for 18 to 24 minutes. (Until loaf is set around edges and center is firm.) 5. Sprinkle top with paprika. Loosen edges and remove to platter. **Note**: If your microwave is 1000 watts, it takes less time.

SHRIMP FACTS

Allow about 1 pound of raw shrimp in the shell for 3 servings (or ½ pound of cooked shrimp without the shells).

To shell shrimp: Wash and let stand in cold water 15 minutes. Holding tail in left hand, lift off shell in segments with other hand. (Shelling may be done before or after boiling shrimp.) Tails may be removed, or left on.

To devein shrimp: With the tip of a small sharp knife, slit each shrimp along outside curvature and lift out the black veins. Rinse with cold water.

To boil fresh shrimp: Add 1 tablespoon salt to 1 quart water; bring to a boil. Add 1 pound shrimp and bring to a boil again. Reduce heat and simmer 3 to 5 minutes, never longer. Drain immediately.

To butterfly shrimp: Peel the shrimp down to the tail, leaving it on; devein. Hold shrimp so the curvature is up. Slice down its length almost clear through. Spread open and flatten to form butterfly shape.

SHRIMP, FRENCH FRIED

Serves 2 to 3 adults

¾ lb. shelled raw shrimp (or 1½ lbs. unshelled)
¼ c. fine cracker crumbs
½ tsp. salt
⅛ tsp. garlic powder or garlic salt

2 T. flour
1 egg + 1 T. water
Olive oil for deep frying

1. Shell and devein shrimp. Leave raw (or, if preferred, boil shrimp in salted water for 5 minutes; drain immediately). 2. Combine cracker crumbs, salt, garlic powder and flour. 3. In small bowl, beat egg with 1 tablespoon water. 4. Dip raw or cooked shrimp in beaten egg, then in crumb mixture. 5. Place several shrimp gently in preheated 365° to 375° oil (in wok, or deep-fat fryer or large kettle). Oil should be at least 2 inches deep. Shrimp must be in single layer. 6. Fry raw shrimp 3 to 5 minutes, depending on size. Fry cooked shrimp 2 to 3 minutes (until golden brown). 7. Drain on absorbent paper.

TARTAR SAUCE

Serve with seafood.

1 c. mayonnaise
1½ T. finely chopped dill pickle
1½ T. finely chopped sweet pickle
2 T. finely chopped onion or 1 T. instant minced dehydrated onion
2 tsp. snipped fresh chives or fresh dill (opt.)
¾ tsp. prepared mustard
4 green olives with pimientos, chopped
½ tsp. dill weed
¼ tsp. garlic salt

1. Combine all ingredients and mix together. **Note**: ¼ cup sweet pickle relish may be used instead of the dill and sweet pickles.

TUNA CAKES, FRIED

Serves 2 to 3 people.

1 (6-oz.) can tuna, drained
1 lg. or 2 sm. eggs
¼ c. fine, dry bread crumbs
⅛ tsp. salt or onion salt
2 T. chopped onion or ½ T. instant minced onion (opt.)
¼ to ⅓ c. diced celery (opt.)
½ to 1 T. olive oil

1. Mix together all ingredients, except oil. 2. Form into 3 to 5 patties. 3. Heat oil in skillet; fry patties for 4 to 5 minutes on each side, or until golden brown, on medium or medium-low heat.

TUNA CAKES, ZUCCHINI

Serves 3.

1 T. olive oil
½ c. finely chopped onion
1 (6½-oz.) can tuna, drained and flaked

1 c. shredded zucchini
2 eggs
3 to 4 T. snipped fresh parsley
1 tsp. lemon juice
½ tsp. salt
⅛ tsp. pepper
1 c. seasoned bread crumbs, divided
2 T. olive oil

1. In small saucepan, heat oil; add onion and cook until tender (not brown). Remove from heat. 2. Add tuna, zucchini, eggs, parsley, lemon juice, seasonings and ½ cup bread crumbs; stir until well combined. 3. Shape into 6 (½-inch-thick) patties; coat with remaining bread crumbs. 4. In medium skillet, heat oil and cook the patties 3 minutes on each side or until golden brown.

TUNA LOAF

2 eggs, beaten
1 c. milk (or part cream)
2 c. soft bread crumbs
¼ c. chopped celery and celery leaves
¼ c. chopped onion
¼ tsp. salt
⅛ tsp. pepper
1 (6½-oz.) can tuna fish, drained

1. In mixing bowl, beat eggs; add milk. 2. Add remaining ingredients, except tuna; let stand until liquid is all absorbed. 3. Add tuna; stir together and place in greased or sprayed loaf pan or small casserole. 4. Set in shallow pan of hot water in center of oven. 5. Bake in preheated 350° oven for 45 minutes, uncovered.

TUNA NOODLE CASSEROLE

For a dash of color, add 1 to 2 tablespoons drained, chopped pimientos and 1 cup frozen peas.

8 oz. (3½ to 4½ c.) uncooked noodles
1 (10¾-oz.) can cream of chicken, mushroom or celery
    soup
¾ c. milk
½ tsp. salt
¼ tsp. onion powder (or 2 T. chopped onion)
⅛ tsp. pepper
⅛ tsp. garlic powder (opt.)
1 (4-oz.) can mushroom stems and pcs., drained (opt.)
2 (6⅛-oz.) cans water-packed tuna, undrained
4 oz. sliced Velveeta cheese or 1 c. shredded yellow cheese
    or 6 slices American cheese
½ to ¾ c. crushed potato chips, cornflakes, cracker
    crumbs or croutons (opt.)

1. Cook noodles in 2 quarts boiling water and ½ tablespoon salt until tender, about 10 to 12 minutes. Drain in colander. 2. In empty noodle pan, add milk gradually to soup; add salt, onion powder, pepper and mushrooms, (if used). 3. Add

drained noodles and undrained tuna; stir gently together. 4. If using crushed topping, stir cheese into noodles. (If not, save cheese for top.) 5. Pour noodle mixture into buttered 13 x 9-inch baking dish or 2-quart round casserole. 6. Sprinkle crushed topping (or cheese) over top of noodles. 7. Bake in preheated 350° oven for 30 to 35 minutes or until bubbly. <u>Substitution</u>: 8 ounces of small pasta shells or 8 ounces of spaghetti (broken into 2-inch lengths, then cooked) may be used instead of noodles. Serves 4 to 6.

TUNA PASTA SKILLET

Something quick.

2 to 3 c. uncooked ziti, spirals or noodles
1 (10¾-oz.) can cream of mushroom soup
1 c. milk
1 to 2 (6-oz.) cans tuna, drained (water packed)
¼ tsp. garlic powder (opt.)
¼ tsp. onion powder
⅛ tsp. pepper
1 T. chopped pimiento (opt., for color) or red sweet pepper
1 c. Cheddar cheese, shredded
½ T. butter

1. Cook noodles in boiling, salted water until tender; drain. 2. Combine soup and milk in heavy iron skillet, blending together. 3. Add drained noodles and remaining ingredients; heat, stirring gently to prevent sticking. <u>Optional Ingredient</u>: 1 or 2 c. frozen peas may be added at the last.

TUNA POT PIE

2 T. butter
3 med. carrots, thinly sliced
1 sm. onion, diced
2 T. flour
1 (12-oz.) can evaporated skimmed milk
1 c. water
1 (9 or 10-oz.) pkg. frozen peas or cut green beans
1 (16-oz.) can whole potatoes, drained and diced
12 to 13 oz. canned solid white tuna in water, drained
¼ tsp. dried dill weed
¼ tsp. salt
Pastry for "Steak & Onion Pie"

1. In 3-quart saucepan over medium heat, in hot melted butter, cook carrots and onion until tender, stirring occasionally. 2. Stir in flour until blended; cook 1 minute. 3. Gradually stir in evaporated skimmed milk and 1 cup water; cook, stirring constantly, until mixture comes to a boil. 4. Add frozen vegetable, stirring to separate; remove saucepan from heat. 5. Stir in diced potatoes, tuna, dried dill weed and salt; pour into a 2-quart casserole. 6. Make pastry and roll to fit over casserole; bake in preheated 400° oven 30 to 35 minutes, until bubbly and golden brown.

Chapter 20

Chicken, Turkey and Dressing

DAVID, STEPHANIE, AND BONNIE SWARTS

CHICKEN, TURKEY AND DRESSING

BAKED CHICKEN, BARBECUED & CRISPY

From Beverly Muir Johnston.

½ c. fine dry bread crumbs
1 tsp. brown sugar
1 tsp. chili powder
½ tsp. garlic powder
¼ tsp. dry mustard
¼ tsp. celery seed
⅛ tsp. cayenne red pepper
2½ to 2¾ lbs. chicken pcs. (remove skin)
Salt and pepper
¼ c. butter, melted

1. Turn oven dial to 375°. 2. Combine dry ingredients in bowl; set aside. 3. Season chicken pieces with salt and pepper on each side. 4. Dip each chicken piece in melted butter; then roll in crumb mixture to coat. 5. Arrange chicken in shallow baking pan so pieces do not touch. 6. Sprinkle with any remaining crumb mixture or butter. 7. Bake, uncovered, in preheated 375° oven about 50 minutes, or until tender. Do not turn.

BAKED CHICKEN BREAST

Beverly Campbell Griffitts. Recipe may be multiplied.

1 lg. chicken breast (or 2 chicken breast halves)
¼ c. (½ stick) butter, melted
Salt
Pepper
Paprika

1. Turn oven dial to 500°. 2. Wash and dry chicken breast; cut in half. 3. Lay breast halves, skin side up, in shallow baking dish. 4. Pour melted butter over top. 5. Sprinkle liberally with salt, pepper and paprika. 6. Bake, uncovered, in preheated 500° oven 15 minutes. 7. Lower oven dial to 450° and bake 15 minutes. 8. Lower oven dial to 350° and bake 15 minutes. Serves 2. **Note**: Do not open oven door until the 45 minutes are up.

BAKED CHICKEN BREASTS, STUFFED

Serves 3 or 4.

3 or 4 split or whole chicken breasts, about 2 lbs. or 5 breast halves
½ c. flour
1 tsp. salt
½ tsp. paprika
⅛ tsp. pepper
1 (10¾-oz.) can cream of chicken soup
1 soup can (1⅓ c.) water

Dressing:
5 to 6 c. soft bread crumbs, firmly measured (8 to 12 oz.)

½ c. chopped celery
¼ c. chopped onion
¼ tsp. salt
¼ tsp. pepper
¼ to ½ tsp. sage or poultry seasoning
½ c. reg. Smart Balance spread or butter, melted

1. Wash chicken, removing fat. (Remove skin, too, if desired.) 2. Combine flour, salt, paprika and pepper in shallow bowl. 3. Dip chicken breasts in flour mixture, coating well. 4. Brown chicken on both sides in skillet with about ⅛ inch oil, or less; place chicken breasts in roaster. 5. In large bowl, combine dressing ingredients, stirring well. 6. Divide dressing and lay over top chicken breasts, molding and pressing together. 7. Combine soup and water gradually, mixing until smooth; pour around chicken. 8. Cover with lid or foil; bake in 325° oven 2½ hours. (Or 250° for 3½ hours.)

BAKED CHICKEN, CRISPY

1 frying chicken, cut up (2½ to 3¼ lbs.)
1 c. fine bread crumbs, cracker crumbs or crushed cornflakes (or a combination of any of these)
1 to 1¼ tsp. salt
¼ tsp. pepper
⅓ c. evaporated milk
¼ c. butter, melted (½ stick)

1. Turn oven dial to 375°. 2. Wash chicken pieces in cold water; if desired, remove skin (and all fat). Drain in colander and pat dry with paper towel. 3. In medium bowl, combine crumbs, salt and pepper. 4. Dip chicken pieces in evaporated milk; then roll in crumbs. 5. Place chicken pieces on foil-lined cookie sheet or 2 foil-lined 13 x 9-inch baking dishes. Do not crowd chicken. (If skin is not removed, place skin side up.) 6. Drizzle melted butter over chicken. 7. Bake in preheated 375° oven 1 hour, uncovered, or until tender. **Note**: If a less-crisp crust is desired, cover loosely with foil.

BAKED CHICKEN, ITALIAN

Serves 2 to 3 people. Recipe may be doubled.

1 c. fine dry bread crumbs, flavored or plain
½ tsp. salt
½ tsp. basil or Italian seasoning
½ tsp. oregano (opt.)
⅛ tsp. garlic powder
¼ c. butter, melted (½ stick)
2¼ to 2½ lbs. frying chicken pcs.

1. Preheat oven to 375°. 2. In medium bowl, combine bread crumbs, salt and seasonings. 3. Melt butter; set aside. 4. Wash chicken pieces in cold water; remove skin and all fat and discard. Dry pieces with paper towel. 5. Dip chicken, one piece at a time, in melted butter; then roll in bread crumb mixture. 6. Place in greased 13 x 9-inch pan or baking dish. 7. Bake, uncovered, in center of preheated 375° oven 1 hour, or until tender.

BAKED CHICKEN, OVEN-FRIED

From Sharon Close. This recipe may be cut in half for two and baked in a smaller pan.

½ c. flour
½ c. fine dry bread crumbs
2½ tsp. salt
¼ tsp. pepper
2 tsp. paprika
¼ c. olive oil
¼ c. butter (½ stick)
1 frying chicken, cut up (about 3 lbs.), washed and drained

1. Turn oven dial to 425°. **2.** Combine flour, bread crumbs, salt, pepper and paprika in paper or plastic bag. **3.** Put oil and butter in 13 x 9-inch pan and place in oven to melt butter. **4.** Shake chicken, 1 or 2 pieces at a time, in bag to coat thoroughly with flour mixture. **5.** Place chicken, skin side down, in single layer in hot oil and butter. **6.** Bake, uncovered, 1 hour, turning chicken pieces over after 30 minutes. Serves 3 or 4.

BAKED CHICKEN, OVEN-FRIED WITH DRESSING

Dressing recipe may be cut in half, if desired. This is enough chicken for 7 to 8 people if you don't use bony pieces.

5 to 6 lbs. frying chicken pieces
1 c. flour
2 tsp. salt
1 tsp. paprika
¼ tsp. pepper
Olive oil

Dressing:
20 oz. soft bread cubes
1 c. celery, diced small or chopped
½ c. onion, diced small or chopped
¼ tsp. salt
¼ tsp. pepper
1 tsp. sage or poultry seasoning
1 c. reg. Smart Balance spread or butter, melted
1 c. cream of chicken or cream of celery soup, not diluted

1. Wash chicken, removing skin and fat. (Leave skin on wings, if desired.) **2.** Combine flour, salt, paprika and pepper in bowl. **3.** Dip chicken pieces in flour mixture, coating well. (If wings need singed, do it with a match after coating with flour.) **4.** Brown chicken on both sides in hot fat (about ⅛ to ¼ inch oil in skillet). **5.** Arrange chicken around the edges of roaster, leaving the center for dressing. **6.** In large bowl, combine dressing ingredients; stir well. Pile the dressing in center of roaster. **7.** Cover tightly; bake in preheated 350° oven for 15 minutes; reduce heat to 300° and continue to bake for 1½ hours. (Or bake at 250° the whole time for 2 to 2½ hours.) **Note**: This recipe may be used without the stuffing.

BAKED CHICKEN, ROSE AVENUE

Crisp, crunchy and delicious. This recipe may be cut in half for 2 people.

1 frying chicken, cut up (2½ to 3¼ lbs.)
2 c. cornflakes (1 c., crushed)
1 T. dried parsley flakes or ¼ c. chopped fresh parsley
¾ tsp. salt
1 tsp. seasoned salt
¼ tsp. pepper
¼ c. grated Parmesan cheese (opt.)
½ c. (1 stick) melted butter

1. Wash chicken pieces and remove skin and all fat; drain in colander. **2.** Crush cornflakes to make 1 cup. (Small food processor does it nicely.) **3.** In medium bowl, combine all dry ingredients (including parsley); mix well. **4.** Dip chicken in melted butter, then in cornflake mixture. **5.** Arrange on one or two baking pans. Allow space between pieces so crust can get crisp. **6.** Bake, uncovered, in preheated 375° oven for 1 hour, or until tender. **Note**: This chicken can be held in a slow oven for latecomers, after it is done (170° to 250°).

CHICKEN A LA KING (Or Turkey)

The easy, shortcut way.

½ c. diced green pepper
2 T. butter
1 (10¾-oz.) can cream of chicken or cream of mushroom soup
½ c. milk
2 c. cubed, cooked chicken or turkey
2 T. diced, canned pimiento, drained
½ c. cooked peas, drained (opt.)

1. In medium saucepan, cook pepper in butter until tender. **2.** Add soup and milk, stirring until blended. **3.** Add chicken, pimiento and peas. **4.** Heat, stirring occasionally; serve over toast, biscuits or rice.

CHICKEN A LA KING, CREAMED (Or Turkey)

Delicious and very easy! Serve over toast, biscuits or rice.

3 T. butter
¼ c. chopped celery
1 T. chopped onion
1 T. diced green pepper (opt.)
⅓ c. flour, packed level
3 c. water, broth, milk or a mixture of these
1 tsp. salt
⅛ tsp. pepper
2 c. cooked chicken or turkey, cubed
1 T. chopped canned pimiento (opt.)
1 to 2 c. frozen peas (opt.)

1. Melt butter in large skillet; add celery, onion and green pepper. Fry until tender. **2.** Add flour and mix well. **3.** Add 3 cups liquid all at once and stir together; add salt and pepper. **4.** Bring to a boil, stirring frequently. **5.** Reduce heat; add chicken, pimiento and peas. **6.** Simmer on low heat 5 minutes.

CHICKEN BAKE & BISCUITS I (Or Turkey)

A delicious recipe from scratch. Serves 4 adults.

½ c. chopped onion
½ c. diced celery
¼ c. butter (½ stick)
¼ c. flour
½ tsp. salt
¼ tsp. pepper
2¼ c. broth or water
2 chicken bouillon cubes (opt.)
1 c. peas, cooked or uncooked
½ c. coarsely diced, cooked carrots (opt.)
¼ c. diced green pepper (opt.)
3 drops yellow food coloring (opt.)
2 c. cooked chicken or turkey, coarsely diced

1. Cook onion and celery in butter until tender in large skillet. **2.** Add flour, salt and pepper, stirring well. **3.** Add broth or water all at once; cook, stirring constantly, until thick and smooth. **4.** Add bouillon cubes, peas, carrots, green pepper and food coloring; simmer 5 minutes on low heat. **5.** Add chicken or turkey, stirring gently. **6.** Pour into a 9 x 13-inch baking dish. **7.** Top with biscuits and bake in preheated 450° oven 12 to 15 minutes.

Biscuits:
1½ c. all-purpose flour
2¼ tsp. baking powder
½ tsp. salt
⅓ c. Smart Balance shortening
½ to ⅔ c. milk

1. Combine flour, baking powder and salt in bowl. **2.** Cut in shortening with pastry blender or fingers until mixture resembles coarse meal. **3.** Add milk to make a soft mixture, stirring only until all flour is dampened. **4.** Drop on top meat filling (or knead on floured surface for 10 seconds; roll to ¼ to ⅓-inch thickness and cut with 2½-inch cutter or top of water glass, making 12 biscuits and placing them on top meat filling). **5.** Bake in preheated 450° oven 12 to 15 minutes, or until biscuits are golden brown. <u>Note</u>: To double this recipe, use a lasagna pan; serves 8 adults. To triple this recipe, use 17 x 11 x 2-inch baking pan; serves 12 adults.

CHICKEN BAKE & BISCUITS II (Or Turkey)

Uses soup and biscuit mix.

½ to 1 onion, chopped
½ c. celery, chopped
2 T. butter
2½ T. flour
1 c. chicken or turkey broth (or 1 c. water and 1 chicken
    bouillon cube)

1 can cream of mushroom or cream of chicken soup
½ c. milk, broth or water
1½ to 2 c. frozen or cooked peas, drained (or 10-oz. pkg.
    frozen peas & carrots)
2 to 4 c. cooked chicken or turkey, cubed
2 c. biscuit mix with ½ c. water

1. Fry onion and celery in butter until tender. **2.** Add flour and stir together. **3.** Add broth and soup, stirring together until smooth. **4.** Add milk and peas; bring to a boil. **5.** Reduce heat and simmer 5 minutes. **6.** Add chicken or turkey, stirring gently. **7.** Pour into casserole or 9 x 13-inch baking pan. **8.** Stir biscuit mix and ½ cup water together with fork just until all flour is dampened. **9.** Drop biscuits on top of hot mixture. **10.** Bake in preheated 450° oven 15 minutes, or until biscuits are golden brown.

CHICKEN, BARBECUED

From Adrienne Hepfner.

2 to 3 lbs. chicken pieces, fat and skin removed
1 (10¾-oz.) can tomato soup
2 cloves garlic, chopped
¾ c. water
½ c. ketchup
¼ c. vinegar
1 T. lemon juice
2 T. prepared mustard
2 T. dried chopped onion
⅓ c. packed brown sugar
⅛ tsp. cayenne red pepper
¾ tsp. salt
¼ tsp. black pepper
1 T. liquid smoke (opt.)
1 T. Worcestershire sauce
1 tsp. chili powder (opt.)

1. Place chicken pieces in roaster, baking pan or casserole. **2.** Make sauce by combining remaining ingredients in saucepan; simmer for 10 to 15 minutes, uncovered. **3.** Pour boiling sauce over chicken; cover and bake in 350° oven for 1½ hours or until chicken is tender. (If in a hurry, bake it in 450° oven for 1 hour.)

CHICKEN CROCK-POT (Rooster)

For an older hen or rooster, this is good.

4½ lbs. chicken pcs. (approx)
3 carrots, peeled and cut in half
½ c. celery, cut in 1-in. pcs.
2½ tsp. salt
¼ tsp. pepper
½ c. hot water

1. In bottom of crock-pot, lay carrots and celery. **2.** Add chicken pieces, then remaining ingredients. **3.** Cover and cook on HIGH 1 hour. **4.** Turn crock-pot to LOW and cook 9 to 12 hours.

CHICKEN CROQUETTES (Or Turkey)

Delicious served with coleslaw or tossed salad. Serves 2 to 3 people but recipe may be doubled or tripled.

1 T. butter
2 T. flour, packed level
¼ tsp. salt
½ c. milk
1 c. finely chopped cooked chicken or turkey
½ T. minced onion
1 T. minced parsley or 1 tsp. dried parsley
1 sm. egg
1 T. lemon juice
¼ c. fine dry bread crumbs
Olive oil for deep-frying

1. Melt butter in small pan; blend in flour and salt. 2. Gradually add milk; cook over low heat until smooth and thick, stirring constantly. 3. Remove from heat; add chicken, onion and parsley; stir together. 4. Spread in a greased or sprayed 8 x 8-inch pan; chill well in refrigerator. 5. Divide mixture into 6 portions and shape into logs. 6. With a fork, lightly beat together egg and lemon juice. 7. Dip croquettes into egg mixture; then roll in crumbs. 8. Deep fry in 1 inch of oil, heated to 365°-370° for about 3 to 5 minutes or until golden brown. 9. Drain on absorbent paper. <u>To Bake:</u> Croquettes may be baked instead of deep-frying. Place on lightly greased baking sheet and bake in preheated 400° oven for 30 minutes or until golden.

CHICKEN & DRIED BEEF (Microwave)

Makes 6 servings in about 30 minutes.

3 whole chicken breasts (1 lb. each), halved
1 (10¾-oz.) can cream of mushroom soup
½ c. sour cream or sour cream alternative
1 (2½-oz.) jar dried beef, cut into pcs.
1 T. dried parsley flakes

1. Wash chicken in cold water and remove skin; place in 12 x 7-inch glass baking dish with thick edges of chicken toward outside. 2. Cover with plastic wrap. 3. Microwave on HIGH 10 minutes; drain. 4. Combine remaining ingredients in medium mixing bowl. 5. Turn chicken over; pour on sauce. Recover. 6. Microwave on MEDIUM HIGH (roast or 70% power) 15 to 18 minutes, or until chicken is fork tender. 7. Let stand, covered, 5 minutes before serving.

CHICKEN & DRIED BEEF WITH GRAVY I

Chicken Supreme, adapted from Rosalie Sankey. Superb!

2½ oz. dried beef (or more)
7 to 10 boneless and skinned chicken breast halves or 5 lb. chicken breast halves
1 to 2 slices uncooked bacon (opt.) cut in pcs.
2 c. sour cream, regular, light or nonfat (16 oz.)
2 (10¾-oz.) cans cream of mushroom or cream of chicken soup (or 1 of each)

Paprika
Pepper

1. Line bottom of greased or sprayed roaster (or large, deep baking pan or dish) with dried beef. 2. Remove skin and fat from chicken pieces and lay on top dried beef. 3. If desired, lay tiny piece of bacon on each chicken piece. 4. In bowl, combine sour cream and soup, mixing well; spoon over and around chicken. 5. Sprinkle with paprika and pepper. 6. Cover pan tightly with lid or foil. 7. Bake in preheated 325° oven 2½ hours, then remove foil and bake for 30 minutes to brown lightly. <u>Substitution</u>: 4 pounds of chicken thighs may be used; do not cut in half. <u>Note</u>: I, II and III can also be baked at 250° for 4 hours, covered.

CHICKEN & DRIED BEEF WITH GRAVY II

2½ oz. dried beef, torn in pcs.
5 to 6 frying chicken thighs (or chicken breast halves)
1 slice uncooked bacon (opt.)
1 sm. can mushrooms, drained (opt.)
1 (10¾-oz.) can cream of mushroom or cream of chicken soup
1 c. (8 oz.) sour cream
Paprika
Pepper

1. Line greased or sprayed baking dish or pan with dried beef. 2. Remove and discard skin and fat from chicken pieces and lay on dried beef. 3. If desired, lay tiny bit of bacon on each piece and drained mushrooms around chicken. 4. In bowl, combine soup and sour cream, mixing well; spoon over and around chicken. 5. Sprinkle with paprika and pepper. 6. Cover pan tightly with lid or foil. 7. Bake in 350° oven 1½ hours, <u>removing lid or foil the last 15 to 20 minutes to lightly brown</u>. <u>Slower Heat</u>: Bake in 275° oven for 3 hours, covered.

CHICKEN & DRIED BEEF WITH GRAVY III

For older chicken beyond the fryer-stage. Serves 8 to 12.

24 pcs. chicken or rooster, boiled until tender
2 (2½-oz.) jars dried beef
8 slices bacon, uncooked
2 cans cream of mushroom soup or cream of chicken soup
2 c. (16-oz.) carton dairy sour cream or low-fat or fat-free sour cream substitute
Pepper and paprika

1. Use good pieces of chicken, not bony pieces. Boil until tender; drain, saving broth for other uses. 2. Grease a large baking pan or roaster and line bottom with dried beef. 3. Remove and <u>discard skin, fat and bones</u> from chicken pieces; lay chicken pieces on dried beef. 4. Cut each slice of bacon in 3 pieces, making 24 pieces; lay bacon on chicken pieces. 5. In bowl, combine soup and sour cream, mixing well; spoon over chicken. 6. Sprinkle with pepper and paprika. 7. Cover pan tightly with foil. 8. Bake in 275° oven for 3 hours; remove foil and bake 15 to 20 minutes longer to brown, turning oven to 350°.

CHICKEN & DUMPLINGS

Adapted from Shirley Kaufman. This recipe serves 3 to 4.

2⅓ to 3 lbs. chicken pcs. (frying or stewing chicken)
6 c. cold tap water
1 med. or small onion, sliced
½ to 1 rib celery, sliced
2 tsp. salt
⅛ tsp. pepper or 6 whole peppercorns
½ bay leaf (opt.)

Gravy:
2 chicken bouillon cubes
4 drops yellow food coloring
½ tsp. dried parsley flakes
⅓ c. all-purpose flour
½ c. chicken broth or water

Dumplings:
1 c. all-purpose flour
2 tsp. baking powder
½ tsp. salt
½ c. milk
2 T. (⅛ c.) olive oil

1. In soup kettle, combine chicken pieces, water, onion, celery, salt, pepper and bay leaf; bring to a boil. 2. Reduce heat and cover with lid; simmer 1 hour for frying chicken (or 2 to 3 hours for stewing chicken), until tender. 3. Remove chicken from broth and cool; remove skin and bones from chicken and cut meat into bite-size cubes. 4. Strain broth through sieve or colander, discarding vegetables and bay leaf. 5. Skim fat from top of broth, discarding fat. 6. Put 4 cups chicken broth in soup kettle. (If not enough broth, add water to make the 4 cups.) 7. Add bouillon cubes, yellow food coloring and dried parsley; bring to a boil. 8. In jar, add flour to ½ cup chicken broth or water and shake together. 9. Set boiling broth off burner and stir in flour mixture. 10. Return mixture to burner, stirring; bring to a boil again. 11. Add chicken and lower heat to keep mixture at a gentle simmer. 12. To make dumplings, combine flour, baking powder and salt in medium bowl, stirring together; make a nest or depression in the middle. 13. Add milk and oil in the nest; stir together just until moistened. 14. Drop from tablespoon atop gently bubbling chicken and gravy, making 9 or 10 dumplings. 15. Cover tightly with lid; simmer 15 minutes without lifting the lid. Note: Frozen mixed vegetables (thawed) may be added to Step 7. Note: Double this recipe (chicken and dumplings) to serve 6 to 8.

CHICKEN, FRIED CRISP, ELLEN'S

A Northerner's version of Southern-fried chicken. Serves 3 to 4 adults.

3 lbs. frying chicken
⅔ c. all-purpose flour
2 tsp. salt
1 tsp. paprika
¼ tsp. pepper
¼ tsp. poultry seasoning or rubbed sage (opt.)

¼ c. milk or less
¼ in. olive oil in electric skillet or heavy skillet

1. If necessary, singe off any hairs on chicken pieces with a match (or natural gas flame on stove). 2. Wash and drain chicken pieces, pulling off any clumps of fat. If breast is too large, cut in half; fold wing tips under. (If desired, remove skin from all chicken pieces, except wings.) 3. Heat oil in large heavy skillet until hot, but not smoking (or set electric skillet at 365° to 375°). 4. While oil is heating, combine flour, salt, paprika and poultry seasoning in medium bowl, stirring well. 5. Put milk in med.-small bowl. 6. Dip chicken, one piece at a time, in milk; let excess milk drop off; then put wet chicken into flour mixture and coat well on all sides. 7. Place chicken in hot oil; repeat until all pieces are in skillet (medium heat if using regular skillet). 8. Brown chicken on both sides (no lid). 9. Reduce heat to 300° (low or medium-low for regular skillet) and cook, uncovered, 25 minutes longer, turning pieces several times. 10. Lay on paper towel-lined platter. Note: If chicken is done before meal is ready, place in shallow baking pan, uncovered, on middle shelf of 250° oven.

CHICKEN, FRIED (OLD-FASHIONED) & GRAVY

Chicken is cooked, then fried.

1 frying chicken, cut up
6 c. water
1½ tsp. salt
Flour
Butter

Gravy:
2½ c. chicken broth, fat removed from top
3 chicken-flavor bouillon cubes
½ c. water
⅓ c. flour, packed level
Yellow food coloring

1. Place chicken pieces, 6 cups water and the salt in large pan and bring to a boil; reduce heat and simmer 15 minutes. 2. Skim off foam and scum; cover and simmer gently over low heat 1 to 1½ hours, until tender. 3. Remove chicken from pan, reserving broth. If desired, remove skin from chicken when cool enough to handle. 4. Dip chicken pieces in flour and brown in skillet in hot butter. 5. While chicken is browning, make gravy by bringing 2½ cups chicken broth and the bouillon to a boil. 6. In jar, shake together ½ cup water and ⅓ cup flour; remove broth from heat and stir in thickening, using as much as is needed. 7. Bring gravy to a boil again; add a few drops of yellow food coloring, if desired.

CHICKEN, FRIED SOFT

Adapted from Marie Stonebraker.
Serves 3 to 4. Use large skillet with tight lid.

2½ to 3 lbs. frying chicken, cut up
⅔ c. flour
2 tsp. salt
2 tsp. paprika
½ tsp. onion powder
¼ tsp. pepper
4 T. butter
¼ c. olive oil

1. If necessary, singe off any hairs on chicken pieces with a match (or natural gas flame on stove). 2. Wash and drain chicken pieces, pulling off any clumps of fat. If breast is too large, cut in half; fold wing tips under. 3. In heavy skillet, over low heat, melt butter with oil. 4. Combine flour, salt, paprika, onion powder and pepper in paper or plastic bag. 5. Drop chicken into bag, 1 or 2 pieces at a time; shake to coat evenly. 6. Place heavy meaty pieces in center of skillet; fit bony pieces around edge. 7. Brown chicken on both sides. 8. Turn chicken again; cover skillet with tight lid. 9. Reduce heat to low or simmer; cook about 1 hour, or until tender. **Note**: Cut recipe in half for 4 chicken breast halves.

CHICKEN & GRAVY CASSEROLE

Adapted from Jean Moyer. Delicious with biscuits,
mashed potatoes or rice. Serves 3 to 4 adults.

2½ to 3½ lbs. frying chicken pcs. (remove skin)
3 to 4 T. butter, melted
1 onion, sliced
3 T. flour (level)
2 c. cold water
1¼ to 1½ tsp. salt
¼ tsp. pepper
2 T. cream, half & half or evaporated milk (or more)

1. Turn oven dial to 350°. 2. Fry chicken pieces in melted butter, browning about 5 or 6 minutes on each side. 3. Remove chicken to 2-quart casserole (ungreased). 4. Fry onion slices in same butter 3 to 5 minutes; lay onion over chicken. 5. Add flour to the melted butter that remains in skillet; stir in cold water, salt and pepper. 6. Bring gravy to a boil, stirring almost constantly. 7. Pour over chicken; cover with lid or foil. 8. Bake in preheated 350° oven 1 hour or until tender. 9. When ready to serve, lift chicken onto a platter; add cream to the gravy (optional). (Do not boil after adding cream.)

CHICKEN & NOODLES

1 (2½ to 3-lb.) stewing or frying chicken pcs.
7 c. water
2 tsp. salt
⅛ tsp. pepper or 6 whole peppercorns
½ bay leaf (opt.)

1 sm. onion, sliced
1 rib celery, sliced
1 carrot (unpeeled), sliced
Chopped fresh parsley or 2 tsp. dried parsley
2 chicken bouillon cubes
4 drops yellow food coloring
4 to 8 oz. uncooked noodles

1. Place chicken pieces, 7 cups water and the salt in large pan and bring to a boil; reduce heat and simmer 15 minutes. 2. Skim off foam; add pepper, bay leaf, onion, celery, carrot, parsley and bouillon cubes. 3. Cover and simmer gently over low heat 1 to 1½ hours, until tender. 4. Remove chicken from broth and cool; strain broth through sieve or colander, discarding vegetables, bay leaf, peppercorns, etc. 5. Skim fat from top of broth, discarding fat. 6. Return broth to large pan; add food coloring and taste for salt. 7. Remove skin and bones from chicken and cut into bite-size cubes; set aside. 8. Bring broth to a boil; add noodles to boiling broth and boil gently 20 minutes or until noodles are tender. 9. Add the chicken meat to noodles and bring just to a simmer. Remove from heat. **Note**: 6 to 7 c. chicken broth are needed in which to cook 8 oz. noodles.

CHICKEN PIE I (Or Turkey)

Serve with leftover gravy.

3 T. olive oil or butter
1 med. onion, chopped
¼ to ½ c. celery, chopped
¼ c. flour, packed level
½ tsp. salt
⅛ tsp. pepper
2 c. water or chicken broth
2 chicken bouillon cubes
3 drops yellow food coloring (opt.)
1 tsp. dried parsley or 1 T. chopped fresh parsley
1¾ to 2½ c. cooked chicken or turkey, cubed
1 c. frozen or canned peas, drained (or ½ c. peas and ½ c. carrots, cooked and drained), or mixed vegetables
Pastry for 9 or 10-inch, double-crust pie

1. Fry onion and celery in butter until tender. 2. Stir in flour, salt and pepper. 3. Add water and bouillon cubes, mashing cubes with back of tablespoon. 4. Bring to a boil, stirring constantly; boil 1 minute. 5. Add food coloring, parsley and chicken. 6. Heat mixture for 2 minutes; add uncooked frozen peas. 7. Pour into unbaked pastry-lined pie pan; arrange top crust over filling. 8. Cut a slit in top crust and seal edges. 9. Bake in preheated 400° to 425° oven for 30 minutes, or until golden brown. 10. Let pie set 10 minutes before serving; serve with chicken or turkey gravy.

CHICKEN PIE II (Or Turkey)

Use recipe for Chicken or Turkey Pie I, except omit the flour, salt, pepper, water and bouillon cubes. Instead, use 1 (10¾-oz.) can cream of chicken soup, diluted with ½ cup water.

CHICKEN POT PIE (Or Turkey)

Serves 6 or more.

3 T. butter
½ c. chopped onion
½ c. diced or chopped celery
⅓ c. all-purpose flour
2¾ c. chicken broth
½ tsp. salt
¼ tsp. pepper
3 to 3½ c. cooked, chopped chicken or turkey
1 (10-oz.) pkg. frozen mixed vegetables, thawed (or peas & carrots)

Pastry:
1½ c. all-purpose flour
¾ tsp. salt
½ c. + 1 T. Earth Balance shortening
4 T. cold water (approx.)

Pastry topping:
1 egg, beaten
1 tsp. water

1. Melt butter in saucepan; add onion and celery. Cook until soft. 2. Add flour; cook 1 minute, stirring. 3. Stir in chicken broth; cook over medium heat, stirring constantly, until mixture is thickened and bubbly. 4. Stir in salt and pepper, chicken and vegetables. 5. Pour chicken mixture into a lightly greased or sprayed 12 x 8-inch baking dish. 6. For pastry, combine flour and salt; cut in shortening with pastry blender until mixture resembles coarse meal. 7. Sprinkle cold water, 1 tablespoon at a time, evenly over surface, while stirring with fork until all ingredients are moistened. 8. On lightly floured surface, roll out pastry to fit top of 12 x 8-inch dish. 9. Combine egg and 1 teaspoon water with fork or small whip; brush pastry lightly with egg mixture (discarding what is not needed). 10. Bake in preheated 400° oven 35 to 40 minutes or until golden.

CHICKEN & RICE, BAKED

1 c. uncooked reg. rice
6 to 8 pcs. frying chicken (preferably only legs, thighs or 5 breast halves)
1 (10¾-oz.) can cream of mushroom or cream of chicken soup or 1⅓ c. chicken gravy
1½ soup cans (2 c.) warm water
1 env. dry onion soup mix (or 4 T. bulk onion soup mix), or less
Paprika and/or pepper (opt.)

1. Turn oven dial to 350°. 2. Grease or spray bottom and sides of 13 x 9-inch baking pan. 3. Sprinkle rice over bottom of pan. 4. Wash chicken pieces, removing skin, if desired; drain and place on top rice without overlapping (skin side up). 5. Gradually combine soup and water, mixing well; pour over chicken and rice. 6. Sprinkle onion soup mix over all, then paprika and/or pepper. 7. Cover with tight lid or foil; bake in preheated 350° oven 1½ hours, or until chicken is

tender; or bake at 325° for 2 hours. **Note**: 4-oz. can of mushrooms, drained, may be added, if desired.

CHICKEN & RICE, BAKED (Larger)

1¾ c. uncooked reg. rice
2 (10¾-oz.) cans cream of chicken, cream of mushroom or cream of celery soup (mix or match)
3 c. warm water
14 frying chicken legs, thighs or breast halves (remove skin, if desired)
2 env. dry onion soup mix (or ½ c. bulk onion soup mix)
Paprika and/or pepper (opt.)

1. Turn oven dial to 325°. 2. Sprinkle rice over bottom of 15 x 11-inch or 17 x 11-inch Pam-sprayed pan. 3. In bowl, combine soups and water; pour over rice carefully. 4. Sprinkle 1 envelope onion soup mix over rice. 5. Place chicken pieces on top rice (skin side up); sprinkle remaining envelope of onion soup mix over chicken. 6. Sprinkle lightly with paprika or pepper; cover tightly with lid or foil. 7. Bake in preheated 325° oven for 2 hours. 8. If chicken needs browned, remove foil and bake 30 minutes longer.

CHICKEN, RICE & BROCCOLI

A quick meal in 30 minutes. Serves 3 to 4.

1 T. olive oil
3 to 4 boneless, skinless chicken breast halves (about 1 lb.)
1 (10¾-oz.) can cream of chicken or cream of mushroom soup
1½ c. water
¼ tsp. paprika
¼ tsp. pepper
1½ c. uncooked Minute Rice
2 to 2½ c. broccoli, fresh or thawed (or 1 can green beans, drained, and 1 can mushrooms, drained)

1. Heat oil in large skillet on med.-high heat; add chicken, sprinkled with a little salt. 2. Cover with lid and turn heat to medium. 3. Cook 10 minutes on each side, until well browned and cooked through. Remove chicken from skillet and discard any oil. 4. Add soup to skillet; gradually add 1½ cups water, stirring until smooth. 5. Add chicken, paprika and pepper; bring to a boil. 6. Cover, turn heat to LOW, and cook 4 minutes. 7. Add Minute Rice and broccoli (or green beans and mushrooms); cover skillet with tight lid and cook on med.-low for 5 minutes, or until done.

CHICKEN, ROASTED & STUFFED (Large)

1 (5 to 7-lb.) roasting chicken
16 to 20 oz. bread, cubed (10 to 13 c.)
1 c. chopped celery
½ c. chopped onion

½ tsp. salt
½ tsp. pepper
1 tsp. ground sage or poultry seasoning
1 c. reg. Smart Balance spread, melted
3½ to 5 c. water
1 or 2 chicken bouillon cubes
Salt
Pepper
Paprika

1. Rinse chicken in cold water and drain; pull off extra chicken fat and discard. 2. In large bowl, combine bread, celery, onion, salt, pepper and sage. 3. Pour melted spread over it and stir together. 4. Tuck wings under chicken, if desired. 5. Place chicken in roaster pan; sprinkle ¼ teaspoon salt inside chicken. 6. Fill chicken with stuffing in neck and body cavities. Any leftover stuffing may be wrapped in foil and placed in roaster with chicken. 7. If needed, rub olive oil over breast and legs of chicken. 8. If desired, slip a rack under chicken; lay giblets around chicken. 9. Pour 3½ to 5 cups water around chicken; add bouillon cubes. 10. Sprinkle chicken and giblets with ¾ teaspoon salt. 11. Sprinkle pepper and paprika lightly over top of chicken. 12. Bake (covered) in 325° oven 4 hours, or until done. (Remove lid last 30 minutes if it needs to brown.) **Note**: Roast a 4-lb. roasting chicken with NO stuffing in it, for 2 to 2½ hours at 300°, or until tender. **Gravy**: 1. Pour broth from roasting pan into a tall, wide-mouthed container and skim all fat off top with gravy ladle. 2. Return broth to roaster or other pan; if there is not enough broth, add some water. 3. Shake together 1¼ cups water and 1 cup flour for thickening. 4. Bring broth to a boil; add as much thickening as desired, stirring constantly. (Turn off heat while adding thickening.) 5. Bring gravy to a boil, stirring almost constantly; reduce heat and boil gently several minutes. 6. For color, 2 to 3 drops yellow food coloring may be added.

CHICKEN, ROASTED & STUFFED (Small)

1 (3 to 3½-lb.) whole frying chicken
3 c. soft bread crumbs
¼ c. chopped celery
2 to 3 T. chopped onion
¼ tsp. poultry seasoning or rubbed sage
⅛ tsp. salt
⅛ tsp. pepper
¼ c. (½ stick) butter, melted
Additional salt and pepper
Paprika

1. Wash chicken in cold water and drain; remove and discard extra chicken fat. 2. In medium bowl, combine bread, celery, onion, poultry seasoning, salt, pepper and melted butter; stir together. 3. Sprinkle salt lightly inside chicken; fill chicken with stuffing. 4. Place chicken in roaster pan; press a small piece of foil over opening to hold stuffing in. 5. Lay giblets and neck around chicken; add ½ cup water to roaster. 6. Sprinkle outside of chicken with salt, pepper and paprika. 7. Cover roaster with lid and roast in 350° oven 2 hours; if not

brown enough, remove lid last 15 minutes and turn oven higher. **Slower Heat:** Roast, covered, in 275° oven for 3½ to 4 hours.

CHICKEN STRATA (or Turkey)

Delectable served with a salad.
(Refrigerate 2 to 9 hours.)

10 slices bread, cubed (about 6½ c.), divided
3 to 4 c. cooked turkey or chicken
¾ c. chopped celery
½ c. chopped onion
2 to 3 c. shredded American or Colby cheese (8 to 12 oz.),
    or 12 slices of cheese, divided
5 eggs, beaten
1 can cream of chicken or cream of mushroom soup
1½ c. milk
1 tsp. poultry seasoning
½ tsp. ground sage
½ tsp. dry mustard
½ tsp. salt or celery salt
1 c. cornflakes or potato chips, partially crushed
¼ c. butter, melted

1. Put 6 slices bread, cubed (or 4 cups soft bread crumbs) over bottom of greased 13 x 9-inch baking dish or cake pan. 2. Cover with cooked, sliced turkey or chicken. 3. Sprinkle celery and onion over poultry. 4. Sprinkle with half the shredded cheese (or lay 6 slices cheese over top). 5. Put remaining bread over cheese. 6. In medium bowl, beat eggs; add undiluted soup and mix together. 7. Add milk, poultry seasoning, sage, dry mustard and salt, stirring into soup. 8. Pour soup mixture over bread layer. 9. Sprinkle with remaining cheese (or lay 6 more slices cheese over top). 10. Cover and refrigerate 2 to 9 hours. 11. When ready to bake, uncover and sprinkle with partially crushed cornflakes or potato chips. 12. Drizzle melted butter over all. 13. Bake in preheated 350° oven 60 minutes, or until bubbly and golden brown.

CHICKEN & STUFFING CASSEROLE

Adapted from Jean Moyer. Makes 6 servings.

3 c. cooked chicken, cut in bite-size pcs. (reserve broth)
1 (10¾-oz.) can mushroom soup
½ c. milk
8 oz. (1 c.) sour cream or sour cream alternative
1 c. chicken broth
2 (6-oz.) boxes Stove Top stuffing mix (or other stuffing
    mix), prepared according to pkg. directions

1. Turn oven dial to 350°. 2. Place chicken in bottom of greased or sprayed 13 x 9-inch baking dish. 3. In bowl, combine soup and milk gradually; add sour cream, then broth, blending well. 4. Pour soup mixture over chicken. 5. Prepare stuffing mix according to package directions and sprinkle over top. 6. Bake in preheated 350° oven 45 to 60 minutes.

CHICKEN, SWEET & SOUR

From Adele Crognale. Serves 4.

¾ lb. chicken breasts, cut in chunks or strips
1 T. olive oil
½ to 1 c. green bell pepper, cut in strips
1 T. cornstarch
¼ c. "lite" soy sauce
1 (8-oz.) can pineapple chunks and juice
3 T. brown sugar
3 T. vinegar
½ tsp. ginger
½ tsp. garlic powder

1. Cook and stir chicken in hot oil in large skillet until browned. 2. Add peppers; cook 3 minutes. 3. In small bowl, stir cornstarch and soy sauce together. 4. Add soy sauce mixture and remaining ingredients to chicken; bring to a boil, stirring constantly. 5. Serve over cooked rice.

CHICKEN TETRAZZINI, MICROWAVE (Or Turkey)

From Debra Patterson.

8 oz. spaghetti, cooked
2 T. butter
⅓ c. seasoned dry bread crumbs
¼ c. (½ stick) butter
¼ c. all-purpose flour
½ tsp. Italian seasoning
½ tsp. salt
¼ tsp. pepper
1 c. chicken broth (can make with bouillon)
1 c. evaporated milk or half & half
2 c. cut-up cooked chicken or turkey
1 (4-oz.) can sliced mushrooms, drained
¼ c. grated Parmesan cheese

1. Cook spaghetti (broken in 4-inch pieces) in 2 quarts boiling water and 2 teaspoons salt until tender; drain, rinse, drain again and set aside. 2. Place 2 tablespoons butter in small bowl; cover with waxed paper and microwave on HIGH for 45 to 60 seconds, or until butter melts. Stir in seasoned bread crumbs. Set aside. 3. In 2-quart casserole, place ¼ cup butter; microwave on HIGH for 45 to 60 seconds (covered with lid), or until butter melts. 4. Blend flour, Italian seasoning, salt and pepper into butter; stir in broth and milk. Microwave on MEDIUM-HIGH, 70% (Number 7) for 8 to 9 minutes, or until mixture thickens, stirring every 2 minutes. 5. Stir in spaghetti, turkey, drained mushrooms and Parmesan cheese. 6. Cover and microwave on MEDIUM-HIGH (Number 7), for 5 to 6 minutes, or until heated through, stirring once. 7. Sprinkle with bread crumb mixture; microwave, uncovered, on HIGH for 2 minutes.

CHICKEN TETRAZZINI, OVEN (Or Turkey)

A spaghetti casserole. Serves 6 adults.

8 oz. uncooked spaghetti (or 4 c. cooked spaghetti)
1 onion, chopped (opt.)
½ c. chopped green and/or red bell pepper (or celery)
1 clove garlic, minced (or ⅛ tsp. garlic powder)
1 (4-oz.) can mushrooms, drained or 8 oz. fresh mushrooms, sliced in half (opt.)
3 T. olive oil
1 T. butter
¼ c. flour
1 c. chicken broth (can make with bouillon)
1 c. milk
1 tsp. salt
⅛ tsp. pepper
1 c. (4 oz.) shredded Cheddar or American cheese
1½ to 2 c. cubed, cooked chicken or turkey
¼ c. broth, milk or water
¼ c. grated Parmesan cheese

1. Break spaghetti into 2-inch pieces; cook in 2 quarts boiling water with 1 teaspoon salt and ½ tablespoon oil until tender (about 14 minutes after coming to a boil). Drain and set aside. 2. In large skillet or Dutch oven, fry onion, green pepper and garlic in the oil and butter until tender. 3. Add mushrooms and fry 1 minute longer. 4. Add flour; stir together well. 5. Add broth and milk all at once, and salt and pepper; cook until thickened, stirring almost constantly. 6. Remove from heat and add shredded cheese; stir until melted. 7. Stir in cooked spaghetti, chicken and ¼ cup broth, milk or water. 8. Turn mixture into 2-quart casserole or 13 x 9-inch baking dish. 9. Sprinkle with grated Parmesan cheese. 10. Bake in preheated 350° oven 30 minutes, covered; remove lid and bake 10 minutes longer. <u>Note</u>: Canned pimiento, drained and diced, may be added when spaghetti is added (for color). Garnish with fresh parsley, if desired. <u>For Crunchy Topping:</u> Omit Parmesan cheese. Combine ¾ cup soft bread crumbs and ¼ cup melted butter; sprinkle over top of casserole and bake, <u>uncovered</u>, 25 to 30 minutes in preheated 350° oven.

CHICKEN WINGS, BUFFALO

Hot and delicious!

20 to 25 chicken wings
Olive oil for deep-frying (opt.)
½ c. butter or reg. Smart Balance spread
2 to 4 T. Durkee red-hot cayenne pepper sauce (or to taste)

1. Cut off and discard the wing tips. 2. Cut main wing bone at joint, separating into 2 pieces; pat dry. 3. In preheated 425° oven, bake wings on rack in roasting pan for 1 hour, turning wings over after first 30 minutes. 4. Or heat oil in a heavy pan or deep fryer until hot (375° to 400°). Deep fry the wings, a few at a time, until cooked through but still juicy. (About 6 to 12 minutes, depending on size.) Transfer to a baking dish and keep warm in oven at 200° or 250° while frying remaining wings. 5. Melt butter; add hot sauce and

stir together. **6.** When wings are cooked, pour sauce over them and stir to coat. **7.** Serves 4 people, each one having at least 10 wing parts. (Serve with celery sticks.)

CHICKEN WINGS, HOT HIDDEN VALLEY

Serve with celery sticks.

12 chicken wings, thawed, cut into 24 pcs. (discarding the tips)
¼ to ½ c. melted butter or reg. Smart Balance spread
2 to 3 T. vinegar
2 to 4 T. hot pepper sauce
1 pkg. Hidden Valley Ranch salad dressing mix (dry)
Paprika

1. Turn oven dial to 400°. **2.** Combine melted butter, vinegar and hot pepper sauce. **3.** Dip chicken pieces in butter mixture; put in sprayed baking pan in single layer. **4.** Sprinkle with package of dry dressing mix. **5.** Bake in preheated 400° oven for 30 minutes; turn wings over and bake another 30 minutes, or until tender and golden brown. **6.** Just before serving, sprinkle with paprika.

CHICKEN-ZUCCHINI STUFFING BAKE
(Or Turkey)

Adapted from Phyllis Overdorff.

6 c. soft bread (or ½ lb.), cubed
½ c. chopped celery
¼ c. chopped onion
½ tsp. poultry seasoning or ground sage
¼ tsp. salt
¼ tsp. pepper
½ c. butter or reg. Smart Balance spread, melted
3 c. cubed zucchini
1 lg. onion, chopped
2 T. olive oil or butter
2 c. cooked, sliced chicken or turkey (or more)
1 (10¾-oz.) can cream of celery or cream of chicken soup
⅔ c. milk, broth or water

1. In large bowl, combine bread crumbs, celery, ¼ cup chopped onion, poultry seasoning, salt and pepper. **2.** Pour melted butter over bread cubes and stir together; set aside. **3.** Fry zucchini and 1 large onion (chopped) in oil until just partially cooked, stirring often. **4.** Put half the stuffing over bottom of 12 x 8½-inch (or 13 x 9-inch) baking dish or pan. **5.** Spread zucchini mixture over stuffing. **6.** Place sliced poultry over zucchini. **7.** To soup, gradually add ⅔ cup liquid, mixing until smooth; pour evenly over all. **8.** Place remaining stuffing over top. **9.** Bake in preheated 350° oven 40 to 45 minutes.

CORNISH GAME HENS, ROCK

Serves 2 to 3 people.

2 (1 to 1½-lb.) Rock Cornish game hens or 1 (2-lb.) hen (fresh or frozen), thawed
Stuffing, prepared
Salt and pepper
2 T. butter, melted
1 tsp. seasoned salt
½ tsp. paprika
½ tsp. ground ginger (opt.)

1. Rinse and drain hens; pat dry with paper towel. **2.** Sprinkle cavities with salt and pepper. **3.** Spoon stuffing lightly in cavities. (Bake any leftover stuffing in covered, greased small casserole during last 30 minutes of roasting time.) **4.** Fold neck skin to back; lift wings toward neck, then tuck them under back of hens so they stay in place. **5.** With string, tie legs and tail of each hen together. **6.** Place hens, breast side up, on small rack in shallow roasting pan; add 1 cup water. Lay giblets in the pan around hens. **7.** In saucepan, melt butter; add seasoned salt, paprika and ginger. **8.** Brush hens with butter mixture, using all of it. **9.** Roast hens in preheated 350° oven, uncovered; baste approximately every 15 minutes with drippings in pan. One-pound hens may be done in 1 hour. 1½-pound hens will take 1½ hours. **10.** To brown the hens, turn oven to 400° during the last 10 minutes, if needed.

GRAVY (CHICKEN OR TURKEY)

Recipe may be cut in half, or multiplied.

4½ c. chicken or turkey broth (fat removed)* or water
4 chicken bouillon cubes or 4 tsp. instant bouillon
1 c. water
⅔ c. flour, packed level
2 to 7 drops yellow food coloring (opt.)

1. Bring broth to a boil with bouillon cubes. **2.** Shake together water and flour in covered jar. **3.** Remove pan from heat; stir in all the thickening. **4.** Return pan to heat and bring gravy to a full boil, stirring almost constantly. **5.** Add food coloring; taste for salt. Simmer on low heat 5 minutes. **6.** If desired, pour gravy through a sieve into serving bowl. ***Note**: To remove fat, pour broth from roasting pan into a wide-mouthed quart jar, or larger. Skim fat off top with gravy ladle, discarding the fat.

GOOSE, WILD, ROASTED

4 lb. wild goose
¼ tsp. salt inside goose
1 tsp. salt sprinkled over outside
2 c. water
Stuffing using 6 or 8 cups of bread in recipe

1. Put foil over the open-end of stuffing in goose. 2. Add water around goose in roaster. 3. Cover and roast in 325°oven for 4 hours; if necessary, cook another hour at 250°.

TURKEY BACKS & NECKS, STUFFED

1 or 2 turkey backs and necks or 6 turkey wings
3 c. water
2 chicken bouillon cubes
½ tsp. salt per pound of meat
Pepper

Stuffing:
3 c. soft bread crumbs (or 4 hot dog buns)
¼ c. celery, chopped
⅛ c. onion, chopped
¼ tsp. sage or poultry seasoning
⅛ tsp. salt
⅛ tsp. pepper
¼ c. (½ stick) butter, melted

1. Place backs and necks in roaster pan with water and bouillon cubes. 2. Sprinkle meat with salt and pepper. 3. Mix stuffing together in order given; pack into turkey back cavities. 4. Put lid on roaster and roast 2½ hours at 325°. (Or at 250° for 3 to 4 hours.) Four Turkey Necks: Wrap stuffing in foil and lay on top necks.

TURKEY BREAST, CROCK-POT

1 turkey breast, thawed
Butter or olive oil or reg. Smart Balance Spread
¼ tsp. salt per pound of meat
Pepper and paprika
¼ c. water
1 t. chicken bouillon granules or 1 cube

1. Put turkey breast on a rack in crock-pot. 2. Rub surface with butter, then add salt, pepper and paprika. 3. Put ¼ cup water in bottom. 4. Turn crock-pot on HIGH for 1 hour; then on LOW for several hours (depending on size), covered with lid. A 6½ pound turkey breast will probably be done after a total of 7 to 9 hours.

TURKEY BREAST, ROASTED I

No lid, no water. Serves 8.

1 turkey breast (5 to 6 lbs., approx.), thawed
Olive oil or melted butter
¼ tsp. salt per pound of turkey
Pepper

1. Turn oven dial to 400°. 2. Wash turkey breast with cold water; pull off any clumps of fat, but leave skin on. 3. Place, skin side up, on rack in shallow roasting pan (like a lasagna pan). 4. Brush breast with olive oil or melted butter; sprinkle with the salt and a little pepper. 5. Turn oven dial to 325° when putting turkey breast in the oven. 6. Roast 3 to 3½ hours at 325° (or until tender). After breast is golden brown, cover loosely with aluminum foil to prevent over-browning. 7. Let stand 10 minutes before slicing. Note: If turkey breast is frozen, it will take at least 30 minutes longer.

TURKEY BREAST, ROASTED II

The old-fashioned method.

6¼ lb. turkey breast, thawed
3 c. water
Olive oil
¼ tsp. salt per pound of meat
3 tsp. chicken bouillon

1. Preheat oven to 400°. 2. Put turkey breast in roaster with 3 c. water; brush with olive oil, then salt it. 3. Add chicken bouillon to water and put lid on. 4. Turn oven to 325°, and bake for 3½ hours. (A 9-lb. turkey breast takes 4 or 5 hours with 4 c. water.)

TURKEY & DRESSING CASSEROLE

Leftover stuffing
Leftover turkey pieces and slices, previously cooked (or chicken)
Leftover turkey or chicken gravy

1. In greased or sprayed casserole (or Crock-Pot) put a layer of dressing over the bottom. 2. Put layer of turkey (or chicken) over the dressing. 3. Pour a little gravy over all. 4. Repeat layers as many times as desired. 5. Bake in preheated 350° oven for 45 miutes to 1 hour. Crock-Pot Method: Layer in crock-pot and cook on LOW, covered, for 3 to 3½ hours.

TURKEY DRUMSTICKS, ROASTED

2 large (or 3 to 4 small) turkey legs
3 c. water
2 chicken bouillon cubes
½ tsp. salt per pound of meat
Pepper
Paprika (opt.)

1. Place turkey legs in roaster pan with water and bouillon cubes. 2. Sprinkle meat with salt, pepper and paprika. 3. Roast in preheated 400° oven, covered loosely, for 30 minutes. 4. Reduce heat to 250° or 325°; cover tightly with lid. Roast for 3 hours, or until tender. (If frozen, it may take a little longer.) Gravy: Skim fat off turkey broth in roaster. Shake together ½ cup water and ⅓ cup flour; add as much thickening as is needed to simmering broth, to make desired consistency. Add 1 drop of yellow food coloring, if desired. Bring gravy to a full boil, stirring.

TURKEY, ROASTED (LARGE) WITH EXTRA DRESSING

19 to 22 lb. turkey, thawed
3 lbs. soft bread, cubed
1½ c. chopped onion
3 c. celery, diced small
3 tsp. rubbed or ground sage or poultry seasoning
1¼ tsp. salt

1¼ tsp. pepper
3 c. butter or reg. Smart Balance spread, melted
4 c. water
3 chicken bouillon cubes
Additional salt and pepper
Paprika

1. Rinse turkey in cool water; drain. 2. Pull off excess fat and discard. 3. In very large bowl or dishpan, combine cubed bread, onion, celery, sage, salt and pepper. 4. Pour melted butter over bread; stir together. 5. Tuck wings under turkey, if desired. 6. Sprinkle inside of turkey with 1 teaspoon salt. 7. Place turkey in roasting pan; fill body cavity with dressing. (Do not pack hard.) 8. Fill neck cavity with stuffing; fold skin over opening and under turkey. 9. Lay turkey neck close by to hold stuffing in. 10. Wash giblets, discarding all fat and lay in pan around turkey. 11. Pour 4 cups water around turkey and put bouillon cubes in the water. 12. Sprinkle ½ teaspoon salt over neck and giblets. 13. Sprinkle 1½ teaspoons salt over turkey. 14. Sprinkle lightly with pepper and paprika. 15. Lay a piece of foil or lid loosely over top of turkey. 16. Roast in 325° oven 6½ to 7½ hours, or until tender, removing foil or lid the last 30 minutes to brown turkey. 17. Put remaining dressing in crock-pot; cover with lid and at proper time, cook on LOW for 3 hours (or longer). 18. Let turkey stand for 15 to 30 minutes after removing from oven, before carving.

TURKEY, ROASTED (14 to 18 Plus Pounds)

Allow a stuffed 14 to 18-PLUS-pound turkey 6 to 7 hours in 325° oven, depending on size, tenderness, etc.

TURKEY, ROASTED (Small)

Allow 1½ hours to prepare onion, celery, cut up bread and get turkey in the oven.

1 (9 to 13-lb.) turkey, thawed
1 to 1¼ lbs. soft bread cubes (about 10 to 13 c.)
½ c. chopped onion
1 c. celery, diced small
1 tsp. rubbed or ground sage or poultry seasoning
½ tsp. salt
½ tsp. black pepper
1 c. butter or reg. Smart Balance spread, melted
4 c. water
2 chicken bouillon cubes
Additional salt and pepper
Paprika

1. Rinse turkey in cool water; drain. 2. Pull off all excess fat and discard; turn oven dial to 400°. 3. In large bowl, combine cubed bread, onion, celery, sage, salt and pepper, stirring together. 4. Pour melted butter slowly over bread, stirring with fork. 5. Tuck wings under turkey. 6. Sprinkle inside of turkey with ½ teaspoon salt. 7. Place turkey in roasting pan; fill neck cavity with stuffing; then fold neck skin over open-

ing and under turkey. 8. Lay neck of turkey close beside neck pouch to hold stuffing in. 9. Fill body cavity with stuffing. (Do <u>not</u> pack hard.) If desired, slip a rack under turkey. 10. Wash giblets, discarding fat and lay in pan around turkey. (If desired, cook liver separately.) 11. Pour 4 cups of water around turkey and put bouillon cubes in water. 12. Sprinkle ¼ teaspoon salt over neck and giblets. 13. Sprinkle 1 teaspoon salt over outside of turkey. 14. Sprinkle lightly with pepper and paprika. 15. Lay a piece of foil or lid loosely over top of turkey. 16. Turn oven dial down to 325°. 17. Roast in 325° oven 5 hours or until tender, removing foil or lid the last 30 minutes to brown turkey. (If it is not tender enough, give it another 30 to 60 minutes.) 18. Let turkey stand for 15 to 30 minutes after removing from oven, before carving. <u>For Extra Stuffing:</u> Double stuffing ingredients: 2 to 2½ pounds soft bread cubes (20 to 26 cups), 1 cup chopped onion, 2 cups chopped celery, 2 teaspoons sage or poultry seasoning, 1 teaspoon salt, 1 teaspoon pepper and 4 sticks (2 cups) butter, melted. After stuffing turkey, put remaining stuffing in crock-pot; cover with lid and cook on LOW for 3 hours or longer.

TURKEY STOCK

Makes about 2 quarts.

Cut up all remaining turkey bones, using strong kitchen shears. Place in large pot with remaining giblets and any remaining bits of turkey. Add enough cold water to cover the bones, about 3 quarts. Cover with lid and bring to a boil. Skim any surface fat and foam. Add 1 teaspoon salt (or to taste) and 1 or 2 chicken bouillon cubes. Simmer, uncovered, 1¼ hours. Strain.

TURKEY & STUFFING CASSEROLE

½ c. melted butter or reg. Smart Balance Spread
½ t. salt
¼ t. pepper
1 t. sage
2 qt. (8 c.) soft bread cubes
⅓ c. milk
⅓ c. chopped onion
⅓ c. chopped celery with leaves
Leftover turkey (cooked)
Gravy (or can use 1 can cream of celery soup and 1 can of cream of mushroom soup, undiluted, and mixed together)

1. Mix together melted butter, salt, pepper and sage; pour over bread crumbs, milk, onion and celery and lightly toss together. 2. Layer the stuffing in bottom of casserole, then layer turkey, then gravy (or soup). 3. Bake in preheated 350° oven for about 45 minutes.

CROCK-POT DRESSING I

Cook for 3 hours on LOW. Delicious. For 3½-quart crock-pot.

20 to 22 oz. (13 to 14 c.) soft bread cubes
1 c. diced or chopped celery
½ c. chopped onion
1 tsp. rubbed or ground sage or poultry seasoning
½ tsp. salt
½ tsp. pepper
1 c. butter or reg. Smart Balance spread, melted

1. In large bowl, combine all ingredients in order given, pouring melted butter over the top while stirring; mix well. **2.** Put dressing in crock-pot; cook on LOW, covered, for 3 hours or longer.

CROCK-POT DRESSING II

Moist and delicious. Makes a lot.

30 oz. (16 to 18 c.) day-old bread cubes
3 c. chopped celery
1½ c. chopped onion
1 to 1½ tsp. ground sage
½ to 1 tsp. salt
½ tsp. pepper
1¼ c. melted butter or reg. Smart Balance Spread

1. In large bowl, combine all ingredients and mix well. The celery and onion may be chopped in a food processor. **2.** Spoon into a 5-quart crock-pot; cover and cook on LOW for 4 hours, stirring once.

SOUTHERN CORNBREAD DRESSING

From Hazel Dawn Ward (Helen Blackwelder's mother).

1 pan of baked cornbread, made without sugar, crumbled (6 c.)
1 (16-oz.) bag Pepperidge Farm Herb Seasoned Stuffing (about 7 c.)
1¼ c. celery, chopped fine
1 c. onion, chopped fine
½ c. green pepper, chopped fine
1½ t. salt
½ t. pepper
2 tsp. sage
3 eggs, beaten
8 c. chicken broth, approximately

1. In large bowl, combine crumbled cornbread, Pepperidge Farm Stuffing, celery, onion, green pepper, salt, pepper and sage. **2.** Combine eggs with some of the broth and add to bowl; continue adding broth until the stuffing is very moist. **3.** Put stuffing in greased 13 x 9-inch baking pan or dish; it will be almost level full. **4.** Bake, uncovered, in preheated 400° oven for 45 minutes or until done.

STEVIE'S CLASSIC STUFFING

From Rita Stevenson.

1 c. finely chopped celery
½ c. chopped onion (1 medium)
½ c. butter or reg. Smart Balance Spread
1 tsp. poultry seasoning or sage
¼ tsp. pepper
⅛ tsp. salt
8 c. dry bread crumbs
1 to 1⅓ c. chicken broth or water

1. Cook celery, onions and butter until tender, but not brown. **2.** Remove from heat and stir in poultry seasoning, pepper and salt. **3.** Drizzle over 8 c. dry bread crumbs in large bowl. **4.** Drizzle with broth or water. **Note:** This stuffs one 8 to 10 lb. turkey, or place stuffing in a Corning casserole with lid and bake in 325° oven for 1 to 1½ hours. Makes 8 cups.

STUFFING BALLS

Adapted from Phyllis Overdorff. Makes 18 balls.

1 c. butter or reg. Smart Balance spread
1 c. chopped celery
½ c. chopped onion
16 oz. (10 to 12 c.) soft bread crumbs
¼ tsp. salt
½ tsp. pepper
1 tsp. poultry seasoning
¼ tsp. ground sage (opt.)
½ can cream of celery, cream of chicken or cream of mushroom soup (½ c. slightly rounded)
1 egg
2 T. water

1. Melt butter in saucepan; add celery and onion, cooking until tender, about 10 to 15 minutes on medium-low heat. **2.** In large bowl, combine bread, salt, pepper, poultry seasoning and sage, stirring together. **3.** Pour melted butter-vegetable mixture over bread; stir together. **4.** In small bowl, combine soup, egg and water; blend together with whisk; then add to bread mixture, stirring well. **5.** Form into 18 balls, using a ¼-cup measure for each ball. **6.** Place balls in greased or sprayed 12 x 8-inch baking dish (or 2½-quart oblong Corning casserole); cover with lid or aluminum foil. **7.** Bake in preheated 325° oven 45 minutes, removing lid the last 15 minutes. **To Microwave:** Cover with glass lid or plastic wrap; cook on HIGH 5 minutes. Uncover and move balls around. Cook, uncovered, on HIGH for a few minutes longer, until hot. If using 1000 watt microwave, cook on #8 power level.

Chapter 21

Cakes

BACK ROW: OPAL BENNINGER, MARC AND RON CHURCHILL
MIDDLE ROW: NANCY BENNINGER, JAN CHURCHILL
FRONT ROW: JIM BENNINGER, CLARENCE BENNINGER

1988

CAKES

In any of these recipes calling for butter, regular Smart Balance Spread or Earth Balance Spread may be substituted. If you wonder why these are substituted, please read Chapter 1.

ANGEL FOOD CAKE DELUXE

This cake takes about 12 to 14 egg whites.

1¾ c. egg whites (room temp.)
1 c. + 2 T. unsifted all-purpose flour
1¾ c. sugar, DIVIDED
¼ tsp. salt
1½ tsp. cream of tartar
1½ tsp. vanilla extract
¼ tsp. almond extract (opt.)

1. Sift flour with ¾ cup sugar; resift 3 times. Set aside. 2. Turn oven dial to 375°. 3. Beat egg whites with salt and cream of tartar at high speed with electric mixer only until soft peaks form. 4. Gradually beat in 1 cup sugar (¼ cup at a time), beating well after each addition; continue beating until stiff peaks form. 5. Add vanilla and almond extract. 6. Sprinkle flour-sugar mixture, ¼ cup at a time, over egg whites. With wire whisk or rubber scraper, gently fold each addition into egg whites, until blended together. 7. With rubber scraper, gently push batter into ungreased 10-inch tube pan.* Cut through batter twice with knife or metal spatula. 8. With rubber scraper, gently spread batter in pan until it touches sides of pan and is smooth on top. 9. Bake on <u>lowest oven shelf</u> 35 minutes in preheated 375° oven, or until top of cake springs back when lightly touched. 10. Invert pan until completely cooled; when cold, loosen cake around sides with metal spatula or knife and remove from pan. *To bake in 13x9-inch pan, bake in 350° oven for 20 minutes, then @ 325° for 10-15 minutes until done.

ANGEL FOOD DAFFODIL CAKE

A marbled white and yellow angel cake.

1 recipe Angel Food Cake Deluxe
5 egg yolks (⅓ c.)
2 T. sugar
2 T. flour
1 T. grated orange peel (or ½ tsp. lemon extract)

1. Follow directions for Angel Food Cake Deluxe as directed through step 6. 2. Beat egg yolks in small bowl with 2 tablespoons sugar and 2 tablespoons flour with portable mixer or rotary eggbeater until thick and lemon-colored. 3. Stir orange peel into egg yolk mixture (or lemon extract). 4. Put ⅓ of angel food cake batter into medium bowl. 5. With rubber scraper or whisk, gently fold egg yolk mixture into ⅓ batter, with about 20 strokes. 6. Spoon white and yellow batters alternately into ungreased 10-inch tube pan, ending with white batter on top. 7. Cut through batter twice with knife or metal spatula. 8. Go to step 8 of "Angel Food Cake Deluxe" and follow remaining directions.

ANGEL FOOD YELLOW CAKE

5 egg yolks
1½ c. sugar
½ c. cold tap water
1½ c. all-purpose flour
½ tsp. baking powder
¼ tsp. salt
1 tsp. vanilla or lemon extract
5 egg whites
¾ tsp. cream of tartar

1. Turn oven dial to 325°. 2. Beat egg yolks well. 3. Add sugar and beat well again. 4. Add water, beating and scraping down sides of bowl. 5. Combine flour, baking powder and salt; add to egg yolk mixture. 6. Add flavoring. 7. In another bowl, beat egg whites with cream of tartar until stiff; fold into yellow batter. 8. Pour into ungreased 10-inch tube pan; cut through batter twice with knife or metal spatula. 9. Gently spread batter in pan until it touches sides of pan and is smooth on top. 10. Bake in lower third of preheated 325° oven for 1 hour. 11. Invert pan until completely cooled; when cold, loosen cake around sides with metal spatula or knife and remove from pan.

APPLE HUMPTY-DUMPTY CAKE

From Luella Henry.

3 eggs
1 c. sugar
⅔ c. olive oil
1 c. chopped nuts
1 (21-oz.) can apple pie filling
3 c. all-purpose flour
1 tsp. baking soda
1 tsp. cinnamon
½ tsp. salt (opt.)

1. Mix all ingredients together with large spoon. 2. Pour into greased or sprayed 13 x 9-inch cake pan. 3. Bake in preheated 350° oven for 35 to 45 minutes, or until center springs back when lightly touched.

APPLE WALNUT CAKE

From Opal Benninger.

4 c. diced apples, peeled or unpeeled
2 eggs
2 c. sugar
½ c. olive oil
1 tsp. vanilla
2½ c. all-purpose flour
2 tsp. baking soda
½ tsp. salt
2 tsp. cinnamon
1 c. coarsely chopped walnuts
½ to 1 c. raisins (opt.)

Cakes

1. Turn oven dial to 325° after preparing apples. 2. Grease or spray 13 x 9 x 2-inch cake pan. 3. In large bowl, combine apples and eggs; stir lightly with fork. 4. Add sugar, oil and vanilla; stir well. 5. Add dry ingredients, stirring together. 6. Fold in nuts (and raisins, if used). 7. Spread in cake pan and bake in preheated 325° oven for 50 to 60 minutes or until center springs back when lightly touched. 8. Cool; serve with whipped topping or frosting or Spicy Sauce. <u>Note</u>: Recipe may be cut in half; bake in 8 x 8-inch greased and floured pan for less time.

APPLESAUCE DATE-NUT CAKE (Eggless)

Jack's once-a-year cake.

1 c. sugar
½ c. olive oil or 1 stick butter
1½ c. unsweetened applesauce
2 tsp. baking soda
2¾ c. all-purpose flour
½ tsp. salt
1 tsp. cinnamon
½ tsp. ground cloves
1¾ to 2 c. chopped dates (about 11 or 12 oz.)
1 to 1½ c. chopped nuts

1. Prepare dates and nuts. 2. Turn oven dial to 325°. 3. Grease and flour angel food tube pan or bundt pan. 4. Cream together sugar and oil or butter. 5. <u>In separate bowl, combine applesauce and soda, stirring until soda is dissolved</u>; add to sugar mixture. (It may curdle, but don't be alarmed.) 6. Add dry ingredients and stir together. 7. Fold in dates and nuts; pour batter into prepared pan. 8. Bake in preheated 325° oven 1 hour, or until cake tests done with wooden pick. 9. Remove from oven and cool in pan 10 minutes. 10. Remove cake from pan to cooling rack. 11. When cool, ice with "Caramel Frosting." <u>Note</u>: Raisins may be substituted for chopped dates, or for part of the dates.

BANANA CUPCAKES

Makes 18 to 21 cupcakes.

1¾ c. all-purpose flour
1 c. sugar
1 tsp. baking soda
½ tsp. salt
½ c. olive oil, or softened butter
1 egg
⅔ c. (5 oz.) evaporated milk or part milk
2 T. vinegar
1 c. mashed bananas
½ c. chopped nuts
2 tsp. vanilla

1. Turn oven dial to 350°. 2. In mixer bowl, add all ingredients in order given; mix together thoroughly. 3. Fill greased or paper-lined muffin cups half to two-thirds full with batter. 4. Bake in preheated 350° oven 20 to 25 minutes or until center springs back when lightly touched.

BANANA NUT CAKE I

Good frosted with "Whipped Soft White Icing."
Moist and delicious.

1 ⅔ c. sugar
½ c. olive oil
2 lg. or 3 sm. eggs
⅔ c. buttermilk or sour milk*, divided
1¼ c. mashed bananas (3 lg. bananas)
1 tsp. vanilla (opt.)
2½ c. all-purpose flour
1½ tsp. baking powder
1¼ tsp. baking soda
½ tsp. salt
⅔ to 1 c. chopped walnuts or pecans

1. Prepare bananas and nuts. 2. Turn oven dial to 350°. 3. Grease 13 x 9-inch cake pan or 2 round 9-inch layer pans; lightly flour pan(s). 4. Cream together sugar and oil. 5. Add eggs; beat well. 6. Add ⅓ cup buttermilk and beat well; add bananas and vanilla. 7. Add dry ingredients alternately with remaining ⅓ cup buttermilk. 8. Fold in nuts. 9. Pour into prepared pan(s); bake on middle shelf of preheated 350° oven 35 to 45 minutes for oblong pan, 25 to 30 minutes for layer pans, or until center springs back when lightly touched. <u>This is essential</u>. 10. For layer pans, cool 5 minutes; then remove from pans to cooling racks. (*To substitute for buttermilk, put 1 teaspoon vinegar in measure and fill with milk to ⅔ cup line; let stand 5 minutes or longer.)

BANANA NUT CAKE II

Moist and delicious, made from a cake mix.

1 yellow cake mix
1 tsp. baking soda
1¼ c. mashed banana (3 lg. bananas)
1 c. water
3 eggs
⅓ c. olive oil
¾ c. chopped nuts

1. Grease and flour 13 x 9-inch cake pan or 2 (9-inch) round layer pans. 2. Prepare bananas and nuts. 3. Turn oven dial to 350°. 4. In mixer bowl, combine cake mix and soda. 5. Add remaining ingredients; beat on medium speed 2 minutes, scraping sides and bottom of bowl once. 6. Pour into prepared pan(s); bake in preheated 350° oven 35 minutes (may take less time in layer pans), until center springs back when lightly touched.

BLACK FOREST CUPCAKES

Chocolate cupcakes with a liquid center of cherries.

1½ c. all-purpose flour
¾ c. sugar
½ c. unsweetened dry cocoa
½ tsp. baking soda

266

1 tsp. baking powder
½ tsp. salt
1¼ c. buttermilk
1 egg (or 2 egg whites)
1 T. olive oil
½ tsp. vanilla
1 (21-oz.) can cherry pie filling (will not use all of it)
⅓ c. chocolate chips (opt.)*

1. Turn oven dial to 375° and line a regular-size muffin tin for 12 cupcakes with paper liners. Lightly spray liners with non-stick cooking spray. 2. In med.-size mixing bowl, combine flour, sugar, cocoa, soda, baking powder and salt, mixing together. 3. Add buttermilk, egg, oil and vanilla all at once; stir together, but do not over mix. 4. Spoon a small amount of chocolate batter into the bottom of prepared muffin cups, until they have about ¾ inch batter in them. 5. Top with pie filling using a scant ⅛ cup in each cupcake. 6. Cover the pie filling with remaining chocolate batter. 7. If desired, sprinkle top of each cupcake with 7 chocolate chips. 8. Bake in center of preheated 375° oven 18 to 20 minutes or until cupcakes are firm to the touch, (*Or omit chocolate chips and frost cupcakes, when cool.)

BLACKBERRY CAKE (Biscuit-Type)

From Mrs. Leota Alberta Benninger.

¼ c. Earth Balance shortening
½ c. sugar
1 egg
2 c. all-purpose flour
4 tsp. baking powder
¼ tsp. salt
¾ c. milk
1½ to 2 c. blackberries (fresh, washed and well drained)

1. Cream together shortening, sugar and egg. 2. Add dry ingredients alternately with milk. 3. With spoon, fold in blackberries gently. 4. Pour into greased and floured 13 x 9-inch cake pan. 5. Bake in preheated 350° oven for 25 minutes or until light golden brown and center springs back when lightly touched. 6. Serve with milk and sugar.

BLACKBERRY CAKE OR RASPBERRY (Cake-Type)

2¼ c. all-purpose flour
1 c. + 1 T. sugar
3 tsp. baking powder
¼ to ½ tsp. salt
¾ c. milk
½ c. olive oil (extra light)
2 eggs (or 4 egg whites)
1 tsp. vanilla extract
1½ to 2 c. blackberries, blueberries or black or red raspberries (fresh or frozen)

1. Grease and flour 13 x 9-inch cake pan. 2. Turn oven dial to 350°. 3. In bowl, mix dry ingredients together. 4. Add milk, oil, eggs and vanilla; mix well. 5. With spoon, gently fold in berries. 6. Pour into prepared pan. 7. Bake in preheated 350° oven for 30 minutes, or until center springs back when lightly touched (325° in glass pan). 8. Serve with milk, if desired.

BOSTON CREAM PIE (Cake)

1 cake mix or cake recipe for yellow or white cake
1 recipe "Vanilla Cream Filling"
1 recipe "Chocolate Glaze"

1. Bake 2 round layers of cake as directed on package or recipe. 2. While layers are baking, make "Vanilla Cream Filling." Cover with tight lid and refrigerate filling. 3. Make "Chocolate Glaze." 4. When filling is lukewarm or cool, spoon onto one cake layer; top with remaining layer. 5. Pour glaze onto top of cake, allowing some to drizzle down sides. 6. Store in refrigerator. **To use only one layer of cake:** Slice layer horizontally to make 2 thin layers. Proceed as directed.

CARROT CAKE

From Shirley Vercamen.

4 lg. eggs
2 c. sugar
2 c. all-purpose flour
3 tsp. baking powder
½ tsp. salt
2 tsp. cinnamon
1 c. olive oil
3 c. grated or shredded carrots
¾ c. chopped walnuts (opt.)

1. Prepare carrots and nuts. 2. Grease or spray 13 x 9-inch cake pan. 3. Turn oven dial to 350°. 4. In mixing bowl, beat together eggs and sugar. 5. Add remaining ingredients and mix together. 6. Pour into prepared pan and bake in preheated 350° oven 40 to 45 minutes or until center springs back when lightly touched. 7. Cool before frosting with "Cream Cheese Frosting." **Note**: Can use 2 c. shredded carrots and 1 c. drained, crushed pineapple.

CHIFFON CAKE

7 lg. or extra-large egg whites
½ tsp. cream of tartar
2 c. all-purpose flour
1½ c. sugar
3 tsp. baking powder
½ tsp. salt
½ c. olive oil (extra light)
¾ c. water
7 lg. or extra-large egg yolks
3 tsp. vanilla

1. Separate eggs; beat egg whites and cream of tartar to very stiff peaks; set aside. **2.** Turn oven dial to 325°. **3.** In another mixing bowl, combine flour, sugar, baking powder and salt; make a well in center. **4.** Add oil, water, egg yolks and flavoring to the well; beat until smooth. **5.** Slowly pour the egg yolk mixture gradually into the beaten egg whites, while folding together gently. **6.** Pour into ungreased 10-inch tube pan (angel food cake pan). **7.** Bake in preheated 325° oven on middle shelf for 75 minutes, or until cake springs back when lightly touched. **8.** Invert cake and cool for at least 1 hour. **9.** Loosen from sides and tube with a spatula to remove cake from pan.

CHIFFON CAKE, LEMON

Follow directions for Chiffon Cake, except instead of ¾ cup water, use ½ cup water and ¼ cup lemon juice. Use 1 teaspoon lemon extract instead of the vanilla.

CHIFFON CAKE, ORANGE

Follow directions for Chiffon Cake, except use orange juice instead of water and use 1 teaspoon orange extract instead of the vanilla.

CHOCOLATE CAKE, DEVIL'S FOOD I

1⅔ c. sugar
2¼ c. all-purpose flour
⅔ c. unsweetened dry cocoa
1¼ tsp. baking soda
¼ tsp. baking powder
½ tsp. salt
⅔ c. olive oil
3 eggs
1 to 2 tsp. vanilla
1⅓ c. cool water

1. Turn oven dial to 350°. **2.** Grease or spray 13 x 9-inch cake pan (or two 9-inch round layer pans); dust with flour or cocoa powder. **3.** In mixing bowl, combine dry ingredients. **4.** Add oil, eggs, vanilla and cool water; mix well, blending only until combined. **5.** Pour into prepared pan(s) and bake in preheated 350° oven 30 to 35 minutes, until center of cake springs back when lightly touched. **6.** For round layer pans, cool 10 minutes before removing from pans. **Note**: All this batter can be put into a 12-inch round Wilton cake pan and baked for 30 minutes or 15 x 11-inch cookie sheet with sides for 28 minutes, or until done. **Cupcakes:** Fill paper-lined muffin cups ⅔ full with batter. Bake in preheated 350° oven 20 to 25 minutes or until center springs back when lightly touched. Makes about 24 cupcakes.

CHOCOLATE CAKE, DEVIL'S FOOD II

From Janet Churchill.

2 c. sugar
½ c. unsweetened dry cocoa
½ c. Earth Balance shortening or olive oil
1 tsp. vanilla
1 c. boiling water
½ c. sour milk, buttermilk (or ½ c. reg. milk mixed with 2 T. vinegar)
2 lg. eggs (or 3 small)
2 c. all-purpose flour
1¼ tsp. baking soda
¼ tsp. salt

1. Turn oven dial to 350° and grease or spray 13 x 9-inch cake pan. **2.** In mixing bowl, cream together sugar, cocoa, shortening (or oil) and vanilla until fluffy. **3.** Add boiling water and stir together. **4.** Add sour milk and eggs; beat together. **5.** In small bowl, combine flour, soda and salt; add half of this mixture to chocolate mixture and beat together. **6.** Add remaining flour mixture, stirring well. (Batter will be thin.) **7.** Pour into prepared pan and bake in preheated 350° oven 30 to 40 minutes, until center springs back when lightly touched.

CHOCOLATE CAKE, EGGLESS BLACK MIDNIGHT

Adapted from Barb Spence. Moist and heavy.

3 c. all-purpose flour
2 c. sugar
½ to ⅔ c. unsweetened dry cocoa, packed level
2 tsp. baking soda
½ tsp. salt
¾ c. olive oil
2 c. cold water
2 T. vinegar
2 tsp. vanilla

1. Turn oven dial to 350°. **2.** Grease and flour 13 x 9-inch cake pan. **3.** Put all ingredients into mixer bowl and beat 3 minutes on medium-low speed of electric mixer, scraping sides of bowl once. **4.** Pour into prepared pan and bake in preheated 350° oven for 10 minutes; then reduce oven thermostat to 300° and bake 35 minutes longer, or until center springs back when lightly touched. **5.** When cake is cool, frost as desired.

CHOCOLATE CAKE, LOLA'S

From Lola Miller. Moist and on the heavy side.

1 c. boiling water
2 tsp. baking soda
⅔ c. Earth Balance shortening or butter
1 c. sugar
1 c. packed brown sugar
2 eggs
1½ tsp. vanilla

2½ c. all-purpose flour
½ c. unsweetened dry cocoa, packed level
½ tsp. salt
1 c. commercial buttermilk
6 to 12 drops red food coloring

1. Turn oven dial to 350° and grease 13 x 9-inch cake pan. 2. Combine boiling water and soda; set aside. 3. Cream together shortening, sugar and brown sugar until fluffy. 4. Add eggs and vanilla; beat. 5. Add dry ingredients alternately with buttermilk. 6. Add red food coloring and the soda-water mixture; pour into prepared pan. 7. Bake in preheated 350° oven for 35 to 40 minutes or until center springs back when lightly touched. 8. When cool, frost with "Chocolate Chip Frosting."

CHOCOLATE CAKE, MOCHA

2 c. all-purpose flour
2 c. sugar
⅔ c. unsweetened dry cocoa
1 tsp. baking powder
2 tsp. baking soda
½ tsp. salt
2 eggs
1 c. milk
⅔ c. olive oil
1 t. vanilla
1 c. brewed coffee, room temperature

1. In mixer bowl, combine dry ingredients. 2. Add eggs, milk, oil and vanilla; beat for 2 minutes. 3. Stir in coffee (batter will be thin). 4. Pour into a greased or sprayed 13x9x2-inch baking pan. Bake in preheated 350° oven for 35 to 40 minutes or until center springs back when lightly touched; cool completely on wire rack.

CHOCOLATE CHERRY CAKE

Tastes like chocolate-covered cherries.

1 devil's food, dark chocolate, fudge or Swiss chocolate
    cake mix
2 large eggs, beaten
1 (21-oz.) can cherry pie filling
1 tsp. almond extract

1. Turn oven dial to 350°. 2. Grease and flour 13 x 9-inch cake pan. 3. In bowl, combine cake mix, beaten eggs, cherry pie filling and almond flavoring with large spoon. (Stir by hand, do not use an electric mixer.) 4. Pour into prepared pan and bake 35 to 40 minutes, or until center springs back when lightly touched. While cake is either warm or cool, frost with "Nell's Chocolate Chip Frosting." **Note**: This cake can be baked in jellyroll pan, 20 to 30 minutes, for bars.

CHOCOLATE CHIP YELLOW CAKE

This is a moist, rather dense cake.

1 c. sugar
1 c. packed brown sugar
¾ c. olive oil (extra light)
1½ tsp. vanilla
3 eggs
3 c. all-purpose flour
2 tsp. baking soda
½ tsp. salt
1 c. milk
1½ c. semi-sweet chocolate mini chips

1. Turn oven dial to 350°. 2. Grease and flour 13 x 9-inch cake pan or 2 (9-inch) round layer pans (grease layer pans and line with waxed paper). 3. Cream together sugar, brown sugar, oil and vanilla, beating well. 4. Add eggs, one at a time, beating well after each addition. 5. Add dry ingredients alternately with milk, beating after each addition. 6. Stir in mini chips with large spoon. 7. Pour into prepared pan(s) and bake in preheated 350° oven 40 to 45 minutes or until center springs back when lightly touched. 8. For layer cakes, cool in pans 10 to 15 minutes before removing from pans to cooling rack. (Loosen around edges first.) __Glaze for Chocolate Chip Cake__: In small saucepan, bring to a boil 2 tablespoons sugar and 2 tablespoons water, stirring until sugar is dissolved. Remove from heat and immediately add ½ cup chocolate mini chips, stirring until chips are melted.

CHOCOLATE MINI-CHIP YELLOW CUPCAKES

Makes 12 wonderful cupcakes.

½ c. (1 stick) Earth Balance spread or butter, softened
¾ c. sugar
1 tsp. vanilla
2 eggs
1¼ c. all-purpose flour
1¼ tsp. baking powder
¼ tsp. salt
½ c. milk
½ c. tiny semi-sweet mini chocolate chips

1. Turn oven dial to 375° and line regular muffin cups with baking papers (or grease and flour muffin cups). 2. In large mixer bowl, beat butter, sugar and vanilla until fluffy, scraping sides of bowl once or twice. 3. Add eggs, one at a time, beating well after each addition. 4. Alternately add dry ingredients and milk, beginning and ending with dry ingredients, beating well after each addition. 5. Stir in mini chocolate chips. 6. Divide batter evenly into 12 prepared muffin cups. 7. Bake in center of preheated 375° oven 18 to 22 minutes, until tops spring back when lightly touched. 8. Cool; frost or sprinkle with powdered sugar.

CHOCOLATE PEPPERMINT CAKE

Make Chocolate Devil's Food Cake, adding ½ cup crushed peppermint candy to the batter. (Candy can be crushed in a food processor or blender.) Or add 1 teaspoon mint extract to the batter, or ¼ teaspoon peppermint extract.

CHOCOLATE ROLL-UP CAKE

Rolled up like a jellyroll.

4 eggs, separated
½ c. sugar
1 tsp. vanilla
⅓ c. sugar
½ c. all-purpose flour
⅓ c. unsweetened cocoa powder
½ tsp. baking powder
¼ tsp. baking soda
⅛ tsp. salt
⅓ c. water
Powdered sugar
1 (8-oz.) carton (or 3 c.) whipped topping, thawed (or 1 qt. softened ice cream)

1. Grease bottom and sides of 15½ x 10½ x 1-inch jellyroll pan; line bottom with waxed paper or foil. Grease bottom again over lining. 2. Turn oven dial to 375°. 3. Beat egg whites until foamy; gradually add ½ cup sugar, beating until stiff peaks form. Set aside. 4. In another bowl, beat egg yolks and vanilla on high speed about 3 minutes; gradually add ⅓ cup sugar, beating 2 minutes more. 5. In small bowl, combine flour, cocoa, baking powder, soda and salt, stirring together. 6. Add dry ingredients to egg-yolk mixture alternately with water. 7. Gently fold chocolate mixture into egg whites. 8. Spread batter evenly into prepared pan, pushing into corners. 9. Bake in preheated 375° oven 12 to 16 minutes, until center of cake springs back when lightly touched. 10. Loosen cake from sides of pan; invert onto towel, sprinkled with powdered sugar. 11. Carefully peel off waxed paper or foil; trim off stiff edges on all 4 sides with sharp knife. 12. Immediately roll cake, rolling towel with it, starting from narrow end; cool on wire rack 1 hour (or longer), seam side down. 13. Gently unroll cake and remove towel; spread with whipped topping or softened ice cream. Carefully re-roll cake. 14. Chill (or if using ice cream, wrap cake roll in foil and freeze at least 3 hours). 15. To serve, drizzle with chocolate sauce or chocolate glaze, or frost, or sprinkle with powdered sugar. Serves 8 or more. For easier slicing, place cake in freezer 20 minutes before serving. <u>Note</u>: To fill with whipped cream, whip 1 cup heavy whipping cream with ¼ cup powdered sugar and ½ teaspoon vanilla until stiff.

CHOCOLATE ZUCCHINI CAKE

Delicious frosted with Chocolate Chip Frosting. This is a moist, heavy cake. Can sprinkle top with 1 cup chocolate chips before baking.

2 c. sugar
2½ c. all-purpose flour
½ c. unsweetened dry cocoa, packed level
1 tsp. baking powder
1 tsp. baking soda
½ tsp. salt
3 eggs
1 c. olive oil
3 tsp. vanilla
2 c. shredded zucchini pulp
1 c. chopped nuts (opt.)

1. Prepare zucchini, peeled or unpeeled, in food processor or shredder. (If zucchini is large, remove seeds and skin.) 2. Grease or spray 13 x 9-inch pan, or bundt or tube pan, or 15 x 10-inch jellyroll pan with sides; dust with flour or dry cocoa. 3. Turn oven dial to 350°. 4. In mixing bowl, combine first 6 dry ingredients, stirring together. 5. Add remaining ingredients, mixing well with large spoon or medium speed of electric mixer. 6. Pour into prepared pan and bake in preheated 350° oven until center springs back when lightly touched, about 40 to 45 minutes for 13 x 9-inch pan, about 60 minutes for bundt or tube pan, or about 40 minutes for 15 x 10-inch jellyroll pan.

COCOA-LIGHT CUPCAKES

Adapted from Bonnie Swarts.

1¼ c. sugar
2 c. all-purpose flour
1 T. unsweetened dry cocoa, packed level
1 tsp. baking soda
½ tsp. salt
2 eggs
½ c. olive oil
1 c. cold water
1 tsp. vanilla
1 c. chocolate chips or peanut butter chips
½ c. chopped nuts (opt.)

1. Grease or spray (or line with paper liners) 16 to 18 muffin cups; turn oven dial to 375°. 2. In mixing bowl, stir together first 5 dry ingredients. 3. Add eggs, oil, cold water and vanilla; beat 1 to 2 minutes. 4. Divide batter into prepared cupcake pans; sprinkle ½ T. chips and nuts over top of each. 5. Bake in preheated 375° oven 22 to 25 minutes, or until center springs back when lightly touched.

COCONUT CAKE, SOUTHERN

From Wanda Marshall. This cake stays moist.

1 package (18¼-oz.) white cake mix, baked according to
  pkg. directions
1½ c. milk
½ c. sugar
1 c. flaked coconut
1 (8-oz.) carton whipped topping, thawed
1 c. flaked coconut for top of cake

1. After baking cake, cool for 15 minutes; poke holes in top of cake with a meat fork. **2.** In saucepan, bring to a boil the milk, sugar and first cup of coconut; reduce heat and simmer 1 minute. **3.** Spoon over the cake, allowing it to soak through; cool completely. **4.** Spread whipped topping over cake; sprinkle with last cup of coconut. **5.** Refrigerate.

COFFEE CAKE, MOTHER B'S

From Mrs. Leota A. Benninger.

¾ c. sugar
¼ c. light olive oil (or butter)
1 egg
2 c. all-purpose flour
3 tsp. baking powder
¼ tsp. salt
1 c. milk
1 tsp. vanilla

Topping:
½ c. packed brown sugar
¼ c. (½ stick) butter
Cinnamon

1. Turn oven dial to 350° and grease or spray 13 x 9-inch cake pan. **2.** Cream together sugar, oil and egg. **3.** Add flour, baking powder and salt alternately with milk and vanilla. **4.** Beat 2 minutes on medium speed of electric mixer (or with large spoon), scraping down sides of bowl at least once. **5.** Pour batter into prepared pan and spread evenly. **6.** Sprinkle brown sugar over top. **7.** Dot with pieces of butter the size of grapes. **8.** Sprinkle cinnamon over all. **9.** Bake in preheated 350° oven 25 to 30 minutes, or until center springs back when lightly touched.

COFFEE CAKE, MOTHER B'S (Larger)

Quick and easy!

1½ c. sugar
3 c. all-purpose flour
½ tsp. salt
4½ tsp. baking powder
⅓ c. light olive oil or soft butter
2 eggs
1½ c. milk
1½ to 2 tsp. vanilla
Topping:
⅔ c. packed brown sugar

⅓ c. butter
Cinnamon

1. Turn oven dial to 350°. **2.** Grease or Pam spray a 15½ x 10½ x 1-inch or 14 x 10-inch pan (or two 8 x 8 or 9 x 9-inch square pans). **3.** In mixer bowl, combine sugar, flour, salt and baking powder; stir together. **4.** Add oil, eggs, milk and vanilla; beat for 2 minutes, scraping sides of bowl once. **5.** Pour batter into prepared pan and spread evenly. **6.** Sprinkle brown sugar over top. **7.** Dot with pieces of butter the size of grapes. **8.** Sprinkle with cinnamon over all. **9.** Bake in preheated 350° oven 25 to 30 minutes, or until center springs back when lightly touched.

FRUIT CAKE, CAROL'S

Thanks to Carol Wells.

1 lb. raisins
2 c. cold water
½ c. butter
2 c. sugar
1 c. liquid (juice from pineapple and cherries)
3 c. all-purpose flour, divided
2 tsp. baking powder
1 tsp. baking soda
1 tsp. salt
3 tsp. cinnamon
1 tsp. nutmeg
1 c. crushed pineapple, drained
½ c. maraschino cherries, drained
1 lb. chopped nuts
1 lb. mixed fruit peels

1. In large pan, simmer raisins in 2 c. water for 15 minutes. **2.** Add butter and sugar to raisins; cool. **3.** Add 1 cup liquid (juice) and 2 cups flour to cooled raisins. **4.** In a small bowl, mix remaining cup of flour, baking powder, soda, salt and spices. **5.** In a large bowl, combine drained crushed pineapple, drained cherries, nuts and peel. **6.** Add flour-spice mixture to fruits and nuts, stirring together. **7.** Add raisin mixture and stir together; pour into greased and floured tube pan. **8.** Bake in preheated 325° oven 2 hours.

FRUIT CAKE, JANET'S

Thanks to Jan Churchill for a date, nut and maraschino cherry fruit cake.

¾ c. flour
¾ c. sugar
½ t. baking powder
½ tsp. salt
1½ c. walnuts, unchopped (or chopped coarsely)
1 (7-oz.) pkg. pitted whole dates
1 (8 to 10-oz.) jar maraschino cherries, drained
3 eggs
1 t. vanilla
Light corn syrup

1. Line a loaf pan (bread pan) with waxed paper or parchment paper on sides and bottom. 2. In mixing bowl combine flour, sugar,baking powder and salt, stirring together. 3. Toss walnuts, dates and drained maraschino cherries into the dry mixture. 4. In separate bowl, beat eggs until foamy; add vanilla to eggs and mix into dry ingredients just until moistened. 5. Pour batter into prepared loaf pan and bake in preheated 300 ° oven 1!/2 hours (90 minutes). 6. Remove from pan and pull off paper gently. 7. While cake is still warm, baste it with light corn syrup on top (to make it shiny). 8. When completely cool, wrap in foil and put in plastic bag; let it age from 12 hours to 1 or 2 weeks.

FRUIT COCKTAIL CAKE

From Doris Andrie.

1½ c. sugar
½ c. light olive oil
2 eggs
2 c. all-purpose flour
2 tsp. baking soda
½ tsp. salt
1 (15 to 17-oz.) can fruit cocktail, including juice

Frosting:
½ c. (1 stick) butter
¾ c. granulated sugar
½ c. evaporated or evaporated skimmed milk
½ c. coconut
½ c. chopped nuts
1 tsp. vanilla

1. Turn oven dial to 350° and grease or spray 13 x 9-inch cake pan. 2. In medium bowl, mix together sugar, oil and eggs (do not use electric mixer with this recipe). 3. In small bowl, stir together flour, soda and salt. 4. Add flour mixture and fruit cocktail with juice; stir gently together. 5. Pour into prepared pan and bake in preheated 350° oven 35 to 45 minutes or until center springs back when lightly touched. 6. In saucepan, combine frosting ingredients, except coconut, nuts and vanilla; bring to a boil. Reduce heat and boil 1 minute. 7. Add remaining ingredients and put on cake while still hot.

GINGERBREAD

From Pat Swarts.

2½ c. all-purpose flour
1 c. sugar
2 tsp. baking soda
½ tsp. salt
1 tsp. cinnamon
1 tsp. ginger
½ tsp. ground cloves
½ tsp. allspice or nutmeg
2 eggs
½ c. olive oil
¾ c. molasses
1 c. hottest tap water

1. Turn oven dial to 350°. 2. Grease or spray 13 x 9-inch baking pan. 3. In mixer bowl, combine dry ingredients, stirring together. 4. Add eggs, oil, molasses and hot water; beat ½ minute. 5. Scrape sides of bowl; beat 1 minute longer. 6. Pour into prepared pan; bake in preheated oven 32 minutes, or until center springs back when lightly touched. **Note**: This recipe may be cut in half and baked in an 8 x 8-inch square pan or 11 x 7-inch pan for 20 to 25 minutes or until done.

GOB CAKE

Something like Ho-Ho's or Twinkies; this serves a crowd, or squares may be wrapped and frozen.

1 chocolate, yellow or lemon cake mix
1 sm. box (four ½-cup serving size) INSTANT chocolate, vanilla or lemon pudding mix (correspond with cake mix)
¼ c. olive oil
1½ c. milk
4 eggs

1. Turn oven dial to 350°. 2. Grease and flour 2 jellyroll pans, approximately 15 x 10 x 1 inches. 3. In mixer bowl, combine ingredients; beat 2 minutes on medium speed, scraping sides of bowl once. 4. Divide batter in prepared pans, spreading evenly. 5. Bake, one at a time, in center of preheated 350° oven about 20 to 25 minutes, until center springs back when lightly touched. 6. Cool in pans; then make "Angel Filling" and spread over one of the cooled cakes. 7. Cut second cake in half; with pancake spatula, loosen around sides and underneath the cake and place each half on top the frosted cake. 8. Cut into 24 to 32 squares. If covering with plastic wrap, sprinkle top with coconut, or candy sprinkles or chopped nuts to prevent cake from sticking to plastic wrap. **Note**: Use chocolate instant pudding with chocolate cake mix.

Angel Filling:
1 egg white
⅔ c. Earth Balance shortening
1 to 1½ tsp. vanilla
2 c. powdered sugar
2 T. flour
2 T. milk
⅛ tsp. salt (or less)

1. Beat egg white in mixer bowl until stiff. 2. Add shortening, vanilla, half the powdered sugar, the flour, milk and salt; beat together. 3. Add remaining powdered sugar. 4. Scrape sides of bowl down and beat 4 to 5 minutes on high speed.

GOLD CAKE I

This is a very good cake-type shortcake for berries.

2 c. all-purpose flour
2 tsp. baking powder
⅛ tsp. salt
½ c. butter, softened

1 c. sugar
4 egg yolks, slightly beaten
¾ c. milk
1 tsp. vanilla

1. Turn oven dial to 375° and grease or spray and flour two (8 or 9-inch) round layer pans or one (13 x 9-inch) cake pan. 2. In medium bowl, combine flour, baking powder and salt, stirring together; set aside. 3. Cream together butter and sugar (added gradually) until fluffy. 4. Add egg yolks, half at a time; beat until very light and fluffy. 5. At low speed of electric mixer, beat in flour mixture alternately with milk, ending with flour; beat just enough to combine. 6. Add vanilla; divide batter into prepared pan(s). 7. Bake in preheated 375° oven 20 to 30 minutes, until center springs back when lightly touched. 8. Cool 5 to 10 minutes; then remove from pan(s) to cooling rack.

GOLD CAKE II

Also makes wonderful shortcake for berries.

⅓ c. light olive oil
¼ c. butter (½ stick), softened
1¼ c. sugar
½ to ⅔ c. egg yolks (about 6 to 10)
2¼ c. all-purpose flour
3 tsp. baking powder
½ tsp. salt
1 c. milk
1½ to 2 tsp. vanilla

1. Grease or spray 2 (9-inch) round layer pans or a 13 x 9-inch cake pan; dust lightly with flour and tap out excess. 2. Turn oven dial to 350°. 3. Cream together oil, butter and sugar. 4. Add egg yolks; beat together at high speed of electric mixer, scraping bowl once, for 2 minutes. 5. Add flour, baking powder and salt alternately with milk and vanilla, beating on low speed. 6. Scrape bowl; beat 1 minute on medium speed. 7. Pour into prepared pan(s); bake layer pans 20 to 25 minutes or until center springs back when lightly touched. Bake 13 x 9-inch pan 30 to 35 minutes, or until done. **Note:** May need a little more milk if only using 6 egg yolks.

HO-HO-HUM CHOCOLATE CAKE

First Layer (chocolate):
1 (18 ¼-oz.) box devil's food cake mix

Cream Filling (white):
½ c. (1 stick) butter (room temp.)
½ c. Earth Balance shortening (room temp.)
1 c. sugar (granulated)
3 T. flour, packed level
1 tsp. vanilla
⅔ c. lukewarm milk (barely lukewarm)

1. Turn oven dial to 350° and grease or spray 15 x 10 or 15 x 11-inch jellyroll pan with sides. 2. Mix cake mix according to package directions and pour into prepared pan. 3. Bake in preheated 350° oven 25 to 30 minutes or until center springs back when lightly touched. 4. Leave cake in pan and cool. 5. To make Cream Filling: cream together butter, shortening, sugar, flour and vanilla until fluffy. 6. Gradually add lukewarm milk (slowly) while beating; beat until consistency is like whipped cream (about 5 minutes) on high speed of electric mixer, scraping down sides of bowl 2 or 3 times. 7. Spread over cooled cake and refrigerate until firm, about 2 hours (or overnight). Frost with "Chocolate Chip Frosting" for Sheet Cake.

HO-HO YELLOW TWINKLY CAKE

Yellow cake, white filling and chocolate frosting.

Follow "Ho-Ho-Hum Chocolate Cake," using a yellow cake mix.

JELLY ROLL

From Anna Limber Stevenson.
This recipe is not as hard as it looks.

3 lg. eggs (⅔ c.), room temp.
1 c. sugar
5 T. water
1 tsp. vanilla
1 c. all-purpose flour
1 tsp. baking powder
¼ tsp. salt
Filling (or 1 c. strawberry or red raspberry jelly or jam)
Powdered sugar

1. Grease or spray and flour jellyroll pan, approximately 15 x 10 x 1 inches. Then line bottom of pan with waxed paper and grease or spray waxed paper. 2. Turn oven dial to 375°. 3. With electric mixer or rotary beater, beat eggs until very thick (high speed of mixer). 4. Gradually add sugar, 2 tablespoons at a time; beat mixture until fluffy, thick and lemon-colored, about 5 minutes. 5. Beat in water and vanilla all at once. 6. In small bowl, combine flour, baking powder and salt; with rubber scraper, gently fold in flour mixture just until batter is smooth. 7. Pour into prepared pan, spreading evenly. 8. Bake in preheated 375° oven about 12 minutes or until center springs back when lightly touched. Do not overbake. 9. Immediately loosen from sides of pan and turn out onto a towel which has been generously sprinkled with powdered sugar or cornstarch. 10. Carefully remove waxed paper; if edges of cake are crisp, stiff or brown, trim them off. 11. Starting at narrow end, roll up cake and towel together; place, seam side down, on cooling rack. 12. Cool at least 30 minutes; gently unroll, remove towel and spread filling or jelly or jam over cake. 13. Roll up again; place, seam side down, on serving platter. 14. Sprinkle with powdered sugar, if desired. Cover with plastic wrap. 15. Let stand at least 1 hour before serving. **To freeze and fill later:** Cooled, rolled cake with towel in it may be frozen. Later, thaw, remove towel, fill and re-roll.

LEMON SUPER CAKE

Adapted from Ruth Leyshon.

1 (3-oz.) pkg. lemon gelatin
1 c. boiling water
1 (18¼-oz.) pkg. yellow or lemon cake mix
⅓ c. light olive oil
3 lg. eggs
1 T. lemon extract (½ T. if lemon cake mix is used)

Glaze:
1 c. powdered sugar
2 T. lemon juice

1. Dissolve gelatin in boiling water; set aside. 2. Turn oven dial to 350° and grease and flour 13 x 9-inch cake pan. 3. On low speed of electric mixer, mix together cake mix and oil. 4. Add eggs, one at a time. 5. Add lemon extract and the gelatin mixture; mix on medium speed. 6. Pour batter into prepared pan; bake in preheated 350° oven 30 to 35 minutes, until center springs back when lightly touched. Do not overbake. 7. While cake is baking, mix together Glaze ingredients. 8. When cake is baked, prick top of cake (all over) with fork; pour glaze over hot cake. Note: If a frosting is preferred, omit pricking cake with fork and omit the glaze.

MANDARIN ORANGE CAKE

Adapted from Louave Hopper.
May also be baked in 9 x 13-inch pan.

1 box yellow cake mix or golden butter cake mix
½ c. light olive oil
4 eggs
1 (11-oz.) can mandarin oranges with juice
½ tsp. orange extract (opt.)

1. Turn oven dial to 350°. 2. Grease and lightly flour 2 or 3 (8 or 9-inch) round layer pans. 3. In mixing bowl, combine all ingredients; beat 2 to 3 minutes at medium-high speed of electric mixer. 4. Pour into layer pans and bake in preheated 350° oven 25 to 30 minutes, until center of cake springs back when lightly touched (9 x 13-inch cake pan needs 35 minutes or until done). 5. Cool 5 minutes; then remove from pans to cooling racks. 6. When completely cool, frost with "Pineapple Fluffy Frosting." 7. Refrigerate cake until serving time. Note: Top of cake may be decorated with additional drained mandarin orange sections, if desired.

MILK CHOCOLATE CAKE

This is a light-chocolate cake.

1¾ c. all-purpose flour
1 ⅔ c. sugar
4 tsp. baking powder
½ tsp. salt
5 T. unsweetened cocoa
⅔ c. soft butter

⅔ c. evaporated milk
⅔ c. water
1½ tsp. vanilla
3 eggs

1. In mixer bowl, combine dry ingredients. 2. Add butter and evaporated milk; beat 2 minutes on high speed. 3. Add water, vanilla and eggs; beat 2 minutes longer on medium speed. (Batter may appear curdled.) 4. Pour into 2 greased and floured 9-inch layer pans. 5. Bake in preheated 350° oven for 30 to 40 minutes, or until center of cake springs back when lightly touched. 6. When cool, frost with "Milk Chocolate Icing."

MISSISSIPPI MUD CAKE

A brownie-type cake that is scrumptious.
No baking powder or soda is used.

1 c. Smart Balance Spread or butter
2 c. sugar
4 eggs
1½ c. all-purpose flour
½ c. unsweetened dry cocoa
¼ tsp. salt
2 tsp. vanilla
1 c. coarsely chopped nuts
1 c. flaked coconut (opt.)
1 (7-oz.) jar (1½ to 2 c.) marshmallow creme (or 4 c. fresh miniature marshmallows)

1. Cream spread, sugar and eggs together. 2. Add remaining ingredients, except marshmallow creme or miniature marshmallows. 3. Mix well and spread in greased 13 x 9-inch cake pan. 4. Bake in preheated 350° oven for 30 to 35 minutes; then remove from oven whether you think it is done or not. 5. Immediately spoon marshmallow creme over top of hot cake; let stand 5 minutes. 6. Spread carefully to evenly cover the entire surface. 7. Frost cake when cool with "Mississippi Mud Cake Frosting."

Mississippi Mud Cake Saucepan Frosting:
½ c. butter, melted
¼ c. milk or evaporated milk
6 T. unsweetened dry cocoa
1 lb. powdered sugar (3½ to 3¾ c.)
1 tsp. vanilla

1. Melt butter in medium saucepan over low heat. 2. Remove from heat and add remaining ingredients, stirring until smooth. Note: If too thick, add a tiny bit more milk; if too thin, add a little more powdered sugar.

OATMEAL CAKE

1¼ c. boiling water
½ c. raisins (opt.)
1 c. uncooked oats (quick or old-fashioned)
½ c. butter or olive oil
1 c. sugar
1 c. packed brown sugar

274

1 ⅓ c. all-purpose flour
1 tsp. baking soda
½ tsp. baking powder
1 tsp. cinnamon
½ tsp. allspice (opt.)
½ tsp. nutmeg (opt.)
½ tsp. salt
2 eggs
1 tsp. vanilla
½ c. chopped nuts (opt.)

1. Pour boiling water over raisins, oats and butter, which has been cut into 6 pieces; stir until butter is melted. Let stand 20 minutes. **2.** Mix dry ingredients in bowl; add eggs, vanilla and oat mixture; mix well. **3.** Pour into greased 13 x 9-inch cake pan. **4.** Bake in preheated 350° oven for 35 to 40 minutes, or until center of cake springs back when lightly touched. <u>Cocoa Oats Cake</u>: Decrease flour to 1 cup. Add 1/3 cup cocoa to dry ingredients.

<u>Microwave Coconut-Caramel Topping (opt):</u>
1 c. flaked coconut
½ c. chopped nuts
½ c. packed brown sugar
½ c. milk
¼ c. butter (½ stick)
Dash of salt

1. In 1-quart microwave-safe dish, combine all ingredients. **2.** Microwave on HIGH 6 minutes, or until thick and bubbly, stirring every 2 minutes.

OATMEAL CHOCOLATE CHIP CAKE

This cake does not need a frosting.

1¾ c. boiling water
1 c. uncooked oatmeal, quick or old-fashioned (but not instant)
1 c. sugar
1 c. lightly packed brown sugar
½ c. olive oil
2 large eggs
1 tsp. vanilla
1¾ c. flour
1 tsp. baking soda
½ tsp. salt
1 T. cocoa, packed level
12 oz. (2 c.) semi-sweet chocolate chips, divided
¾ c. chopped nuts (opt.)

1. Pour boiling water over oatmeal in mixer bowl; let stand 10 minutes. **2.** Add sugars, olive oil, eggs and vanilla; mix well. **3.** Add flour, soda, salt and cocoa; mix well. **4.** Add 1 cup chocolate chips to batter; stir together and pour into a greased or sprayed 9 x 13-inch cake pan. (If desired, flour pan also.) **5.** Sprinkle top of batter with nuts and remaining cup of chocolate chips. **6.** Bake in preheated 350° oven for about 40 minutes or until done.

ORANGE SUPER CAKE

Follow directions for "Lemon Super Cake," using a yellow or orange cake mix, orange gelatin and orange extract. For the glaze, use 1 cup powdered sugar, 2 tablespoons orange juice and ½ teaspoon orange extract. Or frost with "Orange Frosting, Smaller."

PINEAPPLE-NUT CAKE

There is no shortening or salt in this cake.

2 c. all-purpose flour
2 c. sugar
2 tsp. baking soda
1 (20-oz.) can crushed pineapple, including juice (unsweetened)
2 eggs
1 c. chopped nuts
1 tsp. vanilla
1 c. flaked coconut (opt.)

1. Turn oven dial to 350° and grease or spray 13 x 9-inch cake pan. **2.** With large spoon, mix ingredients in bowl, in order given. Do not use electric mixer. **3.** Pour into prepared pan and bake in preheated 350° oven 35 to 45 minutes or until center springs back when lightly touched. **4.** When cake is barely warm (or cool), frost with "Cream Cheese Frosting."

PINEAPPLE UPSIDE-DOWN CAKE

From Patricia Swarts.

½ c. butter or Smart Balance Spread (regular)
1½ c. brown sugar
1 (20-oz.) can crushed pineapple, drained (reserve juice)
1 (20-oz.) can chunk pineapple, drained (reserve juice)
1 yellow, white or lemon cake mix (2-layer size)

1. In a deep iron skillet (10 to 12 inches in diameter), melt butter. **2.** Add brown sugar and stir together. **3.** Add the drained crushed and chunk pineapple; heat in skillet, then turn burner off. **4.** Mix cake as directed except use reserved pineapple juice instead of water. **5.** Pour cake batter over mixture in skillet. **6.** Bake in preheated 350° oven 35 minutes or until center springs back when lightly touched. **7.** Loosen edges; invert onto plate, leaving skillet over the cake. **8.** Wet a towel with cold water, wring it out and place over the skillet; repeat this a second time. **9.** Remove skillet from cake. **Note**: For 10-inch skillet, it may take 45 minutes, because it is a little smaller in diameter, and deeper.

PINEAPPLE YUM-YUM CAKE I

From Kathy DeHaven.

1 (18¼-oz.) pkg. yellow or pineapple cake mix
1 (4-serving size) pkg. instant pudding
1 c. milk
1 (8-oz.) carton whipped topping, thawed
8 oz. cream cheese, softened
1 (20-oz.) can crushed pineapple, drained
Chopped nuts (opt.)
Flaked coconut

1. Mix cake according to package directions and bake in 15 x 10-inch cookie sheet with sides for 15 minutes or until center springs back when lightly touched. Cool. 2. Mix instant pudding with 1 cup milk; set aside. 3. In mixer bowl, beat together whipped topping and cream cheese until well mixed. 4. Add pudding and beat well. 5. Add drained pineapple; spread on cooled cake. 6. Sprinkle with nuts (if desired) and coconut; keep refrigerated.

PINEAPPLE YUM-YUM CAKE II

1 (18¼-oz.) pkg. yellow cake mix
1 can (20-oz.) crushed pineapple, unsweetened
1 c. sugar
1 pkg. (small or lg.) vanilla or coconut cream pudding (instant or cook-kind), prepared
1 c. flaked coconut
8 oz. whipped topping, thawed (or 2 pkgs. Dream Whip, prepared)
1 c. chopped nuts or flaked coconut, slightly toasted

1. Mix yellow cake according to package directions and bake in 13 x 9-inch cake pan in preheated 350° oven. Cool. 2. After cake has cooled, simmer crushed pineapple and sugar in saucepan, boiling gently for 3 minutes; cool slightly. 3. Poke holes in cake with fork and pour pineapple mixture over top; chill. 4. Prepare pudding as directed on package. (If cook-kind, cool.) Add coconut and spread over chilled cake. 5. Spread whipped topping over top of cake. 6. Sprinkle with nuts; chill until served.

POPPY SEED CAKE

From Phillips' Reunion Cookbook.

¼ to ⅓ c. poppy seed
1 c. milk
½ c. (1 stick) butter or light olive oil
1½ c. sugar
2 c. all-purpose flour
1½ tsp. baking powder
1 tsp. vanilla
½ tsp. almond extract
4 egg whites, beaten stiff, but not dry

1. Combine poppy seed and milk; set aside. 2. Turn oven dial to 350° and grease or spray and flour 2 (9-inch) round layer pans (or a 13 x 9-inch cake pan). 3. Cream together butter and sugar until fluffy. 4. In small bowl, combine flour and baking powder; add to butter-sugar mixture alternately with the milk-poppy seed mixture. 5. Add vanilla and almond flavoring. 6. Fold in beaten egg whites. 7. Bake in preheated 350° oven 25 to 30 minutes, or until center of cake springs back when lightly touched.

POUND CAKE, LEMON

1 c. butter (room temp.)
2 c. sugar
4 lg. eggs
1 to 2 tsp. lemon extract
1 tsp. vanilla
3 c. all-purpose flour
½ tsp. baking powder
½ tsp. baking soda
½ tsp. salt
1 c. buttermilk

Glaze:
1 to 1¼ c. powdered sugar
¼ c. butter, softened
2 T. lemon juice
1 tsp. grated lemon peel (opt.)

1. Turn oven dial to 350°. 2. In mixer bowl, cream together butter and sugar until light and fluffy, scraping down sides of bowl twice. 3. Add eggs, one at a time, beating well after each addition. 4. Stir in flavorings. 5. In separate bowl, combine flour, baking powder, soda and salt, stirring together. 6. Add dry ingredients alternately with buttermilk, beginning and ending with flour; beat only long enough to blend well. 7. Pour into greased and lightly floured 9 x 5 x 3-inch loaf pan, bundt pan or 10-inch tube pan. 8. Bake in preheated 350° oven for 70 minutes or until wooden pick inserted in center comes out clean. 9. Cool in pan 15 minutes; then remove cake to cooling rack. 10. When cake is completely cool, frost or glaze.

POUND CAKE, YELLOW

From Martha Estelle Stevenson.

1½ c. (3 sticks) butter
2¾ c. sugar
6 lg. eggs
3 c. all-purpose flour, divided
½ tsp. baking powder
½ tsp. salt
2 tsp. vanilla
⅛ to ¼ tsp. almond extract (opt.)
3 T. cold water

1. Grease and flour 10-inch tube pan (angel food cake pan). 2. Turn oven dial to 325°. 3. In mixer bowl, cream together butter and sugar until light and fluffy, scraping down sides of bowl twice. 4. Add eggs, one at a time, beating well after each addition. 5. Add 2 cups flour, the baking powder and salt; mix together, but do not over beat. 6. Add flavorings and cold water; mix together. 7. Add remaining 1 cup flour; mix together. 8. Pour into prepared pan and bake in preheated 325° oven about 80 minutes, or until wooden pick inserted in center comes out clean. 9. Cool in pan 15 minutes; then remove cake to cooling rack.

PUMPKIN CAKE ROLL

Rolled up like a jellyroll. From Kathy DeHaven.

3 eggs
1 c. sugar
⅔ c. canned pumpkin
1 tsp. lemon juice
¾ c. all-purpose flour
1 tsp. baking powder
2 tsp. cinnamon
1 tsp. ginger
½ tsp. nutmeg
¼ tsp. salt
½ to 1 c. nuts, finely chopped (opt.)

Filling:
1¼ c. powdered sugar, divided
3 to 6 oz. cream cheese (room temp.)
4 T. butter (½ stick)
1 tsp. vanilla

1. Beat eggs in mixer bowl at high speed for 5 minutes. 2. Gradually add sugar, while beating. 3. Stir in pumpkin and lemon juice. 4. Fold in flour, baking powder, spices and salt. 5. In greased and floured jellyroll pan, 15 x 10 x 1 inches or cookie sheet with sides, spread batter. 6. Sprinkle nuts over top of batter, if used. 7. Bake in preheated 375° oven for 15 minutes or until center springs back when lightly touched. 8. Invert on towel, sprinkled with ¼ cup powdered sugar. 9. Quickly roll up towel and cake together like a jellyroll. 10. Place on platter, seam side down, and chill for at least 1 hour (or overnight). 11. Combine remaining 1 cup powdered sugar, cream cheese, butter and vanilla, beating together. 12. Unroll cake, remove towel and spread with the cream cheese filling. 13. Re-roll cake and chill until serving time. **Note**: May be filled with 1 quart butter pecan ice cream, softened. (Spread to within 1 inch of edges.) Roll up, cover and freeze. To serve, let stand a few minutes at room temperature before slicing. Dust with powdered sugar.

RAISIN CUPCAKES

Makes 12 cupcakes.

¼ c. butter
¾ c. sugar
1 egg
1¾ c. all-purpose flour
¼ tsp. salt
3 tsp. baking powder
½ c. milk
1 c. raisins, chopped
1 tsp. lemon extract

1. Turn oven dial to 350° and grease or spray (or line with paper liners) a regular-size muffin tin for 12 cupcakes. 2. In mixing bowl, cream together butter and sugar. 3. Add egg and mix together. 4. Add flour, salt and baking powder; mix together. 5. Add milk, mixing together; add raisins and lemon extract. Blend well. 6. Divide evenly between the 12 muffin cups; bake in preheated 350° oven about 20 minutes, or until center springs back when lightly touched.

RAISIN SPANISH BAR CAKE (LOAF PAN)

1¼ c. water
⅓ c. butter
2 c. raisins
1 c. packed brown sugar (dark brown, preferably)
2 tsp. cinnamon
½ tsp. nutmeg
½ tsp. ground cloves
½ tsp. salt
1 tsp. baking soda
2 tsp. water
2 c. all-purpose flour
1 tsp. baking powder
Buttercream, cream cheese or vanilla frosting

1. In 3-quart saucepan, combine water, butter, raisins, brown sugar and spices; bring to a boil and boil 3 minutes. Cool to room temperature. 2. Dissolve salt and soda in the 2 teaspoons water; blend into saucepan mixture. 3. In small bowl, stir together flour and baking powder; blend into saucepan mixture. 4. Pour into greased and floured loaf pan and bake in preheated 325° oven 55 to 60 minutes or until center springs back when lightly touched. 5. Let cool in pan 10 minutes; then loosen around edges and remove from pan to cooling rack. Frost when cool.

RAISIN SPICE CAKE-BARS (SAUCEPAN)

Delicious! From Sarah Stevenson McIlhany.

1 to 1½ c. raisins (or cut-up dates)
1 c. water
⅓ c. olive oil
1 c. sugar
1¾ c. all-purpose flour, packed level

1 tsp. baking soda
¼ tsp. salt
1 tsp. cinnamon
¼ tsp. nutmeg
¼ tsp. powdered cloves
¼ tsp. allspice (opt.)
¾ c. coarsely chopped nuts
1 egg
Powdered sugar or Vanilla Icing (opt.)

1. Turn oven dial to 350° and grease or spray 13 x 9-inch cake pan. 2. In 2 or 3-quart saucepan, bring raisins and water to a full boil; reduce heat and boil gently ½ to 1 minute. 3. Remove from heat and add oil. 4. Add sugar, flour, soda, salt and spices, stirring well. 5. Add nuts and egg; stir together. 6. Pour into prepared pan and bake in preheated 350° oven 20 to 28 minutes, or until center springs back when lightly touched. 7. When cool, dust with powdered sugar, if desired, or frost with "Vanilla Icing or Glaze." At serving time, cut into bars with pizza cutter and knife.

SHORTCAKE, BISCUIT-TYPE

(Food processor)

2 c. flour
¼ c. sugar
3 t. baking powder
1 t. grated lemon zest (opt.)
¼ t. salt
⅓ c. butter or regular Smart Balance Spread
⅔ c. milk or half 'n half

1. Pulse together dry ingredients. 2. Add butter; process to a coarse meal. 3. Add milk and pulse just until mixture comes together. 4. Pat to a 5 x 8-inch rectangle on floured surface; cut into biscuits. 5. Bake on cookie sheet 15 to 20 minutes in preheated 400° oven or until golden in color. 6. Stir together 4 c. strawberries and ⅓ c. sugar; let set 15 minutes.

SHORTCAKE, BISCUIT-TYPE (Classic)

To double this recipe, bake in greased or sprayed 15 x 11-inch jellyroll pan or large cookie sheet.

2 c. all-purpose flour
2 T. sugar
3 tsp. baking powder
½ tsp. salt
½ c. (1 stick) butter or Earth Balance shortening
1 egg
½ c. milk

1. Turn oven dial to 450°. 2. In bowl, combine dry ingredients; blend in butter with fingers, pastry blender or forks until it resembles coarse cornmeal. 3. In small bowl, beat egg; add milk. 4. Add egg-milk mixture all at once to flour mixture and stir with fork only enough to moisten. 5. Spread dough in greased or sprayed baking pan. (For thin, crispy shortcake, bake in 13 x 9-inch pan. For higher shortcake, bake in one 8 or

9-inch square or round pan.) 6. Bake in preheated 450° oven for 15 minutes (425° in glass pan), until golden brown. **For individual biscuits:** On floured surface, pat dough to ½-inch thickness and cut with 2½-inch round cutter (or top of water glass), floured; place on lightly greased or sprayed baking sheet. Bake 8 to 10 minutes or until golden brown. **Strawberry Shortcake:** 1 quart fresh strawberries, washed, drained and hulled may be sliced or crushed. Add ½ to ⅔ cup sugar and stir together; let stand 1 hour for best taste. Serve with shortcake and milk.

SHORTCAKE, BISCUIT-TYPE (Larger)

Makes 9 to 12 square biscuits! Very good with gravy also.

3 c. all-purpose flour
4½ tsp. baking powder
¾ tsp. cream of tartar
2½ T. sugar (opt.)
¾ tsp. salt
¾ c. Earth Balance shortening
1 egg, beaten
About ¾ c. milk

1. Mix first 6 ingredients with fingers, fork or pastry blender until it resembles coarse cornmeal. 2. Add egg and milk; stir with fork, just until dough forms. 3. Turn dough out onto floured surface; knead gently about 10 strokes with floured fingers. 4. Pat or shape into ½ to 1-inch thick square; cut into biscuits with knife dipped in flour. 5. With spatula, lift squares onto large greased baking sheet. 6. Bake in preheated 425° oven 15 to 20 minutes or until golden brown.

SHORTCAKE, BISCUIT-TYPE (Oil)

2 c. all-purpose flour
3 tsp. baking powder
½ tsp. salt
3 T. sugar (opt.)
1 egg
⅔ c. milk
⅓ c. light olive oil

1. Turn oven dial to 450°. 2. Grease or spray 1 (9-inch) round layer cake pan or 7 x 11-inch pan. 3. Combine dry ingredients in bowl; set aside. 4. In small bowl, beat egg with fork; add milk and oil, beating with fork. 5. Pour over dry ingredients and stir together with fork until soft dough is formed. 6. Place in prepared pan and pat to fit. 7. Bake in preheated 450° oven 14 to 20 minutes, or until golden brown.

SHORTCAKE, CAKE-TYPE

Add 2 to 3 tablespoons sugar to each cup of strawberries; let stand 1 hour.

3 c. all-purpose flour
1½ c. sugar

3 tsp. baking powder
½ tsp. salt
2 eggs
½ c. light olive oil
1¼ c. milk
2 tsp. vanilla

1. Turn oven dial to 350° and grease or spray large jellyroll pan or lasagna pan (or 2 pans, sizes 13 x 9 and 9 x 9 inches). 2. Put all ingredients in mixer bowl and beat for 2 minutes on medium speed. 3. Pour into prepared pan(s) and bake in preheated 350° oven 30 to 40 minutes, or until center springs back when lightly touched.

SPICE CAKE, RAISIN NUT

2⅓ c. all-purpose flour
1 c. sugar
1 tsp. baking soda
½ tsp. salt
1½ tsp. cinnamon
¾ tsp. nutmeg
¾ tsp. cloves
⅔ c. Earth Balance shortening (room temp.)
1 c. packed brown sugar
1 c. buttermilk
2 lg. eggs
1 c. chopped nuts
1 c. raisins

1. Turn oven dial to 350° and grease or spray 13 x 9-inch cake pan (or 2 round layer pans). 2. In mixing bowl, combine flour, sugar, soda, salt and spices. 3. Add shortening, brown sugar and buttermilk; beat 2 minutes. 4. Add eggs; beat 2 minutes. 5. Fold in nuts and raisins; pour into prepared pan(s). 6. Bake in preheated 350° oven 30 to 40 minutes or until center springs back when lightly touched.

SPICE CAKE, STONEBORO

¾ c. (1½ sticks) butter or Earth Balance spread
1½ c. sugar
½ tsp. salt
2¼ c. all-purpose flour
1⅛ tsp. baking soda
1⅛ tsp. cinnamon
1 tsp. cloves
1 c. commercial buttermilk
2 lg. eggs (or 3 small)

1. Grease and flour 2 (8-inch) round layer pans or 1 (13 x 9-inch) cake pan. 2. Turn oven dial to 350°. 3. Cream together butter, sugar and salt until fluffy. 4. Combine flour, soda and spices; add alternately with buttermilk, scraping sides of bowl twice. 5. Add eggs, one at a time, beating after each addition. 6. Pour into prepared pan(s) and bake in preheated 350° oven 30 to 35 minutes or until center springs back when lightly touched.

STRAWBERRY CAKE

Or 24 cupcakes.

1 pkg. white cake mix (2-layer size)
1 pkg. (3 oz.) strawberry Jello, dry
3 T. all-purpose flour, level
⅓ c. light olive oil
4 eggs
1 pkg. (10 to 16 oz.) frozen sweetened strawberries, thawed (1¼ to 1½ c.) or 1 c. mashed, fresh strawberries
½ c. cold water

Frosting:
1 lb. powdered sugar (3½ to 4 c.)
⅓ c. butter or reg. Smart Balance Spread, softened
¼ c. reserved strawberry juice (or ¼ c. mashed, fresh strawberries)
½ to 1 tsp. vanilla (opt.)

1. Grease and flour two 9-inch round layer cake pans or 9 x 13 baking pan. 2. Turn oven to 350°. 3. In mixer bowl, combine cake mix, dry Jello and flour. 4. Drain strawberries, reserving juice; save ¼ cup of juice for frosting. 5. To mixer bowl ingredients, add strawberries and remaining juice, oil, eggs, and ½ cup cold water. Beat until well mixed, but do not overbeat. 6. Pour into prepared pan(s) and bake in middle of preheated 350° oven for 30 to 35 minutes, or until center springs back when lightly touched. 7. Cool on wire racks for 10 minutes, then remove from layer pans to wire racks to cool completely. 8. For frosting, combine all the ingredients and beat until of frosting consistency. If too thick, add a few drops of milk, or a few more berries. If too thin, add a little more powdered sugar.

TEXAS SHEET CAKE

Adapted from Laura Robison and Lola Cramer. This cake freezes well. To omit eggs, use 1 cup buttermilk.

2 c. all-purpose flour
1¾ c. sugar
½ c. dry unsweetened cocoa
½ tsp. salt
2/3 c. light olive oil
1 c. boiling water
2 eggs
1 tsp. vanilla
¾ c. buttermilk, half 'n half, or milk
1 T. vinegar
1 tsp. baking soda

1. Put flour, sugar, cocoa and salt in mixing bowl and stir together. 2. Add olive oil and boiling water; beat until creamy. 3. Add eggs, vanilla, buttermilk, vinegar and baking soda; beat until smooth. (Batter will be thin.) 4. While making cake, preheat oven to 400°. Grease a 15 x 10 x 2-inch cookie sheet (or line bottom with parchment paper). Pour batter into pan. 5. Bake cake for 15 to 20 minutes, or until center of cake springs back when lightly touched.

Frosting:
½ c. butter or reg. Smart Balance Buttery Spread (not light)
⅓ c. dry unsweetened cocoa
¼ c. milk
¼ tsp. salt (opt.)
1 tsp. vanilla
1 lb. (3½ to 4 c.) sifted powdered sugar
½ to 1 c. chopped nuts (opt.)
2 c. miniature marshmallows (opt.)

1. Heat butter, cocoa, milk and salt in 2 or 3-quart saucepan until butter is melted. 2. Remove from heat and add powdered sugar and vanilla; beat until smooth. (If too thick, add a few drops of milk.) 3. Spread frosting over "Texas Sheet Cake;" sprinkle nuts and/or miniature marshmallows over the top, before frosting hardens, if desired.

TURTLE CHOCOLATE CARAMEL CAKE

From Geraldine Tyger. Just scrumptious!

1 (18¼-oz.) pkg. German chocolate or Swiss chocolate cake mix
1 (14-oz.) bag caramels
½ c. evaporated milk (5-oz. can)
⅔ c. butter (1 stick + 2 T.)
1 c. chopped pecans
1 c. chocolate chips
½ c. pecans for top (opt.)

1. Unwrap caramels; grease or spray and flour 13 x 9-inch cake pan. Turn oven dial to 350°. 2. Mix cake mix according to package directions. 3. Pour half of batter into prepared pan and bake in preheated 350° oven for only 15 minutes. 4. While cake is baking, combine caramels, milk and butter in top of double boiler over boiling water; melt together, stirring occasionally. 5. Cool cake 5 minutes; spread melted caramels over baked portion of cake. 6. Sprinkle with 1 cup each of pecans and chocolate chips. 7. Pour remaining cake batter over all, spreading evenly. If desired, sprinkle ½ cup pecans over top of batter. 8. Bake an additional 25 to 30 minutes in preheated 350° oven, or until center springs back when lightly touched. 9. Serve unfrosted with ice cream, or sprinkle powdered sugar over top of cake, or drizzle ½ to 1 cup melted chocolate chips over top. **To melt caramels in microwave**: Melt caramels, butter and evaporated milk together in microwave on HIGH about 10 minutes, stirring a couple times.

WHITE CAKE

All ingredients should be at room temperature.

2¼ c. all-purpose flour
3¼ tsp. baking powder
½ tsp. salt
1½ c. sugar
½ c. Earth Balance shortening (room temp.)
1 c. milk, divided

½ c. egg whites, unbeaten (or 4 egg whites)
1 tsp. vanilla

1. Turn oven dial to 350° and grease and flour 2 (8 or 9-inch) round layer pans (or one 12 x 8 x 2-inch or 13 x 9 x 2-inch cake pan). 2. In mixer bowl, combine dry ingredients. 3. Add shortening and ⅔ cup milk; beat for 2 minutes. (If electric mixer is used, beat on medium-low speed.) 4. Add remaining ⅓ cup milk, then unbeaten egg whites and vanilla; beat 2 minutes. 5. Pour into prepared pan(s) and bake in preheated 350° oven 30 minutes for 8-inch layers, 25 to 30 minutes for 9-inch layers, 40 to 45 minutes for 12 x 8-inch pan, 35 to 40 minutes for 13 x 9-inch pan (or until center springs back when lightly touched). 6. For layers, cool in pans 10 minutes before removing cakes. **Cupcakes:** Divide batter among 18 muffin cups which have been greased and floured (or paper-lined). Bake. **Nut Cake:** Add ¾ cup chopped nuts to batter. **Coconut Cake:** Add 1 cup flaked coconut just before pouring into pan(s).

YELLOW CAKE, 1-2-3-4

1 c. (2 sticks) butter
1 c. milk
2 c. sugar
3 c. all-purpose flour
4 tsp. baking powder
½ tsp. salt
4 eggs
2 tsp. vanilla or almond extract (or ½ tsp. vanilla and ½ tsp. lemon extract)
Few drops yellow food coloring

1. Turn oven dial to 350°. 2. Grease or spray 13 x 9-inch cake pan (or two 8 x 8-inch square pans). 3. Heat butter with milk just until butter is melted; set aside. 4. In medium bowl, combine sugar, flour, baking powder and salt; stir together. 5. In mixer bowl, beat eggs; add dry ingredients, milk mixture and flavoring. Beat all together 2 minutes, scraping sides of bowl once. 6. Pour into prepared pan and bake in preheated 350° oven 35 to 45 minutes, or until center springs back when lightly touched. **Note**: This cake may also be made the conventional way, creaming butter and sugar together (not heating milk). It may take 45 minutes to bake, or until center springs back when lightly touched.

YELLOW CAKE, BUTTERMILK

Delicious!

1½ c. sugar
½ c. (1 stick) butter or ⅓ c. light olive oil
2 eggs, well beaten
2 c. all-purpose or cake flour
1 tsp. baking soda
1 tsp. baking powder
¼ tsp. salt
1¼ c. commercial buttermilk
1½ tsp. vanilla
4 drops yellow food coloring

1. Turn oven dial to 350°. 2. Grease or spray 13 x 9-inch cake pan or 2 round layer pans. (If using layer pans, flour them.) 3. In mixer bowl, cream together sugar and butter until fluffy. 4. Add beaten eggs and mix well. 5. Combine dry ingredients in small bowl; add alternately with buttermilk. 6. Add vanilla and food coloring. 7. Pour into prepared pan(s) and bake in center of preheated 350° oven for 30 to 35 minutes, until center springs back when lightly touched. 8. For layer pans, cool 10 minutes before removing from pans.

YELLOW CAKE, ONE EGG

A good cake for fresh strawberries.

1¾ c. all-purpose flour
1 c. sugar
2½ tsp. baking powder
¼ tsp. salt
1 c. milk (or ⅔ c. evaporated milk and ⅓ c. water)
⅓ c. light olive oil
1 tsp. vanilla
1 egg

1. Grease (or spray) and flour a 9 x 9-inch or 11 x 7-inch pan. 2. Turn oven dial to 350°. 3. Combine dry ingredients in bowl and stir together. 4. Add all remaining ingredients; beat 1 to 2 minutes. 5. Pour batter into prepared pan; bake in preheated 350° oven 30 minutes, or until center springs back when lightly touched.

YELLOW CUPCAKES

Makes 18 cupcakes. So good!

1¾ c. all-purpose flour
3 tsp. baking powder
¼ tsp. salt
1 c. sugar
⅓ c. light olive oil
⅔ c. milk
3 eggs
1 tsp. vanilla or coconut flavoring
1 c. mini chocolate chips (opt.)

1. Turn oven dial to 375° and grease or spray 18 muffin cups, or line with paper liners. 2. In mixer bowl, combine dry ingredients, stirring together. 3. Add remaining ingredients; beat 2 minutes on electric mixer (or 300 strokes by hand). 4. Divide batter into prepared muffin cups and bake in preheated 375° oven 18 minutes or until tops spring back when lightly touched.

YELLOW CUPCAKES, ANNA'S

From Anna Limber Stevenson.
Makes 12 cupcakes; recipe doubles well.

1½ c. all-purpose flour
2 tsp. baking powder
¼ tsp. salt

1 c. sugar
2 eggs
Milk
½ c. additional milk
⅓ c. melted butter or light olive oil
1 tsp. vanilla

1. Turn oven dial to 350° and grease or spray (or line with paper liners) a regular-size muffin tin for 12 cupcakes. 2. In mixing bowl, combine flour, baking powder, salt and sugar (sift together 3 times, if desired). 3. Break eggs into ½-cup measure; add milk to make ½ cup level full. 4. Add egg liquid and additional ½ cup milk, melted butter and vanilla to flour mixture; beat 3 minutes on medium speed. 5. Divide evenly between the 12 muffin cups; bake in preheated 350° oven for 20 minutes, or until center springs back when lightly touched.

ZUCCHINI RAISIN NUT SPICE CAKE

Heavy and delicious . . . needs no frosting.
Adapted from Ruth Melichar.

2 c. sugar
3 c. all-purpose flour
1 tsp. baking powder
1 tsp. baking soda
1 tsp. salt
3 tsp. cinnamon
3 tsp. vanilla
2 c. shredded zucchini (peel if large)
3 eggs
1 c. olive oil
1 c. raisins or cut-up dates (or both)
1 c. coarsely chopped nuts
2 tsp. grated orange rind (opt.)

1. Prepare zucchini in food processor or on coleslaw side of shredder. (Remove seeds and pulp if zucchini is large.) 2. Grease and flour 13 x 9-inch cake pan. 3. Turn oven dial to 350°. 4. In bowl, combine first 6 ingredients (dry ingredients), stirring together. 5. Add remaining ingredients, mixing well with large spoon or medium speed of mixer. 6. Pour into prepared pan and bake in preheated 350° oven 50 to 60 minutes, or until center springs back when lightly touched. 7. May be served plain, or with ice cream, or with "Spicy Sauce."

Chapter 22

Frostings, Glazes and Fillings

JONATHAN AND DAVID SWARTS

1991

FROSTINGS, GLAZES AND FILLINGS

In any of these recipes calling for butter, regular Smart Balance Spread or Earth Balance Spread may be substituted.

ALMOND FROSTING

Enough for top of a 13 x 9-inch cake.

4 T. (½ stick) butter
3 c. powdered sugar, divided
1 tsp. almond extract
1 tsp. vanilla
2 T. cream or evaporated milk (or a bit more if needed)

1. In mixer bowl, combine butter, 1 cup powdered sugar, almond extract and vanilla; beat together. 2. Add remaining powdered sugar alternately with cream; beat on high speed of electric mixer until fluffy.

BANANA FROSTING

For 13 x 9-inch cake, or 18 to 24 cupcakes.

¼ c. butter
⅛ tsp. salt
1 tsp. vanilla
3 c. powdered sugar, divided
⅓ c. mashed banana
1 to 2 drops yellow food coloring (opt.)

1. In mixer bowl, combine butter, salt, vanilla and 1 cup powdered sugar; beat together. 2. Add remaining 2 cups powdered sugar, the mashed banana and food coloring, if used; beat until fluffy.

BANANA-NUT FILLING

Makes enough filling for a two or three-layer cake (only between the layers).

¾ c. sugar
¾ c. evaporated milk
2 egg yolks
3 T. butter
¼ c. mashed banana
¾ c. chopped nuts
1 tsp. vanilla
1 c. flaked coconut (purely opt.)

1. Over medium heat, cook sugar, evaporated milk, egg yolks and butter until very thick, stirring constantly. (About 10 to 12 minutes.) 2. Remove from heat; add banana, nuts and vanilla. 3. Cool, stirring occasionally, until of spreading consistency.

BROWN SUGAR FUDGE FROSTING
(Cooked)

1 tsp. butter
¾ c. white sugar
¾ c. packed brown sugar
½ c. milk or cream
½ tsp. vanilla extract

1. Melt butter in heavy medium pan. 2. Add sugars and milk. 3. Stir while heating to boiling point. 4. Boil without stirring until mixture forms a soft ball in cold water (225° to 228°). 5. Remove from heat and cool to 170° to 190°. 6. Add vanilla; beat with large spoon until proper consistency. It usually stays spreadable long enough to frost cake. If it gets too stiff, add a little milk, or melt over hot water. <u>Note</u>: Double this recipe for a 2-layer cake.

BROWNED BUTTER FROSTING

Makes enough for 8 x 8-inch cake.

3 T. butter
1½ c. powdered sugar
2 T. milk (approx.)
1 to 1½ tsp. vanilla

1. Melt butter in saucepan over medium heat, stirring constantly, until golden brown. 2. Remove from heat; add remaining ingredients. 3. Beat until smooth and of spreading consistency.

BUTTERCREAM FROSTING

For top of 13 x 9-inch cake.

¼ c. (½ stick) butter
⅛ tsp. salt
3 c. powdered sugar, divided
1 to 2 tsp. vanilla
3 T. milk

1. Combine butter, salt, 1 cup powdered sugar and vanilla; beat together. 2. Add remaining powdered sugar alternately with milk; beat until fluffy on high speed of electric mixer 4 or 5 minutes. <u>**Butter Pecan Frosting**</u>: Decrease vanilla to ¾ teaspoon; add ⅔ cup chopped pecans (or toasted pecans, chopped).

BUTTERCREAM HIGH
HUMIDITY FROSTING

This frosts and decorates a 15 x 11-inch cake, baked in a Wilton sheet pan, including borders.

1½ c. Earth Balance shortening
⅛ c. dry Dream Whip powder (½ env.)
1 to 1½ T. white vanilla
2 lbs. powdered sugar

¼ c. all-purpose flour
½ c. milk (approx.)
¼ tsp. salt (opt.)

1. In mixer bowl, beat shortening, Dream Whip powder and vanilla until fluffy. 2. Remove bowl from mixer and stir in powdered sugar, flour, milk and salt with large spoon. 3. Put bowl back on mixer and beat on high speed until fluffy (several minutes). <u>Note</u>: If desired, ¼ teaspoon almond flavoring may also be added.

CARAMEL FROSTING

Enough for top of 13 x 9-inch cake.
Double this recipe for 2-layer cake.

¼ c. butter
2 to 3 T. milk, cream or evaporated milk
½ c. packed brown sugar
½ lb. (about 2 c.) powdered sugar, sifted (or more if needed)
½ tsp. vanilla

1. In saucepan, bring butter, milk and brown sugar to a boil. 2. Remove from heat; add powdered sugar and vanilla. 3. Beat until smooth. If it starts to get too thick, add a few drops of milk.

CHERRY FROSTING

Makes enough to fill and frost a 2-layer cake.

½ c. Earth Balance shortening
1 lb. powdered sugar (sift if lumpy)
¼ tsp. salt
4 tsp. maraschino cherry juice
2 T. milk
2 T. lemon juice
3 T. chopped maraschino cherries

1. Cream together shortening, powdered sugar and salt. 2. Add cherry juice and milk; beat together. 3. Add lemon juice; beat until fluffy. 4. Stir in chopped cherries.

CHERRY FROSTING, SMALLER

Enough for top of 13 x 9-inch cake.

¼ c. butter
⅛ tsp. salt
3 c. powdered sugar, divided (sift if lumpy)
½ tsp. vanilla
2 T. maraschino cherry juice
1 to 2 T. milk

1. Combine butter, salt, half the powdered sugar and the vanilla; blend in cherry juice. 2. Add remaining powdered sugar alternately with milk; beat until fluffy. <u>Note</u>: If needed, add more powdered sugar to thicken, or milk to thin.

CHOCOLATE ANGEL FILLING

1½ c. cold milk
1 pkg. (4-serving size) instant chocolate pudding
1 c. thawed whipped topping (approximately)

1. In mixer bowl, put cold milk; add pudding mix and beat on lowest speed for 3 minutes. 2. Fold in whipped topping.

CHOCOLATE BUTTERCREAM FROSTING

Enough for a two-layer cake.

⅓ c. butter, softened
⅓ c. Earth Balance shortening
⅛ tsp. salt
1 lb. powdered sugar (3¾ c.)
⅓ c. dry unsweetened cocoa
¼ c. milk
1½ to 2 tsp. vanilla

1. Cream together butter, shortening and salt. 2. Gradually add powdered sugar. 3. Add cocoa, then milk and vanilla; beat until fluffy on high speed of electric mixer. <u>Note</u>: The shortening in this recipe may be omitted, if desired.

CHOCOLATE CHIP FROSTING

Enough for a 15½ x 10½-inch sheet cake.

6 oz. (1 c.) chocolate chips
¼ c. butter or olive oil
½ c. sour cream or low-fat or fat-free sour cream substitute
1 tsp. vanilla
⅛ tsp. salt
3 c. sifted powdered sugar

1. In double boiler or heavy pan, melt chips and butter. 2. Remove from heat and blend in sour cream, vanilla and salt. 3. Add powdered sugar, 1 cup at a time, beating after each addition.

CHOCOLATE CHIP FROSTING, LARGER

Makes plenty to fill and frost a 2-layer 9-inch cake.

1¼ c. chocolate chips
⅓ c. evaporated milk
½ c. (1 stick) butter
⅛ tsp. salt
1 lb. (3¾ c.) powdered sugar
2 tsp. vanilla

1. In medium saucepan, melt chips, evaporated milk, butter and salt over medium heat, stirring until smooth. 2. Add powdered sugar and vanilla; beat with large spoon until smooth. (If too thick, add a few drops of milk.)

CHOCOLATE CHIP FROSTING, LOLA MILLER'S

Enough for top of a 13 x 9-inch cake or 2 loaf cakes.

¼ c. (½ stick) butter
3 T. milk
1 c. (6 oz.) chocolate chips
1 tsp. vanilla
2 c. powdered sugar (sift if lumpy)

1. In medium pan, melt butter. **2.** Add milk and chocolate chips; melt over low heat, stirring constantly. **3.** Remove from heat; add vanilla and powdered sugar. **4.** Beat together with large spoon until smooth. (If too thick, add more milk or hot water, a few drops at a time.)

CHOCOLATE CHIP FROSTING, NELL'S

Delicious on the top of a 9 x 13-inch cake.

1 c. granulated sugar
3 T. milk
4 T. (½ stick) butter
6 oz. (1 c.) semi-sweet chocolate chips

1. Combine first 3 ingredients in saucepan and bring to a boil, stirring. **2.** Boil gently 1 minute, stirring constantly. **3.** Remove from heat and add chocolate chips; stir until chips have melted and frosting is smooth.

CHOCOLATE CHIP FROSTING, SMALLER

Enough for top of 1 (8 or 9-inch) square cake or a bundt cake.

3 T. butter
2 T. milk
⅔ c. chocolate chips
1 tsp. vanilla
1½ c. powdered sugar (sift if lumpy)

1. In medium pan, melt butter. **2.** Add milk and chocolate chips; melt over low heat, stirring constantly. **3.** Remove from heat; add vanilla and powdered sugar. **4.** Beat together with large spoon until smooth. (If too thick, add more milk or hot water, a few drops at a time.)

CHOCOLATE FROSTING

Enough for top of 13 x 9-inch cake.
Good frosting for cookies, too, or for 18 cupcakes.

2 ⅔ c. powdered sugar
⅓ c. dry unsweetened cocoa
⅛ tsp. salt
3½ T. milk (approx.)
¼ c. butter, softened or melted
1 tsp. vanilla

1. In mixer bowl, stir together sugar, cocoa and salt. **2.** Add milk, butter and vanilla; beat together until smooth.

CHOCOLATE FROSTING, SMALLER

Enough for top of 8 x 8-inch or 9 x 9-inch square cake.

¼ c. (½ stick) butter
2 c. powdered sugar
3 to 4 T. dry unsweetened cocoa
2 T. milk
1 tsp. vanilla

1. Cream butter until fluffy. **2.** Gradually add powdered sugar and cocoa alternately with milk and vanilla. **3.** Beat at high speed of electric mixer until smooth. **Note**: This recipe makes just enough for filling <u>between</u> 2 (9-inch) layers.

CHOCOLATE FUDGE FROSTING

From Wanda Marsh. Enough for top only,
of a square 9 x 9 cake, or a tube or bundt cake.

1 oz. unsweetened chocolate
1 c. granulated sugar
⅓ c. milk
¼ c. Earth Balance shortening
¼ tsp. salt
1 tsp. vanilla

1. Cut or shave chocolate into medium saucepan. **2.** Add sugar, milk, shortening and salt. **3.** Bring to a boil, stirring constantly; boil gently 1 minute. **4.** Remove from heat and cool until lukewarm. **5.** Add vanilla and beat until thick enough to spread.

CHOCOLATE GLAZE I

Excellent for Boston Cream Pie.

2 T. water
1½ T. butter
2 T. dry unsweetened cocoa
¾ c. powdered sugar
¼ tsp. vanilla

1. In small saucepan, combine water and butter; bring to a boil. **2.** Immediately remove from heat and stir in cocoa. **3.** Beat in powdered sugar and vanilla, using whisk until smooth; cool slightly.

CHOCOLATE GLAZE II

1 (1-oz.) sq. unsweetened chocolate
2 T. milk
2 T. butter
1 c. powdered sugar (sift it lumpy)
½ tsp. vanilla

1. In saucepan, heat chocolate, milk and butter until chocolate melts. **2.** Remove from heat; add powdered sugar and vanilla. 3 Beat until smooth.

CHOCOLATE ICING, DARK & DELICIOUS

¼ c. (½ stick) butter
¼ c. milk
2 oz. (2 sq.) unsweetened chocolate
2½ to 3 c. powdered sugar (sift if lumpy)
1 tsp. vanilla

1. In small pan, heat together butter, milk and chocolate until chocolate melts. **2.** Pour chocolate mixture into mixer bowl; add powdered sugar and vanilla. **3.** Beat until smooth at high speed, using amount of powdered sugar needed for proper consistency.

CHOCOLATE PEPPERMINT FROSTING

Fills and frosts a 2-layer, 8-inch cake.

¼ c. butter
¼ c. unsweetened dry cocoa
3 c. powdered sugar
⅛ tsp. salt
¼ c. hot milk (or more)
¾ tsp. vanilla
1 T. crushed peppermint candy

1. In saucepan, melt butter; stir in cocoa. **2.** Add remaining ingredients, stirring well. **3.** Place pan in bowl of ice and beat frosting until of spreading consistency, about 4 to 6 minutes.

CHOCOLATE ROCKY ROAD FROSTING

From Lola Cramer.

⅓ c. buttermilk or evaporated milk
½ c. (1 stick) butter
¼ c. unsweetened dry cocoa
1 lb. (3½ c.) powdered sugar
1 tsp. vanilla
2 c. miniature marshmallows
½ c. chopped nuts (opt.)

1. In medium pan, bring buttermilk, butter and cocoa to a <u>full boil, stirring</u>. **2.** As soon as butter is melted, remove from heat and add powdered sugar; mix well. **3.** Add vanilla; spread on warm or cold cake. **4.** Immediately sprinkle marshmallows and nuts over frosting. **Note:** If preferred, stir marshmallows and nuts into the frosting.

CHOCOLATE SCRUMPTIOUS FROSTING

Makes plenty for a 9-inch round 2-layer cake.
Adapted from Ruth Campbell.

¼ c. (½ stick) butter
4 oz. (4 sq.) unsweetened chocolate
1 lb. powdered sugar (3¾ c.)
⅛ tsp. salt

⅓ c. hot milk
2 tsp. vanilla

1. In small stainless steel bowl, melt butter and chocolate in a 300° oven. **2.** Meanwhile, put powdered sugar, salt and hot milk in large mixer bowl; beat until sugar is dissolved. (It will be thin.) **3.** Add vanilla and melted chocolate mixture; beat until thick and smooth, scraping down sides of bowl once. **4.** If frosting gets too thick while icing cake, add a few drops of milk at a time until desired consistency is reached.

CHOCOLATE SCRUMPTIOUS FROSTING
(Smaller)

Enough for top of a 13 x 9-inch cake or a small 8-inch round 2-layer cake.

3 T. butter
3 oz. (3 sq.) unsweetened chocolate
⅛ tsp. salt (opt.)
1 tsp. vanilla
3 c. powdered sugar
4 to 6 T. milk (approx.)

1. In medium saucepan, melt butter. **2.** Add chocolate and stir constantly over <u>very low</u> heat until melted. **3.** Add salt and vanilla. **4.** Add powdered sugar alternately with milk; beat until well blended. (If too thick, add a drop of milk at a time.)

CHOCOLATE WHIPPED FROSTING

Makes enough for a 2-layer cake. Cut recipe in half for top of 13 x 9-inch cake. Tastes like chocolate whipped cream.

½ c. (1 stick) butter (room temp.)
½ c. Earth Balance shortening (room temp.)
1 c. sugar (granulated)
¼ c. dry unsweetened cocoa
7 T. flour, packed level
1 tsp. vanilla
⅔ c. lukewarm milk (barely lukewarm)

1. Cream together butter, shortening, sugar, cocoa, flour and vanilla until fluffy. **2.** Gradually (slowly) add lukewarm milk while beating; beat until consistency is like whipped cream (about 5 minutes) on high speed of electric mixer, scraping down sides of bowl 2 or 3 times. **Note:** Make sure flour is packed level and that milk is **<u>barely</u> lukewarm**.

COCONUT-PECAN FILLING

Makes enough filling for between two cake layers, or to fill one cake roll.

2 egg yolks
⅔ c. evaporated milk
½ c. sugar
⅓ c. butter or reg. Smart Balance Spread

¾ t. vanilla
1 c. flaked coconut
⅔ c. chopped pecans, hickory nuts or English walnuts

1. In small saucepan, whisk together egg yolks and evaporated milk. 2. Add sugar, butter and vanilla; cook over med. heat, stirring almost constantly, until mixture thickens (about 10 minutes). 3. Remove from heat; add coconut and nuts. Stir together until of spreading consistency. (Can let cool first, if desired.) Makes about 2 cups.

COOL WHIP FLUFFY FROSTING

1 (4-serving size) pkg. instant pudding mix (any flavor)
1 c. cold milk
1 (8-oz.) carton (3½ c.) whipped topping, thawed (or 2 env. Dream Whip, prepared)

1. Combine pudding mix and milk in mixer bowl; beat at lowest speed of electric mixer about 1 minute. 2. Fold in whipped topping. 3. Keep frosted cake refrigerated.

CREAM CHEESE FROSTING

Enough for top of 13 x 9-inch cake.
Double this recipe for a 2-layer 9-inch cake.

3 to 4 oz. cream cheese, softened
¼ c. (½ stick) butter (room temp.)
2 c. powdered sugar
1 tsp. vanilla
Chopped nuts (opt.)
Coconut (opt.)

1. Cream together cream cheese and butter. 2. Add powdered sugar and vanilla; beat until creamy. 3. Add nuts and/or coconut, if desired; spread on cooled cake. **Chocolate Cream Cheese Frosting**: Add dry unsweetened cocoa to desired color.

IVORY FROSTING

Enough to fill and frost a 9-inch 2-layer cake.
Delicious, cream-colored and creamy.

½ c. (1 stick) butter, softened
½ c. Earth Balance shortening
1 lb. powdered sugar (about 3¾ c.)
⅛ tsp. salt (opt.)
1½ tsp. white vanilla
1 T. milk
2 T. cream or evaporated milk

1. Cream together butter and shortening. 2. Add powdered sugar, ½ cup at a time, on low speed; mix until well blended. 3. Add vanilla, milk and cream; beat on high speed 5 minutes, scraping sides of bowl once or twice. (If too thick, add a tiny amount of milk. If too thin, add a little more powdered sugar.)

IVORY FROSTING, SMALLER

Enough to frost the top of a 13 x 9-inch cake.
Delicious, cream-colored and creamy.

¼ c. (½ stick) butter, softened
¼ c. Earth Balance shortening
2 c. powdered sugar
1/16 tsp. salt (opt.)
¾ tsp. vanilla
1 T. evaporated milk, cream or milk

1. Cream together butter and shortening. 2. Add powdered sugar, ½ cup at a time, on low speed of electric mixer; mix until well blended. 3. Add vanilla and 1 tablespoon liquid; beat at high speed until fluffy, scraping sides of bowl once or twice. (If too thick, add a few drops of milk.)

LEMON FILLING

Nice for a jellyroll or between layers of a cake.

¾ c. sugar
3 T. cornstarch, packed level
⅛ tsp. salt
¾ c. water
1 T. butter
¼ c. lemon juice
3 drops yellow food coloring

1. In saucepan, mix together sugar, cornstarch and salt. 2. Stir in water gradually; cook, stirring constantly, until mixture thickens and boils. Boil and stir 1 minute. 3. Remove from heat; add butter, stirring until it melts. 4. Add lemon juice and food coloring; cover with tight lid and refrigerate until cool. **Note**: If desired, 1 teaspoon grated lemon peel may be added.

LEMON FROSTING

Makes enough for the top of a 13 x 9-inch cake
or top and sides of a chiffon or angel food cake.

¼ c. (½ stick) butter
⅛ tsp. salt
3 c. powdered sugar, divided
3 drops yellow food coloring
1 T. lemon juice (fresh or bottled)
½ tsp. lemon extract
2 T. water

1. Cream butter, salt, 1 cup powdered sugar, yellow food coloring, lemon juice and lemon extract; beat 1 minute on high speed of electric mixer. 2. Add remaining sugar alternately with water; beat until frosting is fluffy.

MAPLE FROSTING

From Linda Deets. For top of 13 x 9-inch cake.

⅓ c. butter
3 c. powdered sugar
½ tsp. maple flavoring
Milk

1. Mix together ingredients (using very little milk) until fluffy and of desired consistency.

MILK CHOCOLATE FROSTING

¼ c. melted butter
⅓ c. dry unsweetened cocoa
⅛ tsp. salt
⅓ c. milk, cream or evaporated milk
1 to 1½ tsp. vanilla
3⅓ c. powdered sugar (sift if lumpy)

1. Combine melted butter, cocoa and salt, stirring together. 2. Add milk and vanilla; gradually add powdered sugar, beating until smooth and creamy. (If too thin, add more powdered sugar. If too thick, add a few drops milk.)

NUT FILLING (For a Banana Cake)

½ c. sugar
2 T. flour
½ c. whole milk or half & half
2 T. butter
½ c. chopped nuts
¼ tsp. salt
1 tsp. vanilla

1. Combine sugar, flour, milk and butter in heavy 2-quart saucepan. 2. Cook, stirring constantly, until thickened. 3. Stir in nuts, salt and vanilla; cool.

NUT ICING, CREAMY

½ c. Earth Balance shortening (or part butter)
2½ T. cake flour or all-purpose flour
¼ tsp. salt
½ c. milk
3 c. sifted powdered sugar
½ tsp. vanilla
½ c. nuts, coarsely chopped

1. Melt shortening in 2-quart saucepan; remove from heat. 2. Blend in flour and salt; stir in milk slowly. 3. Bring to a boil, stirring constantly; boil 1 minute. (If mixture curdles, do not be alarmed.) 4. Remove from heat; stir in powdered sugar. 5. Set saucepan in bowl of cold water; beat until consistency to spread. 6. Stir in vanilla and nuts.

ORANGE FROSTING

Makes enough to frost a 2-layer cake.

½ c. soft butter
1 lb. powdered sugar, divided
⅛ tsp. salt
1 T. orange rind (opt.)
1 tsp. orange extract (opt.)
¼ to ⅓ c. orange juice or milk
A few drops of yellow and red food coloring (opt.)

1. Cream together butter, half the powdered sugar, salt, orange rind and extract until fluffy. 2. Add remaining powdered sugar alternately with orange juice or milk; beat well on high speed of electric mixer. 3. Add a few drops of yellow and red food coloring to make desired shade of light orange. Note: If too thick, add a few more drops of liquid.

ORANGE FROSTING (Smaller)

Makes enough for top of 13 x 9-inch cake or 36 cookies.

¼ c. soft butter
⅛ tsp. salt
2 c. powdered sugar
½ tsp. orange extract
2 T. orange juice or milk
A few drops of yellow and red food coloring (opt.)

1. Cream together butter, salt, half the powdered sugar and orange extract until fluffy. 2. Add remaining powdered sugar alternately with orange juice or milk; beat well on high speed of electric mixer. 3. Add a few drops of yellow and red food coloring to make desired shade of light orange. Note: If too thick, add a few more drops of liquid.

ORANGE GLAZE

Nice for a bundt cake or angel food cake.

⅓ c. butter, melted
2 c. powdered sugar
¼ tsp. orange extract
Orange juice

1. Mix together all ingredients, using just enough orange juice to make the proper consistency. 2. Beat well.

PEANUT BUTTER CREAM CHEESE FROSTING

For the top of a 13 x 9-inch cake.

1 pkg. (3-oz.) cream cheese, softened
¼ c. creamy peanut butter
2 c. powdered sugar
2 T. milk
½ t. vanilla

1. Beat cream cheese and peanut butter in mixing bowl until smooth. 2. Beat in sugar, milk and vanilla and spread over top of cake. 3. Store in refrigerator.

PEANUT BUTTER FROSTING

For the top of a 13 x 9-inch cake.

3 c. powdered sugar, divided
⅓ c. creamy peanut butter
⅓ c. milk (approx)
1 tsp. vanilla

1. In mixer bowl, combine 1½ cups powdered sugar and the peanut butter, mixing together. 2. Alternately add remaining powdered sugar and the milk. 3. Add vanilla; beat until frosting has a smooth spreading consistency. **For top of 8 x 8-inch cake**: Cut recipe in half.

PEANUT BUTTER SELF-FROSTING

It bakes on top the cake as cake bakes.
You may want to double the recipe for a big cake.

¼ c. peanut butter
1 T. butter
½ c. sugar
Dash of cinnamon

1. Mix all ingredients together and sprinkle over cake batter in small chunks; then bake cake as your recipe directs.

PEPPERMINT BUTTERCREAM FROSTING

Makes enough for top of 13 x 9-inch cake or 24 cupcakes.
Peppermint stick may be crushed in food processor.

¼ c. (½ stick) soft butter
⅛ tsp. salt
3 c. powdered sugar, divided
1 tsp. vanilla
1½ to 2 T. milk
A few drops of red food coloring
3 T. crushed peppermint stick candy

1. In mixer bowl, cream together butter, salt, half the powdered sugar and vanilla until fluffy. 2. Add remaining sugar alternately with milk; beat well on high speed of electric mixer. 3. Add a few drops red food coloring to make desired shade of pink. (If too thick, add a few more drops of milk.) 4. Fold in crushed peppermint stick candy.

PINEAPPLE FILLING

Makes enough to put between 2 (9-inch) round cake layers.

½ c. + 2 T. sugar
3 T. cornstarch, packed level
¼ tsp. salt

1 (15¼-oz.) can unsweetened crushed pineapple, including juice
1 tsp. lemon juice
1 T. butter

1. Mix sugar, cornstarch and salt together in small saucepan. 2. Add remaining ingredients and cook, stirring constantly, until mixture comes to a full boil. 3. Reduce heat and boil gently 1 to 2 minutes, stirring. 4. Cool.

PINEAPPLE FILLING & FROSTING, FLUFFY

Wonderful for a sponge or angel food cake.

1 c. milk
1 can (any size) crushed pineapple, <u>well drained</u>
1 env. Dream Whip topping mix (dry)
1 (4-serving size) pkg. instant vanilla pudding (dry)
1 angel food cake

1. In mixer bowl, combine all ingredients (except cake) and beat on high speed of electric mixer several minutes, until a nice fluffy consistency. 2. Slice angel food cake into 2 layers; put pineapple mixture between layers and frost outside of cake with remainder. 3. <u>Refrigerate</u>. <u>Note</u>: Angel food cake may be sliced into 3 layers, using all of the pineapple mixture as filling. Frost outside of cake with Cool Whip and decorate with colored sprinkles.

PINEAPPLE FLUFFY FROSTING

Enough for a 2-layer cake. Makes a lot!

1 (20-oz.) can crushed pineapple, including juice
1 (4 to 6-serving size) box instant vanilla pudding (dry)
1 (12-oz.) carton whipped topping, thawed

1. In mixer bowl, combine all 3 ingredients; mix together well for 2 minutes. 2. Keep frosted cake refrigerated until serving time.

<u>Smaller version for 2-layer cake:</u> *(makes plenty)*
2 c. crushed pineapple, including juice
1 (8-oz.) carton whipped topping, thawed
1 (4-serving size) box instant vanilla pudding (dry)

PINEAPPLE FROSTING

For top of a 13 x 9-inch cake.

2 T. Earth Balance shortening
1 T. butter
⅛ tsp. salt
½ c. powdered sugar
2½ c. powdered sugar
½ c. drained crushed pineapple
1 or 2 drops yellow food coloring (opt.)

1. Beat together first 4 ingredients. 2. Add remaining 2½ cups powdered sugar and the drained crushed pineapple; beat until creamy. 3. Tint with yellow food coloring, if desired; if too thin, add more powdered sugar.

PINEAPPLE SOFT FROSTING

Thanks to Gene Baird.

1 c. milk
2 T. cornstarch
1 c. sugar (granulated)
½ c. soft Earth Balance shortening
1 tsp. vanilla
¼ tsp. salt
½ c. <u>well-drained</u> crushed pineapple

1. Combine milk and cornstarch in small heavy saucepan. 2. Bring to a boil, stirring constantly; cool mixture completely. 3. Cream together sugar, shortening, vanilla and salt in mixer bowl until light and fluffy. 4. Add cooled mixture, one teaspoon at a time, while continuing to beat. 5. Add well-drained crushed pineapple.

SEVEN-MINUTE FROSTING

Using brown sugar, it becomes Sea Foam Frosting.

1½ c. white or packed brown sugar
¼ tsp. cream of tartar or 1 T. corn syrup
⅛ tsp. salt
⅓ c. cold tap water
2 egg whites (¼ c.)
1 tsp. vanilla

1. Combine all ingredients, except vanilla, in top of double boiler and place over boiling water. (Water should not touch bottom of upper pan.) 2. Beat with rotary beater or portable mixer for 7 minutes (or less), until frosting looks fluffy and holds a soft, gentle shape. (With a portable mixer on high speed, it may only take 3 to 4 minutes.) 3. Remove from boiling water and add vanilla; continue to beat until frosting holds definite peaks (about 2 minutes). <u>Note</u>: This is hard to make without a portable mixer.

SEVEN-MINUTE ICING

For a 2-layer 9-inch cake. Cut recipe in half for top of 9 x 13 cake.

1½ c. sugar
½ c. water
¼ tsp. salt
¼ tsp. cream of tartar
3 lg. egg whites (nearly ½ c.)
2 tsp. vanilla

1. Combine sugar, water, salt and cream of tartar in a small saucepan; bring to a boil. (Do not stir.) 2. Boil until mixture

reaches 244° approximately on candy thermometer, or until a small amount of the hot syrup falls threadlike from spoon. 3. While syrup cooks, beat egg whites in a large bowl until stiff peaks form. 4. Pour hot syrup onto egg whites in a very thin stream, while beating at high speed, until frosting is thick and glossy. 5. Beat in vanilla.

SEVEN-MINUTE PINK CLOUD FROSTING

For a 2-layer 9-inch cake, or top of an 11 x 15 sheet cake.

1 c. sugar
⅓ c. light or dark corn syrup
¼ c. maraschino cherry liquid (or water)
¼ tsp. salt
3 to 4 egg whites (nearly ½ c.)
⅛ tsp. cream of tartar
1 to 2 tsp. cherry extract (or 1 tsp. vanilla)
1 to 2 drops red food coloring (opt.)

1. Combine sugar, corn syrup, liquid and salt in small saucepan; cover with lid and heat to boiling. 2. Uncover; boil gently until mixture reaches 242° on candy thermometer, or until a small amount of the hot syrup falls threadlike from spoon. 3. While syrup cooks, <u>beat egg whites with cream of tartar</u> in a large bowl until stiff peaks form when beater is slowly raised. 4. Pour hot syrup onto egg whites in a very thin stream, while beating at high speed, until frosting is thick and glossy. 5. Beat in flavoring and food coloring. <u>Note</u>: Using water and vanilla, instead of cherry juice and cherry extract, this may also be a *White Cloud Frosting*.

STRAWBERRY DREAM WHIP FLUFFY FROSTING

Makes lots for an angel food cake or a 2-layer cake.

1 (10-oz.) pkg. frozen strawberries, thawed
Cold milk
1 env. Dream Whip
1 pkg. INSTANT vanilla pudding mix (4-serving size)
Few drops red food coloring

1. Drain thawed strawberries, reserving syrup. 2. Measure syrup and add cold milk to make 1½ cups liquid. 3. Combine liquid with Dream Whip and instant pudding mix in bowl. 4. Blend together; beat at high speed for 4 minutes or longer, until it forms soft peaks. 5. Add a few drops of red food coloring to make desired shade of pink. 6. Fold in drained strawberries. 7. Frost cake and refrigerate.

STRAWBERRY FROSTING

For 24 cupcakes or a double-layer cake.

½ c. (1 stick) butter or Earth Balance Spread
1 lb. (3¾ to 4 c.) powdered sugar
⅛ tsp. salt

¼ c. frozen strawberries, thawed (with syrup) or ½ c. fresh strawberries, sliced
1 tsp. vanilla

1. In mixer bowl, beat together butter, powdered sugar and salt until crumbly. 2. Add strawberries and vanilla; beat until frosting consistency. If too thick, add a few drops milk, or more strawberries. <u>Smaller amount</u>: For a 9 x 9-inch square cake, or top only of a 9 x 13-inch cake, cut recipe in half.

VANILLA CREAM FILLING I

⅓ c. sugar
2 T. cornstarch (level)
⅛ tsp. salt
2 egg yolks
1½ c. milk
1 T. butter
1½ tsp. vanilla

1. In heavy saucepan, combine sugar, cornstarch and salt. 2. In medium bowl, combine egg yolks and milk with whisk; add to sugar mixture, blending together. 3. Cook and stir until mixture comes to a boil; reduce heat and boil gently 2 minutes, stirring. 4. Remove from heat and add butter, stirring until butter melts. 5. Add vanilla; stir well. 6. Cover with tight lid and cool in refrigerator.

VANILLA CREAM FILLING II

½ c. sugar
1 T. cornstarch
1 c. milk
4 egg yolks, beaten
2 tsp. vanilla

1. In top of double boiler, combine sugar and cornstarch. 2. Stir in milk gradually; cook over boiling water until thickened, stirring often. 3. Cover and cook 10 minutes longer, stirring occasionally. 4. Stir a little of the hot mixture into beaten egg yolks. 5. Slowly stir into remaining hot mixture. 6. Cook over hot water for 2 minutes, stirring constantly. 7. Add vanilla; cool.

VANILLA ICING OR GLAZE

2 T. butter
2 T. milk
2 c. powdered sugar
1⁄16 tsp. salt
½ tsp. vanilla

1. Melt butter; add remaining ingredients in order given. Beat well. If too thick, add a few drops more milk.

WHIPPED BUTTERCREAM LIGHT BROWN FROSTING

A soft icing, not too sweet. Makes plenty for top of a 13 x 9-inch cake

2 T. cornstarch
1 c. milk
1 tsp. vanilla
¾ c. packed brown sugar
⅔ c. soft Earth Balance shortening (or half butter)

1. Mix cornstarch and milk together in saucepan; cook until thick and bubbly, stirring almost constantly. 2. Lower heat and simmer gently 1 minute. 3. Remove from heat; add vanilla and let mixture cool. 4. Cream sugar and shortening together until fluffy, scraping down sides of bowl twice. 5. Add cooled milk mixture and beat until fluffy, again scraping down sides of bowl twice.

WHIPPED BUTTERCREAM SOFT WHITE ICING

Make first part of this icing before baking cake, so it can cool.

1 c. sugar
⅓ c. flour
1 c. milk
½ c. butter
½ c. Earth Balance shortening
1 to 2 tsp. vanilla
½ c. chopped nuts (opt.)

1. In small saucepan, mix together sugar and flour. 2. Add milk, mixing well; cook over medium heat, stirring almost constantly, until mixture comes to a boil. 3. Cool or chill in refrigerator. 4. Cream together butter and shortening until fluffy (at least 3 minutes). 5. Add vanilla and the cooled mixture; beat well, at least 3 minutes longer. 6. If nuts are used, add now or sprinkle on top the cake. <u>Makes enough icing to frost a 2-layer cake.</u>

WHIPPED VANILLA FROSTING

From Hazel Lewis; makes enough for top of a 13 x 9-inch cake. This frosting stays nice indefinitely.

¼ c. (½ stick) butter (room temp.)
¼ c. Earth Balance shortening (room temp.)
½ c. granulated sugar
1½ T. flour, packed level
½ tsp. vanilla
⅓ c. lukewarm milk, barely heated

1. Cream together butter, shortening, sugar, flour and vanilla until fluffy. 2. Gradually (slowly) add lukewarm milk while beating; beat until consistency is like whipped cream (about 5 minutes) on high speed of electric mixer, scraping down sides of bowl 2 or 3 times. <u>Cream filling for cupcakes</u>: Fill cupcakes by injecting pastry bag with round tip into top of

baked cupcakes, using about 1 tablespoon of above recipe. Then frost cupcakes with a chocolate frosting. **For 2-layer cake**: Double this frosting recipe.

WHITE FILLING

From Hazel Schreiner.

¼ c. flour
½ c. milk
¼ c. butter (½ stick)
¼ c. soft Earth Balance shortening
¼ c. granulated sugar
1 tsp. vanilla

1. In small heavy saucepan, combine flour and milk; thicken, stirring constantly, over medium heat. (This will be very thick.) **2.** Cool mixture completely. **3.** Later, cream together butter and shortening; add sugar and beat until fluffy. **4.** Add cooled mixture and vanilla; beat together well, until fluffy. **Note**: This is a white filling to put between 2 chocolate cake layers. Frost top and sides of cake with a chocolate frosting.

WHITE FROSTING, DECORATOR'S

This recipe is enough to fill and frost a 9-inch round 2-layer cake and decorate it with flowers and borders. It is delicious. Double recipe to frost and decorate a 15 x 11 sheet cake.

1 c. Earth Balance shortening
1½ lbs. powdered sugar (about 5½ c.)
¼ tsp. salt
⅓ c. milk (approx.)
1½ tsp. vanilla
¾ tsp. almond flavoring

1. Beat shortening 1 minute. **2.** On lowest speed of mixer add powdered sugar and salt; beat on lowest speed until crumbly. 3 Add milk and flavorings; beat on high speed 5 minutes, scraping sides of bowl once or twice. (If too thick, add a tiny amount of milk.) **Chocolate Frosting**: Add 9 tablespoons unsweetened dry cocoa (level) or 3 squares (3 ounces) unsweetened chocolate, melted. Add a little more milk, if needed. **Note**: To make a small amount of chocolate frosting, add 2 tablespoons unsweetened dry cocoa to 1 cup white frosting and beat well.

WHITE FROSTING, DELICIOUS

For top of a 13 x 9-inch cake, or 18 cupcakes, or 15 x 11-inch sheet cake."

¼ to ⅓ c. Earth Balance shortening
2½ c. powdered sugar
⅛ tsp. salt
1 to 2½ T. milk or cream

2 tsp. vanilla
⅛ to ½ tsp. almond flavoring (opt.)

1. With electric mixer, beat together shortening, powdered sugar and salt. **2.** Add milk and flavoring; beat 5 minutes on high speed, scraping down sides of bowl once. **Chocolate Frosting**: Add dry unsweetened cocoa, 1 T. at a time, until desired color.

WHITE FROSTING, DREAMY

¾ c. Earth Balance shortening
2 T. dry Dream Whip powder
⅛ tsp. salt
1 T. vanilla
¼ tsp. almond flavoring (opt.)
1 lb. (3¾ c.) powdered sugar
2 T. flour (level)
¼ c. milk

1. In mixer bowl, cream together shortening, dry Dream Whip powder, salt and flavoring. **2.** Add powdered sugar, flour and milk; beat on low speed until blended. **3.** Beat on high speed 5 minutes. **Note**: This recipe may also be used for cake decorating.

Chapter 23

Cookies, Bars and Doughnuts

PAUL AND LEOTA REYNOLDS, SAM AND CAROLYN DEETS,
JACK AND ELLEN BENNINGER, BOB AND BARBARA BENNINGER,
JIM AND OPAL BENNINGER
1993

COOKIES, BARS AND DOUGHNUTS

If you wonder why Smart Balance Spread or Earth Balance is substituted for butter, please read Chapter 1.

APPLE-NUT COOKIES, FROSTED

Adapted from Mae Mihleder.

1½ c. packed light brown sugar
½ c. Earth Balance Spread
1 egg
¼ c. milk, apple juice or cider
2½ c. all-purpose flour
1 tsp. baking soda
½ tsp. salt
1 tsp. cinnamon
⅛ to ¼ tsp. cloves (opt.)
½ tsp. allspice (opt.)
½ tsp. nutmeg
1 c. raisins
1 c. chopped nuts
1 c. finely chopped apples, peeled (or unpeeled, if red)

1. In large mixer bowl, cream together brown sugar and spread.
2. Add egg and liquid; mix well together. 3. In another bowl, combine flour, soda, salt and spices. 4. Stir raisins, nuts and apples into flour mixture; add to first bowl and stir together with large spoon. 5. Drop by slightly rounded tablespoonfuls, about 2 inches apart, onto lightly greased or sprayed cookie sheets. 6. Bake in preheated 400° oven about 9 minutes, or until done. 7. Cool on racks and frost, if desired. Makes 3½ dozen.

Frosting:
2½ c. powdered sugar
3 to 4 T. softened butter
1 tsp. vanilla
3 T. milk, or as needed

1. Combine all ingredients and beat until smooth.

APPLESAUCE RAISIN BARS

2 eggs
¾ c. packed brown sugar
¾ c. olive oil
¾ c. applesauce
1 tsp. vanilla
2 c. all-purpose flour
1 tsp. baking powder
¼ tsp. baking soda
¼ tsp. salt
1 tsp. cinnamon
1 tsp. nutmeg
½ c. raisins (or more)
½ c. chopped walnuts (or more)

1. Turn oven dial to 375°. 2. Beat eggs, brown sugar, oil, applesauce and vanilla together in bowl. 3. Add dry ingredients and stir just until moistened. 4. Stir in raisins and nuts; spread evenly in greased or sprayed 13 x 9-inch pan. 5. Bake in preheated 375° oven 20 minutes or until pick inserted in center comes out clean. 6. Cool in pan on rack; cut into bars.

APPLESAUCE-OATMEAL DIET COOKIES

1⅔ c. all-purpose flour
1 tsp. baking soda
½ tsp. salt
1 tsp. cinnamon
½ tsp. nutmeg
¼ tsp. cloves
1 c. quick oats or All-Bran
1⅓ c. raisins (or part sliced dates)
1 T. honey (opt.)
1 c. unsweetened applesauce
½ c. olive oil
1 egg
2 tsp. liquid sweetener
2 tsp. vanilla
⅔ c. chopped nuts (opt.)

1. Turn oven dial to 375°. 2. In mixing bowl, combine all dry ingredients, stirring together. 3. Add raisins and remaining ingredients, beating until smooth. 4. Drop onto greased or sprayed cookie sheet and bake in preheated 375° oven 9 to 10 minutes, or until done. 5. Cool on racks; store in refrigerator in covered container. Makes 35 to 45 cookies.

BLOND BARS, CHOCOLATE CHIP

From Leota Reynolds. Delicious!

½ c. (1 stick) butter
1½ c. packed brown sugar
2 eggs, large
1 tsp. vanilla
1¾ c. all-purpose flour
1½ tsp. baking powder
¼ tsp. salt
1 c. (6 oz.) semi-sweet chocolate chips
⅓ c. chopped nuts or more (opt.)

1. Turn oven dial to 350°. 2. Cream together butter and sugar until smooth. 3. Add eggs and vanilla; beat well. 4. Add dry ingredients and mix well. 5. Stir in chocolate chips and nuts. 6. Spread evenly in greased 13 x 9-inch baking pan. 7. Bake in preheated 350° oven 25 minutes, or until center springs back when lightly touched. 8. While warm, cut into bars; cool in pan before removing. 9. Store in airtight container.

BLOND BARS, CHOCOLATE CHIP, LARGER

½ c. olive oil
1 c. sugar
1 c. packed brown sugar
3 lg. eggs or 4 sm. eggs
1 to 2 tsp. vanilla
2⅔ c. all-purpose flour
2½ tsp. baking powder
½ tsp. salt
1½ c. chocolate chips
¾ to 1 c. chopped nuts (opt.)

1. Turn oven dial to 350°. 2. Beat together oil, sugars, eggs and vanilla until well mixed. 3. Add flour, baking powder and salt, stirring well. 4. Stir in chocolate chips and nuts. 5. Spread evenly on well-greased 15 x 10 x 1-inch cookie sheet or jellyroll pan, or in a 13 x 9-inch cake pan. 6. Bake in preheated 350° oven 20 to 30 minutes, until light golden brown (25 to 30 minutes for 13 x 9-inch pan). 7. When cool, cut into bars and store in airtight container. **Note**: 10 oz. bag of mint chocolate chips may be used instead of regular chocolate chips.

BLOND CHIPPER BARS

Both peanut butter chips and chocolate chips in these.

½ c. (1 stick) butter, softened
¾ c. sugar
¾ c. packed brown sugar
2 lg. eggs
1 to 2 tsp. vanilla
2¼ c. all-purpose flour
2 tsp. baking powder
½ tsp. salt
1 c. semi-sweet chocolate chips
1½ c. peanut butter chips

1. Turn oven dial to 350° and grease or spray 15½ x 10½-inch jellyroll pan. 2. In mixer bowl, cream together butter, the sugars, eggs and vanilla until light and fluffy. 3. Add flour, baking powder and salt, mixing together. 4. Stir in chocolate chips and peanut butter chips. 5. Spread mixture evenly in prepared pan and bake in preheated 350° oven 25 minutes or until light golden brown. Do not overbake. 6. Cool completely; then cut into bars.

BROWNIES CHOCOLATE FROSTING

From Ruth Watral. For 13 x 9-inch pan.

3 T. butter
2 T. unsweetened cocoa, packed level
1½ c. powdered sugar
1 T. milk (approx.)
½ to 1 tsp. vanilla

1. Melt butter in saucepan; remove from heat. 2. Stir in cocoa. 3. Add remaining ingredients; beat with large spoon until smooth. 4. Frost brownies; let set until firm. **Note**: If too thick, add a few drops milk. If too thin, add more powdered sugar.

BROWNIES CHOCOLATE CHIP FROSTING

For 13 x 9-inch pan; cut recipe in half for smaller pan.

1¼ c. sugar
¼ c. (½ stick) butter
¼ c. milk
⅔ c. chocolate chips

1. In saucepan, mix together sugar, butter and milk. 2. Bring to a boil, stirring; boil 30 seconds. 3. Remove from heat and stir in chocolate chips; stir until smooth.

BROWNIES, CHOCOLATE-PEANUT BUTTER

*From Pat Confer. To cut recipe in half,
bake in 8 x 8-inch square dish.*

½ c. olive oil
½ c. peanut butter (creamy or chunky)
1½ c. sugar
2 tsp. vanilla
4 eggs
4 sq. (4 oz.) unsweetened chocolate, melted (or 2/3 c. semi-sweet chocolate chips, melted)
1 c. all-purpose flour
½ tsp. baking powder
1 c. peanuts, slightly chopped (opt.)

1. Turn oven dial to 350° and butter or spray 13 x 9-inch baking dish or pan. 2. In mixer bowl, cream together oil and peanut butter. 3. Add sugar and vanilla, beating until creamy. 4. Add eggs, one at a time, beating after each addition. 5. Remove from mixer and stir in melted chocolate, then flour and baking powder (and nuts, if desired). 6. Pour into prepared pan; bake in preheated 350° oven 20 to 30 minutes, until done.

BROWNIES, FUDGEY

*May be eaten frozen, straight from the freezer!
From Kelly Wells Crouch.*

1½ c. sugar
½ c. olive oil
3 eggs, unbeaten
1 tsp. vanilla
1 c. all-purpose flour, packed level
⅛ tsp. salt
8 T. unsweetened dry cocoa, packed level
½ c. coarsely chopped walnuts or pecans (opt.)

1. Turn oven dial to 325°. 2. Grease or spray 8 x 8-inch square pan (or 9 x 9). 3. In medium bowl, mix together sugar, oil, eggs and vanilla. 4. Add remaining ingredients, stirring with large spoon or low speed of electric mixer. 5. Spread in prepared pan; bake in preheated 325° oven 35 minutes. 6. Cool in pan before cutting into squares; if desired, wrap squares individually and freeze.

BROWNIES, IRRESISTIBLE

Adapted from Tracy Rankin.

4 eggs (large)
2 c. sugar
1 c. olive oil
2 tsp. vanilla
1½ c. flour
¼ tsp. salt
½ c. dry unsweetened cocoa
1 c. coarsely chopped walnuts (opt.)
1 c. chocolate chips (opt.)

1. Chop nuts and grease or spray 9 x 13-inch baking pan, or two 8 x 8-inch pans. 2. Turn oven dial to 325°. (This temperature is for all kinds of pans.) 3. Put eggs, sugar, oil and vanilla in mixer bowl and mix together well. 4. Add flour, salt, cocoa, nuts and chocolate chips (or chocolate chips may be sprinkled over top the batter when in pan). 5. Stir just until moistened; pour into prepared pan, pushing batter into corners and making batter level. 6. Bake in preheated 325° oven for 35 minutes. (About 30 minutes for 8-inch pans.) 7. Cool on rack; when completely cool, cut into squares with pizza cutter and knife. 8. Brownies may be sprinkled with powdered sugar, or frosted if desired. **Note**: This recipe may be cut in half and baked in one 8 x 8-inch pan.

BROWNIES PEANUT BUTTER FROSTING

Enough for 1 (8 x 8-inch or 9 x 9-inch) square pan.
Double recipe for large cake pan.

3 T. butter, softened
¾ c. powdered sugar
2 tsp. milk
½ tsp. vanilla
3 T. creamy or chunky peanut butter

1. In medium mixer bowl, beat butter until fluffy. 2. Gradually add powdered sugar, beating well after each addition. 3. Add milk; beat well. 4. Beat in vanilla and peanut butter.

BROWN SUGAR SAUCEPAN COOKIES

½ c. butter
1 c. packed brown sugar
1 egg (or 2 egg yolks)
1 T. milk or cream
½ tsp. vanilla

2 c. all-purpose flour
1 tsp. baking powder
½ tsp. salt
½ to 1 c. chopped nuts (opt.)

1. Turn oven to 375°. 2. In saucepan, melt butter; remove from burner. 3. Add remaining ingredients; mix well. 4. Drop cookie dough the size of English walnuts, 1 inch apart, on lightly greased cookie sheet. 5. Bake for 8 to 10 minutes, or until done. 6. Cool on wire rack. Makes about 3 dozen.

BUTTERFINGER COOKIES

½ c. butter or reg. Smart Balance spread, softened
¾ c. sugar
⅔ c. packed brown sugar
1 egg (or 2 egg whites)
1¼ c. chunky peanut butter
1½ tsp. vanilla
1 c. all-purpose flour
½ tsp. baking soda
¼ tsp. salt
5 Butterfinger candy bars (2.1 ounces, each), chopped

1. In mixing bowl, cream together butter and sugars. 2. Add egg and beat well. 3. Add peanut butter and vanilla, blending together. 4. Combine flour, soda and salt; add to mixture and beat well. 5. Add chopped candy bars; shape into 1½-inch balls and place on greased baking sheet, 2 inches apart. 6. Bake in preheated 350° oven for 10 to 11 minutes, or until light golden brown. 7. Cool on racks.

BUTTERMILK COOKIES, DROP

4 c. all-purpose flour
2 c. sugar
½ tsp. salt
1 c. Earth Balance shortening
2 eggs
1 c. buttermilk or sour milk
1½ tsp. baking soda
2 tsp. vanilla

1. Turn oven dial to 375°. 2. Mix together flour, sugar and salt; add shortening and cut in with pastry blender, mixer or fingers (as for pie crust) until it resembles coarse meal. 3. In med.-small bowl, beat eggs; add buttermilk. Add soda and stir until foamy. 4. Add egg mixture to flour mixture with vanilla; mix well. 5. Drop by rounded teaspoonfuls about 2 inches apart, onto greased or sprayed cookie sheet. 6. Bake in preheated 375° oven 9 to 10 minutes or until light golden and done. **Options**: Raisins, nuts or chips may be added; or sprinkle cookies with cinnamon-sugar or sprinkles. Also good plain.

BUTTERSCOTCH COCONUT BARS

Adapted from Betty Geneviva. Delicious!
Mix these in a saucepan. Very easy and makes a lot.

½ c. (1 stick) butter
2 c. packed brown sugar
2 lg. eggs
1 to 1½ tsp. vanilla
2 c. all-purpose flour
2 tsp. baking powder
¼ tsp. salt
1 c. flaked coconut
¾ to 1 c. nuts, coarsely chopped (opt.)
1 c. butterscotch or chocolate chips (opt.)

1. Turn oven dial to 350°. 2. Melt butter in 3 or 4-quart sauce-pan over low heat. 3. Remove pan from heat and stir in brown sugar. 4. Add eggs, one at a time, stirring after each addition. 5. Stir in vanilla; add dry ingredients, mixing well. 6. Stir in coconut, then nuts and chips. (Batter will be thick.) 7. Spread evenly in well-greased 15 x 10 x 1-inch jellyroll pan. 8. Bake in preheated 350° oven 20 to 25 minutes, until light golden brown. Do not overbake. 9. Cut into 30 to 35 bars while still warm; cool in pan before removing. Store in airtight container.

CAROB COOKIES

½ c. butter (room temp.)
1 c. turbinado sugar (or reg.)
1 egg or 2 egg yolks
1 T. milk or cream
½ tsp. vanilla
¼ tsp. salt
1 tsp. baking powder
1½ c. flour
⅓ c. carob powder (or cocoa)

1. Cream together butter and sugar thoroughly. 2. Add egg, milk and vanilla; mix together. 3. Add dry ingredients and mix well. 4. Drop from tip of spoon, 1 inch apart, on lightly buttered cookie sheet. 5. Press with fork dipped in cold water. 6. Bake at 325° for 8 minutes or until done. 7. Remove from cookie sheet with spatula and cool on wire rack. Makes 40.

CHOCOLATE CHIP BARS, OATMEAL

¾ c. olive oil
1¼ c. packed brown sugar (or part white sugar)
2 eggs
2 tsp. vanilla
2 T. corn syrup, honey or molasses
1 c. all-purpose flour
1 tsp. baking soda
¼ tsp. salt
⅛ tsp. cinnamon (opt.)
3 c. quick-cooking rolled oats (not instant)
6 to 12 oz. (1 to 2 c.) chocolate (or butterscotch) chips
½ c. chopped nuts (opt.)

1. Turn oven dial to 350°. 2. In large bowl, cream together oil, sugar, eggs and vanilla until fluffy. 3. Add flour, soda, salt and cinnamon, mixing well. 4. Stir in oats, chips and nuts. 5. Spread in lightly greased or sprayed 13 x 9-inch (or 15 x 10 x 1-inch) baking pan. 6. Bake in preheated 350° oven 20 to 28 minutes (until light golden brown and center is set). 7. Cool slightly; then cut into bars (or cut when completely cool).

CHOCOLATE CHIP COOKIES, HONEY

⅓ c. butter
½ c. honey
1 egg
1¼ c. all-purpose flour
½ tsp. baking soda
¼ tsp. salt
1 (6-oz.) pkg. semi-sweet chocolate chips (1 c.)
½ c. chopped nuts (opt.)
1 tsp. vanilla

1. Turn oven dial to 375°. 2. In mixer bowl, cream butter; gradually add honey. Cream until light and fluffy. 3. Add egg; mix well. 4. Add flour, soda and salt, blending together. 5. Stir in chocolate chips, nuts and vanilla. 6. Drop from rounded teaspoonfuls onto lightly sprayed cookie sheet, about 2 inches apart. 7. Bake in preheated 375° oven 10 minutes or until light golden.

CHOCOLATE CHIP COOKIES, PUDDIN'

These cookies stay nice indefinitely.
Makes about 50 cookies.

1 c. (2 sticks) butter, softened
¼ c. sugar
¾ c. packed brown sugar
1 tsp. vanilla
1 sm. pkg. (4-serving size) INSTANT pudding mix (vanilla, chocolate or coconut)
2 eggs
2¼ c. all-purpose flour
1 tsp. baking soda
1½ c. chocolate chips
⅔ to 1 c. nuts, coarsely chopped (opt.)

1. In large mixer bowl, combine butter, sugars, vanilla and instant pudding mix; beat until smooth and creamy, scraping bowl once or twice. 2. Add eggs and beat well. 3. Add flour and baking soda; mix well. 4. Stir in chocolate chips and nuts with large spoon. (Batter will be stiff.) 5. Drop well-rounded teaspoonfuls, about 2 inches apart, on ungreased cookie sheets. 6. Bake in preheated 375° oven for about 9 minutes, or until light golden. (Do not overbake.) Leave on cookie sheet 1 minute before removing. **Note**: If cookies seem too flat after baking first tray, add a small amount of flour.

CHOCOLATE CHIP COOKIES, PUDDIN', LARGER

Makes 75 cookies.

1½ c. (3 sticks) butter
6 level T. sugar
1 c. packed brown sugar
1½ tsp. vanilla
1 lg. pkg. (6-serving size) INSTANT pudding mix (vanilla, chocolate or coconut)
3 eggs
3½ c. all-purpose flour
1½ tsp. baking soda
2 c. (12 oz.) chocolate chips
1 to 1½ c. chopped nuts (opt.)

1. Follow directions for previous recipe.

CHOCOLATE CHIP COOKIES, WINNIE'S

Makes 40 to 50.

¾ c. sugar
¾ c. packed brown sugar
¾ c. olive oil
2 eggs
1 to 1½ tsp. vanilla
2⅓ c. all-purpose flour, packed level
1 tsp. baking soda
¼ tsp. salt
1½ to 2 c. semi-sweet chocolate chips
1 c. chopped nuts (opt.)

1. Turn oven dial to 375°. 2. Cream together sugars, olive oil, eggs and vanilla until fluffy. 3. Add flour, soda and salt. 4. Stir in chips (and nuts, if used). 5. Drop dough almost the size of golf balls, 2 inches apart, on ungreased cookie sheets. 6. Bake in preheated 375° oven for 8 minutes or until light golden brown. Do not overbake. (Bake cookies on middle rack of oven.) 7. Let cool about 1 minute on baking sheet; then remove to cooling racks. **Chocolate Chip Bars**: Spread batter in greased or sprayed 15½ x 10½ x 1-inch jellyroll pan. Bake at 375° for 20 minutes; cool completely; then cut into bars.

CHOCOLATE CHIP CRINKLE COOKIES

2 eggs
1 c. sugar
2 oz. (2 squares) semisweet chocolate or unsweetened chocolate, melted
⅓ c. olive oil
1 tsp. vanilla
1 c. flour
1 tsp. baking powder
1 c. chocolate chips
Confectioners' sugar for rolling

1. In mixer bowl, beat eggs and sugar until light and fluffy. 2. Add melted chocolate, olive oil and vanilla, mixing together well. 3. Add flour and baking powder; mix well. 4. Stir in chocolate chips; cover dough and chill for at least 2 hours, or overnight. 5. Preheat oven to 350°. Grease cookie sheets or line them with parchment paper. 6. Roll chilled dough into 1- to 1½ inch balls and roll each ball in confectioners' sugar, coating generously; place cookies 2 inches apart onto prepared cookie sheets. (Keep dough chilled between batches!) 7. Bake in preheated oven for 11 to 13 minutes (depending on size, etc.). 8. Remove cookies from cookie sheet and cool on wire racks. **Note:** To keep hands from getting sticky, coat hands with a light dusting of confectioners' sugar before forming balls.

CHOCOLATE CHIP OATMEAL COOKIES I

Makes 40 to 50 delicious cookies.

1 c. Earth Balance shortening (or half butter)
¾ c. sugar
¾ c. packed brown sugar
2 eggs
1¾ c. all-purpose flour
1 tsp. baking soda
½ tsp. salt
1 tsp. vanilla
2 c. oatmeal, uncooked
1½ to 2 c. chocolate chips
½ to 1 c. chopped nuts (opt.)

1. Turn oven dial to 375°. 2. Cream together shortening, sugars and eggs until fluffy. 3. Add flour, soda and salt; mix well. 4. Add vanilla and oatmeal. 5. Stir in chocolate chips (and nuts, if used). 6. Drop dough almost the size of golf balls, 2 inches apart, on greased cookie sheets. 7. Bake in preheated 375° oven for 9 minutes or until light golden brown on middle shelf of oven. Do not overbake. 8. Let cool about 1 minute on baking sheet; then remove to cooling racks.

CHOCOLATE CHIP OATMEAL COOKIES II

Makes 52.

¾ c. olive oil
1 c. sugar
1 c. packed brown sugar
1 tsp. vanilla
2 eggs
2½ c. all-purpose flour
1 tsp. baking soda
½ tsp. salt
1⅓ c. oatmeal
1 c. chocolate chips (or more)
1 c. chopped nuts (opt.)

1. Turn oven dial to 375°. 2. Cream the oil and the sugars, beating until creamy. 3. Beat in vanilla and eggs. 4. Add dry ingredients; then stir in chocolate chips and nuts. 5. Drop batter from a teaspoon onto a greased or sprayed cookie sheet, 2 inches apart. 6. Bake in preheated 375° oven for about 9 or 10 minutes. **Note**: Can put this all in a greased 15 x 10 x 1-inch jellyroll pan, using 2¼ c. flour. Bake at 350° for 20 to 25 minutes. Do not overbake.

CHOCOLATE CHIP OATMEAL COOKIES, CHEWY GEMS

Makes 48 to 58 delectable cookies.

2½ c. oatmeal
1 c. butter or Smart Balance spread
1 c. sugar
1 c. packed brown sugar
2 eggs
1 tsp. vanilla
2⅔ c. all-purpose flour
1 tsp. baking powder
1 tsp. baking soda
½ tsp. salt
1½ to 2 c. semi-sweet chocolate chips
1 c. chopped nuts (opt.)
1 (4-oz.) bar milk chocolate, grated (opt.)

1. Measure oatmeal first; then blend oats or put in food processor and process until like flour; set aside. 2. Turn oven dial to 375°. 3. In large mixer bowl, cream together butter and sugars. 4. Add eggs and vanilla, beating well. 5. Add flour, baking powder, soda, salt and blended oats; mix together only until blended. 6. Remove bowl from mixer; with large spoon, stir in chips, nuts and grated chocolate, if used. 7. Drop dough the size of English walnuts or golf balls (about 2 inches apart) on ungreased cookie sheet. 8. Bake in preheated 375° oven about 9 to 10 minutes. Do not overbake! If cookies flatten too much and are too thin, add a little flour to the remaining batter. 9. Leave baked cookies on cookie sheet 1 to 2 minutes; then remove to cooling rack. **To freeze dough**: Roll chilled dough into 5 logs, each 10 inches long and 1½ inches in diameter; wrap in foil or freezer-proof plastic wrap. Freeze up to 2 months.

CHOCOLATE CHIP OATMEAL COOKIES, HEALTHY

2 c. quick or old-fashioned oatmeal, uncooked
2 c. flour
½ c. whole-wheat flour
1 t. baking soda
½ t. salt
1 T. wheat germ, raw or toasted
2 T. flaxseed meal
½ c. reg. Smart Balance Spread
⅓ c. olive oil
1½ c. packed brown sugar

2 eggs
1 t. vanilla
2 T. water
1 c. chopped nuts (opt.)
2 c. (12 oz.) chocolate chips

1. Stir together the first seven dry ingredients in a bowl; set aside. 2. In mixer bowl, cream until fluffy the Smart Balance, olive oil and brown sugar. 3. Add eggs, one at a time, and vanilla. 4. Add dry ingredients alternately with the water; stir in nuts and chocolate chips. 5. Drop on greased cookie sheets, 2 inches apart, and bake about 11 minutes in preheated 350° oven. 6. Cool on cookie sheet two minutes before removing to cooling racks.

CHOCOLATE CHIP OUTER SPACE BARS

From Brenda Rhoades comes a quick and good recipe.

1 yellow cake mix
2 eggs
½ c. light olive oil
2 T. water
1 (12 oz.) pkg. chocolate chips (2 cups, or may use less)
½ bag miniature marshmallows (8 oz.)
½ to 1 c. chopped nuts (opt.)

1. Turn oven dial to 350°; grease a 9 x 13 x 2-inch baking pan. 2. Mix together cake mix, eggs, oil and water; add chocolate chips and mini-marshmallows (and nuts, if used), mixing all together. 3. Put into greased pan and bake for 20 to 30 minutes. 4. Cool completely and cut into bars.

CHOCOLATE CHIP RICE KRISPIES COOKIES

½ c. butter
⅓ c. sugar
⅓ c. packed brown sugar
1 egg
½ tsp. vanilla
1¼ c. flour
½ tsp. baking soda
¼ tsp. salt
1 c. Rice Krispies
½ c. chocolate chips

1. Cream together butter and sugars. 2. Add egg and vanilla; beat well. 3. Stir in dry ingredients, then cereal and chocolate chips. 4. Drop by rounded teaspoonfuls onto greased baking sheet. 5. Bake in preheated 350° oven for 10 minutes or until light golden in color. 6. Cool on wire racks.

CHOCOLATE CHIP TOFFEE BARS (Eggless)

1 c. butter or Smart Balance spread
1 c. packed brown sugar
1 tsp. vanilla
¼ tsp. almond extract
1 to 2 T. instant coffee powder (opt.)
2¼ c. all-purpose flour
½ tsp. baking powder
⅛ tsp. salt
1 c. chocolate chips
½ c. chopped nuts

Almond Glaze:
1 T. soft butter
¾ c. powdered sugar
⅛ tsp. vanilla or almond extract
1 to 2 T. milk

1. Turn oven dial to 350°. 2. Cream together butter and brown sugar; add almond extract and instant coffee. 3. Add dry ingredients and mix together. 4. Stir in chips and nuts. 5. Press into well-greased or sprayed 15 x 10 x 1-inch jellyroll pan. 6. Bake in preheated 350° oven 20 to 25 minutes. 7. While warm, stir together Almond Glaze; drizzle or spread over top (if desired). 8. Cut into bars while warm. **Note**: To cut recipe in half, bake in 11 x 7-inch pan.

CHOCOLATE CHERRY COOKIES

Makes 48. Mint chocolate chips may also be used in the frosting.

½ c. butter
1 c. sugar
1 egg
1½ tsp. vanilla
1½ c. all-purpose flour
⅓ c. unsweetened dry cocoa
¼ tsp. salt
¼ tsp. baking soda
¼ tsp. baking powder
48 maraschino cherries, blotted dry

Frosting:
1 c. (6 oz.) semi-sweet chocolate chips
½ c. sweetened condensed milk
1 to 1½ tsp. maraschino cherry juice

1. Count out 48 cherries and lay on paper towels. 2. Turn oven dial to 350°. 3. In mixer bowl, cream together butter and sugar until fluffy. 4. Beat in egg and vanilla. 5. Add flour, cocoa, salt, soda and baking powder; beat at low speed until dough forms. (Batter will be very firm.) 6. Shape into 48 balls, about 1 inch round. 7. Push 1 cherry halfway into each ball. 8. Place on ungreased cookie sheets and bake in preheated 350° oven 8 to 10 minutes, until puffy. 9. Cool on wire racks; when partly or completely cool, frost. 10. To make frosting, melt chocolate chips and sweetened condensed milk in small saucepan over low heat, stirring constantly. 11. Remove from heat; add cherry juice and stir until smooth. (If too thick, add a few drops additional cherry juice.)

CHOCOLATE COOKIE JAR BROWNIE COOKIES, FROSTED

A chocolate drop cookie that stays moist.

1 c. (2 sticks) butter
1¾ c. sugar
1 c. creamed cottage cheese (or small curd cottage cheese)
2 eggs
1 tsp. vanilla
2½ c. all-purpose flour
½ c. unsweetened dry cocoa
1 tsp. baking powder
1 tsp. baking soda
½ tsp. salt
1 c. chopped pecans or walnuts (or ½ c. each)

1. In large mixer bowl, cream together butter and sugar until fluffy. 2. Beat in cottage cheese. (If using small curd, break up in food processor, or mash with potato masher first.) 3. Add eggs, one at a time, beating well after each addition. 4. Add vanilla. 5. In another bowl, combine dry ingredients and nuts; gradually add to first mixture. 6. Drop by slightly rounded tablespoonfuls, about 2 inches apart, onto lightly greased or sprayed cookie sheets. 7. Bake in preheated 350° oven about 11 minutes, or until done. 8. Cool on racks and frost.

Frosting:
2½ c. powdered sugar
3 to 4 T. softened butter
1 tsp. vanilla
3 T. milk, or as needed

1. Combine all ingredients and beat until smooth. 2. After frosting each cookie, sprinkle with chocolate decors, if desired.

CHOCOLATE FUDGE DROP COOKIES, FROSTED

½ c. (1 stick) butter or Earth Balance shortening
1 c. sugar
1 egg
¾ c. buttermilk or sour milk
1½ tsp. vanilla
2 c. all-purpose flour
⅓ c. unsweetened dry cocoa, packed level
½ tsp. baking soda
½ tsp. salt
½ to 1 c. chopped nuts (walnuts or pecans)

1. Cream together butter and sugar; add egg and beat well. 2. Add buttermilk and vanilla. 3. Add dry ingredients and nuts, stirring together with large spoon. 4. Chill dough 1 hour. 5. Drop on greased or sprayed cookie sheet, about 2 inches apart. 6. Bake in preheated 400° oven about 8 to 10 minutes, or until no imprint remains when touched. 7. Cool on racks; frost with vanilla frosting.

Vanilla Frosting:
2 c. powdered sugar
¼ c. (½ stick) butter, softened
1 tsp. vanilla
2 T. hot milk or cream

1. Beat all ingredients together until smooth.

CHOCOLATE KISS COOKIES

From Adele Crognale. Makes about 41 cookies.

1 c. butter
1 c. sugar
2 egg yolks
1 tsp. vanilla
2 sq. (2 oz.) unsweetened chocolate, melted
2 c. all-purpose flour
½ tsp. salt (or less)
Egg whites
1 c. nuts, finely chopped
1 (9-oz.) bag Hershey milk chocolate kisses

1. Cream together butter and sugar; add egg yolks (reserve egg whites), vanilla, melted chocolate, flour and salt. 2. Chill in refrigerator about 1 hour. 3. Roll into little balls about the size of English walnuts. 4. Dip balls in egg white; then roll in nuts. Place on greased or sprayed cookie sheet and press thumb in middle of cookies. 5. Bake in preheated 350° oven 8 to 10 minutes; when cookies come out of the oven, put chocolate kisses in the indentations while still on cookie sheets. 6. Remove to cooling racks.

CHOCOLATE MALT BARS

Coarsely crush malted milk balls in food processor. The frosting is optional, but good.

⅓ c. butter, softened
½ c. sugar
1 egg
½ c. instant malted milk powder (chocolate or plain)
¼ c. milk
1 tsp. vanilla
1¼ c. all-purpose flour
1 tsp. baking powder
1 c. coarsely crushed malted milk balls

Fudge Frosting:
1¼ c. sifted powdered sugar
2 T. dry unsweetened cocoa
2 T. butter
1 T. very hot water
¼ tsp. vanilla

1. In mixer bowl, beat butter and sugar until fluffy. 2. Add egg, malted milk powder, milk and vanilla; beat for 2 minutes. 3. On low speed of electric mixer, gradually add flour and baking powder, mixing well. 4. Fold in the coarsely crushed

malted milk balls. 5. Spread the mixture into a greased or sprayed 9 x 9 x 2-inch baking pan. 6. Bake in preheated 350° oven for 25 to 30 minutes or until a tooth pick inserted near the center comes out clean. 7. Cool on wire rack. 8. For frosting, combine ingredients and beat together 1 minute on medium speed. 9. Frost cooled bars; then cut into squares.

CHOCOLATE MARSHMALLOW COOKIES, FROSTED

Makes about 70 cookies, but recipe may be cut in half. From Bonnie Bash.

½ c. soft Earth Balance shortening
½ c. butter or Smart Balance spread
2 c. sugar
2 eggs
3½ c. all-purpose flour
1 tsp. baking soda
½ tsp. salt
⅔ c. unsweetened dry cocoa, packed level
1 c. milk
2 tsp. vanilla
1 (10-oz.) bag lg. Marshmallows
Frosting

1. Cream together shortening, butter and sugar until fluffy. 2. Add eggs and beat well. 3. In medium bowl, combine flour, soda, salt and cocoa; stir well. 4. Add flour mixture alternately with milk and vanilla to shortening mixture. 5. Drop by heaping teaspoonfuls, 2 to 3 inches apart on greased cookie sheets; bake about 8 to 12 minutes in preheated 350° oven, or until almost done. (Don't overbake.) 6. Remove from oven and place half a large marshmallow on top of each cookie (cut marshmallows in half across the diameter with sharp, wet knife). 7. Return to oven, baking just until marshmallows are soft, about 2 minutes. (Not long enough for marshmallows to turn tan.) 8. Repeat process until all cookies are baked; cool on cooling racks; then frost.

Chocolate Frosting:
1 lb. powdered sugar (3¾ to 4 c.)
8 T. dry unsweetened cocoa, packed level
⅛ tsp. salt
6 T. butter, melted or softened
6 T. milk or cream (approx.)
1 tsp. vanilla

1. Beat all ingredients together. If too thin, add a little more powdered sugar. If too thick to spread, add a **few drops** of milk. **White Frosting**: Omit cocoa and reduce milk to 5 tablespoons. **Note**: Depending how thickly you spread frosting, cookies may take more frosting than this recipe makes.

CHOCOLATE SNOWBALLS

From Laura Robison.

1¼ c. soft butter
⅔ c. sugar
½ c. unsweetened dry cocoa
1 tsp. vanilla
⅛ tsp. salt
2 c. all-purpose flour
2 c. pecans, chopped rather fine in blender or food processor
Powdered sugar

1. In bowl, cream together butter, sugar, cocoa, vanilla and salt. 2. Work in flour; chill dough. 3. Shape into small balls; bake on lightly greased or sprayed cookie sheets in preheated 350° oven 20 minutes. 4. Roll in powdered sugar.

CHOW MEIN HOPSCOTCH COOKIES

From Deloris Dunkle.

1 (6-oz.) pkg. (1 c.) butterscotch morsels
½ c. peanut butter
1 (3-oz.) can (2 c.) chow mein noodles
1 c. miniature marshmallows

1. Melt butterscotch morsels with peanut butter over hot (not boiling) water. 2. Remove from heat and stir well. 3. Stir in chow mein noodles and marshmallows until well coated. 4. Drop by teaspoonfuls onto waxed paper; chill.

CINNAMON SHORTBREAD COOKIES

A recipe from Kaase's Bakery.

¾ c. sugar
1½ c. butter
¾ tsp. salt
2 tsp. cinnamon
1 tsp. vanilla
½ tsp. maple flavoring
2 eggs
3½ to 4 c. all-purpose flour
1½ c. chopped walnuts
Cinnamon sugar

1. Cream together sugar, butter, salt, cinnamon, vanilla and maple flavoring. 2. Add eggs and mix until smooth. 3. Stir in flour and nuts. 4. Roll out dough on floured surface and cut out with cookie cutters. 5. Sprinkle cookies with cinnamon sugar. 6. Bake on greased cookie sheets in preheated 350° oven for 8 to 10 minutes.

COCONUT COOKIES, CRISP

1 c. sugar
1 c. packed brown sugar
½ c. (1 stick) butter
½ c. Earth Balance shortening
2 eggs
½ tsp. salt
1 T. water
1 tsp. vanilla
3½ c. all-purpose flour (approx.)
1 tsp. baking soda
1 c. flaked coconut

1. Turn oven dial to 375°. 2. Cream together sugars, butter and shortening until fluffy. 3. Add eggs, salt, water and vanilla; mix well. 4. Add flour, soda and coconut; mix well. If dough is not thick enough, add a little more flour. 5. Shape into small balls and place on lightly greased cookie sheet. 6. Flatten cookies with bottom of a water glass (¼ to ⅜--inch thick). 7. If glazed top is desired, brush cookies with milk. 8. Bake in preheated 375° oven 9 minutes, or until light golden brown. 9. Cool on wire racks.

COCONUT MACAROONS

Makes 48 macaroons with 31 calories in each.

Whites from 3 lg. eggs
¼ tsp. cream of tartar
⅛ tsp. salt
¾ c. sugar
¼ tsp. almond extract
¼ tsp. vanilla extract
2 c. flaked coconut
12 candied cherries, quartered to make 48 pcs. (opt.)

1. Turn oven dial to 300°. 2. Beat egg whites, cream of tartar and salt until foamy. 3. Beat in sugar, 1 tablespoon at a time; continue beating 4 minutes, or until stiff, glossy peaks form when beaters are lifted. (Don't underbeat.) 4. Fold in almond and vanilla extracts and coconut. 5. Drop by rounded teaspoonfuls, about 1 inch apart, on greased or sprayed cookie sheets; place a piece of cherry on each. 6. Bake in preheated 300° oven 20 to 25 minutes, just until edges are light brown. 7. Cool on cookie sheet 10 minutes before removing to rack to cool completely.

COOKIE PRESS BROWN SUGAR MAPLE COOKIES

½ c. butter or Earth Balance shortening
1 c. packed brown sugar
2 eggs, well beaten
1 tsp. vanilla
½ tsp. maple flavoring
3 c. all-purpose flour
½ tsp. baking soda
¼ tsp. salt

1. Turn oven dial to 375°. 2. In mixer bowl, cream together butter and sugar until fluffy. 3. Add eggs, vanilla and maple flavoring. 4. Add dry ingredients; mix well; fill cookie press and force on ungreased cookie sheet. 5. Bake in preheated 375° oven for 8 to 10 minutes.

COOKIE PRESS CREAM CHEESE COOKIES I

A not-real-sweet cookie.

½ c. butter or Smart Balance spread
3 oz. cream cheese
⅓ c. sugar
1 egg yolk
1½ tsp. vanilla or orange extract (or other flavoring)
1½ c. all-purpose flour
⅛ tsp. salt
Food coloring (opt.)

1. Cream together butter and cream cheese. 2. Add sugar and mix until fluffy. 3. Add egg yolk and extract. 4. Stir in flour and salt. (If desired, color dough with food coloring.) 5. Force through cookie press onto ungreased cookie sheets. 6. Bake in preheated 375° oven for 8 to 10 minutes.

COOKIE PRESS CREAM CHEESE COOKIES II

From Ruth Watral

2½ c. soft Earth Balance shortening
8 oz. cream cheese
2½ c. sugar
3 eggs
2½ tsp. lemon juice
6¼ c. all-purpose flour
2½ tsp. baking powder
Flavoring, if desired (see directions)

1. Cream together shortening and cream cheese. 2. Add sugar and mix thoroughly. 3. Add eggs and lemon juice; mix well. 4. Add flour and baking powder. (Another ¼ cup flour may be needed to make dough stiff enough.) 5. If desired, dough may be divided in 3 parts. Leave 1 part as is; add 1 teaspoon lemon extract to 1 part; add 1 teaspoon almond extract to 1 part. 6. Put through cookie press onto ungreased, cold cookie sheet. 7. Bake in preheated 375° to 400° oven for 8 to 10 minutes. **Note**: Red or green cherry pieces may be placed in center of cookies before baking. Cookies may be iced after baking, and dipped in chopped nuts.

COOKIE PRESS ORANGE SWEDISH SPRITZ

1 c. (2 sticks) butter
1½ tsp. orange extract
½ c. sugar
1 egg yolk, beaten
2 c. all-purpose flour
¼ tsp. salt

1. Turn oven dial to 375°. 2. In mixer bowl, cream together butter and orange extract. 3. Add sugar and cream until fluffy. 4. Add egg yolk and mix together. 5. Add flour and salt; mix well. 6. Fill cookie press and force onto ungreased cookie sheet. 7. Bake in preheated 375° oven 10 minutes; do not let brown.

COOKIE PRESS PEANUT BUTTER COOKIES

⅓ c. peanut butter
⅔ c. Earth Balance shortening
1 c. sugar
1½ tsp. vanilla
2 eggs, unbeaten
3 c. all-purpose flour
¼ tsp. salt

1. Turn oven dial to 400°. 2. In mixer bowl, cream together peanut butter, shortening, sugar and vanilla. 3. Add eggs and beat well. 4. Mix in flour and salt; fill cookie press and force onto ungreased cookie sheet. 5. Bake in preheated 400° oven 10 to 12 minutes or until set.

COOKIE PRESS SOUR CREAM COOKIES

1 c. Earth Balance shortening
1 c. sugar
2 egg yolks
½ c. thick sour cream
1 tsp. vanilla
4 c. all-purpose flour
½ tsp. salt
1 tsp nutmeg
½ tsp. baking soda

1. Turn oven dial to 375°. 2. In mixer bowl, cream together shortening and sugar. 3. Add egg yolks, sour cream and vanilla. 4. Add dry ingredients, mixing well; fill cookie press and force onto ungreased cookie sheet. 5. Bake in preheated 375° oven 10 to 12 minutes.

COOKIE PRESS SWEDISH SPRITZ

1 c. (2 sticks) butter or Smart Balance spread
½ c. Earth Balance shortening
1 c. sugar
2 eggs
1 tsp. vanilla
½ tsp. almond extract
3½ c. all-purpose flour, packed level
⅛ tsp. baking soda
Food coloring

1. In mixer bowl, cream together butter, shortening and sugar. 2. Add eggs, vanilla and almond extract; mix well. 3. Add flour and soda; mix until smooth. 4. Divide dough into 3 parts; tint ⅓ pink, ⅓ green and leave ⅓ plain. 5. Fill cookie press and force onto ungreased cookie sheet. 6. Bake in preheated 400° oven 8 to 10 minutes or until just set. Do not brown. **Note**: If cookies do not hold their shape, add a little more flour.

DATE BALLS, "CASSEROLE"

Makes about 36 cookie balls.
There is no flour in this recipe.

2 eggs
1 c. sugar
1 c. flaked coconut
1 c. chopped dates
1 c. chopped nuts
1 tsp. vanilla
⅛ tsp. almond extract
⅓ c. powdered sugar, approx. (to roll balls in)

1. Turn oven dial to 350° and grease a 2-quart casserole. 2. Beat eggs well; add sugar gradually, beating until smooth and fluffy. 3. Add remaining ingredients (except powdered sugar) and mix well. 4. Pour into greased 2-quart casserole and bake in preheated 350° oven 30 minutes. 5. Remove from oven and immediately stir well with wooden spoon. 6. Cool completely; then shape into balls about 1 inch in diameter. 7. Roll each ball in powdered sugar. 8. Store in airtight container.

DATE-FILLED DROP COOKIES

1 c. butter or Smart Balance spread
2 c. light brown sugar, packed
2 eggs
½ c. buttermilk
1 tsp. vanilla
3½ c. all-purpose flour
1 tsp. baking soda
½ tsp. salt
¼ tsp. cinnamon

Filling:
11 oz. dates, chopped (or 1¾ c.)
¾ c. sugar
¾ c. water
½ c. walnuts, chopped

1. Make date filling first; combine dates, sugar and water. Cook slowly, stirring until thickened. Remove from heat and add nuts; cool. 2. Turn oven dial to 400°. 3. In mixer bowl, cream together butter and brown sugar; add eggs, buttermilk and vanilla. Mix well. 4. Add dry ingredients; drop 2 inches apart on greased or sprayed cookie sheets. 5. In the center of each cookie, make an indentation and put ½ teaspoon date filling in it. 6. Bake in preheated 400° oven about 10 to 12 minutes, until lightly browned.

DATE HOLIDAY COOKIES

From Bonnie Bash. Makes 3 dozen.

½ c. (1 stick) butter
1 c. packed brown sugar
1 egg
1 tsp. baking soda
¼ tsp. salt
2 c. all-purpose flour

¼ c. buttermilk
1 c. chopped walnuts
1 c. candied cherries, cut up (or candied fruit cake mix)
1 c. dates, chopped

1. Turn oven dial to 400°. 2. In mixer bowl, cream butter; add sugar and eggs. Beat until light and fluffy. 3. Add remaining ingredients; mix well. 4. Drop by spoonfuls onto greased or sprayed cookie sheet about 2 inches apart. 5. Bake in preheated 400° oven for 8 to 10 minutes.

DATE JUMBLES

Makes 54 cookies.

½ c. butter or Earth Balance shortening
1½ c. packed brown sugar
3 eggs
1 tsp. vanilla
3 c. all-purpose flour
½ tsp. salt
1 tsp. baking soda
2 T. hot water
1 c. chopped dates (or candied fruit mix)
1 c. chopped walnuts

1. Turn oven dial to 350°. 2. In mixer bowl, cream together butter and brown sugar. 3. Beat in eggs and vanilla, scraping down sides of bowl. 4. Add flour and salt; mix together. 5. Dissolve soda in hot water; add to cookie dough, stirring well. 6. Stir in dates and nuts; drop on greased or sprayed cookie sheet and bake in preheated 350° oven 10 to 11 minutes, or until done.

DATE-OATMEAL BARS

Date Filling:
16 oz. dates (or use 2¼ to 3 c.), chopped
¼ c. sugar
1½ c. water
½ c. chopped walnuts (opt.)

Dough:
1 c. packed brown sugar
⅔ c. butter
1¾ c. all-purpose flour
½ tsp. baking soda
¼ tsp. salt
1½ c. rolled oats

1. Combine dates, water and sugar in saucepan; cook over low heat, stirring constantly, until thickened, about 10 minutes. 2. Stir in walnuts; cool (or partially cool). 3. Turn oven dial to 400°. 4. In bowl, mix together brown sugar and butter. 5. Add flour, soda and salt, stirring together well. 6. Stir in rolled oats; mix thoroughly. 7. Press half the crumb mixture in greased or sprayed 13 x 9-inch cake pan; press and flatten with hands to cover bottom of pan. 8. Spread with Date Filling; cover with remaining crumbs, patting lightly. 9. Bake in preheated 400° oven 25 to 30 minutes, until lightly browned; while warm, cut into bars and remove from pan.

DATE OATMEAL COOKIES

¾ c. butter or Earth Balance shortening
½ c. sugar
1 c. packed brown sugar
1 egg
¼ c. water
1 tsp. vanilla
1¼ c. all-purpose flour
½ tsp. baking soda
½ tsp. salt
2 c. rolled oats
1 c. chopped dates (or more)
½ c. chopped nuts (or more)

1. Turn oven dial to 350°. 2. Combine butter, sugars, egg, water and vanilla; mix thoroughly. 3. Stir in flour, soda and salt; mix well. 4. Stir in oatmeal, dates and nuts. 5. Drop by spoonfuls onto greased or sprayed cookie sheet, 2 inches apart. 6. Bake in preheated 350° oven 10 to 11 minutes or until done. (Do not overbake.)

DATE PIN WHEELS

From Pat Swarts.

Filling:
1 lb. (2¼ to 2½ c.) pitted chopped dates
1 c. sugar
1 c. water
1 c. chopped nuts

Dough:
1 c. Earth Balance shortening
2 c. packed brown sugar
3 eggs
4 c. all-purpose flour
½ tsp. baking soda
½ tsp. salt

1. For Filling: Cook first 3 ingredients for 10 minutes, stirring almost constantly; remove from heat and add nuts. Cool. 2. Cream shortening, brown sugar and eggs together. 3. Add dry ingredients and mix well. 4. On lightly floured surface, knead dough for a few seconds; divide into 2 balls. 5. Roll each ball of dough out ⅛ to ¼-inch thickness. 6. Divide date filling and spread over dough. 7. Roll up as for jellyroll. 8. Wrap in waxed paper and refrigerate overnight. (If double-wrapped in foil, these will keep a month in the refrigerator, or may be frozen.) 9. Cut into ⅜ to ½-inch slices and bake on greased cookie sheet in preheated 375° oven for 9 to 12 minutes. Cool on wire racks.

DATE SOUR CREAM COOKIES

Also called "Satin Date Drops."
Makes 36 wonderful cookies.

¼ c. (½ stick) butter
¾ c. packed brown sugar

1 egg
½ tsp. vanilla
½ c. dairy sour cream or sour cream alternative
1¼ c. all-purpose flour
½ tsp. baking soda
¼ tsp. baking powder
¼ tsp. salt
8 oz. (1 c.) dates, chopped
½ c. chopped walnuts

1. Turn oven dial to 350°. 2. In mixer bowl, cream together butter and brown sugar until fluffy. 3. Add egg, vanilla and sour cream, mixing on low speed just until blended. 4. Stir in flour, soda, baking powder and salt. 5. Stir in dates and nuts; drop by teaspoon onto lightly greased or sprayed cookie sheet. 6. Bake in preheated 350° oven 10 minutes. **Alternative Method:** Do not stir dates and nuts into batter; instead, drop batter by teaspoon, over a pitted date stuffed with nuts, on greased or sprayed cookie sheet. Bake as directed.

DOUGHNUT BALLS

Makes 36 balls (or more).

3½ c. all-purpose flour
4 tsp. baking powder
½ tsp. salt
¼ tsp. nutmeg or mace
1 c. sugar
2 eggs
1 c. milk
1 tsp. vanilla
2 T. olive oil
Olive oil for deep-frying
Sugar for coating

1. In a mixing bowl, combine dry ingredients. 2. In another bowl, beat eggs; add milk, vanilla and 2 tablespoons oil; pour into dry ingredients. Stir until smooth. 3. Drop by rounded teaspoonfuls into deep fat, heated to 365°. (If spoon is dipped first into hot fat, batter will slip off more easily. Fry-Baby on HIGH.) 4. Fry until brown on under side, about 1½ minutes; turn and fry until brown on other side, another 1½ minutes. 5. Remove from fat with basket or slotted spoon and drain on paper toweling. 6. Sugar-coat by shaking a few at a time, in a paper sack containing several spoonfuls of granulated or powdered sugar.

DOUGHNUTS, YEAST-RAISED

Makes 30 terrific raised doughnuts.

2 pkgs. active dry yeast or 4½ tsp. bulk dry yeast
¼ c. lukewarm water
1½ c. milk, scalded
¼ c. Earth Balance shortening
½ c. sugar
1½ tsp. salt
2 eggs, beaten

5 to 6 c. all-purpose flour, divided
Olive oil for deep-frying

Glaze (optional):
1½ c. powdered sugar
Warm water

1. Soften yeast in lukewarm water; set aside. 2. To scalded milk, add shortening, sugar and salt; stir until thoroughly mixed; then pour into large bowl. 3. When milk mixture is lukewarm, stir in softened yeast, beaten eggs and 2½ cups flour; beat until smooth. 4. Add 2½ to 3 cups flour to make a soft dough and stir thoroughly. 5. Cover dough and let rest 10 minutes. 6. Turn out on floured surface; knead until smooth and satiny, using about ½ cup additional flour for kneading. 7. Place in greased bowl; brush with oil or soft butter. Cover and let rise in draft-free area until double in bulk, about 1 hour. 8. Punch down and let rise again, about 45 minutes. 9. On lightly floured surface, roll out to ⅜ to ½-inch thickness; cut into doughnuts with floured doughnut cutter. 10. Let rise, uncovered, until double in bulk, about 30 minutes (until very light). 11. Drop into deep fat, heated to 365° (3 inches of oil), topside down, about 2 minutes, turning when underside is brown. (Fry no more than 2 or 3 at a time). 12. When both sides are brown, remove from fat and drain on paper towels. 13. If glaze is not wanted, roll the warm dough-nuts in granulated sugar or cinnamon sugar or sifted powdered sugar. 14. For glazing, combine 1½ cups powdered sugar with enough warm water to make a "runny" icing; dip or brush slightly warm doughnuts with glaze; then set on wire rack over waxed paper to dry.

DREAM BARS

Chewy & delicious.

½ c. butter
½ c. packed brown sugar
1 c. all-purpose flour
2 eggs
1 c. packed brown sugar
1 tsp. vanilla
2 T. flour
½ tsp. baking powder
¼ tsp. salt
2 c. walnuts, coarsely chopped

1. Cream first 2 ingredients together. 2. Add 1 cup flour; when mixed, press into 13 x 9-inch cake pan. 3. Bake in preheated 350° oven for 10 minutes; set aside. 4. In large bowl, beat eggs. 5. Add remaining ingredients; spread carefully over hot crust. 6. Return to oven and bake 20 minutes longer. 7. When cool, cut into bars. **Note**: For Nut-Coconut Bars, use 1 cup walnuts or almonds and 1 cup coconut, instead of 2 cups walnuts.

FRUIT COCKTAIL COOKIES

From Margaret Stiffler.

1½ c. sugar (can be part brown sugar, packed)
1 c. Earth Balance shortening
3 eggs
2 T. orange juice
3½ c. all-purpose flour
1 tsp. cinnamon
1 tsp. nutmeg
½ tsp. salt
1 (16-oz.) can fruit cocktail, drained (or 1½ c. drained fruit cocktail)
1 c. chopped walnuts
2 tsp. vanilla
1 tsp. baking soda
1 T. warm water

1. Turn oven dial to 400°. 2. In mixer bowl, cream together sugar, shortening and eggs until fluffy. 3. Add orange juice and dry ingredients, mixing well. 4. With large spoon, stir in drained fruit cocktail, nuts and vanilla. (Do not use mixer.) 5. Dissolve soda in 1 tablespoon warm water; stir in gently. 6. Drop by rounded spoonfuls onto greased or sprayed cookie sheet; bake in preheated 400° oven 9 to 10 minutes.

FUNNEL CAKES

Makes 6 funnel cakes.

1 lg. egg
¾ c. milk
1 c. all-purpose flour
1 tsp. baking powder
¼ tsp. salt
⅛ tsp. cinnamon
Olive oil for deep-frying
Powdered sugar

1. In electric skillet or heavy, wide saucepan or skillet, heat 1½ to 2 inches olive oil to 360° on deep-fat thermometer. 2. In medium bowl, beat egg with milk; stir in flour, baking powder, salt and cinnamon. Mix until smooth. 3. Holding finger under funnel with a ⅓-inch wide opening, pour ¼ cup batter into funnel. 4. Starting in center of skillet, drop batter into hot oil, moving funnel in circular motions, then crisscross motions, to form one funnel cake about 6 inches in diameter. It will rise quickly and expand. 5. Fry to a light golden brown, turning once with slotted spoon (about 2 minutes for each side). 6. Remove from oil, holding over skillet to drain slightly; place on paper towels to drain. 7. While warm, sprinkle with powdered or granulated sugar and serve. (Funnel cakes may be kept in warm oven for a while at a low temperature.) **Note**: If batter thickens upon standing, add a little more milk so batter will flow freely through funnel.

GINGER COOKIES

From Helen Vosler. Thick cookies will be soft.
Thin cookies will be crisp.

½ c. sugar
½ c. (1 stick) butter
½ c. molasses (green label dark Brer Rabbit molasses)
1 egg
1 tsp. vinegar
1 tsp. hot water
3¼ to 3½ c. all-purpose flour
1½ tsp. ginger
1½ tsp. baking soda
½ tsp. salt

1. Cream together sugar and butter. **2.** Add molasses, egg, vinegar and hot water; beat together. **3.** Stir in remaining ingredients, using 3¼ cups flour. If needed, add remaining ¼ cup flour. **4.** Roll dough out on floured surface; cut out with cookie cutters. **5.** Bake in middle of preheated 375° oven about 6 minutes for thin cookies or 10 minutes for thicker cookies.

GINGERSNAP CRINKLES

Makes 36 gingersnaps.

1 c. sugar
½ c. olive oil
¼ c. molasses
1 egg
2 c. all-purpose flour
2 tsp. baking soda
1 tsp. ginger
1 tsp. cinnamon
¼ tsp. powdered cloves
¼ tsp. salt
Additional granulated sugar

1. Turn oven dial to 375°. **2.** In bowl, mix together sugar, oil, molasses and egg. **3.** Add remaining ingredients; chill dough or make immediately. **4.** Form dough into balls the size of English walnuts; roll balls in granulated sugar and place on ungreased cookie sheets, about 2 inches apart. **5.** Bake in middle or upper third of preheated 375° oven about 8 to 10 minutes. **6.** Cool on wire racks. <u>Note</u>: 1 cup raisins may be added to the dough, if desired. If so, use greased cookie sheet.

GINGERSNAPS, ROLLED OUT

Makes 6 dozen or more.

¾ c. sugar
⅓ c. Earth Balance shortening
1 egg
½ c. molasses
2 tsp. baking soda
2 tsp. hot water

2¼ c. all-purpose flour
1 tsp. cinnamon
1 tsp. ginger
¼ tsp. cloves
¼ tsp. salt

1. Cream together sugar and shortening until fluffy. **2.** Add egg and molasses; mix well. **3.** Dissolve soda in 2 teaspoons hot water; add to creamed mixture. **4.** Stir in dry ingredients; chill. **5.** After chilling, roll out on lightly floured surface to ⅛-inch thickness and cut with 2-inch round cookie cutter. **6.** Place cookies on greased or sprayed baking sheet; bake in preheated 350° oven 8 to 12 minutes. (For a crackled surface, brush each cookie with water before baking.)

GOBS

Also called Whoopie Pies.
Makes about 60 singles or 30 when put together.

1 T. vinegar in cup
Milk to fill the cup
2 c. sugar
½ c. (1 stick) butter or Earth Balance Shortening
½ c. olive oil
2 egg yolks (reserve whites for filling)
1 to 2 T. vanilla
4⅔ c. all-purpose flour
1 c. dry unsweetened cocoa
2 tsp. baking soda
1 tsp. baking powder
1 tsp. salt
1 c. hottest tap water

1. Turn oven dial to 375°. **2.** Put vinegar in measuring cup; fill cup with milk and let stand 5 minutes. **3.** Mix sugar and butter together until fluffy. **4.** Add oil and beat together. **5.** Add egg yolks and vanilla; mix well. **6.** Add dry ingredients alternately with the milk and hot water. (If needed, add a bit more flour.) **7.** On greased cookie sheet, drop batter by rounded tablespoonfuls, 2 inches apart. **8.** Bake in preheated 375° oven about 8 minutes (until center of gob springs back when lightly touched). **9.** Cool on racks. **10.** Spread a rounded tablespoon of "Angel Filling" on flat side of half the gobs; top with remaining gobs. **11.** Wrap individually with plastic wrap, waxed paper or plastic "baggies."

<u>Angel Filling for Gobs</u>
2 egg whites
1 c. Earth Balance shortening
2 tsp. vanilla
3 c. powdered sugar, divided
¼ c. flour
¼ c. milk
⅛ tsp. salt

1. Beat egg whites in mixer bowl until stiff. **2.** Add shortening, vanilla, half the powdered sugar, the flour, milk and salt; beat together. **3.** Add remaining powdered sugar. **4.** Scrape sides of bowl down and beat 4 to 5 minutes on high speed.

Another Filling for Gobs
1 c. sugar
½ c. flour
1 c. milk
1 c. soft butter or Smart Balance spread
2 tsp. vanilla

1. In small pan, mix sugar and flour together. **2.** Add milk and cook over low heat, stirring constantly, until thick; cool. **3.** Cream butter until fluffy. **4.** Add cooled mixture and beat well. **5.** Add vanilla and beat until fluffy.

HERMITS

Adapted from R. W. Watral.

¾ c. olive oil
2 c. packed brown sugar (or half white sugar)
2 eggs
½ c. buttermilk, sour milk or cold coffee
3½ c. all-purpose flour
1 tsp. baking soda
1 tsp. baking powder
½ tsp. salt
1 tsp. cinnamon
1 to 2 c. raisins or chopped dates
½ to 1 c. chopped nuts
½ c. coconut (opt.)

1. Turn oven dial to 375°. **2.** Cream together oil, brown sugar and eggs. **3.** Add buttermilk or liquid, then dry ingredients. **4.** Stir in raisins and nuts. (If dough is too soft, add ¼ cup additional flour.) **5.** Drop by spoonfuls, 2 inches apart, on lightly greased or sprayed cookie sheet. **6.** Bake in preheated 375° oven 10 to 12 minutes, or until light golden brown. (Watch carefully after 10 minutes.)

HERSHEY KISS NUT BALLS

From Laura Robison. (White with chocolate kiss inside.)

1 c. butter
½ c. sugar
1 tsp. vanilla
1¾ c. all-purpose flour
1 c. chopped nuts
50 Hershey chocolate kisses (approx.)
Powdered sugar

1. Cream together butter, sugar and vanilla. **2.** Add flour and nuts; cover and chill. **3.** Unwrap kisses; shape a level table-spoon of dough around each kiss. **4.** Roll between palms of hands to form a ball. **5.** Bake in preheated 375° oven 10 to 12 minutes. **6.** Cool and dust with powdered sugar. Makes about 50 cookies.

JELLY BEAN COOKIES

Makes 2½ dozen.

½ c. (1 stick) butter
⅓ c. sugar
⅓ c. packed brown sugar
1 egg
½ tsp. vanilla
1¼ c. all-purpose flour
½ tsp. baking soda
½ tsp. baking powder
¼ tsp. salt
½ c. rolled oats
1 c. jellybeans, cut up

1. Turn oven dial to 375° after cutting up jellybeans. **2.** In mixer bowl, cream together butter and sugars. **3.** Beat in egg and vanilla. **4.** Add flour, soda, baking powder and salt, mixing well. **5.** With spoon, stir in oats, then jelly beans. **6.** Drop on greased or sprayed cookie sheet and bake in preheated 375° oven 10 minutes.

JUMBLES, FROSTED

Adapted from Bonnie Bash. Makes 3 to 4 dozen.

½ c. soft butter or Earth Balance shortening
½ c. sugar
1 c. packed brown sugar
2 eggs
1 c. sour cream or sour cream alternative
1 to 2 tsp. vanilla
3 c. all-purpose flour
½ tsp. baking soda
¼ tsp. salt
1 c. walnuts, coarsely chopped

1. Cream together butter and sugars. **2.** Add eggs and mix well. **3.** Stir in sour cream and vanilla. **4.** Add dry ingredients, then nuts; chill dough 1 hour (or bake immediately). **5.** Drop slightly rounded tablespoonfuls of dough, 2 inches apart, on greased or sprayed cookie sheet. **6.** Bake in preheated 375° oven 9 to 10 minutes, or until almost no imprint remains when touched lightly. **7.** Frost and cool on wire racks.

Browned Butter Frosting:
3 T. butter
2½ c. powdered sugar
½ tsp. vanilla
3 T. evaporated milk or 2 T. hot water

1. In saucepan, melt butter until golden brown. **2.** Add powdered sugar and vanilla. **3.** Add evaporated milk (or hot water) until it reaches desired consistency.

LACY (FRENCH LACE) COOKIES

Really good!

6 T. butter
½ c. packed brown sugar
⅓ c. light corn syrup
¾ c. all-purpose flour
½ tsp. vanilla
¾ c. finely chopped pecans or walnuts

1. Turn oven dial to 375°. 2. In 2-quart saucepan over medium heat, bring butter, brown sugar and corn syrup to boiling (do not use margarine because it separates from sugar during cooking). 3. Remove pan from heat; stir in flour, vanilla and chopped nuts. 4. Drop 1 level teaspoon of mixture onto greased or sprayed cookie sheet, about 3 inches apart. 5. Bake only 8 cookies at a time; bake in preheated 375° oven 5 to 8 minutes, until lightly browned. (Don't let them burn.) 6. Remove cookie sheet from oven; let cool 30 seconds to let cookies set slightly. 7. With pancake turner, quickly loosen cookies and remove to wire rack to cool. 8. Repeat until all batter is used, greasing or spraying cookie sheet each time. 9. Store cooled cookies in tightly covered container.

LEMON BARS, ONE BOWL

From Shirley Stevenson.

1 c. butter or Smart Balance spread
½ c. powdered sugar
2 c. flour
½ tsp. salt
4 eggs
2 c. sugar
¼ c. flour
¼ c. lemon juice

1. Combine butter, powdered sugar, flour and salt. 2. Press with slightly floured fingertips into 13 x 9-inch cake pan. 3. Bake in preheated 325° oven for 20 minutes. 4. In same bowl, beat eggs well. 5. Add sugar, flour and lemon juice, mixing well. 6. Pour lemon mixture over baked crust and bake for 20 minutes or until golden brown. 7. Remove from oven and sprinkle with additional powdered sugar. 8. Cool 30 minutes and cut into bars.

MARASCHINO COOKIES, CHOCOLATE COVERED

Delicious and easy! Makes 20 to 25 cookies.

½ c. butter or reg. Smart Balance spread, softened
¾ c. brown sugar, packed
1 tsp. vanilla
1 T. juice from cherries
1½ c. flour
20 to 25 maraschino cherries, patted dry
20 to 25 chocolate chips plus 1 c. chocolate chips

1. Cream together butter and brown sugar. 2. Add vanilla, 1 tablespoon juice from cherries, and flour; mix well. 3. Chill dough for at least one hour before baking. 4. Pat the cherries dry with paper towels; stuff each cherry with a chocolate chip, then wrap in 1 level tablespoon of dough. 5. Bake on ungreased cookie sheet in preheated 350° oven for 12 to 15 minutes. Cool. 6. When cookies are cool, melt 1 cup chocolate chips in microwavable container at 50% (MED) heat. Ice cookies with melted chocolate.

MIXED-FRUIT CHRISTMAS COOKIES

Makes 35 to 45 moist cookies.

⅔ c. sugar
½ c. (1 stick) butter
½ c. cream-style cottage cheese
1½ c. all-purpose flour, divided
1 egg
2 T. milk
½ tsp. baking powder
¼ tsp. baking soda
½ tsp. vanilla
1 c. diced mixed candied fruits and peels
½ c. chopped walnuts or pecans, coarsely chopped
Pecan halves or sliced candied cherries for top

1. In large mixer bowl, beat together sugar, butter, cottage cheese and half the flour (¾ cup) until fluffy; scrape sides of bowl twice. 2. Add egg, milk, remaining flour (¾ cup), baking powder, soda and vanilla, beating just until combined. 3. Remove from mixer; with large spoon, stir in candied fruit and chopped nuts. 4. Drop dough by rounded teaspoonfuls, 2 inches apart, on ungreased cookie sheet. 5. Onto top of each cookie, press a pecan half or a slice of candied cherry. 6. Bake in preheated 375° oven for 9 minutes or until top of cookie is firm and bottom of cookie is light golden brown. 7. Cool on cookie sheet 1 minute. 8. Remove and cool on wire rack.

MOLASSES BARS (Eggless)

½ c. Earth Balance shortening
⅓ c. packed brown sugar
½ c. molasses
1⅔ c. all-purpose flour
1 tsp. baking soda
¼ tsp. salt
½ tsp. cinnamon
½ tsp. ginger
⅛ tsp. cloves
⅛ tsp. nutmeg
½ c. buttermilk or sour milk

1. Turn oven dial to 375°. 2. Cream together shortening and brown sugar. 3. Add molasses, mixing well. 4. Add dry ingredients alternately with buttermilk. 5. Spread batter in greased or sprayed 15 x 10-inch jellyroll pan. 6. Bake in preheated 375° oven 15 to 20 minutes, until center springs back when lightly touched. 7. Frost with vanilla icing; cut into bars.

MOLASSES COOKIES

From Edith Clark Limber. An old-fashioned cookie.

1 to 1½ c. sugar
1 c. butter or Earth Balance shortening
1 c. molasses
¾ tsp. salt
3 eggs
3½ tsp. baking soda, dissolved in ½ c. boiling water
2 tsp. cinnamon
1 tsp. ground ginger
6 to 7 c. all-purpose flour (start with 5 c.)

1. Turn oven dial to 375°. 2. In large bowl, cream together sugar and butter. 3. Add molasses, salt and eggs; beat well. 4. Dissolve soda in boiling water and stir in. 5. Add cinnamon, ginger and 6 cups flour; stir in more flour, if needed, to make dough stiff enough to roll out. 6. Roll dough out on floured surface; cut out with cookie cutters. 7. Bake in middle of preheated 375° oven 6 to 10 minutes, or until done (depending on thickness of cookies). __Note__: Sugar may be sprinkled over cookies before baking.

MONSTER COOKIES

Makes 100 huge cookies; they freeze well.

1 lb. butter (2 c.)
2 lbs. packed brown sugar (4½ c.)
4 c. white sugar
1 T. vanilla
12 eggs
3 lbs. peanut butter
1 T. light corn syrup
8 tsp. baking soda
18 c. oatmeal (2 lbs. 10 oz.), quick cooking
1 lb. chocolate chips
1 lb. M&M candies

1. Cream butter; gradually add sugar and vanilla, beating well. 2. Add eggs, peanut butter and corn syrup; beat well. 3. Add oats and baking soda, stirring well. 4. Add chocolate chips and candy. 5. Drop dough on ungreased cookie sheets, using an ice cream scoop, placing cookies 4 inches apart. Press flat before baking. 6. Bake in preheated 350° oven for 12 to 18 minutes, or until done. __Note__: This recipe does __not__ use flour.

MONSTER COOKIES, SMALLER RECIPE

__No flour__ in Monster Cookies. Makes 25.

½ c. butter, softened (or olive oil)
1 c. sugar
1 c. + 2 T. packed brown sugar
3 eggs
1½ c. peanut butter
½ tsp. vanilla
1 tsp. light corn syrup

4½ c. oats (reg. or quick)
2 tsp. baking soda
½ c. M&M candies
1 (6-oz.) pkg. semi-sweet chocolate chips

1. Cream butter; gradually add sugar, beating well. 2. Add eggs, peanut butter, vanilla and corn syrup; beat well. 3. Add oats and soda, stirring well. 4. Stir in remaining ingredients. 5. Drop dough by ¼ cupfuls, at least 2 inches apart, onto lightly greased cookie sheets. 6. Bake in 350° preheated oven for 9 to 12 minutes or until done. Centers of cookies should be slightly soft. 7. Cool 2 minutes before removing from cookie sheet to wire racks.

NO-BAKE BUTTERSCOTCH COOKIES

From Frances Craig.

2 c. sugar
⅔ c. evaporated milk
½ c. (1 stick) butter
1 tsp. vanilla
3½ c. quick-cooking rolled oats
1 (4-serving size) box instant butterscotch pudding
½ c. chopped nuts
⅓ c. flaked coconut

1. In 2 or 3-quart saucepan, combine sugar, evaporated milk and butter; cook until mixture comes to boiling. 2. Remove from heat and add remaining ingredients; mix well. 3. Drop by spoonfuls onto waxed paper.

NO-BAKE CHEERIOS CHOCOLATE BARS

½ c. light corn syrup
6 oz. (1 c.) semi-sweet chocolate chips
1 tsp. vanilla
4 c. Cheerios cereal (or part Special K)

1. Butter or spray 9 x 9 x 2-inch (or 8 x 8 x 2-inch) pan. 2. In medium saucepan, heat corn syrup to boiling; remove from heat. 3. Add chocolate chips and vanilla, stirring until chocolate is melted. 4. Add Cheerios; stir until well coated. 5. Turn into prepared pan; spread with buttered back of tablespoon. 6. Cool 1 hour; then cut into bars.

NO-BAKE COCOA OATMEAL COOKIES

2 c. sugar
½ c. (1 stick) butter
½ c. milk
⅓ to ¾ c. unsweetened dry cocoa
½ c. peanut butter
1 to 2 tsp. vanilla
3 c. quick-cooking rolled oats
Nuts, raisins or coconut (opt.)

1. In large saucepan, combine sugar, butter, milk and cocoa; bring to a boil, stirring constantly. **2.** Boil 1½ minutes. **3.** Remove from heat and add peanut butter; blend together well. **4.** Add vanilla, rolled oats and any optional items, if wanted. **5.** Drop by rounded teaspoonfuls onto waxed paper and let stand at room temperature until firm. **6.** Store in cookie jar. **Peanut Butter:** Omit cocoa and increase peanut butter to ¾ cup.

NO-BAKE DATE GRAHAM CRACKER BALLS

Adapted from Laura Robison.

1 c. graham cracker crumbs, firmly packed
1 c. chopped nuts
½ c. coconut, chopped fine in food processor
1 can sweetened condensed milk
1 c. chopped nuts
½ c. chopped or diced dates
3 c. miniature marshmallows
¾ c. ground nuts

1. Combine all ingredients, except ground nuts. **2.** Wet hands with water; shake off excess water and shape date mixture into small balls. **3.** Roll in ground nuts.

NO-BAKE DATE GRAHAM CRACKER LOGS

From Rev. Fred Watson.

10 to 11 oz. dates
8 oz. (2 c.) walnuts or pecans, chopped or cut into sm. pcs.
10 to 10½ oz. miniature marshmallows
½ lb. graham crackers, rolled or crushed
2 T. evaporated milk (approx.)

1. Cut each date into 2 to 4 pieces with scissors or sharp knife. **2.** Reserve ¼ cup graham cracker crumbs. **3.** Put all ingredients, except reserved cracker crumbs, in huge bowl and mix together with hands until dates and marshmallows begin to lose their shape and mixture sticks together. **4.** Form into several logs; roll in reserved crumbs. **5.** Wrap each log in plastic wrap. Slice to serve.

NO-BAKE MARSHMALLOW COOKIES

From Margaret Stiffler.

½ c. butter
1 c. sugar
2 eggs, beaten
1 tsp. vanilla
1½ c. graham cracker crumbs
2 c. miniature marshmallows
½ c. chopped nuts
¼ c. flaked coconut

1. In heavy pan, melt butter; stir in sugar. **2.** Remove from heat; add beaten eggs. **3.** Return to heat; cook and stir constantly over medium heat until thick and bubbly, watching that it does not burn. **4.** Remove from heat and <u>let stand 25 minutes</u> at room temperature, stirring occasionally. **5.** Stir in vanilla, then graham cracker crumbs. **6.** Stir in marshmallows, nuts and coconut. **7.** Drop onto waxed paper and shape with hands. **8.** Let stand until well set; store in tight container.

NO-BAKE PEANUT BUTTER CEREAL BARS

1 c. sugar
1 c. light corn syrup
1 c. peanut butter (creamy or crunchy)
6 c. Cheerios, Special K, Kix, Honey Comb or Rice Krispies or combination of these
1 to 2 c. milk chocolate chips or butterscotch chips (or 1 c. of each), or 10 oz. chunk of milk chocolate

1. Butter or spray 13 x 9-inch pan. **2.** In large pan, bring corn syrup and sugar to a boil, stirring constantly, until sugar is dissolved. **3.** Remove from heat and stir in peanut butter until mixture is smooth. **4.** Add cereal; mix well. **5.** Press into prepared pan. **6.** If frosting is desired, melt chips over medium heat, stirring constantly until smooth. Spread evenly over top. **7.** Refrigerate for at least 15 minutes or until frosting is set; then cut into bars.

NO-BAKE RICE KRISPIES PEANUT BUTTER BARS

No-bake, easy and delicious.

⅓ c. sugar
⅓ c. corn syrup (light or dark)
½ c. peanut butter (smooth or crunchy)
3 c. Rice Krispies cereal
⅓ c. peanuts, coarsely chopped (opt.)
1 c. milk chocolate chips (opt.)

1. Butter an 8 x 8-inch square pan. **2.** In medium saucepan, combine sugar and corn syrup; bring to a soft boil; then remove from heat. **3.** Immediately add peanut butter and stir until smooth. **4.** Add cereal and nuts; stir until evenly coated. **5.** Press mixture into prepared pan, using buttered spatula. **6.** Over low heat, melt chips in heavy saucepan; spread over Rice Krispies mixture. **7.** Cool at room temperature for 2 hours; cut into bars. **8.** Store in airtight container. **To double recipe:** Use 13 x 9-inch pan.

NUT BALLS

"Wedding Cookies" or "Snowballs."
Adapted from Linda Deets and Rita Stevenson.

1 c. (2 sticks) butter
!/3 c. sugar
2¼ c. all-purpose flour

1 T. cold water
1 tsp. vanilla
¼ tsp. almond extract (opt.)
¾ to 1 c. chopped pecans or walnuts
1 c. powdered sugar

1. Cream together butter and sugar. 2. Add remaining ingredients, mixing well. 3. If dough is too soft to make balls, chill 2 hours. 4. Shape into 1-inch balls; place on ungreased cookie sheets. 5. Bake in preheated 325° oven 17 to 20 minutes or until done on bottom, but still white on top. 6. Remove from oven; cool 2 to 5 minutes; then roll in powdered sugar and cool completely. 7. If desired, nut balls may be rolled in additional powdered sugar before serving.

NUT OR DATE HORNS, HUNGARIAN

No eggs or yeast in these individual horns.

2 c. all-purpose flour
¼ tsp. salt
½ c. (1 stick) butter
1 c. commercial sour cream
Powdered sugar

1. Combine flour and salt; cut in butter with pastry blender or hands until it resembles coarse meal. 2. Add sour cream (dough will be sticky). 3. Wrap dough in waxed paper and chill overnight. 4. Next day, roll ⅓ of dough at a time on floured surface to pie crust thickness. 5. Cut into 2½ x 2½-inch squares; put a slightly rounded teaspoon of filling in center of square and spread (not clear to the edges). 6. Bring two opposite corners together in center or roll up into horns. (Moisten dough with water at sealing point.) 7. Bake in preheated 350° oven for 15 minutes or until done. 8. Cool; then sprinkle with powdered sugar.

Nut Filling:
2 c. ground walnuts (or finely chopped in food processor)
¼ c. evaporated milk or light cream
¾ c. sugar

1. Combine ingredients; do not cook.

Date Filling:
1½ c. dates, sliced
½ to ¾ c. chopped walnuts
⅓ c. water
1½ T. butter

1. Combine ingredients and cook 5 minutes, stirring constantly.

NUT ROLLS

Individual nut rolls from Isabella, PA. Makes 54 nut rolls but Edith Reese always doubled this recipe.

1 to 1½ pkgs. dry yeast
¼ c. lukewarm water
4 c. all-purpose flour
¾ tsp. salt

¼ c. sugar
½ c. Earth Balance shortening
½ c. (1 stick) butter
3 eggs
¾ c. evaporated milk

Mix together:
⅔ c. granulated sugar
⅔ c. all-purpose flour

1. Dissolve yeast in lukewarm water in small bowl; set aside. 2. In large bowl, mix flour, salt and ¼ cup sugar together. 3. Add shortening and butter; mix together with pastry blender or hands until it resembles coarse meal. 4. Beat eggs in medium bowl. 5. Add evaporated milk and yeast mixture to eggs. 6. Add milk-yeast liquid to flour mixture and stir together with large spoon. (Dough will be sticky.) 7. Cover bowl with waxed paper and refrigerate at least 4 hours or overnight. 8. When ready to make nut rolls, take a piece of dough the size of a medium orange and roll out to an 8 or 9-inch circle on surface sprinkled with the granulated sugar and flour mixture. 9. The circle will be thin like pie crust; cut each circle into 6 pie wedges. 10. Spread a slightly rounded teaspoonful of Nut Filling on each wedge and roll up, starting at widest edge. (Don't spread filling clear to the edge.) 11. Roll each nut roll in pure granulated sugar (optional). 12. Place on greased or sprayed cookie sheet and bake in preheated 375° oven for 10 to 12 minutes or until light golden in color.

Nut Filling:
¾ lb. shelled English walnuts (3 c.), ground (or chopped fine in food processor)
¾ c. granulated sugar
⅓ c. hot milk
1½ T. melted butter
½ tsp. vanilla

1. Combine all ingredients and stir together.

NUT ROLLS, KIFLE

Filled pastry crescents, claimed by both Hungarians and Yugoslavs.

6¼ c. all-purpose flour
½ lb. (2 sticks) butter
½ lb. (1 c.) Earth Balance shortening
3 egg yolks
2 c. sour cream
2 sm. cakes compressed yeast
⅛ tsp. salt
Granulated sugar

Nut Filling:
½ lb. (2 c.) ground walnuts (or finely chopped in food processor)
1¼ c. sugar
¼ tsp. cinnamon
½ tsp. maple or vanilla flavoring
3 egg whites, beaten stiff
Powdered sugar

1. Cut butter and shortening into flour until mixture is crumbly. 2. Crumble compressed yeast into sour cream; add to flour mixture, with egg yolks and salt. 3. Mix well with electric mixer on low or medium-low speed, until dough is smooth and leaves side of bowl. 4. Shape into a ball; cover and refrigerate 3 hours or overnight. 5. Make Nut Filling by combining walnuts, sugar, cinnamon and flavoring; fold in beaten egg whites. 6. Sprinkle granulated sugar on pastry board. 7. Divide dough into 6 portions (keep unused portions covered and chilled). 8. Roll one portion to ⅛ inch thick, sprinkling top of dough with additional granulated sugar as needed to prevent sticking. 9. Cut into 2 x 2-inch squares; place about ½ teaspoon Nut Filling along one end of each square and start rolling from that end, curving slightly to form crescent. 10. Place, seam side down, on greased or sprayed cookie sheets. 11. Bake in preheated 350° oven 15 to 20 minutes, until light golden in color. 12. When cool, sprinkle lightly with powdered sugar.

OATMEAL COCONUT COOKIES, PRIDE OF IOWA

Makes about 5 dozen.

1 c. sugar
1 c. packed brown sugar
1 c. Earth Balance shortening
2 eggs
2¼ c. all-purpose flour
1 tsp. baking soda
1 tsp. baking powder
¼ tsp. salt
1 tsp. vanilla
1 c. flaked coconut
½ to 1 c. chopped walnuts or pecans (opt.)
3 c. quick-cooking rolled oats

1. Turn oven dial to 375°. 2. In mixer bowl, cream together sugars and shortening until fluffy. 3. Beat in eggs. 4. Add remaining ingredients; roll into 1¼-inch balls (or drop by teaspoon), placing 2 inches apart on lightly greased or sprayed baking sheets. 5. Using your fingers, flatten balls, rounding ragged edges. 6. Bake in preheated 375° oven 8 to 10 minutes or until light golden brown. 7. Cool on wire racks.

OATMEAL COOKIES

Makes 50 to 70 cookies, depending on size.

¾ to 1 c. sugar
¾ to 1 c. packed brown sugar
¾ c. olive oil
2 eggs
1 tsp. vanilla
1 to 1⅓ c. all-purpose flour
1 tsp. baking powder
½ tsp. salt
1 tsp. cinnamon

¼ tsp. nutmeg
3 c. quick or old-fashioned rolled oats
1 c. raisins (opt.)
1 c. chopped nuts (opt.)

1. Turn oven dial to 350°. 2. In mixer bowl, cream together sugars, shortening, eggs and vanilla; beat thoroughly. 3. Add flour, baking powder, salt and spices; mix well. 4. Stir in oats and remaining ingredients. 5. Drop from teaspoon onto greased or sprayed cookie sheets. 6. Bake in preheated 350° oven 10 to 15 minutes, until done. **Chocolate Chip:** Omit spices and raisins; add 6 ounces (1 cup) or more chocolate chips or butterscotch chips.

OATMEAL COOKIES, NELL'S

Makes 30 to 35 cookies.

1 c. all-purpose flour
¼ c. sugar
½ c. packed brown sugar
½ tsp. baking powder
½ tsp. baking soda
¼ tsp. salt
1 egg (or 2 egg whites)
2 T. milk
½ c. olive oil
1 tsp. cinnamon (or vanilla extract)
2 c. quick or old-fashioned oats, uncooked
¾ to 1 c. raisins (or chopped dates)
½ c. chopped walnuts

1. Turn oven dial to 350°. 2. In mixing bowl, combine first 6 ingredients. 3. Add egg, milk, oil and cinnamon or vanilla; beat until smooth. 4. With large spoon, fold in oats, raisins and nuts. 5. Drop from a fork onto lightly greased cookie sheet, making the size of an English walnut. 6. Bake in preheated 350° oven about 11 to 12 minutes, or until done. (Do not overbake.) 7. Let stand 1 minute on cookie sheet before removing to cooling rack.

OATMEAL REFRIGERATOR COOKIES

1 c. sugar
1 c. packed brown sugar
1 c. Earth Balance shortening
2 eggs
1 tsp. vanilla
1½ c. all-purpose flour
½ tsp. salt
2½ c. rolled oats, packed
½ c. chopped nuts (opt.)

1. In mixer bowl, cream together sugars and shortening. 2. Beat in eggs and vanilla. 3. Add remaining ingredients; mix well. 4. Shape dough into a roll (or rolls), wrap in waxed paper and refrigerate overnight. 5. With sharp knife, slice cookies ¼ inch thick. 6. Bake on ungreased (or lightly sprayed) cookie sheet in preheated 350° oven 10 minutes or until done.

OATMEAL REVEL BARS, CHOCOLATE-FILLED

Scrumptious!

1 c. butter, softened
2 c. packed brown sugar
2 eggs
2 tsp. vanilla
½ tsp. salt (opt.)
2½ c. all-purpose flour (or part whole-wheat flour)
1 tsp. baking soda
3 c. quick or old-fashioned rolled oats (not instant)

<u>Fudge Filling:</u>
2 c. semi-sweet chocolate chips
1 (14-oz.) can (or 1¼ c.) sweetened condensed milk
2 T. butter
1 c. coarsely chopped walnuts
2 tsp. vanilla

1. In mixer bowl, cream together 1 cup butter and the brown sugar; add eggs and first vanilla, mixing well. **2.** Add flour and soda, mixing together; stir in oats with large spoon. **3.** Spread ⅔ of the oat mixture into bottom of greased 15 x 10 x 1-inch jellyroll pan. **4.** In medium saucepan, cook chocolate chips, sweetened condensed milk and 2 tablespoons butter over <u>low</u> heat, stirring frequently, until chocolate is melted. **5.** Remove from heat; stir in nuts and vanilla. **6.** Spread chocolate mixture over oat layer in pan; drop remaining oat mixture by small chunks over Fudge Filling. **7.** Bake in preheated 350° oven about 25 to 35 minutes, or until top is lightly golden; cool, then cut into bars.

ORANGE DROP COOKIES, FROSTED

*Makes approximately 60 to 65 cookies.
Adapted from Geraldine Patterson.*

2 c. sugar
1 c. butter (or ¾ c. light olive oil)
2 lg. eggs (or 3 small eggs)
⅔ c. orange juice concentrate, thawed
1½ T. vinegar
Milk to make ⅔ c.*
4½ c. all-purpose flour (or a little more if needed)
2 tsp. baking powder
1 tsp. baking soda
½ tsp. salt
1 tsp. orange extract (opt.)
Grated rind from 2 oranges (or 2 to 3 tsp. McCormick's orange peel), opt.

1. Turn oven dial to 375°. **2.** Cream together sugar and butter until fluffy. **3.** Add eggs and orange juice; mix well. **4.** Put vinegar in a ⅔-cup measure; fill with milk; let stand a few minutes. **5.** Add dry ingredients alternately with milk mixture. **6.** Drop dough the size of an English walnut by teaspoon on greased cookie sheet. **7.** Bake in preheated 375° oven 8 to 9 minutes or until done; cool on racks and frost. *<u>Note</u>: Buttermilk may be substituted for the vinegar and milk.

<u>Orange Frosting for 65 cookies:</u>
1 stick (½ c.) butter, softened
1 lb. powdered sugar (3¾ to 4 c.)
3 T. orange juice concentrate, thawed
1 tsp. orange extract or vanilla

1. Beat all together until fluffy. If too thick, add a few drops milk or orange juice. <u>Note</u>: To make light orange shade, add a few drops of yellow and red food coloring.

PEANUT BUTTER BALLS

Makes 20 to 30 chocolate-covered peanut butter balls; from Rita Stevenson.

½ c. peanut butter, creamy or chunky
3 T. butter, softened
1 c. powdered sugar (sift if lumpy)
8 oz. chocolate chips or chocolate candy coating

1. In mixing bowl stir together peanut butter and butter. **2.** Gradually add powdered sugar, stirring until combined. **3.** Shape into 1 or 1½-inch balls; place on waxed paper and let stand until dry (about 20 minutes). **4.** Melt chocolate coating; cool slightly. **5.** Dip balls, one at a time, into coating. Let excess coating drip off by lifting balls with a fork; draw the fork across the rim of the dish to remove excess coating. **6.** Place on waxed paper; let stand until coating is firm. **7.** Store in tightly covered container.

PEANUT BUTTER BLOSSOMS

With chocolate kisses on top.

½ c. sugar
½ c. packed brown sugar
½ c. creamy peanut butter
¼ c. butter
¼ c. Earth Balance shortening
1 egg, unbeaten
1½ c. all-purpose flour
¾ tsp. baking soda
½ tsp. baking powder
Granulated sugar
1 (9-oz.) bag milk chocolate candy kisses or stars (or chunks of milk chocolate or miniature Reese cups)

1. Turn oven dial to 375°. **2.** Cream together sugar, brown sugar, peanut butter, butter, shortening and egg until fluffy. **3.** Stir in flour, soda and baking powder. **4.** Shape dough into 1-inch balls; roll in granulated sugar. **5.** Place on ungreased cookie sheet about 2 inches apart. **6.** Bake in preheated 375° oven about 8 minutes. **7.** Immediately press a candy kiss or piece of milk chocolate firmly in center of each cookie. **8.** Return to oven; bake 2 to 5 minutes longer.

PEANUT BUTTER CHOCOLATE CHIP COOKIES

⅓ c. butter
¾ c. peanut butter
½ c. sugar
½ c. packed brown sugar
1 tsp. vanilla
1 egg
1½ c. all-purpose flour
½ tsp. baking powder
¼ tsp. baking soda
¼ tsp. salt
½ c. milk
1 c. (6 oz.) semi-sweet chocolate or milk-chocolate chips
½ c. chopped peanuts (opt.)

1. Turn oven dial to 375°. 2. In mixer bowl, cream together butter, peanut butter, the sugars, vanilla and egg until well mixed. 3. Stir in dry ingredients alternately with milk. 4. Fold in chocolate chips; drop by teaspoonfuls onto ungreased baking sheet. 5. Bake in preheated 375° oven 8 to 10 minutes, until done.

PEANUT BUTTER COOKIES

Makes about 30 cookies.

½ c. sugar
½ c. packed brown sugar
½ c. butter, softened
½ c. peanut butter (creamy or crunchy)
1 lg. egg
½ tsp. vanilla
1⅓ c. all-purpose flour
¾ tsp. baking soda
½ tsp. baking powder
¼ tsp. salt

1. Turn oven dial to 350°. 2. In mixer bowl, beat together first 6 ingredients until fluffy. 3. In small bowl, combine flour, soda, baking powder and salt, stirring together; add to first mixture and mix until well blended. 4. Drop by rounded tablespoonfuls onto lightly greased or sprayed cookie sheet, about 2 inches apart. 5. Crisscross gently with fork dipped in flour to flatten. 6. Bake in preheated 350° oven about 10 to 11 minutes, or until light golden brown. 7. Cool slightly before removing to wire rack. 8. Cool completely; store in airtight container.

PEANUT BUTTER CRUNCHY COOKIES

1 c. sugar
1 c. peanut butter, plain or chunky
1 egg

1. Mix the 3 ingredients together in a bowl. 2. Drop on greased cookie sheet and make crisscross design with fork. 3. Bake in preheated 350° oven for 10 minutes, approximately; cool on racks.

PEANUT BUTTER M&M BARS

From Sarah S. McIlhany.

½ c. sugar
⅓ c. packed brown sugar
⅓ c. peanut butter
¼ c. butter, softened
1 tsp. vanilla
2 T. water
1 egg
1¼ c. all-purpose flour
½ tsp. baking soda
⅛ tsp. salt
½ c. chopped peanuts or walnuts
1 c. M&M plain chocolate candies or part chocolate chips

1. Turn oven dial to 350°; grease or spray and flour 13 x 9-inch baking pan or dish. 2. In mixer bowl, cream together sugars, peanut butter, butter and vanilla. 3. Beat in water and egg. 4. Mix in flour, soda and salt. 5. Stir in peanuts and candies; spread dough in prepared pan. 6. Bake in preheated 350° oven 20 minutes, until light golden. 7. Cool completely; then cut into bars.

PEANUT BUTTER-OATMEAL COOKIES

1 c. sugar
⅔ c. packed brown sugar
1 c. (2 sticks) butter or Earth Balance shortening
2 eggs
1 c. peanut butter
1 tsp. vanilla
2 c. all-purpose flour
2 tsp. baking soda
½ tsp. salt
1 c. oats (quick-cooking or old-fashioned, not instant)
½ c. chopped nuts (opt.)
1 to 2 c. semi-sweet chocolate chips (opt.)

1. Turn oven dial to 350°. 2. Cream together the sugars, butter, eggs, peanut butter and vanilla until creamy and well blended. 3. Add remaining ingredients, stirring together. 4. Drop dough by rounded tablespoonfuls onto ungreased cookie sheet, about 2 inches apart. 5. Bake in preheated 350° oven 10 to 12 minutes or until light golden brown. 6. Cool 1 minute; remove from cookie sheet to cooling racks.

PINEAPPLE COOKIES, EGGLESS

From Margaret Stiffler; makes a lot.

1 c. sugar
1 c. packed brown sugar
1 c. butter or Earth Balance shortening
1½ tsp. vanilla
1 (20-oz.) can crushed pineapple, partially drained
1 c. (6 oz.) butterscotch chips (opt.)
4 c. all-purpose flour

1½ tsp. baking soda
½ tsp. baking powder
½ tsp. salt
1 c. chopped nuts (opt.)
1 c. flaked coconut (opt.)

1. Cream together sugars and butter. 2. Add vanilla, partially drained crushed pineapple and butterscotch chips. 3. Add remaining ingredients and mix well. 4. Refrigerate about 1 hour. 5. Drop on ungreased cookie sheet, about 2 inches apart. 6. Bake in preheated 400° oven 8 to 10 minutes, or until done.

PINEAPPLE-FILLED COOKIES

½ c. sugar
1 c. packed brown sugar
1 c. butter
1 egg
3 egg yolks
2 tsp. vanilla
⅓ c. milk
1 T. vinegar
1 tsp. baking soda
5 c. all-purpose flour
¾ tsp. salt
2 tsp. baking powder

1. Cream together sugars and butter. 2. Add eggs and vanilla; beat until fluffy. 3. In a cup, mix together milk, vinegar and soda; add to fluffy mixture. 4. Add 2 cups flour, the salt and baking powder; mix well. 5. Remove bowl from mixer and with large spoon, stir in remaining flour. (Dough may be used immediately, or chilled.) 6. Divide dough into portions; roll ⅛ to ¼ inch thick on lightly floured surface. 7. With 2½-inch cookie cutter (or top of water glass), cut out cookies. 8. Put slightly rounded teaspoonful of filling on center of half the cookies; top with the remaining cookies, using fingers (or tines of fork) to seal edges. 9. Make a hole in top of each cookie to vent. 10. Place 1½ inches apart on lightly greased cookie sheets. 11. Bake on middle shelf of preheated 375° oven 9 to 10 minutes, or until light golden in color. 12. Remove cookies to cooling racks.

Pineapple Filling:
⅔ c. sugar
2 T. cornstarch, packed level
⅛ tsp. salt (opt.)
1 (20-oz.) can crushed pineapple, including juice
1 T. butter
1 T. lemon juice

1. In medium pan, stir together sugar, cornstarch and salt. 2. Add crushed pineapple; bring to a full boil, stirring. 3. Lower heat and simmer 1 minute. 4. Remove from heat and add butter and lemon juice; cool.

PIZZELLES

Adapted from Ruth Flick. Makes about 60.

6 eggs
1½ c. sugar
1 c. olive oil
2 T. anise or lemon extract or vanilla or ½ oz. anise flavoring (or ½ T. oil of anise or 2 to 3 T. anise seed)
3 c. all-purpose flour
⅛ tsp. salt

1. Beat eggs well in mixer bowl. 2. Add sugar gradually, beating together. 3. Add oil gradually, then flavoring and beat until smooth. 4. Add flour, a little at a time, and salt; beat until well blended. 5. Drop by teaspoonfuls onto hot pizzelle iron; cook until done according to manufacturer's directions. <u>Note</u>: Brush pizzelle grids with oil, then close and preheat for 5 minutes before making pizzelles.

PUMPKIN BARS

From Betty Geneviva.

2 c. all-purpose flour
2 tsp. baking powder
1 tsp. baking soda
1½ to 2 tsp. cinnamon or 2 tsp. pumpkin pie spice
½ tsp. salt
1¾ c. sugar
2 c. pumpkin (15 or 16 oz.)
1 c. olive oil
4 eggs
1 c. coarsely chopped nuts

1. Mix ingredients all together. 2. Pour into greased jellyroll pan (15½ x 10½ x 1 inches) or a large cookie sheet with sides. 3. Bake in preheated 325° oven 25 or 30 minutes. 4. Frost with Cream Cheese Frosting.

<u>Cream Cheese Frosting:</u>
3 oz. cream cheese (room temp.)
¼ c. (½ stick) butter (room temp.)
1 tsp. vanilla
1 T. milk or cream
3 c. powdered sugar

1. Combine ingredients and beat until smooth.

PUMPKIN DROP COOKIES, FROSTED

Makes 25 to 30 soft cookies that stay moist.

½ c. sugar
¼ c. olive oil
1 egg
½ c. pumpkin
1 c. flour
2 tsp. baking powder
¼ tsp. salt
1¼ tsp. cinnamon

¼ tsp. nutmeg
⅛ tsp. ginger
½ c. raisins or cut-up dates
⅓ to ½ c. chopped nuts (opt.)

1. Beat sugar, oil, egg and pumpkin together. **2.** Add dry ingredients; then stir in raisins and nuts. **3.** Drop by rounded teaspoonfuls on greased cookie sheets. **4.** Bake in preheated 350° oven for 11 minutes, or until done. **5.** Frost when cool, if desired.

Frosting:
1 T. butter, melted
1 c. powdered sugar
⅛ tsp. salt
½ tsp. vanilla
½ T. milk (approx.)

1. In small container, melt butter. **2.** Add remaining ingredients; add extra milk, drop by drop, until desired consistency is reached.

PUMPKIN OATMEAL COOKIES

Chewy cookie stays soft.

⅔ c. sugar
1 c. packed brown sugar
1 stick (½ c.) butter
½ c. olive oil
1 egg
1 tsp. vanilla
1 c. pumpkin
2½ c. quick or old-fashioned oats, uncooked
1½ c. all-purpose flour
1 tsp. cinnamon
1 tsp. baking soda
½ tsp. salt
1 c. raisins or cut-up dates (opt.)
1 c. coarsely chopped nuts (opt.)
1 c. chocolate chips (opt.)

1. Cream together sugars and butter thoroughly. **2.** Add oil, egg, vanilla and pumpkin; beat well. **3.** Add dry ingredients and nuts; then divide dough in 2 bowls, adding fruit to one part and chocolate chips in the other part, if desired. **4.** Drop by rounded teaspoonfuls on greased cookie sheets. **5.** Bake in preheated 350° oven 11 minutes, or until firm and lightly browned. **Note**: If dough is too soft, add a small amount of flour or oats.

RAISIN-FILLED COOKIES

Makes 60 or more. Don't skimp on the rounded teaspoon of filling.

⅓ c. milk
½ T. vinegar
1 c. sugar
1 c. packed brown sugar
¾ c. olive oil or 1 c. butter

3 eggs (or 2 lg. eggs + 1 egg yolk)
1 tsp. salt
1 tsp. baking soda
2 tsp. baking powder
2 tsp. vanilla
6⅓ c. all-purpose flour, divided (approx.)
Raisin Filling (recipe follows)

1. In small bowl, stir together milk and vinegar; set aside. **2.** Make Raisin Filling; pour into a glass or stainless steel oblong cake pan to partially cool. **3.** Cream together sugars and oil until fluffy; add eggs and sour milk mixture, mixing well. **4.** Add salt, soda, baking powder, vanilla and 3 cups flour; beat well. **5.** Remove bowl from mixer; with large spoon, stir in remaining 3⅓ cups flour. (Dough may be used immediately or chilled.) **6.** On floured surface, place dough the size of a grapefruit; roll out with floured rolling pin to less than ¼-inch thickness. **7.** With 2½-inch cookie cutter (or top of water glass), cut out cookies, re-flouring surface and rolling pin frequently. **8.** Place cookies 1 inch apart on greased cookie sheet. **9.** Put rounded teaspoonful of filling on center of cookies; top with another cookie, sealing edges with fingers (or tines of a fork). **10.** Make a hole in top of each cookie to vent. **11.** Bake on middle shelf of preheated 375° oven 9 minutes, or until light golden in color. **12.** Remove cookies to cooling rack.

Raisin Filling:
1 c. sugar
2 T. cornstarch, packed level
⅛ tsp. salt
2 c. cold water
15 to 16 oz. raisins (2½ c.)
1 T. butter
1 c. chopped nuts (opt.)

1. In medium saucepan, stir together sugar, cornstarch and salt. **2.** Add cold water and stir well. **3.** Add raisins and butter; bring to a boil, stirring frequently. **4.** Simmer gently until raisins are plump and liquid is clear (just a few minutes). **5.** Cool partially; then add nuts.

RAISIN JUMBLE COOKIES

From Bonnie Bash. Makes 60 to 80 cookies, depending on size. Delicious!

2 c. raisins
1 c. water
1 tsp. baking soda
1 c. sugar
1 c. packed brown sugar
¾ c. olive oil or 1 c. Earth Balance shortening
3 eggs
4½ c. all-purpose flour
½ tsp. salt
1 tsp. cinnamon
¼ tsp. nutmeg
¼ tsp. allspice
1 to 1½ c. chopped walnuts
½ c. additional flour, if needed

1. In saucepan, boil raisins and water together for 5 minutes. (Don't let them boil dry.) Cool 15 minutes; then stir in baking soda. Set aside. **2.** Cream together sugars and oil in large bowl. **3.** Add eggs, one at a time, beating after each addition. **4.** Stir in raisin mixture, including liquid. **5.** Add dry ingredients, then nuts; if dough is not thick enough, add the additional ½ cup flour. **6.** Drop by tablespoonfuls onto greased or sprayed cookie sheets, 2 inches apart. **7.** Bake in preheated 350° oven 10 to 12 minutes, until done.

RANGER COOKIES

From Wava Fair.

1 c. sugar
1 c. packed brown sugar
1 c. butter or Earth Balance shortening
2 eggs
1 tsp. vanilla
2½ c. all-purpose flour
½ tsp. baking powder
1 tsp. baking soda
¼ tsp. salt
1 c. flaked coconut
1 c. oats, uncooked
1 c. Rice Krispies or other crisp cereal
1 c. chopped walnuts (opt.)
1 c. butterscotch chips (opt.)

1. Turn oven dial to 350°. **2.** Cream together first 5 ingredients until fluffy. **3.** Add remaining ingredients, stirring together well. **4.** Form into balls the size of an English walnut; place 2 inches apart onto ungreased cookie sheets. **5.** Bake in preheated 350° oven 11 to 12 minutes or until golden in color; let stand ½ to 1 minute before removing to cooling racks. **6.** Cool completely; store in airtight container. **Note**: If cookies are too flat after baking, add a little more flour to remaining dough.

REFRIGERATOR BUTTERSCOTCH COOKIES

Also called "Icebox Cookies."

1 c. (2 sticks) butter or Earth Balance, softened
2 c. packed brown sugar
2 eggs
1 tsp. vanilla
4 c. all-purpose flour
1 tsp. baking soda
1 tsp. cream of tartar
½ tsp. salt
1 c. finely chopped walnuts or pecans

1. In mixer bowl, cream together butter and brown sugar until light and fluffy. **2.** Add eggs and vanilla; beat well. **3.** Add dry ingredients and mix well. **4.** Add nuts; mix well. **5.** Shape into rolls and wrap in waxed paper, plastic wrap or foil. **6.** Refrigerate until firm, several hours or overnight (or store in

refrigerator 7 to 10 days, baking as needed). **7.** Preheat oven to 375°; with sharp knife, cut as many cookies as desired, about ⅛ inch thick. **8.** Place slices, 2 inches apart, on ungreased baking sheets; bake 8 to 10 minutes, or until lightly browned. **9.** Remove to cooling racks.

RICE KRISPIES BARS

Do not use hard, dried-up marshmallows.

¼ c. butter
1 (10½-oz.) pkg. marshmallows (about 40 lg. or 4 c. miniature marshmallows)
5 to 6 c. Rice Krispies, Cocoa Krispies or Honey Comb cereal

1. Melt butter in 3 or 4-quart saucepan over low heat. **2.** Add marshmallows and stir until completely melted; remove from heat. **3.** Add cereal; stir until well coated. **4.** With buttered fingers, press warm mixture evenly into buttered 13 x 9-inch pan. **5.** When cool, cut into squares. **Peanut Butter Bars or Balls**: Use only 2 tablespoons butter; add ¼ cup peanut butter with marshmallows. Follow above recipe, or shape into 12 balls with greased hands (after it cools slightly). **Variation**: 1 cup plain or peanut M & M candies may be added, after adding cereal. **Chocolate Topped**: Melt 2 cups chocolate chips and 1 tablespoon butter together in saucepan over low heat, stirring constantly, until smooth. Spread evenly over cereal mixture. Let stand until firm.

SPRINGERLE COOKIES

Very hard cookies with design on each one.

4 c. all-purpose flour
1 tsp. baking powder
½ tsp. salt (or less)
4 eggs
1½ tsp. anise extract (or ¼ tsp. anise oil)
2 c. granulated sugar
2 tsp. grated lemon peel (opt.)
Powdered sugar or flour (to roll cookies on)

1. Sift flour, baking powder and salt together twice; set aside. **2.** In large mixer bowl, beat eggs at high speed for 5 minutes, until thick and lemon-colored. **3.** Add anise flavoring. **4.** At medium speed, gradually add sugar, ¼ cup at a time, beating after each addition. Continue to beat until thoroughly mixed, about 10 minutes, occasionally cleaning sides of bowl with rubber scraper. **5.** Stir in flour mixture and grated lemon peel (with large spoon), mixing well. **6.** Cover dough and refrigerate 4 hours, or overnight. (Refrigerate springerle rolling pin also.) **7.** Lightly grease 2 large cookie sheets. **8.** Divide dough into 3 portions; keep refrigerated until ready to use. **9.** Roll each portion ¼ to ½ inch thick on surface which has been lightly sprinkled with powdered sugar or flour (or both), with regular rolling pin. **10.** Remove springerle pin from refrigerator; coat lightly with powdered sugar or flour. **11.** Slowly roll pin once, firmly and evenly, to emboss designs.

12. Cut out the little square with floured knife to make individual cookies. **13.** With spatula, lift cookies gently onto prepared cookie sheets, placing ½ inch apart. **14.** Let stand, uncovered, at room temperature <u>overnight</u>. **15.** Next day, preheat oven to 325°. Bake cookies 15 to 30 minutes (one sheet at a time), until just light golden in color. **16.** Remove to wire rack and cool completely. **17.** When cool, store in tightly covered cookie jar or container for 1 to 3 weeks (or can serve immediately). Makes about 54 cookies. <u>Note</u>: Instead of using anise extract or anise oil, 1 tablespoon anise seed may be sprinkled on each greased cookie sheet.

STAINED-GLASS COOKIES (No-Bake)

Also called "Cathedral Window Cookies' and 'Candy Logs."

1 (12-oz.) pkg. chocolate chips
½ c. (1 stick) butter
1 (10½-oz.) pkg. colored miniature marshmallows (5 to 6 c.)
1 c. chopped nuts
1 c. flaked coconut or graham cracker crumbs

1. Melt chocolate chips and butter over medium-low heat. **2.** When melted, remove from heat and cool 10 to 15 minutes. **3.** Pour over marshmallows in bowl; stir in nuts. Divide into 3 portions. **4.** When firm enough to handle, sprinkle coconut or graham cracker crumbs on three separate pieces of waxed paper. **5.** Shape each portion into a long log; roll in coconut or crumbs. **6.** Roll up in waxed paper and refrigerate several hours. **7.** Slice as needed; keep in refrigerator.

SUGAR COOKIES, CHRISTMAS I

A crisp, rolled-out cookie. Really rolls out well.

1 c. butter
2 c. sugar
4 egg yolks
3 c. all-purpose flour
2 tsp. baking powder
¼ tsp. salt
2 T. milk
1 to 1½ tsp. vanilla
½ tsp. almond extract (opt.)

1. In mixer bowl, cream together butter and sugar. **2.** Add egg yolks and mix well. **3.** Add flour, baking powder and salt alternately with milk and flavorings, stirring well. **4.** Place waxed paper or plastic wrap over dough and chill for at least 1 hour. **5.** On lightly floured surface, roll out a portion of dough the size of a grapefruit to ⅛ or ¼ inch thickness. **6.** Cut out with cookie cutters; bake on lightly greased or sprayed cookie sheets in middle or upper third of preheated 350° oven for 10 minutes or until light golden (not brown). **7.** Cool on wire racks; then frost, if desired.

<u>Frosting:</u>
1 lb. (3½ to 4 c.) powdered sugar
⅔ c. butter, softened or melted

4 T. milk
1 tsp. vanilla
Food coloring to tint

1. In mixer bowl, combine all ingredients, except food coloring; beat with electric mixer. **2.** Divide frosting for different colors.

SUGAR COOKIES, CHRISTMAS II

A crisp, rolled-out cookie that rolls out well.

1 c. butter, or Earth Balance shortening
1½ c. sugar
2 eggs
2 tsp. vanilla
3½ c. all-purpose flour
1 tsp. baking powder
½ tsp. salt

1. In mixer bowl, cream together butter and sugar until fluffy. **2.** Add eggs, one at a time, beating after each addition. **3.** Add vanilla; then add dry ingredients gradually, mixing only until blended after each addition. **4.** Chill thoroughly. **5.** On lightly floured surface, roll out a portion of dough the size of a grapefruit to ¼-inch thickness. **6.** Cut out with cookie cutters; bake on lightly greased or sprayed cookie sheets in middle or upper third of preheated 375° oven for 6 to 8 minutes, (Watch carefully to prevent cookies from getting brown.) **7.** Cool on wire racks; then frost, if desired.

SUGAR COOKIES, CHRISTMAS III

These are between a soft and a crisp, rolled-out cookie.

1 c. butter
1 c. sugar
2 eggs
½ c. sour cream
1½ tsp. vanilla
½ tsp. salt
1 tsp. baking powder
1 tsp. baking soda
4 c. all-purpose flour (approx.)

1. In large bowl, cream together butter and sugar. **2.** Add eggs, sour cream and vanilla; mix well. **3.** Add dry ingredients; dough should be rather stiff. **4.** Chill; roll dough ⅛ to ¼-inch thickness on lightly floured surface. Cut out with cookie cutters. **5.** Bake in preheated 375° oven for 8 minutes on lightly greased cookie sheet. **6.** Cool on wire racks. **7.** Ice cookies with frosting, if desired. <u>**Almond or Anise**</u>: Add 1 teaspoon almond or anise flavoring with the vanilla.

SUGAR COOKIES, CHRISTMAS WREATHS

Rolled out.

¾ c. butter
½ c. sugar
1 tsp. grated orange rind
1 egg
2 c. all-purpose flour
¼ tsp. salt
1 egg white
2 T. sugar
Green sugar
Red cinnamon candies (small)

1. In mixer bowl, cream butter; add first sugar, orange rind and egg, beating until creamy. **2.** Add flour and salt; mix well. **3.** Chill for several hours or until firm enough to roll. **4.** Roll to ⅛-inch thickness on lightly floured surface; cut with floured doughnut cutter. **5.** Place wreaths on greased or sprayed cookie sheet. **6.** Beat egg white until foamy; add 2 tablespoons sugar gradually and beat until stiff. **7.** Brush cookies with mixture; sprinkle green sugar over wreaths and decorate with red cinnamon candies. **8.** Bake in preheated 400° oven 10 to 12 minutes.

SUGAR COOKIES, DROP (Jack's)

Chewy-crisp and delicious. Makes 30 cookies.

½ c. (1 stick) butter, or Earth Balance shortening
1 c. sugar
1 egg (or 2 egg yolks)
1 T. milk or cream
½ to 1 tsp. vanilla
1¾ c. all-purpose flour
1 tsp. baking powder
¼ tsp. salt

1. Turn oven dial to 375°. **2.** In mixer bowl, cream together butter, sugar, egg, milk and vanilla. **3.** Add remaining ingredients and mix well; drop dough the size of English walnuts on lightly greased or sprayed cookie sheet, 1 inch apart. **4.** If desired, press with tines of fork dipped in cold water or flatten with bottom of drinking glass dipped in flour. **5.** Bake in preheated 375° oven 8 to 10 minutes; cool on wire rack. **Butterscotch**: Use butter and 1 cup packed brown sugar instead of white sugar. **Chocolate**: Add ¼ to ⅓ cup unsweetened dry cocoa or 2 ounces (2 squares) melted unsweetened chocolate before adding flour. Bake at 325°. **Lemon or Orange**: Use lemon or orange extract instead of vanilla. 1 or 2 teaspoons grated lemon or orange rind may be added and pineapple or orange juice may be used instead of milk, if desired.

SUGAR COOKIES, MELTAWAYS

Makes 45 to 50 cookies that melt in your mouth.

½ c. sugar
½ c. powdered sugar
½ c. (1 stick) butter, softened
½ c. olive oil
1 egg
1 tsp. vanilla
2⅓ c. all-purpose flour
½ tsp. baking soda
½ tsp. cream of tartar
½ tsp. salt
½ c. sugar (opt.)
½ tsp. cinnamon (opt.)

1. In mixer bowl, cream together first 3 ingredients until fluffy. **2.** Add oil, egg and vanilla; beat until creamy. **3.** Add flour, soda, cream of tartar and salt; mix together. **4.** Chill at least 2 hours in refrigerator or 1 hour in freezer. **5.** Shape into balls using 1 level measuring tablespoon dough for each cookie. **6.** If desired, roll in ½ cup sugar (or sugar mixed with cinnamon). **7.** Place balls 2 inches apart on ungreased (or lightly sprayed) cookie sheets; flatten cookies slightly with a fork, meat tenderizer or bottom of a drinking glass. **8.** Bake in preheated 375° oven about 9 to 11 minutes or until set, but not brown. Do not overbake. **Note**: May also be chilled in long rolls; slice and bake.

SUGAR COOKIES, SOFT (Drop)

From Findlay, Ohio. Makes 75 cookies.

1 c. sugar
1 c. packed brown sugar
1 c. (2 sticks) butter or Earth Balance shortening
2 eggs
1 tsp. baking soda
1 c. buttermilk, sour milk or sour cream
4 c. all-purpose flour
2 tsp. baking powder
½ to 1 tsp. salt
¼ tsp. nutmeg
1 tsp. lemon or coconut flavoring
⅓ c. sugar
⅓ c. powdered sugar

1. Turn oven dial to 375°. **2.** In mixer bowl, cream together first 4 ingredients until fluffy. **3.** Dissolve soda in buttermilk; set aside. **4.** In another bowl, combine flour, baking powder, salt and nutmeg. **5.** Add flour mixture to creamed mixture alternately with buttermilk and flavoring. **6.** Combine ⅓ cup sugar and ⅓ cup powdered sugar in a small bowl. **7.** Drop dough by teaspoons into sugar mixture, coating with sugar. **8.** Place on greased or sprayed cookie sheet and bake in preheated 375° oven about 10 to 12 minutes or until done.

SUGAR COOKIES, SOFT (Rolled-out)

From Jean Moyer.

2 c. sugar
1 c. (2 sticks) butter
3 eggs
1 tsp. baking soda, dissolved in ½ c. sour milk (sweet milk with ½ T. vinegar in it)
2 to 3 tsp. vanilla or lemon extract
4 to 5½ c. all-purpose flour
½ tsp. salt
½ tsp. nutmeg (opt.)

1. Cream together sugar, butter and eggs until fluffy, scraping down sides of bowl once. 2. Combine milk and vinegar; dissolve soda in it. 3. Add flour, salt (and nutmeg, if used) alternately with milk and flavoring. 4. Chill dough several hours or overnight. 5. Roll dough on floured surface ¼ to ½ inch thick. 6. Sprinkle rolled-out dough with sugar and cut with cookie cutters. 7. Place cookies on greased or sprayed cookie sheet 1 or 2 inches apart; bake in preheated 350° oven 8 to 10 minutes, or until cookies are set, but not brown. 8. Cool completely; store in airtight container.

SUGAR COOKIES, STIR & DROP

2 eggs
⅔ c. light olive oil
¾ c. sugar
2 t. vanilla
1 t. lemon zest or grated lemon peel (opt.)
2 c. flour
2 t. baking powder
½ t. salt

1. In mixing bowl, beat eggs, olive oil, sugar, vanilla and lemon zest together. 2. Add dry ingredients and stir. 3. Drop dough by rounded teaspoonfuls 2 inches apart onto greased baking sheets. 4. Flatten cookies with the bottom of a drinking glass dipped in water, then in additional sugar (or use colored sprinkles). 5. Bake in preheated 350° oven for 8 to 10 minutes; cool on baking sheets for 2 minutes before removing to cooling racks. 6. Store in airtight containers when cool or freeze. **Note**: If baking cookies one sheet at a time, stir the mixture between each batch.

TASSIES (Pecan Tarts)

Makes 18 to 24.

3 oz. cream cheese, softened
1 stick (½ c.) butter
¼ c. sugar (opt.)
1 c. all-purpose flour

Filling:
1 T. butter
¾ c. packed brown sugar
1 egg

1 tsp. vanilla
⅛ tsp. salt (or less)
⅔ c. chopped pecans or walnuts

1. Combine pastry ingredients, mixing together well. 2. Dough may be chilled for 1 hour or longer, or may be used immediately; put a slightly rounded tablespoon dough in each of 24 miniature muffin cups (dividing dough equally). 3. Press dough against bottom and sides to form tarts; set aside. 4. Turn oven dial to 325°. 5. In small saucepan, melt 1 tablespoon butter; remove from heat. 6. Add remaining filling ingredients and stir together. 7. Put a slightly rounded teaspoon of filling into unbaked shells, dividing equally. 8. Bake in preheated 325° oven for 25 minutes, until light golden brown. 9. Cool 5 minutes; then remove from pans.

TASSIES WALNUT CHOCOLATE FILLING

6 oz. (1 c.) semi-sweet chocolate chips
⅓ c. sugar
1 T. milk
1 T. butter
1 tsp. vanilla
1 lg. egg
½ c. chopped walnuts

1. In top of double boiler over boiling water; melt chocolate chips; stir until smooth. 2. Add sugar, milk, butter and vanilla; stir until butter melts. 3. Remove pan from double boiler. 4. In a mixing bowl, beat egg. 5. Very gradually, stir chocolate mixture into the egg; add nuts. 6. Fill the tart crusts ½ full. (Filling will raise during baking.) 7. Bake in preheated 325° oven 20 to 25 minutes. Do not overbake. 8. Cool tassies about 10 minutes in pan; then remove to wire rack.

TINY TARTS

From Sarah Stevenson McIlhany. Makes 24.

3 oz. cream cheese, softened
½ c. (1 stick) butter
1 c. all-purpose flour
Cherry pie filling

1. Combine cream cheese and butter; blend in flour and chill 1 hour. 2. Shape into balls and press into miniature muffin cups. 3. Bake in preheated 325° oven for 15 minutes. (Keep checking so they don't get too brown.) 4. Fill tarts with cherry pie filling (1 to 3 cherries per tart) and top with a little whipped cream or whipped topping.

TURTLE SNAPPER PECAN COOKIES

Makes 24 turtle cookies.

½ c. (1 stick) butter
½ c. packed brown sugar
1 egg

1 egg yolk (reserve white)
¼ tsp. vanilla
⅛ tsp. maple flavoring (opt.)
1¾ c. all-purpose flour
¼ tsp. baking soda
⅛ tsp. salt
60 pecan halves, cut in half lengthwise

Frosting:
½ c. chocolate chips
3 T. cream or evaporated milk
¼ c. powdered sugar
1 T. butter, softened

1. Cream together butter and brown sugar. 2. Blend in egg, egg yolk and flavorings. 3. Add dry ingredients gradually; mix well. 4. Chill dough. 5. Arrange pecans in groups of five on greased or sprayed cookie sheets to resemble head and legs of turtle. 6. Shape dough by level measuring tablespoonfuls into balls; dip bottom of balls into reserved egg white. 7. Press balls lightly onto nut arrangements so tips will show when baked. 8. Bake in preheated 350° oven about 10 minutes, until light golden; cool; then frost. 9. To make frosting, melt chocolate chips and cream together in small saucepan over low heat. 10. Remove from heat; add powdered sugar and butter, mixing well. Frost tops (or dip tops of cookies into frosting).

YUMMY CHOCOLATE-PECAN BARS

From Sally Coates.

Bottom Layer:
1½ c. flour
¼ c. brown sugar, packed
¼ c. softened butter or reg. Smart Balance Spread

Top Layer:
3 large eggs
¾ c. white sugar
¾ c. light corn syrup
2 T. melted butter
1 tsp. vanilla
1¾ c. semi-sweet chocolate chips
1½ c. coarsely chopped pecans

1. Mix flour, brown sugar and softened butter with electric mixer until well blended. 2. Press into a greased 9x13-inch pan and bake 12 to 15 minutes in 350° preheated oven. 3. Blend eggs with wire whip. 4. Blend in white sugar, corn syrup, melted butter and vanilla. 5. Stir in chips and pecans; pour over cookie crust. 6. Bake in 350° preheated oven 20 to 30 minutes, until set and lightly golden brown. 7. Cut into bars while still slightly warm.

Chapter 24

Pies

JORDYN MCADAMS AND SCHYLER MARCIN

PIES

Smart Balance Shortening or Earth Balance Shortening may be interchanged. If you wonder why we don't use Crisco, please read Chapter 1.

PIE CRUST, AVALON

The nice thing about Avalon Pie crust is that if it breaks up and doesn't roll out right, you can put it back into a ball and roll it out again.

For 1 (9 or 10-inch) pie shell:
1 c. all-purpose flour
1 tsp. sugar
¼ tsp. salt
⅓ c. + 1 T. Earth Balance shortening
½ egg (2 T.)
2 T. very cold water
½ T. vinegar

Follow basic instructions, using 3 tablespoons of the egg-liquid mixture. Only if needed, use a few more drops of egg liquid or ice water.

For 3 (9 or 10-inch) pie shells:
2½ c. all-purpose flour
1 T. sugar
½ tsp. salt
1 c. Earth Balance shortening
1 egg
3 T. very cold water
1 T. vinegar

Follow basic instructions, using all of the egg-liquid mixture. (Sometimes it takes a few drops of additional ice water.)

For 2 (9 or 10-inch) double-crust pies plus 1 small shell:
3 c. all-purpose flour
1 T. sugar
½ tsp. salt
1¼ c. Earth Balance shortening
1 egg (large)
¼ c. very cold water
1 T. vinegar

Follow basic instructions, using all of the egg-liquid mixture, or as much as is needed. If not enough, add a few drops of ice water.

For 5 (9-inch) pie shells:
4 c. all-purpose flour
1½ T. sugar
1 tsp. salt
1¾ c. Earth Balance shortening
1 egg (large)
½ c. very cold water
1½ T. vinegar

Follow basic instructions, using about ⅔ cup of the egg-liquid mixture, or as much as is needed. If not enough, add a few drops of ice water.

For 5 double-crust or 8 or 9 (9-inch) pie shells:
7½ c. all-purpose flour
3 T. sugar
1½ tsp. salt
3 c. Earth Balance shortening
2 eggs
⅔ c. very cold water
3 T. vinegar

Follow basic instructions, using all the egg-liquid mixture. If more is needed, add a few drops of ice water.

BASIC INSTRUCTIONS FOR AVALON PIE CRUST

1. Combine flour, sugar and salt in bowl. 2. Add Earth Balance shortening; mix with pastry blender, fingers or food processor until it resembles coarse meal. 3. In a small bowl, combine egg, cold water and vinegar, mixing together with fork or wire whip. 4. Pour designated amount of egg-liquid mixture over flour-shortening mixture, stirring gently with a fork until dough clings together. Only if needed, use a few more drops of egg-liquid mixture or ice water. 5. Chill 30 minutes, or roll out immediately, on floured surface. (If using a Tupperware pastry sheet, wet underneath side so it will lay flat.) 6. Using a long narrow spatula under dough, lift and turn pie crust over several times, flouring surface and rolling pin each time. Roll until crust is large enough to fit pan for a bottom crust. If making a shell or a top crust, roll it 1 inch larger than the pie plate. 7. For a shell, fit pastry into pie plate, leaving 1-inch rim beyond edge of plate; fold under edge of crust and flute edge all around. 8. For double-crust pie, trim lower crust even with rim of pie plate. Cut slits in top crust. Place over top pie. Trim ½ inch beyond edge; tuck top crust under edge of lower crust. Flute edge all around.

BASIC TIPS FOR AVALON PIE CRUST

1. When baking a pie shell, prick shell several times with a fork. Bake in preheated 450° oven until desired color. Watch carefully; if crust raises up while baking, prick with fork in that area. 2. Use room-temperature Earth Balance shortening. 3. Use either white or cider vinegar. 4. Pie shells may be kept 7 to 10 days in refrigerator before baking. Stack unbaked shells with waxed paper between each pan. Put stack of shells in a large plastic bag and refrigerate (or freeze). 5. To prevent edge of crust from becoming too brown in oven, fold a strip of foil around rim of crust, covering fluted edge. Remove foil the last 15 minutes of baking.

PIE CRUST, CONVENTIONAL

*Makes pastry for 1 (9-inch) double-crust pie
or 2 (9-inch) shells.*

1¾ c. all-purpose flour
½ tsp. salt
⅔ c. Earth Balance shortening
⅓ c. ice cold water

1. In bowl, combine flour and salt; cut in shortening with pastry blender until mixture resembles coarse meal. **2.** Add just enough ice water so that dough holds together. **3.** Roll half the dough out on floured surface dusting rolling pin with flour; roll dough 1 inch larger than pie pan. **4.** Repeat with remaining half of dough.

PIE CRUST, CONVENTIONAL, ONE SHELL

Makes one 9-inch shell.

1 c. all-purpose flour
¼ tsp. salt
⅓ c. Earth Balance shortening
2 to 2½ T. ice cold water

PIE CRUST (Cookie-Sweet Pastry)

*Makes 1 very large pie shell or 2 small 8-inch pie shells.
Rolls out nicely.*

1½ c. all-purpose flour
2 T. powdered sugar, packed level
½ tsp. salt
½ c. Earth Balance shortening
1 egg yolk
2 T. cold water

1. In bowl, combine flour, powdered sugar and salt; work in shortening until very fine. **2.** In small bowl, mix together egg yolk and cold water; add to flour mixture, adding a bit more cold water, if necessary. **3.** Roll lightly on floured surface to fit into pie plate. **4.** Flute edge and prick with fork several places. **5.** Bake in preheated 425° oven 12 to 15 minutes or until golden in color.

PIE CRUST (Food Processor)

*From Mrs. Jean Moyer. Makes enough pastry for 1
double-crust pie and 1 small shell.*

2 c. all-purpose flour
¼ tsp. salt
½ c. (1 stick) butter, cut up (cold)
3 T. Earth Balance shortening or olive oil
¼ c. ice water

1. Put all ingredients in food processor in order given, before turning it on. **2.** Run processor until lumps are formed, watching very carefully; it does not take long! **3.** Remove dough from processor and roll out on floured surface into pie crusts.

PIE CRUST, GRAHAM CRACKER

*Makes 1 (9-inch) crumb shell (or 10-inch shell
or 13 x 9-inch cake pan).*

1 (⅓-lb.) pack graham crackers (about 1½ to 1 2/3 c. crumbs)
¼ c. sugar or honey
¼ c. softened or melted butter

1. Roll graham crackers with rolling pin into fine crumbs (or make crumbs in food processor). **2.** In bowl, combine crumbs, sugar and softened butter; blend well with fingers, fork or pastry blender. **3.** Press crumbs firmly and evenly against bottom and sides of pie plate. Do not spread on rim. **4.** Crust is now ready to fill, or it may be chilled in refrigerator, or frozen. <u>Or for a crisper crust</u>, bake in preheated 375° oven 8 to 10 minutes; cool.

PIE CRUST, GRAHAM CRACKER (Chocolate)

Makes a 9-inch pie shell.

1¼ c. graham cracker crumbs, packed
¼ c. unsweetened cocoa
¼ c. sugar
⅓ c. butter, melted

1. Combine graham cracker crumbs, cocoa and sugar in bowl. **2.** Add melted butter; mix well. **3.** Press firmly onto bottom and up the sides of 9-inch pie plate. **4.** Chill. (Or, bake in preheated 350° oven 8 to 10 minutes; cool.)

PIE CRUST, GRAHAM CRACKER (Microwave)

Makes a 9 or 10-inch crumb shell.

⅓ c. butter
2 T. sugar
1⅓ c. fine graham cracker crumbs or cereal crumbs

1. Melt butter in 9 or 10-inch microwave-safe pie plate on high for 45 seconds. **2.** Stir in sugar and crumbs. **3.** Press crumbs firmly and evenly against bottom and sides of pie plate. **4.** Microwave at high for 1½ minutes; cool.

PIE CRUST, OIL

Makes 1 (9 or 10-inch) double-crust pie.

2½ c. all-purpose flour
½ tsp. salt
¾ c. olive oil
½ c. ice water

1. In large bowl, stir together flour and salt. **2.** In small bowl, combine oil and ice water, beating with a wire whisk or fork until creamy. **3.** Pour into flour mixture, stirring with a fork, until dough holds together. **4.** Gather dough into a ball; divide into 2 portions. **5.** Immediately roll out one portion between two sheets of waxed paper. (If you wet the surface slightly, the bottom piece of waxed paper will stay in place.) **6.** Peel off top sheet of waxed paper and fit crust into pie pan, paper side up; peel off waxed paper. **7.** Roll out second portion between 2 sheets of waxed paper; pull off top sheet. **8.** Put filling in pie; then place remaining crust on pie, paper side up; peel off paper. **9.** Flute edges and slash top crust to vent; follow baking instructions for pie. **Note**: Leave ¼-inch overhang on bottom crust, otherwise it slides down.

PIE CRUST, OIL (One Shell)

Makes 1 (9 or 10-inch) shell.

1⅓ c. all-purpose flour
¼ tsp. salt
⅓ c. olive oil
¼ c. cold water

1. Combine all ingredients; mix until dough clings together in ball. **2.** Place a piece of waxed paper on dampened surface. **3.** Put pie dough on waxed paper; flatten and smooth edges. **4.** Lay another piece of waxed paper over the top; roll out with rolling pin to a circle 1 inch larger than inverted 9 or 10-inch pie pan. **5.** Remove top paper; invert pastry and bottom paper over pie pan. Gently remove paper. **6.** Fit into pie pan; turn excess under the edge and flute edge. **7.** Prick crust with fork several places. **8.** Bake in preheated 400° oven for 10 to 15 minutes, until golden brown.

MERINGUE, MARSHMALLOW

Beat 3 egg whites until soft mounds form. Add 3 heaping tablespoons marshmallow creme (about 1 cup). Continue beating until mixture stands in stiff peaks. Spread meringue over pie filling; bake in preheated 350° oven 12 to 15 minutes or until lightly browned. **Note**: If using 7 oz.-jar or Kraft Marshmallow Creme, it will cover two pies.

MERINGUE, WONDERFUL

A never-fail, lofty meringue, if you make sure all bowls, pans, utensils and rubber scrapers are grease-free.

1 T. cornstarch, packed level
½ c. cool water
3 egg whites or 2 extra-large (⅓ to ½ c.)
6 T. sugar
⅛ tsp. salt
½ to 1 tsp. vanilla

1. In small pan, combine cornstarch and water. **2.** Cook until thickened and bubbly, stirring constantly; remove from heat and set aside. **3.** Beat egg whites in mixer bowl, just until soft white mounds appear. (Not really stiff.) **4.** Add sugar, one tablespoon at a time, one right after the other, while beating at high speed; beat 30 seconds longer. **5.** Add cornstarch mixture all at once (any temperature); beat 30 seconds longer. **6.** Add salt and flavoring; beat 30 seconds longer. **7.** Spread meringue on pie, making swirls and tips. **8.** Bake in preheated 350° oven 15 to 20 minutes, or until meringue is light golden brown. **Note**: Do not use lemon or orange extract to flavor this recipe as they have lemon oil or orange oil in them. Any oils or grease will cause this meringue to fall and become thin. **Note:** Use ⅓ c. egg whites for a commercial graham cracker crust.

TOPPING FOR A FRUIT PIE OR COBBLER

⅓ c. sugar
⅓ c. flour
¼ c. olive oil
1 c. coconut

1. In small food processor, mix together the sugar, flour and olive oil. **2.** Add coconut and mix briefly; sprinkle over top of pie before baking. **Note**: If it is a large pie or cobbler, this recipe should be doubled.

APPLE DANISH PASTRY

From Janet Benninger Churchill.

3 c. flour
½ t. salt
1 c. Smart Balance Shortening
1 egg, large
½ c. milk
6 c. peeled and sliced apples
½ to 1 c. sugar, depending on tartness of apples
¼ c. melted reg. Smart Balance Spread (or butter)
½ to 1 c. English Walnuts, chopped (opt.)
2 T. flour
1 t. cinnamon
For top: Milk and sugar

1. Combine flour and salt; cut in shortening with pastry blender or fingers until it resembles Bisquick. 2. Add egg and milk which have been whisked together; stir just until mixed with dry ingredients into a dough. 3. Divide dough in half and roll out one half on floured surface with floured rolling pin. Lay in bottom of 15 x 10-inch or 9 x 13-inch greased cake pan. 4. Combine apples, sugar, melted butter, flour and cinnamon; spread over dough. 5. Roll out remaining dough; lay over apples. 6. Brush with milk and sprinkle with sugar. 7. Bake in preheated 350° oven for 1 hour, or until light golden brown. 8. When cool or partially cool, combine ½ c. powdered sugar and 2 t. water; drizzle over the top.

APPLE PIE

By using a 10-inch pie pan, pie does not usually boil over.

5 c. peeled and sliced tart apples, packed
1 c. sugar
2 T. flour, packed level
½ to 1 tsp. cinnamon
¼ tsp. nutmeg (opt.)
1 T. lemon juice (unless apples are extremely tart)
2 T. butter (opt.)
Pastry for 1 (10-in.) double-crust pie

1. After preparing apples, turn oven to 400°. 2. In small bowl, combine sugar, flour and cinnamon; stir together and pour over apples. 3. Add lemon juice and stir together; put in unbaked pie crust. 4. Dot top of apples with small chunks of butter. 5. Put top crust in place and seal edges; cut slits in top crust to let steam escape. 6. Bake in 400° oven 10 minutes on middle rack; reduce heat to 375° and bake 35 minutes longer or until apples are tender, juice is bubbling a little, and crust is light golden brown. Note: If crust looks like it is going to get too brown, lay a piece of foil loosely over top of pie while finishing baking. Note: Decrease sugar to ⅔ cup for sweeter apples, or for red or yellow "Delicious" apples. Note: For extremely sour apples, increase sugar to 1¼ cups and flour to 2½ tablespoons.

APPLE PIES, TWO

For 2 apple pies, double the recipe for "Apple Pie,"
using a 3-pound bag of cooking apples.

APPLE PIE, SMALLER

4 c. peeled and sliced cooking apples (1 lb. after peeling)
⅔ c. sugar
4 tsp. flour, packed level
½ tsp. cinnamon
½ T. lemon juice
1 T. butter
Pastry for 8 or 9-in. double-crust pie

1. Follow directions for "Apple Pie."

APPLE PIE, CRUMB TOPPING I

A one-crust pie with crumb topping.

4 c. peeled and sliced tart cooking apples (1 lb. after preparing)
1 tsp. lemon juice (opt.)
½ c. sugar
½ tsp. cinnamon
1 unbaked 9-in. pie shell
¾ c. all-purpose flour
½ c. packed brown sugar
⅓ c. butter

1. In medium-large bowl, combine apples and lemon juice. 2. In small bowl, combine sugar and cinnamon; sprinkle over apples and stir well. 3. Pour apple mixture in unbaked shell. 4. Using empty apple bowl, combine flour, brown sugar and butter, using fingers or pastry blender until crumbly. 5. Sprinkle crumb mixture evenly over apples. 6. Bake in preheated 400° oven 10 minutes; reduce heat to 350° and bake 35 to 40 minutes longer, or until golden brown and bubbly. (If crust starts to get too brown, lay foil loosely over pie to finish baking.)

APPLE PIE, CRUMB TOPPING II

Baked in a brown paper bag.

5 c. apples, peeled and sliced (1¼ lbs. after peeling)
1 T. lemon juice (opt.)
⅔ c. sugar
½ tsp. cinnamon
1 unbaked 10-in. pie shell (large)
1 c. all-purpose flour
½ c. brown sugar, packed
½ c. butter

1. In large bowl, combine apples and lemon juice. 2. In med.-small bowl, combine sugar and cinnamon; sprinkle over apples and stir well. 3. Place apple mixture in large unbaked shell. 4. Using empty med.-small bowl, combine flour, brown sugar and butter; mix together until crumbly. 5. Sprinkle crumb mixture evenly over apples. 6. Slide pie into heavy brown paper bag large enough to cover pie loosely. 7. Fold open-end over twice and fasten with paper clips. 8. Bake in preheated 425° oven for 1 hour; remove from oven and slit bag open immediately.

APPLE PIE, DIET

5 c. peeled and sliced cooking apples (1¼ lbs. after peeling)
2 T. flour, packed level
½ tsp. cinnamon
¼ tsp. nutmeg
¼ tsp. salt (or less)
1 T. lemon juice
1 T. + 1 tsp. liquid sweetener
2 T. butter
Pastry for 9-inch double-crust pie

1. In small bowl, mix together flour, cinnamon, nutmeg and salt. 2. Add lemon juice and liquid sweetener; pour over sliced apples, stirring well. 3. Put mixture into unbaked pie shell; dot with chunks of butter. 4. Put top crust over apples and seal edges; cut slits in top crust to let steam escape. 5. Bake in preheated 375° oven on middle rack about 45 minutes, or until apples are tender, juice is bubbling and crust is golden brown.

BANANA CREAM PIE I

Eggless pie filling.

½ c. sugar
4 T. + 1 tsp. flour
⅛ tsp. salt
2 c. milk
3 drops yellow food coloring
2 T. butter
1 tsp. vanilla
2 to 3 bananas
1 (8 or 9-in.) baked pie shell or graham cracker shell
Whipped topping, thawed, or Dream Whip, prepared

1. In medium saucepan, stir together sugar, flour and salt. 2. Add milk gradually, stirring well. 3. Bring to a boil, stirring almost constantly; lower heat and boil gently 1 minute, stirring. 4. Remove from heat; add yellow food coloring, butter and vanilla, stirring until butter melts. 5. Pour into a bowl and cover surface of pie filling with plastic wrap; refrigerate until cool. 6. When cool, slice bananas over bottom of pie shell; cover bananas with cooled pie filling. 7. Spread whipped topping over filling; refrigerate.

BANANA CREAM PIE II

A 9-inch graham cracker shell may be used instead.

½ c. sugar
⅓ c. cornstarch
¼ tsp. salt
3 c. milk
2 lg. egg yolks
1½ tsp. vanilla
1 T. butter
1 c. whipped topping, thawed, or ½ c. whipping cream, whipped
1 (9-in.) baked pie shell
3 med. or med-large bananas
¼ c. apple jelly

1. In heavy saucepan or black iron skillet, mix together sugar, cornstarch and salt; stir in milk. 2. Cook over medium heat, stirring constantly, until mixture boils. 3. Reduce heat and simmer 1 minute; remove pan from heat. 4. In small bowl, beat egg yolks; stir small amount of hot mixture into egg yolks. 5. Slowly pour egg yolk mixture into hot pudding mixture, stirring continually. 6. Return pan to heat; cook until mixture

boils. Reduce heat and cook 1 minute longer. 7. Remove pan from heat and stir in butter and vanilla. 8. Cover and refrigerate until cool, but not set (about 1 hour or longer). 9. Beat whipping cream until soft peaks form; fold into cooled pie filling. 10. Slice 1 banana and line bottom of graham cracker shell. 11. Pour pie filling over bananas; top with the remaining banana slices. 12. In small saucepan, melt apple jelly over low heat; brush top banana slices with melted jelly. 13. Refrigerate about 2 hours before serving.

BANANA CREAM PIE, CLOUD 9

Delicious.

1 (4-serving size) pkg. vanilla pudding and pie filling (cook-type)
1¾ c. milk
1 c. whipped topping, thawed
1½ c. miniature marshmallows
2 bananas (or 3 sm. bananas)
1 (9-in.) graham cracker crust or reg. baked pie shell

1. Prepare pie filling, using 1¾ cups milk, according to package directions. 2. Cover surface of pie filling with plastic wrap; refrigerate until cool. 3. When cool, stir well; fold in whipped topping and marshmallows. 4. Slice bananas onto crust; cover bananas with pie filling. 5. Refrigerate several hours.

BLACKBERRY PIE I

Let berries partially or fully thaw.

1 (16-oz.) pkg. frozen blackberries (or 3½ c. fresh)
1¼ to 1½ c. sugar
¼ c. flour, packed level
2 T. butter
Pastry for deep 10-in. double-crust pie

1. Mix sugar and flour together; pour over berries and stir gently. 2. Place blackberry mixture in unbaked pie crust. 3. Dot with butter. 4. Cover with top crust and seal edges; cut slits in top crust to let steam escape. 5. Bake in preheated 425° oven for 10 minutes; then reduce heat to 350° and bake 35 minutes until golden brown and bubbling. **Note**: Fresh red raspberries (not frozen) may be used instead of blackberries.

BLACKBERRY PIE II

3 c. blackberries (fresh or frozen)
1 c. sugar
2 T. flour (level)
1½ T. butter
Pastry for 9 or 10-in. double-crust pie

1. Follow directions for preceding recipe.

BLACKBERRY PIE III

2½ c. fresh or frozen blackberries
¾ c. sugar
1 T. flour, packed level
1 T. Minute Tapioca
1 T. butter
Pastry for 9-in. double-crust pie

1. Mix sugar, flour and tapioca together; pour over berries and stir gently. **2.** Place berry mixture in unbaked pie crust. **3.** Dot with butter. **4.** Cover with top crust and seal edges; cut slits in top crust to let steam escape. **5.** Bake in preheated 425° oven for 10 minutes; then reduce heat to 350° and bake 30 minutes longer or until golden brown and bubbling.

BLACKBERRY PIE (Canned Berries)

This is a small 8-inch pie.

1 (17-oz.) can blackberries in syrup (about 2 c.)
⅓ c. sugar
2 T. flour, packed level
1 T. butter
Pastry for 8-in. double-crust

1. Drain berries, saving syrup; set aside. **2.** In small pan, combine sugar and flour. **3.** Add syrup; bring to a boil, stirring constantly. **4.** Remove from heat; add butter, stirring until butter melts. **5.** Add blackberries and stir together very gently. **6.** Pour into pastry-lined pie pan; cover with vented top crust and seal edges. **7.** Bake in preheated 450° oven for 10 minutes, then at 350° for 20 to 25 minutes or until light golden brown.

BLACKBERRY-CHERRY COBBLER PIE

Makes a large, wonderful dessert.

4½ c. thawed blackberries and their juice (can be part blueberries or raspberries)
1½ c. sugar
2 T. all-purpose flour, packed level
2 T. Minute Tapioca, level
2 T. butter
1 (21-oz.) can cherry pie filling and ¼ tsp. almond extract
Pastry recipe using 2½ to 3 cups flour

1. Measure berries and their juice; set aside. **2.** In 3-quart saucepan, combine sugar, flour and tapioca; add berries and bring to a boil, stirring gently, occasionally. **3.** Add butter and let melt. **4.** Add cherry pie filling, stirring together; set aside. **5.** Make pastry and line bottom and sides with rolled-out pie crust in 14 x 10-inch baking pan (2 inches deep), or lasagna pan. **6.** Pour fruit mixture over pastry; make lattice strips of pie crust for top (or make a solid top, cutting slits to let steam escape). **7.** Bake on <u>bottom shelf</u> of preheated 425 oven for 10 to 15 minutes; then reduce heat to 350 and bake 30 minutes longer, or until golden and bubbling. **Note:** If berries have a lot of juice, increase tapioca to 3 tablespoons instead of 2. Filling will thicken as pie cools. If using fresh berries, add ¼ cup water. (For 9 x 13 x 2-inch cake pan, omit cherry pie filling.)

BLUEBERRY PIE

3 c. fresh or frozen blueberries, unsweetened
½ c. blueberry juice or water
¾ c. sugar
1 T. cornstarch (level)
2 T. quick tapioca (level)
1 tsp. lemon juice
1 to 2 T. butter (opt.)
Pastry for 9 or 10-in. double-crust pie, unbaked

1. If berries are frozen, thaw; drain, reserving juice. **2.** Measure juice (if any) and water to measure ½ cup liquid. **3.** In medium saucepan, combine sugar, cornstarch and tapioca; stir ½ cup liquid in and heat quickly until thickened, stirring. (Boiling is not necessary.) **4.** Remove from heat and cool 5 to 10 minutes. **5.** Add blueberries and lemon juice to thickened juice; pour filling into bottom crust. **6.** If desired, add dots of butter over top; cover with top crust, sealing edges and cutting vent design. **7.** Bake in preheated 425° oven <u>on lowest shelf</u> for 30 minutes or until golden brown.

BLUEBERRY PIE, ICEBOX (or CHERRY)

From Mona Stevenson.

8 oz. cream cheese
1 c. powdered sugar
1 tsp. vanilla
1 pt. whipping cream, whipped or 8-oz. carton whipped topping, thawed
1 (21-oz.) can blueberry (or cherry) pie filling
2 T. lemon juice
1 lg. (10-in.) baked pie shell (or one 9-in. and one 8-in. shell)

1. Beat cream cheese, sugar and vanilla until smooth and fluffy. **2.** Fold in whipped cream; pour into baked pie shell(s). **3.** Refrigerate overnight. **4.** Mix together pie filling and lemon juice; spread on top pie before serving. **Note:** Omit lemon juice if using cherry pie filling.

BROWNIE PIE (Crustless)

Quick and delicious.

1 c. sugar
½ c. all-purpose flour
¼ c. dry unsweetened cocoa
⅛ tsp. salt
2 eggs
½ c. olive oil or ½ c. (1 stick) soft butter
1 to 1½ tsp. vanilla
½ c. coarsely chopped nuts

1. Turn oven dial to 325°. 2. Put all ingredients, except nuts, in mixer bowl and beat on low speed 3 minutes, scraping sides of bowl once. 3. Butter or spray 8 or 9-inch pie plate. 4. Add nuts to batter; pour into pie plate, spreading evenly. 5. Bake in preheated 325° oven 30 minutes for 9-inch pie plate (35 minutes for 8-inch pie plate). Do not test pie for doneness because it will not test done in center. 6. Cool. Serve with ice cream (and hot fudge sauce, if desired).

BUTTERSCOTCH PIE

From Mrs. Leota A. Benninger.

1⅓ c. packed brown sugar
½ c. all-purpose flour
¼ tsp. salt
2 c. warm water
3 egg yolks (or 2 lg. egg yolks)
2 tsp. vanilla
2 T. butter
1 (9-in.) baked pie shell
Wonderful Meringue

1. In heavy black iron skillet or heavy saucepan, mix together brown sugar, flour and salt. 2. Add warm water and egg yolks, stirring together well with wire whip. 3. Bring to a boil, stirring almost constantly; lower heat and boil gently 2 minutes, stirring often. 4. Remove from heat; add vanilla and butter, stirring until butter is melted. 5. Pour into baked pie shell; place in preheated 350° oven while making Wonderful Meringue. (This prevents soggy bottom crust.) 6. Cover pie with meringue and bake in 350° oven 15 to 20 minutes, or until golden brown.

BUTTERSCOTCH PIE, ELLEN'S

1 c. brown sugar, packed
4 T. cornstarch, packed level, plus 1 teaspoon
¼ tsp. salt
1 c. cool water
3 egg yolks (or 2 extra-large yolks)
1⅔ c. hot, scalded milk
3 T. butter or regular Smart Balance Spread
1½ t. vanilla
1 (9 or 10-inch) baked pie shell

1. Mix brown sugar, cornstarch and salt in saucepan; gradually add water, then egg yolks, mixing well. 2. Add hot milk and butter; cook over med. heat, stirring constantly, until it thickens and boils. Boil 1 minute. 3. Remove from heat and blend in vanilla; pour into baked pie shell. 4. Top with meringue (or chill, then top with whipped topping or whipped cream).

CHERRY PIE

Make cherry filling before crust, so it can partially cool.

4 c. fresh or frozen unsweetened pitted tart cherries (20-oz. bag)
1¼ c. sugar
¼ c. flour, packed level
⅛ tsp. almond extract
2 T. butter
3 to 7 drops red food coloring
Pastry for 9 or 10-in. double-crust pie

Glaze:
½ to 1 T. milk
½ to 1 tsp. sugar

1. In 3-quart saucepan, cook cherries, sugar and flour, stirring frequently, over medium-high heat until mixture boils; reduce heat and boil 1 minute. 2. Remove from heat and stir in almond extract, butter and red food coloring; set aside to cool while making crust. 3. Pour cherry filling into unbaked bottom crust. 4. Add vented top crust; for glaze, brush top crust with milk and sprinkle with sugar. 5. Bake in preheated 375° oven for 35 to 40 minutes until crust is golden brown and filling is bubbling. 6. If crust browns too quickly, cover edge loosely with a strip of foil to prevent overbrowning.

CHERRY PIE, CREAM CHEESE (New York)

Any graham cracker crust may be used.

1¼ c. graham cracker crumbs
¼ c. sugar
4 T. softened or melted butter
3 to 4 oz. cream cheese, softened
1 c. powdered sugar (or ¼ c. granulated sugar)
1 tsp. vanilla
8 oz. (about 3½ c.) whipped topping, thawed
1 (21-oz.) can cherry pie filling
½ tsp. almond flavoring (opt.)

1. Combine graham cracker crumbs, sugar and butter; press into 9-inch pie plate (or 9 x 9-inch cake pan). Chill. 2. Combine cream cheese, powdered sugar and vanilla, mixing until well blended. 3. Fold in whipped topping; spread mixture over graham cracker crust. 4. Combine cherry pie filling and almond extract; spoon filling over whipped topping layer. 5. Refrigerate.

CHERRY PIE FILLING

1 c. sugar
3 T. cornstarch, packed level
2 (16-oz.) cans pitted tart red cherries
5 to 7 drops red food coloring
½ tsp. almond extract
1 tsp. olive oil (opt.)

1. Combine sugar and cornstarch in saucepan. 2. Drain cherries, reserving ¾ cup juice; stir juice into sugar mixture. 3. Bring to a boil, stirring almost constantly; reduce heat and boil 1 minute. 4. Remove from heat and stir in cherries, red food coloring, almond extract and olive oil. <u>Note</u>: This filling is enough for a 10-inch pie crust. Bake vented double-crust pie in preheated 450° oven for 10 minutes; reduce heat to 350° and bake about 40 minutes longer, until golden brown. If crust browns too quickly, cover edge loosely with a strip of foil to prevent overbrowning during the last 15 to 20 minutes.

CHERRY PIE, SMALL

1 (21-oz.) can cherry pie filling
1½ T. sugar
⅛ tsp. almond flavoring (opt.)
1 T. butter
Pastry for 8-in. double-crust pie

1. Combine pie filling, sugar and almond flavoring; pour into 8-inch pastry-lined pie pan. 2. Dot with butter; add top crust; cut vent design and seal edges. 3. Bake in preheated 425° oven 10 minutes; reduce heat to 350° and bake 30 to 40 minutes, or until bubbly and golden brown. <u>Larger Pie</u>: Use 1 (1 lb., 14-oz.) can cherry pie filling, 3 T. sugar, ¼ tsp. almond flavoring (optional), 1½ T. butter and pastry for 1 (9 or 10-inch) double-crust pie.

CHOCOLATE ANGEL FROZEN PIE

Creamy and delicious, this pie is also easy and quick to make.

1 pkg. (3 to 4 oz.) cream cheese, softened
½ c. sugar
1 tsp. vanilla
⅓ c. baking cocoa
⅓ c. milk
1 carton (8 oz.) frozen whipped topping, thawed
1 baked pie shell (9-inch) or graham cracker shell
Chocolate curls or chips (opt.)

1. In mixing bowl, beat cream cheese, sugar and vanilla until smooth. 2. Add cocoa alternately with milk; mix well. 3. Fold in whipped topping; pour into pie shell. 4. Garnish with chocolate curls or chips, if desired. To make chocolate curls, use a potato peeler and peel from edge of a block of chocolate. 5. Freeze 8 hours or overnight. Serve directly from freezer; pie does not need to thaw.

CHOCOLATE CANDY BAR PIE I

Also called "Milk Chocolate Pie."

6 to 8 oz. milk chocolate or chocolate candy bar (with or without almonds)
¼ c. milk
1 (8-oz.) carton frozen whipped topping, thawed (3½ c.)
1 (8 or 9-in.) baked pie shell or graham cracker shell
For Garnish: mini chocolate chips or chocolate curls

1. Break chocolate into chunks; melt with milk in top of double boiler over hot, not boiling water. 2. <u>Cool to room temperature</u>. 3. Fold whipped topping into cooled chocolate; pour into crust. 4. Garnish with mini chips, chocolate sprinkles or chocolate curls. 5. Chill several hours.

CHOCOLATE CANDY BAR PIE II

15 to 18 lg. marshmallows or 1½ c. miniature marshmallows
½ c. milk
1 (5 to 8-oz.) milk chocolate candy bar (plain or with almonds)
1 env. Dream Whip, prepared (or 2 c. thawed whipped topping)
1 baked 9-in. pie shell or graham cracker shell
Nuts or chocolate curls (opt.)

1. Combine marshmallows, milk and chocolate (broken up) in heavy saucepan. 2. Melt over low heat until melted, stirring frequently. 3. Remove from heat and cool completely. 4. Fold whipped topping into cooled chocolate mixture; pour into pie shell. 5. Sprinkle chopped nuts overtop, if desired; or make chocolate curls with potato peeler or sharp knife to decorate, if desired. 6. Chill several hours, until firm.

CHOCOLATE CHIP PIE

Scrumptious!

½ c. butter or reg. Smart Balance spread, melted and partially cooled
2 eggs
½ c. sugar
½ c. packed brown sugar
½ c. all-purpose flour
¼ c. light olive oil
1 tsp. vanilla
1 c. (6 oz.) semi-sweet chocolate chips
1 to 1½ c. chopped walnuts or pecans
½ c. flaked coconut (opt.)
1 unbaked 9-in. pie shell

1. Melt butter and set aside to partially cool. 2. Turn oven dial to 325°. 3. In medium bowl, beat eggs slightly. (Do not use electric mixer with this recipe.) 4. Add sugar, flour, the butter, the light olive oil and vanilla; with spoon, stir together just until well blended. 5. Stir in chocolate chips, nuts and coconut. 6. Pour filling into unbaked pie shell and bake in preheated 325° oven 35 to 45 minutes, or until golden brown. 7. Serve slightly warm with vanilla ice cream or whipped topping, or serve cold.

CHOCOLATE CHIP PIE, LARGER

Cut this pie into 9 or 10 pieces.

½ c. (1 stick) butter
3 lg. eggs
¾ c. sugar
¾ c. packed brown sugar
¾ c. all-purpose flour
½ c. olive oil
1 tsp. vanilla
1½ c. semi-sweet chocolate chips (or chocolate mint or chocolate mini chips)
1 c. chopped walnuts or pecans
1 unbaked 10-in. (or deep 9-in.) pie shell

1. Melt butter and set aside to cool. 2. Turn oven dial to 325°. 3. In large bowl, beat eggs until foamy. 4. Add sugar and flour, stirring with large spoon until well blended. 5. Add melted butter, oil, vanilla, chocolate chips and nuts; stir together well. 6. Pour into unbaked pie shell and bake in preheated 325° oven 1 hour and 10 minutes (5 minutes longer, if needed). 7. Serve slightly warm with vanilla ice cream or whipped topping, or serve cold.

CHOCOLATE CREAM PIE

¾ c. sugar
4 T. cornstarch (level)
3 T. dry unsweetened cocoa, packed level
¼ tsp. salt
3 egg yolks
2¼ c. milk
1½ to 2 T. butter
1 to 2 tsp. vanilla
1 (9-in.) baked pie shell

1. In deep, black iron skillet or heavy saucepan, combine sugar, cornstarch, cocoa and salt. 2. In medium bowl, combine egg yolks and milk with whisk; add to sugar mixture, blending together. 3. Cook on medium heat until mixture comes to a boil, stirring almost constantly. 4. Reduce heat to medium-low and boil gently for 2 minutes, stirring. 5. Remove from heat and add butter; stir until butter melts. 6. Add vanilla; pour into baked pie shell. 7. For non-soggy bottom crust, place pie in preheated 350° oven for 10 minutes. 8. Remove from oven and cover with meringue (or cool, if serving with whipped topping). **Light Milk Chocolate Pie:** Reduce cocoa to 2 tablespoons.

CHOCOLATE CREAM PIE, EGGLESS

Delicious!

1 c. sugar
4½ T. cornstarch (level)
5 T. unsweetened cocoa (level)
¼ tsp. salt
3 c. milk
2 T. butter
1 to 2 tsp. vanilla
1 (9 or 10-in.) baked pie shell

1. In heavy saucepan, stir together sugar, cornstarch, cocoa and salt. 2. Gradually add milk, blending together with whisk or spoon. 3. Cook until mixture comes to a boil, stirring almost constantly. 4. Reduce heat to low and boil gently for 2 minutes, stirring frequently. 5. Remove from heat and add butter; stir until butter melts. 6. Add vanilla and stir well. 7. Pour into baked pie shell; place pie in preheated 350° oven for 10 minutes to prevent soggy bottom crust. 8. Serve with whipped topping.

CHOCOLATE MOUSSE PIE

1 (12-oz.) can cold evaporated milk or evaporated skimmed milk
1 (4¼ oz.) pkg. chocolate INSTANT pudding and pie filling
1 (8-oz.) carton thawed whipped topping (or less), divided
¼ c. chopped walnuts, pecans or almonds (opt.)
1 (8 or 9-in.) baked pie shell

1. In large mixer bowl, beat cold milk and instant pudding for 2 minutes at medium speed (or with egg beater). 2. Fold in 2 cups whipped topping and nuts. 3. Spoon into baked pie shell; chill 2 to 3 hours or longer. 4. To serve, garnish with remaining whipped topping. Sprinkle with additional nuts, if desired. **Mint Chocolate Mousse Pie:** Add ½ teaspoon peppermint extract after beating pudding 2 minutes. Omit nuts.

COCONUT CUSTARD PIE

3 lg. eggs, slightly beaten (or 4 med. eggs)
2½ c. milk
½ c. sugar
¼ tsp. salt
¼ tsp. nutmeg
1½ tsp. vanilla
1 c. shredded or flaked coconut, divided
1 unbaked 9 or 10-in. pie shell

1. Turn oven dial to 425°. 2. Combine first 6 ingredients and stir well. 3. Reserve ¼ cup coconut; stir remaining coconut into egg mixture. 4. Pour into unbaked pie shell; sprinkle reserved coconut over top. 5. Bake on lowest shelf of preheated 425° oven for 30 minutes, or until filling is set. 6. Cool before serving.

COCONUT IMPOSSIBLE PIE

Makes its own crust.

2 c. milk
¾ c. sugar
½ c. biscuit mix (like Bisquick)
4 eggs
¼ c. butter
1½ tsp. vanilla
1 c. flaked coconut

1. Mix all ingredients, except coconut, in blender on low speed for 3 minutes. **2.** Pour into buttered or sprayed 9-inch pie pan and let it stand 5 minutes while oven preheats to 350°. **3.** Sprinkle coconut over pie. **4.** Bake in preheated 350° oven 45 to 55 minutes, or until set; serve warm or cold.

CREAM PIE, LARGE

¾ c. sugar
5½ T. cornstarch (or ½ c. flour, packed level)
½ t. salt
1 c. cold milk
3 egg yolks (or 2 extra-large egg yolks)
2 c. hot, scalded milk
2 T. butter (opt.)
1½ t. vanilla
1 recipe "Wonderful Meringue" (or whipped topping)

1. In saucepan, mix together sugar, cornstarch, salt; gradually add 1 c. cold milk and egg yolks, mixing well. **2.** Add hot milk and butter; cook over med. heat, stirring constantly, until it thickens and boils. Boil 1 minute. **3.** Remove from heat and stir in vanilla. **4.** Pour into baked pie shell; top with meringue (or chill, then top with whipped topping or whipped cream). **For Coconut Cream Pie:** Add ⅔ to 1 c. flaked coconut and, if desired, add ½ t. coconut flavoring and 1 t. vanilla. Sprinkle ¼ c. flaked coconut over top the meringue before browning.

CREAM PIE, SMALLER

½ c. sugar
3 T. cornstarch (level)
¼ tsp. salt
2 c. milk, divided
2 to 3 lg. (or 4 sm.) egg yolks, slightly beaten
2 T. butter
1 tsp. vanilla
1 baked 8 or 9-in. pie shell
"Wonderful Meringue" (or whipped topping)

<u>Microwave Directions:</u> **1.** In 2-quart casserole or bowl, or 6-cup microwave-safe pitcher, combine sugar, cornstarch, salt and ¼ cup milk. **2.** Stir in remaining milk; microwave at HIGH 8 to 10 minutes, stirring every 2 minutes, or until thickened. **3.** Stir about ½ cup of the hot mixture into egg yolks; blend yolks into remaining pie filling. **4.** Microwave 1 to 2 minutes at HIGH. **5.** Stir in butter, stirring until it melts. **6.** Cool 3 to 5

minutes; then add vanilla. **7.** Pour into baked pie shell; place in preheated 350° oven 10 minutes (to prevent soggy bottom crust) while making meringue. **8.** Follow instructions for meringue (or cool pie; then cover with whipped topping). Refrigerate. <u>Coconut Cream Pie:</u> Add ½ to1 c. flaked coconut to milk mixture before microwaving. After spreading meringue over top pie, sprinkle with ¼ c. flaked coconut before browning.

CUSTARD PIE, DELICIOUS

*Follow baking directions exactly
for a non-soggy bottom crust.*

2½ c. whole or 2% milk
4 lg. eggs
⅔ c. sugar
¼ tsp. salt
3 drops yellow food coloring (opt.)
1 to 2 tsp. vanilla
1 unbaked 10-in. pie shell
Nutmeg

1. Turn oven dial to 400°. **2.** Heat milk until hot, but not boiling. **3.** In medium bowl, beat eggs slightly with fork or whisk. **4.** Add sugar, salt, yellow food coloring, vanilla and hot milk to eggs; stir together. **5.** Pour mixture through fine sieve into unbaked pie shell. **6.** Sprinkle nutmeg over top. **7.** Place pie <u>on lowest shelf</u> of preheated 400° oven and bake 30 minutes, or until knife inserted in center comes out clean.

CUSTARD PIE, DIET

3 c. skim, 1% or 2% low-fat milk
3 lg. eggs
2½ tsp. liquid sweetener, powdered Sweet 'n Low, or ½ c.
  Sprinkle Sweet
¼ tsp. salt
2 tsp. vanilla
Nutmeg
1 unbaked 9 or 10-in. pie shell

1. Turn oven dial to 400°. **2.** Heat milk until hot, but not boiling. **3.** In medium bowl, beat eggs slightly with fork or whisk. **4.** Add sweetener, salt, vanilla and hot milk to eggs. **5.** Pour mixture through fine sieve into unbaked pie shell. **6.** Sprinkle nutmeg over top. **7.** Place <u>on lowest shelf</u> of preheated 400° oven and bake 20 minutes, or until knife inserted in center comes out clean.

ELDERBERRY PIE I

3 c. fresh or frozen elderberries, unsweetened
1 c. elderberry juice or water
1 c. sugar
3 T. flour (level)
1 T. quick tapioca
1 tsp. lemon juice

1 to 2 T. butter
Pastry for 10-in. double-crust pie, unbaked

1. If berries are frozen, thaw and drain, reserving juice. 2. Measure juice (if any) and water to measure 1 cup liquid. 3. In medium saucepan, combine sugar, flour and tapioca, stirring together. 4. Add the 1 cup liquid and the elderberries; bring to a boil, stirring frequently. 5. Remove from heat and add lemon juice and butter. 6. Pour into bottom crust; add top crust, sealing edges and cutting vent design. 7. Bake in preheated 425° oven on lowest shelf for 30 minutes or until golden brown.

ELDERBERRY PIE II

Different method from Elderberry Pie I.

3 c. elderberries (fresh or frozen)
1 c. sugar
1 T. flour, packed level
1 T. Minute Tapioca
1 tsp. lemon juice
1/16 tsp. cinnamon (opt.)
½ T. flour for bottom of pan
2 T. butter
Pastry for 1 (9-in.) double pie crust

1. Put elderberries in large bowl. 2. In small bowl, mix together sugar, first flour, tapioca, lemon juice and cinnamon; pour over berries and gently stir together. 3. Sprinkle ½ tablespoon flour over bottom crust; pour berries into pie crust. 4. Dot butter over berries; add vented top crust and seal. 5. Bake in preheated 425° oven 10 minutes, then at 350° for 30 to 40 minutes longer or until golden in color, and bubbly.

ELDERBERRY PIE, SMALLER

Double this recipe for a 10-inch pie pan.

2¼ to 2½ c. elderberries (fresh or frozen)
½ c. sugar + 2 T.
2 T. flour, packed level
1 tsp. lemon juice
1 T. butter
Pastry for 8 or 9-in. double-crust pie

1. Put elderberries in med.-large bowl. 2. In small bowl, combine sugar and flour. 3. Pour over berries and gently stir together. 4. Fill pastry-lined pie plate with berry mixture. 5. Sprinkle lemon juice over berries. 6. Dot with pieces of butter. 7. Add vented top crust and seal edges. 8. Bake in preheated 425° oven for 10 minutes; reduce heat to 350° and bake 30 to 35 minutes longer, or until golden brown.

ELDERBERRY PIE (Canned Berries)

3/4 c. sugar
3 T. cornstarch
1 pt. canned, unsweetened elderberries
½ tsp. vinegar (opt.)
2 T. butter
Pastry for 9-in. double-crust pie

1. In saucepan, combine sugar and cornstarch, mixing well. 2. Drain elderberries, saving juice. Add enough cold water to juice to make 1¼ cups liquid. 3. Add juice to sugar mixture; bring to a boil, stirring. 4. Add drained elderberries and stir gently together. 5. Remove from heat; add butter and stir together when melted. 6. Pour into pastry-lined pie pan; cover with vented top crust and seal edges. 7. Bake in preheated 425° oven for 10 minutes; reduce heat to 350° and bake 30 minutes longer or until light golden brown.

GERMAN CHOCOLATE PIE I
(Unbaked Pie Shell)

1 (4-oz.) pkg. German sweet cooking chocolate
¼ c. (½ stick) butter
1 (12-oz.) can evaporated milk
1⅓ c. sugar
3 T. cornstarch (level)
⅛ tsp. salt
2 eggs
1 tsp. vanilla
1⅓ c. coconut
1 c. pecans, chopped
1 unbaked deep 9 or 10-in. pie shell

1. Melt chocolate and butter over low heat. 2. Remove from heat and blend in milk; set aside. 3. In medium bowl, mix together sugar, cornstarch and salt. 4. Add eggs and vanilla, beating together. 5. Fold in chocolate mixture. 6. In bottom of unbaked pie shell, put coconut and pecans. 7. Pour chocolate mixture over all. 8. Bake in preheated 350° oven on lowest shelf of oven for 50 to 60 minutes. (Cover top of pie loosely with foil during the last 15 minutes of baking time.) 9. Cool at least 4 hours before cutting to allow filling to set. Serves 8.

GERMAN CHOCOLATE PIE II
(Baked Pie Shell)

Cut pie into 9 or 10 pieces. This is an entirely different method from the previous recipe.

⅓ c. sugar
3 T. cornstarch (level)
1½ c. milk
1 (4-oz.) pkg. German sweet cooking chocolate, cut up
1 T. butter
2 beaten egg yolks
1 tsp. vanilla
1 (9-in.) baked pie shell

Topping:
1 beaten egg
1 (5⅓-oz.) can (or ⅔ c.) evaporated milk
½ c. sugar
¼ c. (½ stick) butter
1⅓ c. flaked coconut (or 3½-oz. can)
½ c. chopped pecans

1. In medium saucepan, combine ⅓ cup sugar and the cornstarch; stir in milk, chocolate and 1 tablespoon butter. 2. Cook, stirring constantly, until thickened and bubbly; reduce heat and cook 2 minutes longer, stirring. 3. Gradually stir about 1 cup of hot mixture into beaten egg yolks. 4. Return mixture to saucepan; cook 2 minutes longer, stirring. 5. Add vanilla; pour into baked pie shell. 6. For topping, combine in another saucepan the beaten egg, evaporated milk, ½ cup sugar and ¼ cup butter. 7. Cook and stir over medium heat just until mixture is thickened and bubbly. 8. Stir in coconut and pecans; spread evenly over chocolate filling. 9. Cool pie on wire rack thoroughly.

GRAPE PIE, DELICIOUS

4 to 4½ c. blue concord grapes
1 c. sugar
3 T. flour, packed level
1 tsp. lemon juice
2 T. butter
Pastry for 9-in. double-crust pie

1. Wash fully ripened grapes and drain. 2. Slip the pulp out of the skins, measuring 2 cups pulp. (Reserve skins.) 3. Cook pulp, without any water, until the seeds separate from pulp. 4. Press pulp through sieve to remove seeds; combine pulp and reserved skins. 5. In small bowl, combine sugar and flour; add to grape mixture. 6. Add lemon juice; pour into pastry-lined pie plate. 7. Dot with butter; add vented top crust and seal. 8. Bake in preheated 450° oven 10 minutes; then lower heat to 350° and bake about 20 minutes longer or until golden brown.

LEMON PIE

A new method for this lemon pie.

1⅔ c. sugar
¼ tsp. salt
6 T. cornstarch, level
½ c. cold water
⅓ c. lemon juice (bottled or fresh)
3 egg yolks, beaten
1½ c. boiling water
1 to 2 T. butter
1 tsp. lemon peel (opt.)
2 drops yellow food coloring (opt.)
1 baked pie shell or graham cracker crust
Meringue or whipped topping

1. In medium saucepan, combine sugar, salt and cornstarch, stirring together well. 2. Add cold water and lemon juice, stirring until well combined. 3. Add beaten egg yolks and stir well. 4. Add boiling water slowly, stirring constantly. 5. On medium heat, bring mixture to a boil, stirring constantly; then reduce heat and simmer 1 minute. 6. Remove from heat and stir in butter (and lemon peel and yellow food coloring, if used). 7. Pour hot filling into baked pie shell or graham cracker pie shell; place in middle of preheated 350 oven for 10 minutes (or while making meringue) to prevent soggy bottom crust. 8. Follow instructions for meringue (or cool pie, then cover with whipped topping and refrigerate).

LEMON SPONGE PIE

From Emma Burnheimer. This pie has a cake-like top and a lemon-filling bottom.

1 c. sugar
2 T. flour
2 T. olive oil (or melted butter)
2 eggs, separated
3 T. lemon juice (or juice and grated rind from 1 lemon)
1 c. milk
1 unbaked 9-in. pie shell

1. Turn oven dial to 325°. 2. Blend together sugar, flour, oil, egg yolks and lemon juice in large bowl. 3. Add milk, a little at a time, until well blended. 4. Beat egg whites until stiff; fold in first mixture. 5. Pour into unbaked pie shell; bake on bottom shelf of preheated 325° oven 45 minutes, until golden brown.

LIME MERINGUE PIE (Microwave)

No sticking, or stirring constantly in the microwave.

1 c. sugar
4 level T. cornstarch
¼ tsp. salt
1¾ c. cool water, divided
3 lg. or 4 sm. egg yolks, slightly beaten
⅓ c. lime juice
2 drops green food coloring
1 baked 9 or 10-in. pie shell or graham cracker shell
Meringue

1. In small mixing bowl or 1½-quart casserole or 4 to 6-cup microwavable pitcher, combine sugar, cornstarch, salt and ¼ cup cool water. 2. Stir in remaining water; microwave at HIGH 6 to 8 minutes, stirring every 2 minutes, until thickened and clear. 3. Mix a little hot mixture into egg yolks; blend yolks into remaining pie filling. 4. Microwave at HIGH 1 minute. 5. Stir in lime juice and green food coloring; cool about 5 minutes. 6. Pour into baked shell; place in preheated 350° oven while making meringue (to prevent soggy bottom crust). 7. Top with meringue and bake in 350° oven 15 to 20 minutes, or until color desired. 8. Refrigerate.

Pies

LIME NO-COOK PIE

From Martha Stevenson. No baking.

Substitute for 4 eggs, like Egg Beaters (1 c.)
1 (14-oz.) can sweetened condensed milk
½ c. lime juice
1¼ tsp. Knox gelatin
6 drops green food coloring
1 (8-inch) graham cracker crust
Whipped topping, thawed, or whipped cream

1. Beat egg substitute well. 2. Slowly add sweetened condensed milk. 3. Heat lime juice and Knox gelatin together slowly to completely dissolve the gelatin. 4. Add lime juice mixture to egg mixture. 5. Add green food coloring; pour into pie shell. 6. Refrigerate 2 hours or overnight; serve with whipped topping.

MINCEMEAT PIES, DELICIOUS

Adapted from Joyce Swearingen. Makes 2 pies.

1¼ to 1½ c. ground-up or finely chopped roast beef (no fat)
1 c. raisins
1 (8-oz.) can (1 c.) crushed pineapple, including juice
1 can cherry pie filling or red sour cherries, including juice
½ c. sugar
¼ c. white corn syrup
1 tsp. orange rind (opt.)
½ tsp. cinnamon
¼ tsp. nutmeg
¼ tsp. allspice
¼ tsp. ginger
⅛ tsp. ground cloves
½ c. applesauce, apple juice or cider
½ c. pineapple juice
2½ c. peeled and chopped apples
2 T. flour
Pastry for 2 lg. double-crust pies
4 T. butter

1. Combine roast beef, raisins, crushed pineapple, cherries, sugar, syrup, orange rind, spices, applesauce and juice. 2. Let set in refrigerator, covered, for a few days before using; when ready to make pies, add apples and flour. 3. Divide mincemeat into 2 large pastry-lined pie pans. 4. Put 2 tablespoons butter, cut into chunks, over top of each pie. 5. Cover with top crust and seal, cutting slits in top crust to let steam escape. 6. Bake on lowest shelf of preheated 425° oven 10 minutes; reduce heat to 350° and bake 30 to 35 minutes longer, or until done.

MULBERRY PIE

From Ruth Deeter.

1 c. sugar
4 T. flour (level)
4 to 4¼ c. mulberries, washed and drained
2 T. butter
Pastry for 10-in. double-crust pie

1. In small bowl, mix together sugar and flour. 2. Pour sugar mixture over mulberries, stirring gently together. 3. Pour into pastry-lined pie pan; dot with butter. 4. Cover with top crust and seal edges; cut slits in top crust to let steam escape. 5. Bake in preheated 400° oven 15 minutes; reduce heat to 350° and bake 30 minutes longer or until golden brown and bubbling.

OATMEAL COCONUT PIE

3 eggs
⅔ c. sugar
⅔ c. packed brown sugar
⅔ c. quick rolled oats (not instant)
⅔ c. shredded or flaked coconut
⅓ c. chopped nuts (opt.)
⅓ c. milk
1 to 2 T. butter, melted
1 tsp. vanilla
1 (8 or 9-in.) unbaked pie shell

1. Beat eggs in bowl; stir in sugars, oats, coconut, nuts, milk, melted butter and vanilla. 2. Pour into unbaked pie shell; bake in preheated 350° oven, in lower third of oven, for about 35 minutes. Cool. 3. Serve with whipped topping, if desired.

PEACH CUSTARD PIE (Fresh Peaches)

No milk in this; it makes its own custard.

4½ to 5 c. fresh, peeled and sliced peaches
1 unbaked 9 or 10-in. pie shell
2 eggs
1 c. sugar
2 T. flour (level)
1 T. butter
Cinnamon

1. Turn oven to 425°. 2. Put peaches in unbaked pie shell. 3. Beat eggs until foamy; add sugar and flour; mix well. 4. Pour egg mixture over peaches; sprinkle with cinnamon and dot with butter. 5. On lower shelf of preheated 425° oven, bake pie 15 minutes; reduce heat to 350° and bake 30 minutes longer, or until mixture is set.

PEACH JELLO PIE (Fresh Peaches)

Delicious!

1 c. sugar
2 T. cornstarch
1½ c. water
1 (3-oz.) pkg. peach gelatin
2½ to 3½ c. fresh peaches, peeled and sliced
1 (10-in.) baked pie shell
Whipped topping or ice cream

1. In medium pan, combine sugar, cornstarch and water. 2. Bring to a boil; lower heat and boil gently 2 minutes, stirring. 3. Remove from heat and add dry gelatin; stir to dissolve. 4. Add peaches; stir gently together to coat peaches. Pour into baked pie shell. 5. Chill. Serve with whipped topping or vanilla ice cream.

PEACH PIE I

5 c. fresh peaches, peeled and sliced (or part nectarines)
1 T. lemon juice
¾ c. + 2 T. sugar
3 T. flour, packed level
⅛ tsp. cinnamon or ¼ tsp. almond flavoring
2 T. butter
Pastry for 1 (10-in.) double-crust pie (or two 8-in. pies)

1. Combine peaches and lemon juice in bowl. 2. In small bowl, combine sugar and flour; add to peaches, stirring together gently. 3. Add cinnamon or almond flavoring; stir. 4. Pour peaches into bottom pie crust. 5. Put butter in small chunks over top. 6. Adjust top crust, cutting slits for escape of steam; fold edge of top crust under edge of bottom crust. Press together and flute. 7. Bake in preheated 450° oven for 10 minutes; then turn oven dial to 375° and bake 25 minutes longer, or until light golden brown and juice begins to bubble through slits in crust.

PEACH PIE II

Luscious, flavored with almond.

4 c. sliced fresh peaches, peeled
1 T. quick tapioca
1 T. lemon juice
¼ tsp. almond flavoring
¾ c. sugar
1 T. butter
Pastry for 9-in. double-crust pie

1. In bowl, combine peaches, tapioca, lemon juice, almond flavoring and sugar; mix together gently. 2. Pour into bottom pie crust. 3. Put butter in small chunks over top. 4. Adjust top crust, cutting slits for escape of steam; fold edge of top crust under edge of bottom crust. Press together and flute. 5. Bake in preheated 450° oven for 10 minutes; then turn oven dial to 375° and bake 25 minutes longer, or until light golden brown and juice begins to bubble through slits in crust.

PEACH PIE (Canned Peaches)

2 (16-oz.) cans peaches, sliced (or 1 qt. home-canned peaches)
½ c. sugar
3 T. flour, packed level
2 T. butter
1 T. lemon juice
⅛ tsp. almond extract (opt.)
Pastry for 9-in. double-crust pie

1. Drain peaches in colander, reserving the syrup. 2. In 2-quart saucepan, combine sugar and flour, mixing well. 3. Add syrup and bring to a boil, stirring constantly. 4. Remove from heat; add butter, lemon juice and almond flavoring, stirring until butter melts. 5. Add peaches and pour into pastry-lined pie pan; cover with top crust, cutting slits for escape of steam. 6. Bake in preheated 400° oven for 40 to 45 minutes.

PEACH PIE, GLAZED

1 c. sugar
3 T. cornstarch (level)
1 c. crushed fresh peaches (about 2 lg. peaches)
¼ c. water
1 T. lemon juice
3 c. sliced peaches, peeled (about 4 lg. peaches)
1 baked 9-in. pie shell
Whipped topping (opt.)

1. In medium pan, combine sugar and cornstarch. 2. Add 1 cup crushed peaches and the water. 3. Cook, stirring constantly, until it boils; lower heat and simmer gently 2 minutes, stirring. 4. Remove from heat and stir in lemon juice. 5. Cover pan and cool to lukewarm. 6. Add 3 cups sliced peaches; stir gently and pour into baked pie shell. 7. Chill; serve with whipped topping, if desired. **Note:** This pie is best when served the same day.

PEANUT BUTTER MERINGUE PIE

From Dolores Lance.

½ c. sugar
⅓ c. flour
¼ tsp. salt
2 lg. egg yolks
2 c. milk
1 T. butter
1½ tsp. vanilla
¾ c. powdered sugar
⅓ c. peanut butter
2 lg. egg whites
2 T. water
½ tsp. vanilla
¼ c. sugar
1 baked 9-in. pie shell

Pies

1. In heavy saucepan or deep black iron skillet, mix together sugar, flour and salt. 2. In medium bowl, beat egg yolks slightly with fork or whisk; add milk, mixing together. 3. Stir milk mixture into sugar-flour mixture; blend well. 4. Cook over medium heat, stirring constantly, until mixture comes to a boil. 5. Reduce heat and boil gently 2 minutes longer. 6. Remove from heat and add butter and 1½ teaspoons vanilla; set aside. 7. In medium bowl, combine powdered sugar and peanut butter until it resembles coarse meal. 8. Reserve 2 or 3 tablespoons for top of pie; sprinkle remaining sugar mixture over bottom of baked pie shell. 9. Make meringue by beating egg whites, 2 tablespoons water and ½ teaspoon vanilla until almost stiff. 10. Gradually add ¼ cup sugar, beating well. 11. Pour hot pie filling into baked pie shell. 12. Pile meringue on top of pie. 13. Sprinkle reserved peanut butter mixture over top meringue. 14. Bake in preheated 300° oven 30 minutes. 15. Cool at room temperature; store in refrigerator.

PEANUT BUTTER PIE (Cream Cheese)

This pie may be frozen or chilled, either one.

4 oz. cream cheese, softened
1 c. powdered sugar
½ c. creamy peanut butter
½ c. milk or half & half
1 (8-oz.) carton whipped topping, thawed
1 graham cracker crust or 9-in. baked pie shell or ready-
    made chocolate pie crust

1. Whip cream cheese until fluffy in mixer bowl. 2. Beat in sugar, then peanut butter. 3. Add milk slowly; blend well. 4. Fold in whipped topping until ingredients are mixed well. 5. Pour into baked or prepared pie shell; freeze until firm or chill 6 hours or longer. 6. Serve plain or with one of the following garnishes: ¼ cup chopped peanuts, peanut butter chips or peanut butter sauce or shavings of milk chocolate or semi-sweet chocolate. **Note:** Take out of freezer 10 to 20 minutes before serving.

PEANUT BUTTER PIE (Instant Pudding)

From Genevieve Jeannerat.

⅓ to ½ c. peanut butter
1 c. powdered sugar
1 baked 9-in. pie shell
1 (4-serving size) pkg. French vanilla instant pudding
Milk for pudding mix
1 (8-oz.) carton whipped topping, thawed (or 1 env. Dream
    Whip, prepared)

1. Cut peanut butter into powdered sugar until it resembles coarse cornmeal; sprinkle ¾ of mixture into bottom of baked pie shell. 2. Prepare pudding according to package directions; pour over peanut butter mixture in pie shell. 3. Chill in refrigerator 30 minutes. 4. Spread whipped topping over pie; sprinkle with remaining peanut butter mixture. 5. Refrigerate.

PEAR PIE WITH CRUMB TOPPING

Has a delicate flavor.

⅔ c. sugar
½ tsp. ground ginger
4 c. fresh pears, peeled and sliced
2 T. lemon juice
10-in. unbaked pie shell

Topping:
1 c. all-purpose flour
½ c. packed brown sugar
½ c. butter or Smart Balance spread

1. Turn oven dial to 450°. 2. In large bowl, combine sugar and ginger. 3. Add sliced pears and lemon juice; stir together well. 4. Place pears in unbaked pie shell. 5. Mix together topping ingredients with fingers or pastry blender. 6. Cover pie with topping. 7. Bake in preheated 450° oven 10 minutes; lower heat to 350° and bake 35 minutes longer, or until bubbly and golden brown.

PECAN PIE

Delicious

½ c. sugar
1 c. dark corn syrup
¼ tsp. salt
1 T. flour
2 lg. Eggs (½ c.)
1 tsp. vanilla
1 T. butter, melted
1¼ to 1½ c. pecan halves
1 unbaked 9-in. pie shell
Evaporated milk for edges

1. Turn oven dial to 325°. 2. Beat together sugar, corn syrup, salt, flour and eggs. 3. Add vanilla, melted butter and pecans; pour into shell. 4. Brush edges of crust with evaporated milk (for a brown crust). 5. Bake in preheated 325° oven 1 hour. 6. Cool. **Substitution:** ½ cup packed brown sugar and 1 cup light corn syrup may be substituted for white sugar and dark corn syrup. **Note:** If it seems to be getting too brown, lightly cover with foil.

PECAN CHEESECAKE PIE

*The cream cheese layer at the bottom
rises during baking.*

8 oz. cream cheese, softened
⅓ c. sugar
1 tsp. vanilla
1 lg. egg
1 unbaked 10-in. pie shell
1¼ c. chopped pecans
3 lg. eggs
1 c. light corn syrup

1 tsp. vanilla
½ c. sugar

1. Turn oven dial to 350°. **2.** In mixer bowl, blend softened cream cheese with ⅓ cup sugar, vanilla and 1 egg; beat until smooth. **3.** Pour mixture into unbaked pie shell; sprinkle with pecans. **4.** In same mixer bowl, blend together 3 eggs, corn syrup, vanilla and ½ cup sugar until smooth. **5.** Gently pour this mixture over pecans. **6.** Bake on center rack (or lower third of oven) in preheated 350° oven 50 to 60 minutes, until center is set and pastry is golden. **7.** Cool on wire rack.

PECAN or WALNUT CHOCOLATE PIE

From Sarah Stevenson McIlhany.

3 large eggs
1 c. light or dark corn syrup
1 c. coarsely chopped walnuts or pecans
6 oz. (1 c.) chocolate chips
½ c. sugar
2 T. butter, melted
1 tsp. vanilla
1 unbaked 9-in. pie shell

1. Turn oven dial to 350°. **2.** In large bowl, beat eggs; add corn syrup, walnuts, chocolate chips, sugar, butter and vanilla. **3.** Mix until well blended; pour into unbaked pie shell. **4.** Bake in preheated 350° oven 50 to 60 minutes. (Filling should be slightly less set in the center than around edges.) **5.** Serve warm or cold with whipped topping, if desired. **6.** This pie may be wrapped well and frozen.

PINEAPPLE PIE

This is an easy two-crust pie.

¾ c. sugar
3 T. cornstarch
⅛ tsp. salt
1 (20-oz.) can crushed pineapple, including juice
1 T. lemon juice
3 T. butter
Pastry for 1 (9-in.) double-crust pie

1. In saucepan, combine sugar, cornstarch and salt, stirring together. **2.** Add crushed pineapple and stir together well. **3.** Add lemon juice and butter. **4.** Cook, stirring almost constantly, until mixture comes to a boil. **5.** Reduce heat; boil gently 1 minute. **6.** Pour into unbaked bottom crust; cover with top crust, slit in several places to allow steam to escape. **7.** Bake in preheated 400° oven 30 minutes or until golden brown.

PUMPKIN PIE, BOSTON-KAY

Makes 2 pies.

4 eggs, slightly beaten
3½ c. (29-oz. can) pumpkin
1 c. sugar
¾ c. packed brown sugar
1 T. molasses (opt.)
1 tsp. salt
2 tsp. cinnamon
1 tsp. ginger
⅛ tsp. ground cloves
2½ c. milk or evaporated milk (or some of each)
2 unbaked 9 or 10-in. pie shells

1. Turn oven dial to 350°. **2.** Mix pie filling ingredients in order given; pour into 2 unbaked pie shells. **3.** Sprinkle top of pies lightly with cinnamon or nutmeg. **4.** Bake <u>on lowest oven rack</u> in preheated 350° oven 1 hour, or until knife inserted in center comes out clean. **Spicier Pumpkin Pie**: Use 3 tsp. cinnamon, 2 tsp. ginger, ¼ tsp. cloves and ¼ tsp. nutmeg. Increase brown sugar to 1 cup. **For speedier baking**: Bake on middle shelf of oven at 425° for 15 minutes, then at 350° for 30 minutes or until knife comes out clean.

PUMPKIN PIE, DIET

2 eggs, slightly beaten (or 3 egg whites)
1¾ to 2 c. (16-oz. can) pumpkin
¼ c. Sprinkle Sweet
1 T. liquid sweetener
1 T. honey
1 tsp. cinnamon
¼ tsp. nutmeg
¼ tsp. ground cloves
¼ tsp. ginger
¼ tsp. salt
¼ c. milk
1½ c. (12-oz. can) evaporated skimmed milk
1 unbaked 9-in. pie shell

1. Turn oven dial to 350°. **2.** Mix pie filling ingredients in order given and pour into unbaked pie shell. **3.** Sprinkle top of pie lightly with additional cinnamon. **4.** Bake <u>on lowest rack</u> in preheated 350° oven for 1 hour and 10 minutes. **5.** Cool on wire rack at room temperature. **6.** When cool, refrigerate.

PUMPKIN PIE, LOW CHOLESTEROL

Makes 1 (9-inch) pie.

3 egg whites, slightly beaten
1½ c. pumpkin
⅓ c. packed brown sugar
⅓ c. granulated sugar
1 tsp. cinnamon
¼ to ½ tsp. ginger
¼ tsp. nutmeg

⅛ tsp. ground cloves
¼ tsp. salt
1 (12-oz.) can evaporated skimmed milk (1½ c.)
1 tsp. vanilla
1 unbaked 9-in. pie shell

1. Turn oven dial to 425°. 2. Mix pie filling in order given and pour into unbaked pie shell. 3. Sprinkle top of pie lightly with additional cinnamon or nutmeg. 4. Bake in lower third of preheated 425° oven for 15 minutes; then turn oven dial to 350° and bake 30 to 40 minutes longer, or until knife inserted in center comes out clean. **Note:** ¼ c. honey may be used instead of the brown sugar and white sugar.

PUMPKIN PIE, LOW SPICE

From Violet McCauley. Makes 2 pies.

3 lg. eggs (or 4 med.), slightly beaten
1 (29-oz.) can pumpkin (3½ to 4 c.)
1½ c. sugar
1 tsp. cinnamon
¼ tsp. cloves
¼ tsp. nutmeg
1 tsp. salt
1½ c. milk
1 (12-oz.) can evaporated milk (1½ c.)
2 unbaked 9 or 10-in. pie shells (or 3 small pie shells)
Nutmeg for top of pie

1. Turn oven dial to 400°. 2. In bowl, combine pie filling ingredients in order given; pour into unbaked pie shells. 3. Sprinkle top of pies lightly with nutmeg. 4. Bake in preheated 400° oven 15 minutes; reduce heat to 300° and bake 45 minutes longer, or until knife inserted in center comes out clean.

PUMPKIN PIES, MARTHA'S

Makes 2 extra-large 10-inch pies or 3 9-inch pies.
From Martha Estelle Stevenson.

5 eggs, slightly beaten
3½ to 4 c. pumpkin (29-oz. can)
1¾ c. sugar
2 tsp. cinnamon
1 tsp. ginger
½ tsp. nutmeg
½ tsp. ground cloves
1 tsp. salt
2 c. milk
1 (12-oz.) can evaporated milk (1½ c.)
2 lg. unbaked 10-in. pie shells

1. Turn oven dial to 400°. 2. Mix pie filling ingredients in large bowl, in order given; pour into 2 large unbaked pie shells. 3. Sprinkle top of pies lightly with cinnamon. 4. Put foil around rim of pie crust to keep crust from browning too much. 5. Bake in preheated 400° oven 50 minutes or until knife inserted in center comes out clean.

PUMPKIN PIE, SUPERB

Makes one pie. Bake on lowest shelf of oven.

3 eggs (or 2 extra-large eggs), slightly beaten
1¾ to 2 c. pumpkin (16-oz. can)
¾ c. + 1 or 2 T. sugar
1 tsp. cinnamon
½ tsp. ginger
¼ tsp. nutmeg (opt.)
¼ tsp. cloves
½ tsp. salt
1 c. milk
⅔ c. evaporated milk
1 unbaked 10-in pie shell
Cinnamon or nutmeg for top of pie

1. Turn oven dial to 375°. 2. In bowl, combine pie filling ingredients in order given; pour into unbaked pie shell. 3. Sprinkle top of pie lightly with cinnamon or nutmeg. 4. Bake on lowest rack in preheated 375° oven for 40 to 50 minutes, or until knife inserted in center comes out clean. **Pecan Topped Pie:** Ten minutes before pie is done, sprinkle ½ cup chopped pecans or pecan halves over pie.

PUMPKIN PIE TOPPING, STREUSEL PECAN

1 (9 or 10-in.) unbaked pumpkin pie
¼ c. all-purpose flour
¼ c. sugar or packed brown sugar
½ tsp. cinnamon (opt.)
¼ tsp. ginger (opt.)
3 T. butter, chilled and cut into sm. pcs.
½ to ¾ c. chopped pecans or walnuts
½ c. shredded coconut (opt.)

1. Disregard baking instructions for the pie. 2. Mix together flour, sugar and spices. 3. Cut butter into flour mixture until crumbly, using pastry blender or fingers. 4. Stir in nuts (and coconut, if desired); set aside. 5. Bake pie in preheated 425° oven for 15 minutes, then at 350° for 30 minutes. 6. Remove pie from oven and sprinkle with topping; bake 10 to 15 minutes longer, or until topping is golden brown. 7. Cool on wire rack.

RAISIN PIE I

Makes 2 (9-inch) pies.

15 or 16 oz. raisins (about 3 c.)
4 c. cold water
1 c. sugar
4 T. cornstarch
¼ tsp. salt
2 T. lemon juice
4 T. butter
Pastry for 2 (9-in.) double-crust pies

1. In pan, combine raisins and water. **2.** In bowl, combine sugar, cornstarch and salt, stirring together. **3.** Pour sugar mixture into raisin mixture and stir together. **4.** Bring to a full boil, stirring often; lower heat and boil gently for 5 minutes. **5.** Remove from heat and add lemon juice and butter, stirring until butter is melted. **6.** Pour into prepared pie crust and put upper crust in place, cutting slits for escape of steam. **7.** Bake at 425° for 15 minutes; reduce heat to 350° and bake 20 minutes longer or until bubbly and golden brown.

RAISIN PIE II

Makes 1 large (10-inch) or 2 small pies.

⅔ lb. raisins (about 2 c.)
3 c. cold water
⅔ c. sugar
3 T. cornstarch
⅛ tsp. salt
1 T. lemon juice
2 T. butter
Pastry for 1 large 10-in. double-crust pie

1. Follow instructions for Raisin Pie I. This filling will seem too thin, but when the pie is baked and cooled, it will be just right.

RHUBARB PIE

Oh, so good!

4 c. fresh rhubarb, cut into 1-in. pcs.
Boiling water
1½ c. sugar
3 T. flour, packed level
1 tsp. Minute Tapioca
1 egg
2 tsp. cold water
1 T. butter
Pastry for 9 or 10-in. 2-crust pie

1. After pastry is made, turn oven dial to 400°. **2.** Put washed and cut-up rhubarb in colander and pour about 4 cups boiling water over it. **3.** Return drained rhubarb to a large bowl. **4.** In small bowl, mix together sugar, flour and tapioca; sprinkle over rhubarb and stir all together. **5.** In the empty small bowl, beat egg and 2 teaspoons cold water together; add to rhubarb. Stir to blend all ingredients. **6.** Turn rhubarb mixture into pastry-lined pie plate; dot with butter. **7.** Adjust top crust, cutting slits for escape of steam; fold edge of top crust under bottom crust; press together and flute. **8.** Bake in preheated 400° oven 15 minutes; reduce heat to 350° and bake 45 minutes longer or until crust is golden brown and juice begins to bubble through slits in crust.

RHUBARB CUSTARD PIE

3 to 3½ c. fresh rhubarb, diced rather small
1 (9 or 10-in.) unbaked pie shell
2 eggs
1⅓ c. sugar
3 T. flour, level
½ tsp. nutmeg
1 T. butter or reg. Smart Balance spread
1 T. evaporated milk, cream or milk

1. Preheat oven to 350°. **2.** Place rhubarb into unbaked pie shell. **3.** Beat eggs slightly in mixing bowl. **4.** Add sugar, flour, nutmeg, butter and evaporated milk; mix well. **5.** Pour mixture over rhubarb. **6.** Bake at 350° for 50 to 60 minutes or until crust is golden brown and filling is bubbly.

RHUBARB-STRAWBERRY PIE

Cool completely before cutting.

3 c. fresh strawberries, halved
2 c. sliced fresh rhubarb
1½ c. sugar
6 T. quick-cooking tapioca
Unbaked pastry for 10-in. double-crust pie
Milk (opt.)
Granulated sugar (opt.)

1. Mix strawberries, rhubarb, 1½ cups sugar and the tapioca together; let stand while making pastry. **2.** Line pie plate with bottom crust; fill with fruit mixture. **3.** Place top crust, trimming ½ to 1 inch beyond edge of pie plate; fold top crust under bottom crust. Seal together and make a standing rim and flute edge. **4.** Cut vents in center of top crust; brush with milk and sprinkle with granulated sugar, if desired. **5.** Bake in preheated 400° oven for about 55 minutes, or until the filling bubbles in the center. **6.** Check pie after first 30 minutes for browning; at that time it may be necessary to lay a piece of aluminum foil loosely over top of pie to prevent excessive browning. Have a piece of foil on bottom of oven in case pie bubbles over. Cool completely before cutting.

STRAWBERRY PIE, GLAZED

1 qt. (4 c.) fresh strawberries, divided
1 c. sugar
3 T. cornstarch, packed level
⅛ tsp. salt
½ c. water
1 T. lemon juice
Whipped topping, thawed, or whipped cream
1 baked 9 or 10-in. pie shell

1. Wash, drain and hull strawberries; slice 2 cups berries into baked pie shell. **2.** In large heavy pan, combine sugar, cornstarch and salt, stirring together. **3.** Stir in water and lemon juice; add remaining strawberries, mashing slightly with a potato masher. **4.** Cook, stirring constantly, until mixture thickens and boils 1 minute. **5.** Remove from heat and cool 10 to 15 minutes; pour over sliced berries in pie shell. **6.** Chill completely; serve with whipped topping or whipped cream.

STRAWBERRY PIE, KATHLEEN'S

4 to 5 c. fresh strawberries
1 c. sugar
3 T. cornstarch
⅛ tsp. salt
1 c. water
½ (3-oz.) pkg. dry strawberry gelatin (about 3 T. + ½ tsp.)
5 drops red food coloring
1 baked 9 or 10-in. pie shell

1. Wash, drain and stem berries; if desired, cut large ones in half. **2.** In 2 or 3-quart saucepan, combine sugar, cornstarch, salt and water; stir well. **3.** Add 1 cup strawberries and crush with potato masher. **4.** Bring mixture to a boil, stirring almost constantly; lower heat and simmer gently 2 minutes. **5.** Remove from heat; add dry gelatin and food coloring, stirring well. **6.** Let mixture cool 10 minutes; then add remaining berries and stir gently together until all berries are coated. **7.** Pour into baked pie shell; refrigerate 2 hours or longer (or overnight). <u>**Note:**</u> Fresh red raspberries and red raspberry gelatin may be used instead of strawberries.

WALNUT PIE

3 eggs, lightly beaten
½ c. sugar
2 T. all-purpose flour
1 c. light or dark corn syrup
2 T. butter, melted
1 tsp. vanilla
1 unbaked 9-in. pie shell
1½ c. lg. pcs. English walnuts

1. Turn oven dial to 400°. **2.** In bowl, combine eggs, sugar, flour, corn syrup, melted butter and vanilla; blend well. **3.** Pour into unbaked pie shell. **4.** Arrange walnuts on top. **5.** Bake on lower shelf of preheated 400° oven for 15 minutes. **6.** Reduce heat to 350° and bake 35 to 45 minutes longer, or until center appears set. **7.** Cool completely.

Chapter 25

Desserts

JONATHAN AND NEOVI SWARTS

1997

DESSERTS

AMBROSIA

4 c. fresh orange sections
⅔ c. flaked coconut
1 lg. (or 2 sm.) bananas, sliced
1 (20-oz.) can pineapple chunks, drained (opt.)
2 T. sugar (opt.)
½ c. orange or pineapple juice
½ c. coarsely chopped nuts (opt.)
1 c. miniature marshmallows (opt.)

1. Combine ingredients; chill.

APPLES, BAKED

From Lola Cramer.

Apples
Brown sugar
Raisins (opt.)
Nuts (opt.)
Cinnamon
Butter
1 c. water

1. Core as many apples as desired and peel one strip around the top of each apple. 2. Place in shallow baking dish; fill cavities with brown sugar. 3. Press brown sugar in; then add raisins and/or nuts, if desired. 4. Sprinkle cinnamon over top. 5. Place a thin slice of butter over each apple. 6. Put 1 cup water in bottom of pan. 7. Bake in 350° oven, uncovered, for 45 minutes or until apples are tender. Serve warm or cold.

APPLE COBBLER

Makes 6 big servings.

5 c. peeled and sliced tart apples
¾ c. sugar
2 T. flour
½ tsp. cinnamon
⅛ tsp. salt
¼ c. water
1 tsp. vanilla
½ T. lemon juice
2 T. butter
½ c. English walnuts, coarsely chopped (opt.)

Batter:
½ c. sugar
2 T. butter, softened
1 egg
½ c. all-purpose flour
½ tsp. baking powder
⅛ tsp. salt

1. After preparing apples, turn oven dial to 375°. 2. In med.-small bowl, combine first sugar, flour, cinnamon and salt, mixing well; sprinkle over apples. 3. Add water, vanilla and lemon juice; stir together. 4. Turn into ungreased 12 x 8-inch baking dish; dot with first butter and sprinkle with nuts. 5. To make batter, combine all batter ingredients in same med.-small bowl (or mixer bowl) and beat until smooth. 6. Drop in 6 portions over apples. (Batter will spread during baking.) 7. Bake in preheated 375° oven 35 to 40 minutes, until golden brown. 8. Serve slightly warm with milk, cream, ice cream or whipped topping.

APPLE CRISP

Serve with ice cream or milk. From Betty Geneviva.

Filling:
1½ lbs. peeled, sliced cooking apples (5 c., firmly packed)
½ c. sugar
1 tsp. cinnamon
¼ tsp. salt

Batter:
1 egg, beaten
1 c. all-purpose flour
¾ c. sugar
1 tsp. baking powder
¼ c. (½ stick) butter, melted

1. Put apples in 13 x 9-inch baking pan. 2. Preheat oven to 350°. 3. In small bowl, combine ½ cup sugar, cinnamon and salt; sprinkle over apples. 4. In same bowl, beat egg; set aside. 5. In medium bowl, combine flour, ¾ cup sugar and the baking powder. 6. Add beaten egg and mix until crumbly. 7. Sprinkle mixture over apples. 8. Drizzle melted butter over top. 9. Bake until light golden brown, about 35 to 45 minutes.

APPLE CRUNCH

From Olive Holt.

1¾ lbs. peeled and thinly sliced apples (6 c., firmly packed)
⅔ c. sugar
1 tsp. cinnamon
1 c. all-purpose flour
½ c. packed brown sugar
⅓ c. butter
1 tsp. cinnamon
½ c. nuts, coarsely chopped

1. Prepare apples; then turn oven dial to 350°. 2. Put sliced apples in greased 12 x 8 x 2-inch baking dish (or 13 x 9-inch baking dish). If apples are not tart, sprinkle 1 tablespoon lemon juice over them. 3. In med.-small bowl, combine sugar and first cinnamon; sprinkle over apples. 4. In same bowl, mix together flour, brown sugar, butter, second cinnamon and nuts; sprinkle over apples. 5. Bake in preheated 350° oven 45 minutes, or until apples are bubbly and top is golden brown. 6. Serve warm or cold with ice cream, whipped topping or milk. **Note:** Do not cover this later, or it will get soggy.

APPLE DUMPLINGS I

Makes 6 apple dumplings. From Lois Perrine.

6 med. whole apples, pared and cored (leave whole)
Sugar, cinnamon and nutmeg

Syrup:
1½ c. sugar
1½ c. water
¼ tsp. cinnamon
¼ tsp. nutmeg
7 drops red food coloring
3 T. butter

Dough:
2 c. all-purpose flour
2 tsp. baking powder
½ tsp. salt
⅔ c. Earth Balance shortening
½ c. milk

1. In saucepan, combine sugar, water, cinnamon, nutmeg and food coloring for syrup and bring to a boil; remove from heat and add butter. Set aside. **2.** For dough, combine dry ingredients in bowl; cut in shortening until mixture resembles coarse crumbs. **3.** Add milk all at once and stir just until flour is moistened. **4.** On lightly floured surface, roll dough ⅛ to ¼ inch thick into 18 x 12-inch rectangle; cut with table knife into 6-inch squares. **5.** Place an apple in each square; sprinkle each apple generously with sugar, cinnamon and nutmeg. **6.** Moisten edges of squares; fold corners to center and pinch edges together. **7.** Place 1 inch apart in ungreased baking pan; pour syrup over dumplings. **8.** Sprinkle with a bit more sugar. **9.** Bake in preheated 375° oven 35 minutes, or until apples are tender. Note: If apples are large, roll dough squares a little larger.

APPLE DUMPLINGS II (Makes 8)

Serve slightly warm with milk or ice cream.

Pastry:
1¾ c. all-purpose flour
½ T. sugar
½ tsp. salt
¾ c. Earth Balance shortening
1 egg
3 T. ice cold water
½ T. vinegar

Syrup:
¾ c. sugar
1 tsp. cinnamon
2 c. water
¼ c. butter

Filling:
4 c. peeled, diced apples
½ c. sugar
1 tsp. cinnamon
Lemon juice

1. Measure flour, sugar and salt into med.-large bowl. **2.** Add shortening; mix with fingers or pastry blender until crumbly. **3.** In small bowl, mix egg, water and vinegar together with wire whip or fork. **4.** Pour as much egg mixture as is needed over flour mixture, stirring with fork only until dough clings together; set bowl in refrigerator. **5.** Put syrup ingredients in medium saucepan and bring to a boil; lower heat and boil gently for 10 minutes; remove from heat. **6.** Peel and dice apples. **7.** In small bowl, mix the remaining ½ cup sugar and 1 teaspoon cinnamon together; set aside. **8.** Turn oven to 375°. **9.** Divide dough evenly into 8 portions (each portion will be about the size of a large egg). If sticky, use a little flour. **10.** Roll each portion on floured surface to a 7 or 8-inch circle or square, approximately. **11.** Place ½ cup diced apples on middle of rolled-out pastry. **12.** Sprinkle 1 tablespoon of the sugar-cinnamon mixture over the ½ cup diced apples. **13.** Add ½ teaspoon lemon juice to each apple dumpling. **14.** Wrap pastry up around the apples; place dumplings in a 13 x 9-inch or 13½ x 8¾-inch baking dish or pan. **15.** Pour hot syrup around dumplings. **16.** Bake, uncovered, in preheated 375° oven for 45 minutes, or until golden in color and bubbly. Makes 8 apple dumplings.

APPLE-OATMEAL KRINKLE

6 c. sliced apples, peeled or unpeeled
½ c. sugar
4 T. flour (level)
1 tsp. cinnamon
1 T. lemon juice
1 c. boiling water
1 c. packed brown sugar
1 c. oats, uncooked (quick or reg.)
1 c. all-purpose flour
¼ tsp. salt
¼ tsp. baking powder
⅔ c. butter
1 tsp. vanilla (opt.)

1. Prepare apples; then turn oven dial to 375°. **2.** Put sliced apples in 13 x 9-inch baking dish, lightly greased or sprayed. **3.** In medium bowl, combine sugar, first flour and cinnamon; sprinkle over apples. **4.** Sprinkle lemon juice over apples. **5.** Pour boiling water over apples. **6.** In same medium bowl, mix together brown sugar, oatmeal, second flour, salt, baking powder, butter and vanilla. **7.** Crumble mixture over apples. **8.** Bake on middle shelf of preheated 375° oven about 35 minutes, or until apples are bubbly and top is golden brown. **9.** Serve warm or cold.

BAKLAVA

From Neovi Karakatsanis and Jonathan Swarts.
A Greek dessert.

8 oz. prepared phyllo pastry leaves
8 oz. finely chopped walnuts
¼ c. sugar
½ tsp. ground cinnamon
½ lb. (2 sticks) pure butter, melted

Syrup:
2¼ c. sugar
1¼ c. water
2 sm. pcs. lemon rind
1 to 1½ cinnamon sticks
3 to 4 whole cloves

1. Let pastry leaves warm to room temperature according to package directions. 2. In small bowl, combine nuts, ¼ cup sugar and ground cinnamon, mixing together. 3. Coat inside of 13 x 9-inch cake pan with butter; turn oven dial to 350°. 4. After opening package of phyllo pastry leaves, keep them covered with damp paper towel, to prevent drying out. Do not stop laying the pastry leaves once you have started because it will quickly dry out and become unworkable. 5. Place 1 sheet of phyllo dough into buttered pan; brush top of sheet with butter. Place second sheet on top of first. Butter top of second sheet. Repeat until you have 6 sheets in pan. Butter top of sixth sheet also. 6. Sprinkle walnut-sugar-cinnamon mixture over entire top, using just part of it. 7. Add 2 sheets of dough, buttering between them and on top of second sheet. 8. Sprinkle another layer of nut mixture over top. 9. Repeat, alternating 2 sheets of dough with a sprinkling of the nut mixture, until there are only 6 sheets of phyllo dough remaining. 10. Finish by topping it with those 6 buttered sheets (the same as the bottom began with 6 sheets). 11. Pour remaining butter over Baklava. 12. Cut the Baklava diagonally into diamond-shape pieces (1½-inch strips). Cut carefully to prevent damaging the layers of soft dough. 13. Sprinkle 2 tablespoons water over Baklava. 14. Bake in preheated 350° oven approximately 1 hour, until golden brown. 15. Allow Baklava to cool completely. 16. To make syrup: In 2-quart saucepan, combine the syrup ingredients and bring to a boil; boil 10 minutes, stirring occasionally. Remove lemon peel, cinnamon sticks and cloves. 17. Pour syrup, while still hot, over the cold Baklava, covering it completely. 18. Allow Baklava to soak in syrup overnight; after soaking, the pieces can be removed from the pan and put in cupcake foils.

BREAD PUDDING, EASY

Delicious served warm or cold!

4 eggs
⅓ c. sugar
⅓ c. packed brown sugar
¼ tsp. salt
4 c. milk (part evaporated milk, if desired)
1 to 2 tsp. vanilla

2 to 2½ c. bread cubes or crumbs (may be stale bread or leftover toast or rolls, cubed)
1 T. butter, cut into pcs.
¼ tsp. cinnamon and/or nutmeg (opt.)
½ c. raisins (opt.)

1. In buttered or sprayed 2-quart casserole, put eggs, sugar, brown sugar, salt, milk and vanilla; beat together with wire whip or whisk. 2. Add remaining ingredients and stir together. 3. Place casserole in 13 x 9-inch cake pan; pour hot water, 1 inch deep, into cake pan. 4. Bake, uncovered, in preheated 325° oven for 1½ hours, or until a knife inserted in pudding comes out clean. (Stir twice after first 45 minutes to get raisins off bottom.)

BREAD PUDDING, PINEAPPLE

10 slices white bread
⅔ c. butter or regular Smart Balance, melted
5 eggs
1 can (20-oz.) crushed pineapple, undrained
½ c. raisins
1 c. sugar
1½ t. vanilla
¾ t. cinnamon

1. Preheat oven to 375°; place bread on a baking sheet and bake 4 minutes. 2. Turn bread over and bake until barely light golden. 3. Cut toasted bread into 1-inch cubes; toss with melted butter and set aside. 4. Reduce oven dial to 350°. 5. In mixer bowl, beat eggs well; add pineapple, undrained, and raisins, sugar and vanilla. Mix together. 6. Fold in bread crumbs; pour into a greased baking dish. Sprinkle with the cinnamon. 7. Bake at 350° for 30 to 35 minutes. Serve slightly warm with whipped topping, if desired.

BROWNIE DELIGHT

From Tammy Wagler.

1 brownie mix for a 13 x 9-inch pan
1 (8-oz.) pkg. cream cheese, softened
1 (8 or 12-oz.) carton whipped topping, thawed (divided)
1 small box instant chocolate pudding
2 c. milk

1. Bake brownies according to package directions; cool completely. 2. Whip cream cheese; fold in 2 cups whipped topping and spread over brownies. 3. Mix together instant pudding and milk; cool in refrigerator 5 minutes. 4. Spread on top the last layer, then spread remaining whipped topping over all.

CHEESECAKE, PINEAPPLE

From Violet Crocker Hilliard.

1 (3-oz.) pkg. lemon gelatin
¾ c. boiling water
8 oz. cream cheese, softened
1 c. sugar
1 tsp. vanilla
1 (16 to 20-oz.) can crushed pineapple, drained well
1 (12-oz.) can evaporated milk, chilled very cold

Crust:
¼ lb. graham crackers, rolled into crumbs
⅓ c. melted butter

1. Combine lemon gelatin and boiling water; cool. 2. Cream together cream cheese, sugar and vanilla. 3. Mix together cooled (but not set) lemon gelatin and cream cheese mixture; add well-drained pineapple. 4. Whip chilled evaporated milk until it will hold a peak; fold into pineapple mixture. 5. To make crust, mix graham cracker crumbs with melted butter; press half the mixture in bottom of 13 x 9-inch pan. 6. Pour pineapple mixture into crust; sprinkle remaining crumbs on top. Chill.
Lemon Cheesecake: Omit pineapple and add 3 T. lemon juice.

CHERRY DELIGHT I

Adapted from Kelly Wells Crouch. Delicious!

1 stick (½ c.) butter, melted
¼ c. sugar
2 c. graham crackers, crushed
1 c. milk
1 c. vanilla ice cream
1 c. whipped topping, thawed
1 lg. or sm. pkg. vanilla instant pudding (6 or 4-serving size)
1 (21-oz. or larger) can cherry pie filling (or blueberry)

1. In saucepan, melt butter; add sugar and stir until sugar dissolves. 2. Remove from heat; add graham cracker crumbs. Mix together and press onto bottom of 13 x 9-inch pan or dish. 3. Chill crust for 15 minutes in refrigerator. 4. In large mixer bowl, combine milk, ice cream, whipped topping and instant pudding mix; beat 2 or 3 minutes with electric mixer. 5. Spread pudding mixture over crust; chill another 15 minutes or until pudding is set. 6. Spread pie filling over pudding layer.

CHERRY DELIGHT II

⅓ to ½ c. butter, melted
1¾ to 2 c. graham cracker crumbs
1 T. sugar
3 to 8 oz. cream cheese, softened a little
⅓ c. powdered or ¼ c. granulated sugar
1 (8-oz.) carton whipped topping, thawed, or 2 env. Dream Whip, prepared
2 (21-oz. each) cans cherry pie filling
½ tsp. almond flavoring*

1. In medium microwave-safe bowl, melt butter (cover with Corelle plate or waxed paper). 2. Add graham cracker crumbs and 1 tablespoon sugar; mix well and press into bottom of 13 x 9-inch dish. 3. In mixer bowl, beat cream cheese; add sugar and beat well. 4. Fold in whipped topping; spread over graham cracker crust. 5. Combine pie filling and almond flavoring; spoon over cream cheese layer. 6. Refrigerate. (*If preparing Dream Whip, add almond flavoring to it instead of to the pie filling, omitting vanilla.) **Blueberry Delight:** Use blueberry pie filling instead of cherry. Omit almond flavoring.

CHOCOLATE ANGEL FILLING

1½ c. cold milk
1 pkg. (4-serving size) instant chocolate pudding
1 c. thawed whipped topping (approximately)

1. In mixer bowl, put cold milk; add pudding mix and beat on lowest speed for 3 minutes. 2. Fold in whipped topping.

CHOCOLATE FILLING
(Eggless, for Cream Puffs)

¾ c. sugar
3 T. cornstarch
3 T. unsweetened dry cocoa
¼ tsp. salt
2 c. milk
1 tsp. vanilla
1 tsp. butter

1. In medium saucepan, mix sugar, cornstarch, cocoa and salt together. 2. Gradually add milk; cook, stirring constantly, until mixture comes to a boil. 3. Lower heat and boil gently 1 minute, stirring. 4. Remove from heat; stir in vanilla and butter.

CHOCOLATE GLAZE I (For Cream Puffs)

½ c. semi-sweet chocolate chips
1 T. Earth Balance shortening
1 T. light corn syrup
1½ T. milk

1. In top of double boiler, combine all ingredients. 2. Place over hot, not boiling, water; stir occasionally, until mixture is smooth. 3. Let cool slightly before frosting or drizzling over tops of cream puffs.

CHOCOLATE GLAZE II (For Cream Puffs)

2 T. cocoa
1 T. + 2 tsp. hot water
1 T. olive oil
1 c. powdered sugar
¼ to ½ tsp. vanilla

1. Dissolve cocoa in hot water. 2. Add oil; then blend in powdered sugar (sift if lumpy). 3. Add more powdered sugar, if needed, to thicken or add a little water to thin for desired consistency. 4. Drizzle over top of 12 cream puffs.

COCONUT, GRATED

One good-sized coconut makes 4 cups.

Pierce* the eyes of the coconut; drain out the liquid and reserve it for another use. Break the coconut with a hammer and remove the flesh from the shell with the point of a strong knife. Peel off the brown membrane and cut the coconut flesh into small pieces. In a blender or food processor, process the pieces, a few at a time. (*With long nail, puncture the 3 indentations at the end of the fresh coconut.)

CREAM PUFF DESSERT

1 c. boiling water
½ c. butter or reg. Smart Balance Spread
1 c. flour
4 eggs

Filling:
3 small pkg. instant vanilla pudding
8 oz. cream cheese, softened
3½ c. milk, divided
1 (8-oz.) carton whipped topping, thawed
Hershey's chocolate syrup

1. Melt butter with boiling water. 2. Add flour and cook slowly until thick; cool. 3. Beat in eggs, one at a time. 4. Pour into greased 9 x 13 x 2-inch pan; bake in preheated 400° oven for 30 to 35 minutes; cool. 5. For filling, beat the cream cheese with 1 cup milk for 2 minutes; then add remaining 2½ c. milk and the instant pudding mixes and beat for 2 minutes longer. 6. Spread over crust; top with whipped topping and drizzle with chocolate syrup. Refrigerate. **Milk Chocolate Flavor:** Use 2 pkg. instant chocolate pudding and 1 pkg. instant vanilla pudding.

CREAM PUFFS

Makes 10.

1 c. water
1 stick (½ c.) butter
¼ tsp. salt
1 c. all-purpose flour
4 lg. eggs, unbeaten
Vanilla Cream Filling
Chocolate Glaze
Powdered sugar

1. In 3-quart saucepan, combine water, butter and salt; bring to a rolling boil. 2. Remove from heat and add flour all at once; stir vigorously. 3. Over low heat, stir until mixture forms a ball, about 1 minute; remove from heat and let cool about 5 minutes. 4. Turn oven dial to 400°. 5. Add eggs, one at a time, and beat with large spoon until very smooth and well blended. 6. Lightly grease or spray one large cookie sheet; spoon batter in 10 even mounds, about 2 to 3 inches apart, on cookie sheet. 7. Bake in preheated 400° oven 35 to 45 minutes, until puffy and golden brown. 8. Carefully remove from cookie sheet to cooling rack; cool completely, away from drafts. 9. Shortly before serving, cut off tops of puffs and remove any soft dough that strings through the inside cavity. 10. Fill puffs with Vanilla Cream Filling (or pudding or ice cream); replace tops. 11. Drizzle with Chocolate Glaze or Fudge Sauce; dust tops with powdered sugar.

Vanilla Cream Filling (eggless):
½ c. sugar
3 T. cornstarch (level)
¼ tsp. salt
2 c. milk
2 T. butter
2 tsp. vanilla
3 drops yellow food coloring

1. In medium saucepan, mix sugar, cornstarch and salt together. 2. Add a small amount of the milk, stirring until blended; add remainder of milk. 3. Cook over medium heat, stirring constantly, until mixture boils; lower heat and boil 1 minute, stirring. 4. Remove from heat; stir in butter, vanilla and food coloring. 5. Cool.

CREPES FROM VIENNA

½ c. olive oil
4 eggs
½ tsp. salt
⅔ c. all-purpose flour
½ c. milk or cream

1. Beat oil, eggs and salt together. 2. Add flour and mix together. 3. Add milk and mix until smooth. (Batter will be thin.) 4. Heat a skillet over medium-high heat. 5. Grease skillet lightly with butter or oil before making each crepe. 6. Pour 2 tablespoons batter into heated, greased skillet, tilting pan quickly so mixture spreads evenly to about 6 or 7 inches in diameter. 7. When light brown on one side, run spatula around edge to loosen; turn and cook other side until light brown. 8. Cook crepes one at a time; cool on wire rack; then stack, with waxed paper between each one. If not using immediately, carefully place stack in a plastic bag or container and refrigerate or freeze. (May be stored in freezer for 3 months.) 9. Fill crepes with creamed meat mixture, roll up and keep warm. Or use as a dessert: fill with cherry pie filling, roll up and sprinkle with powdered sugar or top with whipped cream. Or fill with ice cream, roll up and drizzle hot fudge sauce over top. Makes 14 or 15.

CUSTARD, BAKED

1 T. butter
2½ c. milk
3 eggs, beaten slightly
½ c. sugar
¼ tsp. salt
1 tsp. vanilla
Nutmeg

1. Heat butter and milk together, but do not boil. 2. In medium bowl, beat eggs slightly with fork; add remaining ingredients, except nutmeg. 3. Pour into hot milk; transfer to a casserole and sprinkle nutmeg over top. 4. Place casserole in a shallow pan of hot water. 5. Bake in preheated 350° oven 30 minutes or until knife inserted near the center comes out clean.

DATE PUDDING, AMISH

From Beverly Muir Johnston

1 c. boiling water
1 c. chopped dates
1 c. sugar (or brown sugar)
1 tsp. baking soda
1 T. butter
1 egg
1 c. all-purpose flour
⅛ tsp. salt (opt.)
1 tsp. vanilla
½ to 1 c. chopped walnuts

1. Pour boiling water over dates; add sugar, soda and butter; cool. 2. When cool, add remaining ingredients and stir until combined. 3. Pour into greased (or sprayed) and floured 8 x 8-inch baking pan. 4. Bake in preheated 350° oven 30 minutes or until center springs back when touched. 5. Cut into squares and serve warm or cold with whipped topping. Note: To double this recipe, bake in 13 x 9-inch cake pan. Bake until center springs back when lightly touched, or when wooden pick comes out clean.

DATE PUDDING (Eggless)

From Genevieve Benninger Jeannerat.

Syrup:
1 c. packed brown sugar
1 tsp. butter
3 c. hot water

Batter:
½ c. packed brown sugar
2 T. butter
1½ c. all-purpose flour
2 tsp. baking powder
⅛ tsp. salt
½ c. milk

1 c. diced or chopped dates
½ to 1 c. chopped walnuts

1. Turn oven dial to 350° and grease or spray 13 x 9 x 2-inch baking dish. 2. In saucepan, combine syrup ingredients and boil gently while making batter. 3. For batter, cream together brown sugar and butter; add remaining ingredients. 4. Pour syrup into prepared pan. 5. Drop batter by spoonfuls into hot syrup. 6. Bake in preheated 350° oven 30 minutes. 7. Serve hot or cold with whipped cream.

ÉCLAIR DESSERT

From Berneice Woodward-Pfautz.

Most of one pound graham crackers
2 small boxes instant French Vanilla pudding (or vanilla)
3 c. milk
1 (8-oz.) carton whipped topping, thawed

1. Butter bottom and sides of 9 x 13 x 2-inch pan; line with a single layer of graham crackers (not crumbs). 2. Mix pudding with milk and beat at low or medium speed for two minutes; fold in whipped topping. 3. Pour half of the pudding mixture over crackers, spreading evenly. 4. Place a second layer of crackers over pudding and pour remaining pudding mixture over top, spreading evenly again. 5. Cover with third layer of crackers; refrigerate 1 hour before frosting or frost immediately. Mint Éclairs: After making pudding, but before folding in whipped topping, add ½ t. mint or peppermint extract and 3 to 4 drops green food coloring.

Frosting:
6 T. dry unsweetened cocoa
2 T. olive oil
2 T. corn syrup
2 tsp. vanilla
1½ c. powdered sugar
3 T. softened butter
3 T. milk

1. Put all ingredients into mixing bowl and blend until smooth; spread over dessert. 2. Cover and refrigerate for several hours before serving (up to 24 hours). Makes 10 to 12 servings.

FOUR-LAYER DELIGHT

Also called "Mr. Wonderful," "Slush Cake," "Ice Cream Cake," and many other titles.

1¼ c. all-purpose flour
½ c. (1 stick) butter
½ to 1 c. walnuts, coarsely chopped
8 oz. cream cheese
½ c. sugar (or 1 c. powdered sugar)
½ to 1 tsp. vanilla
1 (8-oz.) carton whipped topping, divided (or larger carton)
2 (4-serving size) boxes INSTANT pudding (chocolate, lemon, butter pecan, pistachio or coconut cream)
3 c. cold milk
Nuts or graham cracker crumbs for top (opt.)

1. With mixer, food processor or hands, mix together flour, butter and nuts. **2.** Press in bottom of ungreased 13 x 9-inch glass baking dish and bake in preheated 350° oven 15 to 20 minutes; cool at least 20 minutes. **3.** For second layer, in mixer bowl, beat together cream cheese, powdered sugar, vanilla and 1 cup whipped topping; spread over cooled crust. **4.** For third layer, in same bowl, sprinkle instant pudding over cold milk; beat on low speed until thick and spread over second layer. **5.** Spread remaining whipped topping carefully over pudding. **6.** If desired, sprinkle crushed or chopped nuts or graham cracker crumbs or flaked coconut over top. (This keeps plastic wrap out of topping.) **7.** Cover with plastic wrap or lid and chill for 2 hours (or overnight). <u>Milk Chocolate Variation</u>: Use 1 package chocolate and 1 package vanilla instant pudding. <u>Pineapple Variation</u>: Put 1 can drained crushed pineapple over cream cheese layer; use pineapple cream instant pudding (or coconut cream). <u>Banana Variation</u>: Lay sliced bananas over cream cheese layer; use banana cream instant pudding. <u>Cherry Variation</u>: Pour 1 can cherry pie filling over cream cheese layer; use vanilla instant pudding. <u>Peach Variation</u>: Lay drained peaches (canned, fresh or frozen) over cream cheese layer; use vanilla instant pudding.

FOUR-LAYER GREEN PISTACHIO DESSERT

From Neovi Karakatsanis. Makes 15 to 20 servings.

1½ c. all-purpose flour
½ c. (1 stick) butter, softened
½ c. chopped pecans or walnuts
8 oz. cream cheese, softened
1 c. powdered sugar
2 (8-oz.) cartons or 1 (12-oz.) carton whipped topping,
    thawed
2 (4-serving size) pkgs. instant pistachio pudding
3 c. milk
½ c. chopped nuts

1. Mix together flour, butter and pecans; pat firmly in the bottom of 13 x 9 x 2-inch baking dish and bake in preheated 350° oven 15 minutes. Cool completely. **2.** Beat cream cheese and powdered sugar together; fold in 8 ounces of whipped topping. **3.** Spread over cooled baked crust; chill in refrigerator. **4.** Mix instant pudding and milk together; pour over cream cheese layer. **5.** Top with remaining whipped topping and sprinkle with nuts; refrigerate.

FRUIT PUDDING-CAKE DESSERT

*Adapted from Jean Dreyer; a very different
and delicious dessert.*

1 c. sugar
2 T. cornstarch, level
¼ t. cinnamon

4 c. apples, sliced, or fresh or frozen sour cherries, or
    fresh or frozen sliced peaches, fresh rhubarb, cut into
    one-inch pieces, or elderberries, fresh or frozen

1 c. sugar
½ c. light olive oil
1 c. milk
½ t. salt
2 t. baking powder
2 c. flour

2 c. boiling water

1. Mix first three ingredients together and set aside. **2.** Put fruit in 9 x 13-inch pan. (If rhubarb or sour cherries are your choice, use glass pan.) **3.** Cream together sugar and oil; then add milk alternately with salt, baking powder and flour. Pour this batter over fruit. **4.** Sprinkle the sugar-cornstarch-cinnamon mixture over the top of batter. **5.** Pour boiling water over all. **6.** Bake in preheated 325 oven for 60 to 70 minutes.

HOT FUDGE PUDDING CAKE

Serve warm with vanilla ice cream or whipped topping.

1 c. all-purpose flour
¾ c. sugar
4 T. unsweetened cocoa
2 tsp. baking powder
¼ tsp. salt
½ c. milk
1 to 1½ tsp. vanilla
2 T. olive oil or melted butter
¾ to 1 c. coarsely chopped nuts or flaked coconut (opt.)
1 c. packed brown sugar
4 T. unsweetened cocoa
1¾ c. hot tap water

1. Turn oven to 350°. **2.** Stir together first 5 ingredients in ungreased 8 x 8-inch or 9 x 9-inch square baking pan (or bowl). **3.** Add milk, vanilla and oil; stir until well blended. **4.** Add nuts or coconut, if desired; spread batter evenly in pan. **5.** Sprinkle brown sugar and last 3 tablespoons cocoa over batter. **6.** Pour hot water over all; do not stir. **7.** Bake in preheated 350° oven 35 to 45 minutes, or until cake springs back when lightly touched. **8.** Let stand 15 minutes; spoon into dessert dishes, spooning sauce from bottom of pan over top. Serves 6 to 9.

ICE CREAM, FRESH PEACH

Makes approximately 2 quarts. No cooking!

½ c. Egg Beaters
1¼ c. sugar
1 c. whole milk or goat's milk
½ to 1 tsp. vanilla
⅛ tsp. almond extract
3 c. peeled and chopped fresh peaches
1 c. goat's milk or whipping cream
1 drop yellow food coloring (opt.)

1. In large mixer bowl, beat eggs until thick and lemon colored. **2.** Beat in sugar. **3.** Stir in milk, vanilla and almond extract; set aside. **4.** Mash peaches with potato masher or puree in food processor or blender; stir into egg mixture. **5.** Stir in the remaining goat's milk or whipping cream. **6.** Pour into ice cream canister; freeze in ice cream maker according to manufacturer's directions.

ICE CREAM, STRAWBERRY

From Martha McKee. No cooking.

1 qt. strawberries (4 c.)
¾ c. sugar
1½ c. evaporated milk, light cream, or evaporated skimmed milk
½ c. whole milk
⅛ tsp. salt
½ tsp. vanilla (opt.)

1. Wash and hull berries; mash well. **2.** Add sugar to berries; let stand 20 minutes. **3.** Add cream, milk, salt and vanilla; pour into freezer container. **4.** Freeze in ice cream maker, according to manufacturer's directions. **Note:** 2 (10-ounce) boxes frozen sliced strawberries, thawed, may be substituted for fresh berries. Add only ½ cup sugar. **Note:** If desired, berries can be forced through a sieve after mashing to remove seeds.

ICE CREAM, VANILLA

Makes 2 quarts.

1⅓ c. sugar
1 T. cornstarch
¼ tsp. salt
3 c. whole milk
2 egg yolks
1 (12-oz.) can evaporated milk (1½ c.)
1 T. white (or dark) vanilla

1. In 2 or 3-quart saucepan, combine sugar, cornstarch and salt. **2.** Stir in whole milk; cook, stirring constantly, over medium heat until mixture comes to a boil. **3.** Reduce heat and simmer 1 minute, stirring; set aside. **4.** In small bowl, beat egg yolks lightly; stir 1 cup hot milk mixture into egg yolks. **5.** Stir egg yolk mixture into remaining hot milk mixture; cook, stirring, over low heat 2 minutes, or until slightly thickened. **6.** Stir in

evaporated milk and vanilla; cool to room temperature. **7.** Pour into ice cream canister; freeze in ice cream maker according to manufacturer's directions. **Note:** 1 cup whipping cream may be substituted for 1 cup of the evaporated milk.

LEMON SPONGE CUPS

Lemon custard on the bottom, and sponge cake on top.

1 c. sugar
2 T. butter
4 T. flour, packed level
⅛ tsp. salt
5 T. lemon juice
Grated rind from 1 lemon (opt.)
3 eggs, separated
1½ c. milk

1. Turn oven dial to 350°. **2.** Grease tops of 6 to 8 custard cups (around rim, mainly). **3.** Cream together sugar and butter. **4.** Add flour, salt, lemon juice and lemon rind; beat well. **5.** In separate bowl, beat egg yolks; add milk and mix well. **6.** Stir together egg mixture and lemon mixture. **7.** Beat egg whites until stiff; fold into lemon mixture with rubber spatula, blending together well until egg whites have disappeared. **8.** Pour into custard cups and set in pan; pour water around cups until it comes halfway up the outside of cups. **9.** Bake about 45 minutes in preheated 350° oven.

NUTTY FRUIT CRISP

5 c. sliced apples, peaches, pears or apricots
3 T. sugar
½ c. uncooked oats
⅓ c. all-purpose flour
1 T. cornstarch
½ c. brown sugar, packed
½ t. cinnamon
⅓ c. Smart Balance 67% Buttery Spread (soften at room temperature for 15 min.)
⅓ c. walnuts or pecans, chopped

1. Place sliced fruit in 8 x 8 x 2-inch baking dish; stir in 3 T. sugar. **2.** In a mixing bowl, combine oats, flour, cornstarch, brown sugar and cinnamon. **3.** Cut in Smart Balance Spread until well mixed. **4.** Stir in chopped nuts and sprinkle over fruit. **5.** Bake at 375° for 30 to 35 minutes or until topping is golden brown. **6.** Serve warm with milk, ice cream, whipped topping or frozen yogurt if desired. Makes 8 servings. **Blueberry variation:** Mix 5 c. blueberries with 3 T. sugar and 4 T. flour; prepare with topping as above and bake.

Desserts

OREO COOKIE DESSERT

Takes cream cheese.

40 Oreo chocolate cookies
½ c. (1 stick) butter
2 (4-serving size) pkgs. instant pudding (pistachio, vanilla or 1 pkg. vanilla and 1 pkg. chocolate)
3 c. cold milk
8 oz. cream cheese (room temp.)
1 c. powdered sugar
1 (8-oz.) carton whipped topping, thawed

1. Crush cookies (in food processor, if available). 2. Melt butter; add crushed cookies, stirring together. 3. Press half the cookie mixture onto bottom of 13 x 9-inch or 12 x 8-inch pan, glass dish or Tupperware container. 4. Combine pudding mixes with 3 cups cold milk; set aside. 5. In another bowl, mix together cream cheese and powdered sugar; add whipped topping, stirring well. 6. Fold in pudding, combining mixtures; pour over cookie crust. 7. Sprinkle remaining half of cookie crumbs over top. 8. Cover with plastic wrap or lid and chill several hours, or overnight.

OREO COOKIE DESSERT, FROZEN

Takes ice cream.

24 Oreo chocolate cookies, coarsely crumbled
6 T. butter, melted
1½ qt. vanilla ice cream, softened slightly
1 c. Hershey chocolate syrup
1 (8-oz.) container whipped topping, thawed
Chopped nuts
3 additional cookies

1. Turn oven dial to 350°. 2. Crumble cookies in 13 x 9-inch pan, using potato masher. 3. Drizzle melted butter over crumbs and stir together; press in bottom of pan. Bake in 350° oven 7 minutes. 4. When crust is cool, cover with softened ice cream; pour syrup over ice cream. 5. Spread whipped topping over all and sprinkle with nuts and 3 additional cookies, crumbled. 6. Freeze.

PARFAIT, CHOCOLATE MINT

So easy, quick and delicious!

3 to 4 oz. cream cheese, softened
1 T. sugar
1 T. milk
¼ tsp. peppermint extract
A few drops of green food coloring
1 carton (8 oz.) whipped topping, thawed (or less)
2 c. milk
1 pkg. (4-serving size) instant chocolate pudding mix

1. With mixer, beat cream cheese, sugar, 1 Tablespoon milk, peppermint extract, and green food coloring together until well blended. 2. Fold in whipped topping; set aside. 3. In another bowl, whisk or beat together 2 c. milk and the pudding mix for 2 minutes. 4. In parfait or glass dishes, layer the pudding and cream cheese mixture (in several layers). **Makes 6 servings.**

PARFAIT, GRASSHOPPER (Microwave)

Easy and delicious.

15 lg. marshmallows
¼ c. milk
½ tsp. vanilla
½ (8-oz.) carton whipped topping, thawed
⅛ tsp. peppermint extract
2 drops green food coloring
4 Oreo-type chocolate cookies (made into crumbs)

1. In 2-quart bowl, microwave marshmallows and milk, covered, on HIGH 1½ to 2 minutes or until melted, stirring halfway through cooking. 2. Stir in vanilla; refrigerate 20 to 25 minutes, until mixture cools and thickens slightly. (Stir occasionally.) 3. Fold whipped topping into marshmallow mixture; divide in half. To one half, add peppermint extract and green food coloring. 4. Spoon into 4 parfait glasses, alternately layering cookie crumbs with white and green marshmallow mixtures. 5. Chill. Makes 4 servings.

PEACH COBBLER I

In Peach Cobbler I and II recipes, either bottom layer may be used with either top layer.

<u>Bottom Layer:</u>
4 to 5 c. peeled, sliced fresh peaches
⅔ c. sugar
1 tsp. cornstarch or quick tapioca
¼ tsp. cinnamon or almond extract
2 T. butter

<u>Cake Topping:</u>
1 c. sugar
¼ c. olive oil
1 egg
1½ c. all-purpose flour
½ tsp. baking powder
¼ tsp. salt
¼ c. milk

1. Turn oven dial to 400°. 2. In 2 or 3-quart saucepan, combine peaches and remaining bottom layer ingredients; bring to a boil. 3. Remove from heat and pour into ungreased 13 x 9-inch baking pan. 4. <u>For cake topping:</u> cream together sugar, oil and egg. 5. Add remaining ingredients and stir together; drop spoonfuls of dough over the peaches. 6. Bake in preheated 400° oven about 25 minutes, or until golden brown. <u>To Cut Recipe In Half:</u> Bake in 8 x 8-inch square pan.

PEACH COBBLER II

Adapted from Laura Robison.

Bottom Layer:
2 (16-oz.) cans sliced peaches, or 1 qt. home-canned
    peaches
¼ c. sugar
1 T. cornstarch
1 T. lemon juice

Biscuit Topping:
1½ c. all-purpose flour
1 T. sugar
3 tsp. baking powder
¼ tsp. salt
⅓ c. Earth Balance shortening
1 egg
½ c. milk
Granulated sugar

1. Turn oven dial to 400°. 2. Drain peaches, reserving liquid. 3. In saucepan, combine sugar and cornstarch; add reserved peach liquid. 4. Cook, stirring almost constantly, until mixture comes to a full boil; remove from heat. 5. Stir in lemon juice and drained peaches; pour into ungreased 13 x 9-inch cake pan or 2-quart baking dish. 6. **For Biscuit Topping:** In medium bowl, combine flour, second sugar, baking powder and salt; cut in shortening with pastry blender or fingers. 7. In small bowl, beat egg and milk together; add to dry ingredients, stirring only until moistened. 8. Drop by spoonfuls over peaches; sprinkle granulated sugar lightly over dough. 9. Bake in preheated 400° oven 20 to 25 minutes, or until golden brown.

PEACH COBBLER III

From Beulah Deeter.

3 c. fresh peaches or 2 c. canned peaches and 1 c. juice
½ c. sugar
2 T. flour
½ T. cinnamon
2 T. butter

Crust:
1 c. flour
¼ c. sugar
1½ t. baking powder
¼ t. salt
¼ c. olive oil
3 T. milk
1 egg

1. Arrange fruit in 8 x 8- or 9 x 9-inch baking pan; combine first sugar, first flour and cinnamon. Sprinkle over fruit. 2. Dot with butter. 3. For crust, combine flour, sugar, baking powder and salt in small bowl; add oil, milk and egg. Stir with fork until blended. 4. Drop by spoonfuls over the fruit; bake in preheated 350° oven 30 to 40 minutes. (Make sure top crust is done underneath.) 5. Serve warm with cream, milk or ice cream.

PEACH MELBA, QUICK

Serves 2 people. A delicious combination!

2 fresh ripe peaches, peeled and halved
4 scoops vanilla ice cream
½ c. Raspberry Sauce (or sugared fresh raspberries)

1. Place 2 peach halves in serving dish. 2. Add 2 scoops of ice cream; drizzle with ¼ cup Raspberry Sauce (or sugared fresh raspberries). Repeat for second dish. 3. Serve immediately.

PEACH OATMEAL CRISP

5 c. fresh peaches, peeled and sliced
½ c. sugar
1 c. quick oats (not instant)
½ c. packed brown sugar
⅓ c. flour
½ tsp. cinnamon
⅓ c. butter
Nuts, chopped (opt.)

1. Turn oven dial to 375° and grease or spray 12 x 8-inch glass cake pan. 2. Combine peaches and ½ cup sugar; pour into prepared pan. 3. In mixing bowl, combine oatmeal, brown sugar, flour and cinnamon. 4. Mix in butter with fork, fingers, pastry blender or electric mixer until crumbly. 5. Sprinkle crumb mixture over peaches; bake in preheated 375° oven about 40 minutes or until bubbly and golden brown.

PEACH OATMEAL CRISP (Smaller)

4½ c. fresh peaches, peeled and sliced
3 T. sugar
¼ tsp. almond flavoring (optional, but good!)
Topping:
½ c. quick oats, uncooked
½ c. packed brown sugar
¼ c. flour, packed, level
¼ tsp. cinnamon
¼ c. butter or regular Smart Balance Spread
¼ c. nuts (or more)

1. Turn oven dial to 375°; combine peaches, 3 T. sugar and the almond flavoring. Pour into a 2-quart 8x8 or 9x9-inch baking dish. 2. In small mixing bowl, combine oatmeal, brown sugar, flour and cinnamon. 4. With pastry blender, fork or fingers cut in butter until mixture resembles coarse crulmbs; stir in nuts. 5. Sprinkle topping over peaches; bake for 30 to 35 minutes or until bubbly and topping is golden.

PINEAPPLE DESSERT

A good way to use leftover cake or even a cake that fell.

6 oz. lemon gelatin
1¼ c. boiling water
¾ to 1 c. sugar
1 (20-oz.) can crushed pineapple, including juice
1 (8-oz.) carton whipped topping, thawed (or 2 env. Dream Whip, prepared)
1 med. angel food cake, broken into pcs. (or 1 layer of white or yellow cake, cut into cubes)
Maraschino cherries or mandarin orange slices, drained

1. Dissolve gelatin in boiling water. 2. Add sugar, stirring until it dissolves. 3. Add crushed pineapple, including juice; chill until partially set. 4. Fold in whipped topping. 5. In 13 x 9-inch Tupperware or glass pan, place half the cake pieces over bottom. 6. Cover with half the pineapple mixture. 7. Repeat process. 8. Garnish with maraschino cherries or mandarin orange slices, drained. 9. Cover with plastic wrap or lid and refrigerate overnight or at least 2 to 3 hours. (This dessert keeps well several days in refrigerator.)

PUDDING, CHOCOLATE (Eggless)

½ c. sugar
2 T. cornstarch (level)
3 T. dry unsweetened cocoa (level)
⅛ tsp. salt
2 c. milk
1 tsp. vanilla

1. In heavy saucepan or deep black iron skillet, combine first 4 ingredients, stirring together well. 2. Add milk; stir or whisk almost constantly, bringing to a full boil over medium heat. 3. Lower heat and simmer 1 minute longer, stirring. 4. Remove from heat and add vanilla; cool before serving. (Press plastic wrap onto surface while hot.)

PUDDING, CHOCOLATE (No-Cook)

2 T. instant chocolate drink mix
2 c. cold milk
1 pkg. (4-serving size) instant chocolate pudding mix
1 banana, sliced (opt.)

1. In mixer bowl, mix together instant chocolate drink mix and cold milk. 2. Add pudding mix; beat on lowest speed of mixer for 3 minutes. 3. Spoon into dessert dishes. (Add banana slices if desired.)

PUDDING, QUICK

Also called "Candy Store Pudding."
Use any flavor of instant pudding.

1 c. cold milk
1 pkg. (4-serving size) instant pudding
4 to 6 oz. frozen whipped topping, thawed

Optional Ingredients:
½ to 1 c. miniature marshmallows
½ to 1 c. miniature chocolate chips
¼ to ½ c. chopped peanuts or pecans
Gumdrops, cut up

1. In a bowl, whisk milk and pudding mix for 2 minutes (or in electric mixer on low speed). 2. Fold in whipped topping and any optional ingredients desired. 3. Refrigerate until serving. Serves 4.

PUDDING, VANILLA (Eggless)

⅓ c. sugar
2½ T. cornstarch (level)
⅛ tsp. salt
2 c. milk
2 tsp. vanilla
3 to 4 drops yellow food coloring

1. In heavy saucepan, combine sugar, cornstarch and salt, stirring together well. 2. Add milk; stir or whisk almost constantly, bringing to a full boil over medium heat. 3. Lower heat and simmer 1 minute longer, stirring. 4. Remove from heat and add vanilla; cool before serving.

RHUBARB CRUNCH

From Margaret Stiffler. Makes a 9 x 9-inch dish.

1 c. all-purpose flour
1 c. oatmeal
1 c. packed brown sugar
½ c. (1 stick) melted butter
3⅔ c. sliced rhubarb
1 c. white sugar
2 T. cornstarch
1 c. water
1 tsp. vanilla
Few drops red food coloring (opt.)

1. Mix flour, oatmeal, brown sugar and melted butter together until crumbly. 2. Press half the crumbly mixture over bottom of 9 x 13-inch (3-quart) glass pan (preferably not aluminum). Butter sides of dish. 3. Sprinkle rhubarb over top. 4. In saucepan, combine white sugar, cornstarch and water; cook until thick and bubbly. 5. Remove from heat and add vanilla. 6. Pour hot mixture over rhubarb. 7. Top with remaining crumbs. 8. Bake in preheated 350° oven 45 minutes, or until golden brown and bubbly.

RHUBARB MERINGUE DESSERT

A three-layer pie-dessert in 13 x 9-inch pan.

<u>Crust:</u>
1½ c. all-purpose flour
2 T. sugar
½ c. (1 stick) butter

<u>Meringue:</u>
4 egg whites
4 T. sugar

<u>Cream Filling:</u>
1¾ c. sugar
3 T. flour, packed level
¼ tsp. nutmeg
4 egg yolks, beaten
⅔ c. milk or cream
4 c. sliced rhubarb

1. Mix together 3 crust ingredients until crumbly and well blended; press into bottom of 13 x 9 x 2-inch glass baking dish. 2. Bake crust in preheated 350° oven 20 minutes. 3. Combine all filling ingredients, including rhubarb, in heavy saucepan or black iron skillet; cook, stirring almost constantly, until mixture comes to a boil. 4. Pour hot filling over crust. 5. Make meringue by beating egg whites until stiff, while adding sugar, 1 tablespoon at a time. 6. Spread meringue over rhubarb filling; bake in 325° oven 15 to 20 minutes, or until golden brown. 7. Cool; refrigerate any leftovers.

RHUBARB SAUCE

7 c. rhubarb, cut up in 1-inch pieces
1 c. sugar
1 c. water
1 T. tapioca, level
7 drops red food coloring (opt.)

1. Put rhubarb, sugar, water and tapioca in a 3-quart pan and stir together. 2. Cook until rhubarb is tender, stirring occasionally. 3. When done, remove from heat and add food coloring if desired. 4. Taste for sweetness; more sugar may be added while it is hot, if needed.

RICE, GLORIFIED

Also called Heavenly Rice.

1 to 2 c. cold cooked rice
1 (20-oz.) can crushed pineapple, drained
⅓ to ½ c. sugar
⅛ to ¼ c. drained, chopped maraschino cherries (or less)
¾ to 1 c. miniature marshmallows
½ c. chopped nuts (opt.)
4 to 8 oz. whipped topping

1. Combine ingredients in bowl, in order given. 2. Chill in refrigerator.

RICE PUDDING CUSTARD

1 c. water
½ c. white rice
½ vanilla bean, split
¼ tsp. salt
2 c. milk
½ c. sugar
1 c. cream, evaporated milk or evaporated skimmed milk
2 lg. eggs
½ c. raisins
¼ tsp. cinnamon for top

1. In 2-quart saucepan, heat water to boiling; add rice, split vanilla bean half and salt; cook 10 minutes. 2. Add milk and bring to boiling again; reduce heat to medium or med.-low; cover and cook until rice is tender, about 20 minutes. 3. Preheat oven to 350°. Lightly butter or spray 1½-quart shallow baking pan or 8 x 8-inch baking dish. 4. In med.-small bowl, combine sugar, cream and eggs; stir into rice mixture. 5. Remove vanilla bean and add raisins; pour mixture into prepared baking dish. Sprinkle cinnamon evenly over top. 6. Place baking dish into a large baking pan; pour boiling water into baking pan to depth of 1 inch. 7. Bake 45 minutes in preheated 350° oven or until pudding is firm. 8. Cool to room temperature on wire rack. 9. Serve at room temperature (or chilled). <u>Note:</u> Instead of vanilla bean, 1 to 2 teaspoons vanilla extract may be added with eggs and sugar.

RICE PUDDING, EASY

3 c. cooked rice
3 c. milk
½ c. sugar
2 T. butter
1 cinnamon stick
½ c. raisins (opt.)
1 t. vanilla

1. Combine all ingredients, except vanilla, in a two-quart saucepan. 2. Cook over medium heat, stirring frequently, for 20 to 25 minutes after it begins to simmer (until thick and creamy). 3. Remove from heat and add vanilla; remove cinnamon stick.

RICE PUDDING, SPECIAL

1 (4-serving size) pkg. vanilla pudding (cook-type or instant)
1 c. cooked rice, chilled
¼ tsp. vanilla
¼ to ⅓ c. raisins
Nutmeg

1. Prepare pudding according to package directions. 2. Add rice, vanilla and raisins, stirring together. 3. Sprinkle nutmeg over top and chill.

RITZY ICE CREAM DESSERT

From Laura Stevenson.
A graham cracker bottom may be used instead.

50 to 60 Ritz crackers, rolled fine
½ c. soft butter
1 c. chopped nuts, divided
1½ c. milk
2 sm. or 1 lg. box instant pudding (any flavor)
4 c. vanilla ice cream, softened
1 or 2 env. Dream Whip, prepared or 1 8-oz. carton Cool
    Whip

1. Combine cracker crumbs, butter and ½ cup nuts. 2. Press into 9 x 13-inch cake pan; set aside. 3. Mix milk and instant pudding together. 4. Add softened ice cream; beat until well blended. 5. Pour into crumb-lined pan; chill for 30 to 60 minutes. 6. Spread whipped topping over the top. 7. Sprinkle with remaining chopped nuts. 8. Cover with lid or plastic wrap; refrigerate. (Keeps for a week or longer in refrigerator.)

STAINED GLASS DESSERT

Serves 15. A beautiful dessert.

2 c. graham cracker crumbs
¼ c. sugar
½ c. (1 stick) butter, melted
1 (3-oz.) pkg. orange gelatin
1 (3-oz.) pkg. lime gelatin
1 (3-oz.) pkg. lemon gelatin
1 (3-oz.) pkg. cherry gelatin
3 c. boiling water, divided
3 c. cold water, divided
1 env. unflavored gelatin
¼ c. cold water
1 c. pineapple juice
1 (8-oz.) carton whipped topping, thawed (or 2 env. Dream
    Whip, prepared)

1. Combine graham cracker crumbs and sugar with melted butter, stirring well; press ⅔ of crumb mixture into bottom of greased 13 x 9 x 2-inch pan; set aside. 2. Reserve remaining crumb mixture for top. 3. Prepare each 3-ounce package of gelatin with ¾ cup boiling water and ¾ cup cold water; pour into separate 8 x 8-inch pans and chill until firm. 4. In small saucepan, soften unflavored gelatin in ¼ cup cold water. 5. Add pineapple juice; cook over low heat, stirring constantly, until gelatin dissolves. 6. Chill pineapple mixture until syrupy (just partially set). 7. Fold whipped topping and pineapple mixture together. 8. Cut the orange, green, yellow and red gelatins into 1-inch cubes; fold into whipped topping mixture. 9. Spoon mixture into crumb-lined pan; sprinkle reserved crumb mixture over top. 10. Chill for 6 to 8 hours. <u>Note:</u> 9 x 9-inch pans make the Jello too thin.

STRAWBERRY ANGEL PARFAIT

From Linda Casburn. A terrific dessert.

½ lg. angel food cake (or 1 sm. angel food cake)
1 c. milk
1 sm. pkg. (4-serving size) instant vanilla pudding
2 c. (1-pt.) vanilla ice cream
1 (3-oz.) pkg. strawberry or wild strawberry gelatin
1 c. boiling water
1 (10 to 16-oz.) pkg. frozen or partially frozen strawber-
    ries, sweetened or unsweetened

1. Tear angel food cake into pieces and put in glass or Tupperware 13 x 9 x 2-inch pan. 2. In mixer bowl, combine milk and instant pudding mix; beat on low speed, until thickened. 3. Add ice cream and beat together on higher speed until smooth. 4. Pour pudding mixture over cake; chill about 1 hour. 5. Dissolve gelatin in 1 cup boiling water; immediately add frozen berries, stirring until berries thaw. 6. Chill gelatin until syrupy (it doesn't take long) and pour over cake-pudding mixture. 7. If desired, cover with plastic wrap or a lid. 8. Refrigerate. Serves 10 to 12. <u>Note</u>: Half of a yellow or white cake may be used instead of angel food cake.

TAPIOCA PUDDING, FLUFFY

Makes a lot! Recipe can be cut in half.

2 eggs, separated (room temp.)
4 c. milk (can be reconstituted powdered milk)
6 T. Minute Tapioca
½ c. sugar
¼ tsp. salt
4 T. sugar
2 tsp. vanilla

1. In 3 or 4-quart saucepan, beat egg yolks slightly. 2. Add just a little of the milk, mixing together gradually until mixed well. 3. Add remaining milk, tapioca, ½ cup sugar and the salt; let stand 5 minutes. 4. Meanwhile, in large mixer bowl, beat egg whites until foamy; then add (1 tablespoon at a time) the 4 tablespoons sugar. 5. Whip until soft peaks form; set aside. 6. Bring tapioca to a full rolling boil, stirring constantly. 7. Remove from burner immediately, and <u>slowly</u> add hot tapioca to egg whites in a slow steady stream. <u>Do not use mixer</u>; stir by tablespoon. 8. Add vanilla; cool for 20 minutes without stirring. 9. Stir after 20 minutes; then chill.

TRIFLE, ENGLISH

From Kathy Heaps, who married an Englishman!

1 (12-oz.) pound cake or one layer of yellow cake, sliced
    (can be leftover cake)
1 (3-oz.) box red Jello
1 small box vanilla pudding (cook-kind, not instant)
8 oz. whipped topping, thawed (may not use it all)
Fruit for top decoration (opt.)

1. Make Jello according to package directions and let cool until syrupy. 2. Cook pudding and let it chill for about 2 hours. 3. Place cake slices in bottom of glass bowl or trifle bowl and pour Jello over it. 4. Pour pudding over Jello and cake. 5. Spread whipped topping over pudding; decorate top with fresh fruit (or canned, well-drained fruit), if desired.

TRIFLE, STRAWBERRY ALOHA

One half of baked chocolate, yellow, white sour cream cake, pound cake or angel food cake; cut into 1-inch pieces
½ c. strawberry preserves (opt)
1 small box vanilla or chocolate pudding (cook-kind or instant)
1 pkg. (10 oz.) frozen strawberries, thawed
1 (20-oz.) can crushed pineapple, drained (opt.)
1 or 2 large bananas
1 (8-oz.) carton whipped topping, thawed
Pecans, walnuts or sliced almonds, toasted, for top

1. Lay half the cake pieces over bottom of 3 or 3½-quart trifle bowl (or glass bowl). 2. Layer half of everything else used (except nuts); repeat layers, ending with whipped topping and nuts. 3. Refrigerate several hours or overnight.

TRIFLE, WITH CHOCOLATE PUDDING SAUCE

Keeps well in refrigerator for several days.

½ of a baked yellow or chocolate cake, cut into 1-in. pcs. (about 2 qt.)
1 (8 to 12-oz.) carton whipped topping, thawed
2½ to 3 c. miniature marshmallows (opt.)
1 recipe Chocolate Pudding Sauce (recipe follows)
Flaked coconut (opt.)

1. In 13 x 9-inch glass pan, place half the cake pieces. 2. Spread half the whipped topping over cake. 3. Sprinkle with 1 cup miniature marshmallows. 4. Repeat entire process. 5. Pour cooled (or lukewarm) Chocolate Pudding Sauce over top of all. 6. Sprinkle with remaining ½ cup (or more) miniature marshmallows (or flaked coconut). 7. Cover with plastic wrap; refrigerate.

Chocolate Pudding Sauce:
¾ c. sugar
¼ c. packed brown sugar
2 T. flour, packed level
4 T. unsweetened cocoa, packed level
⅛ tsp. salt
1½ c. milk
1 T. butter
½ tsp. vanilla

1. In heavy saucepan, combine dry ingredients. 2. Add milk and stir together. 3. Cook, stirring almost constantly, bringing to a full boil; reduce heat and boil gently for 1 minute, stirring. 4. Remove from heat; add butter and vanilla, stirring until butter melts. 5. Cover with tight lid and refrigerate to cool.

YUMMY CHOCOLATE-PEANUT BUTTER ECLAIR DESSERT

From Sally Coates.

1 chocolate cake mix, prepared according to pkg. directions

Peanut butter layer:
¾ c. creamy peanut butter
5 T. Smart Balance shortening
1 c. sifted powdered sugar
½ c. milk
3 T. flour

Chocolate frosting for top:

1. Prepare cake in 9 x 13-inch pan. Cool completely in pan. 2. To make peanut butter layer, mix together peanut butter, shortening, powdered sugar, milk and flour in mixing bowl until well blended. 3. Spread over cooled cake; refrigerate until set, approximately 45 min. 4. Frost with chocolate frosting; refrigerate until frosting is set. 5. Store leftovers in refrigerator.

Chapter 26

Sauces and Toppings for Desserts

JACK AND RUTH BENNINGER

1997

Dessert Sauces & Toppings

BROWN SUGAR SAUCE

Serve warm over cake.

1 c. packed brown sugar
2 T. cornstarch
1½ c. water
½ to 1 T. butter
1 tsp. vanilla

1. In saucepan, mix together brown sugar, cornstarch and water; bring to a boil. **2.** Remove from heat and add butter and vanilla.

BUTTER CRUNCH TOPPING

From Dorothy Bowser. Makes 2½ to 3 cups.

½ c. (1 stick) butter
¼ c. packed brown sugar
1 c. all-purpose flour
½ c. flaked coconut
½ c. coarsely chopped walnuts or pecans

1. Turn oven dial to 400°. **2.** Combine all ingredients, mixing well. **3.** Spoon into 13 x 9-inch pan or jellyroll pan. **4.** Bake in preheated 400° oven 15 minutes, or until golden brown. **5.** Remove from oven and stir with spoon; cool. **6.** Serve over dessert dishes of slightly warm apple pie filling (or other desserts); top with vanilla ice cream, if desired.

BUTTERSCOTCH TOPPING

For cake or ice cream.

¼ c. (½ stick) butter
½ c. sugar
½ c. packed brown sugar
½ c. cream or evaporated milk

1. Heat all ingredients in heavy pan until warm and all the sugar is dissolved. Do not boil.

CHOCOLATE HOT FUDGE SAUCE

From Betty and Dennis Dean. Delicious!

1½ c. sugar
⅓ c. unsweetened cocoa
¼ tsp. cream of tartar
⅛ tsp. salt
2 T. light Karo
½ c. water
1 T. butter
1 tsp. vanilla extract
½ to ⅔ c. evaporated milk (or 5-oz. can)

1. In 2-quart saucepan, cook sugar, cocoa, cream of tartar, salt, Karo and water together, stirring until dissolved. **2.** Bring to a strong boil; boil 3 minutes without stirring. **3.** Remove from heat and add butter and vanilla. **4.** Very slowly, stir in evaporated milk.

CHOCOLATE HOT FUDGE SAUCE, MICROWAVE

So easy! Delicious hot, warm or cold.
Just one step in the Microwave oven.

1 c. sugar
1 T. cornstarch, packed level
3½ T. unsweetened dry cocoa (level)
⅛ tsp. salt
¾ c. milk
1 T. butter
2 T. light or dark corn syrup
1 tsp. vanilla

1. In 8-cup microwave-safe bowl, combine sugar, cornstarch, cocoa and salt; blend thoroughly. **2.** Add milk and stir well. **3.** Add corn syrup and butter. **4.** Microwave on HIGH for 5 minutes. **5.** Stir in vanilla. Note: This can also be made in a saucepan on the stove, boiling gently for 5 minutes. Note: To reheat, cover with plastic wrap and microwave on HIGH, 15 to 20 seconds for each ½ cup sauce.

CHOCOLATE PUDDING SAUCE, VIOLET'S

Nice over yellow cake or ice cream.
From Violet McCauley.

¾ c. sugar
¼ c. packed brown sugar
2 T. flour, level
4 T. unsweetened cocoa, packed level
⅛ tsp. salt
1½ c. milk
1 T. butter
½ to 1 tsp. vanilla

1. In heavy saucepan, combine dry ingredients. **2.** Add milk and stir together. **3.** Cook, stirring constantly, bringing to a full boil; reduce heat and boil gently for 1 minute, stirring. **4.** Remove from heat; add butter and vanilla. **5.** Serve warm (or any temperature) over cake or ice cream.

CLEAR SAUCE

½ c. sugar (or brown sugar, packed)
1 T. cornstarch (level)
¼ c. (½ stick) butter
1 c. hot water
1 to 3 tsp. lemon juice
1 tsp. vanilla

1. In small saucepan, mix together sugar and cornstarch; add butter and hot water; bring to a boil. 2. Remove from heat and add lemon juice and vanilla.

LEMON SAUCE

1 c. sugar
2 T. cornstarch
1½ c. water
¼ c. butter
2 T. lemon juice

1. In small pan, mix sugar and cornstarch together. 2. Add water and butter. 3. Bring to a full rolling boil, stirring constantly. 4. Remove from heat and add lemon juice.

NUTMEG SAUCE

½ c. sugar
1 T. cornstarch
¼ tsp. nutmeg
⅛ tsp. salt
1 c. hot water
2 to 4 T. butter
1 tsp. lemon juice

1. In small pan, mix sugar, cornstarch, nutmeg and salt together. 2. Add hot water and butter; bring to a full rolling boil. 3. Remove from heat and add lemon juice.

PEANUT BUTTER SUNDAE SAUCE

Delicious on vanilla ice cream.

1 c. sugar
1 T. corn syrup
¼ tsp. salt
¾ c. milk
⅓ c. peanut butter (crunchy or creamy)
¼ tsp. vanilla

1. In medium saucepan, cook sugar, corn syrup, salt and milk over medium heat until mixture coats spoon (about 15 minutes). 2. Remove from heat; add peanut butter and vanilla. 3. Beat until smooth; may be stored and reheated as needed.

PRALINE SAUCE I

Makes 1 cup.

1 c. water
⅔ c. chopped pecans
½ c. packed brown sugar
½ c. corn syrup
1 T. butter

1. Bring water to a boil in small saucepan; add chopped pecans. 2. Reduce heat and cook mixture about 5 minutes; drain and set aside. 3. In a heavy saucepan, combine brown sugar, corn syrup and butter; bring mixture to a boil. 4. Reduce heat and simmer 5 minutes, stirring constantly. 5. Stir in pecans. Serve warm over ice cream.

PRALINE SAUCE II

1 c. packed brown sugar
¼ c. light corn syrup
½ c. half & half
2 T. butter
1 tsp. vanilla
⅛ tsp. salt (opt.)
1 c. crushed pecans

1. In saucepan, over medium heat, cook all ingredients, stirring constantly, for about 10 minutes or until sauce is thick and smooth. 2. Cool slightly.

RASPBERRY SAUCE (or BLUEBERRY)

Serve warm or cold.

½ c. sugar
1 T. cornstarch, packed level
⅓ c. water
1 pt. raspberries (about 1¾ c. after washing and draining)

1. In 2-quart saucepan, combine sugar and cornstarch, stirring together. 2. Gradually add water, stirring until smooth. 3. Add raspberries; bring to a boil, stirring almost constantly, over medium-high heat. Boil 1 minute. **Note:** This may be put through a sieve, if desired, to remove seeds.

SPICY SAUCE

1 c. water
3 T. butter
1 c. sugar
1½ T. cornstarch
¼ tsp. cinnamon
¼ tsp. nutmeg
2 tsp. vanilla extract

1. In small pan, bring water and butter to a boil; turn burner off. 2. In small bowl, mix together sugar, cornstarch and spices; add to hot water. 3. Bring to a boil, stirring constantly. 4. Remove from heat and add vanilla. Serve hot or warm over cake.

368

STRAWBERRY SUNDAE SAUCE

Serve over ice cream or angel food cake.

2 c. fresh strawberries, sliced
¼ c. sugar
1½ tsp. cornstarch
¼ tsp. almond extract (opt.)

1. In bowl, stir strawberries and sugar together; cover and refrigerate several hours or overnight. 2. Drain strawberries, reserving juice; set aside. 3. Add enough water to strawberry juice to make ½ cup. 4. Combine juice and cornstarch in small pan, stirring until cornstarch is dissolved. 5. Cook over medium heat, stirring constantly, until smooth and thickened; remove from heat. 6. Stir in strawberries and almond extract. 7. Chill. Makes 1¼ cups sauce.

VANILLA SAUCE

¾ c. sugar
1½ T. cornstarch
1 c. water
¼ c. butter
2 tsp. vanilla extract

1. In small pan, mix sugar and cornstarch together. 2. Add water and butter; bring to a full rolling boil. 3. Remove from heat and add vanilla.

WALNUT CARAMEL SAUCE

¾ c. packed brown sugar
1 tsp. cornstarch
¼ c. water
1 T. butter
Dash of salt
½ c. light corn syrup
⅓ c. chopped walnuts

1. Combine all ingredients, except nuts, in saucepan; bring to a boil, stirring constantly. 2. Remove from heat and cool. 3. Add nuts.

WALNUT SAUCE

1¼ c. packed brown sugar
1¼ c. water
½ c. chopped walnuts or more

1. In saucepan, cook and stir sugar and water until boiling. 2. Reduce heat and boil gently without stirring, 15 minutes. 3. Add nuts; bring to a boil and continue boiling gently another 15 minutes. 4. Cool; then pour into a jar.

WHIPPED CREAM

1 c. heavy heavy (whipping) cream
2 T. confectioners' sugar
½ t. vanilla extract

1. Beat cream in a large bowl with electric mixer at medium speed until it becomes frothy; add sugar and vanilla and continue beating until cream holds soft peaks. Do not overbeat. 2. Refrigerate, if not using immediately.

Chapter 27

Candy, Nuts & Snack Foods

DARREN AND BETH EGGLESTON

2001

CANDY, NUTS, & SNACK FOODS

ALMONDS, ROASTED (Toasted)

Remove shells from almonds. Cover almonds with 4 to 6 cups boiling water; let stand until water is lukewarm or cool. Slip skins off almonds and spread them on a baking sheet lined with paper towels. Dry for several hours, or for 1 or 2 days, stirring occasionally. (If using blanched almonds in a package, omit the previous instructions.) Preheat oven to 325°. In shallow pan or cookie sheet, roast almonds on middle shelf of oven for about 25 minutes, stirring every 10 minutes, until lightly browned (time may differ for various ovens). If almonds are to be used for cooking or baking, remove from oven and cool. If almonds are to be eaten as roasted nuts, add a few dots of butter the size of small peas. Turn oven dial to 300° and continue to roast about 25 minutes longer, stirring occasionally. Remove from oven and salt very lightly. **Note**: Do not let almonds get dark brown in oven.

BUCKEYES

1½ c. peanut butter
½ c. butter or reg. Smart Balance spread
2½ c. powdered sugar, packed level
1 tsp. Vanilla
12 oz. chocolate chips
1 T. Smart Balance shortening (or Earth Balance Short-
    ening)

1. Cream peanut butter, butter, powdered sugar and vanilla together. 2. Roll candy into 1-inch balls and place on cookie sheet lined with waxed paper; chill in refrigerator 2 hours or overnight. 3. Melt chocolate chips and shortening together in top of double boiler. (Keep chocolate mixture in double boiler over low heat while dipping each candy.) 4. Insert a toothpick and dip each one, covering ¾ of the ball. 5. Return candy to cookie sheet to cool. **Note**: Smucker's Natural Peanut Butter works well in this recipe.

CARAMELS, EASY (Microwave)

From Leslie Wallace. Makes 2¾ pounds.

1 c. (2 sticks) butter
2⅓ c. packed brown sugar
1 c. light corn syrup
⅛ tsp. salt
1 (14-oz.) can sweetened condensed milk
1 tsp. vanilla
½ c. chopped walnuts (opt.)

1. Combine all ingredients, except vanilla and chopped nuts, in microwave-safe bowl. 2. Microwave on HIGH 3 to 4 minutes, stirring halfway, until butter is melted; stir well. 3. Microwave on HIGH about 14 minutes or until mixture reaches 245° (firm-ball stage). 4. Stir in vanilla and nuts; remove from

microwave and let stand 10 minutes, stirring well several times. 5. Pour into buttered pan; refrigerate until cool. 6. Invert pan; cut into squares. 7. Wrap in waxed paper and store in refrigerator. **Note**: Can also freeze.

CHOCOLATE CLUSTERS

1 (12-oz.) pkg. chocolate or butterscotch chips (2 c.)
½ can (⅔ c.) sweetened condensed milk (NOT evaporated)
1 tsp. vanilla
2 c. nuts or raisins (or a mixture of both)
2 to 3 c. miniature marshmallows (or more, if desired)

1. Melt chips in saucepan over very low heat. 2. When melted, blend in the milk and vanilla. 3. Add remaining ingredients and stir together. 4. Drop by spoonfuls onto waxed paper-lined cookie sheet. 5. Refrigerate, uncovered, for 1 hour or until firm. **Note**: For dark chocolate clusters, use semi-sweet chocolate chips.

CHOCOLATE-COVERED PEANUT BUTTER BALLS

These can be made with or without the Rice Krispies or graham cracker crumbs.

½ c. (1 stick) butter (room temp.)
2 c. peanut butter
1 lb. powdered sugar
3 to 5 c. Rice Krispies or graham cracker crumbs (opt.)
1 lb. milk chocolate
6 oz. (1 c.) semi-sweet chocolate chips
½ cake (2-oz.) paraffin wax

1. Cream together butter and peanut butter. 2. Add powdered sugar and mix well. 3. In large bowl, combine peanut butter mixture and Rice Krispies; mix well with hands or large wooden spoon. 4. Shape mixture into balls the size of an English walnut. 5. Melt milk chocolate, chocolate chips and paraffin in top of double boiler over simmering water. 6. Plunge a toothpick about halfway into balls; dip into melted chocolate. 7. Place balls on waxed paper until hardened. Makes about 75.

CHOCOLATE DROP TREATS

8 oz. milk chocolate
4 oz. (½ c.) semi-sweet chocolate chips
1 to 2 c. nuts (opt.)
1 c. raisins (opt.)
1 c. Rice Krispies cereal (opt.)
1 c. miniature marshmallows (opt.)
1 c. chow mein noodles (opt.)
1 c. flaked coconut (opt.)

1. Line 2 cookie sheets with waxed paper. 2. Melt chocolate and chips in 1-quart glass measuring pitcher on HIGH in microwave oven 2 to 3 minutes. 3. Stir until smooth; add 2 or 3 of the optional ingredients, stirring until coated. 4. Drop from teaspoon onto waxed paper; let harden at room temperature or chill.

CHOCOLATE ROCKY ROAD CANDY I

So easy and so good!
Do not use stale, dried-up marshmallows.

12 oz. (2 c.) semi-sweet chocolate chips
1 (14-oz.) can sweetened condensed milk (1¼ c.)
2 T. butter
1½ to 2 c. coarsely chopped walnuts or dry roasted peanuts (or some of each)
1 (10½ to 16-oz.) bag miniature white marshmallows (5 to 8 c.)

1. In top of double boiler, over simmering water, melt chips with sweetened condensed milk and butter; stir together well. 2. In large 5 to 8-quart bowl, combine nuts and marshmallows. 3. Stir in chocolate mixture. 4. Spread in buttered or sprayed 13 x 9-inch cake pan or 14 x 10-inch lasagna pan (or drop by rounded spoonfuls onto cookie sheet lined with waxed paper). 5. Chill several hours (or overnight). **Note**: If desired, 1 cup raisins may be added with the nuts.

CHOCOLATE ROCKY ROAD CANDY II

So easy and so good!

12 oz. (2 c.) chocolate chips or milk chocolate
3 c. miniature marshmallows or Rice Krispies
1 to 1½ c. walnuts or other nuts, coarsely chopped (or raisins)

1. In 2-quart microwave-safe bowl, melt chocolate in microwave oven on medium power for a few minutes, stirring occasionally. (Or melt in top of double boiler over very hot water.) 2. When chocolate is melted, add remaining ingredients; stir gently until coated. 3. Line large cookie sheet with waxed paper; drop by rounded tablespoonfuls onto waxed paper. (Or spread mixture into buttered or sprayed 8 x 8-inch pan.) 4. Let harden at room temperature for several hours.

COCONUT BONBONS

Makes 65 to 75 irresistible bonbons.

½ c. (1 stick) butter, melted
1 (14-oz.) can sweetened condensed milk
1 lb. powdered sugar
14 oz. flaked coconut (3 c.)
12 oz. semi-sweet chocolate chips (2 c.)
6 oz. milk chocolate
¼ cake (1 oz.) paraffin

1. In large bowl, mix butter, sweetened condensed milk, powdered sugar and coconut together thoroughly; refrigerate several hours or overnight (or drop by spoonfuls onto buttered cookie sheet; freeze for 15 minutes or until easy to handle.) 2. Roll mixture into balls about the size of small English walnuts. Return to refrigerator (or freezer). 3. Melt chocolate chips, milk chocolate and paraffin together in double boiler over hot water, stirring occasionally. 4. When chocolate and paraffin are melted, turn heat to very low, keeping chocolate over hot water. 5. Put the tip of a wooden pick into cold coconut balls and dip, one at a time, into melted chocolate, letting excess chocolate drip back into pan. 6. Place candy on waxed paper. (Bring only 4 or 5 coconut candies from refrigerator at a time.) 7. When all the candies are covered, fill the pick-hole in the top of each candy with chocolate, using the tip of a paring knife. 8. If there is chocolate left over, nuts or raisins may be mixed in; drop by spoonfuls onto waxed paper.

DATES, STUFFED

Whole dates
Nuts
Sugar

1. Remove seeds from dates. 2. Place a nut in each; pinch opening shut. 3. Roll each date in granulated or powdered sugar.

DIVINITY

Makes 1¼ pounds.

2½ c. sugar
½ c. light corn syrup
½ c. water
¼ tsp. salt
2 egg whites
1 tsp. vanilla
1 c. coarsely chopped nuts (opt.)

1. In saucepan, combine first 4 ingredients; cook over medium heat, stirring constantly, until sugar is dissolved. 2. Cook, without stirring, to firm ball stage (248°) or until a small amount of syrup forms a firm ball which does not flatten when dropped into very cold water. 3. Just before syrup reaches 248°, beat egg whites until stiff, but not dry. 4. Pour about one half of the syrup slowly over egg whites, beating constantly. 5. Cook the remainder of the syrup to soft crack stage (272°) or until a small amount of syrup separates into threads which are hard, but not brittle when dropped into very cold water. 6. Add syrup slowly to first mixture, beating constantly. 7. Continue beating until mixture holds its shape. 8. Add vanilla and nuts; drop from tip of spoon onto waxed paper.

EASTER EGGS (FONDANT) I

Makes 6 wonderful Easter eggs.

3¾ c. granulated sugar
¾ c. light corn syrup
¾ c. water
¼ tsp. salt
3 egg whites
1½ tsp. vanilla
1 lb. milk chocolate

Optional Ingredients:
Nuts
Coarsely chopped candied citrus fruit or fruit and peel mix
Peanut butter
Flaked coconut
Flavorings

1. In saucepan, combine sugar, corn syrup, water and salt; over heat, stir only until sugar is dissolved. 2. Cook to 248° on candy thermometer; before temperature reaches 248°, beat egg whites until stiff. 3. Pour about half of the boiling mixture slowly into beaten egg whites while beating on high speed of electric mixer. 4. Cook remaining syrup to 272° on candy thermometer. 5. Add syrup slowly to egg white mixture while beating on high speed of mixer. 6. Add vanilla; beat at high speed for 5 minutes, or until mixture begins to get thick. 7. If making just one kind, add optional ingredient; divide fondant into 6 mounds on a cookie sheet dusted with cornstarch. 8. If making different kinds, divide fondant into 6 bowls. **For 1 peanut butter egg**, add ¼ cup peanut butter to ⅙ of the fondant. **For 1 coconut egg**, add ½ cup coconut to ⅙ of the fondant. **For 1 fruit and nut egg**, add ⅓ cup candied fruit mix and ⅓ cup nuts to ⅙ of the fondant. **For 1 maple nut egg**, add ½ cup nuts and ⅛ teaspoon maple flavoring to ⅙ of the fondant. **For 1 peppermint egg**, add a few drops oil of peppermint and 1 drop of red food coloring to ⅙ of the fondant to make a pink shade. **For 1 mint egg**, add ⅛ teaspoon mint flavoring and 1 drop of green food coloring (or leave white) to ⅙ of the fondant. 9. Let mixture set for 5 to 20 minutes; then shape each mound into the shape of an egg, using a little cornstarch on hands. 10. Refrigerate eggs several hours or overnight before coating with chocolate. 11. Melt chocolate in microwave oven in microwave-safe dish on MEDIUM (50%), stirring every 30 seconds until chocolate is melted. Or melt in double boiler over hot (not boiling) water. 12. Pick a cold fondant egg up and hold it upside down in one hand; with other hand, coat bottom of egg with melted chocolate, using knife or small spatula. 13. Coat around lower sides of egg; then place egg right side up, on a small piece of waxed paper. 14. Finish coating egg with chocolate; repeat process until all eggs are coated. 15. Refrigerate.

EASTER EGGS (FONDANT) II

From Mrs. Edna Brickell. Makes 5 to 6 eggs.

3 c. sugar
½ c. light corn syrup
½ c. water
¼ tsp. salt
2 egg whites
1 tsp. vanilla
12 oz. milk chocolate

1. Combine sugar, corn syrup, water and salt in pan and cook to 260° on candy thermometer. Do not stir after sugar is dissolved. 2. Before syrup reaches 260°, beat egg whites stiff. 3. Pour syrup slowly into egg whites while beating. 4. Add flavoring and beat until it starts getting thick. 5. Additional ingredients may be added. Form into 5 or 6 eggs; refrigerate overnight. 6. Coat with chocolate using directions in "Fondant Easter Eggs I." **Fruit & Nut Easter Eggs**: Add 1½ to 4 cups coarsely chopped nuts and 8 to 16 ounces fruit and peel or candied citrus fruit. **Coconut Easter Eggs**: Add 14 ounces flaked coconut. **Maple Nut Easter Eggs**: Use ½ teaspoon vanilla and 1 teaspoon maple flavoring. Add 2 to 3 cups coarsely chopped walnuts. **Peanut Butter Easter Eggs**: Add ½ to 1 cup peanut butter immediately after adding vanilla. **Peppermint Easter Eggs**: Add a few drops of oil of peppermint flavoring and a couple drops of red food coloring to make pink. **Mint Easter Eggs**: Add a few drops of mint flavoring and a couple drops of green food coloring.

FUDGE, CHOCOLATE (Old-fashioned)

2 c. sugar
⅓ c. unsweetened cocoa
⅛ tsp. salt
1 c. whole milk
3 T. butter
1 tsp. vanilla
¾ to 1 c. chopped walnuts (opt.)

1. Combine sugar, cocoa and salt in heavy saucepan. 2. Add milk and stir well. 3. Bring to a boil without stirring; cook until candy thermometer reaches 234° (or until small amount of mixture forms soft ball when dropped into cold water). 4. Remove from heat; drop in butter. 5. Cool to lukewarm or 110°. 6. Add vanilla and beat until mixture loses gloss. When it starts to get thick, add nuts and pour onto buttered platter. 7. Cut into squares.

FUDGE, CHOCOLATE FANTASY

Makes about 3 pounds.

3 c. sugar
¾ c. butter or reg. Smart Balance Spread
⅔ c. evaporated milk (5 oz. can)
12 oz. (2 c.) semi-sweet chocolate chips
1 (7-oz.) jar Kraft Marshmallow Creme (1½ c.)
1 to 1½ c. nuts, coarsely chopped
1 tsp. vanilla

1. In heavy 2 or 3-quart saucepan (or deep, black iron skillet), stir together sugar, butter and milk; stirring constantly, bring to a full boil. 2. Over medium heat, boil 5 minutes, stirring constantly (or to 234° F. on candy thermometer). 3. Remove from heat; gradually stir in chips until melted. 4. Add marshmallow creme, nuts and vanilla; mix until well blended. 5. Pour into buttered or sprayed 13 x 9-inch pan. Cool at room temperature.

FUDGE, CHOCOLATE SUPER

This is strictly for chocoholics.

⅔ c. evaporated milk
1 (7-oz.) jar marshmallow creme
4 T. (½ stick) butter
1¾ c. granulated sugar
⅛ tsp. salt
12 oz. semi-sweet chocolate morsels
1 tsp. vanilla
1 c. walnuts or pecans

1. Butter an 8 x 8-inch square pan. 2. In a heavy 2 to 3-quart pan (or deep, black iron skillet) combine evaporated milk, marshmallow creme, butter, sugar and salt. 3. Place over med.-low heat and stir constantly, bringing mixture to a boil. (Lower heat, if necessary, to keep mixture from sticking on bottom of pan.) 4. When mixture comes to a full boil, boil for 5 minutes, stirring constantly. 5. Remove from heat; add chocolate morsels and stir until smooth. 6. Stir in vanilla and nuts; pour into prepared pan. 7. If desired, sprinkle additional nuts on top also, and press them in just a bit. May be wrapped and frozen for longer storage.

FUDGE, IDA BERLIN'S (DARK CHOCOLATE)

3 or 4 c. semi-sweet chocolate chips (or part milk chocolate chips)
1 (14-oz.) can sweetened condensed milk
1½ tsp. vanilla
1 cup chopped walnuts (opt.)

1. In saucepan, over low heat, melt chips with sweetened condensed milk. 2. Remove from heat; stir in vanilla and walnuts. 3. Pour into a wax paper-lined (or aluminum foil-lined) 9 x 9 or 7x11-inch pan. 4. Chill 2 hours or until firm; cut into squares.

FUDGE, PEANUT BUTTER

From Jack Benninger.

1½ c. sugar
½ c. packed brown sugar
1 c. whole milk (or part cream)
2 T. butter, divided
Peanut butter
1 tsp. vanilla

1. In heavy pan, combine both sugars, milk and 1 tablespoon butter. 2. Boil to 234° on candy thermometer, stirring occasionally. (When about half done, add peanut butter the size of a medium egg.) 3. After candy reaches 234°, remove from heat and add another spoonful of peanut butter the size of a medium egg; stir. 4. Add remaining 1 tablespoon butter and the vanilla; set pan in cold water until temperature reaches 110°. 5. When 110° is reached, beat candy until thick.

FUDGE, PEANUT BUTTER FANTASY

3 c. sugar
⅔ c. (5-oz. can) evaporated milk
¾ c. butter (1½ sticks)
1 c. peanut butter (smooth or chunky)
7 oz. (1½ c.) Kraft marshmallow creme
1 tsp. vanilla
1 c. nuts, chopped, or more (opt.)

1. In 2½ to 3-quart heavy pan, combine sugar, milk and butter; heat to full rolling boil, stirring constantly. 2. Stirring occasionally, continue boiling 5 or 6 minutes over medium heat (or until candy thermometer reaches 234°). 3. Remove from heat; add peanut butter and stir until melted. 4. Add marshmallow creme, vanilla and nuts; stir vigorously until well blended. 5. Pour into buttered 13 x 9-inch or 12 x 8-inch pan. 6. Cool at room temperature; then cut into squares.

HARD CANDY

3¾ c. sugar
1½ c. light corn syrup
1 c. water
1 tsp. flavoring oil or 1 T. flavoring extract
5 to 6 drops food coloring (opt.)

1. In large heavy saucepan, stir together sugar, corn syrup and water; cook over medium heat, stirring constantly until sugar dissolves. 2. Boil, without stirring, until temperature registers 310° on candy thermometer (or until small amount of mixture, when dropped into very cold water separates into threads which are hard and brittle). 3. Remove from heat; after boiling has stopped, allow mixture to cool 5 minutes. 4. Stir in flavoring and food coloring; cover and let candy set an additional 5 minutes. 5. Pour candy onto a lightly greased or oiled cookie sheet; as soon as candy can be handled, lift edges around the circle with a spatula and cut into bite-size pieces with kitchen shears. (Or, let cool; then break into pieces.) 6. Allow candy to dry and cool completely; then dust the candies with powdered sugar to prevent pieces from sticking together. Store in airtight containers.

HAYSTACKS (Microwave)

1 (3-oz.) can chow mein noodles (2 c.)
½ to 1 c. nuts
½ to 1 c. miniature marshmallows (opt.)
12 oz. butterscotch chips or MILK CHOCOLATE chips

1. Line 2 cookie sheets with waxed paper. 2. In mixing bowl, toss together noodles, nuts and marshmallows. 3. Melt chips in 1-quart glass measuring pitcher on HIGH in microwave oven for 3 minutes. 4. Stir until smooth. Pour over first mixture; toss gently until coated. 5. Drop from teaspoon onto waxed paper; chill to harden. Makes 30 to 40.

MASHED POTATO-PEANUT BUTTER CANDY

¼ c. leftover mashed potatoes, level
⅛ t. vanilla
Powdered sugar, probably about 2½ to 3 cups
Peanut butter

1. In bowl, add enough powdered sugar to mashed potatoes and vanilla to make a soft dough, but stiff enough to roll out. On board or clean table, sprinkle cornstarch or powdered sugar and roll candy out to ¼-inch thickness. 2. Spread surface with peanut butter; roll up like jelly roll and slice.

NUTS, TOASTED

Spread almonds, pecans or walnuts on baking sheet. Bake in preheated 275° oven until toasted. (Stir several times.)

PEANUT BRITTLE (Microwave)

Make it in 10 minutes.

1 c. sugar
½ c. light corn syrup
⅛ tsp. salt
1 to 1¼ c. peanuts, roasted (preferably unsalted)
1 T. butter
1 tsp. vanilla
1 tsp. baking soda

1. In 2-quart round casserole or mixing bowl (microwave-safe), stir together sugar, corn syrup and salt. 2. Microwave on HIGH 5 minutes, uncovered. 3. Stir in peanuts; microwave 2 to 5 minutes, stirring after 2 minutes, then after 4 minutes, until syrup and peanuts are lightly browned. (Watch that it does not get too brown.) 4. Stir in butter, vanilla and soda until light and foamy. 5. Spread to ¼-inch thickness on large, well-buttered cookie sheet.

STRAWBERRIES, CHOCOLATE-DIPPED

2 c. (1 pt) lg. ripe strawberries with stems
¼ c. semi-sweet chocolate chips
½ T. corn syrup
2½ T. butter

1. Wash strawberries; gently pat dry. 2. In small saucepan, combine chocolate chips, corn syrup and butter; melt chocolate over low heat, stirring constantly. 3. Remove from heat; set saucepan in a pan of hot water to maintain dipping consistency. 4. Dip each strawberry into chocolate mixture, coating ⅔ of each berry; allow excess chocolate to drip back into pan. 5. Place berries, stem side down, on cookie sheet covered with waxed paper. 6. Refrigerate until chocolate is set, 15 to 30 minutes. (Can be refrigerated several hours.) **Another coating**: Melt together 1⅓ c. semi-sweet chocolate chips and 2 tsp. Earth Balance shortening.

TOFFEE, ENGLISH (Easy)

Makes about 3 pounds.

1½ c. coarsely chopped pecans or almonds (opt.)
2 c. (4 sticks) butter
3 c. packed brown sugar
1 tsp. cream of tartar
1½ c. semi-sweet or milk chocolate chips (opt.)

1. In a buttered or sprayed 15 x 10 x 2-inch jellyroll pan, sprinkle nuts over bottom (if using nuts). Set aside. 2. Melt butter in large black iron skillet over medium heat. 3. Add brown sugar and cream of tartar; cook over medium heat, stirring constantly, until mixture reaches 287° to 290° on candy thermometer. (Hard crack.) 4. Quickly pour evenly over nuts in prepared pan. 5. If using chocolate, sprinkle chips over hot toffee; cover with a larger cookie sheet (this helps contain heat so chips will melt). In about 2 minutes, spread melted chocolate over entire surface of toffee. 6. Cool completely; break into pieces. Store airtight in a cool place, up to 2 months. Note: If no candy thermometer is available: hard-crack is when a small amount dropped into ice water forms a brittle mass that snaps easily when pressed between fingers.

WALNUTS, WHITE GLAZED

Delicious! From Carolyn Deets.

½ c. sour cream (can be low-fat)
1½ c. sugar, granulated (not powdered)
1½ tsp. vanilla
4 c. shelled walnuts (do not cut up or chop)

1. Heat sour cream and sugar to 240° or 245° on med. heat, stirring almost constantly so it does not scorch. 2. Remove from heat; add vanilla and walnuts, mixing well. 3. Spread on cookie sheet. 4. When cool, break apart; store in airtight container.

CHEX MUDDY BUDDIES

Recipe may be cut in half.

9 c. any kind of Chex cereal (or a combination)
1 c. semi-sweet chocolate chips
½ c. peanut butter
¼ c. (½ stick) butter
¼ to 1 tsp. vanilla
1½ c. powdered sugar

1. Measure cereal into a large bowl; set aside. 2. In 1-quart microwave-safe bowl or pitcher, combine chocolate chips, peanut butter and butter. 3. Microwave on HIGH 1 minute; stir well. If not smooth, microwave another 30 seconds; then stir. 4. Add vanilla to chocolate mixture; stir. 5. Pour mixture over cereal, stirring well until all pieces are evenly coated. 6. Put powdered sugar and cereal into a large plastic bag; seal bag (or use a twister). 7. Shake bag until all pieces are well coated with powdered sugar. 8. Spread on waxed paper or cookie sheets to cool. 9. Store in airtight container. Makes 9 cups.

CHEX PARTY MIX, CRISP

¼ c. (½ stick) butter
1¼ tsp. seasoned salt
4 to 4½ tsp. Worcestershire sauce
8 c. any kind of Chex cereal (or a combination)
1 c. mixed nuts (or all one kind)
1 c. pretzels

1. Preheat oven to 250°. 2. Melt butter in large open roasting pan. 3. Stir in seasoned salt and Worcestershire sauce. 4. Add cereal, nuts and pretzels, stirring until all pieces are evenly coated. 5. Bake, uncovered, in preheated 250° oven for 1 hour, stirring every 15 minutes. 6. Spread on paper towels to cool. 7. Store in airtight container.

CRISPIX CRUNCH

From Ron Churchill.

1 (12.3-oz.) box Crispix cereal
1 c. semi-sweet chocolate chips
1 c. peanut butter
2 T. (¼ stick) butter
2 c. powdered sugar

1. Pour cereal into large bowl; set aside. 2. In 1-quart microwave-safe bowl or pitcher, combine chocolate chips, peanut butter and butter. 3. Microwave on MEDIUM power (#5) for 2½ to 3 minutes; stir until smooth. 4. Pour mixture over cereal, stirring until all pieces are evenly coated. 5. Put powdered sugar and cereal into a large plastic bag; seal bag (or use a twister). 6. Shake bag until all pieces are well coated with powdered sugar. 7. Spread on waxed paper or cookie sheets to cool. 8. Store in airtight container.

GRANOLA, SUPER

Adapted from Beverly Muir Johnston.
May be eaten as a snack or as a cereal.

2½ to 3 c. old-fashioned or quick rolled oats (not instant)
½ c. flaked coconut
¼ to ½ c. unprocessed bran or Bran Buds or All-Bran
¼ to ½ c. wheat germ (opt.)
½ c. almonds or other nuts (opt.)
¼ c. sesame seeds (opt.)
2 to 3 T. packed brown sugar
1 tsp. cinnamon
¼ c. olive oil
¼ c. honey, corn syrup or molasses
½ tsp. vanilla
½ c. raisins
½ c. dates, chopped (opt.)

1. Turn oven dial to 325°. 2. Lightly grease or spray 13 x 9-inch baking dish or cake pan. 3. In large bowl, combine dry ingredients. 4. In small bowl, combine oil, honey and vanilla; pour over dry ingredients, stirring together well. 5. Spread in prepared pan and bake in preheated 325° oven 30 minutes,

stirring every 10 minutes, until golden brown. 6. Remove from oven and add raisins and dates. 7. Cool completely, stirring occasionally to prevent sticking together; store in tightly covered containers when cool. **Note:** Watch that it does not get too brown toward the end of baking period. For storage beyond 2 weeks, refrigerate or freeze granola. To freshen granola, reheat in 350° oven for 10 to 20 minutes.

POPCORN BALLS

1 c. sugar
⅓ c. light or dark corn syrup
⅓ c. water
¼ tsp. salt
¼ c. (½ stick) butter
2 tsp. vanilla
4 qt. (16 c.) popped corn in a lg. buttered bowl

1. In 2 or 3-quart saucepan, stir together sugar, corn syrup, water, salt and butter. 2. Bring to a boil and cook to 250° to 270° on candy thermometer (without stirring). 3. Immediately remove from heat and add vanilla; pour hot syrup slowly over popcorn. 4. Butter hands (or wet them, shaking off excess water) and form into balls using as little pressure as possible. (Wet hands after every 3 balls.) 5. Balls may be wrapped individually in plastic wrap or waxed paper.

POPCORN, BUTTERED

Makes 3 to 3½ quarts of popped corn.

2 T. olive oil
½ c. popcorn, unpopped
3 to 4 T. butter
Salt

1. Heat oil in 3-quart pan (or larger). It must have a tight lid. 2. When oil is very hot (almost smoking), add popcorn; cover with tight lid and shake pan over hot burner continuously. 3. When corn stops popping, quickly pour into large bowl. 4. Pour melted butter over popcorn, stirring with fork. 5. Sprinkle very lightly with salt. 6. Store any leftover popcorn in airtight container. **Note**: Instead of butter and salt, butter-flavored popcorn salt may be used.

POPCORN, CAJUN

Hot-hot!

5 c. popped popcorn
2 T. butter, melted
½ tsp. paprika
½ tsp. black pepper or lemon pepper
¼ tsp. garlic powder
⅛ tsp. cayenne pepper

1. Pour melted butter over warm popcorn. 2. In small bowl, combine remaining ingredients and sprinkle over popcorn,

tossing to mix. **3.** If crisp popcorn is desired, spread mixture on baking sheet and bake in preheated 300° oven for 5 minutes.

POPCORN, CARAMEL (Microwave)

Quick, easy, chewy and delicious.

8 to 10 c. popped popcorn
¾ c. packed brown sugar
½ c. reg. Smart Balance spread or butter
2 T. light corn syrup
⅛ tsp. salt
¼ tsp. baking soda
¼ to ½ c. nuts (opt.)

1. Place popcorn in large microwave-safe bowl; set aside. **2.** In 1-quart microwave-safe bowl or pitcher, combine brown sugar, butter, corn syrup and salt; microwave on HIGH for 2 minutes. **3.** Stir well; microwave on HIGH again until mixture comes to a full rolling boil (about 30 seconds or more). **4.** Stir in baking soda until well mixed and foamy; add nuts. **5.** Pour foamy mixture over popcorn immediately; stir well. **6.** Microwave on HIGH for 2 minutes. **7.** Spread on waxed paper to cool. **8.** When cool, store in tightly covered container.

POPCORN, CARAMEL (Oven)

Recipe may be cut in half. Very crisp.

6 qt. popped popcorn
1 to 3 c. unsalted or lightly salted peanuts, almonds or
      mixed nuts (opt.)
2 c. packed brown sugar
1 c. reg. Smart Balance spread or butter
½ to ⅔ c. light or dark corn syrup
½ tsp. salt
½ tsp. baking soda
1 tsp. vanilla extract

1. Put popped popcorn and nuts in large roaster or metal dishpan in 250° oven. **2.** In 2 to 3-quart saucepan, stir brown sugar, butter, corn syrup and salt together while bringing to a boil over medium-high heat. **3.** Without stirring, boil 5 minutes on lower heat. **4.** Remove from heat; stir in soda and vanilla. **5.** Pour foamy mixture over warm popcorn, stirring to coat. **6.** Bake in 250° oven, stirring every 15 minutes for 1 hour. **7.** Cool, stirring often during the first 15 minutes of cooling time. **8.** Store in tightly covered containers.

POPCORN, CARAMEL (Larger)

Very crisp, and it stays crisp.

8 to 8½ qt. popped popcorn
¾ c. reg. Smart Balance spread or butter
1½ c. packed brown sugar
¾ c. light or dark corn syrup

½ tsp. cream of tartar
¾ tsp. baking soda
1 to 3 c. almonds or peanuts (opt.)

1. Preheat oven to 225°. **2.** Put popped popcorn in very large roaster or large metal dishpan and place in 225° oven. **3.** In 3-quart (or larger) saucepan, bring butter, brown sugar, corn syrup and cream of tartar to boiling point. **4.** Reduce heat and boil gently for 5 minutes without stirring. **5.** Remove from heat and stir in baking soda. (Watch, as it will foam up.) **6.** Pour mixture over popcorn, stirring until well mixed. **7.** Add nuts, if used, and stir. **8.** Return to 225° oven; bake 2 hours, stirring every 15 minutes with wooden spoon. **9.** Remove from oven and cool, stirring often during the first 15 minutes of cooling period. **10.** Store in tightly covered containers.

POPCORN, ITALIAN-FLAVORED

¼ c. butter, melted
¼ c. Parmesan cheese
½ tsp. garlic salt
½ tsp. oregano
½ tsp. basil
¼ tsp. onion powder
10 c. freshly popped popcorn

1. Combine butter, cheese and seasonings in small bowl, mixing well. **2.** Put popcorn in shallow baking pan. **3.** Pour butter mixture over popcorn, stirring to mix. **4.** Bake in preheated 300° oven for 15 minutes, stirring occasionally.

TRAIL MIX SNACK

2 c. raisins
1 c. banana chips
1 c. chocolate chips or chocolate-covered candies
1 to 2 c. peanuts (or coarsely chopped walnuts or cashews)
1 c. flaked coconut or 1⅓ c. mixed dried fruit

1. Mix together all ingredients; store in airtight container. Makes about 6 cups or more.

Chapter 28

Canning, Preserving & Freezing

BOB BENNINGER, JACK AND ELLEN BENNINGER
AND SARAH MCILHANY
1948 — 1998

JACK AND ELLEN BENNINGER

CANNING, PRESERVING & FREEZING

APPLE BUTTER

Use most any kind of apples. Makes several pints.

6 lbs. apples (4½ to 5 qt.), cored and sliced, peeled or
    unpeeled
1½ to 2 c. water, apple juice or cider
4½ c. sugar
4 tsp. cinnamon
1 tsp. ground cloves
½ tsp. allspice
½ c. vinegar (white or brown)

1. Cook sliced apples in heavy pot with 1½ to 2 cups liquid, turning heat low after mixture begins to boil; cook until apples are soft, stirring occasionally (25 minutes or so). 2. If any liquid remains, drain it off; put apples through food mill or colander to make applesauce. 3. Measure 9¼ to 9½ cups applesauce. **Oven-Baked Method (3 hours)**: Put applesauce in enamel or stainless steel roaster; add sugar, spices and vinegar, mixing well. Place in preheated 350° oven, uncovered. Bake for 3 hours, stirring every 30 minutes. (Stir well.) **Crock-Pot Method (7 hours)**: Put applesauce in crock-pot; add sugar, spices and vinegar, mixing well. Cook on HIGH, covered, for 3 hours, stirring once every hour. Remove lid and cook 4 hours longer on HIGH, stirring once or twice every hour. **To Freeze or Can**: Apple butter may be cooled and frozen, or canned. To can, use water-bath method, processing pints 15 minutes after water comes to a boil. Or use open-kettle method while apple butter is boiling (lids boiling in water for at least 5 minutes).

APPLE PIE FILLING (To Freeze)

Makes 5 to 6 pints to freeze.

6 lbs. apples
2 T. lemon juice
2 c. sugar
¼ c. flour, packed level
1½ tsp. cinnamon
¼ tsp. nutmeg

1. Wash, peel, core and slice apples. (About 4½ to 5 quarts apples after peeling and slicing). 2. Put apples in large cooking pot and add lemon juice. 3. Combine sugar, flour and spices, stirring together; add to apples. 4. Stir all together and let stand 30 to 60 minutes, until juicy. 5. Cook over med.-low heat until mixture begins to thicken, stirring frequently. 6. Cool; freeze in freezer containers. 7. For apple pie, use 2 pints for a 9-inch double-crust pie; cut vents in top pastry and bake on cookie sheet in preheated 425° oven for 40 minutes.

BEETS, PICKLED

Makes approximately 9 pints.

1 peck or about 10 lbs. beets
4 c. sugar
3 c. vinegar
1 c. beet juice or water
Salt (opt.)

1. Wash whole beets, leaving 1 inch of stem (also leave roots on). 2. Cover with boiling water and cook until beets are tender; reserve 1 cup beet liquid. 3. Dip into cold water and slip off skins, stems and root ends. 4. In saucepan, combine sugar, vinegar and 1 cup strained beet juice (or water); simmer gently 15 minutes. 5. Pack beets into clean pint jars, cutting larger beets into chunks. 6. Pour boiling syrup over beets; if desired, add ½ teaspoon salt to each pint. 7. Cap with lids; process both pints and quarts 30 minutes in water-bath canner (count time after water comes to a boil).

BEETS, SWEET 'N SOUR

From Grace Cwynar. Easy and delicious. Makes 12 pints.

11 to 12 lbs. beets, before cooking or 5 qt. diced, cooked
    beets
4 c. sugar
3½ c. white vinegar
8 c. water
4 tsp. salt
1 tsp. black pepper

1. Cook whole beets until tender in large pressure cooker, or however you desire. (No salt.) 2. Put hot beets in cold water and remove skins. Dice the beets to make 5 quarts. 3. In large cooking pot, combine sugar, vinegar, 8 cups water, salt and pepper. 4. Bring to a boil and boil gently for 15 minutes. 5. Add diced beets; bring to a boil and boil 10 minutes. 6. Put in jars and seal. (Open-kettle method, or water-bath pints for 30 minutes in boiling water, counting time after water comes to a boil.)

BREAD & BUTTER PICKLES

Either cucumbers or zucchini may be used in this recipe from Ruth Melichar. Crisp and delicious, this makes 6½ to 7 pints.

4 qt. (1 gal.) zucchini or cucumbers, sliced ⅛ in. thick
8 med. onions, (4 c.), sliced ⅛ in. thick
3 lg. green (or part red) bell peppers, chopped
6 to 8 garlic cloves, peeled and finely sliced or diced
⅓ c. salt
4 c. ice cubes or cracked ice
5 c. sugar
2 tsp. whole mustard seed
1½ tsp. celery seed
1½ tsp. turmeric
3 c. vinegar

1. If using large zucchini or cucumbers, quarter them length-wise before slicing and remove seeds and pulp. It is not necessary to peel them unless skin is tough. 2. Combine zucchini or cucumbers, onions, green peppers, garlic and salt in large container. 3. Cover mixture with ice cubes or cracked ice; stir mixture thoroughly. 4. Let stand 3 hours. 5. Drain well; put vegetables in large cooking pot. 6. Combine sugar and remaining ingredients; pour over vegetables. 7. Bring to a boil, but do not let it continue boiling. 8. Pack in jars and seal (open-kettle method).

CORN, FROZEN

A special recipe from Bonnie Bash which is really good!

4 qt. (16 c.) raw corn, cut off the ears
1 c. sugar
4 c. water
2 tsp. salt

1. In large pan, combine all ingredients, stirring together. 2. Bring to a boil; reduce heat and simmer 15 minutes. 3. Remove from heat and cool overnight in refrigerator. 4. Next morning, drain off any remaining liquid on corn, and freeze in plastic bags or freezer containers.

GRAPE JUICE

Wash and stem grapes; put 2 cups grapes in each empty quart jar. Add ½ cup sugar to each quart and fill with hottest tap water. Seal lids. Process quart jars in "water bath" for 10 minutes after water comes to a boil. Let set a few weeks before drinking. When serving grape juice, discard the grapes.

GREEN BEANS, PICKLED

Makes 5 pints.

2½ to 3 qt. fresh green beans
6 c. water
2 tsp. salt
2 c. sugar
4 c. vinegar
4 c. water

1. Wash beans and remove ends, leaving beans whole. 2. Bring beans to a boil in 6 cups water and the salt, on high heat. 3. After coming to a boil, reduce heat slightly and boil 5 minutes. 4. Drain beans; pack upright in clean jars. 5. In empty bean kettle, combine sugar, vinegar and 4 cups water; bring to a boil and boil 5 minutes. 6. Pour boiling syrup over beans; seal with lids which have been in boiling water for at least 5 minutes. <u>Note:</u> ⅛ teaspoon alum may be added to each pint, if desired.

GREEN TOMATOES, PICKLED

Makes 8 pints.

4 lbs. green tomatoes
4 med. onions, sliced
1 lg. green pepper, chopped (1 c.)
2 qt. white vinegar
5 c. sugar
¼ c. mustard seed
1 T. celery seed
1 tsp. turmeric

1. Wash and core tomatoes; slice ¼ inch thick. (Should have 1 gallon sliced tomatoes.) 2. Combine tomatoes, onions and green pepper; pack into clean pint jars, leaving ½ inch headspace. 3. In saucepan, combine remaining ingredients and bring to a boil; pour boiling syrup over tomatoes, still leaving ½-inch headspace. 4. Cap with lids; process in boiling water 15 minutes (count time after water comes to a boil).

HOT PEPPERS & VEGETABLES

Makes 6 pints.

Hot peppers
Sweet bell peppers
Cucumbers
Onions
Small green tomatoes
Carrots (cook a little first)
Cauliflower (opt.)
Salt
4 c. water
2 c. vinegar

1. Wear plastic gloves to handle hot peppers; cut vegetables in pieces and pack in clean pint jars. 2. Add ½ teaspoon salt to each pint. 3. Heat water and vinegar together; pour over vegetables, leaving ½-inch headspace. 4. Cap with lids; bring to 5 pounds pressure in pressure canner; then immediately turn off heat and let pressure come down by itself.

JAM, CHERRY RHUBARB

6 c. cut-up rhubarb
4 c. sugar
1 (6-oz.) pkg. cherry gelatin or 2 (3-oz.) pkgs.
1 (21-oz.) can cherry pie filling

1. Combine rhubarb and sugar; let stand overnight. 2. Next day, cook mixture until rhubarb is tender, about 30 minutes. 3. Stir in dry gelatin and cherry pie filling; bring to a boil. 4. Remove from heat and cool to lukewarm. 5. Pour into containers and refrigerate or freeze.

JAM, PEACH-JELLO

From Bonnie Bash. Delicious!

5 c. crushed peaches, after peeling
6 c. sugar
1 (20-oz.) can crushed pineapple
1 (8-oz.) can crushed pineapple (1 c.)
6 oz. (1 lg. box or 2 sm. boxes) peach gelatin

1. Boil together crushed peaches, sugar and crushed pine-apple for 15 minutes (after it comes to a boil), stirring occasionally. 2. Remove from heat and add gelatin; stir well. 3. Pour into 6 pint jars within 1½ inches of the top. 4. When jam is cool, cover with lids and put in refrigerator or freezer.

JAM, RED BERRY (Green Tomatoes)

So easy and so good! From Geraldine McMullen.

5 c. green tomato pulp
4 c. sugar
1 (6-oz.) pkg. red raspberry or strawberry gelatin (or 1 sm. box of each flavor)

1. Peel some of the skin off green tomatoes and discard. (Discard core also.) 2. Chop green tomatoes to a pulp in food processor or blender; then measure. 3. Combine green tomatoes and sugar in large pan and boil 20 minutes, stirring occasionally. 4. Remove from heat and stir in gelatin until dissolved. 5. Pour into containers and cool. 6. Cover with lids and freeze or refrigerate.

JELLY, RED RASPBERRY (Beet)

Simply delicious!

4½ c. uncooked beets, peeled and diced
7 c. water
1 box Sure-Jell pectin
¼ c. lemon juice
4 c. sugar
1 (3-oz.) pkg. red raspberry gelatin

1. Peel beets; slice them, then dice. 2. Cook diced beets in 7 cups water until tender, boiling gently. 3. Drain beets, saving juice. (Either discard beets or use them for a vegetable.) 4. Strain beet juice and measure 3 cups into a large cooking pot. 5. Add pectin and lemon juice; bring to a full rolling boil. 6. Remove from heat and add sugar and gelatin; stir well. 7. Return to heat; bring to a full rolling boil and boil 6 minutes. (Watch that it does not boil over.) 8. Remove from heat; skim off foam from top. 9. Pour into containers and cool; cover with lids and freeze or refrigerate.

KETCHUP, ELLEN'S

Adapted from Johnstown, PA, recipe.
Recipe may be cut in half.

4½ to 5 gal. fresh tomatoes, measured after cutting up
2 c. vinegar
5 c. sugar
2 T. salt
1 T. onion salt or onion powder
1 T. celery salt
1 tsp. ground cinnamon
½ tsp. ground allspice
½ tsp. dry mustard
¼ tsp. ground cloves

1. Wash tomatoes; remove core, cut into chunks and measure 5 gallons, pressed down. 2. Cook tomatoes thoroughly (do not add water). 3. Put cooked tomatoes in a cloth bag or pillow case and hang from clothesline, or from a nail, for several hours or overnight, letting juice drain out. Reserve part of juice, if desired. (If using a nail, make 4 holes in hem of pillowcase; put all 4 holes over the nail.) 4. Put tomato pulp through a food mill, sieve or fruit/vegetable strainer attachment to Kitchen Aid mixer. (Should be about 12 to 14 cups of pulp.) 5. Put pulp and vinegar in stainless steel or enamel pot; in separate bowl, combine sugar, salts and spices; add to tomato pulp. If mixture seems too thick for ketchup, add a cup or two of reserved tomato juice (or water). 6. Bring to a boil on medium or low heat, stirring often; boil gently on low heat at least 20 minutes. (A spatter screen over the pot keeps ketchup from splattering.) 7. Put boiling ketchup into sterilized pint jars and seal with boiling hot lids. (Open-kettle method.) Or, water-bath pint jars 45 minutes after water comes to a boil. Or, pressure at 5 or 6 pounds pressure for 10 minutes. Makes 8 to 10 pints.

LIVERWURST, JACK'S

Cut off the good meat from the head of a hog. Add more good lean pork, also some good neck meat. Add liver and heart. Cut all this meat into chunks, discarding the fat. Cover meat with water; add a little salt and cook in large canning pressure cooker for 45 minutes at 10 pounds pressure. (Or boil meat until tender in large pot.) Set meat in refrigerator until fat rises to top and hardens. Lift the rim of fat off and discard. Remove all gristle and fat; grind meat in food chopper or grinder. Strain broth through sieve and add some of the broth to meat to make proper consistency. It will take several cups of broth, depending on how much meat there is. Add salt and pepper to taste, mixing together well. Put in a glass loaf pan and refrigerate; when cold, slice for sandwiches. Or can in pint jars, 15 pounds pressure, for 75 minutes. To serve on pancakes, heat some liverwurst in saucepan with small amount of water or meat broth to make soft consistency.

MARMALADE, GOLDEN APRICOT
(Freezer)

Zucchini is the unknown ingredient.
From Audrey McNutt. Delicious!

6 c. peeled, grated zucchini
Water
6 c. sugar
½ c. lemon juice
1 (20-oz.) can crushed pineapple, drained
2 (3-oz.) boxes apricot gelatin

1. In large kettle, cover grated zucchini with water and bring to a boil; boil 6 minutes. 2. Drain zucchini well. 3. Add sugar, lemon juice and drained pineapple; bring to a boil; then boil 10 minutes. 4. Remove from heat and immediately add apricot gelatin, stirring until dissolved. 5. This will be runny until it is cold; pour 1 cup into each of 8 jars or freezer containers, leaving 1- to 1½-inch headspace for freezer expansion. 6. Cool; then put lids on and freeze. Makes about 8 cups.

MARMALADE, RED MYSTERY

From Lola Cramer. Delicious!

5 c. rhubarb
4 c. sugar
1 (20-oz.) can crushed pineapple
1 (6-oz.) pkg. strawberry gelatin

1. Boil rhubarb, sugar and pineapple 20 minutes or until rhubarb is real soft. 2. Remove from heat and add gelatin; stir until dissolved. 3. Pour into containers; cool. 4. Cover with lids and freeze or refrigerate. Makes 3½ pints.

PICKLES, DILL

Especially good. For best flavor,
do not eat these for 4 weeks. Makes 4 quarts.

4 cloves garlic, sliced
4 heads fresh dill
2 tsp. whole pickling spice
1 tsp. mustard seed
2½ qt. water (10 c.)
2 c. vinegar
¼ c. salt (not iodized)
Pickling cucumbers (6 in. long) to fill 4 quart jars
4 whole cloves garlic
2 bay leaves

1. Fill water bath canner half full of water and place on burner to begin heating; keep the water at a simmer. 2. Combine sliced garlic, dill heads, pickling spice, mustard seed, water, vinegar and salt in enamel or stainless steel pan (not aluminum); bring slowly to boil over med.-low heat. 3. Cut cucumbers lengthwise into quarters, sixths or eighths; pack into clean quart jars. (Cut ⅛ inch off blossom end of each cucumber.) 4. Into each jar, add 1 whole clove garlic, 1 head of dill (from the brine) and ½ bay leaf. 5. Fill jars with brine to within ½ inch of top. 6. Put lids on which have been boiling in a saucepan of water; screw outer bands on firmly. 7. Put filled jars in canner; add additional boiling water until water is 2 inches above tops of jars. 8. Process in water bath 5 minutes, counting processing time as soon as all jars are in the canner. 9. Remove jars from canner and place on a wooden or cloth surface, away from drafts. 10. Allow to stand 12 hours before removing bands.

PICKLES, SHAKE

From Lola Cramer.

Fill a gallon jar ½ full of sliced cucumbers
and 2 to 4 onions, sliced.

Mix together the following:
1½ to 1¾ c. sugar
1½ c. vinegar
2½ T. salt
½ tsp. turmeric
½ tsp. alum
½ tsp. celery seed or celery salt
½ tsp. mustard seed

Pour this mixture over the cucumbers and onions, and place jar in refrigerator. Shake once a day for 6 days. Then pickles are ready for use.

PICKLES, SUNSHINE

A dill-sweet pickle from Marie Leyda. Delicious!

1. Wash pickles and cut ends off; pierce them with end of knife. 2. Pack pickles in a gallon glass jar. Add 2 big cloves garlic (or more if they are smaller) and 2 heads of dill and 4 T. canning or regular iodized salt. 3. Fill with cool tap water and shake to dissolve salt; put one bread crust on top. 4. Set in sun for 7 days. 5. Rinse pickles in cold water; slice them and put back in jar. 6. Add same amount of fresh dill and garlic; then add: ¼ tsp. alum, 3 c. white sugar, ¼ c. vinegar, 1 tsp. celery seed and 1 tsp. mustard seed. 7. Store in refrigerator and shake every day for 1 week. After that, they are ready to eat. Can keep in refrigerator all winter. Note: If cucumbers are BIG, cut into three pieces. If real seedy, remove seeds, then prick on outside.

PICKLES, SWEET CHRISTMAS (Easy)

"These crisp sweet pickles stay in refrigerator.
From Bonnie Bash."

1 gal. pickles, med. (not small and not huge)
4 c. cider vinegar
4 T. salt

4 T. powdered or granulated alum (or 2 T. old-fashioned
    alum)
5 T. pickling spice
Cold tap water

<u>At Christmas Time:</u>
5 c. sugar
½ c. hot water

1. In late summer or fall, wash pickles, prick with fork several places and place in glass gallon jar after slicing ¼ inch thick (or ⅛ inch). 2. Stir together vinegar, salt, alum and pickling spice; pour over pickles. 3. Fill gallon jar with cold tap water; cover with lid and refrigerate until the first or second week in December. 4. Discard vinegar-water that had been on pickles. Wash pickles in several waters. 5. Place pickles back in jar; sprinkle sugar and hot water over them and shake together (with lid on). Refrigerate. 6. Shake pickle jar once a day until Christmas. (Taste them; if you like them sweeter, add more sugar at this time.)

PICKLES, SWEET CINNAMON (Crisp)

Make either red (like cinnamon apple slices) or green.
From Naomi Wieserman.

7 lbs. cucumbers AFTER peeling and removing seeds
    (LARGE cucumbers, even turning yellow, may be used)
1 c. white hydrated lime
1 gal. tap water
Cold water and ice
3 c. distilled white vinegar, divided
4 qt. water
1 T. alum
Either 2 T. red food coloring or ⅛ tsp. (15 drops) green
    food coloring
10 c. sugar
2 c. water
8 cinnamon sticks
1 c. (8 oz.) cinnamon red hot candies (if making red
    pickles)

1. Peel cucumbers; cut in half lengthwise and scrape all the seeds out with a teaspoon. 2. Slice each half into ¼-inch slices crosswise. 3. In large enamel, stainless steel or crock container, combine lime and 1 gallon tap water, stirring together. 4. Add cucumber slices to lime water and soak 24 hours. 5. Drain off lime water; wash 3 times in clean water. 6. Cover with cold water and ice, and let soak 3 hours. Drain. 7. Combine 1 cup white vinegar, 4 quarts water, alum and food coloring; pour over cucumber slices in the large pot. Simmer for 2 hours. 8. Pour off liquid (discard). 9. Combine sugar, remaining 2 cups vinegar, 2 cups water, cinnamon sticks (and cinnamon candies if making red); bring to a boil; then lower heat and simmer 5 minutes. 10. Pour syrup over cucumber slices; let stand 24 hours. 11. Pour syrup off cucumber slices into a pan; bring to a boil again and pour boiling syrup over pickles which have been packed into pint jars. Leave ½-inch headspace at top of each jar. 12. Cap each jar when filled. 13. Process 10 minutes in boiling water bath. Boiling water should

cover jars by 1 inch. Processing time starts when jars are placed in rolling boiling water in canner with tight lid. Leave burner on high heat during processing time. Makes 10 pints.

PICKLES, SWEET LIME (3 Day)

From Ida Burnheimer. Makes 11 or 12 pints.

7 lbs. cucumbers, washed and sliced crosswise, ¼ in. thick
    (6-qt. container level full of slices)
2 c. pickling lime (white hydrated garden lime)
2 gal. cold water
8 c. distilled white vinegar
8 c. sugar (4 lbs.)
1 T. salt
1 T. mixed pickling spice
1 T. celery seed
7 drops green food coloring

1. In crockery, enamel or stainless steel pot, combine lime and 2 gallons of water. (Do not use aluminum.) 2. Soak pickles in lime mixture 12 to 24 hours, or overnight. (Weight pickles down with plate.) 3. Rinse well 3 times in clean water to remove the lime; drain. 4. Cover with cold water and some ice cubes for 3 hours; drain. 5. Combine remaining syrup ingredients and bring to a boil; pour syrup over pickles. Let stand 5 to 6 hours, or overnight. 6. The next morning (third day), simmer pickles in syrup for 35 minutes after coming to a low boil. 7. Fill clean glass jars with pickle slices and pour syrup over pickles, leaving ½ inch headspace. 8. Cap each jar and process 5 minutes in boiling water bath. Boiling water should cover jars by 1 inch. (Start counting time when water comes to a full boil.)

PICKLES, SWEET 6-DAY

Adapted from Bonnie Bash.

5¾ to 6 lbs. med.-sized cucumbers, not large (5-qt. bowl
    level full)
Boiling water
8 c. sugar (4 lbs.)
3 c. vinegar
1 c. water
2 T. mixed pickling spice
2 T. salt (level)

1. Leave cucumbers whole; wash in cool water and drain. Pour boiling water over them to cover. (Weight down with plate so they stay under water.) 2. In 24 hours (second day), drain; cover with fresh boiling water. 3. On third day, repeat process. 4. On fourth day, drain and cut into ¼- to ½-inch slices. Combine syrup ingredients in a pan and bring to a boil; pour over pickles. Let stand 2 days. 5. Drain syrup into a large enamel or stainless steel pot and bring to a boil. 6. Add pickle slices; turn heat lower and let pickles heat through. 7. Pack pickles into clean glass pint jars; reheat syrup to boiling point and pour syrup over pickles, filling almost to tops of jars. Seal (open-kettle method). Makes 7 pints.

PICKLES, SWEET POLISH DILLS

Adapted from Virginia Foster. Makes 6 pints.

1 gal. (4 qt.) cucumbers, washed and cut in ½ to 1-in.
   chunks
2 qt. water
⅓ c. salt
Granulated alum
Fresh dill (or dill seed)

Syrup:
3 c. sugar
¾ tsp. turmeric
¾ tsp. mustard seed
2 to 3 T. celery seed
3 c. vinegar
6 garlic cloves

1. Combine water and salt, stirring until dissolved; pour over cucumber chunks and let stand overnight. 2. Next morning, drain cucumbers and set aside. 3. Combine syrup ingredients in large container and bring to a boil. 4. Put cucumber chunks into syrup, letting them get hot. (Do not boil cucumber chunks, but bring almost to boiling point.) 5. Pack cucumber chunks into pint jars, without syrup, **putting also into each pint:** ⅛ teaspoon granulated alum, 1 clove garlic and 1 head of fresh dill (or 1 teaspoon dill seed). 6. Bring syrup to a boil again and pour over cucumbers, filling jars almost to the top. 7. Put on lids which have been boiling in a pan of water; screw outer band on. No further processing is necessary if domes of lids "seal." Do not take off outer band for 12 hours.

PICKLES, SWEET SLICES (7-Day)

Takes a 6-quart kettle clear full of cucumbers.

7 lbs. med.-sized cucumbers (not large)
Boiling water
2 c. vinegar
4 c. water
10 c. sugar (5 lbs.)
2½ T. salt
2½ T. mixed pickling spice

1. Leave cucumbers whole; wash in cool water and drain. Pour boiling water over them to cover. (Weight down with plate so they stay under water.) 2. In 24 hours (second day), drain; cover with fresh boiling water. 3. On third day, repeat process. 4. On fourth day, repeat process. 5. On fifth day, drain water off pickles and cut into ¼ to ½-inch rings. Combine syrup ingredients in a pan and bring to a boil; pour over pickles. Let stand 24 hours. 6. On sixth day, drain syrup into a pan and bring to a boil; pour over pickles. 7. On seventh day, drain syrup into a large kettle and bring to a boil. Add pickles and bring to boiling point. Put pickles into clean glass pint jars, adding syrup almost to the top. Seal. (Can use either "open-kettle" method or water bath 10 minutes after the water boils.) Makes 11 pints.

REFRIGERATOR PICKLES

From Dawn Boyles.

6 c. thinly sliced cucumbers
1 c. thinly sliced onion
1 c. chopped green pepper
1 c. chopped red pepper

Syrup:
2 c. sugar
1 c. vinegar
1 T. salt
1 t. celery salt
1 t. mustard seed

1. Put vegetables in a bowl. 2. Mix together syrup ingredients in a saucepan and heat just until it is warm and the sugar is dissolved, stirring. 3. Pour syrup over cucumbers; put into a 2-quart jar, cover and refrigerate. 4. **Let set three days**; lasts for months in refrigerator.

RELISH-GREEN TOMATO

Makes 11 pints of delicious relish.

1 peck (2 gal.) green tomatoes
1 c. salt
4 red peppers
4 green peppers
2 qt. onions
1 qt. vinegar
7 c. sugar
4 tsp. celery seed
2 tsp. mustard seed
1 tsp. turmeric
½ tsp. cinnamon
½ tsp. nutmeg
6 drops green food coloring (opt.)

1. Remove cores and quarter green tomatoes. 2. Combine tomatoes and salt; drain in cloth bag overnight (or 6 to 8 hours). 3. Grind tomatoes, peppers and onions; put in colander or sieve for 15 minutes to drain. 4. Combine drained vegetables with remaining ingredients; bring to a boil. 5. Reduce heat and boil gently 30 to 40 minutes. 6. To can, use either open-kettle method while relish is boiling (lids boiling in water for at least 5 minutes); or use water-bath method, processing 5 minutes after water comes to a boil. **Note:** Can omit red peppers and use all green peppers.

RELISH, NELLIE'S ZUCCHINI

This is an excellent recipe from Nellie Johnston.
Makes 6 or 7 pints.

10 c. ground zucchini (if lg., remove seeds and pulp)
4 c. ground onions
6 lg. bell peppers (red or green), ground
5 T. salt

5 c. sugar
1 T. cornstarch
1 T. celery seed
3 tsp. dry mustard
3 tsp. turmeric
2 c. white vinegar

1. Combine ground zucchini, onions and peppers in dishpan or huge bowl. 2. Sprinkle salt over ground mixture. 3. Let stand for 3 hours. 4. Rinse in cold water and drain through a large sieve or fine colander, pressing out liquid. 5. In saucepan, combine sugar and remaining ingredients; bring to a boil and boil 5 minutes. 6. Put ground vegetables in large cooking pot; pour hot syrup over them and bring to a boil; boil 5 minutes. 7. Put in jars and seal. (Open-kettle or process 10 minutes in boiling water bath after water returns to a boil.)

RELISH, SWEET PICKLE

Makes 5 to 6 pints of delicious relish.

10 c. ground cucumbers (remove seeds before grinding)
4 c. ground onions
5 T. salt
1½ to 2 c. ground green and red bell peppers
4½ c. sugar
2 tsp. dry mustard
1 tsp. nutmeg
½ tsp. black pepper
1 T. celery seed
1 T. turmeric
2¼ c. vinegar (white or cider vinegar)

1. Grind cucumbers and onions. (If short on cucumbers, finish with zucchini, removing pulp and seeds before grinding.) 2. Combine cucumbers, onions and salt; let set overnight. 3. Next day, rinse well in cold water; drain. 4. Grind peppers and add to cucumber mixture. 5. Add remaining ingredients, stirring together. 6. Bring mixture to a boil; reduce heat and boil gently for 30 minutes, stirring occasionally. 7. Put into pint jars and seal (open-kettle method). **Note**: If skin is tough on large cucumbers, peel them.

SAUERKRAUT

From Marie Zook.

Grate or shred cabbage. Pack it rather firmly in clean glass quart jars, leaving 1½ inch headspace. Put 2 teaspoons salt (level) in the top of each quart. Fill with hot water, leaving ½ inch headspace. Close with lids and screw bands. Set jars on a pan as the brine may overflow during fermentation. Let stand for 21 days at room temperature, about 70°. Check jars often to make sure cabbage is covered with brine. If necessary, make a brine of 1 quart water and 1½ tablespoons salt; open jars and add more brine. In 21 days (3 weeks), try sauerkraut to see if it is cured sufficiently. The longer the fermentation period, the sharper the flavor. It may take up to 6 weeks. If jars are not too full, they can be frozen when ready.

SOUP, TOMATO

When opening this soup, do not dilute. Just warm it up as it comes out of the can.

2 gal. (8 qt.) washed and quartered tomatoes (do not peel)
3 to 5 lg. onions, sliced
1½ to 2½ c. diced or chopped celery (or more)
2 lg. red peppers (opt.)
3 bay leaves (opt.)
1½ c. sugar
½ c. cornstarch
3 T. salt
½ tsp. pepper (opt.)
4 T. butter (½ stick)

1. Cook tomatoes, onions, celery, red peppers and bay leaves until tender, about 2 hours. 2. Put through Foley Mill, strainer or sieve. 3. Reheat juice and bring to a gentle boil. 4. In bowl, mix together sugar, cornstarch, salt and pepper until thoroughly blended. 5. Remove soup kettle from burner and stir in sugar mixture, stirring well. 6. Return to burner and bring to a boil, stirring frequently. 7. Add butter and boil gently 10 minutes. 8. Fill clean jars with boiling soup to within ⅛ inch of top. 9. Put lids on, which have been boiling in a pan of water; screw outer band on. No further processing is necessary if domes of lids "seal." Do not take off outer bands for 12 hours. (Or pressure at 5 pounds for 10 minutes.) Makes 12 or 13 pints.

SPAGHETTI SAUCE

½ bushel (4 gal.) ripe tomatoes
2 to 3 lbs. peeled and diced onions
4 green bell peppers, de-seeded and diced
4 hot peppers, de-seeded and diced (opt.)
4 to 8 cloves garlic, sliced
4 tsp. oregano
4 tsp. basil
4 tsp. dried parsley flakes (opt.)
⅓ c. salt
1⅓ c. sugar
1 c. olive oil
48 oz. tomato paste

1. Wash and cut tomatoes into chunks. 2. In large pot, simmer tomatoes, onions, peppers and garlic together until soft and well cooked. (If using hot peppers, wear gloves when preparing.) 3. Put cooked tomato mixture through food mill or sieve. 4. Add remaining ingredients and simmer 2 hours, or until desired thickness. 5. Fill clean quart jars; cap with lids and seal. May use open-kettle method with boiling sauce, or process in water-bath canner 20 minutes after water comes to a boil.

STEWED TOMATOES

Delicious!

Fill each quart jar ½ full of peeled and cut fresh tomatoes.

To each jar, add:
1 tsp. salt or celery salt
2 to 3 T. sugar
2 T. chopped celery
2 T. chopped onion
2 T. chopped green pepper or less (opt.)

Fill jars with tomatoes to ½ inch of top. Seal lids and "water bath" for 35 minutes after water comes to a boil. (Or pressure 5 minutes at 5 pounds pressure.)

STRAWBERRY PRESERVES (Low Sugar)

Delicious on toast or on ice cream!

1 env. Knox unflavored gelatin
3 T. cold water
4½ c. hulled strawberries (3 c. crushed strawberries)
½ c. sugar

1. In saucepan, combine gelatin in cold water; heat, stirring constantly, until dissolved. **2.** Add crushed strawberries and sugar. **3.** Bring to a boil over medium heat, stirring constantly; lower heat and simmer 2 minutes. **4.** Pour into jars, leaving 1 to 1½ inches at top for freezer expansion room; cool. **5.** Put lids on and store in freezer or refrigerator.

TOMATO JUICE

From Hazel and Harvey Schreiner.

Cook fresh tomatoes and put through Foley Mill, food mill or strainer. Heat juice; pour into quart jars.

Add to each jar:
½ tsp. garlic salt
1 tsp. onion salt
2 tsp. sugar
½ tsp. Worcestershire sauce
⅛ tsp. Tabasco or Red Hot pepper sauce

Seal lids and process in boiling water bath 20 minutes after water returns to boiling.

TOMATO SAUCE

Fully ripe tomatoes

In each quart jar:
1 tsp. salt
1 tsp. Italian seasoning
1 tsp. minced onion

½ tsp. cornstarch
1 T. sugar
¼ tsp. black pepper
2 sm. cloves garlic, minced

1. Remove stems and cores from washed tomatoes. **2.** Cook until soft; place in colander and drain off clear liquid, discarding it. **3.** Press pulp through colander or food mill. **4.** In each quart jar, add the above ingredients; fill jars with the tomato-pulp juice. **5.** Stir well; cap with lids and cold pack for 30 minutes in water-bath canner. (Count time after water comes to a boil.) **Note**: 2 pecks (½ bushel) tomatoes, before cooking, makes about 5 to 7 quart jars full.

VENISON, OR BEEF, CANNED

Fill clean glass quart jars to within 1 inch of the top of jar with raw venison (deer meat) or beef which has been cut into small serving-size pieces (and washed). Add 1 tsp. salt, level. Do not add any water. Put new (wet) lids on top, and screw bands on tightly.

Put rack in bottom of pressure canner and have water come up to 3 to 4 inches after jars are in the canner.

Turn burner on (<u>NOT</u> on HIGH), and heat until steam comes out of the open petcock freely. Let it steam freely for 7 minutes before closing petcock.

When pressure reaches 10 pounds, keep it right there for 90 minutes (1½ hours). Then let pressure go down <u>by itself</u>. Do not open petcock until it is at zero.

INDEX of RECIPES

YEAST BREADS

BUNS, DINNER ROLLS, AND SWEET ROLLS

CEREAL, FRENCH TOAST, PANCAKES AND WAFFLES

EGGS

SALAD DRESSINGS

SOUP AND CHILI

VEGETABLES

Sauces for Vegetables and Meat

Main Dishes and Meat

FISH

FROSTINGS, GLAZES AND FILLINGS

COOKIES, BARS AND DOUGHNUTS

PIES

DESSERTS

DESSERT SAUCES AND TOPPINGS

CANDY, NUTS & SNACKS FOODS

Canning, Preserving & Freezing